Study Guide

to Accompany

Business Law
Text & Cases—Legal, Ethical, Global, and Corporate Environment
Twelfth Edition

KENNETH W. CLARKSON
University of Miami

ROGER LeROY MILLER
Institute for University Studies
Arlington, Texas

FRANK B. CROSS
Herbert D. Kelleher
Centennial Professor in Business Law
University of Texas at Austin

Prepared by

William Eric Hollowell
Member of
  U.S. Supreme Court Bar
  Minnesota State Bar
  Florida State Bar

Roger LeRoy Miller
Institute for University Studies
Arlington, Texas

SOUTH-WESTERN
CENGAGE Learning

Australia • Brazil • Japan • Korea • Mexico • Singapore • Spain • United Kingdom • United States

SOUTH-WESTERN
CENGAGE Learning

Study Guide to Accompany
Business Law:
TEXT AND CASES
Legal, Ethical, Global, and
Corporate Environment
Twelfth Edition

Kenneth W. Clarkson
Roger LeRoy Miller
Frank B. Cross

Vice President/Editorial Director:
Jack W. Calhoun

Editor-in-Chief:
Rob Dewey

Senior Acquisitions Editor:
Vicky True-Baker

Senior Developmental Editor:
Jan Lamar

Marketing Director:
Lisa L. Lysne

Marketing Manager:
Laura-Aurora Stopa

Marketing Coordinator:
Nicole Parsons

Production Editor:
Bill Stryker

Content Project Manager:
Anne Sheroff

Senior Media Editor:
Kristen Meere

Manufacturing Buyer:
Kevin Kluck

Editorial Assistant:
Patrick Ian Clark

Senior Art Director:
Michelle Kunkler

For product information and technology assistance, contact us at
Cengage Learning Academic Resource Center,
1-800-423-0563
For permission to use material from this text or product, submit all requests online at **www.cengage.com/permissions**
Further permissions questions can be emailed to
permissionrequest@cengage.com

ISBN-13: 978-0-538-47277-7
ISBN-10: 0-538-47277-4

South-Western Cengage Learning
5191 Natorp Blvd.
Mason, OH 45040
USA

Cengage Learning products are represented in Canada by Nelson Education, Ltd.

For your course and learning solutions, visit
www.cengage.com

Purchase any of our products at your local college store or at our preferred online store **www.cengagebrain.com**

Printed in the United States of America
1 2 3 4 5   15 14 13 12 11

Table of Contents

Preface

To the Student

This *Study Guide* is designed to help you read and understand *Business Law,* **Twelfth Edition.**

How the *Study Guide* Can Help You

This *Study Guide* can help you maximize your learning, subject to the constraints and the amount of time you can allot to this course. There are at least six specific ways in which you can benefit from using this guide.

1. The *Study Guide* can help you decide which topics are the most important. Because there are so many topics analyzed in each chapter, many students become confused about what is essential and what is not. You cannot, of course, learn everything; this *Study Guide* can help you concentrate on the crucial topics in each chapter.

2. If you are forced to miss a class, you can use this *Study Guide* to help you learn the material discussed in your absence.

3. There is a possibility that the questions that you are required to answer in this *Study Guide* are representative of the types of questions that you will be asked during examinations.

4. You can use this *Study Guide* to help you review for examinations.

5. This *Study Guide* can help you decide whether you really understand the material. Don't wait until examination time to find out!

6. Finally, the questions in this *Study Guide* will help you develop critical thinking skills that you can use in other classes and throughout your career.

The Contents of the *Study Guide*

Business law sometimes is considered a difficult subject because it uses a specialized vocabulary and also takes most people much time and effort to learn. Those who work with and teach business law believe that the subject matter is exciting and definitely worthy of your efforts. Your text, **Business Law, Twelfth Edition,** and this student learning guide have been written for the precise purpose of helping you learn the most important aspects of business law. We always try to keep you, the student, in mind.

Every chapter includes the following sections:

1. What This Chapter Is About: You are introduced to the main subject matter of each chapter in this section.

2. Chapter Outline: Using an outline format, the salient points in each chapter are presented.

3. True-False Questions: Ten true-false questions are included for each chapter. Generally, these questions test knowledge of terminology and principles. The answers are given at the back of the book. Whenever an answer is false, the reasons why it is false are presented at the back of the book also.

4. Fill-in Questions: Here you are asked to choose between two alternatives for each space that needs to be filled in. Answers are included at the back of the book.

5. Multiple-Choice Questions: Ten multiple-choice questions are given for each chapter. The answers, along with an explanation, are included at the back of this book.

6. Short Essay Questions: Two essay questions are presented for each chapter.

7. GamePoints or RockOn: Unique hypothetical fact problems on key issues.

8. Special Information for CPA Candidates: This section alerts CPA candidates to principles within the chapter that are of special importance for the CPA exam and includes study tips of particular utility to these students.

How to Use this Study Guide

What follows is a recommended strategy for improving your grade in your business law class. It may seem like a lot of work, but the payoffs will be high. Try the entire program for the first three or four chapters. If you then feel you can skip some steps safely, try doing so and see what happens.

For each chapter we recommend you follow the sequence of steps below:

1. Read the What This Chapter Is About and Chapter Outline.

2. Read any of the Concept Summaries that may be included in the chapter you are studying in *Business Law,* **Twelfth Edition.**

3. Read about half the textbook chapter (unless it is very long), being sure to underline only the most important topics (which you should be able to recognize after having read no more than two chapter outlines in this *Study Guide*). Put a check mark by the material that you do not understand.

4. If you find the textbook's chapter easy to understand, you might want to finish reading it. Otherwise, rest for a sufficient period before you read the second half of the chapter. Again, be sure to underline only the most important points and to put a check mark by the material you find difficult to understand.

5. After you have completed the entire textbook chapter, take a break. Then read only what you have underlined throughout the entire chapter.

6. Now concentrate on the difficult material, for which you have left check marks. Reread this material and *think about it*; you will find that it is very exciting to figure out difficult material on your own.

7. Now do the True-False Questions, Fill-In Questions, and Multiple-Choice Questions. Compare your answers with those at the back of this book. Make a note of the questions you have missed and find the pages in your textbook upon which these questions are based. If you still don't understand, ask your instructor.

8. If you still have time, do one or both of the essay questions.

9. Before your examination, study your class notes. Then review the chapter outline in the text. Reread the Chapter Outline in this *Study Guide*, then redo all of the questions within each chapter. Compare your answers with the answers at the back of this *Study Guide*. Identify your problem areas and reread the relevant pages in **Business Law, Twelfth Edition.** Think through the answers on your own.

If you have followed the strategy outlined above, you should feel sufficiently confident and be relaxed enough to do well on your exam.

Study Skills for *Business Law*, Twelfth Edition

Every student has a different way to study. We give several study hints below that we think will help any student to master the textbook **Business Law, Twelfth Edition.** These skills involve outlining, marking, taking notes, and summarizing. You may not need to use all these skills. Nonetheless, if you do improve your ability to use them, you will be able to understand more easily the information in **Business Law, Twelfth Edition.**

MAKING AN OUTLINE

An outline is simply a method for organizing information. The reason an outline can be helpful is that it shows how concepts relate to each other. Outlining can be done as part of your reading or at the end of your reading, or as a rereading of each section within a chapter before you go on to the next section. Even if you do not believe that you need to outline, our experience has been that the act of *physically* writing an outline for a chapter helps most students to improve greatly their ability to retain the material in **Business Law, Twelfth Edition** and master it, thereby obtaining a higher grade in the class, with less effort.

To make an effective outline you have to be selective. Outlines that contain all the information in the text are not very useful. Your objective in outlining is to identify main concepts and to subordinate details to those main concepts. Therefore, your first goal is to *identify the main concepts in each section.* Often the large, first-level headings within your textbook are sufficient as identifiers of the major concepts within each section. You may decide, however, that you want to phrase an identifier in a way that is more meaningful to you. In any event, your outline should consist of several levels written in a standard outline format. The most important concepts are assigned a roman numeral; the second most important a capital letter; the third most important, numbers; and the fourth most important, lower-case letters. Even if you make an outline that is no more than the headings in the text, you will be studying more efficiently than you would be otherwise. As we stated above, the process of physically writing the words will help you master the material.

MARKING A TEXT

From kindergarten through high school you typically did not own your own textbooks. They were made available by the school system. You were told not to mark in them. Now that you own your own text for a course, your learning can be greatly improved by marking your text. There is a trade-off here. The more you mark up your textbook, the less you will receive from your bookstore when you sell it back at the end of the semester. The benefit is a better understanding of the subject matter, and the cost is the reduction in the price you receive for the resale of the text. Additionally, if you want a text that you can mark with your own notations, you necessarily have to buy a new one or a used one that has no markings. Both carry a higher price tag than a used textbook with markings. Again there is a trade-off.

Different Ways of Marking   The most commonly used form of marking is to underline important points. The second most commonly used method is to use a felt-tipped highlighter, or marker, in yellow or some other transparent color. Marking also includes circling, numbering, using arrows, brief notes, or any other method that allows you to remember things when you go back to skim the pages in your textbook prior to an exam.

Why Marking Is Important   Marking is important for the same reason that outlining is—it helps you to organize the information in the text. It allows you to become an *active* participant in the mastery of the material. Researchers have shown that the physical act of marking, just like the physical act of outlining, helps you better retain the material. The better the material is organized in your mind, the more you will remember. There are two types of readers—passive and active. The active reader outlines or marks. Active readers typically do better on exams. Perhaps one of the reasons that active readers retain more is because the physical act of outlining and/or marking requires greater concentration. It is through greater concentration that more is remembered.

Points to Remember When Marking

1. Read one section at a time before you do any extensive marking. You can't mark a section until you know what is important and you can't know what is important until you read the whole section.

2. Don't over mark. Just as an outline cannot contain everything that is in a text (or in a lecture), marking can't be of the whole book. Don't fool yourself into thinking you've done a good job just because each page is filled up with arrows, asterisks, circles, and underlines. When you go back to review the material you won't remember what was important. The key is *selective* activity. Mark each page in a way that allows you to see the most important points at a glance. You can follow up your marking by writing out more in your subject outline.

HOW TO STUDY AND TAKE EXAMS

There is basically one reason why you have purchased the *Study Guide*—to improve your exam grade. By using this *Study Guide* assiduously, you will have the confidence to take your mid-terms and final examinations and to do well. The *Study Guide*, however, should not just be used a day before each exam. Rather, the guide is most helpful if you use it at the time that you read the chapter. That is to say, after you read a chapter in **Business Law, Twelfth Edition** you should directly go to the appropriate chapter in the *Study Guide*. This systematic review technique is the most effective study technique you can use.

Besides learning the concepts in each chapter as well as possible, there are additional strategies for taking exams. You need to know in advance what type of exam you are going to take—essay or objective or both. You need to know which reading materials and lectures will be covered. For both objective and essay exams (but more importantly for the former) you need to know if there is a penalty for guessing incorrectly. If there is, your strategy will be different: you will usually only mark what you are certain of. Finally, you need to know how much time will be allowed for the exam.

FOLLOWING DIRECTIONS

Students are often in a hurry to start an exam so they take little time to read the instructions. The instructions can be critical, however. In a multiple-choice exam, for example, if there is no indication that there is a penalty for guessing, then you should never leave a question unanswered. Even if there only remains a few minutes at the end of the exam, you should guess for those questions about which you are uncertain.

Additionally, you need to know the weight given to each section of an exam. In a typical multiple-choice exam, all questions have equal weight. In some exams, particularly those involving essay questions, different parts of the exam carry different weights. You should use these weights to apportion your time accordingly. If an essay part of an exam accounts for only 20 percent of the total points on the exam, you should not spend 60 percent of your time on the essay.

You need to make sure you are answering the question correctly. Some exams require a No. 2 lead pencil to fill in the dots on a machine-graded answer sheet. Other exams require underlining or circling. In short, you have to look at the instructions carefully.

Lastly, check to make sure that you have all the pages of the examination. If you are uncertain, ask the instructor or the exam proctor. It is hard to justify not having done your exam correctly because you failed to answer all the questions. Simply stating that you did not have them will pose a problem for both you and your instructor. Don't take a chance. Double check to make sure.

TAKING OBJECTIVE EXAMINATIONS

The most important point to discover initially with any objective test is if there is a penalty for guessing. If there is none, you have nothing to lose by guessing. In contrast, if a half-point is subtracted for each incorrect answer, then you probably should not answer any question for which you are purely guessing.

Students usually commit one of two errors when they read objective-exam questions: (1) they read things into the questions that don't exist, or (2) they skip over words or phrases.

Most test questions include key words such as:

- all
- always
- never
- only

If you miss these key words you will be missing the "trick" part of the question. Also, you must look for questions that are only *partly* correct, particularly if you are answering true/false questions.

Never answer a question without reading all of the alternatives. More than one of them may be correct. If more than one of them seems correct, make sure you select the answer that seems the most correct.

Whenever the answer to an objective question is not obvious, start with the process of elimination. Throw out the answers that are clearly incorrect. Even with objective exams in which there is a penalty for guessing, if you can throw out several obviously incorrect answers, then you may wish to guess among the remaining ones because your probability of choosing the correct answer is high.

Typically, the easiest way to eliminate incorrect answers is to look for those that are meaningless, illogical, or inconsistent. Often test authors put in choices that make perfect sense and are indeed true, but they are not the answer to the question under study.

Acknowledgments

We wish to thank Suzanne Jasin of K & M Consulting for her expert design and composition of this guide.

We welcome comments and criticisms to help us make this guide even more useful. All errors are our sole responsibility.

Roger LeRoy Miller
Eric Hollowell

Chapter 1
Introduction to Law and Legal Reasoning

WHAT THIS CHAPTER IS ABOUT

The first chapters in Unit 1 provide the background for the entire course. Chapter 1 sets the stage. From this chapter, you must understand that (1) the law is a set of general rules, (2) in applying these general rules, a judge cannot fit a case to suit a rule, but must fit (or find) a rule to suit the case, and (3) in fitting (or finding) a rule, a judge must also supply reasons for the decision.

CHAPTER OUTLINE

I. WHAT IS LAW?
Law consists of enforceable rules governing relationships among individuals and between individuals and their society.

II. BUSINESS ACTIVITIES AND THE LEGAL ENVIRONMENT
The law is split into different topics to make it easier to study, but more than one of those areas of the law can affect individual business decisions. Whether an activity is ethical is an important part of deciding whether to engage in it, but simply complying with the law may not meet all ethical obligations.

III. SOURCES OF AMERICAN LAW

A. CONSTITUTIONAL LAW
The U.S. Constitution distributes power among the branches of government. It is the supreme law of the land. Any law that conflicts with it is invalid. The states also have constitutions, but the federal constitution prevails.

B. STATUTORY LAW
Statutes and ordinances are enacted by Congress and by state and local legislative bodies. Uniform laws (such as the Uniform Commercial Code) and model codes are created by panels of experts and scholars and adopted at the option of each state's legislature.

C. ADMINISTRATIVE LAW
Administrative law consists of the rules and regulations issued by administrative agencies, which derive their authority from the legislative and executive branches of government.

D. CASE LAW AND COMMON LAW DOCTRINES
Case law includes courts' interpretations of constitutional provisions, statutes, and administrative rules. Because statutes often codify common law rules, courts often rely on the common law as a guide to the intent and purpose of a statute. Case law governs all areas not covered by statutes.

IV. THE COMMON LAW TRADITION

The American legal system, based on the decisions judges make in cases, is a common law system, which involves the application of principles applied in earlier cases with similar facts. This system comes from early English courts, which made a distinction between remedies at law and remedies in equity.

A. REMEDIES AT LAW AND REMEDIES IN EQUITY

As a rule, courts grant an equitable remedy only if the remedy at law is inadequate.

1. Remedies at Law

Remedies at law include awards of land, money, and items of value. A jury trial is available only in an action at law.

2. Remedies in Equity

Remedies in equity include decrees of specific performance, injunctions, and rescission. Decisions to award equitable remedies are guided by equitable maxims.

B. THE DOCTRINE OF *STARE DECISIS*

The use of precedent as binding authority in a common law system is the doctrine of *stare decisis*. *Stare decisis* makes the legal system more efficient, just, uniform, stable, and predictable.

1. Departures from Precedent

A judge may decide that a precedent is incorrect if there have been changes in technology, business practices, or society's attitudes.

2. When There Is No Precedent

When there is no precedent, a court may look at other legal principles and policies, social values, or scientific data.

C. LEGAL REASONING

1. Issue-Rule-Application-Conclusion (IRAC)

Legal reasoning requires learning the facts of a case, identifying the issues and the relevant legal rules, applying the rules to the facts, and coming to a conclusion.

2. Forms of Legal Reasoning

In applying an old precedent or establishing a new one, judges use many forms of reasoning—deductive reasoning, linear reasoning, reasoning by analogy, and others—to harmonize their decisions with earlier cases.

V. SCHOOLS OF JURISPRUDENTIAL THOUGHT

Judges interpret and apply the law. When the law is expressed in general terms, there is some flexibility in interpreting it. This interpretation can be influenced by a judge's personal philosophy. Legal philosophies include the following.

A. THE NATURAL LAW SCHOOL

Natural law is a system of moral and ethical principles that are believed to be inherent in human nature and discoverable by humans through the use of their natural intelligence.

B. THE POSITIVIST SCHOOL

Legal positivists believe that there is no higher law than a nation's positive law (the law created by a particular society at a particular point in time). The law is the law and must be obeyed.

C. THE HISTORICAL SCHOOL

Followers of this school focus on legal principles that have been applied in past cases, emphasizing that those principles should be applied strictly in present cases.

D. LEGAL REALISM

Legal realists believe that in making decisions, judges are influenced by their own beliefs, the application of principles should be tempered by each case's circumstances, and extra-legal sources should be consulted.

VI. CLASSIFICATIONS OF LAW

A. SUBSTANTIVE LAW AND PROCEDURAL LAW

Substantive law includes laws that define, describe, regulate, and create rights and duties. *Procedural law* includes rules for enforcing those rights.

B. PRIVATE LAW AND PUBLIC LAW

Private law concerns relationships between private entities. *Public law* addresses the relationship between persons and their government.

C. CIVIL LAW AND CRIMINAL LAW

Civil law regulates relationships between individuals. *Criminal law* regulates relationships between individuals and society.

D. CYBERLAW

Cyberlaw is the emerging body of law (court decisions, new and amended statutes, etc.) that governs cyberspace transactions.

VII. HOW TO FIND PRIMARY SOURCES OF LAW

A. FINDING STATUTORY LAW

1. Publication of Statutes

Federal statutes are arranged by date of enactment in *United States Statutes at Large*. State statutes are collected in similar state publications. Statutes are also published in codified form (the form in which they appear in the federal and state codes) in other publications.

2. Finding a Statute in a Publication

Statutes are usually referred to in their codified form. In the codes, laws are compiled by subject. For example, the *United States Code* (U.S.C.) arranges by subject most federal laws. Each subject is assigned a title number and each statute a section number within a title.

B. FINDING ADMINISTRATIVE LAW

1. Publication of Rules and Regulations

Rules and regulations adopted by federal administrative agencies are published initially in the *Federal Register*. They are also compiled by subject in the *Code of Federal Regulations* (C.F.R.).

2. Finding a Rule or Regulation in a Publication

In the C.F.R., rules and regulations are arranged by subject. Each subject is assigned a title number and each rule or regulation a section number within a title.

C. FINDING CASE LAW

1. Publication of Court Opinions

State appellate court opinions are often published by the state in consecutively numbered volumes. They may also be published in units of the *National Reporter System*, by West Publishing Company. Federal court opinions appear in other West publications.

2. Finding a Court Opinion in a Publication

After a decision is published, it is usually referred to by the name of the case and the volume, name, and page number of one or more reporters (which are often, but not always, West reporters). This information is called the citation.

VIII. HOW TO READ AND UNDERSTAND CASE LAW

A. THE PARTIES

1. Plaintiff v. Defendant

In the title of a case (*Alpha v. Beta*), the *v.* means versus (against). Alpha is the plaintiff (the party who filed the suit) and Beta the defendant. Some appellate courts place the name of the party appealing a decision first, so this case on appeal may be called *Beta v. Alpha*.

2. Appellant v. Appellee

The appellant is the party who appeals a case to another court or jurisdiction from the one in which the case was originally brought. An appellant may be referred to as a petitioner. The appellee is the party against whom an appeal is taken. An appellee may be referred to as a respondent.

B. THE COURT'S OPINION

The opinion contains the court's reasons for its decision, the rules of law that apply, and the judgment.

1. Unanimous Opinion

When more than one judge (or justice) decides a case, and they all agree, a unanimous opinion is written for the whole court.

2. Majority Opinion

If a decision is not unanimous, a majority opinion outlines the views of the majority.

3. Concurring Opinion

A concurring opinion is one in which a judge emphasizes a point that was not emphasized in the unanimous or majority opinion.

4. Dissenting Opinion

A dissenting opinion may be written by a judge who does not agree with the majority. A dissent may form the basis of arguments used years later in overruling the majority opinion.

TRUE-FALSE QUESTIONS

(Answers at the Back of the Book)

____ 1. Law is a body of enforceable rules governing relationships among individuals and between individuals and their society.

____ 2. Legal positivists believe that law should reflect universal principles that are part of human nature.

____ 3. The doctrine of *stare decisis* obligates judges to follow precedents established within their jurisdictions.

____ 4. Common law develops from rules of law announced in court decisions.

____ 5. Statutory law is legislation.

____ 6. A federal statute takes precedence over the U.S. Constitution.

___ **7.** Congress enacted the Uniform Commercial Code for adoption by the states.

___ **8.** Criminal law covers disputes between persons, and between persons and their governments.

___ **9.** In most states, the same courts can grant legal or equitable remedies.

___ **10.** A citation includes the name of the judge who decided the case.

FILL-IN QUESTIONS
(Answers at the Back of the Book)

The common law system, on which the American legal system is based, involves the application of principles applied in earlier cases _____ (with similar facts/whether or not the facts are similar). This use of previous case law, or _____ (precedent/preeminent), is known as the doctrine of *stare decisis* and _____ (emphasizes a flexible/permits a predictable) resolution of cases.

MULTIPLE-CHOICE QUESTIONS
(Answers at the Back of the Book)

___ **1.** Tonya is a legal positivist. Tonya believes that

a. the law should be applied the same in all cases in all circumstances.
b. the law should reflect universal principles that are part of human nature.
c. the law should strictly follow decisions made in past cases.
d. the written law of a society at a particular time is most significant.

___ **2.** In a suit between Best Products, Inc., and Central Sales Corporation, the court applies the doctrine of *stare decisis*. This means that the court follows rules of law established by

a. all courts.
b. courts of higher rank only.
c. courts of lower rank only.
d. no courts.

___ **3.** In a suit between Delta Fishing Company and Rivermouth Trawlers, Inc., the court applies the doctrine of *stare decisis*. This requires the court to find cases that, compared to the case before it, has

a. entirely different facts.
b. no facts, only conclusions of law.
c. precisely identical facts.
d. similar facts.

___ **4.** In a suit between Retail Sales Company and Shoppers Mall, Inc., the court orders a *rescission*. This is

a. an action to cancel a contract and return the parties to the positions they held before the contract was made.
b. an award of damages.
c. an order to do or refrain from doing a particular act.
d. an order to perform what was promised.

____ **5.** In a given case, most courts may grant

    a. equitable or legal remedies, but not both.
    b. equitable remedies, legal remedies, or both.
    c. equitable remedies only.
    d. legal remedies only.

____ **6.** The U.S. Constitution takes precedence over

    a. a provision in a state constitution or statute only.
    b. a state supreme court decision only.
    c. a state constitution, statute, and court decision.
    d. none of the choices.

____ **7.** Case law includes interpretations of federal and state

    a. administrative rules and statutes only.
    b. administrative rules, statutes, and constitutions.
    c. constitutions only.
    d. none of the choices.

____ **8.** Civil law concerns

    a. disputes between persons, and between persons and their governments.
    b. only laws that define, describe, regulate, and create rights and duties.
    c. only laws that establish methods for enforcing rights.
    d. wrongs committed against society for which society demands redress.

____ **9.** Michael is a judge. To reason by analogy, Michael compares the facts in one case to

    a. an impartial third party's review.
    b. the facts in another case.
    c. the defendant's arguments.
    d. the plaintiff's hypothetical.

____ **10.** A concurring opinion, written by one of the judges who decide a case before a multi-judge panel, is

    a. an opinion that is written for the entire court.
    b. an opinion that outlines only the views of the majority.
    c. a separate opinion that agrees with the court's ruling but for different reasons.
    d. a separate opinion that does not agree with court's ruling.

SHORT ESSAY QUESTIONS

1. What is the primary function of law?

2. What is *stare decisis*? Why is it important?

GAMEPOINTS
(Answers at the Back of the Book)

1. You see a spot in the market for a video game outlet. You open "GameBox" to profit from local sales, rentals, and exchanges. Hott Games Company promises to ship a certain assortment of games and gear for your grand opening. Despite this contract, Hott does not ship as agreed, and your opener is a bust, costing you a lot of money. Into which category of the law does Hott's breach of your contract fall? Which remedies, if any, are available to you?

2.   You're a fan of the "Gods & Warriors" (GW) video game series. On the issue of GWX, you pick up your reserved copy and eagerly put it in your player. Anticipating a great game, you find instead that the graphics are two-dimensional, the response to your commands is slow, and the sound is out of synch. The game has to be rebooted repeatedly in mid-play. Which sources of the law are most likely to afford you an opportunity for relief, and why?

SPECIAL INFORMATION FOR CPA CANDIDATES

Those students planning to sit for the CPA examination will find it most helpful to learn, from the introductory material in this chapter, the terms that designate the different parties to a lawsuit. The general background provided in this chapter is, of course, helpful in understanding the specific concepts and principles set out in subsequent chapters. For that reason—and because much of that material includes information that a successful CPA candidate is expected to know—the background in this chapter is important.

Regarding general preparation for the examination—or for any exam, including ones in this course—CPA candidates and other students may find it helpful to review the significant material weekly. For concepts and principles that will be tested, some students find it helpful to make flashcards. Those cards can be reviewed weekly, together with whatever notes have been taken, and the relevant sections of this study guide.

Chapter 2
Courts and Alternative Dispute Resolution

WHAT THIS CHAPTER IS ABOUT

This chapter explains which courts have power to hear what disputes and when. The chapter also covers alternative dispute resolution, including online dispute resolution. Alternatives to litigation can be as binding to the parties as a court decree.

CHAPTER OUTLINE

I. THE JUDICIARY'S ROLE IN AMERICAN GOVERNMENT

Under the power of judicial review, the courts can decide whether the laws or actions of the executive branch and the legislative branch are constitutional.

II. BASIC JUDICIAL REQUIREMENTS

A. JURISDICTION

To hear a case, a court must have jurisdiction over (1) the defendant or the property involved and (2) the subject matter.

1. Jurisdiction over Persons or Property

A court has *in personam* (personal) jurisdiction over persons within the court's geographic area. Long arm statutes permit courts to exercise jurisdiction over persons and businesses outside that area who have *minimum contacts* within it (e.g., do business there). A court has *in rem* jurisdiction over property within its area.

2. Jurisdiction over Subject Matter

A court of general jurisdiction can decide virtually any type of case. A court's jurisdiction may be limited by the subject of a suit, the amount of money in controversy, or whether a proceeding is a trial or appeal.

3. Jurisdiction of the Federal Courts

a. Federal Questions

Any suit based on the Constitution, a treaty, or a federal law can originate in a federal court.

b. Diversity of Citizenship

Federal jurisdiction covers cases involving (1) citizens of different states, (2) a foreign government and citizens of a state or of different states, or (3) citizens of a state and citizens or subjects of a foreign government. The amount in controversy must be more than $75,000.

4. Exclusive v. Concurrent Jurisdiction

Exclusive: when cases can be tried only in federal courts or only in state courts. Concurrent: When both federal and state courts can hear a case.

9

B. JURISDICTION IN CYBERSPACE

Whether a court can compel the appearance of a party outside the geographic area of the court's jurisdiction depends on the amount of business the party transacts over the Internet with parties within the court's area ("sliding scale" test). Internationally, the minimum contacts test mentioned above generally applies.

C. VENUE

Venue is concerned with the most appropriate location for a trial.

D. STANDING TO SUE

Standing is the interest (injury or threat) that a plaintiff has in a case. A plaintiff must have standing to bring a suit, and the controversy must be justiciable (real, as opposed to hypothetical or purely academic).

III.   THE STATE AND FEDERAL COURT SYSTEMS

A. THE STATE COURT SYSTEM

1. Trial Courts

Trial courts are courts in which trials are held and testimony is taken.

2. Appellate Courts

Courts that hear appeals from trial courts look at *questions of law* (what law governs a dispute) but not *questions of fact* (what occurred in the dispute), unless a trial court's finding of fact is clearly contrary to the evidence. Decision of a state's highest court on state law is final.

B. THE FEDERAL COURT SYSTEM

1. U.S. District Courts

The federal equivalent of a state trial court of general jurisdiction. There is at least one federal district court in every state. Other federal trial courts include the U.S. Tax Court and the U.S. Bankruptcy Court.

2. U.S. Courts of Appeals

The U.S. (circuit) courts of appeals for twelve of the circuits hear appeals from the federal district courts located within their respective circuits. The court of appeals for the thirteenth circuit (the federal circuit) has national jurisdiction over certain cases.

3. United States Supreme Court

The highest level of the federal court system. The Supreme Court can review any case decided by any of the federal courts of appeals, and it has authority over some cases decided in state courts.

4. Appeals to the Supreme Court

To appeal a case to the Supreme Court, a party asks for a writ of *certiorari*. Whether the Court issues the writ is within its discretion.

IV.   ALTERNATIVE DISPUTE RESOLUTION (ADR)

A. NEGOTIATION

Parties come together informally, with or without attorneys, to try to settle or resolve their differences without involving independent third parties.

B. MEDIATION

Parties come together informally with a mediator, who is expected to propose solutions. A mediator is often an expert in a particular field.

C. ARBITRATION

An arbitrator—the third party hearing the dispute—decides the dispute. If the parties agree, the decision may be legally binding.

1. Arbitration and the Courts

Many courts require parties to try to settle their differences through arbitration before going to trial. The arbitrator's decision is not binding—if either party rejects the award, the case goes to trial.

2. The Arbitration Process

At an arbitration hearing, the parties make their arguments, present evidence, and call and examine witnesses, and the arbitrator makes a decision. The decision is called an **award,** even if no money is involved.

3. Arbitration Clauses

Disputes are often arbitrated because of an arbitration clause in a contract entered into before the dispute. Courts enforce such clauses.

4. Arbitration Statutes

Most states have statutes under which arbitration clauses are enforced. The Federal Arbitration Act (FAA) enforces arbitration clauses in contracts involving interstate commerce.

D. OTHER TYPES OF ADR

1. Early Neutral Case Evaluation

Parties select a neutral third party (generally an expert) to evaluate their positions, with no hearing and no discovery. The evaluation is a basis for negotiating a settlement.

2. Mini-trial

A private proceeding in which attorneys briefly argue each party's case. A third party indicates how a court would likely decide the issue.

3. Summary Jury Trial (SJT)

Like a mini-trial, but a jury renders a nonbinding verdict. Negotiations follow. If no settlement is reached, either side can seek a full trial.

E. PROVIDERS OF ADR SERVICES

ADR services are provided by government agencies and private organizations, such as the American Arbitration Association.

F. ONLINE DISPUTE RESOLUTION

Many Web sites offer online dispute resolution (ODR) services to help resolve small- to medium-sized business liability claims. Some cities use ODR as a means to resolve claims against them.

V. INTERNATIONAL DISPUTE RESOLUTION

To protect themselves, parties to international contracts may include special clauses, including a forum-selection clause (stating which jurisdiction will hear a dispute), a choice-of-law clause (stating which law applies), and an arbitration clause (stating that a dispute must go first to arbitration).

TRUE-FALSE QUESTIONS

(Answers at the Back of the Book)

____   **1.**   Under a long arm statute, a state court can compel someone outside the state to appear in the court.

_____ **2.** Doing substantial business in a jurisdiction over the Internet can be enough to support a court's jurisdiction over a nonresident defendant.

_____ **3.** The United States Supreme Court is the final authority for any case decided by a state court.

_____ **4.** Suits involving federal questions originate in federal district courts.

_____ **5.** Most lawsuits go to trial.

_____ **6.** In mediation, a mediator makes a decision on the matter in dispute.

_____ **7.** A party to an arbitration agreement may never be compelled to arbitrate a dispute.

_____ **8.** The jury verdict, in a summary jury trial, is binding.

_____ **9.** A major similarity between negotiation and mediation is that no third parties are involved.

_____ **10.** In binding arbitration, an arbitrator's decision is usually the final word.

FILL-IN QUESTIONS

(Answers at the Back of the Book)

Courts of original jurisdiction are _____ (trial/reviewing) courts. Courts of appellate jurisdiction are _____ (trial/reviewing) courts. Trial courts resolve disputes through determining _____ (factual issues/the law) and applying _____ (the facts to the law/ the law to the facts). Reviewing courts most commonly reverse cases on the basis of errors _____ (of law but not of fact/of fact and of law) committed by lower courts within the same system.

MULTIPLE-CHOICE QUESTIONS

(Answers at the Back of the Book)

_____ **1.** Matrix Corporation, which is based in Texas, advertises on the Web. A court in Illinois would be most likely to exercise jurisdiction over Matrix if the firm

   a. conducted substantial business with Illinois residents at its site.
   b. interacted with any Illinois resident through its Web site.
   c. only advertised passively at its Web site.
   d. all of the choices.

_____ **2.** Kim and Lou agree to dissolve their partnership but cannot agree on the division of assets and profits. They decide to mediate their dispute. The advantages of mediation include

   a. lower cost than arbitration.
   b. resolutions that benefit both sides.
   c. the speed with which a dispute can be resolved, compared to arbitration.
   d. all of the choices.

_____ **3.** Centre Hotels Corporation was incorporated in Delaware, has its main office in New Jersey, and does business in New York. Centre is subject to the jurisdiction of

   a. Delaware, New Jersey, or New York.
   b. Delaware or New Jersey only.
   c. Delaware or New York only.
   d. New Jersey or New York only.

____ 4. Saf-T Packaging, Inc., loses its suit against Medico Equipment Corporation. Saf-T's best ground for an appeal is the trial court's interpretation of

a. the conduct of the witnesses during the trial.
b. the credibility of the evidence that Top presented.
c. the dealings between the parties before the suit.
d. the law that applied to the issues in the case.

____ 5. Jon files a suit against Keyes, and loses. Jon appeals, and loses again. The United States Supreme Court is

a. required to hear the case if Jon appeals again.
b. required to hear the case if Jon lost in a federal court.
c. required to hear the case if Jon lost in a state court.
d. not required to hear the case.

____ 6. Gabriella files a suit against Huey. Before going to trial, the parties meet with their attorneys to represent them, to try to resolve the dispute without involving a third party. This is

a. arbitration.
b. litigation.
c. mediation.
d. negotiation.

____ 7. Cobb and Roberts submit their dispute to binding arbitration. A court can set aside the arbitrator's award if

a. Cobb is not satisfied with the award.
b. Roberts is not satisfied with the award.
c. the award involves at least $75,000.
d. the award violates public policy.

____ 8. Sean files a suit against Tifa. They meet, and their attorneys present the case to a jury. The jury renders a non-binding verdict, after which the parties try to reach an agreement. This is

a. a mini-trial.
b. arbitration.
c. a summary jury trial.
d. early neutral case evaluation.

____ 9. Gulf Coast Realty Company, which is based in Florida, owns commercial property in Georgia. A dispute arises over the ownership of the property with Naomi, a resident of Alabama. Naomi files a suit against Gulf Coast Realty in Georgia. In this suit, Georgia has

a. diversity jurisdiction.
b. *in personam* jurisdiction.
c. *in rem* jurisdiction.
d. no jurisdiction.

____ 10. Levonne sues Mica in a state trial court. Levonne loses the suit. If Levonne wants to appeal, the most appropriate court in which to file the appeal is

a. the state appellate court.
b. the nearest federal district court.
c. the nearest federal court of appeals.
d. the United States Supreme Court.

SHORT ESSAY QUESTIONS

1. What is jurisdiction? How does jurisdiction over a person or property differ from subject matter jurisdiction?

2. What permits a court to exercise jurisdiction based on contacts over the Internet?

GAMEPOINTS

(Answers at the Back of the Book)

1. You're playing "AniMax," a video game in which you assume the identity of "Max," a resident of New Jersey with the power to morph into vicious animals to battle a variety of super- and sub-human beings. As a Siberian tiger, you confront a series of deadly reptiles released into the wilds of New York City by "The Trainer." If you were to file a lawsuit against your opponent, in which type of court could you initiate the action?

2. You're a game designer with the Xcite Now Games Corporation. Your company moves from Colorado to Texas to take advantage of the technical talent available in the Austin area. You sell your house and relocate your family, but Xcite Now discharges you less than two months later. You file a suit against the employer for reinstatement or at least damages. You lose the trial and appeal. The appellate court affirms the decision of the trial court. You want to appeal to the United States Supreme Court. Can the Court refuse to hear the case?

SPECIAL INFORMATION FOR CPA CANDIDATES

The procedural steps in a civil trial in an American court are not specifically tested on the CPA examination. A general understanding of the legal system will prove helpful, however, to comprehending other materials that are tested on the exam.

Chapter 3
Court Procedures

WHAT THIS CHAPTER IS ABOUT

After the decision to take a dispute to court, one of the most important parts of the judicial process is the application of procedural rules in the case. The goal of this chapter is to outline what happens before, during, and after a civil trial.

CHAPTER OUTLINE

I.   PROCEDURAL RULES

The Federal Rules of Civil Procedure govern trials in federal district court. Each state has its own rules of procedure that apply in its courts, as well as to the federal courts within the state.

A. STAGES OF LITIGATION

The litigation process has three phases: pretrial, trial, and posttrial.

B. THE FIRST STEP: CONSULTING WITH AN ATTORNEY

An attorney tells a client about a lawsuit, including the probability of success, and the procedures, money, and time involved. The time and expense of litigation are important considerations when deciding what course to pursue. Another factor is the defendant's ability to pay any damages. Attorney fees can be fixed, may accrue on an hourly or a contingency basis, or may be set by a judge.

II. PRETRIAL PROCEDURES

A. THE PLEADINGS

The pleadings inform each party of the claims of the other and specify the issues in the case. They include the complaint and answer (and counterclaim and reply).

1. The Plaintiff's Complaint

Filed by the plaintiff with the clerk of the trial court (with the proper venue). The complaint contains (1) a statement alleging the facts necessary for the court to take jurisdiction, (2) a short statement of the facts necessary to show that the plaintiff is entitled to a remedy, and (3) a statement of the remedy the plaintiff is seeking.

a. Service of Process

The complaint is delivered to the defendant, with a summons. The summons tells the defendant to answer the complaint and file a copy of the answer with the court and the plaintiff within a specified time (usually twenty to thirty days).

b. Method of Service

Corporations receive service through their officers or registered agents.

c. Waiver of Service

In federal cases, service can be waived.

2. The Defendant's Response

15

a. Answer

An answer admits the allegations in the complaint or denies them and sets out any defenses.

1) Affirmative Defense

This exists when the defendant admits the truth of the complaint but raises new facts to dismiss the action (for example, the time period for raising the claim has passed).

2) Counterclaim

This is the defendant's claim against the plaintiff, who will have to answer it with a reply, which has the same characteristics as an answer.

b. Motion to Dismiss

This motion alleges that even if the facts in the complaint are true, their legal consequences are such that there is no reason to go on with the suit and no need for the defendant to present an answer.

1) Denial of the Motion

If the court denies the motion, and the defendant does not file a further pleading, a judgment will be entered for the plaintiff.

2) Grant of the Motion

If the court grants the motion, the defendant is not required to answer the complaint. If the plaintiff does not file an amended complaint, a judgment will be entered for the defendant.

c. No Response

Results in a default judgment for the plaintiff (who is awarded the relief sought in the complaint).

B. DISMISSALS AND JUDGMENTS BEFORE TRIAL

1. Motion to Dismiss

(See above.) Either party may file a motion to dismiss if they have agreed to settle the case. A court may file such a motion on its own.

2. Motion for Judgment on the Pleadings

Any party can file this motion (after the complaint, answer, and any counterclaim and reply have been filed), when no facts are disputed and only questions of law are at issue. A court may consider only those facts stated in the pleadings.

3. Motion for Summary Judgment

Any party can file this motion, if there is no disagreement about the facts and the only question is which laws apply to those facts. A court can consider evidence outside the pleadings (for example, sworn statements by witnesses).

C. DISCOVERY

1. What Discovery Is

Discovery is the process of obtaining information from the opposing party or from witnesses. Privileged material is safeguarded and only relevant matters are discoverable.

a. Discovery Rules

Discovery is allowed concerning any information that is relevant to any party's claim or defense. Of course, parties are protected from undue harassment, and privileged or confidential information is protected from disclosure.

b. Depositions

Sworn testimony, recorded by a court official. Can be used as testimony, if a witness is unavailable, or to impeach (challenge the credibility of) a party or witness who testifies differently at trial.

   c. **Interrogatories**
    A series of written questions for which written answers are prepared and signed under oath. Interrogatories are directed to the plaintiff or the defendant.

   d. **Request for Admissions**
    A written request to a party for an admission of the truth of matters relating to the trial. Any matter admitted is considered to be true.

   e. **Request for Documents, Objects, and Entry on Land**
    A written request to examine documents and other items not in the party's possession.

   f. **Request for Examinations**
    Granted when a party's physical or mental condition is in question.

   g. **Electronic Discovery**
    Relevant information stored electronically can be the subject of a discovery request.

  2. **What Discovery Does**
   Discovery allows both parties to learn as much as they can about what to expect at a trial and helps to narrow the issues so that trial time is spent on the main questions.

D. PRETRIAL CONFERENCE
After discovery, the attorneys may meet with the judge to discuss resolving the case or at least to clarify the issues and agree on such things as the number of expert witnesses or the admissibility of certain types of evidence.

E. THE RIGHT TO A JURY TRIAL
The Seventh Amendment to the U.S. Constitution guarantees the right to a jury trial for cases at law in federal courts when the amount in controversy exceeds $20. Most states have similar guarantees in their own constitutions (with a higher dollar-amount). The right to a trial by jury does not have to be exercised.

F. JURY SELECTION
Most civil matters can be heard by six-person juries. Some trials must be heard by twelve persons.

  1. *Voir Dire*
   The process by which a jury is selected. The parties' attorneys ask prospective jurors questions to determine whether any are biased or have a connection with a party or a witness.

  2. **Challenges**

   a. **Peremptory Challenge**
    Asking, without providing a reason, for an individual not to be sworn in as a juror.

   b. **Challenge for Cause**
    Asking, for a specific reason, for an individual not to be sworn in as a juror.

III. THE TRIAL

A. OPENING STATEMENTS
Each side sets out briefly his or her version of the facts and outlines the evidence that will be presented. The plaintiff goes first.

B. RULES OF EVIDENCE
These rules ensure that evidence presented during a trial is fair and reliable.

C. PRESENTATION OF EVIDENCE

  1. **Burden of Proof**
   In a civil case, a plaintiff must prove his or her case by a **preponderance of the evidence** (the claim is more likely to be true than the defendant's). Some claims (such as fraud) must be

proved by **clear and convincing evidence** (the truth of the claim is highly probable). Evidence includes the testimony of witnesses.

2. Admissible Evidence
Evidence that is relevant to the matter in question (tends to prove or disprove a fact in question or to establish that a fact or action is more probable or less probable than it would be without the evidence).

3. Inadmissible Evidence
Relevant evidence whose probative value is substantially outweighed by other considerations (the issue has been proved or disproved, or the evidence would mislead the jury, or cause the jury to decide the issue on an emotional basis). Hearsay is not admissible.

4. Examination of Witnesses

a. Plaintiff's Evidence
After the opening statements, the plaintiff calls and questions the first witness (direct examination); the defendant questions the witness (cross-examination); the plaintiff questions the witness again (redirect examination); the defendant follows (recross-examination). The plaintiff's other witnesses are then called.

b. Defendant's Evidence

1) Motion for a Directed Verdict
At the conclusion of the plaintiff's case, the defendant can ask the judge to direct a verdict for the defendant on the ground that the plaintiff presented no evidence that would justify granting the plaintiff relief. The judge grants the motion if there is insufficient evidence to raise an issue of fact.

2) Defendant's Witnesses
If the motion is denied, the defendant calls the witnesses for his or her side of the case (and there is direct, cross-, redirect, and recross-examination). At the end of the defendant's case, either side can move for a directed verdict.

c. Rebuttal
At the conclusion of the defendant's case, the plaintiff can present a rebuttal (additional evidence to refute the defendant's case).

d. Rejoinder
The defendant can refute the plaintiff's rebuttal in a rejoinder.

D. CLOSING ARGUMENTS
Each side summarizes briefly his or her version of the facts, outlines the evidence that supports his or her case, and reveals the shortcomings of the points made by the other party. The plaintiff goes first.

E. JURY INSTRUCTIONS
In a jury trial, the judge instructs (charges) the jury in the law that applies to the case. The jurors may disregard the facts as stated in the charge, but they are not free to ignore the statements of law. (A reviewing court ordinarily remands a case for a new trial if a judge misstates the law in the jury instructions.)

F. JURY VERDICT
In a jury trial, the jury specifies the factual findings and the amount of damages to be paid by the losing party. This is the verdict. After it is announced, the trial is ended, and the jurors are discharged.

IV.   POSTTRIAL MOTIONS

A. MOTION FOR A JUDGMENT IN ACCORDANCE WITH THE VERDICT
The prevailing party usually files this motion.

B. MOTION FOR A NEW TRIAL
This motion is granted if the judge believes that the jury erred but that it is not appropriate to grant a judgment for the other side (for example, the jury verdict resulted from a misapplication of the law or misunderstanding of the evidence, or there is newly discovered evidence, misconduct by the parties, or error by the judge).

C. MOTION FOR JUDGMENT *N.O.V.*
The defendant can file this motion, if he or she previously moved for a directed verdict (*n.o.v.* is from the Latin *non obstante veredicto,* "notwithstanding the verdict;" federal courts use "motion for judgment as a matter of law"). The judge will grant this motion if the jury's verdict was unreasonable and erroneous.

V. THE APPEAL

A. FILING THE APPEAL
The papers to be filed include—

1. Notice of Appeal
The appellant (the losing party—or the winning party, if that party is dissatisfied with the relief obtained) must file a notice of appeal with the clerk of the trial court within a certain period of time.

2. Record on Appeal
The appellant files in the reviewing court: (1) the pleadings, (2) a transcript of the trial and copies of the exhibits, (3) the judge's rulings on the parties' motions, (4) the arguments of counsel, (5) the jury instructions, (6) the verdict, (7) the posttrial motions, and (8) the judgment order from which the appeal is taken.

3. Brief
The appellant files with the abstract a brief, which contains (1) a short statement of the facts; (2) a statement of the issues; (3) the rulings by the trial court that the appellant contends are erroneous and prejudicial; (4) the grounds for reversal of the judgment; (5) a statement of the applicable law; and (6) arguments on the appellant's behalf, citing applicable statutes and relevant cases.

4. Reply
The appellee (respondent) may file an answering brief.

B. APPELLATE REVIEW
Appellate courts do not usually reverse findings of fact unless they are contradicted by evidence at the trial. An appellate court can **affirm, reverse,** or **modify** a trial court's decision, or **remand** the case to the trial court for further proceedings consistent with the appellate court's opinion.

C. HIGHER APPELLATE COURTS
If the reviewing court is an intermediate appellate court, the case may be appealed to the state supreme court. The state supreme court can affirm, reverse, or remand. If a federal question is involved, the case may be appealed to the United States Supreme Court, which may agree to hear it. Otherwise, the case is ended.

VI. ENFORCING THE JUDGMENT
The court can order a sheriff to seize property owned by the defendant and hold it until the defendant pays the judgment owed to the plaintiff. If the defendant fails to pay, the property can be sold at an auction and the proceeds given to the plaintiff, or the property can be transferred to the plaintiff in lieu of payment.

TRUE-FALSE QUESTIONS

(Answers at the Back of the Book)

____ 1. Pleadings consist of a complaint, an answer, and a motion to dismiss.

____ 2. In ruling on a motion for summary judgment, a court cannot consider evidence outside the pleadings.

____ 3. At a pretrial conference, the parties and the judge may set ground rules for the trial.

____ 4. An answer may admit or deny the statements or allegations in a complaint.

____ 5. Before a trial, if there are no issues of fact, a court may grant a summary judgment.

____ 6. Only a losing party may appeal to a higher court.

____ 7. To obtain documents from an opposing party in anticipation of a trial, a party uses the appeal process.

____ 8. In a jury trial, the parties have a right to conduct *voir dire*.

____ 9. In a civil case, a plaintiff must establish his or her case beyond a reasonable doubt.

____ 10. A motion for a new trial is granted if a jury verdict is the obvious result of a misapplication of the law.

FILL-IN QUESTIONS

(Answers at the Back of the Book)

A motion _____(to dismiss/for summary judgment) alleges that even if the facts in the complaint are true, their legal consequences are such that there is no reason to go on with the suit and no need for the defendant to present an answer. A motion _____ (to dismiss/for judgment on the pleadings) is properly filed after the complaint, answer, and any counterclaim and reply have been filed, when no facts are disputed and only questions of law are at issue. A motion for _____ (summary judgment/a new trial) is proper if there is no disagreement about the facts and the only question is which laws apply to those facts.

MULTIPLE-CHOICE QUESTIONS

(Answers at the Back of the Book)

____ 1. Black Steel, Inc., is considering a suit against Copper Foundry. Important considerations include

   a. alternatives to settling the dispute without going to court.
   b. the cost of going to court.
   c. the patience to follow a case through the judicial system.
   d. all of the choices.

____ 2. Digital Corporation initiates a lawsuit against Electra Company. Digital's complaint should contain

   a. a statement alleging jurisdictional facts.
   b. a statement asking for a specific remedy.
   c. a statement of facts entitling the complainant to relief.
   d. all of the choices.

____   **3.** Fast-Food Company files a suit against Giant Serving Corporation. Before the trial, Fast-Food can obtain from Giant Serving

    a. access to related documents in Giant Serving's possession.
    b. accurate information about Giant Serving's trade secrets.
    c. an admission of the truth of matters not related to the trial.
    d. all of the choices.

____   **4.** In Doug's suit against Evelyn, Evelyn may file a motion to dismiss

    a. only if the court lacks jurisdiction.
    b. only if the complaint does not state a claim for which relief can be granted.
    c. if the court lacks jurisdiction or if the complaint does not state a claim for which relief can be granted.
    d. under no circumstances.

____   **5.** Cris serves a complaint on Dru, who files a motion to dismiss. If the motion is denied

    a. Cris will be given time to file an amended complaint.
    b. Cris will have a judgment entered in her favor.
    c. Dru will be given time to file another response.
    d. Dru will have a judgment entered in his favor.

____   **6.** Jasmine and Kedric are involved in an automobile accident. Lyle is a passenger in Kedric's car. Jasmine wants to ask Lyle, as a witness, some questions concerning the accident. Lyle's answers to the questions are given in

    a. a deposition.
    b. a response to interrogatories.
    c. a response to a judge's request at a pretrial conference.
    d. none of the choices.

____   **7.** Rapido Manufacturing, Inc., loses its suit against Slowdown Products, Inc., and files an appeal. The appellate court is most likely to review the trial court's

    a. application of the law.
    b. consideration of the credibility of the evidence.
    c. findings of fact.
    d. interpretation of the conduct of the witnesses.

____   **8.** Ronny files a suit against Salazar. At the trial, after Ronny calls and questions Timor

    a. Ronny calls his second witness.
    b. Ronny questions Timor again.
    c. Salazar calls her first witness.
    d. Salazar questions Timor.

____   **9.** The jury returns a verdict against Natural Reserve Corporation (NRC), in its suit against Overflow Waste, Inc. NRC can file a motion for

    a. a directed verdict.
    b. a judgment on the pleadings.
    c. a new trial or for a judgment notwithstanding the verdict.
    d. summary judgment.

_____ **10.** ABC Sales Company wins its suit against DEF Products, Inc. After the entry of a judgment, an appeal may be filed by

a. ABC only.
b. DEF only.
c. either ABC or DEF.
d. neither ABC nor DEF.

SHORT ESSAY QUESTIONS

1. What is the primary consideration in deciding whether to settle a dispute or take the dispute to court?

2. What evidence is, and what evidence is not, admissible in a trial?

GAMEPOINTS

(Answers at the Back of the Book)

1. You're playing "Judgment Day," a video game in which your avatar acts to protect "J-Day," a video game that you launched after hours of careful, creative development. Among action that includes battles of brawn and wars of wit against Canis Major—a corporate entity intent on copying your success by copying your game—your avatar files a suit to end-run round the entity's thievery. You believe that the law and the facts are on your side. At the end of the game trial, however, the judge rules issues a judgment in Canis's favor. If you are unwilling to accept this result, what are your avatar's options?

2. In the course of legal action against Canis Major in the previous question, on an appeal, the court overturns the lower court's decision and rules in your avatar's favor, On remand there is an award of damages. How can your avatar enforce this judgment?

SPECIAL INFORMATION FOR CPA CANDIDATES

The procedural steps in a civil trial in a U.S. court are not specifically tested on the CPA examination, but it is assumed that some of these details are familiar. Also, as noted in the previous chapter, a general understanding of the legal system will prove helpful to comprehending other materials that are tested on the exam. In particular, understanding the procedural course of a trial will help in reading the case excerpts in this textbook and in understanding the course of trials and judgments in general.

Chapter 4

Constitutional Authority to Regulate Business

WHAT THIS CHAPTER IS ABOUT

This chapter emphasizes that the Constitution is the supreme law in this country and discusses some of the constitutional limits on the law. Neither Congress nor any state may pass a law in conflict with the Constitution. To sustain a federal law or action, a specific federal power must be found in the Constitution. A state has the inherent power to enact laws that have a reasonable relationship to the welfare of its citizens.

CHAPTER OUTLINE

I. THE CONSTITUTIONAL POWERS OF GOVERNMENT

A. A FEDERAL FORM OF GOVERNMENT
In a federal form of government (the United States), the states form a union and sovereign power is divided between a central authority and the states.

1. Relation between State and Federal Powers
Neither the national government nor a state government is superior to the other except within areas of exclusive authority granted under the Constitution. The courts determine the nature and scope of state and federal powers.

2. The Regulatory Powers of the States
States possess police powers (the right to regulate private activities to protect or promote the public order, health, safety, morals, and general welfare). Statutes covering almost every aspect of life have been enacted under the police powers.

3. Relations among the States

a. The Privileges and Immunities Clauses
Each state must provide the citizens of other states the same privileges and immunities it provides its own citizens. A state cannot treat nonresidents engaged in basic, essential activities differently without substantial justification.

b. The Full Faith and Credit Clause
Property and contract rights established by law in one state must be honored by other states.

B. THE SEPARATION OF THE NATIONAL GOVERNMENT'S POWERS
Under the Constitution, the legislative branch makes the laws, the executive branch enforces the laws, and the judicial branch interprets the laws. Under a checks and balances system, each branch has some power to limit the actions of the other two.

C. THE COMMERCE CLAUSE

The Constitution (Article I, Section 8) gives Congress power to regulate commerce among the states.

1. The Commerce Power Today

The national government can regulate every commercial enterprise in the United States. The United States Supreme Court has held, however, that this does not justify regulation of areas that have "nothing to do with commerce."

2. The "Dormant" Commerce Clause

When state laws impinge on interstate commerce, courts balance the state's interest in regulating a certain matter against the burden on interstate commerce. State laws that *substantially* interfere with interstate commerce violate the commerce clause.

D. THE SUPREMACY CLAUSE AND FEDERAL PREEMPTION

The Constitution (Article IV) provides that the Constitution, laws, and treaties of the United States are the supreme law of the land.

1. When Federal and State Laws Are in Direct Conflict

The state law is rendered invalid.

2. Federal Preemption

If Congress chooses to act exclusively in an area in which states have concurrent power, Congress preempts the area (the federal law takes precedence over a state law on the same subject).

E. THE TAXING AND SPENDING POWERS

1. The Taxing Power

The Constitution (Article I, Section 8) gives Congress the power to levy taxes, but Congress may not tax some states and exempt others. Any tax that is a valid revenue-raising measure will be upheld.

2. The Spending Power

The Constitution (Article I, Section 8) gives Congress the power to spend the money it raises with its taxing power. This involves policy choices, with which taxpayers may disagree. Congress can spend funds to promote any objective, so long as it does not violate the Bill of Rights.

II.   BUSINESS AND THE BILL OF RIGHTS

The first ten amendments to the Constitution protect individuals and businesses against some interference by the federal government. Under the due process clause of the Fourteenth Amendment, many rights also apply to the states. In other words, many of the limits apply to both the federal and state governments.

A. LIMITS ON FEDERAL AND STATE GOVERNMENTAL ACTIONS

Under the due process clause of the Fourteenth Amendment, many rights also apply to the states. In other words, many of the limits apply to both the federal and state governments.

B. FREEDOM OF SPEECH

The First Amendment guaranty of freedom of speech applies to the federal and state governments.

1. Reasonable Restrictions

Any form of expression is subject to reasonable restrictions. If a restriction is content neutral (not aimed at suppressing expressive conduct or its message), it will likely be upheld.

2. Protected Speech

This includes symbolic speech—nonverbal expressions, such as gestures, articles of clothing, some acts and so on. Governments can regulate the time, place, and manner of speech.

3. Speech with Limited Protection

a. Corporate Political Speech
States can prohibit corporations from using corporate funds for independent expressions of opinion about political candidates.

b. Commercial Speech
A state restriction on commercial speech, such as advertising, is valid as long as it (1) seeks to implement a substantial government interest, (2) directly advances that interest, and (3) goes no further than necessary to accomplish its objective.

4. Unprotected Speech

a. Defamatory Speech
This is speech that harms the good reputation of another. It can take the form of libel (if it is in writing) or slander (if it is oral).

b. "Fighting Words"
These are words that are likely to incite others to violence.

c. Obscene Speech
States can ban child pornography. Bans on other materials are often disputed.

d. Online Obscenity
Attempts to regulate obscene materials on the Internet have been challenged, and some have been struck as unconstitutional.

C. FREEDOM OF RELIGION
Under the First Amendment, the government may not establish a religion (the establishment clause) nor prohibit the exercise of religion (the free exercise clause).

1. The Establishment Clause
The government cannot show a preference for, or promote or inhibit one religion over another, but must accommodate all religions.

2. The Free Exercise Clause
A law that infringes on the free exercise of religion in public places must be justified by a compelling state interest. A person cannot be compelled to do something contrary to his or her religious practices unless those practices contravene public policy or public welfare.

D. SEARCHES AND SEIZURES
Under the Fourth Amendment, law enforcement and other government officers cannot conduct unreasonable searches or seizures.

1. Search Warrant Required
An officer must obtain a search warrant before searching or seizing private property. It must describe what is to be searched or seized.

a. Non-business Contexts
To obtain a warrant, the officer must convince a judge that there is **probable cause** (evidence that would convince a reasonable person a search or seizure is justified).

b. Business Premises
To obtain a warrant to inspect business premises, government inspectors must have probable cause, but the standard is different: a general and neutral enforcement plan is enough.

2. No Search Warrant Required
No warrant is required for seizures of spoiled or contaminated food or searches of businesses in highly regulated industries. The same standard sometimes applies in other contexts (such as airline screenings). General manufacturing is not considered a highly regulated industry.

E. SELF-INCRIMINATION
Under the Fifth Amendment, no person can be compelled to give testimony that might subject him or her to a criminal prosecution.

1. Sole Proprietors
Individuals who own their own businesses and have not incorporated cannot be compelled to produce their business records.

2. Partnerships and Corporations
Partnerships and corporations *can* be compelled to produce their business records, even if the records incriminate the persons who constitute the business entity.

III. DUE PROCESS AND EQUAL PROTECTION

A. DUE PROCESS
Both the Fifth and the Fourteenth Amendments provide that no person shall be deprived "of life, liberty, or property, without due process of law."

1. Procedural Due Process
Any government decision to take away the life, liberty, or property of an individual must include procedural safeguards to ensure fairness.

2. Substantive Due Process
Substantive due process focuses on the content (substance) of legislation.

a. Compelling Interest Test
A statute can restrict an individual's fundamental right (such as all First Amendment rights) only if the statute promotes a compelling or overriding governmental interest.

b. Rational Basis Test
Restrictions on rights not regarded as fundamental must relate rationally to a legitimate government purpose. Most business regulations qualify.

B. EQUAL PROTECTION
The Fourteenth Amendment prohibits a state from denying any person "the equal protection of the laws." The due process clause of the Fifth Amendment applies the equal protection clause to the federal government.

1. What Equal Protection Means
Equal protection means that the government must treat similarly situated individuals in a similar manner. If a law distinguishes among individuals, the basis for the distinction (classification) is examined.

a. Strict Scrutiny
A law that inhibits some persons' exercise of a fundamental right or a classification based on a suspect trait must be necessary to promote a compelling state interest.

b. Intermediate Scrutiny
Laws using classifications based on gender or legitimacy must be substantially related to important government objectives.

c. The "Rational Basis" Test
In matters of economic or social welfare, the classification will be considered valid if there is any conceivable rational basis on which it might relate to any legitimate government interest.

2. The Difference between Substantive Due Process and Equal Protection
A law that limits the liberty of *all* persons to do something may violate substantive due process. A law that limits the liberty of only *some* persons may violate equal protection.

IV.   PRIVACY RIGHTS

There is no specific guarantee of this right, but it is derived from guarantees in the First, Third, Fourth, Fifth, and Ninth Amendments. There are a number of federal statutes that protect privacy in certain areas, including medical information. Pretending to be someone else or to make false representations—pretexting—to obtain another's confidential phone records is a federal crime.

TRUE-FALSE QUESTIONS

(Answers at the Back of the Book)

____   1. A federal form of government is one in which a central authority holds all power.

____   2. The president can hold acts of Congress and of the courts unconstitutional.

____   3. Congress can regulate any activity that substantially affects commerce.

____   4. A state law that substantially affects interstate commerce is unconstitutional.

____   5. When there is a direct conflict between a federal law and a state law, the federal law is invalid.

____   6. Some constitutional protections apply to businesses.

____   7. The Bill of Rights protects against various types of interference by the federal government only.

____   8. Any restriction on commercial speech is unconstitutional.

____   9. Due process and equal protection are different terms for the same thing.

____ 10. A right to privacy is not specifically guaranteed in the U.S. Constitution.

FILL-IN QUESTIONS

(Answers at the Back of the Book)

Police power is possessed by the _____ (federal government/states). Police power refers to the right of the _____ (federal government/states) to regulate private activities to protect or promote the public order, health, safety, morals, and general welfare. Building codes, licensing requirements, and many other _____ (federal/state) statutes have been enacted under the police power.

MULTIPLE-CHOICE QUESTIONS

(Answers at the Back of the Book)

____   1. Of the three branches of the federal government provided by the Constitution, the branch that makes the laws is

a. the administrative branch.
b. the executive branch.
c. the judicial branch.
d. the legislative branch.

____ **2.** Tristate Business Corporation markets its products in three states. Under the commerce clause, Congress can regulate

   a. any commercial activity in the United States.
   b. only commercial activities that are in interstate commerce.
   c. only commercial activities that are local.
   d. only activities that have nothing to do with commerce.

____ **3.** Southeast Shipping Company challenges an Alabama statute, claiming that it unlawfully interferes with interstate commerce. A court will likely

   a. balance Alabama's interest in regulating the matter against the burden on interstate commerce.
   b. balance the burden on Alabama against the merit and purpose of interstate commerce.
   c. strike the statute.
   d. uphold the statute.

____ **4.** A Nevada statute bans business entities from making political contributions that individuals can make. A court would likely hold this statute to be

   a. an unconstitutional restriction of speech.
   b. constitutional under the First Amendment.
   c. justified by the need to protect individuals' rights.
   d. necessary to protect state interests.

____ **5.** An Ohio statute bans certain advertising to prevent consumers from being misled. A court would likely hold this statute to be

   a. an unconstitutional restriction of speech.
   b. constitutional under the First Amendment.
   c. justified by the need to protect individuals' rights.
   d. necessary to protect state interests.

____ **6.** Procedures used in Oklahoma and other states in making decisions to take life, liberty, or property are the focus of constitutional provisions covering

   a. equal protection.
   b. procedural due process.
   c. substantive due process.
   d. the right to privacy.

____ **7.** A Vermont statute that limits the liberty of *all* persons to engage in a certain activity may violate constitutional provisions covering

   a. equal protection.
   b. procedural due process.
   c. substantive due process.
   d. the right to privacy.

____ **8.** A Harbor City ordinance restricts most vendors from doing business in a heavily trafficked area. This might be upheld under constitutional provisions covering

   a. equal protection.
   b. procedural due process.
   c. substantive due process.
   d. the right to privacy.

___ **9.** If South Carolina enacts a statute that directly conflicts with a federal law

    a. both laws are invalid.
    b. both laws govern concurrently.
    c. South Carolina's statute takes precedence.
    d. the federal law takes precedence.

___ **10.** The First Amendment protects Nancy and others from

    a. dissemination of obscene materials and speech that harms their good reputations or violates state criminal laws.
    b. dissemination of obscene materials only.
    c. speech that harms their good reputations or violates state criminal laws only.
    d. neither dissemination of obscene materials nor speech that harms their good reputations or violates state criminal laws.

SHORT ESSAY QUESTIONS

1. What is the effect of the supremacy clause?

2. What is the significance of the commerce clause?

GAMEPOINTS
(Answers at the Back of the Book)

1. In the video game "Brainiac," each player solves puzzles and answers questions based on information displayed on the screen. The quicker and more accurate answers score more points. As the creator, developer, and seller of "Brainiac," you hope to sell millions of copies. How does the Constitution affect what you can say in the game's ads?

2. "Trader Vex" is a video game that involves commerce among virtual worlds and their inhabitants in the midst of an intergalactic conflict. The goal is to amass the most goods and money, or their equivalent, and store them in a safe location. If these worlds were the states of the United States, could the national government regulate their trade? Could the states regulate affairs within their borders? If so, and these regulations were in conflict, what would be the result?

SPECIAL INFORMATION FOR CPA CANDIDATES

In the past, most of the information covered in this chapter has not been included in the CPA examination. Those who sit for the exam are expected to know, however, that states base their regulation of professional licensing on their police powers. Test-takers will also be expected to know that the Securities Exchange Commission bases its regulation of securities on the Constitution's commerce clause.

When confronted with a multiple-choice question on the exam that covers these areas of the law, it is important to attempt to answer the question, even if it is not clear what the answer is. This is because in grading the multiple-choice portion of the exam, there is no deduction for wrong answers. Scores are based only on the total number of correct answers.

Chapter 5
Ethics and Business Decision Making

WHAT THIS CHAPTER IS ABOUT

The concepts set out in this chapter include the nature of business ethics and the relationship between ethics and business. Ultimately, the goal of this chapter is to provide you with basic tools for analyzing ethical issues in a business context.

CHAPTER OUTLINE

I. BUSINESS ETHICS

Ethics is the study of what constitutes right and wrong behavior. Ethics focuses on morality and the application of moral principles in everyday life. Business ethics focuses on what constitutes ethical behavior in the world of business. Business ethics is *not* a separate kind of ethics.

A. WHY IS BUSINESS ETHICS IMPORTANT?
An understanding of business ethics is important to the long-run viability of a business, the well being of its officers and directors, and the welfare of its employees.

B. THE MORAL MINIMUM
The minimal acceptable standard for ethical business behavior is compliance with the law. The minimal acceptable standard for ethical business behavior is compliance with the law. But the law does not, and cannot, codify all ethical requirements. An action that is legal may not be ethical. Standards in a company's policies or codes of ethics must also guide decisions.

C. "GRAY AREAS" IN THE LAW
The legality of a particular action is not always clear. Because there are many laws regulating business, it is possible to violate one without realizing it. And there are "gray areas" of the law in which it is difficult to predict how a court will rule. Sometimes, the test may be whether a consequence was "foreseeable." Or a case may involve the law in a new context. The best course is to act responsibly and in good faith.

D. SHORT-RUN PROFIT MAXIMIZATION
In the short run, unethical behavior may lead to increased profits. In the long run, such behavior can lead to costly lawsuits, settlements and other payments, and bad publicity, undercutting profits.

E. THE IMPORTANCE OF ETHICAL LEADERSHIP
Management must set and apply ethical standards to which they are committed. Employees will likely follow their example.

1. Attitude of Top Management
Ethical conduct can be furthered by not tolerating unethical behavior, setting realistic employee goals, and periodic employee review.

31

2. Behavior of Owners and Managers
Those who actively foster unethical or illegal conduct encourage it in others.

F. CREATING ETHICAL CODES OF CONDUCT
Most large corporations have codes of conduct that indicate the firm's commitment to legal compliance and to the welfare of those who are affected by corporate decisions and practices.

1. Ethics Training to Employees
Large firms may emphasize ethics in training programs.

2. The Sarbanes-Oxley Act
The Sarbanes-Oxley Act of 2002 requires firms to set up confidential systems for employees to report suspected illegal or unethical financial practices.

II. ETHICAL TRANSGRESSIONS BY FINANCIAL INSTITUTIONS

A. STOCK BUYBACKS
If the management of a company believes that its stock price is too low, or below "fair value," company funds can be used to buy shares, boosting the price. This benefits corporate executives who have stock options through which they can buy shares at a lower price and sell at the higher price. This is not illegal, but can appear to be improper.

B. EXECUTIVE DECISIONS
A business's decision to overextend itself risks failure and, with an ill-timed expenditure of company funds, can appear to be unethical. For example, American International Group's issuance of policies to guarantee financial contracts led to the company's near failure when too many of the insured events occurred. Its executives' simultaneous spending of company funds on an expensive conference added to the appearance of impropriety.

C. EXECUTIVE BONUSES
Company commissions and bonuses can be paid for conduct that ultimately results in negative consequences for the company. For example, a commission may be paid on the purchase of a risky asset—such as a loan with a significant possibility of default—even after the risk materializes. Such payments contributed to the subprime mortgage crisis of 2007.

III. APPROACHES TO ETHICAL REASONING
Ethical reasoning is the process by which an individual examines a situation according to his or her moral convictions or ethical standards. Fundamental ethical reasoning approaches include the following.

A. DUTY-BASED ETHICS

1. Religious Ethical Standards
Religious standards provide that when an act is prohibited by religious teachings, it is unethical and should not be undertaken, regardless of the consequences. Religious standards also involve compassion.

2. Kantian Ethics
Immanual Kant believed that people should be respected because they are qualitatively different from other physical objects. Kant's *categorical imperative* is that individuals should evaluate their actions in light of what would happen if everyone acted the same way.

3. The Principle of Rights
According to the principle that persons have rights (to life and liberty, for example), a key factor in determining whether a business decision is ethical is how that decision affects the rights of others, including employees, customers and society.

B. OUTCOME-BASED ETHICS: UTILITARIANISM
Utilitarianism is a belief that an action is ethical if it produces the greatest good for the greatest number. This approach is often criticized, because it tends to reduce the welfare of people to plus and minus signs on a cost-benefit worksheet.

C. CORPORATE SOCIAL RESPONSIBILITY

1. Stakeholder Approach
Under this approach, a firm's duty to its shareholders should be weighed against duties to others (employees, etc.) who may have a greater stake in a particular decision.

2. Corporate Citizenship
This theory argues that business firms should pursue goals that society deems important, because firms have so much wealth and power. Some companies publish annual corporate social responsibility—or sustainability, or citizenship—reports to highlight their activities.

3. A Way of Doing Business
Some argue that corporate promotion of social goals should be pursued as a "way of doing business" rather than as a special program. Some suggest that such activities should be relevant and significant to a firm's stakeholders.

4. Employee Recruiting and Retention
A focus on corporate social responsibility can help a firm retain its employees, especially altruistic younger workers.

IV. MAKING ETHICAL DECISIONS
The goal is to ensure that all corporate actors think more broadly about how their decisions and actions will affect other employees, shareholders, customers, and the community. Guidelines include the following.

A. THE LAW
Is the proposed action legal?

B. BUSINESS RULES AND PROCEDURES
Is the proposed action consistent with company policies and procedures?

C. SOCIAL VALUES
Is the proposed action consistent with the "spirit" of the law, even if it is not expressly prohibited?

D. AN INDIVIDUAL'S CONSCIENCE
How does the actor's or decision maker's conscience regard the plan of action? Could the plan survive in the glare of publicity?

E. PROMISES TO OTHERS
Will the action satisfy commitments that have been made to others, inside and outside the corporation?

F. HEROES
How would the actor's or decision maker's hero regard the action?

V. PRACTICAL SOLUTIONS TO CORPORATE ETHICS QUESTIONS
A practical method to investigate and solve ethics problems might include five steps—

A. INQUIRY
Who are the parties, what is the problem, and what are the relevant ethical principles?

B. DISCUSSION
What are the options for action? What are the goals to be attained?

C. DECISION
Can a consensus be reached on the options for action? If so, what is the plan?

D. JUSTIFICATION
What are the reasons for the proposed actions? Will the corporate stakeholders accept those reasons?

E. EVALUATION
Will the solution satisfy corporate, community, and individual values?

VI.   BUSINESS ETHICS ON A GLOBAL LEVEL

There are important ethical differences among, and within, nations. Some countries, for example, largely reject any role for women professionals, which may cause difficulties for American women attempting to do business in those countries.

A. THE MONITORING OF EMPLOYMENT PRACTICES OF FOREIGN SUPPLIERS

Concerns include the treatment of foreign workers who make goods imported and sold in the United States by U.S. firms. Should a U.S firm refuse to deal with certain suppliers or monitor their workplaces to make sure that the workers are not being mistreated?

B. THE FOREIGN CORRUPT PRACTICES ACT

Payments to government officials in exchange for government contracts are not unusual in some countries and are not always considered to be unethical.

1. Prohibition against the Bribery of Foreign Officials

The Foreign Corrupt Practices Act (FCPA) of 1977 prohibits U.S. businesspersons from bribing foreign officials to secure favorable contracts.

2. Accounting Requirements

Accountants may be subject to penalties for making false statements business records or accounts.

3. Penalties

Firms: fines up to $2 million. Individuals: fines up to $100,000 (cannot be paid by the company); imprisonment up to five years.

TRUE-FALSE QUESTIONS

(Answers at the Back of the Book)

_____ **1.** Ethics is the study of what constitutes right and wrong behavior.

_____ **2.** A background in business ethics is as important as knowledge of specific laws.

_____ **3.** The _minimal_ acceptable standard for ethical behavior is compliance with the law.

_____ **4.** According to utilitarianism, it does not matter how many people benefit from an act.

_____ **5.** The best course towards accomplishing legal and ethical behavior is to act responsibly and in good faith.

_____ **6.** The ethics of a particular act is always clear.

_____ **7.** To foster ethical behavior among employees, managers should apply ethical standards to which they are committed.

_____ **8.** If an act is legal, it is ethical.

_____ **9.** The roles that women play in other countries can present ethical problems for U.S. firms doing business internationally.

_____ **10.** Bribery of public officials is only an ethical issue.

FILL-IN QUESTIONS

(Answers at the Back of the Book)

_____ (Religious standards/ Kantian ethics/ The principle of rights) provide(s) that when an act is prohibited by religious teachings, it is unethical and should not be undertaken, regardless of the consequences. According to _____ (religious standards/ Kantian ethics/ the principle of rights), individuals should evaluate their actions in light of what would happen if everyone acted the same way. According to _____ (religious standards/ Kantian ethics/ the principle of rights), a key factor in determining whether a business decision is ethical is how that decision affects the rights of others.

MULTIPLE-CHOICE QUESTIONS

(Answers at the Back of the Book)

____   1. Trent is a marketing executive for Unique Appliance Company. Compared to Trent's personal choices, his actions in the business world require the application of

    a. more complex ethical standards.
    b. simpler ethical standards.
    c. the same ethical standards.
    d. no ethical standards.

____   2. Darby, an employee of Equipment Sales, Inc., takes a duty-based approach to ethics. Under this standard, Darby believes that she must

    a. achieve the greatest good for the most people.
    b. avoid unethical behavior regardless of the consequences.
    c. conform to society's standards.
    d. place Equipment Sales's interests first.

____   3. Mikayla, chief financial officer of Napoli Pasta Company, adopts religious ethical standards. These involve an element of

    a. compassion.
    b. cost-benefit analysis.
    c. discretion.
    d. utilitarianism.

____   4. Reba, an employee of Sterling Credit Bank, takes an outcome-based approach to ethics. With this approach, Reba believes that she must

    a. achieve the greatest good for the most people.
    b. avoid unethical behavior regardless of the consequences.
    c. conform to society's standards.
    d. place Sterling Credit's interests first.

____   5. Don is a manager with Engineering Aviation Systems. At a company ethics meeting, Don's most effective argument against utilitarianism is that it

    a. gives profits priority over costs.
    b. ignores the practical costs of a given set of circumstances.
    c. justifies human costs that many persons find unacceptable.
    d. requires complex cost-benefit analyses of simple situations.

___   **6.** In resolving an ethical problem, in most cases a decision by Oil Production Services, or any business firm, will have a negative effect on

    a. one group as opposed to another.
    b. the firm's competitors.
    c. the government.
    d. none of the choices.

___   **7. Based on a Sample CPA Exam Question.** Ethical standards would most likely be considered violated if Light & Sound Services, Inc., represents to Studio Film Production Company that certain services will be performed for a stated fee, but it is apparent at the time of the representation that

    a. Light & Sound cannot perform the services alone.
    b. the actual charge will be substantially higher.
    c. the actual charge will be substantially lower.
    d. the fee is a competitive bid.

___   **8.** Stefanie, the president of Thruway Trucking, Inc., tries to ensure that Thruway's actions are legal and ethical. To ensure this result, the best course of Stefanie and Thruway is to act in

    a. good faith.
    b. ignorance of the law.
    c. regard for the firm's shareholders only.
    d. their own self interest.

___   **9.** Pew, an executive with Black Spot Corporation, follows the "principle of rights" theory, under which an action may be ethical depending on how it affects

    a. the right determination under a cost-benefit analysis.
    b. the right of Pew to maintain his dignity.
    c. the right of Black Spot to make a profit.
    d. the rights of others.

___   **10.** Treasure Trove, Inc., a U.S. corporation, makes a side payment to the minister of commerce of Tuvalu (an island country in the Pacific Ocean) for a favorable business contract. In the United States, this payment would be considered

    a. illegal and unethical.
    b. illegal only.
    c. neither illegal nor unethical.
    d. unethical only.

SHORT ESSAY QUESTIONS

1. What is ethics?

2. What is the difference between legal and ethical standards? How are legal standards affected by ethical standards?

GAMEPOINTS

(Answers at the Back of the Book)

1. You're playing "Sun Ascendant," a video game in which the sun has burned out, and your goal is to accomplish certain tasks, advance to different levels, collect eight "Golden Orbs," and ultimately restart the fire in our sun. The difficulty of mastering the tasks increases at each level. At the fifth level—Mars—you become stalled. There are Web sites on which players reveal the steps to win the game. Is it ethical to consult these sites? Why or why not?

2. Still playing "Sun Ascendant," you advance no farther than Venus, the seventh level. Frustrated, you purposely damage the game disk and attempt to return it to the game outlet where you bought it. If the seller won't take it back, you vow to complain about the game and the vendor on every gamers' site on the Internet. What are the ethics in this situation? Discuss.

SPECIAL INFORMATION FOR CPA CANDIDATES

Ethics is tested in the auditing and attestation, and regulation sections of the CPA examination. The general outline provided in this chapter can serve as a jumping-off point for a more specific study of professional ethics. In the past, the CPA has covered the legal implications to CPAs, of certain business transactions, as well as the CPA's professional responsibility to clients and the accounting profession. The Foreign Corrupt Practices Act has been tested in the securities portion of the exam.

Specific topics in the area of professional responsibility can be divided into two categories: (1) the code of conduct and other professional responsibilities and (2) the law relating to CPA responsibilities. The first category can be further split into such topics as the code of professional conduct; proficiency and due care; consulting responsibilities; and tax practice responsibilities. The second category includes such topics as potential common law liability to clients and third parties, liability under federal statutes, and liability relating to working papers, privileged communications with clients, and confidentiality. These topics are covered in Chapter 48.

CUMULATIVE HYPOTHETICAL PROBLEM FOR UNIT ONE—INCLUDING CHAPTERS 1–5

(Answers at the Back of the Book)

Computer Data, Inc. (CDI), incorporated and based in California, signs a contract with Eagle Managememnt Corporation, incorporated and based in Arizona, to make and sell customized software to Eagle for resale to consumers. CDI ships defective software to Eagle, which causes losses estimated at $100,000.

____ **1.** Eagle and CDI enter into mediation. In mediation, the parties

    a. may come to an agreement by mutual consent.
    b. must accept a winner-take-all result.
    c. settle their dispute without the assistance of a third party.
    d. submit their dispute to a mediator for a legally binding decision.

____ **2.** Eagle could file a suit against CDI in

    a. Arizona only.
    b. California only.
    c. a federal court only.
    d. Arizona, California, or a federal court.

____ **3.** Eagle files a suit against CDI, seeking the amount of its losses as damages. Damages is a remedy

    a. at law.
    b. in equity.
    c. at law or in equity, depending on how the plaintiff phrases its complaint.
    d. at law or in equity, depending on whether there was any actual "damage."

____ **4.** Federal authorities file charges against CDI, alleging that the shipment of defective software violated a federal statute. CDI asks the court to exercise its power of judicial review. This means that the court can review

    a. the actions of the federal authorities and declare them excessive.
    b. the charges against CDI and declare them unfounded.
    c. the statute and declare it unconstitutional.
    d. the totality of the situation and declare it unethical.

____ **5.** Arizona enacts a statute that restricts certain kinds of advertising by Eagle and other businesses to protect consumers from being misled. A court would most likely hold this statute to be

    a. an unconstitutional restriction of speech.
    b. constitutional under the First Amendment.
    c. justified by the need to protect individual rights.
    d. necessary to protect state interests.

QUESTIONS ON THE FOCUS ON ETHICS FOR UNIT ONE— ETHICS AND THE LEGAL ENVIRONMENT OF BUSINESS

(Answers at the Back of the Book)

____ **1.** The managers of Standard Products Company (SPC) evaluate its sale of possibly defective goods in terms of its ethical obligations, if any. In other words, the managers are considering SPC's

    a. legal liability.
    b. maximum profitability.
    c. moral minimum.
    d. right or wrong behavior.

____ **2.** If SPC conducts its operations ethically, there will be a likely increase in its

    a. future profits, goodwill, and reputation.
    b. future profits only.
    c. good will only.
    d. reputation only.

____ **3.** If SPC pursues a certain course because its managers believe in the "rightness" of a cause, rather than because the action will increase corporate profits, SPC's position could arguably be

    a. illegal.
    b. maximal.
    c. socially irresponsible.
    d. unethical.

Chapter 6
Intentional Torts and Privacy

WHAT THIS CHAPTER IS ABOUT

The law of **torts** is concerned with wrongful conduct by one person that causes injury to another. *Tort* is French for "wrong." For acts that cause physical injury or that interfere with physical security and freedom of movement, tort law provides remedies, typically damages (money).

This chapter outlines intentional torts, including torts that are more specifically related to business. Negligence and strict liability, other parts of tort law, are outlined in Chapter 7.

CHAPTER OUTLINE

I. THE BASIS OF TORT LAW

Two notions serve as the basis of all torts: wrongs and compensation. Tort law recognizes that some acts are wrong because they cause injuries to others. A tort action is a *civil* action in which one person brings a personal suit against another, usually for damages.

A. THE PURPOSE OF TORT LAW
The purpose is to provide remedies for the violation of protected interests, including personal safety, property, privacy, family relations, reputation, and dignity.

B. DAMAGES AVAILABLE IN TORT ACTIONS
Compensatory damages compensate a person for actual losses. Punitive damages are intended to punish a wrongdoer and deter others from similar wrongdoing.

1. Compensatory Damages
Special damages cover quantifiable losses, such as medical expenses, lost wages, irreplaceable items, and damaged property. *General damages* are for non-monetary harm, such as pain and suffering, loss of reputation, and loss or impairment of mental or physical capacity.

2. Punitive Damages
These are awarded only when wrongful conduct is particularly egregious or reprehensible. Punitive damages are subject to the limits of the due process clause of the U.S. Constitution.

C. TORT REFORM
The tort law system has been criticized as encouraging trivial and unfounded lawsuits, excessive damage awards, and costly changes in response (such as doctors' ordering unnecessary tests).

1. Federal Level
At the federal level, the Class Action Fairness Act (CAFA) of 2005 shifted jurisdiction over cases involving large numbers of plaintiffs and large amounts of potential awards to the federal courts.

2. State Level
At the state level, about half of the states have limited damages—or banned punitive damages—especially in medical malpractice cases.

II.   INTENTIONAL TORTS AGAINST PERSONS

These torts involve acts that were intended or could be expected to bring about consequences that are the basis of the tort. A tortfeasor (one committing a tort) must intend to commit an act, the consequences of which interfere with the personal or business interests of another in a way not permitted by law.

A.   ASSAULT AND BATTERY

1.   Assault
Assault is an intentional act that creates in another person a reasonable apprehension or fear of immediate harmful or offensive contact.

2.   Battery
Battery is an intentional and harmful or offensive physical contact. Physical injury need not occur. The reasonable person standard determines whether the conduct is offensive.

3.   Compensation
A plaintiff may be compensated for emotional harm or loss of reputation resulting from a battery, as well as for physical harm.

4.   Defenses to Assault and Battery
An individual who is defending his or her life or physical well-being can claim self-defense. An individual can claim defense of others if he or she acted reasonably to protect others who were in real or apparent danger.

B.   FALSE IMPRISONMENT

1.   What False Imprisonment Is
False imprisonment is the intentional confinement or restraint of another person without justification. Confinement can be by physical barrier, physical restraint, or threat of physical force.

2.   Merchants' Privilege to Detain
In some states, a merchant is justified in delaying suspected shoplifters if there is probable cause. The detention must be done in a reasonable manner and for only a reasonable time.

C.   INTENTIONAL INFLICTION OF EMOTIONAL DISTRESS

This consists of an act that amounts to extreme and outrageous conduct resulting in severe emotional distress in another. Stalking is one way to commit it. Repeated annoyance, with threats, is another.

D.   DEFAMATION

Defamation is wrongfully hurting another's good reputation through false statements of fact. Doing it orally is slander. Doing it in writing is libel.

1.   The Publication Requirement
The statement must be published (communicated to a third party). Anyone who republishes or repeats a defamatory statement is liable.

2.   Damages for Libel
Because libelous statements are written, can be circulated widely, and are typically a result of deliberation, general damages are presumed. Showing an actual injury is not required.

3.   Damages for Slander
Because slander has a temporary quality, special damages must be proved. Proof of injury—actual economic loss—is required. The exceptions are when one falsely states that a person has a loathsome disease, has committed improprieties in a profession or trade, has committed or been imprisoned for a serious crime, or is unchaste or has engaged in serious sexual misconduct.

4.   Defenses to Defamation

a. Truth
The statement is true. It must be true in whole, not in part.

b. Privileged Speech
The statement is privileged: absolute (made in a judicial or legislative proceeding) or qualified (for example, made by one corporate director to another and was about corporate business).

c. Public Figures
The statement is about a public figure, made in a public medium, and related to a matter of general public interest. To recover damages, a public figure must prove a statement was made with actual malice (knowledge of its falsity or reckless disregard for the truth).

E. INVASION OF PRIVACY
A person must have a reasonable expectation of privacy. The invasion must be highly offensive. Four acts qualify:

1. The use of a person's name, picture, or other likeness for commercial purposes without permission. (This is appropriation—see below.)

2. Intrusion on an individual's affairs or seclusion.

3. Publication of information that places a person in a false light.

4. Public disclosure of private facts about an individual that an ordinary person would find objectionable.

F. APPROPRIATION
This is the use of one person's name or likeness by another, without permission and for the benefit of the user. An individual's right to privacy includes the right to the exclusive use of his or her identity.

1. Degree of Likeness
The use of a person's name may be enough to impose liability.

2. Right of Publicity as a Property Right
A person's financial interest in the commercial exploitation of his or her identity is protected.

G. FRAUDULENT MISREPRESENTATION
Fraud is the use of misrepresentation and deceit for personal gain. Opinions and puffery (seller's talk) are not fraud. The elements of fraudulent misrepresentation—

1. **Misrepresentation** of material facts or conditions with knowledge that they are false or with reckless disregard for the truth.

2. **Intent** to induce another to rely on the misrepresentation.

3. **Justifiable reliance** by the deceived party.

4. **Damages** suffered as a result of reliance.

5. **Causal connection** between the misrepresentation and the injury.

H. ABUSIVE OR FRIVOLOUS LITIGATION
Persons have a right not to be sued unless there is a legally just and proper reason. Torts related to abusive litigation include malicious prosecution (suing out of malice without probable cause) and abuse of process (using a legal process in an improper manner or to accomplish a purpose for which it was no t designed). The latter does not require proof of malice or a loss in a prior legal proceeding.

III.   BUSINESS TORTS
Torts involving wrongful interference with business rights generally fall into these two categories.

A. WRONGFUL INTERFERENCE WITH A CONTRACTUAL RELATIONSHIP

1. The Intent Factor
Any lawful contract can be the basis for this action. The plaintiff must prove that the defendant actually induced the breach of a contractual relationship, not merely that the defendant reaped the benefits of a broken contract.

2. Requirements
There are three elements: (1) a valid, enforceable contract between two parties, (2) a third party's knowledge of the contract, and (3) the third party's intentionally causing one of the parties to break the contract.

B. WRONGFUL INTERFERENCE WITH A BUSINESS RELATIONSHIP

1. An Example
If there are two yogurt stores in a mall, placing an employee of Store A in front of Store B to divert customers to Store A constitutes the tort of wrongful interference with a business relationship.

2. Requirements
The elements of this action are (1) an established business relationship, (2) a third party's use of predatory methods to end the relationship, and (3) damages.

C. DEFENSES TO WRONGFUL INTERFERENCE
There is no liability if the interference was permissible. Bona fide competitive behavior is a privileged interference even if it results in the breaking of a contract. The public policy that favors free competition in advertising outweighs the instability that competitive activity might cause in contractual relations.

IV. INTENTIONAL TORTS AGAINST PROPERTY

A. TRESPASS TO LAND
This occurs if a person, without permission, enters onto, above, or below the surface of another's land; causes anything to enter onto the land; or remains on the land or permits anything to remain on it.

1. Trespass Criteria, Rights, and Duties
Posted signs *expressly* establish trespass. Entering onto property to commit an illegal act *impliedly* does so. Trespassers are liable for any property damage. Owners may have a duty to post notice of any danger.

2. Defenses against Trespass to Land
Defenses against trespass include that the trespass was warranted or that the purported owner had no right to possess the land in question.

B. TRESPASS TO PERSONAL PROPERTY
This occurs when an individual unlawfully harms the personal property of another or interferes with an owner's right to exclusive possession and enjoyment. Defenses include that the interference was warranted.

C. CONVERSION
Conversion is an act depriving an owner of personal property without permission and without just cause. Conversion is the civil side of crimes related to theft. Buying stolen goods is conversion.

D. DISPARAGEMENT OF PROPERTY
Disparagement of property occurs when economically injurious falsehoods are made about another's product or ownership of property. It is a general term for torts that can be specifically referred to as slander of quality (product) or slander of title (ownership of property).

V. CYBER TORTS

Cyber torts are torts committed in cyberspace.

A. IDENTIFYING THE AUTHOR OF ONLINE DEFAMATION

To discover the identity of a person who posts a defamatory remark, a party generally must obtain a court order.

B. LIABILITY OF INTERNET SERVICE PROVIDERS

Under the Communications Decency Act (CDA) of 1996, Internet service providers (ISPs) are not liable for the defamatory remarks of those who use their services.

C. THE SPREAD OF SPAM

Spam is junk e-mail.

1. State Regulation

Most states regulate spam. Many of these require the senders to tell recipients how to opt out of future mailings. Increasingly, states are passing laws to prohibit spam.

2. The Federal CAN-SPAM Act

a. What Is Preempted

The Controlling the Assault of Non-Solicited Pornography and Marketing (CAN-SPAM) Act preempts state antispam statutes except for those that prohibit deceptive e-mailing practices.

b. What Is Permitted

The CAN-SPAM Act permits the use of unsolicited commercial e-mail.

c. What Is Prohibited

The act prohibits certain spamming activities, including the use of false return addresses and other misleading or deceptive information. Also prohibited are "dictionary attacks"—sending messages to randomly generated e-mail addresses—and "harvesting" e-mail addresses from Web sites.

3. The U.S. Safe Web Act

a. Cooperation

The Undertaking Spam, Spyware, and Fraud Enforcement with Enforcers Beyond the Borders (U.S. Safe Web) Act of 2006 allows the Federal Trade Commission (FTC) to cooperate and share information with foreign agencies investigating and prosecuting Internet fraud, spamming, and spyware.

b. Safe Harbor

Internet service providers (ISPs) have a "safe harbor"—immunity from liability—for supplying information to the FTC concerning unfair or deceptive conduct in foreign jurisdictions.

TRUE-FALSE QUESTIONS

(Answers at the Back of the Book)

____ 1. To commit an intentional tort, a person must intend the consequences of his or her act or know with substantial certainty that certain consequences will result.

____ 2. A reasonable apprehension or fear of harmful or offensive contact in the distant future is an assault.

____ 3. A defamatory statement must be communicated to a third party to be actionable.

____ 4. Puffery is fraud.

____ 5. Malicious prosecution occurs when a party files a suit out of malice, with or without probable cause.

____ 6. Conversion is wrongfully taking or retaining an individual's personal property and placing it in the service of another.

____ 7. Disparagement of property is another term for appropriation.

____ 8. Bona fide competitive behavior can constitute wrongful interference with a contractual relationship.

____ 9. An Internet service provider is not normally liable for its users' defamatory remarks.

____ 10. The government does not regulate spam.

FILL-IN QUESTIONS

(Answers at the Back of the Book)

An individual who is defending his or her life or physical wellbeing may use _____ _____ (any force/ no force/ whatever force is reasonably necessary to prevent harmful contact). This defense extends to _____ (apparent danger only/ real danger and apparent danger/ real danger only) but force cannot be used _____ _____ (after the danger has passed/ at any time/ before offensive contact occurs/ during the danger). Revenge is _____ (always/ never/ sometimes) permitted. Individuals may also use force _____ (in no other circumstances/ to defend others only/ to defend property only/ to defend others or property).

MULTIPLE-CHOICE QUESTIONS

(Answers at the Back of the Book)

____ 1. Melvin, a wholesale dairy products salesperson, follows Nadine, another wholesale dairy products salesperson, as he contacts his customers. Melvin solicits each of Nadine's customers. Melvin is most likely liable for

a. appropriation.
b. assault.
c. conversion.
d. wrongful interference with a business relationship.

____ 2. Vern, the security guard for WiFi Communications, detains Yao, a customer, whom Vern suspects of shoplifting. This is false imprisonment if

a. Vern detains Yao for an unreasonably long time.
b. Yao did not shoplift.
c. Yao has probable cause to suspect Vern of deceit.
d. Yao protests her innocence.

____ 3. Bio Box Company advertises so effectively that Product Packaging, Inc., stops doing business with Styro Cartons, Inc. Bio is liable for

a. appropriation.
b. conversion.
c. wrongful interference with a business relationship.
d. none of the choices.

____ 4. Ricardo sends a letter to Stefanie in which he falsely accuses her of embezzling from her employer Teeth & Gums Dental Clinic. This is defamation only if the letter is read by

   a. a public figure.
   b. any third person.
   c. Stefanie.
   d. Stefanie's employer.

____ 5. Internet Services, Inc. (ISI), is an Internet service provider. ISI does not create, but disseminates, a defamatory statement by Jason, its customer, about Kelly. Liability for the remark may be imposed on

   a. ISI.
   b. ISI and Jason.
   c. Jason.
   d. Kelly.

____ 6. Lonnie drives across Myra's land. This is a trespass to land only if

   a. Lonnie damages the land.
   b. Lonnie does not have Myra's permission to drive on her land.
   c. Lonnie makes disparaging remarks about Myra's land.
   d. Myra is aware of Lonnie's driving on her land.

____ 7. Online World (OW) is an Internet service provider. Publicity Now!, Inc., spams OW's customers, some of who then cancel OW's services. Publicity Now! may be liable for

   a. battery.
   b. conversion.
   c. infliction of emotional distress.
   d. trespass to personal property.

____ 8. Petra believes that Quinn is about to hit her. To prevent harmful contact, Petra hits Quinn. If Quinn sues Petra, she can most likely successfully claim

   a. defense of others.
   b. intentional infliction of emotional distress.
   c. self-defense.
   d. no defense.

____ 9. Ricky accuses Sara of fraud. Normally, the reliance giving rise to fraud is based on a statement of

   a. delusion.
   b. fact.
   c. opinion.
   d. puffery.

____ 10. Meryl shoves Ninotchka, who falls and suffers a concussion. This is an intentional tort

   a. if Meryl had a bad motive for shoving Ninotchka.
   b. if Meryl intended to shove Ninotchka.
   c. if Ninotchka was afraid of Meryl.
   d. only if Meryl intended that Ninotchka suffer a concussion.

SHORT ESSAY QUESTIONS

1. What is a *tort*?

2. What is a cyber tort, and how are tort theories being applied in cyberspace?

GAMEPOINTS

(Answers at the Back of the Book)

1. The game "StreetFight" features martial contests between two or more players, with the winner of the bouts "owning the street." You're playing the game with Tom, who's losing every bout, when he suddenly grabs the playing device from your hands, raises it as if to strike you, and says, "If I lose one more time, we're gonna take this outside." Which torts set out in this chapter, if any, might Tom have committed? Why?

2. From **gameexchange.com/free**, you download a beta version of "Pirates Cove," a game of hidden treasure and maritime battles across the Seven Seas. With that bit of software, you also unknowingly download a computer virus that soon wreaks havoc with your operating system and other files. What tort has the party who originated this virus most likely committed? What are its elements and how do they apply to these facts?

SPECIAL INFORMATION FOR CPA CANDIDATES

In the past, the CPA examination has tested knowledge of torts in such situations as the following:

- Liability for damages and injuries caused by defective products (see Chapter 22).
- Employers' liability for the torts of their employees (see Chapter 33).
- Liability for the torts of corporate officers and directors committed in the course of their corporate duties (see Chapter 40).
- Liability of auditors, accountants, and other professionals (see Chapter 48).

Chapter 7
Negligence and Strict Liability

WHAT THIS CHAPTER IS ABOUT

Negligence involves acts that depart from a reasonable standard of care, creating an unreasonable risk of harm to others. Strict liability is liability for injury imposed for reasons other than fault.

CHAPTER OUTLINE

I. NEGLIGENCE

An act that does not constitute an intentional tort because the element of intent is missing may constitute negligence.

A. THE DEFINITION OF NEGLIGENCE

1. What Negligence Is

Negligence is a party's failure to live up to a required duty of care, causing another to suffer injury. The breach of the duty must create a risk of certain harmful consequences, whether or not that was the intent of the party who committed the breach.

2. The Elements of Negligence

(1) A duty of care, (2) breach of the duty of care, (3) damage or injury as a result of the breach, and (4) the breach causes the damage or injury.

B. THE DUTY OF CARE AND ITS BREACH

A failure to comply with a duty of care may consist of an act or its omission.

1. The Reasonable Person Standard

The measure of the duty of care is the reasonable person standard (how a reasonable person would have acted in the same circumstances).

2. The Duty of Landowners

Owners, including retailers and other businesspersons, are expected to use reasonable care (guard against some risks and warn of others) to protect persons, such as customers and other invitees, coming onto their property. Obvious risks may provide an exception.

3. The Duty of Professionals

A professional's duty is consistent with his or her knowledge, skill, and intelligence, including what is reasonable for that professional. These include accountants, attorneys, and physicians.

4. Factors for Determining a Breach of the Duty of Care

These factors include the nature of the act (whether it is outrageous or commonplace), the manner in which the act is performed (cautiously versus heedlessly), and the nature of the injury (whether it is serious or slight).

5. No Duty to Rescue

Failing to rescue a stranger in peril is not a breach of a duty of care.

47

C. CAUSATION

1. Causation in Fact
The breach of the duty of care must cause the injury—that is, "but for" the wrongful act, the injury would not have occurred.

2. Proximate Cause
There must be a connection between the act and the injury strong enough to justify imposing liability. Generally, the harm or the victim of the harm must have been foreseeable in light of all of the circumstances.

D. THE INJURY REQUIREMENT AND DAMAGES
To recover damages, a party must have suffered a loss, harm, wrong, or invasion of a protected interest. Compensatory damages are the norm, but punitive damages may be awarded if a defendant was grossly negligent (acted with reckless disregard for the consequences).

II.   DEFENSES TO NEGLIGENCE
Besides the following defenses, a defendant might assert that a plaintiff failed to prove one of the required elements of negligence.

A. ASSUMPTION OF RISK
A person who voluntarily enters into a risky situation, aware of the risk, cannot recover. This does not include a risk different from or greater than the risk normally involved in the situation. This defense does not apply in emergencies or when a statute protects a class of people from harm and a member of the class is injured by the harm (such as a workers' compensation statute).

B. SUPERSEDING CAUSE
A superseding intervening force breaks the connection between the breach of the duty of care and the injury or damage. Taking a defensive action (such as swerving to avoid an oncoming car) does not break the connection. Nor does someone else's attempt to rescue the injured party.

C. CONTRIBUTORY OR COMPARATIVE NEGLIGENCE

1. Contributory Negligence
In a few states, a plaintiff cannot recover for an injury if he or she was negligent.

2. "Pure" Comparative Negligence
In most states, the plaintiff's and the defendant's negligence is compared and liability prorated.

3. Modified Comparative Fault
Under a "50 percent" rule, a plaintiff recovers nothing if he or she is determined to have been more than 50 percent at fault. Under a "51 percent" rule, a plaintiff recovers nothing if he or she is determined to have been more than half (51 percent or more) at fault.

III.   SPECIAL NEGLIGENCE DOCTRINES AND STATUTES

A. RES IPSA LOQUITUR
If negligence is very difficult to prove, a court may infer it, and the defendant must prove he or she was not negligent. This is only if the event causing the harm is one that normally does not occur in the absence of negligence and is caused by something within the defendant's control.

B. NEGLIGENCE PER SE
A person who violates a statute providing for a criminal penalty is liable when the violation causes another to be injured, if (1) the statute sets out a standard of conduct, and when, where, and of whom it is expected; (2) the injured person is in the class protected by the statute; and (3) the statute was designed to prevent the type of injury suffered.

C. **"DANGER INVITES RESCUE" DOCTRINE**
A person who endangers another is liable for injuries to third persons attempting to rescue the endangered party.

D. **SPECIAL NEGLIGENCE STATUTES**
Good Samaritan statutes protect persons (especially medical personnel) who aid others from being sued for negligence. Dram shop acts impose liability on tavern owners or bartenders for injuries caused by intoxicated persons who are served by them. A statute may impose liability on social hosts for acts of their guests.

IV. STRICT LIABILITY
Under this doctrine, liability for injury is imposed for reasons other than fault.

A. **ABNORMALLY DANGEROUS ACTIVITIES**
The basis for imposing strict liability on an abnormally dangerous activity is that the activity creates an extreme risk. Balancing the risk against the potential for harm, it is fair to ask the person engaged in the activity to pay for injury caused by that activity. Abnormally dangerous activities—

1. Involve potentially serious harm to persons or property.
2. Involve a high degree of risk that cannot be completely guarded against by the exercise of reasonable care.
3. Are activities not commonly performed in the area in which damage or an injury occurs.

B. **OTHER APPLICATIONS OF STRICT LIABILITY**
A person who keeps a dangerous animal is strictly liable for any harm inflicted by the animal. Strict liability is also a theory applicable in product liability (Chapter 22) and bailment (Chapter 49) cases.

TRUE-FALSE QUESTIONS
(Answers at the Back of the Book)

____ 1. A wrongful act need not actually be the cause of an injury for liability on a theory of negligence.

____ 2. A *reasonable* person standard determines whether allegedly negligent conduct breached a duty of care.

____ 3. Negligence requires a failure to exercise due care.

____ 4. Strict liability is liability strictly for intended results.

____ 5. Strict liability requires a failure to exercise due care.

____ 6. In many states, the plaintiff's negligence is a defense that may be raised in a negligence suit.

____ 7. Assumption of risk can be raised as a defense in a negligence suit.

____ 8. Strict liability applies only to abnormally dangerous activities.

____ 9. Good intentions are *not* a defense against a charge of negligence.

____ 10. An unforeseeable superseding event can break the connection between a wrongful act and an injury.

FILL-IN QUESTIONS

(Answers at the Back of the Book)

1. Basic defenses to _____ (negligence/intentional torts) include comparative negligence, contributory negligence, and assumption of risk.

2. One who voluntarily and knowingly enters into a risky situation normally cannot recover damages. This is the defense of _____ (contributory negligence/ assumption of risk).

3. When both parties' failure to use reasonable care combines to cause injury, in some states the injured party's recovery is prorated according to his or her own negligence. This is _____ (comparative/ contributory) negligence.

MULTIPLE-CHOICE QUESTIONS

(Answers at the Back of the Book)

____ **1.** Driving a car negligently, Rollo crashes into a phone pole. The pole falls, smashing through the roof of a house, killing Silky. But for Rollo's negligence, Silky would not have died. Regarding the death, the crash is the

    a. cause in fact.
    b. intervening cause.
    c. proximate cause.
    d. superseding cause.

____ **2.** Hortense, a salesperson for Idling Corporation, causes a car accident while on business. Hortense and Idling are liable to

    a. all those who were injured.
    b. only those who were uninsured.
    c. only those whose injuries could have been reasonably foreseen.
    d. only those with whom Hortense was doing business.

____ **3.** Resource Mining Company (RMC) engages in blasting operations. This is subject to strict liability because

    a. blasting is a dangerous activity.
    b. blasting is a negligent activity.
    c. mining can be done without blasting.
    d. RMC is a mining company.

____ **4.** To protect its customers and other business invitees, Grocers Market must warn them of

    a. all dangers.
    b. hidden dangers.
    c. obvious dangers.
    d. no dangers.

____ **5.** Major Construction, Inc. (MCI), uses dynamite in its projects. Neil stores household chemicals in the garage. Most likely liable for any injury caused by an abnormally dangerous activity is

    a. MCI and Neil.
    b. MCI only.
    c. Neil only.
    d. neither MCI nor Neil.

____ 6. Curt owns Destruction Corporation (DC), a demolition company. A demolition by a DC crew injures Elise, a passerby. Under the doctrine of strict liability, Curt must pay for Elise's injury

    a. only if the injury was not reasonably foreseeable.
    b. only if the injury was reasonably foreseeable.
    c. only if the crew was at fault.
    d. whether or not the crew was at fault.

____ 7. Stefano, an engineer, supervises the construction of a new house. When the house collapses due to faulty construction, the injured parties sue Stefano. As a professional, he is held to the same standard of care as

    a. ordinary persons.
    b. other engineers.
    c. other professionals, including accountants, attorneys, and physicians.
    d. the injured parties.

____ 8. Gail hires Harry to design an office building. Dissatisfied with the look of the building, Gail sues Harry for negligence. Harry can successfully defend against the suit by showing that he

    a. designed the building as attractively as any ordinary person could.
    b. designed the building as attractively as Gail could.
    c. did not injure Gail.
    d. does not know much about art.

____ 9. Lara enters Marathon, an athletic competition. Regarding the risk of injury, Lara assumes

    a. all of the risks normally associated with the event.
    b. all of the risks different than those normally associated with the event.
    c. only the risks greater than those normally associated with the event.
    d. only the risks lesser than those normally associated with the event.

____ 10. Nina is injured in a truck accident and sues Owen, alleging negligence. Owen claims that Nina was driving carelessly. Comparative negligence may reduce Nina's recovery

    a. even if Nina was only slightly at fault.
    b. only if Nina was as equally at fault as Owen.
    c. only if Nina was less at fault than Owen.
    d. only if Nina was more at fault than Owen.

SHORT ESSAY QUESTIONS

1. What is meant by strict liability? In what circumstances is strict liability applied?

2. What are the elements of a cause of action based on negligence?

GAMEPOINTS

(Answers at the Back of the Book)

1. "RaceCar2010" is a video game that features races in virtual locations throughout the United States—in the clouds above Hawaii, down the slopes of the Rockies, along the length of the Appalachian Trail, among others. In each contest, your opponent drives too fast, smashing into the other racing vehicles, including yours. What tort is most likely being committed? What is your opponent's best defense?

2. You're playing "Prince of Peril," a video game in which your avatar travels the universe, engaging nasty villains and taking on fantastic risks at incredible odds to "honor the imperial duty of care." In one

encounter, your avatar leaps from his space cruiser to battle a pair of Saturnian Neanderthals. The cruiser collides with an orbiting space station that veers off course, enters the Earth's atmosphere, bursts into flames, and crashes into an oil refinery in Louisiana. The earth-shaking concussion causes a nearby silo to collapse onto Twyla, a bystander. Applying the principles set out in this chapter, can Twyla recover from the Prince of Peril?

SPECIAL INFORMATION FOR CPA CANDIDATES

The CPA examination has traditionally tested on negligence as one of three kinds of product liability actions (see Chapter 22).

Chapter 8
Intellectual Property and Internet Law

WHAT THIS CHAPTER IS ABOUT

Intellectual property consists of the products of intellectual, creative processes. The law of trademarks, patents, copyrights, and related concepts protect many of these products (such as inventions, books, software, movies, and songs). This chapter outlines these laws, including their application in cyberspace.

CHAPTER OUTLINE

I. TRADEMARKS AND RELATED PROPERTY

A. STATUTORY PROTECTION OF TRADEMARKS
The Lanham Act protects trademarks at the federal level. Many states also have statutes that protect trademarks.

1. What Is a Trademark?
A distinctive mark, motto, device, or emblem that a manufacturer stamps, prints, or otherwise affixes to the goods it produces to distinguish them from the goods of other manufacturers.

2. The Federal Trademark Dilution Act of 1995
Prohibits dilution (unauthorized use of marks on goods or services, even if they do not compete directly with products whose marks are copied).

B. TRADEMARK REGISTRATION
A trademark may be registered with a state or the federal government. Trademarks do not need to be registered to be protected.

1. Requirements for Federal Registration
A trademark may be filed with the U.S. Patent and Trademark Office on the basis of (1) use or (2) the intent to use the mark within six months (which may be extended to thirty months).

2. Renewal of Federal Registration
Between the fifth and sixth years and then every ten years (twenty years for marks registered before 1990).

C. TRADEMARK INFRINGEMENT
This occurs when a trademark is copied to a substantial degree or used in its entirety by another.

D. DISTINCTIVENESS OF THE MARK
The extent to which the law protects a trademark is normally determined by how distinctive it is, with the purpose of reducing the likelihood that consumers will be confused by similar marks.

1. **Strong Marks**
Fanciful, arbitrary, or suggestive marks are considered most distinctive.

2. **Descriptive Terms, Geographic Terms, and Personal Names**
Descriptive terms, geographic terms, and personal names are not inherently distinctive and are not protected until they acquire a secondary meaning (which means that customers associate the mark with the source of a product)

3. **Generic Terms**
Terms such as *bicycle* or *computer* receive no protection, even if they acquire secondary meaning.

E. **SERVICE, CERTIFICATION, AND COLLECTIVE MARKS**
Laws that apply to trademarks normally also apply to—

1. **Service Marks**
Used to distinguish the services of one person or company from those of another. Registered in the same manner as trademarks.

2. **Certification Marks**
Used by one or more persons, other than the owner, to certify the region, materials, mode of manufacture, quality, or accuracy of the owner's goods or services.

3. **Collective Marks**
Certification marks used by members of a cooperative, association, or other organization.

F. **TRADE DRESS**
Trade dress is the image and appearance of a product, and has the same protection as trademarks.

G. **COUNTERFEIT GOODS**
Counterfeit goods copy or imitate trademarked goods but are not genuine.

1. **The Stop Counterfeiting in Manufactured Goods Act**
This act makes it a crime to intentionally traffic in counterfeit goods or services, or use a counterfeit mark on or in connection with goods or services. The act covers counterfeit labels, stickers, packaging, and similar items, whether or not they are attached to goods.

2. **Counterfeiting Penalties**
These include fines of up to $2 million and imprisonment of up to ten years (more for repeat offenders). Forfeiture of counterfeit products and the payment of restitution to a trademark holder or other victim can be imposed.

H. **TRADE NAMES**
These indicate a business's name. Trade names cannot be registered with the federal government but may be protected under the common law if they are used as trademarks or service marks.

II.   CYBER MARKS

A. **DOMAIN NAME REGISTRATION**
The Internet Corporation for Assigned Names and Numbers (ICANN) oversees the Internet domain registration system and facilitates the resolution of domain name disputes. To protect genuine marks, businesses sometimes register thousands of misspelled names.

B. **ANTICYBERSQUATTING LEGISLATION**
Disputes over domain names often involve cybersquatting or typosquatting. The Anticybersquatting Consumer Reform Act (ACRA) of 1999 amended the Lanham Act to make cybersquatting clearly illegal. Damages may be awarded.

1. **Cybersquatting**
   Cybersquatting occurs when a person registers a domain name that is the same as, or confusingly similar to, another's mark and offers to sell it to the authentic mark's owner.

2. **Typosquatting**
   This occurs when a person registers a misspelling of a mark that he or she does not own.

C. **META TAGS**
   Meta tags are words in a Web site's key-word field that determine the site's appearance in search engine results. Using others' marks as tags without permission constitutes trademark infringement.

D. **DILUTION IN THE ONLINE WORLD**
   Using a mark, without permission, in a way that diminishes its distinctive quality is dilution. Tech-related cases have concerned the use of marks as domain names and spamming under another's logo.

E. **LICENSING**
   Licensing is permitting a party to use a mark, copyright, patent, or trade secret for certain purposes, which may need to include the maintenance of quality to protect the licensor's rights. Use for other purposes is a breach of the license agreement.

III. PATENTS

A. **WHAT A PATENT IS**
   A grant from the federal government that conveys and secures to an inventor the exclusive right to make, use, and sell an invention for a period of twenty years (fourteen years for a design).

B. **SEARCHABLE PATENT DATABASES**
   Searchable patent databases are important to a business to inventory its assets or to study trends in an industry or a technology, which may help to develop a business strategy or evaluate a job applicant.

C. **WHAT IS PATENTABLE?**
   An invention, discovery, or design must be genuine, novel, useful, and not obvious in light of the technology of the time to be patented. A patent is given to the first person to invent a product, not to the first person to file for a patent.

1. **Patents for Software**
   The basis for software is often a mathematical equation or formula, which is not patentable, but a patent can be obtained for a process that incorporates a computer program.

2. **Patents for Business Processes**
   Business processes are patentable (laws of nature, natural phenomena, and abstract ideas are not).

D. **PATENT INFRINGEMENT**
   Making, using, or selling another's patented design, product, or process without the patent owner's permission is infringement. (Making and selling a patented product in another country is not.)

E. **REMEDIES FOR PATENT INFRINGEMENT**
   A patent owner may obtain an injunction, damages, an order for destruction of all infringing copies, attorneys' fees, and court costs.

IV. COPYRIGHTS

A. **WHAT A COPYRIGHT IS**
   An intangible right granted by statute to the author or originator of certain literary or artistic productions. Protection is automatic; registration is not required.

B. COPYRIGHT PROTECTION

Protection lasts for the life of the author plus 70 years. Copyrights owned by publishing houses expire 95 years from the date of publication or 120 years from the date of creation, whichever is first. For works by more than one author, copyright expires 70 years after the death of the last surviving author.

C. WHAT IS PROTECTED EXPRESSION?

To be protected, under Section 102 of the Copyright Act a work must meet these requirements—

1. Fit a Certain Category

It must be a (1) literary work; (2) musical work; (3) dramatic work; (4) pantomime or choreographic work; (5) pictorial, graphic, or sculptural work; (6) film or other audiovisual work; or (7) a sound recording. The Copyright Act also protects computer software and architectural plans.

2. Be Fixed in a Durable Medium

From which it can be perceived, reproduced, or communicated.

3. Be Original

A compilation of facts (formed by the collection and assembling of preexisting materials of data) is copyrightable if it is original.

D. WHAT IS NOT PROTECTED

Ideas, facts, and related concepts are not protected. If an idea and an expression cannot be separated, the expression cannot be copyrighted.

E. COPYRIGHT INFRINGEMENT

A copyright is infringed if a work is copied without the copyright holder's permission. A copy does not have to be exactly the same as the original—copying a substantial part of the original is enough.

1. Penalties

Actual damages (based on the harm to the copyright holder); damages under the Copyright Act, not to exceed $150,000; and criminal proceedings (which may result in fines or imprisonment).

2. Exception—Fair Use Doctrine

The Copyright Act permits the fair use of a work for purposes such as criticism, news reporting, teaching (including multiple copies for classroom use), scholarship, or research. Factors in determining whether a use is infringement include the effect of the use on the market for the work.

F. COPYRIGHT PROTECTION FOR SOFTWARE

The Computer Software Copyright Act of 1980 protects the binary object code (the part of a software program readable only by computer); the source code (the part of a program readable by people); and the program structure, sequence, and organization. Protection does not extend to a program's "look and feel"—the general appearance, command structure, video images, menus, windows, and other displays.

V. COPYRIGHTS IN DIGITAL INFORMATION

Copyright law requires the copyright holder's permission to sell a "copy" of a work. This is important in cyberspace because the nature of the Internet means that data is "copied" before being transferred online—loading a file or program into a computer's random access memory (RAM) is making a "copy."

A. PIRACY, PROFIT, AND CRIME

It is a crime to exchange pirated, copied, copyrighted materials, even if no profit is realized from the exchange, and to copy works for personal use without the owners' authorization.

B. THE DIGITAL MILLENNIUM COPYRIGHT ACT OF 1998
This act imposes penalties on anyone who circumvents encryption software or other technological anti-piracy protection. Also prohibits the manufacture, import, sale, or distribution of devices or services for circumvention. ISPs are not liable for their customers' violations.

C. MP3 AND FILE-SHARING TECHNOLOGY
MP3 file compression and music file sharing occur over the Internet through peer-to-peer (P2P) networking. Doing this without the permission of the owner of the music's copyright is infringement.

VI. TRADE SECRETS

A. WHAT A TRADE SECRET IS
Trade secrets include customer lists, formulas, plans, research and development, pricing information, marketing techniques, production techniques, and generally anything that provides an opportunity to obtain an advantage over competitors who do not know or use it.

B. TRADE SECRET PROTECTION
Protection of trade secrets extends both to ideas and their expression. Liability extends to those who misappropriate trade secrets by any means. Trade secret theft is a violation of the common law and most states' statutes (based on the Uniform Trade Secrets Act), and a federal crime (under the Economic Espionage Act of 1996).

C. TRADE SECRETS IN CYBERSPACE
The nature of technology (especially e-mail) undercuts a firm's ability to protect its confidential information, including trade secrets.

VII. INTERNATIONAL PROTECTION

A. THE BERNE CONVENTION
The Berne Convention is an international copyright treaty.

1. For Citizens of Countries That Have Signed the Berne Convention
If, for example, an American writes a book, the copyright in the book is recognized by every country that signed the convention.

2. For Citizens of Other Countries
If a citizen of a country that has not signed the convention publishes a book first in a country that has signed, all other countries that have signed recognize that author's copyright.

B. THE TRIPS AGREEMENT
Trade-Related Aspects of Intellectual Property Rights (TRIPS) Agreement is part of the agreement creating the World Trade Organization (WTO). Each member nation must not discriminate (in administration, regulation, or adjudication of intellectual property rights) against the rights' owners.

C. THE MADRID PROTOCOL
Under this treaty, a U.S. company wishing to register its trademark abroad can submit a single application and designate other member countries in which they would like to register the mark.

TRUE-FALSE QUESTIONS

(Answers at the Back of the Book)

____ 1. To obtain a patent, an applicant must show that an invention is genuine, novel, useful, and not obvious in light of current technology.

____ 2. To obtain a copyright, an author must show that a work is genuine, novel, useful, and not a copy of a current copyrighted work.

____   **3.**   In determining whether the use of a copyrighted work is infringement under the fair use doctrine, one factor is the effect of that use on the market for the copyrighted work.

____   **4.**   A personal name is protected under trademark law if it acquires a secondary meaning.

____   **5.**   A formula for a chemical compound is not a trade secret.

____   **6.**   A trade name, like a trademark, can be registered with the federal government.

____   **7.**   A copy must be exactly the same as an original work to infringe on its copyright.

____   **8.**   Only the *intentional* use of another's trademark is trademark infringement.

____   **9.**   Using another's trademark in a domain name without permission violates federal law.

____   **10.**   Trademark dilution requires proof that consumers are likely to be confused by the unauthorized use of the mark.

FILL-IN QUESTIONS

(Answers at the Back of the Book)

Copyright protection is automatic for the life of the author of a work plus _____ (70/95/120) years. Copyrights owned by publishing houses expire _____ (70/95/120) years from the date of the publication of a work or _____ (70/95/120) years from the date of its creation, whichever is first. For works by more than one author, a copyright expires _____ (70/95/120) years after the death of the last surviving author.

MULTIPLE-CHOICE QUESTIONS

(Answers at the Back of the Book)

____   **1.**   Johnnycakes, Inc., uses Pattycake Corporation's patented formula in Johnnycakes's recipe for a similar product, without Pattycake's permission. This is

a. copyright infringement.
b. patent infringement.
c. trademark infringement.
d. none of the choices.

____   **2.**   Omega, Inc., uses a trademark on its products that no one, including Omega, has registered with the government. Under federal trademark law, Omega

a. can register the mark for protection.
b. cannot register a mark that has been used in commerce.
c. is guilty of trademark infringement.
d. must postpone registration until the mark has been out of use for three years.

____   **3.**   Tony owns Tonio's, a pub in a small town in Iowa. Universal Dining, Inc., opens a chain of pizza places in California called "Tonio's" and, without Tony's consent, uses "toniosincalifornia" as part of the URL for the chain's Web site. This is

a. copyright infringement.
b. cybersquatting.
c. trademark dilution.
d. none of the choices.

___ **4.** The graphics used in "Grave Raiders," a computer game, are protected by

   a. copyright law.
   b. patent law.
   c. trademark law.
   d. trade secrets law.

___ **5.** Production techniques used to make "Grave Raiders," a computer game, are protected by

   a. copyright law.
   b. patent law.
   c. trademark law.
   d. trade secrets law.

___ **6.** Tech Corporation uses USA, Inc.'s trademark in Tech's ads without USA's permission. This is

   a. copyright infringement.
   b. patent infringement.
   c. trademark infringement.
   d. none of the choices.

___ **7.** Clothes made by workers who are members of the Clothes Makers Union are sold with tags that identify this fact. This is

   a. a certification mark.
   b. a collective mark.
   c. a service mark.
   d. trade dress.

___ **8.** Isabel invents a new type of light bulb and applies for a patent. If Isabel is granted a patent, the invention will be protected

   a. for 10 years.
   b. for 20 years.
   c. for the life of the inventor plus 70 years.
   d. forever.

___ **9.** Data Corporation created and sells "Economix," financial computer software. Data's copyright in Economix is best protected under

   a. the Berne Convention.
   b. the Madrid Protocol.
   c. the Paris Convention.
   d. the TRIPS Agreement.

___ **10.** National Media, Inc. (NMI), publishes *Opinion* magazine, which contains an article by Paula. Without her permission, NMI puts the article into an online database. This is

   a. copyright infringement.
   b. patent infringement.
   c. trademark infringement.
   d. none of the choices.

SHORT ESSAY QUESTIONS

1. What does a copyright protect?

2. What is a trade secret and how is it protected?

GAMEPOINTS

(Answers at the Back of the Book)

1. You create a new video game-playing device that you call "The Gem." Its revolutionary twist on other game devices is that The Gem can respond to a player's eye movements, making a handheld joystick or similar control almost unnecessary. At this point, is The Gem protected by trademark, patent, or copyright law? If not, how could this protection be obtained?

2. For The Gem, you write and develop "Rock Roles," a game that allows players to perform in a virtual rock band. Can "Rock Roles" be marketed with a thousand songs uploaded without the copyright owners' permission? Would this be "fair use"? Explain.

SPECIAL INFORMATION FOR CPA CANDIDATES

The material in this chapter has not traditionally been part of the CPA examination.

When studying for the CPA exam, many students integrate their review of business law topics with their review of other topics that make up distinct subject matter on the exam. For example, when reviewing the law behind business organizations, it can be most helpful to review the accounting and reporting details behind businesses' financial statements. Which topics to integrate and how much time to spend on each depends in part on each student's knowledge and understanding of the individual topics, as well as the emphasis that should be placed on a topic because of its importance for the exam.

Chapter 9
Criminal Law and Cyber Crime

WHAT THIS CHAPTER IS ABOUT

This chapter defines what makes an act a crime, describes crimes that affect business (including cyber crimes), lists defenses to crimes, and outlines criminal procedure. Sanctions for crimes are different from those for torts or breaches of contract. Another difference between civil and criminal law is that an individual can bring a civil suit, but only the government—through a district attorney, for example— can prosecute a criminal.

CHAPTER OUTLINE

I. CIVIL LAW AND CRIMINAL LAW

A. CIVIL LAW
Civil law consists of the duties that exist between persons or between citizens and their governments, excluding the duty not to commit crimes.

B. CRIMINAL LAW
A crime is a wrong against society proclaimed in a statute and, if committed, punishable by society through fines, imprisonment, or death. Crimes are offenses against society as a whole (some torts are also crimes) and are prosecuted by public officials, not victims. In a criminal trial, the state must prove its case beyond a reasonable doubt.

C. CLASSIFICATION OF CRIMES
Felonies are serious crimes punishable by death or by imprisonment in a federal or state penitentiary for more than a year. A crime that is not a felony is a misdemeanor—punishable by a fine or by confinement (in a local jail) for up to a year. Petty offenses are minor misdemeanors.

II. CRIMINAL LIABILITY
Two elements must exist for a person to be convicted of a crime—

A. THE CRIMINAL ACT (*ACTUS REUS*)
A criminal statute prohibits certain behavior—an act of commission (doing something) or an act of omission (not doing something that is a legal duty).

B. STATE OF MIND (INTENT TO COMMIT A CRIME, OR *MENS REA*)
The mental state required to establish criminal guilt depends on the crime.

1. Criminal Negligence or Recklessness
Criminal recklessness is conscious disregard for a substantial and justifiable risk. Criminal negligence is a deviation from the standard of care that a reasonable person would use under the same circumstances—an unjustified, substantial, foreseeable risk that results in harm.

2. Strict Liability and Overcriminalization
Strict liability crimes do not require a wrongful mental state. These include environmental crimes, drug offenses, and other violations affecting public health, safety, and welfare. Critics

contend that strict liability is the wrong theory to apply to social problems such as drug abuse.

C. CORPORATE CRIMINAL LIABILITY

1. Liability of the Corporate Entity

A corporation is liable for crimes committed by its agents and employees within the course and scope of employment if the corporation authorized or could have prevented the crime. A corporation may also be liable for failing to perform a duty imposed by law.

2. Liability of Corporate Officers and Directors

Directors and officers are personally liable for crimes they commit and may be liable for the actions of employees under their supervision.

III. TYPES OF CRIMES

A. VIOLENT CRIME

These include murder, rape, assault and battery (see Chapter 6), and *robbery* (forcefully and unlawfully taking personal property from another). They are classified by degree, depending on intent, use of weapons, and the victim's suffering.

B. PROPERTY CRIME

Robbery could also be in this category.

1. Burglary

Burglary is the unlawful entry into a building with the intent to commit a felony.

2. Larceny

Wrongfully taking and carrying away another's personal property with the intent of depriving the owner permanently of the property (without force or intimidation, which are elements of robbery).

a. Property

The definition of property includes computer programs, computer time, trade secrets, cellular phone numbers, long-distance phone time, Internet service, and natural gas.

b. Grand Larceny and Petit Larceny

In some states, grand larceny is a felony and petit larceny a misdemeanor. The difference depends on the value of the property taken.

3. Arson

Arson is the willful and malicious burning of a building (and in some states, personal property) owned by another. Every state has a statute that covers burning a building to collect insurance.

4. Receiving Stolen Goods

The recipient need not know the identity of the true owner of the goods.

5. Forgery

Forgery is fraudulently making or altering any writing in a way that changes the legal rights and liabilities of another is forgery.

6. Obtaining Goods by False Pretenses

This includes, for example, buying goods with a check written on an account with insufficient funds.

C. PUBLIC ORDER CRIME

Examples: public drunkenness, prostitution, gambling, and illegal drug use.

D. WHITE-COLLAR CRIME

1. **Embezzlement**
   Embezzlement is fraudulently appropriating another's property or money by one who has been entrusted with it (without force or intimidation). Withholding taxes collected from employees can constitute embezzlement. Intending to return embezzled property is not a defense.

2. **Mail and Wire Fraud**

   a. **The Crime**
      It is a federal crime to (1) mail or cause someone else to mail something written, printed, or photocopied for the purpose of executing (2) a scheme to defraud (even if no one is defrauded). Also a crime to use wire, radio, or television transmissions to defraud.

   b. **The Punishment**
      Fine of up to $1,000, imprisonment for up to five years, or both. If the violation affects a financial institution, the fine may be up to $1 million, the imprisonment up to thirty years, or both.

3. **Bribery**

   a. **Bribery of Public Officials**
      This is attempting to influence a public official to act in a way that serves a private interest by offering the official a bribe. The crime is committed when the bribe (anything the recipient considers valuable) is offered.

   b. **Commercial Bribery**
      Commercial bribery is attempting, by a bribe, to obtain proprietary information, cover up an inferior product, or secure new business is commercial bribery.

   c. **Bribery of Foreign Officials**
      A crime occurs when attempting to bribe foreign officials to obtain business contracts. The Foreign Corrupt Practices Act of 1977 (see Chapter 5) makes this a crime.

4. **Bankruptcy Fraud**
   Filing a false claim against a debtor; fraudulently transferring assets to favored parties; or fraudulently concealing property before or after a petition for bankruptcy is filed.

5. **Insider Trading**
   Using inside information (information not available to the general public) about a publicly traded corporation to profit from the purchase or sale of the corporation's securities (see Chapter 41).

6. **Theft of Intellectual Property**
   It is a federal crime to steal trade secrets, or to knowingly buy or possess another's stolen secrets. Penalties include up to ten years' imprisonment, fines up to $500,000 (individual) or $5 million (corporation), and forfeiture of property. Piracy—the unauthorized copying of intellectual property—is also a federal crime, punishable by five years' imprisonment and $500,000 or more.

E. **ORGANIZED CRIME**

1. **Money Laundering**
   Transferring the proceeds of crime through legitimate businesses. Financial institutions must report transactions of more than $10,000.

2. **The Racketeer Influenced and Corrupt Organizations Act (RICO) of 1970**
   RICO incorporates by reference twenty-six federal crimes and nine state felonies. Two offenses constitute "racketeering activity."

a. Activities Prohibited by RICO

(1) Use income from racketeering to buy an interest in an enterprise, (2) acquire or maintain such an interest through racketeering activity' (3) conduct or participate in an enterprise through racketeering activity, or 4) conspire to do any of the above.

b. Criminal Liability

RICO can be used to attack white-collar crime. Penalties include fines of up to $25,000 per violation, imprisonment for up to 20 years, or both.

c. Civil Liability

Civil penalties include divestiture of a defendant's interest in a business or dissolution of the business. Private individuals can recover treble damages, plus attorneys' fees.

IV. DEFENSES TO CRIMINAL LIABILITY

A. JUSTIFIABLE USE OF FORCE

People can use as much nondeadly force as necessary to protect themselves, their dwellings, or other property or to prevent a crime. Deadly force can be used in self-defense if there is a reasonable belief that imminent death or serious bodily harm will otherwise result, if the attacker is using unlawful force, and if the defender did not provoke the attack.

B. NECESSITY

A defendant may be relieved of liability if his or her criminal act was necessary to prevent an even greater harm.

C. INSANITY

1. The Model Penal Code Test

Most federal courts and some states use this test: a person is not responsible for criminal conduct if at the time, as a result of mental disease or defect, the person lacks substantial capacity either to appreciate the wrongfulness of the conduct or to conform his or her conduct to the law.

2. The *M'Naughten* Test

Some states use this test: a person is not responsible if at the time of the offense, he or she did not know the nature and quality of the act or did not know that the act was wrong.

3. The Irresistible Impulse Test

Some states use this test: a person operating under an irresistible impulse may know an act is wrong but cannot refrain from doing it.

D. MISTAKE

1. Mistake of Fact

This is a defense if it negates the mental state necessary to commit a crime.

2. Mistake of Law

A person not knowing a law was broken may have a defense if (1) the law was not published or reasonably made known to the public or (2) the person relied on an official statement of the law that was wrong.

E. DURESS

Duress occurs when a threat induces a person to do something that he or she would not otherwise do. Duress can be a defense if the threat is of a danger that is immediate and inescapable.

F. ENTRAPMENT

This occurs when a law enforcement agent suggests that a crime be committed, pressures or induces an individual to commit it, and arrests the individual for it.

G. STATUTES OF LIMITATIONS
A statute of limitation provides that the state has only a certain amount of time to prosecute a crime. Most statutes of limitations do not apply to murder.

H. IMMUNITY
A state can grant immunity from prosecution or agree to prosecute for a less serious offense in exchange for information. This is often part of a plea bargain between the defendant and the prosecutor.

V. CRIMINAL PROCEDURES

A. CONSTITUTIONAL SAFEGUARDS
Most of these safeguards apply not only in federal but also in state courts by virtue of the due process clause of the Fourteenth Amendment.

1. **Fourth Amendment**
   This amendment provides protection from unreasonable searches and seizures. No warrants for a search or an arrest can be issued without probable cause.

2. **Fifth Amendment**
   No one can be deprived of "life, liberty, or property without due process of law." No one can be tried twice (double jeopardy) for the same offense. No one can be required to incriminate themselves.

3. **Sixth Amendment**
   This amendment guarantees a speedy trial, trial by jury, a public trial, the right to confront witnesses, and the right to a lawyer in some proceedings.

4. **Eighth Amendment**
   This amendment prohibits excessive bail and fines, and cruel and unusual punishment.

B. THE EXCLUSIONARY RULE
Evidence obtained in violation of the Fourth, Fifth, and Sixth Amendments, as well as all "fruit of the poisonous tree" (evidence derived from illegally obtained evidence), must be excluded from trial. The purpose is to deter police misconduct.

C. THE *MIRANDA* RULE

1. **Rights**
   A person in custody to be interrogated must be informed (1) he or she has the right to remain silent, (2) anything said can and will be used against him or her in court, (3) he or she has the right to consult with an attorney, and (4) if he or she is indigent, a lawyer will be appointed.

2. **Exceptions**
   These rights can be waived if the waiver is knowing and voluntary. "Public safety" may warrant admissibility. If other evidence justifies a conviction, it will not be overturned if a confession was coerced. A suspect must assertively state that he or she wants a lawyer, to exercise that right.

D. CRIMINAL PROCESS

1. **Arrest**
   An arrest requires a warrant based on probable cause (a substantial likelihood that the person has committed or is about to commit a crime). To make an arrest without a warrant, an officer must also have probable cause.

2. **Indictment or Information**
   A formal charge is called an **indictment** if issued by a grand jury and an **information** if issued by a government prosecutor.

3. **Trial**

Criminal trial procedures are similar to those of a civil trial, but the standard of proof is higher: the prosecutor must establish guilt beyond a reasonable doubt.

4. **Federal Sentencing Guidelines**

These guidelines cover possible penalties for federal crimes. A sentence is based on a defendant's criminal record, seriousness of the offense, and other factors.

VI. CYBER CRIME

Computer crime is a violation of criminal law that involves knowledge of computer technology for its perpetration, investigation, or prosecution.

A. CYBER FRAUD

Fraud (a misrepresentation knowingly made with the intent to deceive another and on which a reasonable person relies to his or her detriment) occurs online via e-mail by false promises of funds or notices of a relative's distress.

1. **Online Auction Fraud**

This occurs when a buyer pays for an auctioned item but does not receive it, or receives something worth less than the promised article. It can be difficult to pinpoint a fraudulent seller, who may assume multiple identities.

2. **Online Retail Fraud**

This occurs when a consumer pays for, but does not receive, an item, which may be nonexistent or worthless.

B. CYBER THEFT

Cyber theft occurs when a thief steals data from a computer via the Internet.

1. **Identity Theft**

Identity theft occurs when a form of identification is stolen and used to access the victim's financial resources. Identity theft is a federal crime. Victims have rights to work with creditors and credit bureaus to remove negative information from credit reports, among other things.

2. **Phishing**

This occurs when a criminal posing as a legitimate business e-mails an unsuspecting individual to update or confirm personal banking, credit, or other information.

3. **Vishing**

This variation of phishing involves voice communication—an e-mail requesting a phone call, for example, to relate a credit account password and number.

4. **Employment Fraud**

A criminal may claim to be an employer to obtain personal information from job seekers who post their resumes online.

5. **Credit-Card Crime on the Web**

Stolen credit cards are more likely to hurt merchants and issuers because consumers whose cards are stolen are not liable for the costs of subsequent purchases made with the cards. Businesses take further risks by electronically storing customers' credit account numbers, which can be stolen.

C. HACKING

A hacker uses one computer to break into another, often without the knowledge of either computer's owner. A hacker might appropriate a number of computers by secretly installing a program on each to operate as a robot, or bot, and forward a transmission to more computers, creating a botnet.

1. **Malware**
   A bot program, or any software harmful to a computer or its user, is malware. Other examples include a worm, which can reproduce itself and spread from computer to another, and a virus, which can reproduce but must be attached to a host file to travel between computers.

2. **New Service-Based Hacking Available at Low Cost**
   The business trend of software as a service (SAAS) has been adopted by hackers who rent their crimeware as a service (CAAS) through various Web sites. Those who hire CAAS can target individual groups, if desired, for minimal cost.

3. **Cyberterrorism**
   A cyberterrorist exploits a computer for a serious impact, such as exploding an internal data "bomb" to shut down a central computer or spreading a virus to cripple a computer network. A business might be targeted to steal a customer list or business plans, to sabotage products or services, or to disrupt operations.

D. **PROSECUTING CYBER CRIMES**
   Jurisdictional issues and the anonymous nature of technology can hamper the investigation and prosecution of cyber crimes. For example, a person who commits an act that constitutes a crime in one jurisdiction may have acted from a different jurisdiction, where the act is not a crime. If the act is committed via e-mail, there may not be "sufficient contacts" to support a prosecution.

E. **THE COMPUTER FRAUD AND ABUSE ACT**
   The Counterfeit Access Device and Computer Fraud and Abuse Act of 1984 prohibits cyber theft. The crime consists of (1) accessing a computer without authority and (2) taking data. Penalties include fines and imprisonment for up to twenty years (and civil suits).

TRUE-FALSE QUESTIONS

(Answers at the Back of the Book)

____ 1. Only the government prosecutes criminal defendants.

____ 2. A crime punishable by imprisonment is a felony.

____ 3. Burglary involves taking another's personal property from his or her person or immediate presence.

____ 4. Embezzlement requires physically taking property for another's possession.

____ 5. Stealing computer time is larceny.

____ 6. Offering a bribe is only one element of the crime of bribery.

____ 7. Receiving stolen goods is a crime only if the recipient knows the true owner.

____ 8. Using a fabricated identity to access online funds is identity theft.

____ 9. The appropriate location for a trial can be a key issue in a case involving a cyber crime.

____ 10. A business takes no risk by electronically storing its customers' credit account numbers.

FILL-IN QUESTIONS

(Answers at the Back of the Book)

Specific constitutional safeguards for those accused of crimes apply in all federal courts, and most of them also apply in state courts under the due process clause of the Fourteenth Amendment. The safeguards include (1) the Fourth Amendment protection from _____ (unexpected/unreasonable) searches and seizures, (2) the Fourth Amendment requirement that no warrants for a search or an arrest can be issued without _____ (probable/possible) cause, (3) the Fifth Amendment requirement that no one can be deprived of "life, liberty, or property without _____ (consent/due process of law)," (4) the Fifth Amendment prohibition against double _____ (immunity/jeopardy), (5) the Sixth Amendment guaranties of a speedy _____ (appeal/trial), _____ _____ (appeal to/trial by) a jury, a public trial, the right to confront _____ (counsel/witnesses), and the right to legal counsel, and (6) the Eighth Amendment prohibitions against excessive _____ (bail/bail and fines) and cruel and unusual punishment.

MULTIPLE-CHOICE QUESTIONS

(Answers at the Back of the Book)

____ **1.** Loren is charged with criminal theft. For a conviction, like most crimes, theft requires

a. a guilty conscience and physical symptoms such as sweaty palms.
b. a personal ethics code and a failure to follow its standards.
c. a specified state of mind and performance of a prohibited act.
d. a desire or an ambition, a plan to accomplish a goal, and the motivation to act.

____ **2.** Gwen signs Heidi's name, without her consent, to the back of a check. This is

a. burglary.
b. embezzlement.
c. forgery.
d. larceny.

____ **3.** Newt, a bank teller, deposits into his account checks that bank customers give to him to deposit into their accounts. This is

a. burglary.
b. embezzlement.
c. forgery.
d. larceny.

____ **4.** Grover posts an electric piano for bids on iSell, a Web auction site. Hyapatia makes the highest bid and sends the payment, which Grover receives, but he does not ship the piano. This is online

a. auction fraud.
b. puffery.
c. retail fraud.
d. trickery but not fraud.

____ **5.** Posing as Deft Credit Company, Milo e-mails Lovey, asking her to verify her credit card information through a link in the e-mail. She clicks on the prompt and enters the data. This is

a. employment fraud.
b. phishing.
c. piracy.
d. vishing.

____ **6.** Crissy uses her computer and an online connection to break into Bargain Discount Store's computer network. Crissy is

a. a virus.
b. a hacker.
c. a worm.
d. malware.

___   7. Jody, a government agent, arrests Kevin for the commission of a crime. Kevin claims that Jody entrapped him. This is a valid defense if Jody

       a. did not tell Kevin that she was a government agent.
       b. pressured Kevin into committing the crime.
       c. set a trap for Kevin, who was looking to commit the crime.
       d. was predisposed to commit a crime.

___   8. Perla is arrested on suspicion of the commission of a crime. Individuals who are arrested must be told of their right to

       a. confront witnesses.
       b. protection against unreasonable searches.
       c. remain silent.
       d. trial by jury.

___   9. While away from her business, Kate is arrested on suspicion of commission of a crime. At Kate's trial, under the exclusionary rule

       a. biased individuals must be excluded from the jury.
       b. business records must be excluded from admission as evidence.
       c. illegally obtained evidence must be excluded from admission as evidence.
       d. the arresting officer must be excluded from testifying.

___   10. Eve is arrested on suspicion of commission of a crime. A grand jury issues a formal charge against her. This is

       a. an arraignment.
       b. an indictment.
       c. an information.
       d. an inquisition.

SHORT ESSAY QUESTIONS

1. What are some of the significant differences between criminal law and civil law?

2. What constitutes criminal liability under the Racketeer Influenced and Corrupt Organizations Act, and what are the penalties?

GAMEPOINTS

(Answers at the Back of the Book)

1. In the video game "Xtreme Climb," your avatar is making an ascent up the highest peak in the United States, when a yeti—an abominable snowman—leaps from an outcropping and tosses your climbing companion from the precipice. The yeti howls into the wind and stomps along the ledge towards your avatar. Which crimes described in this chapter, if any, has the yeti committed? Explain.

2. You're playing "Not Me," a video game in which your identity has been stolen and is in use by someone else. Your credit is being depleted and your bank accounts are being bled dry. What methods are most likely being used to rob you?

SPECIAL INFORMATION FOR CPA CANDIDATES

    In the past, the CPA examination has not tested knowledge of specific crimes. Instead, the exam has asked for responses concerning liability in the context of corporate crime and in the area of accountants' liability. The first topic is covered in part in this chapter and in part in Chapter 39. Depending on the circumstances, corporate officers or directors may be liable for corporate crimes. An employer may also be liable for the crimes of his or her employees, although probably not in the absence of a specific statute setting out that liability. Accountants' criminal liability is covered in Chapter 48.

CUMULATIVE HYPOTHETICAL PROBLEM FOR UNIT TWO—INCLUDING CHAPTERS 6–9

(Answers at the Back of the Book)

Computer Data, Inc. (CDI), incorporated and based in California, signs a contract with Digital Products Corporation (DPC), incorporated and based in Arizona, to make and sell customized software for DPC to, in turn, sell to its clients.

____   1. To protect the rights that CDI has in the software it produces, CDI's best protection is offered by

    a. criminal law.
    b. intellectual property law.
    c. tort law.
    d. none of the choices.

____   2. CDI ships defective software to DPC, which sells it to a customer, Eagle Distribution Corporation. The defective software causes losses that Eagle estimates at $100,000. With respect to Eagle, CDI has likely violated

    a. criminal law.
    b. intellectual property law.
    c. tort law.
    d. none of the choices.

____   3. DPC's officers order some employees to access CDI's computers online to obtain its data without CDI's permission. This is

    a. fraud.
    b. theft.
    c. trespass.
    d. unethical but not criminal.

____   4. During an investigation into DPC's activities, some of its officers are suspected of having committed crimes. As a corporation, DPC can

    a. be fined or denied certain privileges if it is held criminally liable.
    b. be imprisoned if it is held criminally liable.
    c. be fined, denied privileges, or imprisoned if it is held criminally liable.
    d. not be found to be criminally liable.

____   5. DPC's officers who are suspected of having committed crimes can

    a. be fined or denied certain privileges if they are held criminally liable.
    b. be imprisoned if they are held criminally liable.
    c. be fined, denied privileges, or imprisoned if they are held criminally liable.
    d. not be held criminally liable.

QUESTIONS ON THE FOCUS ON ETHICS FOR UNIT TWO— ETHICS AND TORTS AND CRIMES

(Answers at the Back of the Book)

____ 1. Quality Info Company collects and sells personal data about individuals to businesses. This may violate

   a. businesses' copyrights.
   b. companies' freedom of speech.
   c. individuals' privacy rights.
   d. marketers' trademarks.

____ 2. Macro Corporation makes and sells software. Nick operates a Web site under the domain name "macrosoftwaresucks.com." In Macro's suit against Nick, his best defense is that this domain is protected by

   a. copyright law.
   b. Nick's freedom of speech.
   c. Nick's privacy rights.
   d. trademark law.

____ 3. Lee posts computer code that allows its users to de-encrypt and copy Movie Corporation's (MC's) copyright-protected DVDs. In MC's suit against Lee, the court is most likely to rule that the posting is

   a. a "fair use."
   b. a misappropriation of trade secrets.
   c. a privacy right.
   d. "pure speech."

Chapter 10
Nature and Terminology

WHAT THIS CHAPTER IS ABOUT

Contract law concerns the formation and keeping of promises, the excuses our society accepts for breaking such promises, and what promises are considered contrary to public policy and therefore legally void. This chapter introduces the basic terms and concepts of contract law, including the rules for interpreting contract language.

CHAPTER OUTLINE

I. **AN OVERVIEW OF CONTRACT LAW**

   A. **SOURCES OF CONTRACT LAW**
   Contract law is common law, which governs all contracts except when statutes or administrative regulations have modified or replaced it. Statutory law—particularly the Uniform Commercial Code (UCC)—governs all contracts for sales of goods.

   B. **THE FUNCTION OF CONTRACT LAW**
   Contract law ensures compliance with a promise and entitles a nonbreaching party to relief when a contract is breached. All contractual relationships involve promises, but all promises do not establish contractual relationships. Most contractual promises are kept, because keeping a promise is generally in the mutual self-interest of the promisor and the promisee.

   C. **THE DEFINITION OF A CONTRACT**
   A **contract** is a promise for the breach of which the law gives a remedy or the performance of which the law recognizes as a duty (that is, an agreement that can be enforced in court). A contract may be formed when two or more parties promise to perform or to refrain from performing some act now or in the future. A party who does not fulfill his or her promise may be subject to sanctions, including damages or, in some circumstances, being required to perform the promise.

   D. **THE OBJECTIVE THEORY OF CONTRACTS**
   Intent to enter into a contract is judged by objective (outward) facts as interpreted by a reasonable person, rather than by a party's subjective intention. Objective facts include (1) what the party said when entering into the contract, (2) how the party acted or appeared, and (3) the circumstances surrounding the transaction.

II. **ELEMENTS OF A CONTRACT**

   A. **REQUIREMENTS OF A VALID CONTRACT**

     1. **Agreement**
     This requirement includes an offer and an acceptance. One party must offer to enter into a legal agreement, and another party must accept the offer.

     2. **Consideration**
     Promises must be supported by legally sufficient and bargained-for consideration.

3. **Contractual Capacity**
These include characteristics that qualify the parties to a contract as competent.

4. **Legality**
A contract's purpose must be to accomplish a goal that is not against public policy.

B. DEFENSES TO THE ENFORCEABILITY OF A CONTRACT

1. **Voluntary Consent**
The apparent consent of both parties must be genuine.

2. **Form**
A contract must be in whatever form the law requires (some contracts must be in writing).

III.   TYPES OF CONTRACTS
Each category signifies a legal distinction regarding a contract's formation, performance, or enforceability.

A. CONTRACT FORMATION

1. **Bilateral versus Unilateral Contracts**

   a. **Bilateral Contract**
   This is a promise for a promise—to accept the offer, the offeree need only promise to perform.

   b. **Unilateral Contract**
   This is a promise for an act—the offeree can accept only by performance. A problem arises when the promisor attempts to revoke the offer after the promisee has begun performance but before the act has been completed.

      1) **Revocation—Traditional View**
      The promisee can accept only by performing fully. Offers are revocable until accepted.

      2) **Revocation—Present-Day View**
      The offer cannot be revoked once performance begins.

2. **Formal versus Informal Contracts**
   A formal contract requires a special form or method of creation to be enforceable (such as such as a negotiable instruments, which include checks and other drafts, promissory notes, and certificates of deposit). All contracts that are not formal are informal, and except for certain contracts that must be in writing, no special form is required.

3. **Express versus Implied Contracts**
   An express contract fully and explicitly states the terms of the agreement in words (oral or written). An implied contract is implied from the conduct of the parties.

   a. **Express Contract**
   An express contract fully and explicitly states the terms of an agreement in words (oral or written).

   b. **Implied Contract**
   An implied contract is implied from the conduct of the parties.

   c. **Requirements for an Implied Contract**
   To establish an implied-in-fact contract—

      1) The plaintiff must have furnished some service or property.
      2) The plaintiff must have expected to be paid and the defendant knew or should have known that payment was expected.
      3) The defendant had a chance to reject the service or property and did not.

B. CONTRACT PERFORMANCE

1. Executed Contract
This is a contract that has been fully performed on both sides.

2. Executory Contract
This is a contract that has not been fully performed by one or more parties.

C. CONTRACT ENFORCEABILITY

1. Valid Contract
A valid contract has all the elements necessary for contract formation.

2. Voidable Contract
This is a valid contract that can be avoided by one or more parties (for example, contracts by minors are voidable at the minor's option).

3. Unenforceable Contract
An unenforceable contract cannot be enforced because of certain legal defenses (for example, if a contract that must be in writing is not in writing).

4. Void Contract
This has no legal force or binding effect (for example, a contract is void if its purpose was illegal).

IV. QUASI CONTRACTS

In the absence of an actual contract, a court may impose a quasi contract to avoid the unjust enrichment of one party at the expense of another

A. LIMITATIONS ON QUASI-CONTRACTUAL RECOVERY
Persons are not normally liable for benefits thrust on them.

B. WHEN AN ACTUAL CONTRACT EXISTS
A quasi contract cannot be imposed if there is an actual contract that covers the area in controversy.

V. INTERPRETATION OF CONTRACTS

Rules of contract interpretation provide guidelines for determining the meaning of contracts. The primary purpose of these rules is to determine the parties' intent from the language of their agreement and to give effect to that intent.

A. PLAIN-LANGUAGE LAWS
The federal government and most states require an agreement and other legal documents and forms to be written clearly, coherently, and in words of common, everyday meaning.

B. THE PLAIN MEANING RULE
When the writing is clear and unequivocal, it will be enforced according to its plain terms. The meaning of the terms is determined from the written document alone.

C. OTHER RULES OF INTERPRETATION
When the writing contains unclear terms, courts use the following rules. If the terms are still unclear, a court will consider extrinsic evidence to prove what the parties intended.

1. A reasonable, lawful, and effective meaning is given to all terms.

2. A contract is interpreted as a whole; individual, specific clauses are considered subordinate to the contract's general intent. All writings that are part of the same transaction are interpreted together.

3. Terms that were negotiated separately are given greater consideration than standard terms and terms that were not negotiated separately.

4. A word is given its ordinary, common meaning, and a technical word its technical meaning, unless the parties clearly intended otherwise.

5. Specific, exact wording is given greater weight than general language.

6. Written or typewritten terms prevail over preprinted ones.

7. When the language has more than one meaning, it is interpreted against the party who drafted the contract.

8. Evidence of usage of trade, course of dealing, and course of performance may be admitted to clarify meaning.

TRUE-FALSE QUESTIONS

(Answers at the Back of the Book)

____ 1. All promises are legal contracts.

____ 2. A contract is formed when two parties agree to perform an act in the future.

____ 3. A promisor is a person who makes a promise.

____ 4. A unilateral contract is accepted by a promise to perform.

____ 5. An oral contract is an implied contract.

____ 6. An unenforceable contract is a valid contract that can be avoided by at least one of the parties to it.

____ 7. Under the plain meaning rule, a court will enforce a contract in which the writing is clear and unequivocal.

____ 8. When the language in a contract has more than one meaning, it will be interpreted against the party who drafted the contract.

____ 9. An executed contract is one that has been fully performed.

____ 10. A quasi contract arises from a mutual agreement between two parties.

FILL-IN QUESTIONS

(Answers at the Back of the Book)

Whether or not a party intended to enter into a contract is determined by the _____ (objective/subjective) theory of contracts. The theory is that a party's intention to enter into a contract is judged by _____ (objective/subjective) facts as they would be interpreted by a reasonable person. Relevant facts include: (1) what the party said; (2) what the party _____ (did/secretly believed); and (3) the _____ (circumstances surrounding/party's personal thoughts concerning) the transaction.

MULTIPLE-CHOICE QUESTIONS

(Answers at the Back of the Book)

____ **1.** Molecular Vision, Inc., and Nano Products Corporation enter into a contract to market jointly developed biotech products. The freedom to enter into contracts is

a. a concept that underlies the application of international law.
b. a fundamental public policy in the United States.
c. an ambiguous business goal that is irrelevant in terms of the law.
d. a principle that describes contracting parties' intent.

____ **2.** Speedy Delivery, Inc., agrees to deliver paper to Thespian Script Company, which promises to pay for the service. Speedy delivers the paper. This contract is

a. executory on Speedy's part.
b. executory on Thespian's part.
c. fully executed.
d. fully non-executed.

____ **3.** Mariah enters into an implied-in-fact contract with Noel. The parties' conduct

a. defines the contract's terms.
b. determines the facts.
c. factors in the implications of the contract.
d. is irrelevant in terms of the facts.

____ **4.** Dan, a doctor, renders aid to Edwina, who is injured. Dan can recover the cost of from Edwina

a. even if Edwina was not aware of Dan's help.
b. only if Edwina was aware of Dan's help.
c. only if Edwina was *not* aware of Dan's help.
d. under no circumstances.

____ **5.** Fay claims that she and Gio entered into a contract. The intent to enter into a contract is determined with reference to

a. the conscious theory of contracts.
b. the objective theory of contracts.
c. the personal theory of contracts.
d. the subjective theory of contracts.

____ **6.** Rowan calls Shary on the phone and agrees to buy her laptop computer for $500. This is

a. an express contract.
b. an implied-in-fact contract.
c. an implied-in-law contract.
d. a quasi contract.

____ **7.** Ogden enters into a contract with Pam to review her financial status. They later dispute the meaning of their contract. If the terms are unclear, the rules of contract interpretation will give effect to

a. the parties' intent as expressed in their contract.
b. what the defendant claims was the parties' intent.
c. what the plaintiff claims was the parties' intent.
d. what the parties now agree they intended.

___ 8. Laura enters into a contract with Midge for landscape design services. The contract's express terms have

    a. less priority than the parties' prior dealing.
    b. less priority than the trade usage in the industry.
    c. less priority than the parties' course of performance.
    d. more priority than the prior dealing, course of performance, and trade usage.

___ 9. Bo's contract with Cris is voidable. If the contract is avoided

    a. both parties are released from it.
    b. neither party is released from it.
    c. only Bo is released from it.
    d. only Cris is released from it.

___ 10. Marlon "declares that something will or will not happen in the future." This is

    a. an ethical principle.
    b. a plain language law.
    c. a plain meaning rule.
    d. a promise.

SHORT ESSAY QUESTIONS

1. What are the basic elements of a contract?

2. What is the function of contract law?

RockOn

(Answers at the Back of the Book)

1. You own a small club—Sammy D's—that features local musicians. On Tuesday night, you post a notice promising to pay $100 to any musician who takes to the stage for one hour. Tyler steps up to the mic and opens a sixty-minute set with a cover of the Beatles tune "I Saw Her Standing There." Do you have to pay Tyler $100? Explain.

2. Suppose, in the previous question, that your notice did not promise to pay but simply publicized "Tuesday Tune Night" and offered stage time to any musician who wished to perform. Uri entertains your patrons for an hour with a polished, professional hip hop repertoire, and then asks you for a percentage of the club's receipts for that hour. Do you have to pay?

SPECIAL INFORMATION FOR CPA CANDIDATES

Among the attributes for success on the CPA examination is a positive attitude. Preparation for the exam is a long process, and it can be difficult to keep one's mind focused on a successful conclusion. Because a positive attitude can make the difference between passing and failing, however, it is important that you stay refreshed, confident, and optimistic. To accomplish this, take time off from your studies once in a while. Spend an evening or an afternoon with friends; get some exercise; do some leisure reading; go to a movie—or do whatever else it takes, when your spirits sag, to regain a positive attitude.

Chapter 11:
Agreement in Traditional and E-Contracts

WHAT THIS CHAPTER IS ABOUT

An agreement is the essence of every contract. The parties to a contract are the **offeror** (who makes an offer) and the **offeree** (to whom the offer is made). If, through the process of offer and acceptance, an agreement is reached, and the other elements are present (consideration, capacity, legality), a valid contract is formed.

E-contracts include any contract entered into in e-commerce, whether business to business (B2B) or business to consumer (B2C), and any contract involving the computer industry. This chapter reviews some of the problems of e-contracts.

CHAPTER OUTLINE

I. **AGREEMENT**

The elements of an agreement are offer and acceptance—one party offers a bargain to another, who accepts.

A. **REQUIREMENTS OF THE OFFER**

An **offer** is a promise or commitment to do or refrain from doing some specified thing in the future. An offer has three elements—

1. **Intention**

The offeror must intend to be bound by the offer.

   a. **How to Determine the Offeror's Intent**

   The offeror's intent is what a reasonable person in the offeree's position would conclude the offeror's words and acts meant. Words in anger, jest, or undue excitement do not qualify.

   b. **Expressions of Opinion**

   These are not offers. For example, a doctor's opinion that a hand will heal within a few days of an operation is not an offer.

   c. **Statements of Future Intent**

   No offer is made when a party says that he or she plans to do something.

   d. **Preliminary Negotiations**

   A request or invitation to negotiate is not an offer. An invitation to submit bids is not an offer. Thus, when contractors are invited to bid on a job, the party to whom the bid is submitted is not bound. (The bid is an offer, however, and the contractor is bound by its acceptance.)

   e. **Advertisements**

   Ads, catalogs, and so on are invitations to negotiate. A price list is not an offer; it invites a buyer to offer to buy at that price. If an ad makes a promise so definite in character

79

that it is apparent the offeror is binding himself or herself to the conditions stated, however, the ad is an offer.

f. Auctions
An auction is not an offer (the owner is only expressing a willingness to sell).

g. Auctions with and without Reserve
In an auction with reserve, the owner may withdraw an item before the auctioneer closes the sale. A bidder is an offeror and may revoke a bid, or an auctioneer may reject it before he or she strikes the hammer, which constitutes acceptance. An auction is assumed to be with reserve, unless it is stated to be without reserve, in which goods cannot be withdrawn and must be sold to the highest bidder.

h. Agreements to Agree
Agreements to agree serve valid commercial purposes and can be enforced if the parties clearly intended to be bound and agreed on all essential terms, and no disputed issues remain. The emphasis is on the parties' intent rather than on form.

2. Definiteness of Terms
All of the major terms must be stated with reasonable definiteness in the offer (or, if the offeror directs, in the offeree's acceptance).

3. Communication
The offeree must know of the offer.

B. TERMINATION OF THE OFFER

1. Termination by Action of the Parties

a. Revocation of the Offer by the Offeror
The offeror usually can revoke the offer (even if he or she promised to keep it open), by express repudiation or by acts that are inconsistent with the offer and that are made known to the offeree.

1) Communicated to the Offeree
A revocation becomes effective when the offeree or offeree's agent receives it.

2) Offers to the General Public
An offer made to the general public can be revoked in the same manner the offer was originally communicated.

b. Irrevocable Offers

1) When an Offeree Changes Position in Justifiable Reliance
The offer may not be revoked, under the doctrine of promissory estoppel (see Chapter 12).

2) A Merchant's Firm Offer
The offer may be irrevocable (see Chapter 19).

3) Option Contract
An option contract is a promise to hold an offer open for a period of time. If no time is specified, a reasonable time is implied.

c. Rejection of the Offer by the Offeree
The offeree may reject an offer by words or conduct evidencing intent not to accept. A rejection is effective on receipt. Asking about an offer is not a rejection.

d. Counteroffer by the Offeree
The offeree's attempt to include different terms is a rejection of the original offer and a simultaneous making of a new offer. The **mirror image rule** requires the acceptance to match the offer exactly.

2. Termination by Operation of Law

a. Lapse of Time
An offer terminates automatically when the period of time specified in the offer has passed.

1) When the Time Begins to Run
Time begins to run when the offeree receives an offer. If there is a delay, time runs from the date the offeree would have received it (if the offeree knows or should know of the delay).

2) If No Time Is Specified
If no time is specified, a reasonable time is implied.

b. Destruction of the Subject Matter
An offer is automatically terminated.

c. Death or Incompetence of the Offeror or Offeree
An offeree's power of acceptance is terminated. Exceptions include irrevocable offers (see above).

d. Supervening Illegality of the Proposed Contract
When a statute or court decision makes an offer illegal, the offer is automatically terminated.

C. ACCEPTANCE

1. Who Can Accept?
Usually, only the offeree (or the offeree's agent) can accept.

2. Unequivocal Acceptance
The offeree must accept the offer unequivocally. This is the mirror image rule (see above).

3. Silence as Acceptance
Ordinarily, silence cannot operate as an acceptance. Silence or inaction can constitute acceptance in the following circumstances—

a. Receipt of Offered Services
If an offeree receives the benefit of offered services even though he or she had an opportunity to reject them and knew that they were offered with the expectation of compensation.

b. Prior Dealings
The offeree had prior dealings with the offeror that lead the offeror to understand silence will constitute acceptance.

4. Communication of Acceptance

a. Bilateral Contract
A bilateral contract is formed when acceptance is communicated. The offeree must use reasonable efforts to communicate acceptance.

b. Unilateral Contract
Communication is normally unnecessary, unless the offeror requests it or has no way of knowing the act has been performed.

5. Mode and Timeliness of Acceptance (in Bilateral Contracts)
Acceptance is timely if it is made before the offer is terminated.

a. The Mailbox Rule
Acceptance is effective when it is sent by whatever means is authorized by the offeror. This is the *mailbox rule*.

b. Authorized Means of Communication

1) Express

When an offeror specifies how acceptance should be made and the offeree uses that mode, the acceptance is effective even if the offeror never receives it.

2) Implied

When an offeror does not specify how acceptance should be made, the offeree may use the same means the offeror used to make the offer or a faster means.

3) Not Express or Implied

An acceptance sent by means not expressly or impliedly authorized is not effective until it is received.

c. Substitute Means of Communication

If an offeree uses a mode of communication that was not authorized by the offeror, acceptance is effective when received.

II.   AGREEMENT IN E-CONTRACTS

Disputes arising from contracts entered into online concern the terms and the parties' assent to those terms.

A. ONLINE OFFERS

Terms should be conspicuous and clearly spelled out. On a Web site, this can be done with a link to a separate page that contains the details. Subjects include remedies, dispute resolution, payment, taxes, refund and return policies, disclaimers, and privacy policies. A click-on acceptance box should also be included.

B. ONLINE ACCEPTANCES

Generally, a contract can be made and agreed to in any words or conduct sufficient to show agreement.

1. Click-On Agreements

A *click-on agreement* is when a buyer, completing a transaction on a computer, indicates his or her assent to be bound by the terms of the offer by clicking on a button that says, for example, "I agree." The terms may appear on a Web site through which a buyer obtains goods or services, or on a computer screen when software is loaded.

2. Shrink-Wrap Agreements

A *shrink-wrap agreement* is an agreement whose terms are expressed inside a box in which a product is packaged. Usually, the agreement is not between a seller and a buyer, but a manufacturer and the product's user. Terms generally concern warranties, remedies, and other issues.

a. Shrink-Wrap Agreements and Enforceable Contract Terms

Courts often enforce shrink-wrap agreements, reasoning that the seller proposed an offer that the buyer accepted after an opportunity to read the terms. Also, it is more practical to enclose the full terms of sale in a box.

b. Shrink-Wrap Terms That May Not Be Enforced

If a court finds that the buyer learned of the shrink-wrap terms *after* the parties entered into a contract, the court might conclude that those terms were proposals for additional terms, which were not part of the contract unless the buyer expressly agreed to them.

3. Browse-Wrap Terms

Browse-wrap terms do not require a user to assent to the terms before going ahead with an online transaction. Offerors of these terms generally assert that they are binding without the user's active consent. Critics argue that a user should at least be required to navigate past the terms before they should be considered binding.

C. E-SIGNATURE TECHNOLOGIES
Methods for creating and verifying e-signatures include—

1. Digitized Handwritten Signatures
These are graphical images of handwritten signatures that can be created by, for example, a digital pen and pad.

2. Public-Key Infrastructure-Based Digital Signatures
Asymmetric cryptographic keys provide private code for one party and public software for another party, who reads the code to verify the first party's identity. A cybernotary issues the keys.

D. STATE LAWS GOVERNING E-SIGNATURES
Most states have laws governing e-signatures, although the laws are not uniform. The Uniform Electronic Transactions Act, issued in 1999, was an attempt by the National Conference of Commissioners on Uniform State Laws and the American Law Institute to create more uniformity.

E. FEDERAL LAW ON E-SIGNATURES AND E-DOCUMENTS
In 2000, Congress enacted the Electronic Signatures in Global and National Commerce (E-SIGN) Act to provide that no contract, record, or signature may be denied legal effect solely because it is in an electronic form. Some documents are excluded (such as those governed by UCC Articles 3, 4, and 9.)

F. PARTNERING AGREEMENTS
Through a partnering agreement, a seller and a buyer agree in advance on the terms to apply in all transactions subsequently conducted electronically. These terms may include access and identification codes. A partnering agreement, like any contract, can prevent later disputes.

III. THE UNIFORM ELECTRONIC TRANSACTIONS ACT
The UETA removes barriers to e-commerce by giving the same legal effect to e-records and e-signatures as to paper documents and signatures.

A. THE SCOPE AND APPLICABILITY OF THE UETA
The UETA applies only to e-records and e-signatures in a transaction (an interaction between two or more people relating to business, commercial, or government activities).

1. The Parties Must Agree to Conduct Their Transaction Electronically
This agreement may be implied by the circumstances and the parties' conduct (for example, giving out a business card with an e-mail address on it). Consent may also be withdrawn.

2. The Parties Can "Opt Out"
Parties can waive or vary any or all of the UETA but it applies absent an agreement to the contrary.

3. The UETA Does Not Apply to All Laws
The UETA does not apply to laws governing wills or testamentary trusts, the UCC (except Articles 2 and 2A), and other laws excluded by the states that adopt the UETA.

B. THE FEDERAL E-SIGN ACT AND THE UETA

1. Does the E-SIGN Act Preempt the UETA?
If a state enacts the UETA without modifying it, the E-SIGN Act does not preempt it. The E-SIGN Act preempts modified versions of the UETA to the extent that they are inconsistent with the E-SIGN Act.

2. Can the States Enact Alternative Procedures or Requirements?
Under the E-SIGN Act, states may enact alternative procedures or requirements for the use or acceptance of e-records or e-signatures if—

  a. The procedures or requirements are consistent with the E-SIGN Act.
  b. The procedures do not give greater legal effect to any specific type of technology.
  c. The state law refers to the E-SIGN Act if the state adopts the alternative after the enactment of the E-SIGN Act.

C. ATTRIBUTING ELECTRONIC SIGNATURES

If a person types his or her name at the bottom of an e-mail purchase order, that typing qualifies as a "signature." Any relevant evidence can prove that the e-signature is, or is not, attributable to a certain person. If issues arise that relate to agency, authority, forgery, or contract formation, state laws other than the UETA apply.

D. THE EFFECT OF ERRORS

If the parties agree to a security procedure and one party does not detect an error because he or she did not follow the procedure, the conforming party can avoid the effect of the error. If the parties do not agree on a security procedure, other state laws determine the effect of the mistake. To avoid the effect of an error, a party must (1) promptly notify the other party and (2) return any benefit received.

E. TIMING

1. When Is an E-Record "Sent"?

When it is directed from the sender's place of business to the intended recipient in a form readable by the recipient's computer at the recipient's place of business with the closest relation to the deal (or either party's residence, if there is no place of business). Once an e-record leaves the sender's control or comes under the recipient's control, it is sent.

2. When Is an E-Record "Received"?

When it enters the recipient's processing system in a readable form—even if no person is aware of it.

IV. INTERNATIONAL TREATIES AFFECTING E-COMMERCE

International organizations have created their own regulations for global Internet transactions. For example, the United Nations Convention on the Use of Electronic Communications in International Contracts of 2005 provides standards to determine an Internet user's location and to give the same legal effect to e-records and e-signatures as to paper documents and signatures.

TRUE-FALSE QUESTIONS

(Answers at the Back of the Book)

_____ **1.** An agreement is normally evidenced by an offer and an acceptance.

_____ **2.** A contract does not need to contain reasonably definite terms to be enforced.

_____ **3.** A counteroffer terminates an offer.

_____ **4.** There are no irrevocable offers.

_____ **5.** The mirror image rule does not require an acceptance to match an offer to create a contract.

_____ **6.** State e-signature laws are not uniform.

_____ **7.** The Uniform Electronic Transactions Act (UETA) is a federal law.

_____ **8.** Under the UETA, a name typed at the bottom of an e-mail note can qualify as an e-signature.

_____ **9.** Under the UETA, a contract is enforceable even if it is in electronic form.

_____ **10.** An e-record is considered received under the UETA only if a person is aware of its receipt.

FILL-IN QUESTIONS

(Answers at the Back of the Book)

The elements necessary for an effective offer are (1) a _____ (serious/subjective) intent by the _____ (offeror/offeree) to be bound by the offer; (2) _____ (detailed/reasonably definite) terms; and (3) communication of the offer to the _____ (offeror/offeree).

MULTIPLE-CHOICE QUESTIONS

(Answers at the Back of the Book)

____ 1. Dill offers to buy from Connie a used computer, with a monitor and printer, for $400. Connie says, "OK, but $200 more for the monitor and printer." Connie has

    a. accepted the offer.
    b. made a counteroffer without rejecting the offer.
    c. rejected the offer and made a counteroffer.
    d. rejected the offer without making a counteroffer.

____ 2. Lexi offers to sell her car to Kim, stating that the offer will stay open for thirty days. Lexi may revoke the offer

    a. before Kim accepts the offer.
    b. before thirty days have expired, whether or not Kim has accepted the offer.
    c. only after Kim accepts the offer.
    d. only after thirty days.

____ 3. Leo offers to sell Mona a video game player. Mona sends an acceptance via the mail. This acceptance is effective when it is

    a. in transit.
    b. received.
    c. sent.
    d. written.

____ 4. **Based on a Sample CPA Exam Question.** Before opening her new sports merchandise store, Jade places an ad in the newspaper showing cross-training shoes at certain prices. Within hours of opening for business, the store is sold out of some of the shoes. In this situation

    a. Jade has made an offer to the people reading the ad.
    b. Jade has made a contract with the people reading the ad.
    c. Jade has made an invitation seeking offers.
    d. Any customer who demands goods advertised and tenders the money is entitled to them.

____ 5. Plasticorp, Inc., includes a shrink-wrap agreement with its products. A court would likely enforce this agreement if a buyer used the product

    a. after having had an opportunity to read the agreement.
    b. before having had an opportunity to read the agreement.
    c. only after actually reading the agreement.
    d. none of the choices.

____ **6.** BroadBand Company agrees to sell software to Ally from BroadBand's Web site. To complete the deal, Ally clicks on a button that, with reference to certain terms, states, "I agree." The parties have

    a. a binding contract that does not include the terms.
    b. a binding contract that includes only the terms to which Holly later agrees.
    c. a binding contract that includes the terms.
    d. no contract.

____ **7.** Rapido Delivery Company and Stateside Trucking, Inc., attempt to enter into a contract in electronic form. Under the Electronic Signatures in Global and National Commerce Act (E-SIGN Act), because this contract is in electronic form, it

    a. may be denied legal effect.
    b. may not be denied legal effect.
    c. will be limited to certain terms.
    d. will not be enforced.

____ **8.** Digital Tec, Inc., e-mails an e-record, as part of a business deal, to Custom Work Corporation. Under the UETA, an e-record is considered sent

    a. only when it leaves the sender's control.
    b. only when it comes under the recipient's control.
    c. when it leaves the sender's control or comes under the recipient's control.
    d. when it is midway between the sender and recipient.

____ **9.** NuSoftware, Inc. (NSI), and Olde Company (OC) agree to follow a certain security procedure in transacting business. NSI fails to follow the procedure and, for this reason, does not detect an error in its deal with OC. OC can avoid the effect of the error

    a. only if NSI's name is affixed to the e-record evidencing the error.
    b. only if OC takes reasonable steps to return any benefit received.
    c. under any circumstances.
    d. under no circumstances.

____ **10.** Direct2U Sales Company and eDeals, Inc., engage in e-commerce without expressly opting in or out of the UETA. The UETA covers

    a. none of the contract.
    b. only the part of the contract that does not involve e-commerce.
    c. only the part of the contract that involves e-signatures.
    d. the entire contract.

SHORT ESSAY QUESTIONS

1. What is an offer? What are the elements necessary for an effective offer?

2. Are shrink-wrap and click-on agreements enforceable?

ROCKON

(Answers at the Back of the Book)

1. In your capacity as talent coordinator for Ideal Concert Promotions, Inc., you offer the James Brothers, a new, suddenly popular pop group, a certain price to play the Luminous Center Stadium on a certain date.

The offer states that it will expire thirty days from June 1. The James Brothers categorically rejects the offer on June 10. Can the group change their mind and validly accept the offer within what remains of the thirty days? Explain.

2. Jay posts an ad on his Web site—BamSlam!.com—to sell a series of digital video lessons to aspiring percussionists who want to learn to "Drum like the Masters!" The ad is flashy, splashy, colorful, and loud. The terms are on a separate page on which a "Future Master!" must click "Okay!" before being transferred to yet another page on which to pay for the lessons and click on a link to download the videos. Are the terms binding? Why or why not?

SPECIAL INFORMATION FOR CPA CANDIDATES

One of the points covered in this chapter that has often been tested on the CPA examination is the mailbox rule. Sometimes, the examination has included a problem in which the offeror specifies that an acceptance must be received before it is effective. In that circumstance, of course, the mailbox rule does not apply. It might be helpful to remember, too, that the mailbox rule is the only exception to the rule that a communication is effective only on receipt—offers, revocations, rejections, counteroffers, and acceptances not subject to the mailbox rule must be received to be effective.

The CPA examination covers information technology (IT) topics, but does not, as of this writing, cover the details of the law discussed in this chapter. The exam may require review of business information systems and the personnel within an IT department. Those systems consist, of course, of hardware, software, and network components. Their use includes data structure, analysis, and manipulation, as well as transaction and application processing. It may also be useful to review IT control objectives, control activities and design, physical access controls and security, and disaster recovery and business continuity.

Chapter 12
Consideration

WHAT THIS CHAPTER IS ABOUT

Good reasons for enforcing promises have been held to include something given as an agreed exchange, a benefit that the promisor received, and a detriment that the promisee incurred. These are referred to as consideration. No contract is enforceable without it.

Consideration is the value given in return for a promise. For example, the value can consist of money given in return for a promise to deliver certain goods. Thus, when Roy pays for a computer to be delivered by Sam, there is consideration. This chapter outlines the concepts and principles of consideration.

CHAPTER OUTLINE

I. ELEMENTS OF CONSIDERATION
There are two elements to consideration—something of legal value and a bargained-for exchange.

A. SOMETHING OF LEGAL VALUE
Something of legal value must be given in exchange for a promise. The "something" may be (1) a promise to do something that one had no legal duty to do, (2) performing an act that one had no legal duty to perform, or (3) refraining from doing something that one could otherwise do.

B. BARGAINED-FOR EXCHANGE
The consideration given by the promisor must induce the promisee to incur legal detriment, and the detriment incurred must induce the promisor to make the promise. A gift does not have this element.

II. ADEQUACY OF CONSIDERATION
Adequacy of consideration refers to the fairness of a bargain.

A. COURTS TYPICALLY WILL NOT CONSIDER ADEQUACY
Normally, a court will not question adequacy because parties are free to bargain as they wish.

B. WAS VOLUNTARY CONSENT LACKING?
Grossly inadequate or absent consideration may indicate fraud, duress, incapacity, undue influence, or a lack of a bargained-for exchange. A contract may be unconscionable (and unenforceable) if consideration is so one-sided under the circumstances as to be unfair. In these cases, a court may look more closely at the exchange of values.

III. AGREEMENTS THAT LACK CONSIDERATION
Situations in which promises or acts do not qualify as consideration include—

A. PREEXISTING DUTY
A promise to do what one already has a duty to do is not consideration. For example, if a builder contracts to build something, that duty cannot be consideration for a second contract to raise the price.

1. **Exception—Unforeseen Difficulties**
When a party runs into extraordinary difficulties that were unforeseen at the time the contract was formed, some courts will enforce an agreement to pay more. Unforeseen difficulties often arise under construction contracts and relate to soil conditions. Ordinary business risks are not included.

2. **Exception— Rescission and New Contract**
Two parties can agree to rescind their contract to the extent that it is executory.

  a. **Preexisting Duties Discharged by Rescission**
  There are three separate agreements—the initial agreement, the rescission agreement, and the later agreement. Preexisting duties are discharged by the rescission.

  b. **When Rescission and New Contract Occur at the Same Time**
  Some courts hold that the new agreement is unenforceable, on the ground that the parties had a preexisting duty under the previous contract. Other courts hold that the consideration for the original agreement carries over into the new agreement.

B. **PAST CONSIDERATION**
Promises made with respect to events that have already taken place are unenforceable.

C. **ILLUSORY PROMISES**
If the terms of a contract express such uncertainty of performance that the promisor has not definitely promised to do anything, the promise is illusory—without consideration and unenforceable.

1. **Option-to-Cancel Clauses**
Reserving, in a contract, the right to cancel or withdraw at any time can be an illusory promise. If the right is at all restricted, however—such as by requiring thirty days' notice—there is consideration.

2. **Requirements and Output Contracts**
Problems of consideration may arise in these circumstances because of the uncertainty of performance. For example, Tio's Café promises to buy from Pizza King, Inc., "such ingredients as we require." Tio's promise may be illusory—it could depend solely on the buyer's discretion.

D. **SETTLEMENT OF CLAIMS**

1. **Accord and Satisfaction**
A debtor may offer to pay, and a creditor may agree to accept, less than the amount of a debt. For such an accord and satisfaction, the amount of the debt must be in dispute.

  a. **Accord**
  The agreement under which one of the parties undertakes to give or perform, and the other to accept, in satisfaction of a claim, something other than what was originally agreed on.

  b. **Satisfaction**
  This occurs when an accord is executed. There can be no satisfaction without an accord.

  c. **Liquidated Debt—No Consideration**
  Acceptance of less than the entire amount of a liquidated debt is not satisfaction, and the balance of the debt is still owed. No consideration is given by the debtor, because the debtor has a preexisting obligation to pay the entire debt.

  d. **Unliquidated Debt—Consideration**
  When the amount of the debt is in dispute, acceptance of a lesser sum discharges the debt. Consideration is given by the parties' giving up a legal right to contest the amount of debt.

2. **Release**

A release (a promise to refrain from suing on a valid claim) bars any further recovery beyond the terms stated in the release. Releases will generally be binding if they are (1) given in good faith, (2) stated in a signed writing, and (3) accompanied by consideration.

3. **Covenant Not to Sue**

The parties substitute a contractual obligation for some other type of legal action based on a valid claim. If the obligation is not met, an action can be brought for breach of contract.

IV. EXCEPTIONS TO THE CONSIDERATION REQUIREMENT

A. PROMISSORY ESTOPPEL

Under the doctrine of promissory estoppel (detrimental reliance), a person who relies on the promise of another may be able to recover in the absence of consideration.

1. **Requirements to State a Claim for Promissory Estoppel**

   a. The promise was clear and definite.
   b. The promisor knew or had reason to believe that the promisee would likely rely on the promise.
   c. The promisee acted or refrained from acting in reasonable reliance on the promise.
   d. The promisee's reliance resulted in substantial detriment.
   e. Justice will be better served by enforcement of the promise.

2. **Application of the Doctrine**

   This doctrine is applied in many situations, including business transactions.

B. PROMISES TO PAY DEBTS BARRED BY A STATUTE OF LIMITATIONS

Creditors must sue within a certain period to recover debts. If a debtor promises to pay a debt barred by a statute of limitations (promise can be implied if debtor acknowledges debt by making part payment), a creditor can sue to recover the entire debt, or at least the amount promised.

C. CHARITABLE SUBSCRIPTIONS

Subscriptions to religious, educational, and charitable institutions are promises to make gifts, which are not supported by consideration, but such gifts are often enforced under the doctrine of promissory estoppel or consideration is found as a matter of public policy.

TRUE-FALSE QUESTIONS

(Answers at the Back of the Book)

____ 1. Inadequate consideration may indicate fraud, duress, or undue influence.

____ 2. A promise to do what one already has a legal duty to do is not legally sufficient consideration.

____ 3. Past consideration is consideration.

____ 4. Rescission is the unmaking of a contract and the parties' return to their pre-contract positions.

____ 5. A promise has no legal value as consideration.

____ 6. If, in a contract, a promisor does not definitely promise to do anything, the promise is illusory.

____ 7. A covenant not to sue always bars further recovery.

____ 8. Only a liquidated debt can serve as consideration for an accord and satisfaction.

____ 9. Consideration is the value given in return for a promise.

____ 10. The doctrine of promissory estoppel requires a clear and definite promise.

FILL-IN QUESTIONS

(Answers at the Back of the Book)

The doctrine of promissory estoppel, or detrimental reliance, involves a _____ (promise/performance) given by one party that induces another party to rely on it to his or her _____ (benefit/detriment). When the _____ (promisor/promisee) can reasonably have expected the reliance, and injustice cannot otherwise be avoided, the _____ (promise/benefit) will be _____ (enforced/awarded). In other words, the _____ (promisor/promisee) must have acted with justifiable reliance. Generally, the act must have been of a _____ (substantial/inconsequential) nature.

MULTIPLE-CHOICE QUESTIONS

(Answers at the Back of the Book)

____ 1. Gayla questions whether there is consideration for her contract with Julius. Consideration has two elements—there must be a bargained-for exchange and the value of whatever is exchanged must be

   a. economically fair.
   b. grossly inadequate.
   c. legally sufficient.
   d. reasonably reliable.

____ 2. Dave offers to buy a book owned by Lee for $40. Lee accepts and hands the book to Dave. The transfer and delivery of the book constitute performance. Is this performance consideration for Dave's promise?

   a. No, because Lee already had a duty to hand the book to Dave.
   b. No, because performance never constitutes consideration.
   c. Yes, because Dave sought it in exchange for his promise, and Lee gave it in exchange for that promise.
   d. Yes, because performance always constitutes consideration.

____ 3. **Based on a Sample CPA Exam Question.** Jay is seeking to avoid performing a promise to pay Karen $150. Jay is claiming a lack of consideration on Karen's part. Jay will win if he can show that

   a. before Jay's promise, Karen had already performed the requested act.
   b. Karen's only claim of consideration was the relinquishment of a legal right.
   c. Karen's asserted consideration is only worth $50.
   d. the consideration to be performed by Karen will be performed by a third party.

____ 4. Hillcrest Office Company promises to pay Gerard $1,000 to repair the roof on Hillcrest's building. Gerard fixes the roof. The act of fixing the roof

   a. imposes a moral obligation on Hillcrest to pay Gerard.
   b. imposes no obligation on Hillcrest unless it is satisfied with the job.
   c. is not sufficient consideration because it is not goods or money.
   d. is the consideration that creates Hillcrest's obligation to pay Gerard.

____ 5. Delite Pastries, Inc., contracts with Elron to deliver its products. Later, the parties decide to cancel their contract. They

   a. may rescind their entire contract.
   b. may rescind their contract to the extent that it is executory.
   c. must perform their entire contract.
   d. must perform the part of their contract that is executory.

___ **6.** Idle Contractor Corporation begins constructing a building for Haute Apartments, Inc. In mid-project, Idle asks for $150,000 more, claiming an increase in ordinary business expenses. Haute agrees. This agreement is

   a. enforceable as an accord and satisfaction.
   b. enforceable because of unforeseen difficulties.
   c. unenforceable as an illusory promise.
   d. unenforceable due to the preexisting duty rule.

___ **7.** Sawyer causes an accident in which Reese is injured. Reese accepts Sawyer's offer of $5,000 to release Sawyer from further liability. Later, Reese learns that his injuries are more serious than he realized. The release will

   a. bar further recovery from Sawyer.
   b. not bar further recovery from Sawyer if Sawyer is insured.
   c. not bar further recovery from Sawyer if Reese is insured.
   d. not bar further recovery from Sawyer under any circumstances.

___ **8.** Mikayla promises to pay Lauren to work for her. Lauren agrees and quits her job, but Mikayla does not hire her. Mikayla is liable to Lauren based on

   a. the concept of accord and satisfaction.
   b. the doctrine of promissory estoppel.
   c. the preexisting duty rule.
   d. the principle of rescission.

___ **9.** Owen hires Paula under a contract that reserves to Owen the right to cancel the contract on thirty days' notice at any time after Paula begins work. This promise is

   a. enforceable.
   b. illusory.
   c. imaginary.
   d. unforeseen.

___ **10.** Blakely has a cause to sue Carly in a tort action, but agrees not to sue her if Carly will pay for the damage. If Carly fails to pay, Blakely can bring an action against her for breach of contract. This is

   a. a covenant not to sue.
   b. an accord and satisfaction.
   c. an unenforceable contract.
   d. a release.

SHORT ESSAY QUESTIONS

1. When is consideration legally sufficient?

2. What are the circumstances in which a court will question whether consideration is adequate?

ROCKON

(Answers at the Back of the Book)

1. Gerard, an events promoter and coordinator, promises to stage a concert for the benefit of Kids Care, a charitable organization dedicated to helping disadvantaged youth. In reliance on the anticipated receipts, Kids Care contracts for the construction of a residence for homeless teens. After the concert, Gerard tells

Kids Care that he has decided not to donate the receipts to the organization. Is Gerard's promise enforceable despite the lack of consideration? Explain.

2.   You sign a contract with Lewis to play saxophone on six consecutive nights, for a certain price, during the Marina Harbor Jazz Festival in August. The day before the festival begins, Lewis asks for your price to be reduced 15 percent because "ticket sales have not been as good as I'd like." You agree and play as promised, but later sue for the difference in price. Is your agreement to the reduction enforceable? Why or why not?

SPECIAL INFORMATION FOR CPA CANDIDATES

On the CPA examination, questions concerning consideration have often concentrated on the modification of contracts. You might find it helpful to review those rules. In particular, remember that an agreement to pay less than the amount that is owed for an unliquidated debt is not binding without consideration. Under the UCC, however, consideration is not required to modify a contract (for a sale of goods). Other important points to keep in mind include that the consideration exchanged by the parties does not have to have equal value—it does not even have to be reasonable or fair.

Chapter 13
Capacity and Legality

WHAT THIS CHAPTER IS ABOUT

If a party to a contract lacks capacity, an essential element for a valid contract is missing, and the contract is void. Some persons have capacity to enter into a contract, but if they wish, they can avoid liability under the contract. Also, to be enforceable, a contract must not violate any statutes or public policy.

CHAPTER OUTLINE

I. **CONTRACTUAL CAPACITY**

A. **MINORS**
A minor can enter into any contract that an adult can enter into, as long as it is not prohibited by law (for example, the sale of alcoholic beverages).

1. **Age of Majority, Marriage, and Emancipation**
A person who reaches the age of majority (eighteen, in most states) is not a minor for contractual purposes. In some states, marriage terminates minority status. Minors, over whom parents have relinquished control, have full contractual capacity.

2. **A Minor's Right to Disaffirm**
A minor can disaffirm a contract by manifesting an intent not to be bound. A contract can ordinarily be disaffirmed at any time during minority or for a reasonable time after a minor comes of age. (An adult cannot disaffirm a contract with a minor on the ground that the minor can.)

3. **A Minor's Obligation on Disaffirmance**
A minor cannot disaffirm a fully executed contract without returning whatever goods have been received or paying their reasonable value.

a. **What the Adult Recovers**

1) **In Most States**
If the goods (or other consideration) are in the minor's control, the minor must return them (without added compensation).

2) **In a Growing Number of States**
If the goods have been used, damaged, or ruined, the adult must be restored to the position he or she held before the contract.

b. **What the Minor Recovers**
A minor can recover all property that he or she transferred to an adult as consideration, even if it is in a third party's hands. If it cannot be returned, the adult must pay the minor its value.

4. **Exceptions to the Minor's Right to Disaffirm**

95

a. Misrepresentation of Age
In most states, a minor who misrepresents his or her age can still disaffirm a contract. In others, this is enough to prohibit disaffirmance.

b. Doing Business as an Adult
Some states prohibit minors who engage in business as adults from disaffirming related contracts.

c. Contracts for Necessaries
Necessaries are food, clothing, shelter, medicine, and hospital care—whatever a court believes is necessary to maintain a person's status. A minor may disaffirm a contract for necessaries but will be liable for the reasonable value.

5. Ratification
Ratification is the act of accepting and thereby giving legal force to an obligation that was previously unenforceable.

a.   Express Ratification
When a person, after reaching the age of majority, states orally or in writing that he or she intends to be bound by a contract.

b. Implied Ratification
When a minor performs acts inconsistent with disaffirmance or fails to disaffirm an executed contract within a reasonable time after reaching the age of majority.

6. Parents' Liability
Generally, parents are not liable for contracts made by their minor children acting on their own.

B. INTOXICATION

1. If a Person Is Sufficiently Intoxicated to Lack Mental Capacity
Any contract he or she enters into is voidable at the option of the intoxicated person, even if the intoxication was voluntary. On sobriety, the person can ratify the contract.

2. If a Person Understands the Legal Consequences of a Contract
Despite intoxication, the contract is usually enforceable.

C. MENTAL INCOMPETENCE

1. Persons Adjudged Mentally Incompetent by a Court—Void Contracts
If a person has been adjudged mentally incompetent by a court of law and a guardian has been appointed, a contract by the person is void.

2. Incompetent Persons Not So Adjudged by a Court

a. Voidable Contracts
A contract is voidable (at the option of the person) if a person does not know he or she is entering into the contract or lacks the capacity to comprehend its nature, purpose, and consequences.

b. Valid Contracts
If a mentally incompetent person understands the nature and effect of entering into a certain contract, the contract will be valid.

II. LEGALITY

A. CONTRACTS CONTRARY TO STATUTE

1. Contracts to Commit a Crime
A contract to commit a crime is illegal. If the contract is rendered illegal by statute after it has been entered into, the contract is discharged.

2. **Usury**

   Every state sets rates of interest charged for loans (exceptions are made for certain business deals). Charging a higher rate is usury—most states limit the interest that may be collected on the contract to the lawful maximum. Federal law limits the interest and fees on credit cards.

3. **Gambling**

   All states regulate gambling (any scheme that involves distribution of property by chance among persons who pay for the chance to receive it).

4. **Online Gambling**

   Federal law bars electronic payments, such as credit-card transactions, to online gambling sites.

5. **Licensing Statutes**

   In some states, the lack of a required business or professional license bars the enforcement of work-related contracts.

   a. **Illegal Contracts**

      If a licensing statute's purpose is to protect the public from unauthorized practitioners, a contract with an unlicensed individual is illegal.

   b. **Enforceable Contracts**

      If the purpose of the statute is to raise revenue, a contract entered into with an unlicensed practitioner is enforceable.

B. **CONTRACTS CONTRARY TO PUBLIC POLICY**

1. **Contracts in Restraint of Trade**

   Competition in the economy is favored so contracts that restrain trade or violate an antitrust statute (see Chapter 47) are prohibited.

   a. **Covenant Not to Compete**

      This is enforceable if it is reasonable, determined by the length of time and the size of the area in which the party agrees not to compete.

   b. **Reformation of an Unreasonable Covenant Not to Compete**

      A court may reform an unreasonable covenant not to compete by converting its terms into reasonable ones and enforcing the covenant.

2. **Unconscionable Contracts or Clauses**

   A bargain that is unfairly one-sided is unconscionable.

   a. **Procedural Unconscionability**

      This relates to a party's lack of knowledge or understanding of contract terms because of small print, "legalese," etc. An adhesion contract (drafted by one party for his benefit) may be held unconscionable.

   b. **Substantive Unconscionability**

      This relates to the parts of a contract that are so unfairly one-sided they "shock the conscience" of the court.

3. **Exculpatory Clauses**

   Contract clauses attempting to release parties of negligence or other wrongs. Sometimes enforced, particularly if the party seeking enforcement is a private business not considered important to the public interest, such as an amusement park. In most real property leases, however, these clauses are held to be contrary to public policy.

4. **Discriminatory Contracts**

   Contracts in which a party promises to discriminate in terms of color, race, religion, national origin, disability, or gender are illegal.

C. EFFECT OF ILLEGALITY

Generally, an illegal contract is void. No party can sue to enforce it and no party can recover for its breach. Exceptions include—

1. **Justifiable Ignorance of the Facts**
   A party who is innocent may recover benefits conferred in a partially executed contract or enforce a fully performed contract.

2. **Members of Protected Classes**
   When a statute is designed to protect a certain class of people, a member of that class can enforce a contract in violation of the statute (the other party to the contract cannot enforce it).

3. **Withdrawal from an Illegal Agreement**
   If the illegal part of an agreement has not been performed, the party rendering performance can withdraw and recover the performance or its value.

4. **Contracts Illegal through Fraud, Duress, or Undue Influence**
   A party induced to enter into an illegal bargain by fraud, duress, or undue influence can enforce the contract or recover for its value.

5. **Severable, or Divisible Contracts**
   If a contract can be divided into parts, a court may enforce a legal portion but not an illegal part.

TRUE-FALSE QUESTIONS

(Answers at the Back of the Book)

____ 1. A minor may disaffirm a contract entered into with an adult.

____ 2. Some states impose a duty of restitution on minors who disaffirm contracts.

____ 3. An intoxicated person who enters into a contract can void it.

____ 4. A parent is always liable for a minor's contract.

____ 5. A lender who makes a loan at a rate above the lawful maximum commits usury.

____ 6. A contract that exculpates one party for negligence will usually be held unconscionable.

____ 7. A contract in which the stronger party dictates the terms is an adhesion contract.

____ 8. A contract that calls for the performance of an illegal act may be enforceable.

____ 9. A contract with an unlicensed practitioner is always enforceable.

____ 10. A covenant not to compete is never enforceable.

FILL-IN QUESTIONS

(Answers at the Back of the Book)

The act of accepting and giving legal force to an obligation that previously was not enforceable is _____ (disaffirmance/ratification). In relation to contracts entered into by minors or persons who are intoxicated or mentally incompetent, this is an act or an expression in words by which the person, on or after reaching majority or regaining sobriety or mental competence, indicates intent to be bound by a contract.

Disaffirmance or ratification may be express or implied. For example, a person's continued use and payments on something bought when he or she was incompetent is inconsistent with a desire to _____ (disaffirm/ratify) and _____ (indicates/does not indicate) an intent to be bound by the contract. In general, any act or conduct showing an intent to affirm the contract will be deemed _____ (disaffirmance/ratification).

MULTIPLE-CHOICE QUESTIONS

(Answers at the Back of the Book)

____ 1. **Based on a Sample CPA Exam Question.** Tom is a minor who enters into a contract with Diane. All of the following are effective methods for Tom to ratify the contract EXCEPT

    a. expressly ratifying the contract after Tom reaches the age of majority.
    b. failing to disaffirm the contact within a reasonable time after Tom reaches the age of majority.
    c. ratifying the contract before Tom reaches the age of majority.
    d. impliedly ratifying the contract after Tom reaches the age of majority.

____ 2. While intoxicated, Konrad agrees to sell his warehouse for half its assessed value. The contract is

    a. enforceable even if Konrad did not understand its legal consequences.
    b. enforceable only if Konrad understood its legal consequences.
    c. unenforceable because it obviously favors the buyer.
    d. unenforceable under any circumstances.

____ 3. Vincenzo is adjudged mentally incompetent. Sophia is appointed to act as Vincenzo's guardian. Vincenzo signs a contract to sell his house. The contract is

    a. enforceable if Vincenzo comprehended the consequences.
    b. enforceable if Vincenzo knew he was entering into a contract.
    c. enforceable if the house was entirely paid for.
    d. void.

____ 4. Ewa, a sixteen-year-old minor, buys a car from Downtown Autos and wrecks it. To disaffirm the contract and satisfy a duty of restitution, Ewa must

    a. return the car without paying for the damage.
    b. pay for the damage without returning the car.
    c. return the car and pay for the damage.
    d. keep the car and not pay for the damage.

____ 5. Bosley bets Finster on the outcome of the SuperBowl. Gambling on sports events is illegal in their state. Before the game is over, Bosley's attempt to withdraw from the bet is

    a. invalid if it comes in the second half.
    b. invalid unless Bosley's team was ahead at the time of the withdrawal.
    c. invalid without Finster's consent.
    d. valid.

____ 6. Jaime sells his business to Isabella and, as part of the agreement, promises not to engage in a business of the same kind within thirty miles for one year. This promise is

    a. an unreasonable restraint of trade.
    b. unreasonable in terms of geographic area and time.
    c. unreasonable in terms of Isabella's "goodwill" and "reputation."
    d. valid and enforceable.

____ 7. Luke is an unlicensed contractor in a state that requires a license to protect the public from unauthorized contractors. Kirkpatrick hires Luke to build an office building. This contract is

  a. enforceable only after Kirkpatrick learns of Luke's status.
  b. enforceable only before Kirkpatrick learns of Luke's status.
  c. enforceable only if no problems arise.
  d.   unenforceable.

____ 8. Franz signs a covenant not to compete with his employer, Gifts 'n More Corporation. This covenant is enforceable if it

  a. is not ancillary to the sale of a business.
  b. is reasonable in terms of geographic area and time.
  c. is supported by consideration.
  d. requires both parties to obtain business licenses.

____ 9. Sam leases real property from Regina under an agreement that includes an exculpatory clause. This clause is likely unenforceable

  a. as a matter of public policy.
  b. if either party is in a business important to the public interest.
  c. if the lease involves commercial property.
  d. none of the choices.

____ 10. Leigh contracts with Klausen, a financial planner who is required by the state to have a license. Klausen does not have a license. Their contract is enforceable if

  a.   Leigh does not know that Klausen is required to have a license.
  b. Klausen does not know that he is required to have a license.
  c. the purpose of the statute is to protect the public from unlicensed practitioners.
  d. the purpose of the statute is to raise government revenue.

SHORT ESSAY QUESTIONS

1. Who has protection under the law relating to contractual capacity and what protection do they have?

2. What makes an agreement illegal? What is the effect of an illegal agreement?

ROCKON

(Answers at the Back of the Book)

1.   A state statute requires that criminal activity be reported to the authorities. Denny and you are employees of Euphonious Warehouse, an online seller of music paraphernalia. Flo, your supervisor, catches Denny pilfering some of the goods, but promises not to report the crime if Denny pays her half the value of the stolen merchandise. Denny agrees and pays. If Flo later reports Denny, can he sue to enforce or rescind their agreement? Why or why not?

2.   On May 1. Franco sells you, a minor, an electric guitar and amplifier. On June 1, you attain the age of majority. On June 5, Franco is offered a considerably larger sum of money by Garth for the instrument that he sold to you. Franco offers to return your money and demands that you return the guitar and amp. You refuse. Franco argues that because you were a minor at the time of the deal, he has a right to disaffirm the contract and rescind the sale. Is Franco correct? Discuss.

SPECIAL INFORMATION FOR CPA CANDIDATES

The CPA examination has not generally tested heavily on capacity. Those points that it may be important to keep in mind include that a minor can disaffirm a contract for a reasonable time after reaching majority. The CPA exam recognizes the rule that for a minor to disaffirm, he or she must return whatever the minor received under the contract. Also, on the CPA exam, intoxication qualifies as a defense only if it was involuntary.

The CPA exam has often asked questions relating to covenants not to compete and to contracts that violate licensing statutes. A covenant not to compete is usually legal if it is part of the sale of a business. A covenant not to compete between an employer and an employee is legal if it is reasonable in length of time and geographic scope.

If a contracting party failed to comply with a licensing statute that has as its purpose the raising of revenue, the contract will likely still be enforceable. If the purpose of the statute is to regulate members of the profession of which the noncomplying party claims to be a part, however, the contract is not enforceable.

Chapter 14
Mistakes, Fraud, and Voluntary Consent

WHAT THIS CHAPTER IS ABOUT

A contract may be unenforceable if the parties have not genuinely assented to its terms. Assent may be lacking because of mistakes, misrepresentation, undue influence, or duress. A party who has not truly assented can choose to avoid the transaction—lack of assent is both a defense to the enforcement of a contract and a ground for rescission (cancellation) of a contract. An injured party can also opt to enforce the deal.

CHAPTER OUTLINE

I. MISTAKES

It is important to distinguish between mistakes made in judgment as to value or quality and mistakes made as to facts. Only the latter have legal significance.

A. MISTAKES OF FACT

1. Bilateral (Mutual) Mistake of Fact
If *both* parties are mistaken as to a *material fact,* either party can rescind the contract. This is also true if they attach different meanings to a term subject to more than one reasonable interpretation.

2. Unilateral Mistake of Fact
When *one* contracting party makes a mistake as to some material fact, he or she is *not* entitled to relief from the contract. Exceptions are—

a. Other Party's Knowledge
A contract may not be enforceable if the other party to the contract knows or should have known that a mistake was made.

b. Mathematical Mistakes
A contract may not be enforceable (or may be reformed) if a significant mistake in addition, subtraction, division, or multiplication was inadvertent and made without gross negligence.

B. MISTAKES OF VALUE
When *one or both* parties make a mistake as to the *market value* or quality of the object of a contract, either party can *enforce* the contract.

II. FRAUDULENT MISREPRESENTATION
When an innocent party is fraudulently induced to enter into a contract, the contract normally can be avoided because that party has not voluntarily consented to its terms.

103

A. THE ELEMENTS OF FRAUD

These are (1) misrepresentation of a material fact, (2) an intent to deceive, and (3) an innocent party's justifiable reliance on the misrepresentation.

1. Misrepresentation Has Occurred

Misrepresentation can occur through words or conduct.

a. Statements of Opinion

Statements of opinion generally are not subject to claims of fraud. But when a naïve purchaser relies on an expert's opinion, the innocent party may be entitled to rescission or reformation (an alteration of the terms of the contract to reflect the parties' true intent).

b. Misrepresentation by Conduct

Misrepresentation can occur by conduct, including concealing a fact material to the contract.

c. Misrepresentation of Law

Misrepresentation of law does not entitle a party to relief, unless the misrepresenting party is in a profession known to require greater knowledge of the law than a layperson has.

d. Misrepresentation by Silence

Generally, no party to a contract has a duty to disclose facts. Exceptions include—

1) Latent Defects

If a serious defect is known to the seller but could not reasonably be suspected by the buyer, the seller may have a duty to speak.

2) Fiduciary Relationships

In a fiduciary relationship, if one party knows facts that materially affect the other's interests, they must be disclosed.

2. Intent to Deceive (*Scienter*)

A misrepresenting party must know that facts are falsely represented.

a. When *Scienter* Exists

If a party (1) knows a fact is not as stated; (2) makes a statement he or she believes not to be true or makes it recklessly, without regard to the truth; or (3) says or implies that a statement is made on a basis such as personal knowledge when it is not.

b. Innocent Misrepresentation

This occurs when a person misrepresents a material fact without the intent to defraud (he or she believes the statement to be true). A party who relies on the statement to his or her detriment can rescind the contract.

c. Negligent Misrepresentation

This occurs when a person misrepresents a material fact by failing to exercise reasonable care in uncovering or disclosing the facts, or not using the skill and competence that his or her business or profession requires. In effect, this is treated as fraudulent misrepresentation.

3. Reliance on the Misrepresentation

The misrepresentation must be an important factor in inducing the party to contract. Reliance is not justified if the party knows the truth or relies on obviously extravagant statements, or the defect is obvious.

B. INJURY TO THE INNOCENT PARTY

To rescind a contract, most courts do not require proof of injury. To recover damages, proof of injury is required. In actions based on fraud, punitive damages are often granted, on the public-policy ground of punishing the defendant or setting an example to deter similar wrongdoing by others.

III. UNDUE INFLUENCE

If a contract enriches a party at the expense of another who is dominated by the enriched party, the contract is voidable.

A. HOW UNDUE INFLUENCE MAY OCCUR

A confidential or fiduciary relationship in which one party can greatly influence another (attorney-client, parent-child) provides an opportunity for undue influence. The essential feature is that the party taken advantage of does not exercise free will.

B. THE PRESUMPTION OF UNDUE INFLUENCE

In a confidential or fiduciary relationship, the dominant party is held to the utmost good faith in dealing with the subservient party. When a dominant party is enriched from the relationship, undue influence is presumed. To rebut the presumption, the dominant party must show that there was full disclosure, adequate consideration, and independent, competent advice for the subservient party.

IV. DURESS

Duress involves conduct of a coercive nature.

A. WHAT DURESS IS

Forcing a party to enter into a contract by threatening the party with a wrongful or illegal act—threatening blackmail or extortion, for example—is committing duress.

B. WHAT DURESS IS NOT

Threatening to exercise a legal right or taking advantage of another's economic need (unless the party exacting the price also creates the need) does not give rise to duress.

V. ADHESION CONTRACTS AND UNCONSCIONABILITY

A. WHAT AN ADHESION CONTRACT IS

An adhesion contract is written exclusively by one party (usually a seller or creditor) and presented to the other (buyer or borrower) on a take-it-or-leave-it basis.

B. STANDARD-FORM CONTRACTS

These often contain fine-print provisions that shift a risk ordinarily borne by one party to the other. To be deemed unconscionable, the contract must be between parties with substantially unequal bargaining power and its enforcement must be unfair or oppressive.

C. UNCONSCIONABILITY

UCC 2–302, which applies to sales of goods, gives courts discretion to invalidate unconscionable clauses and contracts. Many courts apply UCC 2–302 to situations other than sales of goods. Some states have not adopted UCC 2–302, applying instead traditional fraud, undue influence, or duress.

TRUE-FALSE QUESTIONS

(Answers at the Back of the Book)

____ 1. A unilateral mistake does not generally afford the mistaken party a right to relief from the contract.

____ 2. If both parties are mistaken as to the same material fact, neither party can rescind the contract.

____ 3. To commit fraud, one party must intend to mislead another.

____ 4. To rescind a contract for fraud, a plaintiff must prove that he or she suffered an injury.

____ 5. Threatening a civil suit does not normally constitute duress.

___ **6.** A contract entered into under undue influence is voidable.

___ **7.** Adhesion contracts are always enforced.

___ **8.** If a person believes a statement to be true, he or she cannot be held liable for misrepresentation.

___ **9.** A seller has no duty to disclose a defect that he or she knows of but of which a buyer is unaware.

___ **10.** If both parties are mistaken as to the market value of their contract, either party can rescind it.

FILL-IN QUESTIONS

(Answers at the Back of the Book)

Believing something is worth more than it is a mistake of _____(fact/value). When parties contract, their agreement establishes the worth of the object of their contract for the moment. The next moment, the worth may change. Either party may be mistaken as to what the change may be. This is a mistake of _____ (fact/value). Under such a mistake, a contract _____ (cannot/may) be avoided. Mistakes as to _____ (value/fact) will almost never justify voiding a contract.

MULTIPLE-CHOICE QUESTIONS

(Answers at the Back of the Book)

___ **1. Based on a Sample CPA Exam Question.** Subprime Properties, LLC, asks for bids on a construction project. Subprime estimates that the cost will be $200,000. Most bids are about $200,000, but Restoration Construction Company (RCC) bids $150,000. In adding figures, RCC mistakenly omitted a $50,000 item. Because Subprime had reason to know of the mistake

　　a. RCC can avoid the contract because Subprime knew of the errors.
　　b. RCC can avoid the contract because the errors were the result of negligence.
　　c. Subprime can enforce the contract because the errors were unilateral.
　　d. Subprime can enforce the contract because the errors were material.

___ **2.** Krista persuades Jonna to contract for her company's services by asserting that her employees are the "best and the brightest." Krista's statement is

　　a. duress.
　　b. fraud.
　　c. puffery.
　　d. undue influence.

___ **3.** LaRue sells to Milly ten shares of NHance Corporation stock. Milly believes that it will increase in value, but it later drops in price. From LaRue, Milly can most likely recover

　　a. nothing.
　　b. the difference between the stock's purchase price and its later value.
　　c. the stock's later value only.
　　d. the stock's purchase price only.

___ **4.** Clark sells Lena a parcel of land, claiming that it is "perfect" for commercial development. She later learns that it is not zoned for commercial uses. Lena may rescind the contract

　　a. only if Clark knew about the zoning law.
　　b. only if Lena did not know about the zoning law.
　　c. only if the zoning law was not common knowledge.
　　d. under no circumstances.

5. In offering to install a 3D projection system in Phoenix's movie theater, Quimby deliberately misstates what he has done and what he can do. In reliance, Phoenix contracts for Quimby's services. Quimby's statement is

a. duress.
b. fraud.
c. puffery.
d. undue influence.

6. Fran is an eighty-year-old widow with no business experience. Fran's nephew Mark urges her to sell some of her stock at a price below market value to Tim, Mark's "business" partner. Fran, relying on Mark, agrees to sell the stock to Tim. She may avoid the contract on the ground of

a. duress.
b. fraud.
c. mistake.
d. undue influence.

7. InteliSource, a chain of computer stores, presents its customer Hubert with a form contract on a take-it-or-leave basis to finance his purchase. The contract is

a. enforceable under all circumstances.
b. not enforceable if enforcement would be unfair or oppressive.
c. not enforceable if the terms are fair but Hubert would prefer not to pay.
d. not enforceable in states that have not adopted UCC 2–302.

8. Ren contracts with Salvatore under what Ren later learns to have been misrepresented facts. Ren has not yet suffered an injury. Ren can

a. either obtain damages or rescind the contract.
b. neither obtain damages nor rescind the contract.
c. only obtain damages from Salvatore.
d. only rescind the contract.

9. To sell his house to Rosemary, Sage does not tell her that the foundation was built on unstable pilings. Rosemary may later avoid the contract on the ground of

a. duress.
b. fraud.
c. mistake.
d. undue influence.

10. Dennae and Mai enter into a contract. Dennae later tells Mai that if she does not perform her part of the deal, Dennae will sue her. Mai can

a. avoid the contract on the basis of duress.
b. avoid the contract on the basis of fraudulent misrepresentation.
c. avoid the contract on the basis of undue influence.
d. not avoid the contract.

SHORT ESSAY QUESTIONS

1. Why are mistakes of value not accorded the same relief as mistakes of fact?

2. What are the elements of fraudulent misrepresentation?

ROCKON

(Answers at the Back of the Book)

1.   You own Chords, a music store. You have a basic knowledge of bookkeeping—you can balance a checkbook—but you are not an accountant. Dana, a local bass guitarist and entrepreneur, offers to buy Chords and asks about its finances. Using bills and receipts, you prepare a simple financial statement. You suggest that Dana have an accountant review the store's records. He says no and makes an offer in reliance on your statement, which mistakenly inflates Chords's assets and income. Unaware of the mistakes, you accept the offer. Can Dana later sue you successfully for misrepresentation? Explain.

2.   As a musician with Grass Roots, a folk and blues group, you supplement your income by working as an electrical subcontractor. In this capacity, you submit a bid for work on Honey Tones, a new recording studio. Your bid includes material mathematical mistakes, which overstate your costs. Idle Builders, Inc., the project's general contractor, notices the errors but accepts your bid. Are you liable for the mistakes? Why or why not?

SPECIAL INFORMATION FOR CPA CANDIDATES

The CPA examination has traditionally covered at least four of the types of conduct mentioned in this chapter—fraudulent misrepresentation, nonfraudulent misrepresentation, undue influence, and duress. You may want to review the elements of those types of conduct, keeping in mind that each of these is interpreted according to the person defrauded, unduly influenced, or under duress (they are not interpreted according to what a reasonable person in the position of the innocent party would have believed). Remember, too, that the conduct must relate to a material fact, or otherwise be material, and it must truly result in the innocent party's assent.

Chapter 15
The Statute of Frauds— Writing Requirement and Electronic Records

WHAT THIS CHAPTER IS ABOUT

Under the Statute of Frauds, certain types of contracts must be in writing to be enforceable. If there is no written evidence of a contract that falls under this statute, it is not void, but it may not be enforceable. This chapter covers contracts that fall under the Statute of Frauds and the parol evidence rule, which concerns the admissibility at trial of evidence that is external to written contracts.

CHAPTER OUTLINE

I. THE ORIGINS OF THE STATUTE OF FRAUDS
The English passed the Statute of Frauds in 1677. Today, every state has a statute that stipulates what types of contracts must be in writing (or evidenced by a writing) to be enforceable. If one of these contracts is not in writing, the contract is not void but the Statute of Frauds is a defense to its enforcement.

Pg. 296

II. CONTRACTS THAT FALL WITHIN THE STATUTE OF FRAUDS

A. CONTRACTS INVOLVING INTERESTS IN LAND
Land includes all objects permanently attached, such as trees. Contracts to transfer interests in land (such as leases; see Chapters 48 and 49) must be in writing.

B. THE ONE-YEAR RULE

1. Performance Objectively Impossible Must Be in Writing
A contract must be in writing if performance is objectively impossible within one year of the date after the contract's formation.

2. Possibility of Performance Need Not Be in Writing
A contract need not be in writing if performance within one year is possible—even if it is improbable, unlikely, or takes longer.

C. COLLATERAL PROMISES
A collateral promise is a secondary promise, or a promise ancillary to a principal transaction.

1. Primary versus Secondary Obligations
A primary obligation does not need to be in writing to be enforceable. A promise by a third party to assume the debts or obligations of a primary party, if the primary party does not perform, is a secondary obligation and must be in writing to be enforceable.

2. An Exception—The "Main Purpose" Rule

An oral promise to answer for the debt of another is enforceable if the guarantor's main purpose is to secure a personal benefit.

D. PROMISES MADE IN CONSIDERATION OF MARRIAGE

Prenuptial and postnuptial agreements must be in writing to be enforceable. (As with other contracts, consideration and voluntary consent are also required.)

E. CONTRACTS FOR SALES OF GOODS

The Uniform Commercial Code (UCC) requires a writing for a sale of goods priced at $500 or more [UCC 2–201] (see Chapter 20). A written memo or a series of writings may satisfy the requirement.

F. EXCEPTIONS TO THE STATUTE OF FRAUDS

1. Partial Performance

a. Contracts for the Transfer of Interests in Land

If a buyer pays part of the price, takes possession, and makes permanent improvements and the parties cannot be returned to their pre-contract status quo, a court may grant specific performance.

b. Contracts Covered by the UCC

Under the UCC, an oral contract is enforceable to the extent that a seller accepts payment or a buyer accepts delivery of the goods.

2. Admissions

In some states, if a party admits in pleadings, testimony, or in court that a contract was made, the contract will be enforceable. A contract subject to the UCC will be enforceable only to the extent of the quantity admitted.

3. Promissory Estoppel

An oral contract may be enforced if (1) a promisor makes a promise on which the promisee justifiably relies to his or her detriment, (2) the reliance was foreseeable to the promisor, and (3) injustice can be avoided only by enforcing the promise.

4. Special Exceptions under the UCC

Oral contracts that may be enforceable under the UCC include those for customized goods and those between merchants that have been confirmed in writing (see Chapter 20).

III. SUFFICIENCY OF THE WRITING

There must be at least a memo, confirmation, invoice, sales slip, check, fax, several documents, or electronic evidence that includes—

A. THE SIGNATURE OF THE PARTY TO BE CHARGED

The writing must be signed (initialed) by the party against whom enforcement is sought (the party who refuses to perform). The signature can be anywhere in the writing. Electronic signatures, which can be consist of a name at the end of an e-mail note, are discussed in Chapter 11.

B. THE ESSENTIAL TERMS

1. Contracts Covered by the UCC

The writing must include a quantity term. Other terms need not be stated exactly, if they adequately reflect the parties' intentions.

2. Other Contracts

The writing must include the identity of the parties, subject matter, consideration, and essential terms (in a sale of land these would include the price and a legal description of the property).

Pg. 300

IV. THE PAROL EVIDENCE RULE

A. THE RULE FOR INTEGRATED CONTRACTS

If the parties' written contract is integrated (the final expression of their agreement), evidence of their prior negotiations, prior agreements, or contemporaneous oral agreements that contradicts or varies the terms of the contract is not admissible at trial.

B. EXCEPTIONS TO THE RULE

Parol evidence is admissible to show—

1. A Contract Was Subsequently Modified

Evidence of subsequent modification (oral or written) of a written contract is admissible (but oral modifications may not be enforceable if they bring the contract under the Statute of Frauds).

2. A Contract Is Voidable or Void

3. The Meaning of Ambiguous Terms

4. An Essential Term Is Lacking in an Incomplete Contract

5. Prior Dealing, Course of Performance, or Usage of Trade

Under the UCC, evidence can be introduced to explain or supplement a contract by showing a prior dealing, course of performance, or usage of trade (see Chapter 20).

6. An Orally Agreed-on Condition Precedent

Proof of such a condition does not modify the written terms but involves the enforceability of the written contract.

7. An Obvious or Gross Clerical Error

V. THE STATUTE OF FRAUDS IN THE INTERNATIONAL CONTEXT

The Convention on Contracts for the International Sale of Goods (CISG) does not include a Statute of Frauds or any other requirements as to form [Article 11]. This is in line with the law in most countries.

TRUE-FALSE QUESTIONS

(Answers at the Back of the Book)

____ 1. A contract that cannot by its own terms be performed within a year must be in writing to be enforceable.

____ 2. A promise to answer for the debt of another must always be in writing to be enforceable.

____ 3. A promise on which a promisee justifiably relies to his or her detriment will not be enforced unless it is in writing.

____ 4. If a party admits in pleadings that a contract was made, it may be enforceable even if it was oral.

____ 5. Oral contracts that are *not* enforceable under the UCC include those for customized goods.

____ 6. A contract for a transfer of an interest in land need not be in writing to be enforceable.

____ 7. To be enforceable, a contract for a sale of goods priced at $300 or more must be in writing.

____ 8. An oral contract that should be in writing to be enforceable may be enforceable if it has been partially performed.

___ 9. The only writing sufficient to satisfy the Statute of Frauds is a printed form, with the heading "Contract," signed at the bottom by all parties.

___ 10. The parol evidence rule permits the introduction at trial of evidence of the parties' negotiations or agreements that contradicts or varies their contract.

FILL-IN QUESTIONS

(Answers at the Back of the Book)

A collateral promise is a promise that is _____ (superior/ancillary) to a _____ (primary/secondary) contractual relationship.

A promise by one person to pay the debts or discharge the duties of another person if the other fails to perform _____ (must/need not) be in writing to be enforceable under the Statute of Frauds. If the main purpose of a promise to pay another's debts or perform another's duties is to benefit the promisor, however, the agreement _____ (must/need not) be in writing to be enforceable.

MULTIPLE-CHOICE QUESTIONS

(Answers at the Back of the Book)

___ 1. Marci orally promises to work for Lions Share Oil Company, whose representative orally promises to employ Marci at a rate of $1,000 a week. This contract must be in writing to be enforceable if Marci promises to work for

a. at least five years.
b. five years but either party can terminate the contract on two weeks' notice.
c. less than a year.
d. life.

___ 2. Sham Rock Mining & Sales Company agrees to hire Leif as a sales representative for six months. Their contract is oral. This contract is enforceable by

a. neither Sham Rock nor Leif.
b. Sham Rock only.
c. Sham Rock or Leif.
d. Leif only.

___ 3. **Based on a Sample CPA Exam Question.** Under a written agreement, Rosalie sells a motel to Felix. When Rosalie removes the furniture, Felix sues. The court decides the written agreement includes everything the parties intended. Which of the following agreements about the furniture will be admissible?

a. A prior written agreement only
b. A subsequent oral agreement only
c. Either a prior written agreement or a subsequent oral agreement
d. Neither a prior written agreement nor a subsequent oral agreement

___ 4. Polyhedron Engineering Company and Omega Imaging Corporation enter into an oral contract for the sale of a warehouse. Before Omega takes possession, this contract is enforceable by

a. Polyhedron only.
b. Polyhedron or Omega.
c. neither Polyhedron or Omega.
d. Omega only.

____ **5.** Warehouses, Inc., orally contracts for a lease of its storage facilities to Valu Storage Company. Valu Storage pays part of the price, takes possession, and makes permanent improvements to the property. The contract is most likely enforceable against

   a. neither Warehouses nor Valu Storage.
   b. Warehouses and Valu Storage.
   c. Warehouses only.
   d. Valu Storage only.

____ **6.** Music Rental & Sales Company contracts with Band Together, Inc., to buy seventy-six trombones and on assortment of other musical instruments. The contract is most likely enforceable against Band Together if Music Rental & Sales offers as proof of the agreement

   a. an ad placed in the media by Band Together.
   b. a purchase order signed by Music Rental & Sales.
   c. a sales slip signed by Band Together.
   d. testimony by a Music Rental & Sales agent.

____ **7.** Casual Investors, Inc., contracts with Formal Properties to buy one of Formal's office buildings. The contract is most likely enforceable against Formal if Casual offers as proof of the agreement

   a. a blank sheet of Formal's letterhead stationery.
   b. Formal's business card.
   c. photos of the building taken by a Casual employee.
   d. none of the choices.

____ **8.** Jeb and Keri enter into a contract for Jeb's sale to Keri of seven telescopes for $500 each. After Keri takes possession, but before she makes payment, this contract is enforceable

   a. only if it is in writing.
   b. only if it is oral.
   c. whether it is oral or in writing.
   d. under no circumstances.

____ **9.** Eiger borrows $1,000 from Front Street Bank. Giselle orally promises the bank that she will repay the debt if Eiger does not. This promise is enforceable by

   a. Eiger only.
   b. Eiger or Front Street Bank.
   c. Front Street Bank only.
   d. neither Eiger nor Front Street Bank.

____ **10.** Jane agrees to make kitchen cabinetry for Henny, who tells Enoch that she will guarantee payment for whatever supplies Jane orders from Enoch for the shelves. Henny's promise is enforceable

   a. only if it is in writing.
   b. only if it is oral.
   c. whether it is oral or in writing.
   d. under no circumstances.

SHORT ESSAY QUESTIONS

1. What is required to satisfy the writing requirement of the Statute of Frauds?

2. What is *not* admissible under the parol evidence rule?

ROCKON

(Answers at the Back of the Book)

1. You begin your career in music as a keyboardist, writing songs for Lifelong, a faith-based rock group. With success comes the opportunity to record for Masterworx Studios, where you pick up the skills of a recording engineer. Now, as a sought-after producer, you are hired by Masterworx to remix Nightingale's new album. The terms of your oral agreement provides that you are to finish the album within sixteen months. But the work could be done within one year. Is this agreement enforceable? Discuss.

2. To become more proficient, your heavy-metal rock group Axme devotes long hours to rehearsing. For this purpose, and the storage of your amps and other gear, you negotiate with Brick on behalf of Corporate Properties, Inc., to lease a warehouse. Brick orally agrees that Corporate Properties will pay the utilities, but the written lease provides that Axme pay the utilities. In a later suit to rescind the lease, can you introduce evidence of the oral agreement about the utilities? Why or why not?

SPECIAL INFORMATION FOR CPA CANDIDATES

Among the details covered in this chapter, the CPA examination has asked questions about the types of contracts that fall within the Statute of Frauds, the enforceability of oral contracts that come under the Statute of Frauds, and the effect of an oral acceptance of a written offer. Sometimes, these details have been woven into questions are less direct. For example, a question might ask for a calculation of damages for the breach of an oral contract, which requires a consideration of the types of contracts subject to the Statute of Frauds.

Chapter 16
Third Party Rights

Concept Summary Pg. 310 (handwritten)

WHAT THIS CHAPTER IS ABOUT

A party to a contract can assign the rights arising from it to another or delegate the duties of the contract by having another perform them. A third party also acquires rights to enforce a contract when the contract parties intend the contract to benefit the third party (who is an intended beneficiary). When a contract only incidentally benefits a third party, he or she is an incidental beneficiary and cannot enforce it.

CHAPTER OUTLINE

I. ASSIGNMENTS AND DELEGATIONS

Assignment and delegation occur after the original contract is made, when one of the parties transfers to another party an interest or duty in the contract.

A. ASSIGNMENTS

1. What an Assignment Is
Parties to a contract have rights and duties. One party has a *right* to require the other to perform, and the other has a *duty* to perform. The transfer of the *right* to a third person is an assignment. *In privity* (handwritten)

2. How Assignments Function
Assignments are involved in much business financing. The most common contractual right that is assigned is the right to the payment of money.

3. The Effect of an Assignment
(1) Rights of the assignor are extinguished; (2) assignee has a right to demand performance from the obligor; and (3) assignee's rights are subject to defenses the obligor has against the assignor.

4. Form of the Assignment
An assignment can be oral or written. Assignments covered by the Statute of Frauds must be in writing to be enforceable. Most states require contracts for the assignment of wages to be in writing.

5. Rights That Cannot Be Assigned

a. When a Statute Prohibits Assignment
(For example, statutes often prohibit assignment of future workers' compensation benefits.)

b. When a Contract Is Personal in Nature
The rights under the contract cannot be assigned unless all that remains is a money payment. (Personal services are unique to the person rendering them. Rights to receive personal services are likewise unique and cannot be assigned.)

c. When an Assignment Will Significantly Change the Risk or Duties of Obligor

115

    d. When a Contract Prohibits Assignment
    Exceptions: a contract cannot prevent an assignment of—

      1) A right to receive money.
      2) Rights in real estate (restraint against alienation).
      3) Rights in negotiable instruments (see Chapter 24).
      4) A right to receive damages for breach of a sales contract or for payment of amount owed under it (even if contract prohibits it).

  6. Notice of Assignment
  An assignment is effective immediately, with or without notice.

    a. Same Right Assigned to More Than One Party
    If the assignor assigns the same right to different persons, in most states, the first assignment in time is the first in right. In some states, priority is given to the first assignee who gives notice.

    b. Discharge before Notice
    Until an obligor has notice, his or her obligation can be discharged by performance to the assignor. Once the obligor has notice, only performance to the assignee can act as a discharge.

B. DELEGATIONS
Duties are delegated. The party making the delegation is the delegator; the party to whom the duty is delegated is the delegatee.

  1. Form of Delegation
  No special form is required.

  2. Duties That Cannot Be Delegated

    a. When the Duties Are Personal in Nature
    A duty cannot be delegated, if its performance depends on the personal skill or talents of the obligor, or special trust has been placed in the obligor.

    b. When Performance by a Third Party Will Vary Materially from That Expected by the Obligee
    The obligee is the one to whom performance is owed under a contract.

    c. When the Contract Prohibits Delegation

  3. Effect of a Delegation
  The obligee (to whom performance is owed) must accept performance from the delegatee, unless the duty is one that cannot be delegated. If the delegatee fails to perform, the delegator is liable.

  4. Liability of the Delegatee
  If the delegatee makes a promise of performance that will directly benefit the obligee, there is an "assumption of duty." Breach of this duty makes the delegatee liable to the obligee, and the obligee can sue both the delegatee and the delegator.

C. ASSIGNMENT OF "ALL RIGHTS"
A contract that provides in general words for an assignment of all rights (for example, "I assign the contract") is both an assignment of rights and a delegation of duties.

II.   THIRD PARTY BENEFICIARIES   Pg. 313

Only intended beneficiaries acquire legal rights in a contract.

A. INTENDED BENEFICIARIES
An intended beneficiary is one for whose benefit a contract is made. If the contract is breached, he or she can sue the promisor.

1. **Types of Intended Beneficiaries**

   a. **Creditor Beneficiaries**
   A creditor beneficiary benefits from a contract in which a promisor promises to pay a debt that the promisee owes to him or her.

   b. **Donee Beneficiaries**
   A donee beneficiary benefits from a contract made for the express purpose of giving a gift to him or her. The "modern view" is not to distinguish between types of intended beneficiaries.

2. **When the Rights of an Intended Beneficiary Vest**
   To enforce a contract against the original parties, the rights of the third party must vest (take effect). The rights vest when (1) the third party materially alters his or her position in justifiable reliance, (2) the third party files a suit on the promise, or (3) the third party manifests assent to the contract.

3. **Modification or Rescission of the Contract**
   Until a third party's rights vest, the others can modify or rescind the contract without the third party's consent. If a contract reserves the power to rescind or modify, vesting does not terminate the power.

B. **INCIDENTAL BENEFICIARIES**
The benefit that an incidental beneficiary receives from a contract between other parties is unintentional. An incidental beneficiary cannot enforce a contract to which he or she is not a party.

C. **INTENDED OR INCIDENTAL BENEFICIARY?**

1. **Reasonable Person Test**
   A beneficiary is intended if a reasonable person in his or her position would believe that the promisee intended to confer on the beneficiary the right to sue to enforce the contract.

2. **Other Factors Indicating an Intended Beneficiary**
   (1) Performance is rendered directly to the third party, or (2) the third party is expressly designated as beneficiary in the contract.

TRUE-FALSE QUESTIONS

(Answers at the Back of the Book)

_____ 1. Third parties do not have rights under contracts to which they are not parties.

_____ 2. The party who makes an assignment is the assignee.

_____ 3. Rights under a personal service contract normally can be assigned.

_____ 4. All rights can be assigned.

_____ 5. With notice of an assignment, an assignee can compel an obligor to perform.

_____ 6. A right to the payment of money may be assigned.

_____ 7. An assignment is not effective without notice.

_____ 8. No special form is required to create a valid delegation of duties.

_____ 9. Only intended beneficiaries acquire legal rights in a contract.

_____ 10. If a delegatee fails to perform, the delegator must do so.

FILL-IN QUESTIONS

(Answers at the Back of the Book)

The transfer of rights to a third person is _____ (an assignment/a delegation) and the transfer of duties to a third person is _____ (an assignment/a delegation). Probably the most common contractual right that is _____ (assigned/delegated) is the right to the payment of money. For instance, Digital Computer Corporation sells its computers on credit. Digital has the right to installment payments from its customers. To obtain funds to buy more inventory, Digital can _____ (assign/delegate) the right to the payments to a financing agency, which will pay Digital for the right.

MULTIPLE-CHOICE QUESTIONS

(Answers at the Back of the Book)

____ 1. Chelsea enters into a contract with Donato that indirectly benefits Emily, although neither Chelsea nor Donato intended that result. Emily is

a. a delegatee.
b. an assignee.
c. an incidental beneficiary.
d. an intended beneficiary.

____ 2. Olinka and Nadine sign a contract under which Olinka agrees to repair Nadine's computer for $150. Later, they agree that Nadine will pay the $150 directly to Olinka's creditor, Mainstay Bank. The bank is

a. a delegatee.
b. an assignee.
c. an incidental beneficiary.
d. an intended beneficiary.

____ 3. Joe and Kit enter into a contract that intentionally benefits Larue. Larue's rights under this contract will vest

a. if Larue manifests assent to it or materially alters her position in justifiable reliance on it.
b. only if Larue manifests assent to it.
c. only if Larue materially alters her position in justifiable reliance on it.
d. under no circumstances.

____ 4. Sharon insures her warehouse under a policy with Riders Insurance Company. Sharon assigns the policy to Polly, who also owns a warehouse. Rider's best argument against the assignment of the policy is that

a. it did not consent to the assignment.
b. it was not paid for the assignment.
c. the assignment will materially alter its risk.
d. this is a personal service contract.

____ 5. Norm signs a contract to provide lawn-mowing services to Orin. Norm delegates his duty under the contract to Palucci. Orin can compel performance from

a. neither Norm nor Palucci.
b. Norm only.
c. Palucci only.
d. Palucci or, if Palucci does not perform, Norm.

___ **6.** Rhonda and Shirley sign a contract. Tim, a third party, is an intended beneficiary to the contract

   a. only if performance is rendered directly to Tim.
   b. only if there is an express designation in the contract.
   c. only if Tim has the right to control the details of performance.
   d. any of the choices.

___ **7. Based on a Sample CPA Exam Question.** Dana assigns to Evon a contract to buy a used car from Francine. To be valid, the assignment must

   a. be in writing and be signed by Dana.
   b. be supported by adequate consideration from Evon.
   c. not be revocable by Dana.
   d. not materially increase Francine's risk or duty.

___ **8.** A contract for a sale of goods between Laramie and Michelle provides that the right to receive damages for its breach cannot be assigned. This clause

   a. is effective only before the contract is executed.
   b. is effective only after the contract is executed.
   c. is effective under all circumstances.
   d. is not effective.

___ **9.** Ellen assigns to Fern her rights under a contract with Gibby. Ellen's rights under the contract

   a. are extinguished.
   b. continue until the contract is fully executed.
   c. continue until Gibby performs his obligations under the contract.
   d. continue until Fern receives Gibby's performance.

___ **10.** Mia has a right to receive payment under a contract with Neil. Without notice, Mia assigns the right first to Jozie and then to Pace. In most states, the party with priority to the right would be

   a. Mia.
   b. Neil.
   c. Jozie.
   d. Pace.

SHORT ESSAY QUESTIONS

1. What is a third party beneficiary contract? What are the circumstances under which a third party can bring an action to enforce it?

2. Who are the parties in an assignment? What are their rights and duties?

ROCKON

(Answers at the Back of the Book)

1. You and your country group Haze perform before an enthusiastic crowd at the Idyll County Fair. Jack, the owner of a local club, sees you perform and likes what he sees. Without a written contract, Jack begins to support your group, arranging gigs, collecting payment, paying bills, and generally managing its career. Later, Mega Entertainment Agency enters into a written management contract with you and your group. The contract provides that Mega will pay the debts that your band has accrued with Jack plus a "gratuity" for his efforts on your behalf. Can Jack enforce the agreement between you and Mega? Why or why not.

2.   Rolling River City contracts with you to repair a stage and construct a set in Sandy Beach Theater for an upcoming series of concerts by Townhall Symphony. The contract specifies details that affect the acoustic properties of the set. The contract does not expressly restrict its assignment. Without informing Rolling River City, you assign the stage repair and set construction to Wellworth Building Company. Wellworth does not build the set according to the specifications in the contract between Rolling River City and you. Are you liable? Explain.

SPECIAL INFORMATION FOR CPA CANDIDATES

It is important to remember for the CPA examination that only a creditor or donee beneficiary may recover from a promisor who fails to perform according to the contract—an incidental beneficiary has no enforceable rights under the contract. It is also important to remember that generally any contract can be assigned (unless the contract expressly prohibits it). There are more restrictions on delegations of duties. The point to remember in regard to delegation of duties is that when a duty is personal, it cannot be assigned.

Finally, it should be remembered that unless there is a release or a novation, the assignor remains liable on the contract despite its assignment. A party who, without notice of an assignment, pays an assignor will not later be liable to the assignee: the assignee should notify the obligor of the assignment.

Chapter 17
Performance and Discharge in Traditional and E-Contracts

WHAT THIS CHAPTER IS ABOUT

This chapter discusses performance and discharge of contracts. Performance of a contract (when the parties do what they agreed to do) discharges it. Discharging a contract terminates it. Discharge usually results from performance but can occur in other ways: (1) the occurrence or failure of a condition on which a contract is based, (2) breach of the contract, (3) agreement of the parties, and (4) operation of law.

CHAPTER OUTLINE

I. CONDITIONS

A **condition** is a possible future event, occurrence or nonoccurrence of which triggers performance of an obligation or terminates an obligation. If performance is contingent on a condition that is not satisfied, neither party has to perform.

A. CONDITION PRECEDENT

A condition precedent must be fulfilled before a party's performance can be required. Such conditions are common. For example, a real estate contract is usually conditioned on a buyer's ability to get financing.

B. CONDITION SUBSEQUENT

A condition subsequent operates to terminate an obligation to perform. The condition follows a duty to perform. Such conditions are rare.

C. CONCURRENT CONDITION

This is when each party's duty to perform is conditioned on the other party's duty to perform. It occurs only when the parties are to perform their duties simultaneously (for example, paying for goods on delivery). No party can recover for breach unless he or she first tenders performance.

D. EXPRESS AND IMPLIED CONDITIONS

1. Express Condition

An express condition is a condition provided in the parties' agreement, and is usually prefaced by the word "if," "provided," "after," or "when."

2. Implied-in-Fact Condition

An implied-in-fact condition is understood to be part of the agreement but not found in its express language. A court infers these conditions from the promises (for example, notice is an implied condition to correct a defect under warranty).

II. DISCHARGE BY PERFORMANCE   *Pg. 330*

Most contracts are discharged by performance—the parties' doing what they promised to do.

121

A. TENDER OF PERFORMANCE

Tender (an unconditional offer to perform by one who is ready, willing, and able to do so) can accomplish performance. If performance has been tendered and the other party refuses to perform, the party making the tender can sue for breach.

B. TYPES OF PERFORMANCE

1. Complete Performance

Complete performance occurs when express conditions are fully satisfied in all aspects.

2. Substantial Performance

a. Confers Most of the Benefits Promised

To qualify as substantial, performance must not vary greatly from that promised in the contract and must create substantially the same benefits.

b. Entitles the Other Party to Damages

Substantial performance by one party entitles the other party to damages for the failure to comply with the contract.

3. Performance to the Satisfaction of Another

a. Personal Satisfaction of One of the Parties

When the subject matter of the contract is personal, performance must actually satisfy the party (a condition precedent).

b. Satisfaction of a Reasonable Person

Most contracts need only be performed to the satisfaction of a reasonable person.

c. Satisfaction of a Third Party

When the satisfaction of a third party is required, most courts require the work to be satisfactory to a reasonable person. Some require the personal satisfaction of the third party.

C. MATERIAL BREACH OF CONTRACT

A breach of contract is the nonperformance of a contractual duty. It is material when performance is not at least substantial; the nonbreaching party is excused from performing. If a breach is minor (not material), the nonbreaching party's duty to perform may be suspended until the breach is remedied.

D. ANTICIPATORY REPUDIATION

This is when, before either party has a duty to perform, one party refuses to perform.

1. Damages and a Similar Contract

Anticipatory repudiation can discharge the nonbreaching party, who can sue to recover damages immediately and can also seek a similar contract elsewhere.

2. Retraction Is Possible

Until the nonbreaching party treats a repudiation as a breach, the repudiating party can retract his or her repudiation by proper notice.

E. TIME FOR PERFORMANCE

If a specific time is stated, the parties must usually perform by that time. If time is stated to be vital or construed to be "of the essence," it is a condition of the contract. If no time is stated, a reasonable time is implied, and a delay will not affect the performing party's right to payment.

III. DISCHARGE BY AGREEMENT

A. DISCHARGE BY RESCISSION

Rescission is the process by which a contract is canceled and the parties are returned to the positions they occupied prior to forming it.

1. Executory Contracts
Contracts that are executory on both sides can be rescinded.

a. Requirements for Rescission
The parties must make another agreement, which must satisfy the legal requirements for a contract. Their promises not to perform are consideration for the second contract.

b. Form of Rescission
Rescission is enforceable if oral (even if the original agreement was in writing), unless it is subject to the UCC and the contract requires written rescission.

2. Executed Contracts
Contracts that are executed on one side can be rescinded only if the party who has performed receives consideration to call off the deal.

B. DISCHARGE BY NOVATION
This occurs when the parties to a contract and a new party get together and agree to substitute the new party for one of the original parties. Requirements are (1) a previous valid obligation, (2) an agreement of all the parties to a new contract, (3) the extinguishment of the old obligation (discharge of the prior party), and (4) a new, valid contract.

C. DISCHARGE BY SETTLEMENT AGREEMENT
Parties to a contract can execute a new agreement with different terms. The new agreement can expressly or impliedly revoke and discharge the previous contract's obligations.

D. DISCHARGE BY ACCORD AND SATISFACTION
To discharge by accord and satisfaction, the parties must agree to accept performance that is different from the performance originally promised.

1. Accord
An accord is an executory contract to perform an act that will satisfy an existing duty. An accord suspends, but does not discharge, the duty.

2. Satisfaction
Satisfaction is the performance of the accord, and discharges the original contract.

3. If the Obligor Refuses to Perform
The obligee can sue on the original obligation or seek specific performance of the accord.

IV. DISCHARGE BY OPERATION OF LAW

A. ALTERATION OF THE CONTRACT
An innocent party can treat a contract as discharged if the other party materially alters a term (such as quantity or price) without consent.

B. STATUTES OF LIMITATIONS
Statutes of limitations limit the period during which a party can sue based on a breach of contract. An action for the breach of a contract for a sale of goods must be commenced within four years after the breach occurs, whether the innocent party knows of the breach [UCC 2–725]. The parties can shorten this period to one year but cannot extend it.

C. BANKRUPTCY
A discharge in bankruptcy (see Chapter 30) will bar enforcement of most of a debtor's contracts.

D. IMPOSSIBILITY OR IMPRACTICABILITY OF PERFORMANCE

1. Objective Impossibility of Performance
Performance is objectively impossible in the unforeseeable event of—

a. A party's death or incapacity.

    b. Destruction of the specific subject matter.

    c. A change in law that makes performance illegal.

2. Temporary Impossibility
An event that makes it temporarily impossible to perform will suspend performance until the impossibility ceases.

3. Commercial Impracticability
Performance may be excused if it becomes significantly more difficult or expensive than contemplated when the contract was formed.

4. Frustration of Purpose
A contract will be discharged if unforeseeable, supervening circumstances make it impossible to attain the purpose the parties had in mind.

TRUE-FALSE QUESTIONS

(Answers at the Back of the Book)

____ **1.** A promise to perform subject to obtaining financing is a condition precedent.

____ **2.** Complete performance occurs when a contract's conditions fully occur.

____ **3.** A material breach of contract does not excuse the nonbreaching party from further performance.

____ **4.** An executory contract cannot be rescinded.

____ **5.** Objective impossibility discharges a contract.

____ **6.** A condition can trigger the performance of a legal obligation.

____ **7.** If a contract does not require a certain time for performance, a reasonable time will be implied.

____ **8.** A party can treat a contract as discharged if the other party materially alters it without consent.

____ **9.** Before either party to a contract has a duty to perform, if one party refuses to do so, there is nothing the other party can do.

____ **10.** There is no time limit for a party to file a suit against another based on a breach of contract.

FILL-IN QUESTIONS

(Answers at the Back of the Book)

Most contracts are discharged by performance—by doing what was promised. Any contract can be discharged by agreement of the parties. _____ (Rescission/Novation) is the process by which a contract is canceled and the parties are returned to the positions they occupied before forming it. _____ (Rescission/Novation) substitutes a new party for an original party by agreement of all the parties. _____ (Substitution of a new contract/Accord and satisfaction) revokes and discharges a prior contract. _____ (A substitution/An accord) suspends a contractual duty that has not been discharged. Once the _____ (substitution/accord) is performed, the original contractual obligation is discharged.

MULTIPLE-CHOICE QUESTIONS

(Answers at the Back of the Book)

____ 1. Sandra and Terry want to discharge their obligations under a prior contract by executing and performing a new agreement. They must execute and perform

   a. an accord and satisfaction.
   b. an assignment.
   c. a novation.
   d. a nullification.

____ 2. Gina enters a contract with Han. Before either party performs, rescission of their contract requires

   a. additional consideration.
   b. a mutual agreement to rescind.
   c. performance by both parties.
   d. restitution.

____ 3. Rod contracts to repair Stu's building for $30,000. Payment is to be made "on the satisfaction of Tina, Stu's architect." Stu tells Tina not to approve the repairs. Rod sues Stu for $30,000. Rod will

   a. not recover, because Rod is not acting reasonably, honestly, and in good faith.
   b. not recover, because Tina has not expressed satisfaction with the work.
   c. recover, because Stu is not acting reasonably.
   d. recover, because Tina is Stu's architect.

____ 4. Dion contracts to build a store for Ellis for $500,000, with payments to be in installments of $50,000 as the work progresses. Dion finishes the store except for a cover over a compressor on the roof. A cover can be installed for $500. Ellis refuses to pay the last installment. If Dion's breach is not material

   a. both parties have claims against each other.
   b. Dion has a claim against Ellis for $50,000, but Ellis has no claim against Dion.
   c. Ellis has a claim against Dion for the failure to cover the compressor, but Dion has no claim against Ellis.
   d. neither party has a claim against the other.

____ 5. On May 1, Ula agrees to work for Vital Corporation for four months beginning June 1. On May 15, Vital tells Ula that it doesn't need her after all. Ula's duty to work for Vital

   a. was discharged on May 15.
   b. was discharged on May 16.
   c. will be discharged on June 1.
   d. will be discharged on September 30.

____ 6. Kyle and Liu contract for the sale of 500 computers. The agreement states, "The obligations of the parties are conditional on Liu obtaining financing from Main Street Bank by August 1." This is

   a. a concurrent condition.
   b. a condition precedent.
   c. a condition subsequent.
   d. not a condition.

____ 7. Finnegan and Ewan want Dribble to replace Finnegan as a party to their contract. They can best accomplish this by agreeing to

a. an accord and satisfaction.
b. an assignment.
c. a novation.
d. a nullification.

____ 8. Town Delivery Service contracts with Pizza! Pie! to deliver its goods to customers. This contract will, like most contracts, be discharged by

a. accord and satisfaction.
b. agreement.
c. operation of law.
d. performance.

____ 9. **Based on a Sample CPA Exam Question.** Carlotta contracts with Darlene to act as her personal financial planner. Carlotta's duties under this contract will be discharged if

a. Darlene declares bankruptcy.
b. it becomes illegal for Carlotta to provide the service.
c. the cost of providing the service doubles.
d. none of the choices.

____ 10. Ric and Skye contract for the sale of Ric's business. Skye makes a down payment, and Ric gives her the keys to one of his stores. Before the contract is fully performed, however, they agree to return the money and keys, and cancel the sale. This is

a. a material breach.
b. an accord and satisfaction.
c. a novation.
d. a rescission.

SHORT ESSAY QUESTIONS

1. How are most contracts discharged?

2. What effect does a material breach have on the nonbreaching party? What is the effect of a nonmaterial breach?

ROCKON

(Answers at the Back of the Book)

1. With the profits from *Sportz!,* a successful pop-rock album, you make a down payment on an isolated ranch on which you arrange for the construction of a sports park. The park includes grassy fields and paved courts, indoor and outdoor pools, and skate and bike ramps and trails. The property is subject to a loan from Titan Bank. Five years later, after two unsuccessful albums, you find it difficult to make payments on the loan. You offer the property to United Funds, LLC., a group of local investors, who accept. United assumes the loan and Titan releases you. What is the transaction between United, Titan, and you? Explain.

2. You're the owner of Joystick Productions, a recording company with an eclectic catalog of musical and dramatic works. The artists can present unique challenges to Joystick's technology—even the classical and spoken-word performers often push the envelope to its limits. You contract with Outside the Box, Inc., to build and program a digital recording system that doesn't require pushing buttons, clicking switches, or manipulating a mouse, but responds instead to gestures and voices. Images are to be selected on a screen by the movement of your hand in the air. Operations are to be controlled by such commands as, "Record now"

and "Cut." The system that Outside the Box delivers nearly meets the specifications—only its voice recognition capability fails to perform as promised. What effect does this failure have on Joystick's obligation to pay?

SPECIAL INFORMATION FOR CPA CANDIDATES

In the past, the CPA examination has tested heavily on discharge, agreements to discharge, and discharge by operation of law. For this reason, it would be good to review those topics. In particular, releases and novations are covered in connection with assignments (discussed in the previous chapter), and accord and satisfaction is tested. Discharge by operation of law should not be confused with termination of an offer by operation of law. For example, the death of an offeror will terminate an offer, but the death of a party to a contract will not necessarily discharge the contract. Other important points to remember, among those covered in this chapter, include what will discharge a party by frustration of purpose. Only something that was not expected will qualify (unusual weather, for example). A statute of limitations begins to run from the time of a breach, or when the breach should have been discovered.

Chapter 18
Breach of Contract and Remedies

336 à 347

WHAT THIS CHAPTER IS ABOUT

Breach of contract is the failure to perform what a party is under a duty to perform. When this happens, the nonbreaching party can choose one or more remedies. Unless damages would be inadequate, that is usually what a court will award.

CHAPTER OUTLINE

I. DAMAGES

Damages compensate a nonbreaching party for the loss of a bargain and, under special circumstances, for additional losses. Generally, the party is placed in the position he or she would have occupied if the contract been performed.

A. TYPES OF DAMAGES

1. Compensatory Damages
These damages compensate a party for the *loss* of a bargain.

a. Standard Measure
The measurement of compensatory damages varies by type of contract. The standard measure is the difference between the value of the promised performance and the value of the actual performance, less any loss that the injured party could have avoided.

b. Sale of Goods
The usual measure is the difference between the contract price and the market price. When a buyer breaches and the seller has not yet produced the goods, the measure is instead normally lost profits on the sale.

c. Sale of Land
In most states, the measure of damages is the difference between the contract and market prices of the land. In some states, when a seller breaches a contract and the breach is not deliberate, the buyer recovers only the down payment and expenses, placing him or her in the position occupied before the sale, not the benefit of the bargain.

d. Construction Contracts
The measure depends on which party breaches and when.

1) **Owner's Breach Before, During, or After Construction**
Contractor can recover (1) before construction: only profits (contract price, less cost of materials and labor); (2) during construction: profits, plus cost of partial construction; (3) after construction: the contract price, plus interest.

2) **Contractor's Breach**
Owner can recover for (1) failing to begin: cost, above contract price, to complete; (2) stopping mid-project: cost of completion; (3) late completion: costs related to loss of use; (4) substantial performance: cost of completion, if there would be no substantial economic waste (if cost to complete does not exceed value the extra work contributes.)

129

e. Incidental Damages
These are expenses caused directly by a breach of contract (such as those incurred to obtain performance from another source). Incidental damages are added to compensatory damages.

2. Consequential Damages
These are damages giving an injured party the entire *benefit* of the bargain—foreseeable losses caused by special circumstances beyond the contract. The breaching party must know (or have reason to know) that special circumstances will cause the additional loss.

3. Punitive Damages
These damages punish a guilty party and make an example to deter similar, future conduct. Awarded for a tort, but not for a contract breach (which is not a crime and may not harm society).

4. Nominal Damages
These damages (such as $1) establish that a defendant acted wrongfully even if no loss resulted.

B. MITIGATION OF DAMAGES
An injured party has a duty to mitigate damages. For example, persons whose jobs have been wrongfully terminated have a duty to seek other jobs. The damages they receive are their salaries, less the income they received (or would have received) in similar jobs.

C. LIQUIDATED DAMAGES VERSUS PENALTIES

1. Liquidated Damages Provision—Enforceable
This specifies a certain amount to be paid on a breach *to compensate for the loss to the nonbreaching party.*

2. Penalty Provision—Unenforceable
This specifies a certain amount to be paid on a breach *to penalize the breaching party.*

3. How to Determine If a Provision Will Be Enforced
Ask (1) when a contract was made, was it clear damages would be difficult to estimate on a breach, and (2) was the amount set as damages reasonable? If either answer is "no," a provision will not be enforced.

II. EQUITABLE REMEDIES

A. RESCISSION AND RESTITUTION
Rescission is an action to undo, or cancel, a contract—to return a nonbreaching party to the position he or she occupied before the transaction. Rescission is available if fraud, mistake, duress, or failure of consideration is present. The rescinding party must give prompt notice to the breaching party.

1. Restitution
To rescind a contract, the parties must make restitution by returning to each other goods, property, or money previously conveyed.

2. Restitution Is Not Limited to Rescission Cases
Restitution is available in other actions, such as when money or property is transferred due to a mistake, incapacity, or fraud.

B. SPECIFIC PERFORMANCE
This remedy calls for the performance of the act promised in the contract.

1. When Specific Performance Is Available
Damages must be an inadequate remedy. If goods are unique, a court will grant specific performance. Specific performance is usually granted to a buyer on the breach of a contract for the sale of land (every parcel of land is unique).

2. When Specific Performance Is Not Available
Contracts for sales of goods (other than unique goods) rarely qualify, because substantially identical goods can be bought or sold elsewhere. Courts normally refuse to grant specific performance of personal service contracts.

C. REFORMATION
This remedy is used when the parties have imperfectly expressed their agreement in writing. Reformation allows the contract to be rewritten to reflect the parties' true intentions.

1. When Reformation Is Available
(1) In cases of fraud or mutual mistake; (2) on proof of the correct terms of an oral contract; (3) if a covenant not to compete is for a valid purpose (such as the sale of a business), but the area or time constraints are unreasonable, some courts will reform the restraints.

2. When Reformation Is Not Available
If the area or time constraints in a covenant not to compete are unreasonable, some courts will throw out the entire covenant.

III. RECOVERY BASED ON QUASI CONTRACT
When there is no enforceable contract, quasi contract prevents unjust enrichment. The law implies a promise to pay the reasonable value for benefits received.

A. WHEN QUASI CONTRACTS ARE USED
This remedy is useful when a party has partially performed under a contract that is unenforceable. The party may recover the reasonable value (fair market value).

B. THE REQUIREMENTS OF QUASI CONTRACT
A party seeking recovery must show (1) he or she conferred a benefit on the other party, (2) he or she had the reasonable expectation of being paid, (3) he or she did not act as a volunteer in conferring the benefit, and (4) the other party would be unjustly enriched by retaining it without paying.

IV. ELECTION OF REMEDIES
To prevent double recovery, a nonbreaching party must choose which remedy to pursue. (The pleadings may seek more than one remedy and a choice may be made or imposed later in the proceedings.) This doctrine has been eliminated in contracts for sales of goods—UCC remedies are cumulative.

V. WAIVER OF BREACH
A waiver occurs when a nonbreaching party accepts defective performance.

A. CONSEQUENCES OF A WAIVER
A waiver keeps a contract going. A party waiving a breach cannot take later action based on the breach. In effect, the waiver erases the past breach. But the breaching party is liable for damages for the breach.

B. SUBSEQUENT BREACHES
A waiver extends only to the matter waived and not to the whole contract nor generally to future breaches. It extends to future breaches, however, if a reasonable person would conclude that similar defective performance would be acceptable in the future.

VI. CONTRACT PROVISIONS LIMITING REMEDIES

A. LIMITATION-OF-LIABILITY CLAUSES
These provide that the only remedy for breach is replacement, repair, or refund of the purchase price (or some other limit). Such clauses may be enforced.

B. EXCULPATORY CLAUSES

A provision excluding liability for fraudulent or intentional injury or for illegal acts will not be enforced. An exculpatory clause for negligence contained in a contract made between parties (such as large corporations) who have roughly equal bargaining power usually will be enforced.

C. CONTRACTS FOR SALES OF GOODS

Remedies can be limited (see Chapter 21).

TRUE-FALSE QUESTIONS

(Answers at the Back of the Book)

____ 1. Damages are designed to compensate a nonbreaching party for the loss of a bargain.

____ 2. Punitive damages are usually not awarded in breach of contract actions.

____ 3. Nominal damages establish that a defendant acted wrongfully.

____ 4. Liquidated damages are uncertain in amount.

____ 5. On rescission, the parties essentially return to the positions they were in before the contract.

____ 6. Rescission is not available in a case involving fraud.

____ 7. On a breach of contract, a nonbreaching party has a duty to mitigate damages.

____ 8. Quasi-contractual recovery is possible only when there is an enforceable contract.

____ 9. Consequential damages are foreseeable damages that arise from a party's breach of a contract.

____ 10. Specific performance is the usual remedy when one party has breached a contract for a sale of goods.

FILL-IN QUESTIONS

(Answers at the Back of the Book)

The usual measure of compensatory damages under a contract for a sale of goods is the difference between _____ (the contract price and the market price/the market price and lost profits on the sale). The usual remedy for a seller's breach of a contract for a sale of real estate is _____ (specific performance/rescission and restitution). If this remedy is unavailable or if the buyer breaches, in most states the measure of damages is the difference between _____ (the contract price and the market price/the market price and lost profits on the sale).

MULTIPLE-CHOICE QUESTIONS

(Answers at the Back of the Book)

____ 1. Dani pays Esteban $1,000 to design an intranet for her business office. The next day, Eli tells Dani that he has accepted a job with E-Services, Inc., and cannot design her network, but he does not return her payment. Dani can recover

a. $1,000.
b. Eli's pay from E-Services.
c. $1,000 plus Eli's pay from E-Services.
d. nothing.

____ 2. Cavendish contracts to deliver Bagels & More's products to its customers for $1,500, payable in advance. Bagels pays the money, but Cavendish fails to perform. Bagels can

    a. rescind the contract.
    b. obtain restitution of the $1,000 but not rescind the contract.
    c. rescind the contract and obtain restitution of the $1,000.
    d. recover nothing nor rescind the contract.

____ 3. Soda Fountain Supplies Corporation contracts to sell to Tasty Malts, Inc., six steel mixers for $5,000. When Soda Fountain fails to deliver, Tasty Malts buys mixers from Dairy Appliance Company, for $6,500. Tasty Malts' measure of damages is

    a. $6,500.
    b. $5,000.
    c. $1,500 plus incidental damages.
    d. nothing.

____ 4. General Construction contracts to build a store for Home Stores for $1 million. In mid-project, Home repudiates the contract, and General stops working. General incurred costs of $600,000 and would have made a profit of $100,000. General's measure of damages is

    a. $1 million.
    b. $700,000.
    c. $100,000.
    d. nothing.

____ 5. Olivia contracts with Pinky to buy a credenza for $1,500. Olivia tells Pinky that if the goods are not delivered on Monday, she will lose $2,000 in business. Pinky ships the credenza late. Olivia can recover

    a. $3,500.
    b. $2,000.
    c. $1,500.
    d. nothing.

____ 6. Jay agrees to sell an acre of land to Cliburn for $5,000. Jay fails to go through with the deal, when the market price of the land is $7,000. If Cliburn cannot obtain the land through specific performance, he may recover

    a. $7,000.
    b. $5,000.
    c. $2,000.
    d. nothing.

____ 7. Hunter orally agrees to build three barns for Glade. She builds the first barn, but Glade fails to pay. As a remedy for the breach, Hunter's best option is

    a. quasi-contractual recovery.
    b. reformation.
    c. rescission.
    d. specific performance.

____ 8. Jake agrees to sell an office building to Ivy. Their contract provides that if Jake fails to close the deal on a certain day, he will pay a fee equal to half of the price of the finished building. This is

    a. a liquidated damages clause.
    b. a mitigation of damages clause.
    c. an exculpatory clause.
    d. a penalty clause.

____ **9.** Les agrees to deliver two tons of copper to Metalworks, Inc. The contract states that delivery is to be within "15" days when the parties intend "50" days. If Metalworks will not amend the contract, Les may obtain

   a. reformation.
   b. rescission.
   c. specific performance.
   d. nothing.

____ **10. Based on a Sample CPA Exam Question.** Eagle Manufacturing, Inc., contracted with Digital Repair Services to maintain Eagle's computers. A "Liquidated Damages Clause" provides that Digital will pay Eagle $500 for each day that Digital is late in responding to a service request. If Digital is three days late in responding, and Eagle sues to enforce this clause, Eagle will

   a. lose, because liquidated damages clauses violate public policy.
   b. lose, unless the liquidated damages clause is determined to be a penalty.
   c. win, because liquidated damages clauses are always enforceable.
   d. win, unless the liquidated damages clause is determined to be a penalty.

SHORT ESSAY QUESTIONS

1. What are damages designed to do in a breach of contract situation?

2. What must parties do to rescind a contract?

ROCKON

(Answers at the Back of the Book)

1. You and your heavy metal band Rigid contract with Blitz Festivals, Inc., a regional concert promoter, to perform June 16 in an amphitheatre at the McCloud County Fair for a total of $8,500. The community pressures the fair sponsors to stage acts with broader name-recognition than your band, despite the greater expense, in an effort to draw larger crowds. Blitz then reneges on its deal with you—"What can we do? Our hands are tied. You guys aren't big enough." You find another gig for that date, playing in Tavern on the Commons, a small club, for $4,250. If you successfully sue Blitz for breach, how much might you recover?

2. Richly Entertainment Corporation contracts to sell you Savoire Faire—a dining, dancing, and musical theater venue—for $1.3 million. The contract requires you to pay the entire amount on July 1, when title to the property will be transferred to you. On that date, however, Richly refuses to complete the sale. If you file a suit against the seller, are you entitled to relief? If so, in what form?

SPECIAL INFORMATION FOR CPA CANDIDATES

   One of the points in this chapter covered in the past on the CPA examination has been that if damages are appropriate, specific performance will not be granted. Specific performance is granted most typically in cases involving unique goods. Also remember that liquidated damages must be reasonable in light of what could have been expected when the contract was made.

CUMULATIVE HYPOTHETICAL PROBLEM FOR UNIT THREE—INCLUDING CHAPTERS 10–18

(Answers at the Back of the Book)

Doe & Roe is a small accounting firm that provides bookkeeping, payroll, and tax services for small businesses. Java, Inc., is a small manufacturing firm, making and selling commercial espresso machines.

____ 1. Java sends e-mail to Doe & Roe, offering to contract for Doe & Roe's services for a certain price. The offer is sent on June 1 and is seen by Doe on June 2. The offer states that it will be open until July 1. This offer

  a. cannot be revoked because it is a firm offer.
  b. cannot be revoked because it is an option contract.
  c. could have been revoked only before Doe saw it.
  d. may be revoked any time before it is accepted.

____ 2. Java and Doe & Roe discuss terms for a contract, but nothing is put in writing. If a dispute develops later, and one party files a suit against the other, alleging breach of contract, the court will determine whether or not there is a contract between the parties by looking at

  a. the fairness of the circumstances.
  b. the offeree's subjective intent.
  c. the parties' objective intent.
  d. the parties' subjective intent.

____ 3. Java and Doe & Roe sign a written contract for Doe & Roe's services. The contract includes a large arithmetical error. Java later files a breach of contract suit against Doe & Roe, which asserts the mistake as a defense. Doe & Roe will win

  a. if Java wrote the contract.
  b. if the mistake was unilateral and Java knew it.
  c. only if the mistake was due to Java's negligence.
  d. only if the mistake was mutual.

____ 4. Java and Doe & Roe sign a written contract for Doe & Roe's services. Java later files a breach of contract suit against Doe & Roe. Doe & Roe could avoid liability on the contract

  a. if the contract has been assigned.
  b. if there is an unexecuted accord between the parties.
  c. if Java has been discharged by a novation.
  d. in none of these circumstances.

____ 5. Java and Doe & Roe sign a written contract for Doe & Roe's services. Java later files a suit against Doe & Roe. Doe & Roe is held to be in breach of contract. The court is most likely to grant relief to Java in the form of

  a. damages only.
  b. specific performance only.
  c. damages and specific performance.
  d. neither damages nor specific performance.

QUESTIONS ON THE FOCUS ON ETHICS FOR UNIT THREE— CONTRACT LAW AND THE APPLICATION OF ETHICS

(Answers at the Back of the Book)

____ 1. Ilse and Jem enter into a contract for Kirby's services. Whether this contract is unconscionable is determined by

   a. a court.
   b. Ilse only.
   c. Jem only.
   d. UCC 2–302.

____ 2. Satin offers goods to Thelma at less than half their market price, of which Satin is not aware. Thelma knows the goods' value, but says nothing. Thelma's silence could be justified by

   a. a covenant not to compete.
   b. the concept of unconscionability.
   c. the doctrine of promissory estoppel.
   d. the principle of freedom of contract.

____ 3. To bid on a job, General Contractor, Inc. (GCI), relies on the promise of Standard Subcontracting Company (SSC) to perform certain work at a certain price. If SSC fails to perform, GCI may recover from SSC under

   a. a covenant not to compete.
   b. the concept of unconscionability.
   c. the doctrine of promissory estoppel.
   d. the principle of freedom of contract.

Chapter 19
The Formation of Sales and Lease Contracts

WHAT THIS CHAPTER IS ABOUT

This chapter introduces two parts of the Uniform Commercial Code: Article 2, which covers sales of goods, and Article 2A, which covers leases. The chapter also includes a section on contracts for international sales of goods.

Article 3, 4, 9

CHAPTER OUTLINE

I. THE UNIFORM COMMERCIAL CODE

The UCC provides rules to deal with all phases of a commercial sale: Articles 2 and 2A cover contracts for sales or leases of goods; Articles 3, 4, and 4A cover payments by checks, notes, and other means; Article 7 covers warehouse documents; and Article 9 covers transactions that involve collateral.

II. THE SCOPE OF ARTICLE 2—SALES

Article 2 governs contracts for sales of goods.

  A. WHAT IS A SALE?

  A **sale** is "the passing of title from the seller to the buyer for a price" [UCC 2–106(1)]. The price may be payable in money, goods, services, or land.

  B. WHAT ARE GOODS?

  Goods are tangible and movable. Legal disputes concern the following—

    1. Goods Associated with Real Estate

    Goods include minerals or the like and structures, if severance from the land is by the seller (but not if the buyer is to do it); growing crops or timber to be cut; and other "things attached" to realty but capable of severance without material harm to the land [UCC 2–107].

    2. Goods and Services Combined

      a. General Rule

      Services are not included in the UCC. If a transaction involves both goods and services, a court determines which aspect is dominant under the predominant-factor test.

      b. Special Cases

      Serving food or drink is a sale of goods [UCC 2–314(1)]. Other goods include unborn animals and rare coins.

  C. WHO IS A MERCHANT?

  UCC 2–104: Special rules apply to those who (1) deal in goods of the kind involved; (2) by occupation, hold themselves out as having knowledge and skill peculiar to the practices or goods involved in the transaction; (3) employ a merchant as a broker, agent, or other intermediary.

137

III. THE SCOPE OF ARTICLE 2A—LEASES

Article 2A governs contracts for leases of goods.

A. DEFINITION OF A LEASE AGREEMENT

A **lease agreement** is the bargain of the lessor and lessee, in their words and deeds, including course of dealing, usage of trade, and course of performance [UCC 2A–103(k)].

B. CONSUMER LEASES

Special provisions apply to leases involving (1) a lessor who regularly leases or sells, (2) a lessee who leases for a personal, family, or household purpose, and (3) total payments of less than $25,000 [UCC 2A–103(1)(e)].

C. FINANCE LEASES

A finance lease involves a lessor (financier) who buys or leases goods from a supplier and leases or subleases them to a lessee [UCC 2A–103(g)]. The lessee must perform, whatever the financier does [UCC 2A–407].

IV. THE FORMATION OF SALES AND LEASE CONTRACTS

The following summarizes how the UCC *changes* the common law of contracts.

A. OFFER

An agreement sufficient to constitute a contract can exist even if verbal exchanges, correspondence, and conduct do not reveal exactly when it became binding [UCC 2–204(2), 2A–204(2)].

1. Open Terms

A sales or lease contract will not fail for indefiniteness even if one or more terms are left open, as long as (1) the parties intended to make a contract and (2) there is a reasonably certain basis for the court to grant an appropriate remedy [UCC 2–204(3), 2A–204(3)].

a. Open Price Term

1) If the parties have not agreed on a price, a court will determine "a reasonable price at the time for delivery" [UCC 2–305(1)].

2) If either the buyer or the seller is to determine the price, the price is to be fixed in good faith, which means honesty in fact and the observance of reasonable commercial standards of fair dealing in the trade [UCC 2–103(1)(b), 2–305(2)].

3) If a price is not fixed through the fault of one party, the other can cancel the contract or fix a reasonable price [UCC 2–305(3)].

b. Open Payment Term

When parties do not specify payment terms—

1) Payment is due at the time and place at which the buyer is to receive the goods [UCC 2–310(a)].

2) The buyer can tender payment in cash or a commercially acceptable substitute (a check or credit card) [UCC 2–511(2)].

c. Open Delivery Term

When no delivery terms are specified—

1) The buyer normally takes delivery at the seller's place of business [UCC 2–308(a)]. If the seller has no place of business, the seller's residence is used. When goods are located in some other place and both parties know it, delivery is made there.

2) If the time for shipment or delivery is not clearly specified, a court will infer a "reasonable" time [UCC 2–309(1)].

d. Duration of an Ongoing Contract
A party who wishes to terminate an indefinite but ongoing contract must give reasonable notice to the other party [UCC 2–309(2), (3)].

e. Options and Cooperation Regarding Performance

1) When no specific shipping arrangements have been made but the contract contemplates shipment of the goods, the seller has the right to make arrangements [UCC 2–311].

2) When terms relating to an assortment of goods are omitted, the buyer can specify the assortment [UCC 2–311].

f. Open Quantity Term
If parties do not specify a quantity, there is no basis for a remedy. Exceptions include [UCC 2–306]—

1) **Requirements Contract**
The buyer agrees to buy and the seller agrees to sell all or up to a stated amount of what the buyer needs or requires. There is consideration: the buyer gives up the right to buy from others.

2) **Output Contract**
The seller agrees to sell and the buyer agrees to buy all or up to a stated amount of what the seller produces. Because the seller forfeits the right to sell goods to others, there is consideration.

3) **The UCC Imposes a Good Faith Limitation**
The quantity under these contracts is the amount of requirements or output that occurs during a normal production year.

2. Merchant's Firm Offer

a. When Does a Merchant's Firm Offer Arise?
If a merchant gives assurances in a signed writing that an offer will remain open, the offer is irrevocable, without consideration, for the stated period, or if no definite period is specified, for a reasonable period (neither to exceed three months) [UCC 2–205, 2A–205].

b. Requirements
The offer must be in writing and signed by the offeror. When a firm offer is contained in a form contract prepared by the offeree, a separate firm offer assurance must be signed.

B. ACCEPTANCE

1. Methods of Acceptance

a. Any Reasonable Means
When an offeror does not specify a means of acceptance, acceptance can be by any reasonable means [UCC 2–206(1), 2A–206(1)].

b. Promise to Ship or Prompt Shipment

1) **Promise or Shipment of Conforming Goods**
An offer to buy goods for current or prompt shipment can be accepted by a promise to ship or by a prompt shipment [UCC 2–206(1)(b)].

2) **Shipment of Nonconforming Goods**
Prompt shipment of nonconforming goods is both an acceptance and a breach, unless the seller (1) seasonably notifies the buyer that it is offered only as an accommodation and (2) indicates clearly that it is not an acceptance.

2. Communication of Acceptance
To accept a unilateral offer, the offeree must notify the offeror of performance if the offeror would not otherwise know [UCC 2–206(2)].

3. Additional Terms
If the offeree's response indicates a definite acceptance of the offer, a contract is formed, even if the acceptance includes terms in addition to, or different from, the original offer [UCC 2–207(1)]. This is contrary to the common law mirror image rule.

a. When the Seller or Buyer Is a Nonmerchant
Additional terms are considered proposals and not part of the contract. The contract is on the offeror's terms [UCC 2–207(2)].

b. When Both Parties Are Merchants
Additional terms are part of the contract unless (1) the offer expressly states no other terms; (2) they materially alter the original contract; or (3) the offeror objects to the modified terms in a timely fashion [UCC 2–207(2)].

c. Conditioned on the Offeror's Assent
If the additional terms are conditioned on the offeror's assent, the offeree's response is not an acceptance.

d. Additional Terms May Be Stricken
Regardless of what parties write down, they have a contract according to their conduct [UCC 2–207(3)]. If they do not act in accord with added terms, the terms are not part of a contract.

C. CONSIDERATION
An agreement modifying a sales or lease contract needs no consideration to be binding [UCC 2–209(1), 2A–208(1)].

1. Modification Must Be Made in Good Faith [UCC 1–203]

2. When Modification without Consideration Requires a Writing

a. Contract prohibits changes except by a signed writing.

b. If a consumer (nonmerchant) is dealing with a merchant, and the merchant's form prohibits oral modification, the consumer must sign a separate acknowledgment [UCC 2–209(2), 2A–208(2)].

c. Any modification that brings a *sales* contract under the Statute of Frauds must be in writing to be enforceable [UCC 2–209(3)].

D. THE STATUTE OF FRAUDS
To be enforceable, a sales contract must be in writing if the goods are $500 or more and a lease if the payments are $1,000 or more [UCC 2–201, 2A–201].

1. Sufficiency of the Writing
A writing is sufficient if it indicates the parties intended to form a contract and is signed by the party against whom enforcement is sought. A sales contract is not enforceable beyond the quantity stated. A lease must identify and describe the goods and the lease term.

2. Special Rules for Contracts between Merchants
The writing requirement is met if one merchant sends a signed written confirmation.

a. Contents of the Confirmation
The confirmation must indicate the terms of the agreement, and the merchant receiving it must have reason to know of its contents.

   b. Objection Within Ten Days

   Unless the merchant who receives the confirmation objects in writing within ten days, the confirmation is enforceable [UCC 2–201(2)].

3. Exceptions

An oral contract for a sale or lease that should otherwise be in writing will be enforceable in cases of [UCC 2–201(3), 2A–201(4)]—

   a. Specially Manufactured Goods

   The seller (or lessor) makes a substantial start on the manufacture of the goods, or makes commitments for it, and the goods are unsuitable for resale to others in the ordinary course of the business.

   b. Admissions

   The party against whom enforcement of a contract is sought admits in pleadings or court proceedings that a contract was made.

   c. Partial Performance

   Some payment has been made and accepted or some goods have been received and accepted (enforceable to that extent).

E. PAROL EVIDENCE — *Similar to common law*

1. The Rule

If parties to a contract set forth its terms in a writing intended as their final expression, the terms cannot be contradicted by evidence of any prior agreements or contemporaneous oral agreements.

2. Exceptions [UCC 2–202, 2A–202]

A court may accept evidence of the following—

   a. Consistent Additional Terms

   Such terms clarify or remove ambiguities in a writing.

   b. Course of Dealing and Usage of Trade

   The meaning of an agreement is interpreted in light of commercial practices and other surrounding circumstances [UCC 1–205].

   c. Course of Performance

   Conduct that occurs under the agreement indicates what the parties meant by the words in their contract [UCC 2–208(1), 2A–207(1)].

3. Rules of Construction

Express terms, course of performance, course of dealing, and usage of trade are to be construed together when they do not contradict one another. If that is unreasonable, the priority is: (1) express terms, (2) course of performance, (3) course of dealing, and (4) usage of trade [UCC 1–205(4), 2–208(2), 2A–207(2)].

F. UNCONSCIONABILITY *court can ignore, throw out part, or throw out entire contract*

1. What an Unconscionable Contract (or Clause) Is

An unconscionable contract or clause is a contract or clause so one-sided and unfair (at the time it was made) that enforcing it would be unreasonable.

2. What a Court Can Do

A court can (1) refuse to enforce the contract, (2) enforce the contract without the unconscionable clause, or (3) limit the clause to avoid an unconscionable result [UCC 2–302, 2A–108].

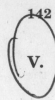

V. CONTRACTS FOR THE INTERNATIONAL SALE OF GOODS

The 1980 United Nations Convention on Contracts for the International Sale of Goods (CISG) governs contracts for the international sale of goods.

A. APPLICABILITY OF THE CISG

The CISG is to international sales contracts what UCC Article 2 is to domestic sales contracts (except the CISG does not apply to consumer sales). The CISG applies when the parties to an international sales contract do not specify in writing the precise terms of their contract.

B. A COMPARISON OF CISG AND UCC PROVISIONS

1. **The Mirror Image Rule**

   The terms of the acceptance must mirror those of the offer [Art. 19].

2. **Irrevocable Offers**

   An offer is irrevocable if the offeror states that it is or if the offeree reasonably relies on it as being irrevocable. The offer is irrevocable even without a writing and consideration [Art. 16(2)].

3. **The Statute of Frauds**

   Article 11 does not include the requirements of the Statute of Frauds. (This accords with the law of most nations, in which contracts no longer need to meet formal requirements to be enforceable.)

4. **Time of Contract Formation**

   When an acceptance is sent, an offer becomes irrevocable, but the acceptance is not effective until it is received. Acceptance by performance does not require notice to the offeror.

C. SPECIAL PROVISIONS IN INTERNATIONAL CONTRACTS

1. **Choice of Language**

   Designates official language for interpreting contract in the event of disagreement. May indicate language for translations and arbitration.

2. **Choice of Forum**

   Designates forum, including specific court, for litigating a dispute. Clause is invalid if it denies one party an effective remedy, is the product of fraud or unconscionable conduct, causes substantial inconvenience to one party, or violates public policy.

3. **Choice of Law**

   Designates the applicable law. Under international law, there is no limit on parties' choice of law. If a choice is not specified, the governing law is that of the country of the seller's place of business.

4. *Force Majeure* **("Impossible or Irresistible Force")**

   Stipulates that acts of God and other eventualities (government orders, regulations, embargoes, shortages of materials) may excuse a party from liability for nonperformance.

TRUE-FALSE QUESTIONS

(Answers at the Back of the Book)

____ 1. Article 2 of the UCC governs sales of goods.

____ 2. Under the UCC, a sale occurs when title passes from a seller to a buyer for a price.

____ 3. The UCC governs sales of services and real estate.

____ 4. Under the UCC, an agreement modifying a contract needs new consideration to be binding.

____ **5.** If a contract for a sale of goods is missing a term, it will not be enforceable.

____ **6.** An unconscionable contract is a contract so one-sided and unfair, at the time it is made, that enforcing it would be unreasonable.

____ **7.** The CISG is to international sales contracts what Article 2 of the UCC is to domestic sales contracts.

____ **8.** Under the UCC, an offer to buy goods can be accepted only by a prompt shipment of the goods.

____ **9.** A lease agreement is the lessor and lessee's bargain.

____ **10.** No oral contract is enforceable under the UCC.

FILL-IN QUESTIONS

(Answers at the Back of the Book)

_____ (Course of dealing/Usage of trade) is a sequence of conduct between the parties that occurred before their agreement and establishes a common basis for their understanding. _____ (Course of dealing/Usage of trade) is any practice or method of dealing having regularity of observance in a place, vocation, or _____ (deal/trade) so as to justify an expectation that it will be observed with respect to the transaction in question. The express terms of an agreement, the course of dealing, and the usage of trade will be construed to be _____(consistent/ inconsistent) with each other whenever reasonable. When that is not possible, the _____ (course of dealing/usage of trade/terms in the agreement) prevail.

MULTIPLE-CHOICE QUESTIONS

(Answers at the Back of the Book)

____ **1.** Ernestine pays a Discount City store $1,500 for a 3D LED HD-TV. Under the UCC, this is

a. a service.
b. a merchant's offer.
c. a lease.
d. a sale.

____ **2.** Chips n' Digits Electronics, Inc., sells computers, and some computer accessories, to persons who order them. Chips n' Digits is a merchant with respect to

a. computer accessories only.
b. computers and computer accessories.
c. computers only.
d. nonc of the choices.

____ **3.** MediQuip Corporation and LiquiClean Products, Inc., enter into a contract for a sale of goods that does not include a price term. In a suit between MediQuip and LiquiClean over this contract and the price, a court will

a. determine a reasonable price.
b. impose the lowest market price for the goods.
c. refuse to enforce the agreement.
d. return the parties to the positions they held before the contract.

___   4.   Builders Supply Company sells two construction cranes to Contractors, Inc., which leases one crane to Design Worx Corporation and gives the other to Equipment, Inc. Article 2A of the UCC applies to

    a.   the gift.
    b.   the lease.
    c.   the sale.
    d.   the gift, the lease, and the sale.

___   5.   Rugged Boots, Inc., and Strata Shoe Company orally agree to a sale of 100 pair of hiking boots for $5,000. Rugged gives Strata a check for $500 as a down payment. At this point, the contract is

    a.   enforceable to at least the extent of $500.
    b.   fully enforceable because it is for specially made goods.
    c.   fully enforceable because it is oral.
    d.   unenforceable.

___   6.   Mall Stores Corporation sends its purchase order form to Neat Displays, Inc., for shelving. Neat responds with its own form. Additional terms in Neat's form automatically become part of the parties' contract

    a.   under any circumstances.
    b.   under no circumstances.
    c.   unless Mall objects to the new terms within a reasonable period of time.
    d.   unless Neat indicates otherwise before shipping the goods.

___   7.   Gina and Hootie dispute the interpretation of an ambiguous clause in their contract. In a suit to determine the meaning of the clause, the court may accept evidence of

    a.   consistent additional terms only.
    b.   consistent additional terms and contradictory terms.
    c.   contradictory terms only.
    d.   anything extrinsic to the contract.

___   8.   **Based on a Sample CPA Exam Question.** Eagle Products, Inc., assures Fine Retail Corporation that its offer to sell its products at a certain price will remain open. This is a firm offer only if

    a.   Fine (the offeree) gives consideration for the offer.
    b.   Fine (the offeree) is a merchant.
    c.   the offer is made by Eagle (a merchant) in a signed writing.
    d.   the offer states the time period during which it will remain open.

___   9.   Kelly enters a contract with Jersey Appliances, Inc. In a later suit, Kelly claims that a clause in the contract is unconscionable. If the court agrees, it may

    a.   enforce, limit, or refuse to enforce the contract or the disputed clause.
    b.   enforce the contract without the disputed clause only.
    c.   limit the application of the disputed clause only.
    d.   refuse to enforce the contract only.

___   10.   Mac's Service Station agrees to buy an unspecified quantity of ethanol from NuFuel Corporation. NuFuel breaches the contract. Mac's can most likely

    a.   enforce the agreement to the amount of a reasonable quantity.
    b.   enforce the agreement to the amount of Mac's requirements for ethanol.
    c.   enforce the agreement to the amount of NuFuel's output of ethanol.
    d.   not enforce the agreement.

STARBUCKS COFFEE COMPANY
INTERNATIONAL SALES CONTRACT
APPLICATIONS

(Answers at the Back of the Book)

The following hypothetical situation and multiple-choice questions relate to your text's fold-out exhibit of the international sales contract used by Starbucks Coffee Company. In that contract, Starbucks orders five hundred tons of coffee at $10 per pound from XYZ Co.

____ 1. Starbucks and XYZ would have an enforceable contract even if they did *not* state in writing

    a. the amount of coffee ordered.
    b. the price of the coffee.
    c. both a and b.
    d. none of the above.

____ 2. If Starbucks and XYZ did not include a "DESCRIPTION" of the coffee as "High grown Mexican Altura," then the delivered coffee must meet

    a. Starbuck's subjective expectations of their quality.
    b. Starbuck's description of the goods in ads, on labels, and so on.
    c. XYZ's description of the goods in ads, on labels, and so on.
    d. XYZ's subjective belief in their quality.

____ 3. Starbucks's incentive to pay on time, according to the terms of this contract, is the clause titled

    a. CLAIMS.
    b. GUARANTEE.
    c. PAYMENT.
    d. PRICE.

____ 4. XYZ's incentive to deliver coffee that conforms to the contract is the clause titled

    a. CLAIMS.
    b. GUARANTEE.
    c. PAYMENT.
    d. PRICE.

____ 5. Under this contract, until the coffee is delivered to its destination, the party who bears the risk of loss is

    a. Bonded Public Warehouse.
    b. Green Coffee Association
    c. Starbucks.
    d. XYZ.

SHORT ESSAY QUESTIONS

1. For purposes of UCC Article 2, what is a sale? What are goods?

2. Who, for the purposes of UCC Article 2, is a merchant?

ROCKON

(Answers at the Back of the Book)

1. As a beginning songwriter and performer, you are convinced that a certain model of electric guitar is what you need to turn the musical world on its ear. Chick's Music Store advertises the item but because the

store is sold out of the guitars when you get there, you accept a rain check signed by Daria, one of the store's employees. You return to the store one month later, but Chick refuses to honor the rain check. Would you win a suit to enforce it? Why or why not?

2.   On May 1, you contract orally with Johnny, a salesperson with Keyboards Emporium, to buy for $450 an electric organ for your personal enjoyment with delivery to occur on July 1. On May 15, you ask for delivery on June 1 and Johnny agrees. But delivery does not occur on June 1. The store later tells you that delivery will be on July 1 as agreed in the first place. Which delivery date is binding? Discuss.

SPECIAL INFORMATION FOR CPA CANDIDATES

Concepts introduced in this chapter that are important to keep in mind for the CPA examination include the differences between common law and the UCC. The UCC rules that apply in transactions between merchants have also been on the exam in the past (questions covering firm offers, for instance), as have questions about which contracts must be in writing and what satisfies the writing requirement. Remember, too, that although the UCC applies to any sale of goods, regardless of the amount, an agreement for a sale of goods priced under $500 need not be in writing to be enforceable.

Chapter 20
Title, Risk, and Insurable Interest

WHAT THIS CHAPTER IS ABOUT

The UCC has special rules involving title, which may determine the rights and remedies of the parties to a sales contract. In most situations, however, issues concerning the rights and remedies of parties to sales or lease contracts are controlled by three other concepts: (1) identification, (2) risk of loss, and (3) insurable interest.

CHAPTER OUTLINE

I. IDENTIFICATION

For an interest in goods to pass from seller to buyer or lessor to lessee, the goods must (1) exist and (2) be identified as the goods subject to the contract. Identification occurs when specific goods are designated as the subject matter of the contract.

A. WHY IDENTIFICATION IS SIGNIFICANT
Identification gives the buyer (1) the right to obtain insurance and (2) the right to obtain the goods from the seller.

B. WHEN IDENTIFICATION OCCURS
Identification occurs according to the parties' agreement [UCC 2–501, 2A–217]. If they do not specify a time and the goods are—

1. Existing Goods
Identification occurs when the contract is made.

2. Future Goods
If a sale involves unborn animals or crops to be harvested within twelve months of the contract (or, for crops, during the next harvest season, whichever is further in the future), identification occurs when the goods are conceived, planted, or begin to grow.

3. Goods That Are Part of a Larger Mass
Identification occurs when—

a. Goods Are Marked, Shipped, or Otherwise Designated

b. Exception—Fungible Goods
A buyer can acquire rights to goods that are alike by physical nature, agreement, or trade usage and that are held by owners in common by replacing the seller as owner [UCC 2–105(4)].

II. WHEN TITLE PASSES

Parties can agree on when and under what conditions title will pass. If they do not specify a time, title passes on delivery [UCC 2–401(2)]. Delivery terms determine when this occurs.

A. SHIPMENT CONTRACTS
If the seller is required or authorized to ship goods by carrier, title passes at time and place of shipment [UCC 2–401(2)(a)]. All contracts are shipment contracts unless they say otherwise.

147

B. DESTINATION CONTRACTS

If the seller is required to deliver goods to a certain destination, title passes when the goods are tendered there [UCC 2–401(2)(b)].

C. DELIVERY WITHOUT MOVEMENT OF THE GOODS

If a buyer is to pick up goods, passing title turns on whether a seller must give a document of title (bill of lading, warehouse receipt).

1. When a Document of Title Is Required

Title passes when and where the document is delivered. The goods do not need to move (for example, they can stay in a warehouse).

2. When No Document of Title Is Required

If the goods have been identified, title passes when and where the contract was made. If the goods have not been identified, title does not pass until identification [UCC 2–401(3)].

D. SALES OR LEASES BY NONOWNERS

Generally, a buyer acquires whatever title the seller has to the goods sold [UCC 2–402, 2–403]. A lessee acquires whatever title a lessor could transfer, subject to the lease [UCC 2A–303, 2A–304, 2A–305].

1. Void Title

If the seller or lessor stole the goods, the buyer or lessee acquires nothing, and the real owner can reclaim the goods.

2. Voidable Title

A seller or lessor has voidable title if the goods were obtained by fraud, paid for with a check that is later dishonored, bought on credit from an insolvent seller, or bought from a minor. The real owner can reclaim the goods except from a good faith purchaser or lessee for value [UCC 2–403(3)].

3. Entrustment Rule

Entrustment includes both delivering goods to a merchant and leaving goods with a merchant for later delivery or pickup [UCC 2–403(3)].

a. Entrusting Goods to a Merchant Who Deals in Goods of the Kind

The merchant can transfer all rights to a buyer or sublessee in the ordinary course of business [UCC 2–403(2), 2A–305(2)].

b. What a Buyer or Sublessee in the Ordinary Course Gets

Only those rights held by the person who entrusted the goods.

III. RISK OF LOSS

The question of who suffers a financial loss if goods are damaged, destroyed, or lost (who bears the *risk of loss*) is determined by the parties' contract. If the contract does not state who bears the risk, the UCC has rules to determine it.

A. DELIVERY WITH MOVEMENT OF THE GOODS—CARRIER CASES

When goods are to be delivered by truck or other paid transport—

1. Contract Terms

a. F.O.B. (Free on board)—delivery is at seller's expense to a specific location. Risk passes at the location [UCC 2–319(1)].

b. F.A.S. (Free alongside)—seller delivers goods next to the ship that will carry them, and risk passes to buyer [UCC 2–319(2)].

c. C.I.F. or C.&F. (Cost, insurance, and freight)—seller puts goods in possession of a carrier before risk passes [UCC 2–320(2)].

    d. **Delivery Ex-ship** (From the carrying vessel)—risk passes to buyer when goods leave the ship or are unloaded [UCC 2–322].

2. **Shipment Contracts**
Risk passes to the buyer or lessee when the goods are delivered to a carrier [UCC 2–509(1)(a), 2A–219(2)(a)].

3. **Destination Contracts**
Risk passes to the buyer or lessee when the goods are tendered to the buyer at the destination [UCC 2–509(1)(b), 2A–219(2)(b)].

B. **DELIVERY WITHOUT MOVEMENT OF THE GOODS**
When goods are to be picked up by the buyer or lessee—

1. **If the Seller or Lessor Is a Merchant**
Risk passes only on the buyer's or lessee's taking possession of the goods.

2. **If the Seller or Lessor Is Not a Merchant**
Risk passes on tender of delivery [UCC 2–509(3), 2A–219(c)].

3. **If a Bailee Holds the Goods**
Risk passes when (1) the buyer receives a negotiable document of title for the goods, (2) the bailee acknowledges the buyer's (or in the case of a lease, the lessee's) right to the goods, or (3) the buyer receives a nonnegotiable document of title, presents the document to the bailee, and demands the goods. If the bailee refuses to honor the document, the risk remains with the seller [UCC 2–503(4)(b), 2–509(2), 2A–219(2)(b)].

C. **CONDITIONAL SALES**

1. **Sale on Approval**
A seller offers to sell goods, and the buyer takes them on a trial basis. Title and risk remain with the seller until the buyer accepts the goods.

    a. **What Constitutes Acceptance**
Any act inconsistent with the trial purpose or the seller's ownership; or by the buyer's choice not to return the goods on time.

    b. **Return**
Return is at the seller's expense and risk [UCC 2–327(1)]. Goods are not subject to the claims of the buyer's creditors until acceptance.

2. **Sale or Return**
A seller delivers goods to a buyer who may retain any part and pay accordingly. The balance is returned or held by the buyer as a bailee.

    a. **Title and Risk Pass to the Buyer with Possession**
Title and risk stay with the buyer until he or she returns the goods to the seller within the specified time. Goods in the buyer's possession are subject to claims of the buyer's creditors.

    b. **Sale**
A sale is final if the buyer fails to return the goods in time.

D. **CONSIGNMENTS**
A consignment is similar to a sale or return. UCC Article 9 (see Chapter 29) governs consignments except for those involving goods defined as "consumer goods" before consignment.

1. **Title to Consigned Goods**
Title to consigned goods remains with the consignor who can retake them at any time. If the consignee sells them, he or she receives a commission. Unsold goods are returned.

2. Creditors' Claims

If the owner files a financing statement covering the goods, his or her creditors can assert claims against them. If the owner does not file a financing statement, the consignee's creditors can assert claims against the goods unless they know the consignee is in the business of selling others' goods on consignment [UCC 9–102(20)].

E. RISK OF LOSS WHEN A SALES OR LEASE CONTRACT IS BREACHED

Generally, the party in breach bears the risk of loss.

1. When the Seller or Lessor Breaches

Risk passes to the buyer or lessee when the defects are cured or the buyer or lessee accepts the goods in spite of the defects. If, after acceptance, a buyer discovers a latent defect, acceptance can be revoked and the risk goes back to the seller [UCC 2–510(2), 2A–220(1)].

2. When the Buyer or Lessee Breaches

Risk shifts to the buyer or lessee (if the goods have been identified), where it stays for a commercially reasonable time after the seller or lessor learns of the breach. The buyer or lessee is liable to the extent of any deficiency in seller or lessor's insurance [UCC 2–510(3), 2A–220(2)].

IV. INSURABLE INTEREST   *Key employer, Hollywood Actors*

A party buying insurance must have a "sufficient interest" in the insured item. More than one party can have an interest at the same time.

A. INSURABLE INTEREST OF THE BUYER OR LESSEE

A buyer or lessee has an insurable interest in goods the moment they are identified, even before risk of loss passes [UCC 2–501(1), 2A–218(1)].

B. INSURABLE INTEREST OF THE SELLER OR LESSOR

A seller or lessor has an insurable interest in goods as long as he or she holds title or a security interest in the goods [UCC 2–501(2), 2A–218(3)].

TRUE-FALSE QUESTIONS

(Answers at the Back of the Book)

____ 1. Before an interest in specific goods can pass from a seller to a buyer, the goods must be identified.

____ 2. Under all circumstances, title passes at the time and place that the buyer accepts the goods.

____ 3. Unless a contract provides otherwise, it is normally assumed to be a shipment contract.

____ 4. In a sale on approval, the buyer can set aside the deal by returning the goods.

____ 5. A buyer and a seller cannot both have an insurable interest in the same goods at the same time.

____ 6. If a buyer breaches a contract, the risk of loss shifts to the buyer.

____ 7. In a sale on approval, the risk of loss passes to the buyer as soon as the buyer takes possession.

____ 8. An innocent buyer can acquire title to goods as a good faith purchaser from a thief.

____ 9. Under a destination contract, title passes at time and place of shipment.

____ 10. If a seller is a merchant, the risk of loss passes when a buyer takes possession of the goods.

FILL-IN QUESTIONS

(Answers at the Back of the Book)

_____ (F.A.S./F.O.B.) means that delivery is at a seller's expense to a specific location—the place of shipment or a place of destination. When the term is _____ (F.A.S./F.O.B.) place of _shipment_, risk passes when the seller puts the goods into a carrier's possession. When the term is _____ (F.A.S./F.O.B.) place of _destination_, risk passes when the seller tenders delivery. _____ (F.A.S./ F.O.B.) requires a seller at his or her own expense and risk to deliver goods alongside the ship that will transport them at which point risk passes.

MULTIPLE-CHOICE QUESTIONS

(Answers at the Back of the Book)

____ 1. Ron agrees to sell 1,000 pens to State University Book Store. Before an interest in the pens can pass from Ron to the bookstore, the pens must be

a. in existence only.
b. identified as the specific goods designated in the contract only.
c. in existence and identified as the goods in the contract.
d. none of the choices.

____ 2. **Based on a Sample CPA Exam Question.** Calibrate Corporation agrees to ship one hundred scientific calculators to GR8 Equations, Inc. Before the calculators arrive at GR's laboratory, they are lost. The most important factor in determining who bears the risk of loss is

a. how the calculators were lost.
b. the contract's shipping terms.
c. the method by which the calculators were shipped.
d. title to the calculators.

____ 3. Sid buys an MP3 player from Tom, his neighbor, who agrees to keep the player until Sid picks it up. Before Sid can get it, the player is stolen. The loss is suffered by

a. neither Sid nor Tom.
b. Sid and Tom.
c. Sid only.
d. Tom only.

____ 4. Slick Floor Stores buys tile from Smooth Tile Corporation. Snug Storage holds the tile in a warehouse. The tile is delivered to Retail by the transfer of a negotiable warehouse receipt. A fire later damages the tile. The loss is suffered by

a. not Slick, Smooth, or Snug.
b. Slick.
c. Smooth.
d. Snug.

____ 5. Omni Architects buys ten drafting desks from Precision Supply, Inc. They agree to ship the computers "F.O.B. Omni" via Quik2U Trucking Company. The desks are lost in transit. The loss is suffered by

a. Omni (the buyer).
b. Precision (the seller).
c. Quik2U (the carrier).
d. not Omni, Precision, or Quik2U.

____ 6. NuProdux Inc. (NPI), agrees to sell 100 cell phones to MyTalk Cell Service. NPI identifies the goods by marking the crate with red stripes. Before the crate is shipped, an insurable interest exists in

   a. not NPI or MyTalk.
   b. NPI and MyTalk.
   c. NPI only.
   d. MyTalk only.

____ 7. Spiffymade, Inc., ships fifty defective heaters to Thermal Products Corporation. Thermal rejects the heaters and ships them back to Spiffymade, via Unwieldy Transport, Inc. The heaters are lost in transit. The loss is suffered by

   a. not Spiffymade, Thermal, or Unwieldy.
   b. Spiffymade.
   c. Thermal.
   d. Unwieldy.

____ 8. Red Apples Corporation agrees to sell forty cases of apples to Sweet Fruit, Inc., under a shipment contract. Red gives the apples to Refrigerated Trucking, Inc. (RTI), which delivers them to Sweet. Title passed when

   a. Red agreed to sell the goods.
   b. Red gave the goods to RTI.
   c. RTI delivered the goods to Sweet.
   d. Sweet exercised dominion over the goods.

____ 9. Nora leaves her car with OK Auto Sales & Service for repairs. OK sells the car to Pete, who does not know that OK has no right to sell the car. Nora can recover from

   a. not OK or Pete.
   b. OK and Pete.
   c. OK only.
   d. Pete only.

____ 10. Lorena buys a scooter from Mooch's Motor Sales, which agrees to keep the scooter until Lorena picks it up. Before she gets it, it is stolen. The loss is suffered by

   a. Lorena and Mooch's.
   b. Lorena only.
   c. Mooch's only.
   d. neither Lorena nor Mooch's.

SHORT ESSAY QUESTIONS

1. What is "risk of loss" under the UCC?

2. When does risk pass (a) under a shipment contract? (b) under a destination contract? (c) when the buyer is to pick up the goods and the seller is a merchant? (d) when the buyer is to pick up the goods and the seller is not a merchant? (e) when a bailee holds the goods?

ROCKON

(Answers at the Back of the Book)

1. Sassy Brass Instrument Co. owns a warehouse where it stores its inventory of band and orchestral instruments. In your capacity of band director for a school district, you order seventy-six trombones from

Sassy. The seller identifies the goods to be shipped, but before they are loaded onto a truck for delivery, the warehouse and its inventory is destroyed in a fire. Before the fire, did your district—the buyer—have title and an insurable interest in the trombones? Explain.

2. You are the producer of the first annual "May Day Bay City Blues & Jazz Festival." On April 1, you contract to buy speakers, amplifiers, and other sound equipment from Venue Sound Systems and pay 30 percent of the price. On April 7, before the seller has separated the goods for your festival from the rest of its inventory, it becomes insolvent. Can you recover the equipment you ordered? Why or why not?

SPECIAL INFORMATION FOR CPA CANDIDATES

The most important concept in this chapter to master for the CPA examination is passage of the risk of loss. In most of the problems on the CPA examination, the party who bears the loss has traditionally been the party who breached the contract. You should bear in mind, however, that who ultimately bears the risk of loss is not necessarily the same party who has title or an insurable interest, nor does it depend on whether the buyer has paid for the goods or on whether some action by a party outside the contract contributed to the loss of the goods.

Other concepts discussed in this chapter may occur on the CPA exam. The concept of title is often tested in a context involving stolen goods, voidable title, or entrustment. The passage of title and risk may be at issue in questions on sales on approval and sales or return. Questions are also sometimes asked about bulk sales.

Chapter 21:
Performance and Breach of Sales and Lease Contracts

WHAT THIS CHAPTER IS ABOUT

This chapter examines the basic obligations of a seller and a buyer under a sales contract, and a lessor and a lessee under a lease contract, and the remedies each party has if the contract is breached. The general purpose of the remedies is to put a nonbreaching party "in as good a position as if the other party had fully performed."

CHAPTER OUTLINE

merchants held to a higher standard

I. **PERFORMANCE OBLIGATIONS**

The obligations of good faith and commercial reasonableness underlie every contract within the UCC [UCC 1–203]. There is a higher standard for merchants: honesty in fact and the observance of reasonable commercial standards of fair dealing in the trade [UCC 2–103, 2A–516(1)].

II. **OBLIGATIONS OF THE SELLER OR LESSOR**

A seller or lessor must have and hold conforming goods at the disposal of the buyer or lessee and give whatever notice is reasonably necessary to enable the buyer or lessee to take delivery [UCC 2–503(1), 2A–508(1)].

A. **TENDER OF DELIVERY**

Tender must occur at a reasonable hour, in a reasonable manner, and the goods must be available for a reasonable time [UCC 2–503(1)(a)]. Goods must be tendered in a single delivery unless parties agree otherwise [UCC 2–612, 2A–510] or a party can request delivery in lots [UCC 2–307].

B. **PLACE OF DELIVERY**

Parties may agree on a particular destination, or the contract or circumstances may indicate a place.

1. **Noncarrier Cases**

   a. **Seller's Place of Business**

   If the contract does not designate a place of delivery, and the buyer is to pick up the goods, the place is the seller's place of business or if none, the seller's residence [UCC 2–308].

   b. **Identified Goods That Are Not at the Seller's Place of Business**

   Wherever they are is the place of delivery [UCC 2–308].

2. **Delivery via Carrier**

   a. **Shipment Contract**

   The seller must [UCC 2–504]—

155

1) Put the goods into the hands of a carrier.

2) Make a contract for the transport of the goods that is reasonable according to their nature and value.

3) Tender to the buyer any documents necessary to obtain possession of the goods from the carrier.

4) Promptly notify the buyer that shipment has been made.

5) If a seller fails to meet these requirements, and this causes a material loss or a delay, the buyer can reject the shipment.

b. Destination Contract
The seller must give the buyer appropriate notice and necessary documents of title [UCC 2–503].

C. THE PERFECT TENDER RULE   *(not under common law)*
A seller or lessor must deliver goods in conformity with every detail of the contract. If goods or tender fail in any respect, the buyer or lessee can accept the goods, reject them, or accept part and reject part [UCC 2–601, 2A–509].

D. EXCEPTIONS TO THE PERFECT TENDER RULE

1. Agreement of the Parties
Parties can agree in their contract that, for example, the seller can repair or replace any defective goods within a reasonable time.

2. Cure

a. Within the Contract Time for Performance
If nonconforming goods are rejected, the seller or lessor can notify the buyer or lessee of an intention to repair, adjust, or replace the goods and can then do so within the contract time for performance [UCC 2–508, 2A–513].

b. After the Time for Performance Expires
The seller or lessor can cure if there were reasonable grounds to believe the nonconformance would be acceptable. ("Reasonable grounds" include nonconforming tender with a price allowance.)

c. Substantially Restricts the Buyer's Right to Reject
If the buyer or lessee refuses goods but does not disclose the nature of the defect, he or she cannot later assert the defect as a defense if it is one that could have been cured [UCC 2–605, 2A–514].

3. Substitution of Carriers
If, through no fault of either party an agreed manner of delivery is not available, a substitute is sufficient [UCC 2–614(1)].

4. Installment Contracts

a. Substantial Nonconformity
A buyer or lessee can reject an installment only if a nonconformity substantially impairs the value of the installment and cannot be cured [UCC 2–612(2), 2–307, 2A–510(1)].

b. Breach of the Entire Contract
A breach occurs if one or more nonconforming installments substantially impair the value of the whole contract. If the buyer or lessee accepts a nonconforming installment, the contract is reinstated [UCC 2–612(3), 2A–510(2)].

5. **Commercial Impracticability**
   No breach if performance is impracticable due to the occurrence of an unforeseen contingency. This does not include problems that could have been foreseen, such as cost increases due to inflation. If the event allows for partial performance, the seller or lessor must do so, in a fair manner (with notice to the buyer or lessee) [UCC 2–615, 2A–405].

6. **Destruction of Identified Goods**
   When goods are destroyed (through no fault of a party) before risk passes to the buyer or lessee, the parties are excused from performance [UCC 2–613, 2A–221]. If goods are only partially destroyed, a buyer can treat a contract as void or accept damaged goods with a price credit.

7. **Assurance and Cooperation**
   A party with reasonable grounds to believe that the other will not perform may demand adequate assurance, suspend his or her own performance, and with no assurance within thirty days treat the contract as repudiated [UCC 2–609, 2A–401]. When required cooperation is not forthcoming, the other party can do whatever is reasonable, including holding the uncooperative party in breach [UCC 2–311(3)(b)].

III. OBLIGATIONS OF THE BUYER OR LESSEE

The buyer or lessee must make payment at the time and place he or she receives the goods unless the parties have agreed otherwise [UCC 2–310(a), 2A–516(1)].

A. PAYMENT
Payment can be by any means agreed on between the parties [UCC 2–511].

B. RIGHT OF INSPECTION
The buyer or lessee can verify, before making payment, that the goods are what were contracted for. There is no duty to pay if the goods are not as ordered [UCC 2–513(1), 2A–515(1)]. Inspection can be in any reasonable place, time and manner, determined by custom of the trade, practice of the parties, and so on [UCC 2–513(2)].

C. ACCEPTANCE
Acceptance is presumed if a buyer or lessee has a reasonable opportunity to inspect and fails to reject in a reasonable time [UCC 2–606, 2–602, 2A–515]. A buyer or lessee can accept by words or conduct. Under a sales contract, a buyer can accept by any act (such as using or reselling the goods) inconsistent with the seller's ownership [UCC 2–606(1)(c)].

D. PARTIAL ACCEPTANCE
If some of the goods do not conform to the contract, and the seller or lessor has failed to cure, a buyer or lessee can accept only the conforming goods, but not less than a single commercial unit [UCC 2–601(c), 2A-509(1)].

IV. ANTICIPATORY REPUDIATION

The nonbreaching party can (1) treat the repudiation as a final breach by pursuing a remedy or (2) wait, hoping that the repudiating party will decide to honor the contract [UCC 2–610, 2A–402]. If the party decides to wait, the breaching party can retract the repudiation [UCC 2–611, 2A–403].

V. REMEDIES OF THE SELLER OR LESSOR

A. WHEN THE GOODS ARE IN POSSESSION OF THE SELLER OR LESSOR

1. **The Right to Cancel the Contract**
   A seller or lessor can cancel a contract (with notice to the buyer or lessee) if the other party breaches it [UCC 2–703(f), 2A–523(1)(a)].

2. **The Right to Withhold Delivery**
   A seller or lessor can withhold delivery if a buyer or lessee wrongfully rejects or revokes acceptance, fails to pay, or repudiates [UCC 2–703(a), 2A–523(1)(c)]. If a buyer or lessee is

insolvent, a seller or lessor can refuse to deliver unless a buyer pays cash [UCC 2–702(1), 2A–525(1)].

3. The Right to Resell or Dispose of the Goods

The seller or lessor can hold the buyer or lessee liable for any loss [UCC 2–703(d), 2–706(1), 2A–523(1)(e), 2A–527(1)]. The seller must timely notify the buyer unless the goods are perishable or will rapidly decline in value [UCC 2–706(2), (3)].

a. Unfinished Goods

If the goods are unfinished at the time of the breach, the seller or lessor can either stop or complete their manufacture before reselling (or re-leasing) them.

b. Measure of Damages

The buyer or lessee is responsible for the difference between the contract and resale (or re-lease) prices, as well as incidental damages [UCC 2–706(1), 2–710, 2A–527(2)].

4. The Right to Recover the Purchase Price or Lease Payments Due

A seller or lessor can bring an action for the price if the buyer or lessee breaches after the goods are identified to the contract and the seller or lessor is unable to resell [UCC 2–709(1), 2A–529(1)].

5. The Right to Recover Damages for the Buyer's Nonacceptance

If a buyer or lessee repudiates a contract or wrongfully refuses to accept, the seller or lessor can recover the difference between the contract price and the market price (at the time and place of tender), plus incidental damages. If the market price is less than the contract price, the seller or lessor gets lost profits [UCC 2–708, 2A–528].

B. WHEN THE GOODS ARE IN TRANSIT

A seller or lessor can stop delivery of goods if (1) buyer or lessee is insolvent or (2) buyer or lessee is solvent but in breach (if the quantity shipped is a carload, a truckload, or larger) [UCC 2–705, 2A–526]. This right is lost if—

must be full container ↓ not if sharing load with someone else

1. The buyer or lessee has the goods.
2. The carrier or a bailee acknowledges that the goods are being held for the buyer or lessee.
3. In the case of a sale, a document of title has been negotiated to the buyer [UCC 2–705(2), 2A–526(2)].

C. WHEN THE GOODS ARE IN POSSESSION OF THE BUYER OR LESSEE

1. The Right to Recover the Purchase Price or Lease Payments Due

A seller or lessor can bring an action for the price, plus incidental damages, if the buyer or lessee accepts the goods but refuses to pay [UCC 2–709(1), 2A–529(1)].

2. The Right to Reclaim the Goods

a. Sales Contracts—Buyer's Insolvency

If an insolvent buyer gets goods on credit, the seller can (within ten days) reclaim them. A seller can reclaim any time if a buyer misrepresents solvency in writing within three months before delivery [UCC 2–702(2)].

b. Sales Contracts—A Buyer in the Ordinary Course of Business

A seller cannot reclaim goods from such a buyer.

c. Lease Contracts

A lessor can reclaim goods from a lessee in default [UCC 2A–525(2)].

VI. REMEDIES OF THE BUYER OR LESSEE

A. WHEN THE SELLER OR LESSOR REFUSES TO DELIVER THE GOODS

1. **The Right to Cancel the Contract**
   The buyer or lessee can rescind (cancel) the contract. On notice to the seller, the buyer or lessee is discharged [UCC 2–711(1), 2A–508(1)(a).

2. **The Right to Recover the Goods**
   A buyer or lessee who paid for goods in the hands of the seller or lessor can recover them if the seller or lessor is insolvent or becomes insolvent within ten days of receiving payment and the goods are identified to the contract. Buyer or lessee must tender any unpaid balance [UCC 2–502, 2A–522].

3. **The Right to Obtain Specific Performance**
   A buyer or lessee can obtain specific performance if goods are unique or damages would be inadequate [UCC 2–716(1), 2A–521(1)].

4. **The Right of Cover**
   A buyer or lessee can obtain cover (substitute goods) and then sue for damages. The measure of damages is the difference between the cost of cover and the contract price, plus incidental and consequential damages, minus expenses saved by the breach [UCC 2–712, 2–715, 2A–518, 2A–520].

5. **The Right to Replevy Goods**
   A buyer or lessee can use, against a seller or lessor, replevin (an action to recover goods from a party wrongfully withholding them) if the buyer or lessee is unable to cover [UCC 2–716(3), 2A–521(3)].

6. **The Right to Recover Damages**
   The measure of damages is the difference between the contract price and, when the buyer or lessee learned of the breach, the market price (at the place of delivery), plus incidental and consequential damages, less expenses saved by the breach [UCC 2–713, 2A–519].

B. **WHEN THE SELLER OR LESSOR DELIVERS NONCONFORMING GOODS**

1. **The Right to Reject the Goods**
   A buyer or lessee can reject the part of goods that fails to conform to the contract (and rescind the contract or obtain cover) [UCC 2–601, 2A–509].

   a. **Timeliness and Reason for Rejection Required**
   Notice must be timely, and a buyer or lessee must tell the seller or lessor what the defect is [UCC 2–602(1), 2–605, 2A–509(2), 2A–514].

   b. **Duties of a Merchant Buyer or Lessee**
   Follow the seller or lessor's instructions about the goods [UCC 2–603, 2A–511]. Without instructions, perishable goods can be resold; otherwise they must be stored or returned.

2. **The Right to Revoke Acceptance of the Goods**

   a. **Substantial Impairment**
   Any nonconformity must substantially impair the value of the goods *and* either not be seasonably cured or be difficult to discover [UCC 2–608, 2A–517].

   b. **Notice of a Breach Must Be within a Reasonable Time**
   Before the goods have undergone substantial change (not caused by their own defects, such as spoilage) [UCC 2–608(2), 2A–517(4)].

3. **The Right to Recover Damages for Accepted Goods**
   Notice of a breach must be within a reasonable time. The measure of damages is the difference between value of goods as accepted and value if they had been as promised [UCC 2–714(2), 2A–519(4)].

VII. ADDITIONAL PROVISIONS AFFECTING REMEDIES

Parties can provide for remedies in addition to or in lieu of those in the UCC, or they can change the measure of damages [UCC 2–719, 2A–503].

A. EXCLUSIVE REMEDIES

Any remedy can be made exclusive (at least until it fails in its essential purpose) [UCC 2–719(2), 2A–503(2)].

B. CONSEQUENTIAL DAMAGES

If a buyer or lessee is a consumer, limiting consequential damages for personal injuries on a breach of warranty is *prima facie* unconscionable.

C. LEMON LAWS   *— usually within 1 year*

If a car under warranty has a defect that significantly affects the vehicle's value or use, and the seller does not fix it within a specified number of opportunities, the buyer is entitled (after following certain procedures) to a new car, replacement of defective parts, or return of all consideration paid.   *3 tries within 12 months or you can return*

VIII. DEALING WITH INTERNATIONAL CONTRACTS

A. LETTER-OF-CREDIT TRANSACTIONS   *— good for 1 time deals with people you don't know or trust*

1. A Simple Transaction

The issuer (a bank) agrees to issue a letter of credit and to ascertain whether the beneficiary (seller) performs certain acts. The account party (buyer) promises to reimburse the issuer for amounts paid to the beneficiary. The issuer is bound to pay the beneficiary when he or she complies with the terms of the letter (by presenting required documents—typically a bill of lading).

2. The Basic Principle

The basic principle is that payment is made against the documents presented by the beneficiary and not against the facts that the documents purport to reflect. The issuer does not police the underlying contract; the letter is independent of it.

B. REMEDIES FOR BREACH OF INTERNATIONAL SALES CONTRACTS

The United Nations Convention on Contracts for the International Sale of Goods (CISG) provides remedies similar to the UCC's, including, in appropriate circumstances, damages (difference between contract and market prices), the right to avoid a contract, and the right to specific performance.

TRUE-FALSE QUESTIONS

(Answers at the Back of the Book)

_____ 1. The duties and obligations of the parties to a contract include those specified in the agreement.

_____ 2. Generally, under a sales or lease contract, all goods must be tendered in a single delivery.

_____ 3. If goods fail to conform to a contract in any way, a buyer or lessee can accept or reject the goods.

_____ 4. Unless the parties agree otherwise, a buyer or lessee must pay for goods in advance.

_____ 5. If a contract does not specify otherwise, the place for delivery of goods is the buyer's place of business.

_____ 6. A buyer or lessee who accepts a delivery of goods cannot withdraw the acceptance.

___ 7. A seller or lessor cannot consider a buyer or lessee in breach until the time for performance has past.

___ 8. In an installment contract, a buyer can reject any installment for any reason.

___ 9. If a buyer or lessee wrongfully refuses to accept or pay for conforming goods, the seller or lessor can cancel the contract and recover damages.

___ 10. If a seller or lessor wrongfully refuses to deliver conforming goods, the buyer or lessee can cancel the contract and recover damages.

FILL-IN QUESTIONS

(Answers at the Back of the Book)

A seller's obligations include holding _____ (conforming/nonconforming) goods at a buyer's disposal _____ (and/or) giving notice reasonably necessary for the buyer to take delivery. Unless the parties have agreed otherwise, the _____ (seller/buyer) must provide facilities reasonably suited for _____ (delivery/receipt) of the goods. Also, unless the parties have agreed otherwise, a buyer must pay at the time and place of receipt, _____ (even if/unless) the place of shipment is the place of delivery.

MULTIPLE-CHOICE QUESTIONS

(Answers at the Back of the Book)

___ 1. **Based on a Sample CPA Exam Question.** Desktop Office Products orders 100 computers from Inventory Supply Company. Unless the parties agree otherwise, Inventory's obligation to Desktop is to

  a. deliver the computers to a common carrier.
  b. deliver the computer's to Desktop's place of business.
  c. hold conforming goods and give notice for Desktop to take delivery.
  d. set aside conforming goods for Desktop's inspection before delivery.

___ 2. Engineering, Inc. (EI), agrees to sell specially made parts to Precision Manufacturing Company. EI does not deliver. Due to a market shortage, Precision cannot obtain cover. The buyer's right to recover the parts from EI is

  a. novation.
  b. replevin.
  c. rescission.
  d. specific performance.

___ 3. Delta Grocers, Inc., agrees to buy 10,000 potatoes from Bayou Farms. Only half of the shipment conforms to the contract, but conforming potatoes are in short supply in the market. Bayou's best course is to

  a. accept the entire shipment.
  b. accept the conforming goods and sue for the difference between the contract price and the cost of cover.
  c. reject the entire shipment and sue for specific performance.
  d. suspend payment and wait to see if Eagle will tender conforming goods.

____ 4. Kyle contracts to sell five laser printers to Lora under a shipment contract. Kyle must

   a. make a reasonable contract to transport the goods and tender documents needed to obtain them.
   b. neither make a reasonable contract to transport the goods nor tender documents needed to obtain them.
   c. only make a reasonable contract for the transport of the goods.
   d. only tender to Lora the documents needed to obtain possession of the goods.

____ 5. Video Stores, Inc., refuses to buy 1,000 DVD players for $80 each from WOW Products Company under their contract, due to a drop in the market price for the players, which can be bought for $40 each. As damages, WOW can recover

   a. $120,000.
   b. $80,000.
   c. $40,000.
   d. $0.

____ 6. Excel Corporation agrees to sell the latest version of its Go! video game to Gamers Outlet. Excel delivers an outdated version of Go! (nonconforming goods). Gamers's remedies may include

   a. recovering damages only.
   b. rejecting part or all of the goods, or revoking acceptance only.
   c. recovering damages, rejecting goods, or revoking acceptance.
   d. none of the choices.

____ 7. City Soccer League contracts to buy goods from Del's Sports. Del's wrongfully fails to deliver the goods. City can recover damages equal to the difference between the contract price and the market price

   a. at the time the contract was made.
   b. at the time and place of tender.
   c. when City learned of the breach.
   d. when City filed a suit against Del's.

____ 8. **Based on a Sample CPA Exam Question.** LiveWire Software Company agrees to sell to Motor Parts Manufacturing, Inc., a customized software system. If Motor Parts materially breaches the contract, the remedies available to LiveWire include the right

   a. to cancel the contract only.
   b. to recover damages only.
   c. to cancel the contract and recover damages.
   d. none of the choices.

____ 9. Orchard Farms contracts for a sale of fruit to Pik-It Market. Orchard can enforce its right to payment

   a. only after Pik-It has inspected the goods.
   b. only after Pik-It has had an opportunity to inspect the goods.
   c. only before Pik-It has inspected the goods.
   d. whether or not Pik-It has had the opportunity to inspect the goods.

____ 10. Frozen Cow, Inc., agrees to sell ice cream to Pricey Stadium Concessions. Before the time for performance, Frozen Cow tells Pricey that it will not deliver. This is

   a. anticipatory repudiation.
   b. perfect tender.
   c. rejection of performance.
   d. revocation of acceptance.

SHORT ESSAY QUESTIONS

1. What is a seller's right to cure and how does it affect a buyer's right to reject?

2. What is a buyer's right of cover?

ROCKON

(Answers at the Back of the Book)

1. For the Summer Solstice Symphonic Symposia—a series of workshops for composers and musicians—you order fifty Tundra-brand cellos from The String Instrument Source, Inc. The Source confirms your order in writing. On the last day to ship the order, the seller realizes that it does not have enough Tundra cellos in stock and ships Unitone cellos instead, with a note stating that the Unitone instruments are an accommodation. Is The Source in breach? Discuss.

2. As a sound engineer, you agree orally to custom design and build a system for Cato, the newest pop star, for his upcoming European tour at the price of $250,000. You complete the project for $180,000, but Cato says that he no longer needs the system and refuses to pay for it. Unable to sell the unique system, you incur storage costs of $6,000. Can you recover damages? If so, how much?

SPECIAL INFORMATION FOR CPA CANDIDATES

A number of the concepts in this chapter often arise in the CPA examination, sometimes intertwined with the rules set out in other chapters covering Article 2 of the UCC. For example, a seller who does not tender delivery of conforming goods is in breach of the contract. Such a tender is also necessary for the risk of loss to pass.

It may be easiest to remember all of these rules by imagining a real sales contract situation and applying them to that situation. In particular, it can be helpful to sort out the rules in Article 2 that apply when one of the parties is a merchant and when both parties are merchants. The following topics (discussed in this chapter), as they relate to merchants, are often tested in the part of the CPA exam covering the UCC: risk of loss, the buyer's responsibility regarding rejected goods, the buyer's obligation to designate defects, sales on approval and sales or returns, and either party's right to assurance of performance.

Chapter 22:

Warranties and Product Liability

WHAT THIS CHAPTER IS ABOUT

Warranties that impose duties on sellers cover most goods. A breach of a warranty is a breach of the seller's promise. Manufacturers, processors, and sellers may also be liable to consumers, users, and bystanders for physical harm or property damage caused by defective goods. This is product liability.

CHAPTER OUTLINE

I. TYPES OF WARRANTIES

A. WARRANTIES OF TITLE

1. Good Title
Sellers warrant that they have good and valid title and that the transfer of title is rightful [UCC 2–312(1)(a)].

2. No Liens
Sellers warrant that goods are free of a security interest of which the buyer has no knowledge [UCC 2–312(1)(b)]. Lessors warrant no third party will interfere with the lessee's use of the goods [UCC 2A–211(1)].

3. No Infringements
Sellers warrant that the goods are free of any third person's patent, trademark, or copyright claims [UCC 2–312(3)].

    a. Sales Contract—If the Warranty Is Breached and the Buyer Is Sued
    The buyer must notify the seller. If the seller agrees in writing to defend and bear all costs, the buyer must let the seller do it (or lose all rights against the seller) [UCC 2–607(3)(b), (5)(b)].

    b. Lease—If the Warranty Is Breached and the Lessee Is Sued
    Same as above, except that a consumer who fails to notify the lessor within a reasonable time does not lose any rights against the lessor [UCC 2A–516(3)(b), (4)(b)].

4. Disclaimer of Title Warranties
These warranties can be disclaimed or modified by specific language in the contract [UCC 2–312(2), 2A–214(4)].

B. EXPRESS WARRANTIES

1. When Express Warranties Arise
A seller or lessor warrants that goods will conform to affirmations or promises of fact, descriptions, samples or models [UCC 2–313, 2A–210].

2. Basis of the Bargain

An affirmation, promise, description, or sample must be part of the basis of the bargain: it must come at such a time that the buyer could have relied on it when agreeing to the contract [UCC 2–313, 2A–210].

3. Statements of Opinion

a. Opinions

A statement relating to the value of goods or a statement of opinion or recommendation about goods is not an express warranty [UCC 2–313(2), 2A–210(2)], unless the seller or lessor who makes it is an expert and gives an opinion as an expert.

b. Puffery

Whether a statement is a warranty or puffery is not easy to determine. Factors include the specificity of the statement and the reasonableness of the buyer's reliance on it. Clearly improbable claims and oral statements are less likely to qualify.

C. IMPLIED WARRANTIES

An implied warranty is derived by implication or inference from the nature of a transaction or the relative situations or circumstances of the parties.

1. Implied Warranty of Merchantability

A warranty automatically arises in every sale or lease of goods by a merchant who deals in such goods that the goods are merchantable [UCC 2–314, 2A–212].

a. Reasonably Fit for Ordinary Purposes

Goods that are merchantable are "reasonably fit for the ordinary purposes for which such goods are used." Merchantable food is food that is fit to eat.

b. Characteristics of Merchantable Goods

Average, fair, or medium-grade quality; pass without objection in the market for goods of the same description; adequate package and label, as provided by the agreement; and conform to the promises or affirmations of fact made on the container or label.

2. Implied Warranty of Fitness for a Particular Purpose

Arises when a seller or lessor (merchant or nonmerchant) knows or has reason to know the purpose for which a buyer or lessee will use goods and knows he or she is relying on the seller to select suitable goods [UCC 2–315, 2A–213]. Goods can be merchantable but unfit for a particular purpose.

3. Implied Warranties from Prior Dealings or Trade Customs

When the parties know a well-recognized trade custom, it is inferred that they intended it to apply to their contract [UCC 2–314, 2A–212].

D. MAGNUSON–MOSS WARRANTY ACT

No seller is required to give a written warranty for consumer goods, but if a seller chooses to do so and the cost of the goods is more than $25, the warranty must be clearly labeled—

1. "Full" or "Limited"

A full warranty requires free repair or replacement of defective parts, and if not done within a reasonable time, the buyer can choose a refund or replacement at no charge. A limited warranty is any warranty that is not full.

2. Required Information

The seller must state (fully and conspicuously in a single document in "readily understood language") the seller's name and address, what is warranted, procedures for enforcing the warranty, any limitations on relief, and that the buyer has legal rights.

II. OVERLAPPING WARRANTIES

A. WHEN WARRANTIES ARE CONSISTENT

They are cumulative [UCC 2–317, 2A–215].

B. WHEN WARRANTIES CONFLICT

1. Express warranties displace inconsistent implied warranties (except fitness for a particular purpose).

2. Samples take precedence over inconsistent general descriptions.

3. Technical specs displace inconsistent samples or general descriptions.

III. WARRANTY DISCLAIMERS AND LIMITATIONS ON LIABILITY

A. EXPRESS WARRANTIES
A seller can avoid making express warranties by not promising or affirming anything, describing the goods, or using of a sample or model [UCC 2–313].

1. Oral Warranties
Oral warranties made during bargaining cannot be modified later without consent.

2. Negating or Limiting Express Warranties
A written disclaimer—clear and conspicuous—can negate all warranties not in the written contract [UCC 2–316(1), 2A–214(1)].

B. IMPLIED WARRANTIES

1. General Disclaimer
Implied warranties can be disclaimed by the expression "as is" or a similar phrase [UCC 2–316(3)(a), 2A–214(3)(a)]. (Some states do not allow such disclaimers.)

2. Specific Disclaimer
Fitness for a particular purpose: disclaimer must be in writing and conspicuous (word *fitness* is not required). Merchantability: disclaimer must mention *merchantability*; if in writing, must be conspicuous.

3. What Is Conspicuous?
A term or clause that a reasonable person would notice (such as larger or contrasting type) is considered conspicuous [UCC 1–201(10)].

C. BUYER'S OR LESSEE'S EXAMINATION OR REFUSAL TO INSPECT
If a buyer examines the goods before entering a contract, there is no implied warranty with respect to defects that a reasonable examination would reveal [UCC 2–316(3)(b), 2A–214(2)(b)]. The same is true if the buyer refuses to examine over the seller or lessor's demand.

D. UNCONSCIONABILITY
Courts view disclaimers with disfavor, especially when consumers are involved, and have sometimes held disclaimers unconscionable [UCC 2–302, 2A–108].

E. STATUTES OF LIMITATIONS

1. When an Action for Breach of Contract Must Be Brought
An action for breach of contract under the UCC must be brought within four years after the cause of action accrues. In their contract, the parties can change the period to not less than one, and not more than four, years [UCC 2–725(1)].

2. When a Cause of Action for Breach of Warranty Accrues
When the seller tenders delivery, even if the nonbreaching party is unaware the cause has accrued [UCC 2–725(2)]. Notice of the breach to the breaching party is required to pursue a remedy.

IV. PRODUCT LIABILITY
Product liability may be based on negligence, misrepresentation, strict liability, or warranty law.

A. PRODUCT LIABILITY BASED ON NEGLIGENCE

If the failure to exercise reasonable care in the making or marketing of a product causes an injury, the basis of liability is negligence.

1. Manufacturer's Duty of Care

Due care must be exercised in designing, assembling, and testing a product; selecting materials; inspecting and testing products bought for use in the final product; and placing warnings on the label to inform users of dangers of which an ordinary person might not be aware.

2. Privity of Contract between Plaintiff and Defendant Is Not Required

B. PRODUCT LIABILITY BASED ON MISREPRESENTATION

There may liability for a misrepresentation if it (1) is of a material fact, (2) is intended to induce a buyer's reliance, (3) the buyer relies on it, and (4) there is an injury. Fraudulent misrepresentation occurs when the misrepresentation is done knowingly or with reckless disregard for the facts.

V.   STRICT PRODUCT LIABILITY

A defendant may be liable for the result of his or her act regardless of intention or exercise of reasonable care (see Chapter 7).

A. STRICT PRODUCT LIABILITY AND PUBLIC POLICY

Public policy assumes that (1) consumers should be protected from unsafe products, (2) manufacturers and distributors should not escape liability solely for lack of privity, and (3) sellers and lessors are in a better position to bear the cost of injuries caused by their products.

B. THE REQUIREMENTS FOR STRICT PRODUCT LIABILITY

Under the *Restatement (Second) of Torts*, Section 402A—

1. Product Is in a Defective Condition When the Defendant Sells It

2. Defendant Is Normally in the Business of Selling the Product

3. Defect Makes the Product Unreasonably Dangerous

A product may be so defective if either—

a. Product Is Dangerous beyond the Ordinary Consumer's Expectation

There may have been a flaw in the manufacturing process that led to some defective products being marketed, or a perfectly made product may not have had adequate warning on the label.

b. There Is a Less Dangerous, Economically Feasible Alternative That the Manufacturer Failed to Use

A manufacturer may have failed to design a safe product.

4. Plaintiff Incurs Harm to Self or Property by Use of the Product

5. Defect Is the Proximate Cause of the Harm

6. Product Was Not Substantially Changed after It Was Sold

Between the time the product was sold and the time of the injury.

C. PRODUCT DEFECTS

The *Restatement (Third) of Torts: Products Liability* categorizes defects as—

1. Manufacturing Defects

A manufacturing defect occurs when a product departs from its intended design even though all possible care was taken (strict liability).

2. **Design Defects**

A design defect exists when a foreseeable risk of harm posed by a product could have been reduced by use of a reasonable alternative design and the omission makes the product unreasonably unsafe. A court considers such factors as consumer expectations and warnings.

3. **Inadequate Warnings**

A warning defect occurs when a reasonable warning could have reduced a product's foreseeable risk of harm and the omission makes the product unreasonably unsafe. Factors include the content and comprehensibility of a warning, the obviousness of a risk, and the expected users.

D. MARKET-SHARE LIABILITY

In some cases, some courts hold that all firms that manufactured and distributed a certain product during a certain period are liable for injuries in proportion to the firms' respective shares of the market.

E. OTHER APPLICATIONS OF STRICT PRODUCT LIABILITY

1. **Strict Liability Protects Bystanders**

All courts extend strict liability to cover injured bystanders (limited in some cases to those whose injuries are reasonably foreseeable).

2. **Strict Liability Extends to Suppliers**

Suppliers of component parts may be liable for injuries caused by defective products.

VI. DEFENSES TO PRODUCT LIABILITY

A. ASSUMPTION OF RISK

In some states, this is a defense if (1) plaintiff knew and appreciated the risk created by the defect and (2) plaintiff voluntarily engaged in the risk, event though it was unreasonable to do so.

B. PRODUCT MISUSE

The use must not be the one for which the product was designed, and the misuse must not be reasonably foreseeable.

C. COMPARATIVE NEGLIGENCE (FAULT)

Most states consider a plaintiff's actions in apportioning liability.

D. COMMONLY KNOWN DANGERS

Failing to warn against such a danger is not ground for liability.

E. KNOWLEDGEABLE USER

Failing to warn a *knowledgeable* user of a danger that is commonly known to such users is not ground for liability.

F. STATUTES OF LIMITATIONS AND REPOSE

A statute of limitations provides that an action must be brought within a specified period of time after the cause of action accrues (after some damage occurs or after a harmed party discovers the damage). A statute of repose limits the time in which a suit can be filed. It runs from an earlier date and for a longer time than a statute of limitations.

TRUE-FALSE QUESTIONS

(Answers at the Back of the Book)

____ 1. Promises of fact made during the bargaining process are express warranties.

____ 2. A contract cannot include both an implied warranty and an express warranty.

____ 3. A merchant cannot disclaim an implied warranty of merchantability.

___ **4.** An express warranty can be limited.

___ **5.** Privity of contract is required to bring a product liability suit based on negligence.

___ **6.** One requirement for a product liability suit based on strict liability is a failure to exercise due care.

___ **7.** In many states, the plaintiff's negligence is a defense that may be raised in a product liability suit based on strict liability.

___ **8.** A warranty of title can be disclaimed or modified only by specific language in a contract.

___ **9.** A manufacturer has a duty to warn about risks that are obvious or commonly known.

___ **10.** Assumption of risk can be raised as a defense in a product liability suit.

FILL-IN QUESTIONS

(Answers at the Back of the Book)

An express warranty _____ (can/cannot) be disclaimed in writing if it is called to the buyer's attention. An implied warranty of fitness for a particular purpose _____ (can/cannot) be disclaimed in writing. An implied warranty of merchantability _____ (can/cannot) be disclaimed in writing. A disclaimer of the implied warranty of fitness for a particular purpose _____ (must/need not) use the word "fitness." A disclaimer of the implied warranty of merchantability _____ (must/need not) include the word merchantability.

MULTIPLE-CHOICE QUESTIONS

(Answers at the Back of the Book)

___ **1.** Falcon Skis, Inc., makes and sells skis. In deciding whether the skis are merchantable, a court would consider whether

   a. Falcon violated any government regulations.
   b. the skis are a quality product.
   c. the skis are fit for the ordinary purpose for which such goods are used.
   d. the skis are made in an efficient manner.

___ **2.** Wildwood Furniture Company makes and sells furniture. To avoid liability for most implied warranties, their sales agreements should note that their goods are sold

   a. "as is."
   b. by a merchant.
   c. for cash only.
   d. in perfect condition.

___ **3.** **Based on a Sample CPA Exam Question.** Daphne, a sales representative for Ergo Office Furniture shows swatches of upholstery fabric to Floyd, a customer, who says he needs chairs for an office reception area. An example of an express warranty is a warranty of

   a. conformity of goods to a sample.
   b. fitness for a particular purpose.
   c. merchantability.
   d. usage of trade.

____   4. Jupiter Auto Sales sells cars, trucks, and other motor vehicles. A Jupiter salesperson tells potential customers, "This is the finest car ever made." This statement is

   a. an express warranty.
   b. an implied warranty.
   c. a warranty of title.
   d. puffery.

____   5. The design of a bridge built by Suspension Engineering, Inc., is defective and soon after completion it begins to sway in the wind. Everyone stays off, except Rory, who wants to show off. Rory falls from the bridge and sues Suspension, who can raise the defense of

   a. assumption of risk.
   b. commonly known danger.
   c. product misuse.
   d. knowledgeable user.

____   6. Kitchensharp Products, Inc. (KPI), makes knifes and other utensils. Louella is injured while using a KPI knife, and sues KPI for product liability based on negligence. KPI could successfully defend against the suit by showing that

   a. Louella's injury resulted from a commonly known danger.
   b. Louella misused the knife in a foreseeable way.
   c. KPI did not sell the knife to Louella.
   d. the knife was not altered after KPI sold it.

____   7. StandUp Tools, Inc., makes and sells tools. Tifa is injured as a result of using a StandUp tool. She sues StandUp for product liability based on strict liability. To succeed, Tifa must prove that StandUp

   a. was in privity of contract with Tifa.
   b. did not use care with respect to the tool.
   c. misrepresented a material fact regarding the tool on which Tifa relied.
   d. none of the choices.

____   8. Yard Work, Inc., makes and sells garden tools. Under the *Restatement (Second) of Torts*, a tool could be unreasonably dangerous

   a. only if, in making the tool, Yard Work failed to use a less dangerous but economically feasible alternative.
   b. only if the tool is dangerous beyond the ordinary consumer's expectation.
   c. if, in making the tool, Yard Work failed to use a less dangerous but economically feasible alternative or if the tool is dangerous beyond the ordinary consumer's expectation.
   d. none of the choices.

____   9. Misha is in a Sip n' Snak store when a bottle of Hi Cola on a nearby shelf explodes, injuring her. She can recover from the manufacturer of Hi Cola only if she can show that

   a. she did not assume the risk of the explosive bottle of Hi Cola.
   b. she intended to buy the explosive bottle of Hi Cola.
   c. she was injured due to a defect in the product.
   d. the manufacturer failed to use due care in making the bottle of Hi Cola.

____   10. Vivid Vid, Inc., designs and manufacturers DVD players. In a product liability suit based on negligence, Vivid could be liable for violating its duty of care with respect to

   a. a player's design only.
   b. a player's design or manufacture.
   c. a player's manufacture only.
   d. neither a player's design nor its manufacture.

SHORT ESSAY QUESTIONS

1. What is the difference between the implied warranty of merchantability and the implied warranty of fitness for a particular purpose?

2. How defective must a product be to support a cause of action in strict liability in a product liability suit?

RockOn

(Answers at the Back of the Book)

1. OptiAmp Corp. promises you that its electrical equipment will meet the needs of any venue from a stadium to a café. You buy the equipment for Playtime, your urban rap club, but it is not sufficient to power the lighting, heating, and refrigeration systems of the club's facilities, much less meet the entertainers' needs. Has OptiAmp violated a warranty? If so, which one?

2. You buy a grand piano from Piano Showcase that was sold to the retailer by Quality Wholesale, Inc., which bought it from its manufacturer Raven Corp. While you are adjusting a rug under one of the piano's feet, it collapses on you, causing bodily injuries. You file a suit in strict product liability against the seller, the wholesaler, and the maker. Can you recover damages without proof of negligence? Explain.

SPECIAL INFORMATION FOR CPA CANDIDATES

The CPA examination does not cover the Magnuson–Moss Warranty Act (or similar state consumer protection legislation). The CPA exam has covered, however, the UCC's rules on warranty. These rules may be better applied if they are actually understood. That is, a rote memorization of the rules may not prove as useful as actual comprehension. To this end, it may be helpful to imagine their application in a real sales contract situation. In particular, remember that UCC warranty actions require privity of contract and that the warranty of merchantability applies only to merchants.

The CPA examination has also traditionally tested on three kinds of product liability actions: (1) UCC warranties, (2) negligence, and (3) strict liability. In particular, in a negligence or strict liability action, remember that no privity of contract is required. Keep in mind that the negligence may occur at any stage in a product's development, manufacture, and sale. Review the elements for an action in strict product liability. Also, don't forget relevant defenses, including assumption of risk and foreseeable misuse.

Chapter 23
International Law in a Global Economy

WHAT THIS CHAPTER IS ABOUT

This chapter notes sources of international law, some of the ways in which U.S. businesspersons do business in foreign countries, and how that business is regulated. The chapter concludes with a look at some aspects of national legal systems.

CHAPTER OUTLINE

I. **INTERNATIONAL LAW**

To facilitate commerce, sovereign nations agree to be governed in certain respects by international law.

A. SOURCES OF INTERNATIONAL LAW

1. **International Customs**
These are customs that evolved among nations in their relations with each other. "[E]vidence of a general practice accepted as law" [Article 38(1) of the Statute of the International Court of Justice].

2. **Treaties and International Agreements**
A treaty is an agreement or contract between two or more nations that must be authorized and ratified by the supreme power of each nation. A bilateral agreement occurs when only two nations form an agreement; multilateral agreements are those formed by several nations.

3. **International Organizations**
Composed mainly of nations (such as the United Nations); usually established by treaty; such entities adopt resolutions that require particular behavior of nations (such as the 1980 United Nations Convention on Contracts for the International Sale of Goods).

B. COMMON LAW AND CIVIL SYSTEMS
Legal systems are generally divided into common law and civil law systems.

1. **Common Law Systems**
Common law systems are based on case law. These systems exist in countries that were once a part of the British Empire (such as Australia, India, and the United States). *Stare decisis* requires following precedent unless otherwise necessary.

2. **Civil Law Systems**
Civil law systems are based on codified law (statutes). Courts interpret the code and apply the rules without developing their own laws. Civil law systems exist in most European nations, and in Latin American, African, and Asian countries.

3. **Islamic Law Systems**
In an Islamic legal system, the law is influenced by *sharia*, the religious law of Islam. Some Middle Eastern countries have codified *sharia* and enforce it through national court systems.

173

C. INTERNATIONAL PRINCIPLES AND DOCTRINES

The following are based on courtesy and respect and are applied in the interest of maintaining harmony among nations.

1. The Principle of Comity

One nation defers and gives effect to the laws and judicial decrees of another country, so long as those laws and judicial decrees are consistent with the law and public policy of the accommodating nation.

2. The Act of State Doctrine

The judicial branch of one country will not examine the validity of public acts committed by a recognized foreign government within its own territory. This doctrine applies in cases of—

a. Expropriation

This occurs when a government seizes a privately owned business or goods for a proper public purpose and pays just compensation.

b. Confiscation

This occurs when a government seizes private property for an illegal purpose or without just compensation. In a suit on this ground, the defendant must show that a taking was an expropriation, not a confiscation.

3. The Doctrine of Sovereign Immunity

This doctrine exempts foreign nations from the jurisdiction of domestic courts. In the United States, the Foreign Sovereign Immunities Act (FSIA) of 1976 exclusively governs the circumstances in which an action may be brought against a foreign nation. Generally, the plaintiff must show that the defendant is not entitled to sovereign immunity.

a. When Is a Foreign State Subject to U.S. Jurisdiction?

When it has waived its immunity, when the action is based on commercial activity in the U.S. by the foreign state, or when the foreign state has committed a tort or violated certain international laws [Section 1605].

b. What Entities Fall within the Category of Foreign State?

A political subdivision and an instrumentality (an agency or entity acting for the state) [Section 1603].

c. What Is a Commercial Activity?

Courts decide whether an activity is governmental or commercial.

II. DOING BUSINESS INTERNATIONALLY

A. EXPORTING

The simplest way to do business internationally is to export to foreign markets. Direct exporting: signing a sales contract with a foreign buyer. Indirect exporting: selling directly to consumers through a foreign agent or foreign distributor.

B. MANUFACTURING ABROAD

A domestic firm can establish a manufacturing plant abroad by—

1. Licensing

A firm may license its technology to a foreign manufacturer to avoid the process, product, or formula being pirated. The foreign firm agrees to keep the technology secret and to pay royalties for its use.

2. Franchising

Franchising (see Chapter 35) is a form of licensing in which the owner of a trademark, trade name, or copyright conditions its use in the selling of goods or services.

3. Investing in a Wholly Owned Subsidiary or a Joint Venture
When a wholly owned subsidiary is established, the domestic firm retains ownership of the foreign facilities and control over the entire operation. In a joint venture, a domestic firm and one or more foreign firms share ownership, responsibilities, profits, and liabilities.

III. REGULATION OF SPECIFIC BUSINESS ACTIVITIES

A. INVESTMENT PROTECTIONS
When a government confiscates property without just compensation, few remedies are available. Many countries guarantee compensation to foreign investors in their constitutions, statutes, or treaties. Some countries provide insurance for their citizens' investments abroad.

B. EXPORT CONTROLS

1. Restricting Exports
Under the U.S. Constitution, Congress cannot tax exports, but may set export quotas. Under the Export Administration Act of 1979, restrictions can be imposed on the flow of technologically advanced products and technical data.

2. Stimulating Exports
Devices to stimulate exports include export incentives and subsidies.

C. IMPORT CONTROLS
Laws prohibit, for example, importing illegal drugs and agricultural products that pose dangers to domestic crops or animals.

1. Quotas and Tariffs
Quotas limit how much can be imported. Tariffs are taxes on imports (usually a percentage of the value, but can be a flat rate per unit).

2. Antidumping Duties
A tariff (duty) may be assessed on imports to prevent *dumping* (sales of imported goods at "less than fair value," usually determined by prices in the exporting country).

D. TRADE AGREEMENTS THAT MINIMIZE TRADE BARRIERS

1. The World Trade Organization (WTO)
This the principal instrument for regulating international trade. Each member country agrees to grant *normal-trade-relations (NTR) status* to other members (the most favorable treatment with regard to trade).

2. The European Union (EU)
The EU is a regional trade association that minimizes trade barriers among its member nations.

3. The North American Free Trade Agreement (NAFTA)
NAFTA created a regional trading unit consisting of Mexico, the United States, and Canada. The goal is to eliminate tariffs in the region on substantially all goods over a period of fifteen to twenty years, while retaining tariffs on goods imported from other countries.

4. The Central American-Dominican Republic Free Trade Agreement (CAFTA-DR)
CAFTA-DR aims to reduce tariffs and improve market access among Costa Rica, Dominican Republic, El Salvador, Guatemala, Honduras, Nicaragua, and the United States.

IV. U.S. LAWS IN A GLOBAL CONTEXT

A. U.S. ANTITRUST LAWS
For U.S. courts to exercise jurisdiction over a foreign entity under U.S. antitrust laws, a violation must (1) have a substantial effect on U.S. commerce or (2) constitute a *per se* violation (see

Chapter 31). Foreign governments and persons can also sue U.S. firms and persons for antitrust violations.

B. INTERNATIONAL TORT CLAIMS
The Alien Tort Claims Act (ATCA) of 1789 allows foreign citizens to bring suits in U.S. courts for injuries allegedly caused by violations of international tort law. Some cases have involved violations of human rights, including torture and discrimination. Some have alleged environmental crimes.

C. ANTIDISCRIMINATION LAWS
U.S. employers must abide by U.S. employment discrimination laws (see Chapter 34) unless to do so would violate the laws of the country in which their workplace is located.

TRUE-FALSE QUESTIONS

(Answers at the Back of the Book)

____ 1. All nations must give effect to the laws of all other nations.

____ 2. Under the act of state doctrine, foreign nations are subject to the jurisdiction of U.S. courts.

____ 3. Under the doctrine of sovereign immunity, foreign nations are subject to the jurisdiction of U.S. courts.

____ 4. The Foreign Sovereign Immunities Act states the circumstances in which the United States can be sued in foreign courts.

____ 5. A member of the World Trade Organization must usually grant other members most-favored nation status, with regard to trade.

____ 6. U.S. courts cannot exercise jurisdiction over foreign entities under U.S. antitrust laws.

____ 7. Legal systems are generally divided into criminal law and civil law systems.

____ 8. U.S. employers with workplaces abroad must generally comply with U.S. discrimination laws.

____ 9. Foreign citizens can bring suits in U.S. courts for injuries allegedly caused by violations of international tort law.

____ 10. Congress cannot tax exports.

FILL-IN QUESTIONS

(Answers at the Back of the Book)

_____ (A confiscation/An expropriation) occurs when a national government seizes a privately owned business or privately owned goods for a proper public purpose. _____(A confiscation/An expropriation) occurs when the taking is made for an illegal purpose. When _____ (a confiscation/an expropriation) occurs, the government pays just compensation. When _____ (a confiscation/an expropriation) occurs, the government does not pay just compensation.

MULTIPLE-CHOICE QUESTIONS

(Answers at the Back of the Book)

____ **1.** Lightspeed, Inc., makes supercomputers that feature advanced technology. To inhibit Lightspeed's export of its products to other countries, Congress can

a. confiscate all profits on exported supercomputers.
b. expropriate all profits on exported supercomputers.
c. set quotas on exported supercomputers.
d. tax exported supercomputers.

____ **2.** Kenya issues bonds to finance the construction of an international airport. Kenya sells some of the bonds in the United States to Lacy. A terrorist group destroys the airport, and Kenya refuses to pay interest or principal on the bonds. Lacy files suit in a U.S court. The court will hear the suit

a. if Kenya's acts constitute a confiscation.
b. if Kenya's acts constitute an expropriation.
c. if Kenya's selling bonds is a "commercial activity."
d. under no circumstances.

____ **3.** To obtain new computers, Liberia accepts bids from U.S. firms, including Macro Corporation and Micro, Inc. Macro wins the contract. Alleging impropriety in the awarding of the contract, Micro files a suit in a U.S. court against Liberia and Macro. The court may decline to hear the suit under

a. the act of state doctrine.
b. the doctrine of sovereign immunity.
c. the Export Administration Act.
d. the World Trade Organization.

____ **4.** An Australian seller and a U.S. buyer form a contract that the buyer breaches. The seller sues in an Australian court and wins damages, but the buyer's assets are in the United States. If a U.S. court enforces the judgment, it will be because of

a. the act of state doctrine.
b. the doctrine of sovereign immunity.
c. the principle of comity.
d. the World Trade Organization.

____ **5.** General Auto Corporation makes cars in the United States. To boost the sales of General Auto and other domestic automakers, Congress can

a. neither set quotas nor tax imports.
b. only set quotas on imports.
c. only tax imports.
d. set quotas and tax imports.

____ **6.** Global Construction, Inc., is a U.S. firm. Helen, a U.S. citizen, works for Global in a country outside the United States. Inez, a citizen of a foreign country, also works for Global outside the United States. Helen and Inez believe that they are being harassed on the job, in violation of U.S. law. This law protects

a. Helen and Inez.
b. Helen only.
c. Inez only.
d. neither Helen nor Inez.

_____ 7. The United States has a common law legal system. Common law systems are based on

    a. administrative rules and regulations.
    b. case law.
    c. codified law.
    d. executive pronouncements.

_____ 8. France has a civil law legal system. Civil law systems are based on

    a. administrative rules and regulations.
    b. case law.
    c. codified law.
    d. executive pronouncements.

_____ 9. United Oil, Inc., is a U.S. firm, doing business in the United States and in other nations, including Venezuela. Venezuela seizes the property of United Oil, without paying just compensation. This is

    a. a confiscation.
    b. a dumping.
    c. a licensing.
    d. an expropriation.

_____ 10. High Sierra Lumber Company, a U.S. firm, signs a contract with Izo, Ltd., a Japanese company, to give Izo the right to sell High Sierra's products in Japan. This is

    a. a distribution agreement.
    b. a joint venture.
    c. direct exporting.
    d. licensing.

SHORT ESSAY QUESTIONS

1. In what ways may a company conduct international business?

2. How does the Foreign Sovereign Immunities Act affect commercial activities by foreign governments?

GAMEPOINTS

(Answers at the Back of the Book)

1. In the video game "Business Planet," your avatar flies in a private jet around the world, making deals. The play involves the application of legal doctrines, economic principles, and cultural values to outwit competitors in global markets and profit handsomely. In an Asian city, Won Thieu Tre, Ltd., offers your avatar a deal that promises a 200 percent profit. Your avatar immediately accepts. Won Thieu Tre fails to pay, however, and you file a suit in the game in a U.S. court. The defendant claims "sovereign immunity." What does this mean?

2. Still playing "Business Planet," you warehouse a variety of raw materials and other resources on your firm's property in Indonesia in anticipation of enterprising contracts with local outfits in the economically booming Far East. A political party hostile to Western influence ascends to power and seizes these assets. Your avatar protests, asking for compensation. The government responds that if you were entitled to anything, the profit that you have already accrued is enough. Could you recover more in a U.S. court? Why or why not?

SPECIAL INFORMATION FOR CPA CANDIDATES

Most of the material in this chapter is not covered in the CPA examination (although in the business world, an accountant will likely encounter many aspects of international business and law). The Foreign Corrupt Practices Act has been tested in the securities portion of the exam.

The CPA examination is designed to test technical competence in at least three areas: (1) technical knowledge and the application of this knowledge, (2) an understanding of professional responsibilities, and (3) the exercise of good judgment. The material in this chapter can contribute to an understanding of the law as it applies in all three of these areas. This chapter provides background to a study of business law by underscoring the point that the law is not static. This material illustrates that the law changes—from time to time and from place to place within a given time. Basic principles may change only slowly and over relatively long periods of time, but there is otherwise the same fluidity in the law as there is in any other field of knowledge.

Overall, in the past, the CPA exam has tested heavily in the following areas of business law: contracts, sales, commercial paper, bankruptcy, agency, partnerships, corporations, securities, accountant's professional liability, and property. The CPA exam has tested less heavily in these areas: documents of title, secured transactions, guaranty and suretyship, employment laws, insurance, and trusts.

CUMULATIVE HYPOTHETICAL PROBLEM FOR UNIT FOUR—INCLUDING CHAPTERS 19–23

(Answers at the Back of the Book)

Drake, Egon, and Flip pool their resources to create and sell video game software. They do business under the name "Game Life."

_____ 1. Game Life buys inventory—game cases—from Plastique Products. Plastique tenders delivery of the cases. Game Life says that it cannot take possession immediately but will do so later in the day. Before this happens, the goods are destroyed in a fire. The risk of loss

    a. passed to Game Life at the time the contract was formed.
    b. passed to Game Life on Plastique's tender of delivery.
    c. remained with Plastique, because Game Life had not yet taken possession.
    d. remained with Plastique, because title had not yet passed to Game Life.

_____ 2. Game Life contracts with Fong, Ltd., a Hong Kong firm, allowing Fong to use and profit from Game Life's patented software. A dispute arises between Game Life and Fong, and Game Life obtains a judgment in a U.S. court against Fong. Whether the judgment will be enforced by a court in China depends on the Chinese court's application of

    a. the act of state doctrine.
    b. the doctrine of sovereign immunity.
    c. the principle of comity.
    d. the World Trade Organization.

_____ 3. I2I Game Centers writes to Game Life to order Game Life's most popular games, which I2I plans to sell to its customers. Game Life writes to accept but adds a clause providing for interest on any overdue invoices (a common practice in the industry). If there is no further communication between the parties

    a. Game Life has made a counteroffer.
    b. there is a contract but without Game Life's added term.
    c. there is a contract that includes Game Life's added term.
    d. there is no contract because I2I did not expressly accept the added term.

____   **4.** Game Life ships defective games to I2I, which sells them to its customers. The defective games damage some of the customers' computers and game players. With respect to those individuals, Game Life likely violated principles of

a. lease law.
b. international law.
c. no law.
d. product liability law.

____   **5.** As a result of publicity concerning the defective games, Game Life loses business when its customer Jump-In Inc. says that it has decided not to buy what it had previously ordered. In Game Life's suit against Jump-In to enforce their contract, Game Life can most likely recover the contract price if

a. Game Life does not seek any damages in addition to the contract price.
b. Game Life identified the goods to the contract and a reasonable effort to resell them would not succeed.
c. specific performance is not possible.
d. the goods have been destroyed and Game Life's insurance is inadequate.

QUESTIONS ON THE FOCUS ON ETHICS FOR UNIT FOUR— DOMESTIC AND INTERNATIONAL SALES AND LEASE CONTRACTS

(Answers at the Back of the Book)

____   **1.** Lark and Keith enter into a contract for the sale of a Mito game player and a dozen compatible games. Even if not expressly stated, read into this contract is the concept of

a. advantage.
b. good faith.
c. impracticability.
d. unconscionability.

____   **2.** Gina and Harvey enter into a contract for the sale of a 3D HD TV. Either party's nonperformance may be excused, because of unforeseen circumstances, under the doctrine of commercial

a. advantage.
b. good faith.
c. impracticability.
d. unconscionability.

____   **3.** Ivan and Josey enter into a contract for the sale of a personal data assistant. If the contract includes a clause that is perceived as grossly unfair to one party, its enforcement may be challenged under the doctrine of

a. advantage.
b. good faith.
c. impracticability.
d. unconscionability.

Chapter 24
The Function and Creation of Negotiable Instruments

WHAT THIS CHAPTER IS ABOUT

A **negotiable instrument** can function as a substitute for money or as an extension of credit. To do so, it must be easily transferable without danger of being uncollectible. Thus, a negotiable instrument is a signed writing that contains an unconditional promise or order to pay an exact sum of money, when demanded or at an exact future time. This chapter outlines types of negotiable instruments and the requirements for negotiability.

CHAPTER OUTLINE

I. TYPES OF NEGOTIABLE INSTRUMENTS

A. DRAFTS AND CHECKS (ORDERS TO PAY)
The person who signs or makes an order to pay is the drawer. The person to whom the order is made is the drawee. The person to whom payment is ordered is the payee.

1. Draft
An unconditional written order by one person to another to pay money. The drawee must be obligated to the drawer either by an agreement or through a debtor-creditor relationship to honor the order.

a. Time Draft
Payable at a definite future time.

b. Sight Draft (Demand Draft)
Payable on sight (when presented for payment). A draft payable at a stated time after sight is both a time and a sight draft.

c. Trade Acceptance
A draft in which the seller is both the drawer and the payee. The draft orders the buyer to pay a specified sum of money to the seller, at a stated time in the future.

d. Banker's Acceptance
A draft drawn by a creditor against his or her debtor, who must pay it at maturity. Typically, the term is short.

2. Check
A draft drawn on a bank and payable on demand. A cashier's check is a draft in which the bank is both the drawer and drawee. A teller's check is a draft drawn by one bank on another bank [UCC 3–104(h)].

B. PROMISSORY NOTES (PROMISES TO PAY)
A person who promises to pay is a maker. A person to whom the promise is made is a payee. A promissory note is a written promise by one party to pay money to another party.

181

C. CERTIFICATES OF DEPOSIT (PROMISES TO PAY)

A certificate of deposit (CD) is a note made by a bank promising to repay a deposit of funds with interest on a certain date [UCC 3–104(j)].

II. REQUIREMENTS FOR NEGOTIABILITY

To be negotiable, an instrument must meet all of the following requirements [UCC 3–104(a)]. The instrument must be—

A. IN WRITTEN FORM

A writing can be on anything that (1) is permanent and (2) has portability [UCC 3–103(a)(6)].

B. SIGNED BY THE MAKER OR DRAWER

A signature can be any place on an instrument and in any form (a mark or rubber stamp) that purports to be a signature and authenticates the writing [UCC 1–201(39), 3–401(b)].

C. AN UNCONDITIONAL PROMISE OR ORDER

1. Promise or Order

A promise must be an affirmative written undertaking—more than a mere acknowledgment of a debt (an I.O.U. does not qualify; use of the words "I promise" or "Pay" qualifies) [UCC 3–103(a)(9)].

a. Certificates of Deposit

The bank's acknowledgment of a deposit and the other terms indicates a promise to repay a sum of money [UCC 3–104(j)].

b. More Than One Payee

An order may be addressed to more than one person, either jointly ("Pay Joe and Jan") or alternatively ("Pay Joe or Jan") [UCC 3–103(a)(6)].

2. Unconditionality

Payment cannot be conditional, and the promise or order cannot be subject to or governed by another writing, or be subject to rights or obligations stated in another writing [UCC 3–104(a), 3–106(a)]. Negotiability is not affected by—

a. References to Other Writings [UCC 3–106(a)]

b. Payments Only out of a Particular Fund or Source [UCC 3–106(b)(ii)]

D. AN ORDER OR PROMISE TO PAY A FIXED AMOUNT OF MONEY

A negotiable instrument must state a fixed amount of money to be paid when the instrument is payable.

1. Fixed Amount

a. References to Outside Sources

Interest may be determined with reference to information not contained in the instrument but readily ascertainable by reference to a source described in the instrument [UCC 3–112(b)].

b. Variable Interest Rate Notes Can Be Negotiable

The fixed-amount requirement applies only to principal [UCC 3–104].

2. Payable in Money

Only instruments payable in money (not bonds, stock, gold, or goods) are negotiable [UCC 3–104(a)(3)]. *Money* is a medium of exchange recognized as the currency of a government [UCC 1–201(24)].

E. PAYABLE ON DEMAND OR AT A DEFINITE TIME

1. Payable on Demand
An instrument that is payable on sight or presentment or that does not state any time for payment [UCC 3–108(a)]. A check is payable on demand [UCC 3–104(f)]. Presentment occurs when a person presents an instrument to a person liable on it for payment or when a person presents a draft to a drawee for acceptance.

2. Payable at a Definite Time
Payable on or before a stated date or within a fixed period after sight, or on a date or time ascertainable at the time the instrument is issued [UCC 3–108(b)].

3. Acceleration Clause
Allows a holder to demand payment of entire amount due if a certain event occurs. Does not affect negotiability [UCC 3–108(b)(ii)]. A holder is "the person in possession if the instrument is payable to bearer, or in the case of an instrument payable to an identified person, if the identified person is in possession" [UCC 1–201(20)].

4. Extension Clause
The period of the extension must be specified if the right to extend is given to the maker. If the holder has the right, no period need be specified [UCC 3–108(b)(iii), (iv)].

F. PAYABLE TO ORDER OR TO BEARER
When it is issued or first comes into a holder's possession [UCC 3–104(a)(1)].

1. Order Instrument
May be payable "to the order of an identified person" or to "an identified person or order" (the person must be identified with certainty) [UCC 3–109(b)].

2. Bearer Instrument
Does not designate a specific payee (but an instrument payable to a nonexistent entity is not bearer paper) [UCC 3–109(a) and Comment 3]: "Payable to the order of bearer," "Pay to the order of cash," "Pay cash"

III. FACTORS THAT DO NOT AFFECT NEGOTIABILITY

A. NO DATE
Negotiability is affected only if a date is necessary to determine a definite time for payment [UCC 3–113(b)].

B. POSTDATING
Postdating (antedating) an instrument does not affect negotiability [UCC 3–113(a)].

C. HANDWRITTEN WORDS
Handwritten words prevail typewritten words, which prevail over those that are printed (such as preprinted forms) [UCC 3–114].

D. DISCREPANCY BETWEEN WORDS AND NUMBERS
An amount stated in words outweighs a contradictory number [UCC 3–114].

E. UNSPECIFIED INTEREST RATE
If a rate is unspecified, interest will be at the *judgment rate* [UCC 3–112(b)].

F. NOTATION ON A CHECK THAT IT IS NONNEGOTIABLE
This has no effect on a check, but any other instrument is made nonnegotiable by the maker or drawer adding such a notation [UCC 3–104(d)].

TRUE-FALSE QUESTIONS

(Answers at the Back of the Book)

____   1.   The person who signs or makes an order to pay is the drawer.

____   2.   A negotiable instrument serves as a substitute for money.

____ **3.** A bearer instrument is payable to whoever possesses it.

____ **4.** To be negotiable, an instrument must be in writing.

____ **5.** An instrument can be negotiable even if it is not payable on demand or at a definite time.

____ **6.** An instrument including a clause that permits the date of maturity to be extended by the *maker* for "no more than a reasonable time" is negotiable.

____ **7.** An instrument payable to the order of a specific person is not negotiable.

____ **8.** To be negotiable, the terms of a promise or order must be included on the instrument.

____ **9.** To be negotiable, an instrument must include an unconditional promise to pay.

____ **10.** An instrument is not negotiable if reference must be made to foreign exchange rates when payment is due.

FILL-IN QUESTIONS

(Answers at the Back of the Book)

The person who signs or makes an order to pay is a _____ (drawer/drawee). The person to whom an order to pay is made is a _____ (drawee/payee). The person to whom payment is ordered is a _____ (payee/maker). A person who promises to pay a note is a _____ (payee/maker). A person to whom the promise to pay a note is made is a _____ (payee/drawee).

MULTIPLE-CHOICE QUESTIONS

(Answers at the Back of the Book)

____ **1. Based on a Sample CPA Exam Question.** Dieter makes out an instrument that states he promises to pay $600 and gives it to Erica. To be negotiable, this instrument must

   a. be payable to order or to bearer.
   b. be signed by the payee.
   c. contain references to all agreements between the parties.
   d. contain necessary conditions of payment.

____ **2.** Oberon makes out a check "Pay to the order of bearer." This is

   a. a bearer instrument and an order instrument.
   b. a bearer instrument only.
   c. an order instrument only.
   d. none of the choices.

____ **3.** Craig signs a promissory note payable to the order of Debit Loan Company. The note states simply that it is payable "with interest." This note is

   a. negotiable.
   b. nonnegotiable, because it does not specify a particular rate of interest.
   c. nonnegotiable, because it is payable to a specific party.
   d. nonnegotiable, because it states only that it is payable "with interest."

____ 4. To pay for a new truck, Tri-state Transport Company issues a draft in favor of Uno Motor Sales, Inc. A draft is

a. a conditional promise to pay money.
b. an unconditional written order to pay money.
c. a promise to pay money.
d. a promise to deliver goods at a future date.

____ 5. Loren writes a check for $100 payable to Jana on Loren's account at Corn County Bank. Loren is

a. the drawee.
b. the drawer.
c. the holder.
d. the payee.

____ 6. To pay for an office building, Keysha executes a negotiable instrument in favor of Leah. They are the only two parties to the instrument. This is

a. a certificate of deposit.
b. a check.
c. a draft.
d. a promissory note.

____ 7. Macro Mart Industries, Inc., issues an instrument in favor of National Credit Corporation. To be negotiable, the instrument need *not*

a. be an unconditional promise or order to pay.
b. be payable on demand or at a specific time.
c. be signed by Macro Industries.
d. recite the consideration given in exchange for it.

____ 8. Riza executes an instrument is favor of Pauline. For the instrument to be negotiable, Riza's signature

a. may be anywhere on the instrument.
b. must be in the lower right hand corner.
c. must be on the back.
d. must not be on the instrument.

____ 9. Quality Products, Inc., signs an instrument payable to Regional Distributors, Inc., that includes the notation "as per contract." This instrument is

a. negotiable.
b. nonnegotiable, because an obligation with respect to it is stated in another writing.
c. nonnegotiable, because it is governed by another writing.
d. nonnegotiable, because it states a condition to payment.

____ 10. Timor signs a check payable to Vid Vu Corporation. The check does not include a date. This check is

a. negotiable.
b. nonnegotiable, because it does not include a date.
c. nonnegotiable, because it is payable to a specific party.
d. nonnegotiable, because it is signed by its issuer.

SHORT ESSAY QUESTIONS

1. What are the primary functions of negotiable instruments?

2. What are the requirements for an instrument to be negotiable?

GAMEPOINTS

(Answers at the Back of the Book)

1. You are playing "Kill 'Em Again Incorporated," a video game in which your avatar "Nick" drives the streets of Urban City to spot and duel zombies. To cruise the streets, the game requires you to buy a ride, and to pay for it, you sign the following on-screen instrument.

> May 1, 2011
>
> I promise to pay to the order of Urban City Car Co.
> $20,000 (Twenty thousand dollars) with interest at the
> rate of 7% per annum.
>
> *Nick*
> Nick

What type of instrument is this? Assuming an on-screen item otherwise qualifies, does this instrument meet the requirements for negotiability under the UCC?

2. The video game "Pita Pizza Pi" revolves around the antics in a café run by a sandwich, a slice of pizza, and a mathematical anomaly. When you play the game, your character is Pete, the pie vendor. To pay for a delivery of your wares, you give Pita a draft drawn by you ordering the three buyers to pay you the price of the goods at a specified future date. The buyers sign the draft and give it back to you. What type of draft is this?

SPECIAL INFORMATION FOR CPA CANDIDATES

For the CPA examination, the two most important concepts in the area of negotiable instruments are negotiability and holder in due course (HDC) (which is discussed in the next chapter). You should fully understand both concepts to be able to answer questions involving UCC Article 3. The significance of negotiability is that it facilitates the transfer and payment of money using a contractual obligation instead of cash. As you'll learn in the next chapter, if an instrument is negotiable, a holder can be an HDC. This is an important status because of the protection it provides.

Chapter 25
Transferability and Holder in Due Course

See page 508 Ex. 26-2 for "backfill" info on this chaptr

WHAT THIS CHAPTER IS ABOUT

A negotiable instrument is transferred more easily than a contract, and a person who acquires it is subject to less risk than the assignee of a contract. This chapter outlines the types and the effect of indorsements, defines *holder in due course* (HDC), and describes how a holder becomes an HDC.

CHAPTER OUTLINE

I. NEGOTIATION

On a transfer by negotiation, the transferee becomes a holder and receives the rights of the previous possessor (and possibly more) [UCC 3–201(a), 3–202(b), 3–203(b), 3–305, 3–306].

A. NEGOTIATING ORDER INSTRUMENTS *(checks, etc)*
Order instruments are negotiated by delivery with indorsement [UCC 3–201(b)].

B. NEGOTIATING BEARER INSTRUMENTS *(cash)*
Bearer instruments are negotiated by delivery only [UCC 3–201(b)].

II. INDORSEMENTS

Indorsements are required to negotiate an order instrument. The person who indorses an instrument is an indorser; the person to whom the instrument is transferred is an indorsee.

A. WHAT AN INDORSEMENT IS
An indorsement is a signature with or without additional words or statements. Usually written on the back of an instrument but can be written on a separate piece of paper (an allonge) affixed (stapled) to it [UCC 3–204(a)].

B. BLANK INDORSEMENT
Specifies no particular indorsee and can consist of a mere signature [UCC 3–205(b)]. Converts an order instrument to a bearer instrument.

C. SPECIAL INDORSEMENT
Names the indorsee [UCC 3–205(a)]. No special words are needed. Converts a bearer instrument into an order instrument.

D. QUALIFIED INDORSEMENT
A qualified indorsement disclaims or limits contract liability (see Chapter 18) (the notation "without recourse" is commonly used) [UCC 3–415(b)]. Often used by persons in a representative capacity.

1. No Payment Guarantee
A qualified indorsement does not guarantee payment, but does transfer title. (Most blank and special indorsements are unqualified, guaranteeing payment and transferring title).

2. Further Negotiation
A *special* qualified indorsement makes an instrument order paper (and requires indorsement and delivery for negotiation). A *blank* qualified indorsement creates bearer paper (and requires only delivery).

187

E. RESTRICTIVE INDORSEMENTS

1. Indorsement Prohibiting Further Indorsement
Does not destroy negotiability [UCC 3–206(a)]. Has the same effect as a special indorsement.

2. Conditional Indorsement
Specifying an event on which payment depends does not affect negotiability. A person paying or taking the instrument for value can disregard the condition [UCC 3–206(b)]. (Conditional language on the face of an instrument, however, does destroy negotiability.)

3. Indorsement for Deposit or Collection
Making the indorsee (usually a bank) a collecting agent of the indorser (such as "For deposit only") locks the instrument into the bank collection process [UCC 3–206(c)].

4. Trust Indorsement (Agency Indorsement)
An indorsement by one who is to hold or use the funds for the benefit of the indorser or a third party [UCC 3–206(d), (e)]. To the extent the original indorsee pays or applies the proceeds consistently with the indorsement, he or she is a holder and can become a holder in due course (HDC). Any subsequent purchaser can qualify as an HDC (unless he or she knows the instrument was negotiated in breach of fiduciary duty).

F. CONVERTING ORDER INSTRUMENTS TO BEARER INSTRUMENTS AND VICE VERSA

An instrument can be converted from a bearer to an order instrument, or vice versa, by indorsement. A check payable to "cash" subsequently indorsed "Pay to Bob" must be negotiated as an order instrument (by indorsement and delivery) [UCC 3–205(a)]. An instrument payable to a named payee ("Bob") and indorsed in blank is a bearer instrument [UCC 3–205(b)].

III. MISCELLANEOUS INDORSEMENT PROBLEMS

A. FORGED OR UNAUTHORIZED SIGNATURES OR INDORSEMENTS
See Chapters 26 and 27.

B. MISSPELLED NAMES
An indorsement should be the same as the name on the instrument. An indorsee whose name is misspelled can indorse with the misspelled name, the correct name, or both [UCC 3–204(d)].

C. AGENTS OR OFFICERS
An instrument payable to an entity ("Pay to the order of the YWCA") can be negotiated by the entity's representative. An instrument payable to a public officer ("Pay to the order of the County Tax Collector") can be negotiated by whoever holds the office [UCC 3–110(c)].

D. MULTIPLE PAYEES
An instrument payable in the alternative ("Pay to the order of Bill or Joan") requires the indorsement of only one. An instrument payable jointly ("Pay to the order of Bill and Joan") requires the indorsements of both. If it is not clear how it is payable, it requires the indorsement of only one [UCC 3–110(d)].

IV. HOLDER VERSUS HOLDER IN DUE COURSE (HDC)

A. HOLDER *has legal right to paper*
A holder is "the person in possession if the instrument is payable to bearer, or in the case of an instrument payable to an identified person, if the identified person is in possession" [UCC 1–201(20)]. A holder is subject to the same defenses that could be asserted against the transferor (the party from whom the holder obtained the instrument).

B. HOLDER IN DUE COURSE *ex. bank*
A holder who meets certain requirements becomes a holder in due course (HDC), and takes an instrument free of all claims to it and most defenses against payment that could be successfully asserted against the transferor.

C. REQUIREMENTS FOR HDC STATUS

A person must be a holder and take an instrument (1) for value; (2) in good faith; and (3) without notice that it is overdue, that it has been dishonored, that any person has a defense against it or a claim to it, or that the instrument contains unauthorized signatures, alterations, or is so irregular or incomplete as to call into question its authenticity [UCC 3–302].

1. Taking for Value

a. What Constitutes Value

A holder gives value by [UCC 3–303(a)]—

1) Performing a promise for which an instrument was issued or transferred.

2) Acquiring a security interest or other lien in the instrument (other than a lien obtained by a judicial proceeding).

3) Taking instrument in payment of, or as security for, an antecedent debt.

4) Giving a negotiable instrument as payment.

5) Giving an irrevocable commitment as payment.

b. Special Situations

A holder does not give value by receiving an instrument as a gift or inheriting it. A holder can be limited to ordinary holder's rights by buying an instrument at a judicial sale or taking it under legal process; acquiring it when taking over an estate; or buying it as part of a corporate purchase of assets [UCC 3–302(c)].

2. Taking in Good Faith

a. What Constitutes Good Faith

"Honesty in fact and the observance of reasonable commercial standards of fair dealing."

b. How to Apply this Requirement

A purchaser must honestly believe that an instrument is not defective and observe reasonable commercial standards. This applies only to the holder—a person who in good faith takes an instrument from a thief may become an HDC.

3. Taking without Notice

A holder must acquire an instrument without knowing, or having reason to know, it is defective.

Protects HDC

a. What Constitutes Notice

Notice is (1) actual knowledge of a defect, (2) receipt of notice about a defect, or (3) reason to know that a defect exists [UCC 1–201(25)]. Knowledge of certain facts does not constitute notice [see UCC 3–302(b)].

b. Overdue Demand Instruments

A holder has notice if he or she takes an instrument knowing demand was made or takes it an unreasonable time after its issue (ninety days for a check; other instruments depend on the circumstances [UCC 3–304(a)]).

c. Overdue Time Instruments

A holder has notice if he or she takes an instrument after its expressed due date. If, on an installment note or on a series of notes, the maker defaults on an installment or one of the notes [UCC 3–304(b)].

d. Dishonored Instruments

A holder has notice if he or she knows an instrument has been dishonored or knows of facts that would lead him or her to suspect an instrument has been dishonored [UCC 3–302(a)(2)].

e. Notice of Claims or Defenses

A holder cannot be an HDC if he or she knows of a claim to the instrument or defense against it [UCC 3–302(a)]—if a claim or defense is apparent on the face of the instrument or if the purchaser otherwise had reason to know it from facts surrounding the transaction. Knowing of one defense bars HDC status to all defenses.

f. Incomplete Instruments
A holder has notice if an instrument is so incomplete that an element of negotiability is lacking (e.g., amount not filled in). Accepting an instrument without knowing it was incomplete when issued is not notice.

g. Irregular Instruments
A holder has notice if an irregularity on the face of an instrument calls into question its validity or terms of ownership, or creates ambiguity as to who to pay.

V. HOLDER THROUGH AN HDC

A. THE SHELTER PRINCIPLE
A person who does not qualify as an HDC but who acquires an instrument from an HDC or from someone with HDC rights receives the rights and privileges of an HDC [UCC 3–203(b)].

B. LIMITATIONS TO THE SHELTER PRINCIPLE
A holder who was a party to fraud or illegality affecting an instrument or who, as a prior holder, had notice of a claim or defense cannot improve his or her status by repurchasing it from a later HDC [UCC 3–203(b)].

TRUE-FALSE QUESTIONS

(Answers at the Back of the Book)

____ 1. A holder in due course (HDC) takes a negotiable instrument free of most defenses and claims to it.

____ 2. Indorsements are required to negotiate order instruments.

____ 3. A promise to give value in the future makes a holder an HDC

____ 4. Indorsements are required to negotiate bearer instruments.

____ 5. Every person who possesses an instrument is a holder.

____ 6. For HDC status, good faith means "honesty in fact and the observance of reasonable commercial standards of fair dealing."

____ 7. A holder has only those rights that his or her transferor had in the instrument.

____ 8. All claims to an instrument can be successfully asserted against an HDC.

____ 9. Taking a check knowing that the drawee dishonored it prevents a holder from becoming an HDC.

____ 10. A holder who has knowledge of a defense against payment on an instrument can become an HDC.

FILL-IN QUESTIONS

(Answers at the Back of the Book)

A person who does not qualify as an HDC _____ (can/cannot) acquire the rights of an HDC if a person who does not qualify as an HDC acquires an instrument from an HDC. A holder who was a party to fraud or illegality affecting an instrument _____ (can/cannot) improve his or her status by repurchasing the instrument from a later HDC. A holder who, as a prior holder, had notice of a claim or defense against the instrument _____ (can/cannot) improve his or her status by repurchasing it from a later HDC.

MULTIPLE-CHOICE QUESTIONS

(Answers at the Back of the Book)

____ 1. Ferris signs and delivers to Erin a $5,000 negotiable note payable to "Erin or bearer." Erin negotiates it to Grendel, indorsing it on the back by signing "Erin." The note is now

a. a bearer instrument, and Grendel can convert it to order paper by writing "Pay to the order of Grendel" above Erin's signature.
b. a bearer instrument, and it cannot be converted to an order instrument.
c. an order instrument, and it cannot be converted to a bearer instrument.
d. a nonnegotiable instrument.

____ 2. Ollie makes out a check "Pay to the order of Paco." Paco indorses the check on the back. The check can now be negotiated by

a. delivery only.
b. indorsement only.
c. only delivery and indorsement.
d. neither delivery nor indorsement.

____ 3. **Based on a Sample CPA Exam Question.** Leah accepts a promissory note from Mikayla. For Leah to be a holder in due course (HDC) of the note

a. all prior holders must have HDCs.
b. Leah must be the payee of the note.
c. the note must be negotiable.
d. the note must be "Payable to Bearer."

____ 4. Bathsheba writes out a check for $500, but does not specify a payee. Ciara steals the check and makes it payable to herself. She negotiates the check to Debra, who takes it in good faith and without notice. Regarding payment, Bathsheba is

a. liable to Ciara and Debra.
b. liable to Ciara, but not Debra.
c. liable to Debra, but not Ciara.
d. not liable to Ciara or Debra.

____ 5. Judith contracts with Ivan to fix her roof, and she writes Ivan a check, but he never makes the repairs. Ivan transfers the check to Hurtado, who knows that Ivan breached the contract, but decides to cash the check anyway. Hurtado can attain HDC status as to

a. any defense Judith might have against payment.
b. only any personal defense Judith might have against payment.
c. only Ivan's breach, which is Judith's personal defense against payment.
d. none of the choices.

____ 6. River contracts with Sebastian for monthly $2,000 shipments of coffee to River's Flow, A Coffee Shop. River pays in advance with a $12,000 note. One month later, Sebastian sells the note to Truly for $11,000. When the note is sold, Sebastian is

a. an HDC for $12,000.
b. an HDC for $2,000.
c. an HDC for $1,000.
d. not an HDC.

____ **7.** Demosthenes opens an account at College Bank with a $4,000 check drawn on another bank and payable to him. He indorses the check in blank. The bank credits his account and allows him to draw on the $4,000 immediately. The bank knows of no defense to the check. The bank is

a. an HDC to the extent that Demosthenes draws against the $4,000 balance.
b. an HDC for the full amount of the check.
c. an HDC to the extent of any amount that is collected on the check.
d. not an HDC.

____ **8.** Teon signs a note that states, "Payable in thirty days." Ursa buys the note on the thirty-first day. Ursa is on notice that the note

a. has been dishonored.
b. is no longer negotiable.
c. is overdue.
d. is payable immediately.

____ **9.** Joelle writes out a check payable to the order of Kristen. Kristen receives the check but wants to negotiate it further to her friend Lucas. Kristen can negotiate the check further by

a. delivery only.
b. indorsement only.
c. only delivery and indorsement.
d. neither delivery nor indorsement.

____ **10.** Robin indorses a check, "Pay to Highway Equipment Corporation if they deliver the backhoe by June 1, 2012." This indorsement is

a. a blank indorsement.
b. a qualified indorsement.
c. a restrictive indorsement.
d. a special indorsement.

SHORT ESSAY QUESTIONS

1. How are instruments negotiated?

2. How is a person who acquires a time instrument or a demand instrument put on notice that the instrument is overdue?

GAMEPOINTS

(Answers at the Back of the Book)

1. You're playing the video game "In Due Course." Your avatar, Holder, operates enterprises of your choice in Urban City. Holder's objective is to collect payments from your customers by ferreting out the bad instruments from the good—those that can be negotiated further. Urban City is a haven for unseemly characters, particularly those inclined to commit crimes with negotiable instruments. Forger is an accountant with Quiescent Corporation, but has no authority to sign corporate checks. Forger gives Holder "for goods rendered" a Quiescent check, signed "Q. Corp. by Forger." If Holder accepts it, can Quiescent refuse to pay it?

2. Still playing the video game "In Due Course," your avatar, Holder, attains a level captioned "Check It Out." In this sequence, the goal is to skillfully handle the myriad of instruments that Holder collected from your customers, patrons, associates, and others to reap the greatest benefit for your enterprises. Some of the instruments are notes and drafts "payable to bearer" or to the order of a named payee, and indorsed on the back with the signatures of the parties who gave the instruments to Holder. To avoid the risk of loss from the theft of these items—which in Urban City is a common occurrence—what could Holder add to these indorsements?

SPECIAL INFORMATION FOR CPA CANDIDATES

On the CPA exam, questions concerning negotiability and holders in due course are asked nearly every time. When testing on negotiability, the exam often includes instruments with a number of different indorsements. The CPA exam will not explain the indorsements for you. You will need to work through them and determine what they mean to respond to the question. (Remember that an indorsement in blank does not mean that there is no indorsement.) Negotiability is determined from the face of an instrument; whether an instrument is order paper or bearer paper can be affected by the front and the back of the instrument (and remember that this status can change). As regards holders in due course, memorize the requirements (holder, value, good faith, no notice). Review, too, the shelter rule, which is frequently covered on the exam.

Chapter 26
Liability, Defenses, and Discharge

WHAT THIS CHAPTER IS ABOUT

Two kinds of liability are associated with negotiable instruments: signature liability and warranty liability. This chapter outlines this liability, as well as the effects of certain defenses against holders and holders in due course (HDCs) and the ways in which parties can be discharged from liability on negotiable instruments.

CHAPTER OUTLINE

I.   SIGNATURE LIABILITY
Every party (except a qualified indorser) who, or whose agent, signs an instrument is either primarily or secondarily liable when it comes due [UCC 3–401(a)]. Each party is liable for the full amount to any later indorser or to any holder.

A. WHAT IS A SIGNATURE?
A signature can consist of any name, including a trade or assumed name, or a word, mark, or symbol "executed or adopted by a person with the present intention to authenticate a writing" [UCC 1–209(39), 3–401(b)].

B. PRIMARY LIABILITY
A person who is primarily liable is absolutely required to pay, subject to certain defenses [UCC 3–305]. Primarily liable parties include—

1. Maker of a Note
If an instrument is incomplete when the maker signs it, the maker must pay it as completed if authorized or, if unauthorized, as completed to an HDC [UCC 3–407, 3–412, 3–413].

2. Acceptor of a Draft
When a drawee accepts a draft (by signing it), he or she becomes an acceptor and is primarily liable to all subsequent holders [UCC 3–409(a)]. (A drawee that refuses to accept a draft requiring the drawee's acceptance has dishonored the instrument.)

C. SECONDARY LIABILITY
Drawers and unqualified indorsers are secondarily liable—they pay only if a party who is primarily liable does not pay. A drawer pays if a drawee does not; an indorser pays if a maker defaults. Secondary liability is triggered by proper presentment, dishonor, and notice of dishonor.

1. Proper Presentment

a. To the Proper Person
A note or CD is presented to the maker; a draft to the drawee for acceptance, payment, or both (whatever is required); a check to the drawee [UCC 3–501(a), 3–502(b)].

b. In the Proper Manner
Depending on the instrument, presentment can be made by any commercially reasonable means [UCC 3–501(b)]. A bank can date a presentment that occurs after a certain time (after 2 P.M.) to the next business day.

195

2. Timely Presentment

Failure to present within a reasonable time (for an ordinary check, within thirty days after its date, or for an indorser's liability, within thirty days after indorsement) is the most common reason for improper presentment [UCC 3–414(f), 3–415(e), 3–501(b)(4)]. A reasonable time is determined by the nature of the instrument, banking or trade usage, and other circumstances.

3. Dishonor

Dishonors occurs when payment or acceptance is refused or cannot be obtained within the prescribed time, or when required presentment is excused and the instrument is not accepted or paid [UCC 3–502(e), 3–504].

4. Proper Notice

On dishonor, to hold secondary parties liable, notice must be given within thirty days following the day on which a person receives notice of the dishonor (except a bank, which must give notice before midnight of the next banking day after receipt) [UCC 3–503].

D. ACCOMMODATION PARTIES

An accommodation party signs an instrument to lend his or her name as credit to another party on the instrument [UCC 3–419(a)]. An accommodation party has primary liability if he or she signs on behalf of a maker, but secondary liability if he or she signs on behalf of a payee or other holder.

E. AGENTS' SIGNATURES

Agents can sign negotiable instruments and thereby bind their principals [UCC 3–401(a)(ii), 3–402(a)].

1. Authorized Agent—Liability of the Parties

a. When the Agent Clearly Names the Principal

The principal is liable. The agent is not—if the signature shows that it is on behalf of the principal [UCC 3–402(b)(1)].

b. Other Situations

(1) If an agent signs his or her name only; (2) if an instrument is signed in both agent's and principal's names, but does not indicate agency relation; or (3) if an agent indicates agency status but fails to name the principal [UCC 3–402(b)(2)]—

1) Agent's Liability

The agent is personally liable to an HDC who has no notice that the agent was not intended to be liable. Agent is not liable to others if the original parties did not intend it.

2) Principal's Liability

The principal is liable if a party entitled to enforce the instrument can prove the agency.

2. Unauthorized Agent—Liability of the Parties

The agent's signature is ineffective except as the signature of the unauthorized signer [UCC 3–403(a)].

F. UNAUTHORIZED SIGNATURES

An unauthorized signature does not bind the person whose name is forged. (For liability of banks paying under forged signatures, see Chapter 27.)

1. Two Exceptions

(1) An unauthorized signature is binding if the person whose name is signed ratifies it [UCC 3–403(a)]; (2) a person can be barred, on the basis of negligence, from denying liability [UCC 3–115, 3–406, 4–401(d)(2)].

2. Liability of the Signer

An unauthorized signature operates as the signature of the *signer* (the forger) in favor of an HDC [UCC 3–403(a)].

G. SPECIAL RULES FOR UNAUTHORIZED INDORSEMENTS

Generally, the loss falls on the first party to take the instrument. The loss falls on the maker or drawer in cases involving—

1. Imposters

An imposter is one who induces a maker or drawer to issue an instrument in the name of an impersonated payee.

2. Effect of an Imposter's Indorsement

Effective against the drawer, if the instrument is transferred to an innocent party [UCC 3–404(a)].

3. Fictitious Payees

A fictitious payee is one to whom an instrument is payable but who has no right to receive payment. (Dishonest employees may issue such instruments or deceive employers into doing so.)

4. Effect of a Fictitious Payee's Indorsement

Not treated as a forgery; the employer can be held liable by an innocent holder [UCC 3–404(b)(2)]. The employer has recourse against the dishonest employee.

5. Comparative Negligence Standard

Comparative negligence applies in cases involving imposters and fictitious payees (thus, a bank may be partially liable) [UCC 3–404(d), 3–405(b)].

II. WARRANTY LIABILITY

A. TRANSFER WARRANTIES

1. The Warranties

Any person who transfers an instrument for consideration warrants to the transferee and, if the transfer is by indorsement, to all later transferees and holders who take the instrument in good faith [UCC 3–416]—

a. The transferor is entitled to enforce the instrument.

b. All signatures are authentic and authorized.

c. The instrument has not been altered.

d. The instrument is not subject to a defense or claim that can be asserted against the transferor.

e. The transferor has no knowledge of any insolvency proceedings against the maker, the acceptor, or the drawer of the instrument.

2. To Whom the Warranties Extend

With order instruments, the warranties run to any subsequent holder who takes the instrument in good faith. With bearer instruments, the warranties run only to the immediate transferee [UCC 3–416(a)].

3. When to Sue for Breach of Warranty

As soon as a transferee or holder who takes an instrument in good faith has reason to know of it [UCC 3–416(b), (c), (d)]. Notice of the claim must be given to the warrantor within thirty days.

4. Disclaimer

With respect to any instrument, except a check, include in the indorsement such words as "without warranties" [UCC 3–416(c)].

B. PRESENTMENT WARRANTIES

1. The Warranties

Any person who obtains payment or acceptance of an instrument warrants to any other person who in good faith pays or accepts the instrument [UCC 3–417(a), (d)]—

a. The person obtaining payment or acceptance is entitled or authorized to enforce the instrument (that is, there are no missing or unauthorized indorsements).

b. The instrument has not been altered.

c. The person obtaining payment or acceptance has no knowledge that the signature of the issuer of the instrument is unauthorized.

2. The Last Two Warranties Do Not Apply in Certain Cases

It is assumed, for example, that a drawer or a maker will recognize his or her own signature and that a maker or an acceptor will recognize whether an instrument has been materially altered.

3. When to Sue for Breach of Warranty

As soon as a transferee or holder who takes an instrument in good faith has reason to know of it [UCC 3–417(e)]. Notice of the claim must be given to the warrantor within thirty days.

4. Disclaimer

Valid with respect to any instrument except a check.

III. DEFENSES AND LIMITATIONS

A. UNIVERSAL DEFENSES

Valid against all holders, including HDCs and holders who take by HDCs.

1. Forgery

Forgery of a maker's or drawer's signature cannot bind the person whose name is used (unless that person ratifies the signature or is precluded from denying it) [UCC 3–403(a)].

2. Fraud in the Execution

This defense is valid if a person is deceived into signing an instrument, believing that it is something else. This defense is not valid if reasonable inquiry would have revealed the nature of the instrument [UCC 3–305(a)(1)(iii)].

3. Material Alteration

An alteration is material if it changes the contract terms between any two parties in any way (making any change in an unauthorized manner that relates to a party's obligation) [UCC 3–407(a)].

a. **Complete Defense against an Ordinary Holder**

A holder recovers nothing [UCC 3–407(a)]. (If an alteration is visible, a holder has notice and cannot be an HDC [UCC 3–302(a)(1)].)

b. **Partial Defense against an HDC**

If an instrument was originally incomplete and later completed in an unauthorized manner, an HDC can enforce it as completed [UCC 3–407(b)].

4. Discharge in Bankruptcy

Absolute defense [UCC 3–305(a)(1)].

5. **Minority**
   A defense to the extent that state law recognizes it as a defense to a contract [UCC 3–305(a)(1)(i)] (see Chapter 13).

6. **Illegality**
   A defense if the law declares that an instrument executed in connection with illegal conduct is *void* [UCC 3–305(a)(1)(ii)].

7. **Mental Incapacity**
   An instrument issued by a person who has been adjudicated mentally incompetent by state proceedings is void [UCC 3–305(a)(1)(ii)].

8. **Extreme Duress**
   Extreme duress is an immediate threat of force or violence [UCC 3–305(a)(1)(ii)].

B. PERSONAL DEFENSES
Personal defenses avoid payment to an ordinary holder (but not an HDC).

1. **Breach of Contract or Breach of Warranty**
   If there is a breach of a contract for which an instrument was issued or a breach of warranty (see Chapter 23), the maker or drawer may not pay.

2. **Lack or Failure of Consideration [UCC 3–303(b), 3–305(a)(2)]**
   For example, when there is no consideration for the issuing of a note.

3. **Fraud in the Inducement (Ordinary Fraud)**
   If one issues an instrument based on false statements by the other party.

4. **Illegality**
   When a statute makes an illegal transaction *voidable*.

5. **Mental Incapacity**
   If a person drafts an instrument while mentally incompetent but before a court declares him or her so, the instrument is voidable.

6. **Others**
   Discharge by payment or cancellation; unauthorized completion of an incomplete instrument; nondelivery of an instrument; ordinary duress or undue influence.

C. FEDERAL LIMITATIONS ON HDC RIGHTS
A Federal Trade Commission rule (FTC Rule 433) effectively abolished HDC protection in consumer transactions.

1. **When the Rule Applies**
   As part of a consumer credit contract, a seller or lessor of consumer goods or services receives a promissory note from a consumer or arranges with a third party for a loan for a consumer to pay for the goods or services.

2. **What the Rule Requires**
   The seller or lessor must include in the contract a notice that all holders take subject to any defenses the debtor has against the seller or lessor.

3. **Effect of the Rule**
   There can be no HDC of an instrument that contains the notice (or a similar statement required by law) [UCC 3–106(d)]. A consumer can assert any defense he or she has against the seller of a product against a subsequent holder as well.

IV. DISCHARGE

A. DISCHARGE BY PAYMENT OR TENDER OF PAYMENT

All parties are discharged if the party primarily liable pays to a holder the amount due in full [UCC 3–602, 3–603]. Payment by any other party discharges only that party and subsequent parties.

1. Paying in Bad Faith

A party is not discharged when paying in bad faith to a holder who got the instrument by theft or from someone who got it by theft (unless the holder has the rights of an HDC) [UCC 3–602(b)(2)].

2. When Tender Is Refused

Indorsers and accommodation parties with recourse against the party making tender are discharged to the extent of the tender [UCC 3–603(b)].

B. DISCHARGE BY CANCELLATION OR SURRENDER

A holder can discharge any party by intentionally destroying, mutilating, or canceling an instrument, canceling or striking out a party's signature, or adding words (such as "Paid") to the instrument indicating discharge [UCC 3–604]. A holder can also discharge by surrendering it to the person to be discharged.

C. DISCHARGE BY REACQUISITION

A person who reacquires an instrument that he or she held previously discharges all intervening indorsers against subsequent holders who do not qualify as HDCs [UCC 3–207].

D. DISCHARGE BY IMPAIRMENT OF RECOURSE OR OF COLLATERAL

If a holder adversely affects an indorser's right to recover payment from prior parties, the indorser is discharged [UCC 3–605].

TRUE-FALSE QUESTIONS

(Answers at the Back of the Book)

____ 1. Signature liability extends to any person who signs a negotiable instrument.

____ 2. Every party who signs an instrument is primarily liable for payment of it when it comes due.

____ 3. An authorized agent may be personally liable on an instrument on which the agent signs the agent's name but not the principal's name.

____ 4. Warranty liability does not bind parties who only present instruments for payment.

____ 5. An accommodation party has primary liability if he or she signs on behalf of a maker.

____ 6. Universal defenses can be raised to avoid payment to an HDC.

____ 7. A drawer can stop payment on a check in the possession of an innocent holder if the drawer was induced by an imposter to issue the check in the name of an impersonated payee.

____ 8. Personal defenses can be raised to avoid payment to an HDC.

____ 9. An unauthorized signature usually binds the person whose name is forged.

____ 10. A drawer is secondarily liable on an instrument.

FILL-IN QUESTIONS

(Answers at the Back of the Book)

There are three _____ (presentment/transfer) warranties. Any person who seeks payment or acceptance of a negotiable instrument impliedly warrants to any other person who in good faith pays or accepts the instrument that: (1) the _____ (presenter/transferor) has good title to the instrument or is authorized to obtain payment or acceptance on behalf of a one who has good title; (2) the _____ (presenter/transferor) has no knowledge that the signature of _____ (any indorsee/the maker or the drawer) is unauthorized; and (3) the instrument has not been _____ (materially altered/materially altered by the presenter/ materially altered by the transferor).

MULTIPLE-CHOICE QUESTIONS

(Answers at the Back of the Book)

____   1.   **Based on a Sample CPA Exam Question.** First National Bank is an HDC of a note for $1,000 on which there is the signature "Gridley Addams." Gridley has a defense against payment on the note to the bank if

   a. Gridley's signature was forged.
   b. the note was issued based on the false statements of another party.
   c. there was no consideration for issuing the note.
   d. there was a breach of the contract for which the note was issued.

____   2.   Rondel writes out a check for $50 to Samantha, who alters the amount to $500. Although the alteration is clearly visible, Timor cashes the check for $500. Rondel is liable to pay Timor for

   a. $50.
   b. $500.
   c. $550.
   d. $0.

____   3.   Debit Company writes a check to EZ Credit, Inc., that is drawn on Debit's account at First Federal Bank. If the bank does not accept the check, liability for its amount is on

   a. Debit.
   b. EZ.
   c. First Federal.
   d. the party holding the draft.

____   4.   Farley signs a note payable to the order of Gabriella. Gabriella indorses the note and gives it to Heather as payment for a debt. Heather presents it to Farley, who pays it. Farley's payment discharges

   a. all of the parties.
   b. only Farley.
   c. only Gabriella.
   d. only Heather.

____   5.   Mariena who cannot read English, signs a note after Nimrod tells her that it is a credit application. If later sued by an HDC, Mariena's best defense would be

   a. duress.
   b. mistake.
   c. fraud in the inducement.
   d. fraud in the execution.

____ 6. Linwood Company writes a check to Maxime Corporation drawn on Linwood's account at Neighborly Bank. Maxime presents the check to the bank for payment. If the bank accepts the check, the bank is

   a. not liable for payment.
   b. primarily liable for payment.
   c. secondarily liable for payment.
   d. simultaneously liable for payment.

____ 7. Jenna gives a $500 note to Keyton to deliver a load of fresh seafood to Jenna's store. On delivery, the seafood is spoiled. Jenna may defend her decision not to pay the note based on

   a. breach of warranty.
   b. fraud in the inducement.
   c. lack of consideration.
   d. undue influence.

____ 8. Hamish writes a check on his account at Indigo Bank to Jada to pay a preexisting debt. Jada negotiates the check to Kendra by indorsement. Before Hamish or Jada may be liable on the check, it must be

   a. lost and unpaid.
   b. presented for payment and dishonored, for which notice must be given.
   c. presented for payment and dishonored, without notice.
   d. presented for payment and paid.

____ 9. Giana writes a check on her account at Harbor Bay Bank to Itzak, a famous investor. The person purporting to be Itzak is an imposter, however, named Jeno. Jeno negotiates the check to the bank. Liability for the check is on

   a. Harbor Bay Bank.
   b. Giana.
   c. Itzak.
   d. Jeno.

____ 10. Undertow Plumbing Products, Inc., authorizes Vitor to use company checks to buy plumbers' tools. Vitor writes a check to Wholesale Hardware, Inc., for $100 over the price of a purchase, for which the seller returns cash. When Wholesale presents the check for payment, it may recover

   a. nothing.
   b. the amount stated in the check.
   c. the amount of the overpayment only.
   d. the price of the tools only.

SHORT ESSAY QUESTIONS

1. What are the similarities and differences between transfer and presentment warranties?

2. What are the two situations in which, when there is a forged or unauthorized indorsement, the burden of loss falls on the maker or drawer?

GAMEPOINTS

(Answers at the Back of the Book)

1. In the video game "Bills & Coins," each player tracks income, spending, investments, and taxes in a simulated real-world environment to exceed the net worth of the other players with whom business is transacted. Your character, "Money Man," is given the following instrument:

Silky   <u>July 14</u>
2011
Gametown, Ohio

Pay to the order of <u>Money Man   </u>
<u>$1,500.00</u>
<u>One thousand five hundred and 00/100</u>   dollars

United Bank   *Silky*
Lake City, Ohio

Under the principles of the UCC, who is primarily liable on this item? Who is secondarily liable? If United Bank does not pay it, from whom can you seek payment and what steps must you take to obtain it?

2.   You work in the warehouse of Entrée Entertainment, Inc., which distributes video games, including the best-selling "Fettuccini Alfredo." Your job requires you to match deliveries to invoices. You notice that several Glowworm Packaging Co. invoices were double-paid. With a little sleuthing, you learn that half of the checks were indorsed by Holly, Entrée's bookkeeper, and deposited in her personal account. Assuming that Holly was not entitled to the checks, who is likely liable on them and why?

SPECIAL INFORMATION FOR CPA CANDIDATES

Questions can be constructed so that an apparently good faith party is liable on an instrument. This is particularly true in situations involving imposters, fictitious payees, and untrustworthy agents. You may find it helpful to review the rules concerning these culprits, and remember that a good faith party can be liable for a loss. There's one point that you may be able to forget, however: FTC Rule 433 has never been on the CPA exam.

Chapter 27
Checks and Banking in the Digital Age

WHAT THIS CHAPTER IS ABOUT

This chapter outlines the duties and liabilities that arise when a check is issued and paid. UCC Articles 3 and 4 govern checks. If there is a conflict between the articles, Article 4 controls. This outline also covers electronic fund transfers, e-money, and online banking.

CHAPTER OUTLINE

I. CHECKS

A check is a draft drawn on a bank, ordering the bank to pay a fixed amount of money on demand [UCC 3–104(f)]. If a bank wrongfully dishonors any of the following special types of checks, the holder can recover expenses, interest, and consequential damages [UCC 3–411].

A. CASHIER'S CHECK

A cashier's check is a check drawn by a bank on itself; negotiable on issue [UCC 3–104(g)].

B. TELLER'S CHECK

A teller's check is a draft drawn by a bank on another bank, or if drawn on a nonbank, payable at or through a bank [UCC 3–104(h)].

C. TRAVELER'S CHECK

A traveler's check is a check on which a financial institution is both drawer and drawee. The buyer must sign it twice (buying it and using it) [UCC 3–104(i)].

D. CERTIFIED CHECK

A check accepted by the bank on which it is drawn is a certified check [UCC 3–409(d)]. When a bank certifies a check, it immediately charges the drawer's account and transfers those funds to its account. The effect of certification is to discharge the drawer and prior indorsers [UCC 3–414(c), 3–415(d)]. *money still technically in your account*

II. THE BANK-CUSTOMER RELATIONSHIP

A. WHAT A BANK IS

A "person engaged in the business of banking, including a savings bank, savings and loan association, credit union or trust company" [UCC 4–105(1)]. Rights and duties of bank and customer are contractual.

B. WHAT A CUSTOMER IS

A customer is a creditor of the bank (and the bank, a debtor of the customer) when the customer deposits funds in his or her account. A bank acts as an agent for the customer when he or she writes a check drawn on the bank or deposits a check in his or her account for the bank to collect [UCC 4–201(a)].

III. THE BANK'S DUTY TO HONOR CHECKS

If a bank dishonors a check for insufficient funds, it has no liability. The customer is liable to the payee or holder of the check in a civil suit. If intent to defraud is proved, the customer is also subject to criminal prosecution. If a bank wrongfully dishonors a check, however, it is liable to the customer [UCC 4–402].

A. OVERDRAFTS

1. Pay or Dishonor?

If there are insufficient funds in a customer's account, the bank can pay an item drawn on the account or dishonor it. If the bank pays, it can charge the customer's account (if the customer has authorized payment) [UCC 4–401(a)]. If a check "bounces," a holder can resubmit it but must notify any indorsers of the first dishonor (or they are discharged).

2. Bank's Liability for Agreeing to Pay Overdrafts

Once a bank agrees to accept overdrafts, refusal to honor checks on an overdrawn account is wrongful dishonor [UCC 4–402(b)].

B. POSTDATED CHECKS

A bank can charge a postdated check against a customer's account if the customer does not give the bank enough notice. If the bank has notice but charges the check anyway, the bank is liable [UCC 4–401(c)].

C. STALE CHECKS

A bank is not obliged to pay an uncertified check presented for payment more than six months after its date [UCC 4–404]. If a bank pays in good faith, it can charge the customer's account for the amount.

D. DEATH OR INCOMPETENCE OF A CUSTOMER

Until a bank knows of the situation and has time to act, it is not liable for paying items [UCC 4–405]. If a bank knows of a death, for ten days after the date of death it can pay items drawn on or before the date of death (unless a person claiming an interest in the account orders a stop payment).

E. STOP-PAYMENT ORDERS

1. Who Can Order a Stop Payment and When It Must Be Received

Only a customer or person authorized to draw on the account. Must be received in a reasonable time and manner [UCC 4–403(a), 4–405].

2. How a Stop Payment Can Be Given and How Long It Is Effective

In most states, it can be given orally, but it is binding for only fourteen calendar days unless confirmed in writing. In writing, it is effective for six months, when it may be renewed [UCC 4–403(b)].

3. If the Bank Pays over an Order

It must recredit the customer's account for any loss, including damages for the dishonor of subsequent items [UCC 4–403(c)].

4. The Customer's Risks

Possible liability to payee for the amount of the item (and damages). Defense against payment to a payee may not prevent payment to a subsequent HDC [UCC 3–305, 3–306].

F. FORGED DRAWERS' SIGNATURES

1. The General Rule

A forged signature on a check has no legal effect as the signature of a drawer [UCC 3–403(a)]. If the bank pays, it must recredit the account.

2. Customer Negligence

If the customer's negligence substantially contributed to the forgery, the bank is not obligated to recredit the account [UCC 3–406(a)].

a. Reducing a Customer's Liability
A customer's liability may be reduced by a bank's negligence (if it substantially contributed to the loss) [UCC 3–406(b)].

b. Timely Examination of Bank Statements Required
The customer must examine the bank statement and canceled checks promptly and report any forged signatures [UCC 4–406(c)].

1) When There Is a Series of Forgeries by the Same Wrongdoer
To recover for all items, a customer must report the first forgery to the bank within *thirty* calendar days of receiving the statement and canceled checks [UCC 4–406(d)(2)].

2) When the Bank Is Also Negligent
If the bank fails to exercise ordinary care ("reasonable commercial standards"), it may have to recredit the customer's account for a portion of the loss (on the basis of comparative negligence) [UCC 4–406(e)].

c. Absolute Time Limit
A customer must report a forged signature within one year of the date the statement and canceled checks were available [UCC 4–406(f)].

3. Other Parties from Whom the Bank May Recover

a. The Forger
A forged signature is effective as the signature of the unauthorized signer [UCC 3–403(a)].

b. The Customer or Collecting Bank Who Cashed the Check
The bank may recover from "the person to whom or for whose benefit payment was made" [UCC 4–207(a)(2), 3–418(a)(ii)]. The bank cannot recover from "a person who took the instrument in good faith and for value or who in good faith changed position in reliance on the payment or acceptance" [UCC 3–418(c)].

G. CHECKS BEARING FORGED INDORSEMENTS

1. The General Rule
If the bank pays a check with a forged indorsement, it must recredit the account (or be held liable for breach of contract) [UCC 4–401(a)].

2. Timely Examination of Bank Statements Required
The customer must examine the bank statement and canceled checks and report forged indorsements promptly. Failure to do so within three years relieves the bank of liability [UCC 4–111].

3. Parties from Whom the Bank May Recover
The bank can recover for breach of warranty from the bank that cashed the check [UCC 4–207(a)(2)]. Ultimately, the loss usually falls on the first party to take the instrument.

H. ALTERED CHECKS
If the bank fails to detect an alteration, it is liable to its customer for the loss [UCC 4–401(d)(1)].

1. The Customer's Negligence
If a bank traces its loss to the customer's negligence or, on successive altered checks, to the customer's failure to discover the first alteration, its liability is reduced (unless it was negligent) [UCC 4–401, 4–406].

2. Other Parties from Whom the Bank May Recover
The bank can recover from the transferor, for breach of warranty. Exceptions involve cashier's checks, teller's checks, and certified checks [UCC 3–417(a)(2), 4–208(a)(2), 4–207(a)(2)].

IV.   THE BANK'S DUTY TO ACCEPT DEPOSITS

A. AVAILABILITY SCHEDULE FOR DEPOSITED CHECKS
Under the Expedited Funds Availability Act of 1987 and Regulation CC—

1. Funds That Must Be Available the Next Business Day after Deposit

a. The First $100 of Any Deposit and the Next $400 of a Local Check
The first $100 must be available for withdrawal on the opening of the next business day. The next $400 of a local check must be available by no later than 5:00 P.M. the next business day.

b. Cash Deposits, Wire Transfers, and Certain Checks
Funds must be available on the next business day for cash deposits, wire transfers, government checks, the first $100 of a day's check deposits, cashier's checks, certified checks, and checks for which the depositary and payor banks are the same institution.

2. Funds That Must Be Available within Five Business Days
All nonlocal checks and nonproprietary ATM deposits, including cash.

3. Funds That Can Be Held for Eight Days or an Extra Four Days
Eight days: funds in new accounts (open less than thirty days). Four days: deposits over $5,000 (except government and cashier's checks), accounts with many overdrafts, checks of questionable collectibility (the bank must tell the depositor it suspects fraud or insolvency).

B. INTEREST-BEARING ACCOUNTS
Under the Truth-in-Savings Act of 1991 and Regulation DD—

1. When Must a Bank Pay Interest?
On the full balance of a customer's account each day.

2. What Must a Bank Tell New Customers?
New customers must be told, in writing, the minimum to open an interest-bearing account, the interest in terms of the annual percentage yield, whether interest is calculated daily, and fees and other charges.

3. What Must Be Included in a Monthly Statement?
Interest earned, any fees that were charged, how the fees were calculated, and the number of days that the statement covers.

C. THE TRADITIONAL COLLECTION PROCESS

1. Banks Involved in the Collection Process
Depositary bank: first bank to receive a check for payment. *Payor bank*: bank on which a check is drawn. *Collecting bank*: bank (except payor bank) that handles a check for collection. *Intermediary bank*: any bank (except payor and depositary banks) involved in the collection process.

2. Check Collection between Customers of the Same Bank
An item payable by a depositary bank that is also the payor bank is an "on-us item." If the bank does not dishonor it by the second banking day, it is considered paid [UCC 4–215(e)(2)].

3. Check Collection between Customers of Different Banks
A depositary bank must arrange to present a check either directly or through intermediary banks to the appropriate payor bank.

a. Midnight Deadline
Each bank in the collection chain must pass a check on before midnight of the next banking day (on which the bank is open for substantially all its functions) following receipt [UCC 4–202(b)].

   b. **Deferred Posting and the Midnight Deadline**
      Posting of checks received after a certain time can be deferred until the next day [UCC 4–108].

   c. **Electronic Check Presentment**
      Can be done the same day a check is deposited. The check may be kept at the place of deposit with only information about the check presented for payment under a Federal Reserve agreement, clearinghouse rule, or truncation agreement [UCC 4–110].

D. CHECK CLEARING AND THE CHECK 21 ACT
   The Check Clearing in the 21st Century Act (which took effect in 2004) facilitates the use of electronic check processing.

   1. **Digital Images and Substitute Checks**
      Under the act, a substitute check (a paper copy of a check) can be created from a digital image. The originals can be destroyed (which saves space and prevents more than one payment on a check).

   2. **Reduced "Float" Time**
      The "float" is the time between when a check is written and when the account is deducted from an account. Under Check 21, banks can exchange checks digitally (which speeds collection) and this time is substantially reduced.

   3. **Faster Access to Funds**
      As check-processing speeds up, the Federal Reserve Board will revise the availability schedule for funds from deposited checks to correspond to reductions in processing time.

V. ELECTRONIC FUND TRANSFERS

A. TYPES OF ELECTRONIC FUND TRANSFER (EFT) SYSTEMS

   1. **Automated Teller Machines (ATMs)**
      Connected online to bank computers, ATMs accept deposits, dispense funds from accounts, make credit-card advances, and receive payments.

   2. **Point-of-Sale Systems**
      Connected online to bank computers, these systems allow consumers to transfer funds to pay merchants. The merchant inserts a customer's card into a terminal to read the card's coded data.

   3. **Direct Deposits and Withdrawals**
      Through a terminal, a deposit may be made directly to a customer's account. An institution at which a customer's funds are on deposit can also make payments electronically to a third party.

   4. **Pay-by-Internet Systems**
      These systems provide access to a financial institution's computer system over the Internet to direct a transfer of funds.

B. CONSUMER FUND TRANSFERS
   Under the Electronic Fund Transfer Act (EFTA) of 1978 and Regulation E (issued by the Federal Reserve Board of Governors)—

   1. **Who Is Subject to the EFTA?**
      Financial institutions that offer electronic fund transfers (EFTs) involving customer asset accounts established for personal, family, or household purposes.

   2. **Disclosure Requirements**
      The terms and conditions of EFTs involving a customer's account must be disclosed in readily understandable language at the time the customer contracts for services. Disclosures include—

a. Customer Liability

If a debit card is lost or stolen, and misused, a customer is liable for (1) $50—if he or she notifies the bank within two business days of learning of the loss; (2) $500—if he or she does not tell the bank until after the second day; or (3) unlimited amounts—if notice does not occur within sixty days after the transfer appears on the customer's statement.

b. Errors on Monthly Statements

Customer's and bank's responsibilities with respect to monthly statements: customer has sixty days to report an error, bank has ten days to respond or return any disputed amounts.

c. Receipts

Bank must furnish receipts for transactions made through electronic terminals,

d. Periodic Statements

1) How Often They Must Be Provided

A monthly statement is required for every month in which there is an electronic transfer.

2) What They Must Include

The amounts and dates of transfers, the fees, identification of the terminals, names of third parties involved, and an address and phone number for inquiries and error notices.

e. Stopping Preauthorized Transfers

A customer may stop a transfer by notifying the institution orally or in writing up to three business days before the scheduled date of the transfer. The institution may require the customer to provide written confirmation with fourteen days of oral notification.

3. Stopping Payment and Reversibility

Except for preauthorized transfers, the EFTA does not provide for the reversal of an electronic transfer of funds, once it has occurred.

4. Unauthorized Transfers

a. What an Unauthorized Transfer Is

(1) A transfer is initiated by a person who has no actual authority to initiate the transfer; (2) the consumer receives no benefit from it; and (3) the consumer did not furnish the person "with the card, code, or other means of access" to his or her account.

b. Criminal Sanctions

Unauthorized use of an EFT system access device is a federal felony, subject to fines up to $10,000 and imprisonment up to ten years.

5. Violations and Damages

Banks are held to strict compliance. Penalties include—

a. Civil

A customer may recover actual damages, as well as punitive damages of not less than $100 and more than $1,000. In a class action suit, the punitive damages limit is the lesser of $500,000 or 1 percent of the institution's net worth.

b. Criminal

Sanctions included subjecting an institution or its officials to fines of up to $5,000 and imprisonment up to one year.

C. COMMERCIAL FUND TRANSFERS

In most states, UCC Article 4A clarifies the rights and liabilities of parties involved in fund transfers not subject to the EFTA or other federal or state statutes. In those states that have not adopted Article 4A, commercial fund transfers are governed by contract law and tort law.

E-MONEY AND ONLINE BANKING

E-money has the potential to replace physical cash with virtual cash (e-money) in the form of electronic impulses, or digital cash.

A. STORED-VALUE CARDS

Plastic cards embossed with magnetic stripes containing encoded data. Can be used to buy specific goods and services offered by the issuer.

B. SMART CARDS

Contain microchips that hold more information than a magnetic stripe. Less prone to error, and carry and process security programming (such as a digital signature). Debits and credits are automatic and can be immediate.

C. ONLINE BANKING SERVICES

These include bill consolidation and payment, transferring funds among accounts, and applying for loans. Depositing and withdrawing is not yet generally available over the Internet, but virtual banks do business through physical delivery systems.

D. PRIVACY PROTECTION

1. **Electronic Communication Privacy Act of 1986**
   This act prohibits any person from knowingly divulging the contents of an electronic communication while that communication is in transmission or in electronic storage.

2. **Right to Financial Privacy Act of 1978**
   An issuer of e-money may be subject to this act if the issuer is deemed to be (1) a bank by virtue of its holding customer funds or (2) an entity that issues a physical card similar to a credit or debit card.

3. **Financial Services Modernization Act (Gramm-Leach-Bliley Act) of 1999**
   This act proscribes the disclosure of financial institutions' customer data without notice and an opt-out opportunity.

TRUE-FALSE QUESTIONS

(Answers at the Back of the Book)

____ 1. A check is a draft drawn on a bank.

____ 2. If a bank fails to honor a customer's stop-payment order, it may be liable to the customer for more than the amount of the loss suffered by the drawer because of the wrongful payment.

____ 3. A bank's duty to honor its customer's checks is absolute.

____ 4. Generally, funds must be available on the next business day for cash deposits.

____ 5. A bank that fails to investigate an error and report its conclusion promptly to the customer is in violation of the Electronic Fund Transfer Act (EFTA).

____ 6. A customer must examine the statements provided by the institution handling his or her account and notify it of any errors within sixty days.

____ 7. The rights and duties of a bank and its customers are contractual.

____ 8. All funds deposited in all bank accounts must be available for withdrawal no later than the next day.

____ 9. A bank that pays a customer's check bearing a forged indorsement must recredit the customer's account.

____ 10. A forged drawer's signature on a check is effective as the signature of the person whose name is signed.

FILL-IN QUESTIONS

(Answers at the Back of the Book)

A depositor is the _____ (drawee/drawer) of a check. The depositor is the bank's _____ (creditor/debtor) as to the amount on deposit in the depositor's account. The depositor is the bank's _____ (agent/principal) in the deposit contract. The bank is the _____ (drawee/drawer) of a check. The bank is the depositor's _____ (creditor debtor) as to the amount on deposit in the depositor's account. The bank is the depositor's _____ (agent/principal) in the handling of the account and in the collection process.

MULTIPLE-CHOICE QUESTIONS

(Answers at the Back of the Book)

____ 1. Fleet National Bank pays a check on which has been forged the signature of the drawer, Gunhilde, who is the bank's customer. The bank must recredit her account for the entire amount of the check if

   a. Gunhilde's negligence substantially contributed to the forgery.
   b. the amount of the check was less than $50.
   c. the amount of the check was more than $5,000.
   d. the bank's negligence substantially contributed to the forgery.

____ 2. Hometown Bank's cutoff hour is 2 P.M. The bank receives a check drawn on the account of Icicle Treats Corporation, one of its customers, at 4 P.M. Monday, presented by Jaclyn, not a bank customer. The bank uses deferred posting. The bank may timely dishonor the check by midnight

   a. Monday.
   b. Tuesday.
   c. Wednesday.
   d. Thursday.

____ 3. Koko buys three television sets from Laszlo, paying with a check. When the sets prove defective, Koko orders Metro Bank, the drawee, to stop payment on the check. This order is valid for fourteen

   a. years.
   b. months.
   c. weeks.
   d. days.

____ 4. Newville Bank mistakenly pays one of Oswald's checks with a forged indorsement. Oswald can recover his loss from the bank if, after receipt of the bank statement, he notifies the bank within three

   a. years.
   b. months.
   c. weeks.
   d. days.

____ 5. **Based on a Sample CPA Exam Question.** Jillian is the holder and payee of check drawn by Kerri on Laramie Bank. Jillian takes the check to the bank to have it certified. After certification

   a. Kerri is discharged on the check.
   b. Kerri is primarily liable on the check.
   c. the bank is discharged on the check.
   d. the bank is secondarily liable on the check.

___ **6.** Pixie writes a check for $600 drawn on her account at Quest Bank and presents it to Rocco. When Rocco presents the check for payment, the bank dishonors it. Rocco may sue

  a. the bank for dishonoring the check.
  b. Pixie on the underlying obligation.
  c. both the bank and Pixie.
  d. none of the choices.

___ **7.** Salty Snax Company issue a payroll check to Trevor drawn on its account at Unity Bank. This check will be stale if Trevor presents it for payment six

  a. months after it is issued.
  b. months after he indorses.
  c. weeks after he receives it.
  d. weeks after the pay period that it covers.

___ **8.** Regine issues a check to Super Discount Store in payment on her account. Tisha, Super Discount's accountant, forges the store's indorsement and deposits the check in her bank account. Urban Bank, Regine's bank, pays the check. Regine can recover from

  a. no one.
  b. Tisha, but not Urban Bank.
  c. Urban Bank, which can recover from Tisha.
  d. Urban Bank, which cannot recover from Tisha.

___ **9.** Devon loses his bank access card. He realizes his loss the next day but waits a week to call Estuary Bank, his bank. Meanwhile, Floria finds and uses Devon's card to withdraw $5,000 from his account. Devon is responsible for

  a. 0.
  b. $50.
  c. $500.
  d. $5,000.

___ **10.** Web Funds, Inc., an e-money issuer, may be subject to the Right to Financial Privacy Act if Web Funds

  a. does not accept deposits.
  b. does not hold customer funds, whether or not the funds qualify as "deposits."
  c. investigates its customers' credit backgrounds.
  d. issues a physical card similar to a debit card.

SHORT ESSAY QUESTIONS

1. Under what circumstances might a customer be unable recover from a bank that pays on a forged check drawn on the customer's account?

2. What are the principal features of the Electronic Fund Transfer Act (EFTA)?

GAMEPOINTS

(Answers at the Back of the Book)

1. "Credit Check" is a video game that charges its players with accurately identifying and correcting problems with checks and bank accounts. You choose to play the game as the character "Financial Wizard." You are shown the following item, on which the signature of Jacky is a forgery:

Jacky   <u>June 12</u>
<u>2011</u>
Harbor City, Virginia

Pay to the order of <u>Knuckles Mahoney</u> $9,000.00
<u>Nine thousand and 00/100</u>   dollars

First State Bank   *Jacky*
Harbor City, Virginia

To advance to the game's Level 2, outline the possible liability of the parties on this instrument.

2. You create and design "Little League World Series," a video game that focuses on local youth league athletes. The game can be updated each season through a dedicated Web site. You sell the game and the site to Major Players, Inc., a game company that agrees to pay semi-annual royalties. The first check that Major Players gives you—for $5,000—is drawn on an out-of-state branch of your bank. You deposit the check in your account. If your bank processes checks according to the traditional schedule, how soon can you withdraw the funds? Under Check 21, how soon could you withdraw the full amount?

SPECIAL INFORMATION FOR CPA CANDIDATES

Typically, banking questions on the CPA exam concern the relationship between a bank and its customer. Remember in particular that there is no primarily liable party among the original three parties on a check; only the drawer can sue a drawee for wrongful dishonor (a payee cannot enforce a check against the drawee); and a drawee does not have to pay a stale check. Another specific matter tested on the exam has been the liability surrounding stop-payment orders. In that context, remember that a personal defense is no good against a holder in due course.

Electronic fund transfers are not tested on the CPA exam.

CUMULATIVE HYPOTHETICAL PROBLEM FOR UNIT FIVE—INCLUDING CHAPTERS 24–27

(Answers at the Back of the Book)

On May 15, 2011, Eve bought the following instrument from Beta Corporation for $1,700. Eve paid for the instrument with check. Eve knew that Alpha, Inc., disputed its liability on the instrument because of Beta's alleged breach of the computer purchase contract referred to on the face of the instrument. On May 20, First National Bank bought the instrument from Eve for $1,900. First National did not know that Alpha disputed its liability. On the back of the instrument is the indorsement "Pay to the order of First National Bank, without recourse [signed] *Eve*".

May 1, 2011

Alpha, Inc., promises to pay to Beta Corp. or bearer $2,000 on June 1, 2011, with interest at the rate of 8 % per year. Alpha may elect to extend the due date to July 1, 2011.

Alpha, Inc.

By <u>*C.D. Jones*</u>

C.D. Jones, president

Re: computer purchase order no. 123, dated May 1, 2008

___ **1.** This instrument is

a. a check.
b. a promissory note.
c. a sight draft.
d. a trade acceptance.

___ **2.** This instrument is

a. negotiable because it refers to the computer purchase agreement.
b. negotiable even though Alpha has the right to extend the due date.
c. nonnegotiable because Alpha has the right to extend the due date.
d. nonnegotiable because it refers to the computer purchase agreement.

___ **3.** First National Bank can negotiate the instrument

a. by delivery without indorsing it.
b. only by canceling Eve's indorsement.
c. only by indorsing it.
d. only by making it payable to the order of a specific individual.

___ **4.** First National demands payment on the instrument from Alpha. Alpha refuses, claiming that Beta breached the computer purchase agreement. First National

a. can collect from Alpha because First National is an HDC.
b. can collect from Eve, but not Alpha, because Eve knew of Alpha's claim.
c. cannot collect from Alpha because Eve was not an HDC.
d. cannot collect from Alpha because of Beta's breach.

___ **5.** Beta presents Eve's check for payment, but City Bank, the drawee, refuses to pay. The party with primary liability for payment of the check is

a. Beta.
b. City Bank.
c. Eve.
d. not Beta, City Bank, or Eve.

QUESTIONS ON THE FOCUS ON ETHICS FOR UNIT FIVE— NEGOTIABLE INSTRUMENTS

(Answers at the Back of the Book)

___ **1.** Carol signs a promissory note in reliance on Don's assurance that it is not a note. Don negotiates the note to Friendly Collection Company, which takes it for value, in good faith, and without knowledge or notice of the circumstances by which it was executed. When Friendly tries to collect, Carol refuses to pay. Under the holder-in-due-course (HDC) doctrine, the loss falls on

a. Carol only.
b. Carol and Friendly equally.
c. Carol or Friendly, depending on who can most easily afford the loss.
d. Friendly only.

___ **2.** First State Bank wrongfully dishonors a check issued by Greg, its customer, to Holly. On wrongful dishonor of a customer's check, a bank's liability may include

a. compensatory damages only.
b. consequential damages.
c. nominal damages only.
d. the amount of the check only.

____   **3.** City Bank fails to verify all customer signatures on all of the checks that the bank processes each month. Instead, like most banks, City Bank verifies the signatures on checks less than $2.500 on a random basis. Under the UCC, this practice may constitute

     a. ordinary care.
     b. ordinary failure.
     c. ordinary malfeasance.
     d. ordinary negligence.

Chapter 28
Creditors' Rights and Remedies

WHAT THIS CHAPTER IS ABOUT

This chapter sets out the rights and remedies available to a creditor, when a debtor defaults, under laws other than UCC Article 9. Among those remedies are rights afforded by liens, and surety and guaranty agreements.

CHAPTER OUTLINE

I. LAWS ASSISTING CREDITORS

A. LIENS
A lien is a claim against property to satisfy a debt or to protect a claim for payment of a debt.

1. Mechanic's Liens
A creditor can file this lien on real property when a person contracts for labor, services, or materials to improve the property but does not pay.

a. When a Creditor Must File a Mechanic's Lien
A creditor must file the lien within a specific period, measured from the last date on which materials or labor was provided (usually within 60 to 120 days).

b. If the Owner Does Not Pay
The property can be sold to satisfy the debt. Notice of the foreclosure and sale must be given to the debtor in advance.

2. Artisan's Liens
This is a security device by which a creditor can recover from a debtor for labor and materials furnished in the repair of personal property.

a. The Creditor Must Possess the Property
The lien terminates if possession is voluntarily surrendered, unless the lienholder records notice of the lien in accord with state statutes.

b. If the Owner Does Not Pay
The property can be sold to satisfy the debt. Notice of the foreclosure and sale must be given to the debtor in advance.

3. Judicial Liens

a. Writ of Attachment
Attachment is a court-ordered seizure and taking into custody of property before the entry of a final judgment for a past-due debt.

1) **After a Court Issues a Writ of Attachment**
A sheriff or other officer seizes nonexempt property. If the creditor prevails at trial, the property can be sold to satisfy the judgment.

217

2) Limitations
The due process clause of the Fourteenth Amendment limits a court's power to authorize seizure of a debtor's property without notice to the debtor or a hearing on the facts.

b. Writ of Execution
A writ of execution is an order, usually issued by a clerk of court, directing the sheriff to seize and sell any of the debtor's nonexempt property within the court's geographical jurisdiction.

1) First, the Creditor Must Obtain a Judgment against the Debtor
If the debtor does not pay, proceeds from the sale pay the judgment. The debtor can redeem the property any time before it is sold.

2) Limitations
Because of laws that exempt a debtor's homestead and designated items of personal property, many judgments are uncollectible.

B. GARNISHMENT
Garnishment occurs when a creditor collects a debt by seizing property of the debtor (such as wages or money in a bank account) that a third party (such as an employer or a bank) holds.

1. Garnishment Proceedings
The creditor obtains a judgment against the debtor and serves it on the third party (the garnishee) so that, for example, part of the debtor's paycheck will be paid to the creditor.

2. Laws Limiting the Amount of Wages Subject to Garnishment
In some states, a creditor must go back to court for a separate order of garnishment for each pay period. Both federal and state laws limit the amount of money that can be garnished from a debtor's weekly take-home pay. State limits are often higher.

C. CREDITORS' COMPOSITION AGREEMENTS
A *creditors' composition agreement* is a contract between a debtor and his or her creditors for discharge of the debtor's liquidated debts on payment of a sum less than that owed.

II. SURETYSHIP AND GUARANTY

A. SURETYSHIP
Suretyship is a promise by a third person to be responsible for a debtor's obligation. The promise does not have to be in writing. A surety is primarily liable—a creditor can demand payment from the surety the moment the debt is due.

B. GUARANTY
A guaranty is a promise to be secondarily liable for the debt or default of another. A guarantor pays only after the debtor defaults and the creditor has made an attempt to collect from the debtor. A guaranty must be in writing unless the main-purpose exception applies (see Chapter 15). A guaranty may be continuing (to cover a series of transactions), unlimited or limited in time and amount, and absolute (immediate liability on the debtor's default) or conditional (liability only a certain event).

C. ACTIONS RELEASING THE SURETY AND THE GUARANTOR

1. Material Change to the Contract between Debtor and Creditor
Without obtaining the consent of the surety (guarantor), a surety is discharged completely or to the extent the surety suffers a loss.

2. Principal Obligation Is Paid or Valid Tender Is Made

3. Surrender or Impairment of Collateral
Without the surety's (guarantor's) consent, this action on the part of the creditor releases the surety to the extent of any loss suffered.

D. DEFENSES OF THE SURETY AND THE GUARANTOR

1. Most of the Principal Debtor's Defenses
Defenses that cannot be used: debtor's incapacity, bankruptcy, and statute of limitations.

2. Surety or Guarantor's Own Defenses

E. RIGHTS OF THE SURETY AND THE GUARANTOR
If the surety (guarantor) pays the debt—

1. The Right of Subrogation
A surety (guarantor) may seek any remedies that were available to the creditor against the debtor.

2. The Right of Reimbursement
A surety is entitled to receive from a debtor all outlays made on behalf of the suretyship arrangement.

3. The Right of Contribution
A surety who pays more than his or her proportionate share on a debtor's default is entitled to recover from co-sureties.

 III PROTECTION FOR DEBTORS

A. EXEMPTED REAL PROPERTY
Each state allows a debtor to keep the family home (in some states only if the debtor has a family) in its entirety or up to a specified amount. The Bankruptcy Abuse Prevention and Consumer Protection Act of 2005 limits the use of these exemptions.

B. EXEMPTED PERSONAL PROPERTY
This includes household furniture up to a specified dollar amount; clothing and other possessions; a vehicle (or vehicles); certain animals; and equipment that the debtor uses in a business or trade.

TRUE-FALSE QUESTIONS

(Answers at the Back of the Book)

____ **1.** A mechanic's lien involves personal property.

____ **2.** An employer can dismiss an employee due to garnishment.

____ **3.** A creditor's composition agreement discharges only debts owed to creditors who agree.

____ **4.** An artisan's lien involves personal property.

____ **5.** A writ of attachment is a court order to seize a debtor's property *before* the entry of a final judgment in a creditor's lawsuit against the debtor.

____ **6.** A writ of execution is a court order to seize a debtor's property *after* the entry of a final judgment in a creditor's lawsuit against the debtor.

____ **7.** Each state permits a debtor to retain all of the family home, free from unsecured creditor's claims.

____ **8.** A guarantor is discharged from his or her obligation when the principal debtor pays the debt.

____ **9.** A surety cannot use defenses available to the debtor to avoid liability on an obligation to a creditor.

____ **10.** A surety cannot use a debtor's bankruptcy as a defense against the surety's payment of a debt.

FILL-IN QUESTIONS

(Answers at the Back of the Book)

A _____ (contract of suretyship/guaranty contract) is a promise to a creditor made by a third person to be responsible for a debtor's obligation. A _____ (guarantor/surety) is primarily liable: the creditor can hold the _____ (guarantor/surety) responsible for payment of the debt when the debt is due, without first exhausting all remedies against the debtor. A _____ (contract of suretyship/guaranty contract) also includes a promise to answer for a principal's obligation, but a _____ (guarantor/surety) is secondarily liable—that is, the principal must first default, and ordinarily, a creditor must have attempted to collect from the principal, because ordinarily a debtor would not otherwise be declared in default.

MULTIPLE-CHOICE QUESTIONS

(Answers at the Back of the Book)

____ 1. Fiona leaves her ruby red dancing shoes with GoGo's Footwear Fix to be repaired. When Fiona returns for the shoes, she says, "I'll pay for the repair later." To obtain payment, GoGo's can use

    a. a mechanic's lien.
    b. an artisan's lien.
    c. a writ of attachment.
    d. a writ of execution.

____ 2. Davy borrows money from EZ Credit, Inc. Davy defaults. To use attachment as a remedy EZ must first

    a. be unable to collect the amount of a judgment against Davy.
    b. file a suit against Davy.
    c. lose a suit against Davy.
    d. succeed in a suit against Davy.

____ 3. **Based on a Sample CPA Exam Question.** Niles's $2,500 debt to Otmar is past due. To collect money from Niles's wages to pay the debt, Otmar can use

    a. an order of receivership.
    b. a writ of attachment.
    c. a writ of execution.
    d. garnishment.

____ 4. Eli owes Fatima $200,000. A court awards Fatima a judgment in this amount. To satisfy the judgment, Eli's home is sold at public auction for $150,000. The state homestead exemption is $50,000. Fatima gets

    a. 0.
    b. $50,000.
    c. $100,000.
    d. $150,000.

____ 5. Eager Biz Company wants to borrow money from Finance Bank. The bank insists that Gwen, Eager's president, agree to be personally liable for payment if Eager defaults. Gwen agrees. She is

    a. a garnishee.
    b. a guarantor.
    c. a lienor.
    d. a creditor.

____ 6. Ismail and Jody agree to act as guarantors on a loan made by Keenan. Keenan defaults on the payments and Jody refuses to pay. If Ismail pays the debt, he can recover from

    a. Keenan and Jody under the right of reimbursement.
    b. Keenan and Jody under the right of proportionate liability.
    c. Keenan under the right of subrogation and Jody under the right of contribution.
    d. neither Keenan nor Jody.

____ 7. Aaron owes Babs $500 but he refuses to pay. To collect, Babs files a suit against Aaron and wins. Aaron still refuses to pay. To collect the amount of the judgment, Babs can use

    a. a creditor's composition agreement.
    b. a homestead exemption.
    c. a writ of attachment.
    d. a writ of execution.

____ 8. Robin contracts with Safe & Stolid Roofing to replace the ceramic tiles on Robin's roof for $8,000. Robin pays half of the contract price in advance. Safe & Stolid complete the project. Robin says, "Thanks," but refuses to pay the rest of the price. To obtain payment, Safe & Stolid can use

    a. a mechanic's lien.
    b. an artisan's lien.
    c. a writ of attachment.
    d. a writ of execution.

____ 9. Gracie agrees to act, without compensation, as a surety for Hershel's loan from InstaCredit. Later, without Gracie's knowledge, Hershel and InstaCredit agree to extend the time for repayment and to increase the interest rate. Gracie's obligation

    a. changes to match Hershel's obligation.
    b. does not change.
    c. is discharged to the extent of any loss caused by the extension of time.
    d. is discharged completely.

____ 10. Lobo agrees to act, without compensation, as a guarantor for Marion's loan from Nichelle. Collateral for the loan is Marion's car, which Marion gives to Nichelle. Later, without Lobo's knowledge, Marion and Nichelle agree to increase the interest rate and Nichelle returns the car to Marion. Lobo's obligation

    a. does not change.
    b. is discharged to the extent of the additional interest.
    c. is discharged to the extent of any loss caused by surrender of the car.
    d. is discharged completely.

SHORT ESSAY QUESTIONS

1. What is a lien? What are the four ways in which a lien can arise? What is a lienholder's priority compared to other creditors?

2. What are the differences between contracts of suretyship and guaranty contracts?

GAMEPOINTS

(Answers at the Back of the Book)

1. The story and the art of the video game "Erase against Time" imitates a graphic novel. Players are required to quickly find and obliterate each other's weapons, which are non-traditional in appearance and

operation. You find the game so compelling that you ignore everything else, including the payment of your debts. Eventually, your creditors take action, levying mechanic's and artisan's liens. How can they recover payment through these liens? Do they have to notify you?

2. You are playing the video game "Medieval Nights," in which the object is to amass wealth, prestige, and points by battling and defeating foes, rescuing others in distress, and currying favor with royalty. Your character Knight Light co-signs King Gambol's loan from Squire Merchant. The king's chancellor later adjudicates Gambol to be mentally incompetent. Without asking the king to pay, the lender seeks payment of the loan only from you. Before you respond, Queen Gambit pays the loan in full. Are you released from your obligation to pay? Explain.

SPECIAL INFORMATION FOR CPA CANDIDATES

Suretyship is usually tested on the CPA examination in the section covering the relationship between debtors and creditors. Questions regarding suretyship have also been included in the contracts section as part of a Statute of Frauds question or a question concerning consideration. One common fact situation presented on the exam has involved a surety who is not paid for his or her suretyship. Consideration is usually present elsewhere in the question, however, and thus, its lack is not a defense for that surety. Another frequent scenario involves co-sureties—be certain that you grasp the rights of the parties in such circumstances.

Chapter 29
Secured Transactions

UCC Article 9 (handwritten)

WHAT THIS CHAPTER IS ABOUT

This chapter covers transactions in which the payment of a debt is secured (guaranteed) by personal property owned by the debtor or in which the debtor has a legal interest. The importance of being a secured creditor cannot be overemphasized—secured transactions are as basic to modern business as credit.

CHAPTER OUTLINE

I. THE TERMINOLOGY OF SECURED TRANSACTIONS
UCC Article 9 applies to secured transactions.

A. SECURED TRANSACTION
A secured transaction is a transaction in which payment of a debt is guaranteed by personal property owned by the debtor or in which the debtor has a legal interest.

B. SECURITY INTEREST, SECURED PARTY, COLLATERAL, AND DEBTOR
A *security interest* is the interest in the collateral that secures payment or performance of an obligation [UCC 1–201(37)]. A *secured party* is a creditor in whose favor there is a security interest in the debtor's collateral [UCC 9–102(a)(72)]. *Collateral* is the subject of a security interest [UCC 9–102(a)(12)]. *Debtor* is the party who owes payment [UCC 9–102(a)(28)].

II. CREATION OF A SECURITY INTEREST *(Attachment)* (handwritten)

A. TWO CONCERNS
A creditor's main concerns are, if a debtor fails to pay, (1) satisfaction of the debt through possession or sale of the collateral and (2) priority over other creditors to the collateral.

B. THREE REQUIREMENTS *Attachment* (handwritten)
A creditor's rights attach to collateral, creating an enforceable security interest against a debtor if the following requirements are met [UCC 9–203].

1. Written or Authenticated Security Agreement
(1) It must be written or authenticated (which includes electronic media, or records), (2) describe the collateral, and (3) be signed or authenticated by the debtor [UCC 9–102, 9–108]. Or the secured party must possess the collateral. If the debtor's name changes, the financing statement must be amended within four months to include the change and continue in effect.

2. Secured Party Must Give Value
Value is any consideration that supports a contract [UCC 1–201(44)].

3. Debtor Must Have Rights in the Collateral
The debtor must have an ownership interest or right (current or future legal interest) to obtain possession of the collateral.

III. PERFECTION OF A SECURITY INTEREST *(Perfection)* *Perfection trumps attachment* (handwritten)
Perfection is the process by which secured parties protect themselves against the claims of others who wish to satisfy their debts out of the same collateral.

223

A. PERFECTION BY FILING

Filing is the most common means of perfecting a security interest.

1. What a Financing Statement Must Contain

It must contain (1) the names of the debtor and the creditor (a trade name is not sufficient), and (3) a description of the collateral [UCC 9–502, 9–503, 9–506, 9–521].

2. Where to File a Financing Statement

Depending on how collateral is classified, filing is with a county (timber, fixtures, etc.) or a state (other collateral) [UCC 9–301(3), 9–502(b)]. The specific office depends on the debtor's location—

1) Individual debtors: the state of the debtor's residence.
2) Chartered entity (corporation): state of charter or filing.
3) Other: state in which business or chief executive office is.

B. PERFECTION WITHOUT FILING

1. Perfection by Possession

A creditor can possess collateral and return it when the debt is paid [UCC 9–310, 9–312(b), 9–313]. For some securities, instruments, and jewelry, this is the only way to perfect.

2. Perfection by Attachment

[handwritten: Perfection occurs at same time as attachment]

a. Purchase-Money Security Interest (PMSI)

A PMSI is (1) retained in, or taken by a seller of, goods to secure part or all of the price, or (2) taken by a lender, such as a bank, as part of a loan to enable a debtor to buy the collateral [UCC 9–103(a)(2)]. *[handwritten: or car sale]*

b. Perfection of a PMSI

A PMSI in consumer goods is perfected automatically when it is created. The seller need do nothing more.

c. Exceptions

Security interests subject to other federal or state laws that require additional steps are excepted. For example, to perfect a PMSI in a car requires filing a certificate of title.

C. EFFECTIVE TIME DURATION OF PERFECTION

A financing statement is effective for five years [UCC 9–515]. A continuation statement filed within six months before the expiration date continues the effectiveness for five more years (and so on) [UCC 9–515(d), (e)].

[handwritten margin note: only applies to consumer goods — all other cases must file for PMSI]

IV. THE SCOPE OF A SECURITY INTEREST

A. PROCEEDS

Proceeds include whatever is received when collateral is sold or otherwise disposed of. A secured party has an interest in proceeds that perfects automatically on perfection of the security interest and remains perfected for twenty days after the debtor receives the proceeds. The interest remains perfected for more than twenty days if—

1. A filed financing statement covers the original collateral and the proceeds [UCC 9–315(c), (d)].
2. There is a filed statement that covers the original collateral and the proceeds are identifiable cash proceeds [UCC 9–315(d)(2)].

B. AFTER-ACQUIRED PROPERTY

A security agreement may provide for coverage of **after-acquired property** [UCC 9–204(a)]—collateral acquired by a debtor after execution of a security agreement.

C. FUTURE ADVANCES

A security agreement may provide that future advances against a line of credit are subject to a security interest in the collateral [UCC 9–204(c)].

D. THE FLOATING-LIEN CONCEPT

A *floating lien* is a security agreement that provides for the creation of a security interest in any (or all) of the above. The concept can apply to a shifting stock of goods—the lien can start with raw materials and follow them as they become finished goods and inventories and as they are sold, turning into accounts receivable, chattel paper, or cash.

V. PRIORITIES

When several creditors claim a security interest in the same collateral of a debtor, which interest has priority?

A. SECURED PARTIES V. OTHER SECURED PARTIES

1. The General Rule

The first interest to be filed or perfected has priority over other filed or perfected security interests. If none of the interests has been perfected, the first to attach has priority [UCC 9–322(a)(1), (3)].

2. Exception—Commingled or Processed Goods

When goods have lost their identity into a product or mass, security interests attach in a ratio of the cost of the goods to which each interest originally attached to the cost of the total product or mass [UCC 9–336].

3. Exception—Purchase-Money Security Interest (PMSI)

a. Inventory

A perfected PMSI prevails over a previously perfected security interest if the holder of the PMSI perfects and gives the holder of the other interest written notice of the PMSI before the debtor takes possession of the new inventory [UCC 9–324(b)].

b. Software

If software is used in goods subject to a PMSI, priority is according to the classification of the goods [UCC 9–103(c), 9–324(f)].

c. Other Collateral

A perfected PMSI prevails over a previously perfected security interest if the holder of the PMSI perfects before the debtor takes possession of the collateral or within twenty days [UCC 9–324(a)].

B. SECURED PARTIES V. UNSECURED PARTIES

Secured parties (perfected or not) prevail over unsecured creditors and creditors who have obtained judgments against the debtor but who have not begun the legal process to collect on those judgments [UCC 9–201(a)].

C. SECURED PARTIES V. BUYERS

1. The General Rule

A security interest in collateral continues even after the collateral has been sold unless the secured party authorized the sale.

2. Exception—Buyer in the Ordinary Course of Business

Takes goods free of any security interest (unless the buyer knows that the purchase violates a third party's rights) [UCC 9–320(a)].

3. Exception—Buyers of Consumer Goods Purchased outside the Ordinary Course of Business

The buyer must give value and not know of the security interest; the purchase must occur before the secured party perfects by filing [UCC 9–320(b)].

4. Exception—Buyers of Instruments, Documents, or Securities

A holder in due course, a holder to whom a negotiable instrument has been negotiated, and a bona fide purchaser of securities have priority over a previously perfected security interest [UCC 9–330(d), 9–331(a)].

5. Exception—Buyers of Farm Products
A buyer from a farmer has priority over a perfected security interest unless, in some states, the secured party has filed centrally an effective financing statement or the buyer has notice before the sale.

VI.   RIGHTS AND DUTIES OF DEBTORS AND CREDITORS

A. INFORMATION REQUESTS
When filing, creditors and debtors can ask the filing officer to furnish a copy of the statement with the file number, the date, and the hour [UCC 9–523(a)]. Others (such as prospective creditors) can ask the filing officer to provide a certificate that gives information on possible perfected financing statements [UCC 9–523(c), 9–525(d)].

B. RELEASE, ASSIGNMENT, AND AMENDMENT
A secured party can release all or part of the collateral [UCC 9–512, 9–521(b)], or assign part or all of the security interest [UCC 9–514, 9–521(a)]. A filing can be amended, if both parties agree [UCC 9–512(a)].

C. CONFIRMATION OR ACCOUNTING REQUEST BY DEBTOR
When the debtor asks, the secured party must tell the debtor the amount of the unpaid debt (within two weeks of the debtor's request) [UCC 9–210].

D. TERMINATION STATEMENT
When a debt is paid, the secured party can send a termination statement to the debtor or file it with the original financing statement.

1. If the Collateral Is Consumer Goods
The statement must be filed within one month after the debt is paid, or—if the debtor requests the statement in writing—within twenty days of receipt of the request, whichever is earlier [UCC 9–513(b)].

2. If the Collateral Is Other Goods
The statement must be filed or furnished to the debtor within twenty days after a written request is made by the debtor [UCC 9–513(c)].

VII.   DEFAULT

Default is whatever the parties stipulate in their agreement [UCC 9–601, 9–603]. Occurs most often when debtors fail to make payments or go bankrupt.

A. BASIC REMEDIES

1. Repossession of the Collateral—The Self-Help Remedy
A secured party can take possession of the collateral without a court order, if it can be done without a breach of the peace, [UCC 9–609(b)] and retain it for satisfaction of the debt [UCC 9–620] or resell it and apply the proceeds toward the debt [UCC 9–610] (see below).

2. Execution and Levy
A secured party can give up the security interest and proceed to judgment on the debt (this is done if the value of the collateral is less than the debt and the debtor has other assets) [UCC 9–601(a)].

B. DISPOSITION OF COLLATERAL

1. Retention of Collateral by the Secured Party

a. Notice
A secured party must give written notice to the debtor. In all cases except consumer goods, notice must also be sent to any other secured party from whom the secured party has received notice of a claim.

b. If Debtor or Other Secured Party Objects within Twenty Days
The secured party must sell or otherwise dispose of the collateral [UCC 9–620(a), 9–621].

2. **Consumer Goods**
    If the collateral is consumer goods with a PMSI and the debtor has paid 60 percent or more on the price or loan in a non-PMSI, the secured party must sell within ninety days [UCC 9–620(e), (f)].

3. **Disposition Procedures**
    (1) Disposition must be in a commercially reasonable manner and (2) the debtor must be notified of the sale [UCC 9–610(b)].

    a. **Disposition**
        After default, a secured party may sell, lease, license, or otherwise dispose of any or all of the collateral. "Commercially reasonable" means the method, manner, time, place, and other terms.

    b. **The Secured Party Must Give Written Notice to the Debtor**
        In all cases except consumer goods, notice must also be sent to any other secured party from whom the secured party has received notice of a claim [UCC 9–611(b), (c)], unless the collateral is perishable or is customarily sold in a recognized market.

    c. **Failure to Act in a Commercially Reasonable Manner or Give Proper Notice**
        Any deficiency of the debtor can be reduced to the extent the creditor's failure affected the rice received on the sale [UCC 9–626(a)(3).

4. **Proceeds from Disposition**
    Must be applied to (1) expenses stemming from retaking, storing, or reselling, (2) balance of the debt, (3) junior lienholders, and (4) surplus to the debtor [UCC 9–608(a); 9–615(a), (e)].

5. **Noncash Proceeds**
    The value of noncash proceeds received on a disposition of collateral must be applied in a commercially reasonable manner [UCC 9–608(a)(3), 9–615(c)].

6. **Deficiency Judgment**
    In most cases, if a sale of collateral does not repay the debt, the debtor is liable for any deficiency. A creditor can obtain a judgment to collect.

7. **Redemption Rights**
    Before the secured party retains or disposes of the collateral, the debtor or any other secured party can take the collateral by tendering performance of all secured obligations and paying the secured party's expenses [UCC 9–623].

TRUE-FALSE QUESTIONS

(Answers at the Back of the Book)

____   1. A financing statement is not effective if it is filed electronically.

____   2. Attachment gives a creditor an enforceable security interest in collateral.

____   3. A secured creditor's right to proceeds exists for only ten days after the debtor's receipt of the proceeds.

____   4. To be valid, a financing statement does not need to contain a description of the collateral.

____   5. When a secured debt is paid, the secured party does not need to file a termination statement in all cases.

____   6. A security agreement determines most of the parties' rights and duties concerning the security interest.

____   7. A secured party can release the collateral described in a financing statement at any time.

_____ 8. Default occurs most commonly when a debtor fails to repay the loan for which his or her property served as collateral.

_____ 9. After a default, and before a secured party disposes of the collateral, a debtor cannot exercise the right of redemption.

_____ 10. When two secured parties have perfected security interests in the same collateral, generally the most recent to perfect has priority.

FILL-IN QUESTIONS

(Answers at the Back of the Book)

1. Generally, in a secured transaction, the _____ (creditor/debtor) files a financing statement with the appropriate state office. When the debt is paid, the _____ (creditor/debtor) may also send a termination statement to the officer with whom the financing statement was filed.

2. When two or more secured parties have perfected security interests in the same collateral, generally the _____ (first/last) to perfect has priority. When two conflicting security interests are unperfected, the _____ (first/last) to attach has priority.

MULTIPLE-CHOICE QUESTIONS

(Answers at the Back of the Book)

_____ 1. Careful Credit Corporation files a financing statement regarding a transaction with Design Services Company. To be valid, the financing statement must contain all of the following *except*

   a. a description of the collateral.
   b. the debtor's name.
   c. the reason for the transaction.
   d. the secured party's name.

_____ 2. Storage Warehouse, Inc., buys a forklift, but does not make a payment on it for five months. The seller, Tool & Equip Company, repossesses it by towing it from a public street. Storage Warehouse sues Tool & Equip for breach of the peace. The plaintiff will likely

   a. not prevail because Tool & Equip did not use judicial process.
   b. not prevail because Tool & Equip's repossession was not a breach of the peace.
   c. prevail because Storage Warehouse did not default on the loan.
   d. prevail because Tool & Equip's repossession was a breach of the peace.

_____ 3. Benny owns Caffeine Café, which he uses as collateral to borrow $10,000 from Community Bank. To be effective, the security agreement must include

   a. a description that reasonably identifies the collateral only.
   b. a description that reasonably identifies the collateral and Benny's signature.
   c. Benny's signature only.
   d. neither a description that reasonably identifies the collateral nor Benny's signature.

_____ 4. Business Lenders, Inc., asks Craft Works Company to sign a security agreement that provides for coverage of the proceeds from the sale of after-acquired property. This is

   a. a first-in, first-out rule.
   b. a floating lien.
   c. a funds guaranty.
   d. a future advance.

____ 5. Grande Trucks, Inc., repossesses a truck (not a consumer good subject to a purchase-money security interest) from Hiway Transport Company, and decides to keep it instead of reselling it. Grande sends written notice of this intent to the debtor. Grande must also send notice to

    a. any junior lien claimant who has filed a statutory lien or security interest and any secured party from whom Grande has received notice.
    b. only a junior lien claimant who has filed a statutory lien or security interest in the truck.
    c. only a secured party from whom Grande has received notice of a claim in the truck.
    d. none of the choices.

____ 6. Cheep Credit, Inc., has a security interest in the proceeds from the sale of collateral owned by Dazzle Stores Company. This interest may remain perfected for longer than twenty days after Dazzle receives the proceeds

    a. if a filed financing statement covers the proceeds or the proceeds are identifiable cash proceeds.
    b. only if a filed financing statement covers the proceeds.
    c. only if the proceeds are identifiable cash proceeds.
    d. under none of these circumstances.

____ 7. Levon borrows $5,000 from Money Company, which files a financing statement on May 1, but does not sign a security agreement until it disburses the funds on May 5. Levon also borrows $5,000 from Newtown Bank, which advances funds, files a financing statement, and signs a security agreement on May 2. He uses the same property as collateral for both loans. On his default, in a dispute over the collateral, Money Company will

    a. lose because Newtown Bank perfected first.
    b. lose because Newtown Bank's interest attached first.
    c. win because Money Company filed first.
    d. win because Money Company's interest attached first.

____ 8. Whiz Electronics Stores sell consumer products. To create a purchase-money security interest in a 3D HD TV bought by Yang, Whiz must

    a. assign to a collection agent a portion of Whiz's accounts payable
    b. assign to a collecting agent a portion of Whiz's accounts receivable
    c. extend credit for part or all of the purchase price of the computer.
    d. refer Yang to Zippee Cash Company, a third-party lender.

____ 9. Safe-T Loans, Inc., wants to perfect its security interest in collateral owned by Tech Products Corporation. Most likely, Safe-T should file a financing statement with

    a. the city manager.
    b. the county clerk.
    c. the federal loan officer.
    d. the secretary of state.

____ 10. Unbound Sales Company is incorporated in Virginia, with its chief executive office in the state of Washington. Using its equipment as collateral, Unbound borrows $5,000 from XtraCredit, Inc. To perfect its security interest, XtraCredit needs to file its financing statement in

    a. any convenient state.
    b. Virginia only.
    c. Virginia and Washington.
    d. Washington only.

SHORT ESSAY QUESTIONS

1. What is the floating lien concept?

2. What are a secured party's rights on a debtor's default?

GAMEPOINTS

(Answers at the Back of the Book)

1. You are the chief executive officer of Money Games Inc. (MGI), which has begun to market "Borrow & Spend," a video game set in the world of finance. To buy ads, MGI borrows $50,000 from First Savings Bank. On MGI's behalf, you sign a note for the loan and offer its accounts receivable as collateral. You sign a security agreement that describes the collateral. The bank does not file a financing statement. Has the bank's security interest attached? If so, when?

2. In the video game "Fun with Fund$," the goal is to correctly calculate debt, identify the debtors' assets, prioritize the creditors' interests, and accurately balance these categories to come to a financial resolution. In one segment, Agile Corporation borrows $1 million from Hi Finance Company (HFC). Agile signs a financing statement that describes the collateral—its inventory and proceeds—and HFC files the statement in the appropriate state office. Using the same collateral, Agile later borrows $500,000 from Metro Bank, which files its financing statement. Agile defaults on the loans. Metro claims that at the time of its loan it was unaware of HFC's interest. Between these parties, who has priority to the collateral? Why?

SPECIAL INFORMATION FOR CPA CANDIDATES

The importance of the material in this chapter is evident in the number of questions that have been devoted to it on the CPA examination. Traditionally, the UCC made up about 25 percent of the exam, and of that 25 percent, about a third of the questions covered secured transactions. These percentages have been decreased, but these topics are still important. The focus has been on four basic topics: attachment; perfection; priorities; and the rights of debtors, creditors, and others. Also covered: purchase money security interests and the classification of goods as consumer goods, inventory, equipment, or farm products. All of these topics may be touched on in a single problem (or series of questions). To have a good grasp of how these topics interrelate, it may help to keep a diagram of the typical secured transaction in mind.

Chapter 30
Bankruptcy Law *— Always Federal*

WHAT THIS CHAPTER IS ABOUT

This chapter covers bankruptcy law. Congressional authority to regulate bankruptcies comes from Article I, Section 8, of the U.S. Constitution. Bankruptcy law has two goals: (1) protect a debtor by giving him or her a fresh start and (2) ensure equitable treatment to creditors competing for a debtor's assets.

CHAPTER OUTLINE

I. BANKRUPTCY PROCEEDINGS

A. BANKRUPTCY COURTS
Bankruptcy proceedings are held in federal bankruptcy courts under the authority of the federal district courts, to which rulings can be appealed. Anyone liable to a creditor can declare bankruptcy (insolvency is not required).

B. TYPES OF BANKRUPTCY RELIEF
United States Code

The Bankruptcy Code is in Title 11 of the U.S.C.. Chapters 1, 3, and 5 include definitions and provisions governing case administration, creditors, debtors, and estates. Chapter 7 provides for liquidation. Chapter 11 governs reorganizations. Chapters 12 and 13 provide for the adjustment of debts by parties with regular incomes (family farmers under Chapter 12).

C. SPECIAL REQUIREMENTS OF CONSUMER DEBTORS
A clerk of court must provide consumer-debtors (those whose debts arise primarily from purchases of goods for personal or household use) with certain information (details in the text).

II. LIQUIDATION PROCEEDINGS (CHAPTER 7)
This is the most familiar type of bankruptcy proceeding. A debtor declares his or her debts and gives all assets to a trustee, who sells the nonexempt assets and distributes the proceeds to creditors.

A. WHO CAN FILE FOR A LIQUIDATION
Any "person"—individuals, partnerships, and corporations (spouses can file jointly)—except railroads, insurance companies, banks, savings and loan associations, and credit unions.

B. VOLUNTARY BANKRUPTCY

1. **The Debtor Receives Credit Counseling**
A debtor must receive credit counseling from an approved nonprofit agency within 180 days (six months) before filing a petition.

2. **The Debtor Files a Petition with the Court**
A husband and wife may file jointly.

3. **The Debtor Files Schedules (Lists) with the Court**
Within 45 days, a debtor must file forms that list (1) creditors and the debt to each, (2) the debtor's financial affairs, (3) the debtor's property, (4) current income and expenses, (5) payments from employers within the previous 60 days, (6) a certificate proving the receipt of

credit counseling, (7) an itemized calculation of monthly income, and (8) the debtor's most recent federal tax return.

4. The Debtor's Attorney Files an Affidavit
The debtor's attorney, if there is one, must attest to a reasonable attempt to verify the accuracy of the debtor's petition and schedules.

5. The Court or Other Party "of Interest" Asks for More Information
Copies of later federal tax returns may be required. A debtor may need to verify his or her identity.

6. The Court May Dismiss a Petition for Substantial Abuse under the "Means Test"

a. If the Debtor's Family Income Exceeds the Median Family Income in the Geographic Area
Abuse may be presumed, and a creditor can file a motion to dismiss the petition, under this "means test." A debtor can rebut the presumption by showing "special circumstances."

b. If the Debtor's Family Income Does *Not* Exceed the Median Family Income in the Geographic Area
A court can dismiss a petition for bad faith or another factor—for example, that the debtor seeks only an advantage over creditors and his or her financial situation does not warrant a discharge of debts.

7. Other Grounds on which the Court May Dismiss a Petition
If the debtor has been convicted of a crime of violence or drug trafficking, a victim can file a motion to dismiss. Failing to pay post-petition domestic support may also result in a dismissal.

8. Filing of the Petition Constitutes an Order for Relief
The clerk of the court must give the trustee and creditors notice within twenty days.

C. INVOLUNTARY BANKRUPTCY
A debtor's creditors can force the debtor into bankruptcy proceedings.

1. Who Can Be Forced into Involuntary Proceedings
A debtor with twelve or more creditors, three or more of whom (with unsecured claims of at least $13,475) file a petition. A debtor with fewer than twelve creditors, one or more of whom (with a claim of $13,475) files. Not a farmer or a charitable institution.

2. When an Order for Relief Will Be Entered
If the debtor does not challenge the petition, the debtor is generally not paying debts as they come due, or a receiver, assignee, or custodian took possession of the debtor's property within 120 days before the petition was filed.

D. AUTOMATIC STAY
When a petition is filed, an automatic stay suspends all action by creditors against the debtor.

1. Exceptions
These include domestic support obligations (owed to a spouse, former spouse, debtor's child, child's parent or guardian, or the government), related proceedings, securities regulation investigations, property tax liens, prior eviction actions, and withholding to repay retirement account loans.

2. Limitations

a. Request for Relief
A creditor or other party "in interest" can ask for relief from the automatic stay, which then expires in 60 days, unless the court extends it.

b. Secured Debts—Adequate Protection Doctrine
This doctrine protects secured creditors by requiring payments, or other collateral or relief, to the extent that the stay may cause the value of their collateral to decrease.

c. Secured Debts—Other Protection
The stay on secured debts may expire within 30 days of a petition if the debtor had a petition dismissed within the prior year. Two dismissed petitions require a finding of good faith in the current filing before the stay takes effect. A stay on secured property terminates 45 days after the creditors' meeting if the debtor does not redeem the property or reaffirm the debt.

created after stay

E. BANKRUPTCY ESTATE

non-exempt

1. What Property Is Included in the Debtor's Estate
Interests in property presently held; community property; property transferred in a transaction voidable by the trustee; proceeds and profits; certain after-acquired property; interests in gifts, inheritances, property settlements, and life insurance death proceeds to which the debtor becomes entitled within 180 days after filing.

exempt

2. What Property Is Not Included
Property acquired after the filing of the petition except as noted above. Also, withholdings for employee benefit plan contributions are excluded.

F. THE TRUSTEE
After the order for relief, an interim trustee is appointed to preside over the debtor's property until the first meeting of creditors, when a permanent trustee is elected. A trustee's duty is to collect and reduce to money the property of the estate and distribute the proceeds.

1. The Trustee's Duties

a. Initial Duties
A trustee must state whether a filing constitutes substantial abuse under the "means test" (see above) within ten days of the creditors' meeting, notify creditors within five days, and file a motion to dismiss or convert to Chapter 11 (or explain why not) within forty days).

b. Duty with Respect to Domestic Support Obligations
A trustee must provide a party to whom this support is owed with certain information.

2. The Trustee's Powers

a. The Right to Possession of the Debtor's Property
The trustee also can require persons holding a debtor's property when a petition is filed to give the property to the trustee.

b. The Strong-Arm Power
The trustee's position is equivalent in rights to that of certain other parties. A trustee has strong-arm power—the same right as a lien creditor who could have levied execution on the debtor's property.

c. Avoidance Powers
A trustee has specific powers to set aside a transfer of the debtor's property. These powers include any voidable rights and the power to avoid preferences, certain statutory liens, and fraudulent transfers.

d. Liens on the Debtor's Property
A trustee can avoid the fixing of certain statutory liens on a debtor's property.

e. The Debtor Shares Most of the Avoidance Powers
If a trustee does not act to enforce a right, the debtor can.

3. Voidable Rights

A trustee can use any ground—including fraud, duress, incapacity, and mutual mistake—that a debtor can use to obtain return of the debtor's property.

4. Preferences

A trustee can recover a debtor's payment or transfer of property made to a creditor within ninety days before the petition in preference to others.

a. Preferences to Insiders

Transfers to insiders within a year of the petition can be recovered, but the debtor's insolvency at the time of the transfer must be proved.

b. Transfers That Do Not Constitute Preferences

Payment for services rendered within ten to fifteen days before payment is not considered a preference. A consumer-debtor can transfer any property to a creditor up to a certain amount without it constituting a preference. Domestic-support debts and transfers under a credit-counseling service's negotiated schedule are excepted.

5. Fraudulent Transfers

A trustee can avoid fraudulent transfers made within two years of a petition's filing or if they were made with intent to delay, defraud, or hinder a creditor. Transfers for less than reasonably equivalent consideration may also be avoided if, by making them, a debtor became insolvent, was left in business with little capital, or intended to incur debts that he or she could not pay.

G. EXEMPTIONS

1. Federal Law

Federal law exempts such property as interests in a residence to $21,625, a motor vehicle to $3,450, certain household goods to $11,525, tools of a trade to $2,175, and retirement and education savings accounts, and the rights to receive Social Security, domestic support, and other benefits.

2. State Law

Most states preclude the use of federal exemptions; others allow a debtor to choose between state and federal. State exemptions may include different value limits and exempt different property.

H. THE HOMESTEAD EXEMPTION

To use this exemption, a debtor must have lived in the state for two years before filing a petition. If the home was acquired within the previous three and a half years, the exemption is limited to $146,450. In certain cases of substantial abuse and criminal or tortuous acts, no amount is exempt.

I. CREDITORS' MEETING

The trustee calls the creditors' meeting within twenty and forty days of the petition. The debtor must attend (unless excused by the court) and submit to examination under oath. At the meeting, the trustee ensures that the debtor is advised of the potential consequences of bankruptcy and of his or her ability to file for bankruptcy under a different Chapter.

J. CREDITORS' CLAIMS

Within ninety days of the meeting, a creditor must file a proof of claim if its amount is disputed. If the debtor's schedules list a claim as liquidated, proof is not needed.

K. DISTRIBUTION OF PROPERTY   *orderly payout to creditors*

Any amount remaining after the property is distributed to creditors is turned over to the debtor.

1. Secured Creditors

If collateral is surrendered, a secured party can accept it in full satisfaction of the debt or sell it, apply the proceeds to the debt, and become an unsecured creditor for the difference.

2. **Unsecured Creditors**
Paid in the order of priority. Each class is paid before the next class is entitled to anything. The order of priority is—

a. Claims for domestic support obligations (subject to certain administrative costs).
b. Administrative expenses (court costs, trustee and attorney fees).
c. In an involuntary bankruptcy, expenses incurred by a debtor in the ordinary course of business.
d. Unpaid wages, salaries, and commissions earned within ninety days of a petition.
e. Unsecured claims for contributions to employee benefit plans.
f. Claims by farmers and fishers against storage or processing facilities.
g. Consumer deposits.
h. Taxes due to the government.
i. Claims of general creditors.

L. DISCHARGE

1. Exceptions—Debts That May Not Be Discharged
Claims for back taxes, amounts borrowed to pay back taxes, goods obtained by fraud, debts that were not listed in a petition, domestic support, student loans, certain cash advances, and others.

2. Objections—Debtors Who May Not Receive a Discharge
Those who conceal property with intent to hinder, delay, or defraud creditors; who fail to explain a loss of assets; who have been granted a discharge within eight years prior to filing a petition; or who fail to attend a debt management class (unless no class is available).

3. Effect of a Discharge
A discharge voids any judgment on a discharged debt and prohibits any action to collect a discharged debt. A co-debtor's liability is not affected.

4. Revocation of a Discharge
A discharge may be revoked within one year if the debtor was fraudulent or dishonest during the bankruptcy proceedings.

M. REAFFIRMATION OF DEBT
A debtor's agreement to pay a dischargeable debt can be made only after certain disclosures and before a discharge is granted, usually requires court approval, and will be denied if it will cause undue hardship. The debtor can rescind a reaffirmation within sixty days or before a discharge is granted, whichever is later.

III. REORGANIZATIONS (CHAPTER 11)
The creditors and debtor formulate a plan under which the debtor pays a portion of the debts, is discharged of the rest, and continues in business.

A. WHO IS ELIGIBLE FOR RELIEF UNDER CHAPTER 11
Any debtor (except a stockbroker or a commodities broker) who is eligible for Chapter 7 relief is eligible under Chapter 11. With some exceptions, the same principles apply that govern liquidation proceedings (automatic stay, etc.).

B. WHY A CASE MAY BE DISMISSED
A case may be dismissed if this is in the creditors' best interest, there is no reasonable likelihood of rehabilitation, a debtor is unable to affect a plan, or there is an unreasonable delay. Creditors may prefer a *workout* (a privately negotiated settlement) to bankruptcy.

C. DEBTOR IN POSSESSION

On entry of an order for relief, a debtor continues in business as a debtor in possession (DIP).

1. If Gross Mismanagement Is Shown
The court may appoint a trustee (or receiver) to operate the business. This may also be done if it is in the best interests of the estate.

2. The DIP's Role Is Similar to That of a Trustee in a Liquidation

The DIP can avoid pre-petition preferential payments and fraudulent transfers and decide whether to cancel pre-petition executory contracts.

D. CREDITORS' COMMITTEES

A committee of unsecured creditors is appointed to consult with the trustee or DIP. Other committees may represent special-interest creditors. Some small businesses can avoid creditors' committees.

E. THE REORGANIZATION PLAN

1. Who Can File a Plan

Only a debtor can file within the first 120 days (180 days in some cases) after the date of an order for relief. Any other party can file if a debtor does not meet the deadline or fails to obtain creditor consent within 180 days. A court may extend these time periods.

2. What the Plan Must Do

Be fair and equitable ("in the best interests of the creditors"); designate classes of claims and interests; specify the treatment to be afforded the classes; and provide an adequate means for execution; and provide for the payment of tax claims over a fine-year period.

3. The Plan Is Submitted to Creditors for Acceptance

Each class adversely affected by a plan must accept it (two-thirds of the total claims must approve). If only one class accepts, the court may confirm it under the Code's cram-down provision if the plan does not discriminate unfairly against any creditors.

4. Discharge

A plan is binding on confirmation. Claims are not discharged if they would be denied in a liquidation proceeding. An individual debtor is not discharged until a plan's completion.

IV. INDIVIDUALS' REPAYMENT PLANS (CHAPTER 13)

A. WHO IS ELIGIBLE

Individuals (not partnerships or corporations) with regular income and unsecured debts of less than $360,475 or secured debts of less than $1,081,400 are eligible.

B. FILING THE PETITION

A Chapter 13 case can be initiated by voluntary filing of a petition or by conversion of a Chapter 7 case. A debtor must act in good faith at the time of the filing of the plan and the petition. A trustee is appointed.

C. AUTOMATIC STAY

The automatic stay applies to consumer debts but not business debts or domestic-support obligations.

D. THE REPAYMENT PLAN

Only a debtor can file a plan, which must provide for (1) turnover to the trustee of the debtor's future income, (2) full payment of all claims entitled to priority, and (3) the same treatment of each claim within a particular class.

1. Confirming the Plan

A court will confirm a plan (1) if the secured creditors accept it, (2) if it provides that secured creditors retain their liens until there is full payment or a discharge, or (3) if a debtor surrenders property that secures claims to the creditors. Also, a creditor with a purchase-money security interest in a car bought within 910 days before a filing must be paid in full.

2. Payments under the Plan

The time for payment is five years if a debtor's income exceeds the state's median under the "means test" (see above) and three years if it does not. Payments must be timely, or the court can convert the case to a liquidation or dismiss the petition.

E. DISCHARGE
After completion of payments, debts provided for by the plan are discharged. Many debts (tax claims, domestic support obligations, student loans, and others) are not dischargeable. A discharge obtained by fraud can be revoked within one year.

V. FAMILY-FARMER AND FAMILY-FISHERMAN PLANS (CHAPTER 12)
The procedures and requirements under Chapter 12 are nearly identical to those under Chapter 13. Eligible debtors include family farmers and fishermen.

A. FAMILY FARMERS
A family farmer is one whose gross income is at least 50 percent farm dependent and whose debts are at least 50 percent farm related (total debt must not exceed $3,792,650). A partnership or closely held corporation (at least 50 percent owned by a farm family) can also qualify.

B. FAMILY FISHERMEN
A family fisherman is one whose gross income is at least 50 percent dependent on commercial fishing and whose debts are at least 80 percent related to commercial fishing (total debt must not exceed $1,757,475). A partnership or closely held corporation (at least 50 percent owned by a farm family) can also qualify.

TRUE-FALSE QUESTIONS
(Answers at the Back of the Book)

____ 1. A debtor must be insolvent to file a voluntary petition under Chapter 7.

____ 2. The filing of a petition for bankruptcy will not stay most legal actions against the debtor.

____ 3. Generally, in a bankruptcy proceeding, any creditor's claim is allowed.

____ 4. With some exceptions, the same principles cover liquidations and reorganizations.

____ 5. Under Chapter 13, a bankruptcy may be commenced by voluntary petition only.

____ 6. Under Chapter 13, the automatic stay applies only to consumer debts, not business debts.

____ 7. Under Chapter 13, a discharge obtained by fraud can be revoked within one year.

____ 8. A business debtor who files for Chapter 11 protection cannot continue in business.

____ 9. No small business can avoid creditors' committees under Chapter 11.

____ 10. Bankruptcy proceedings are held in state bankruptcy courts under state law.

FILL-IN QUESTIONS
(Answers at the Back of the Book)

Liquidation is the purpose of Chapter _____ (7/11/13). Reorganization is the purpose of Chapter _____ (7/11/13). Adjustment is the purpose of Chapter _____ (7/11/13). Under Chapter _____ (7/11/13), nonexempt property is sold, with proceeds distributed in a certain priority to classes of creditors, and dischargeable debts are terminated. Under Chapter _____ (7/11/13), a plan for reorganization is submitted, and if it is approved and followed, debts are discharged. Under Chapter _____ (7/11/13), a plan must be approved if the debtor turns over all disposable income for a five-year period, after which debts are discharged. The advantages of Chapter _____ (7/11/13) include the debtor's opportunity for a fresh start. The advantages of Chapter _____ (7/11/13) include the debtor's continuation in business under a plan that allows for reorganization of debts. The advantages of Chapter ____ (7/11/13) include the debtor's continuation in business and discharge of many debts.

MULTIPLE-CHOICE QUESTIONS

(Answers at the Back of the Book)

____ 1. Ciera is the sole proprietor of Caliente Café, which owes debts in an amount more than Ciera believes she and the café can repay. The creditors agree that liquidating the business would not be in their best interests. To file for bankruptcy yet stay in business, Ciera's best option is

a. Chapter 7 (liquidation).
b. Chapter 9 (municipalities).
c. Chapter 11 (reorganization) or Chapter 13 (adjustment).
d. Chapter 12 (family farmers or fishermen).

____ 2. Wilder's monthly income is $3,500, his monthly expenses are $3,000, and his debts are nearly $25,000. If he applied the difference between his income and expenses to pay off the debts, they could be eliminated within five years. This situation is covered by

a. Chapter 7 (liquidation).
b. Chapter 11 (reorganization).
c. Chapter 13 (adjustment).
d. no chapter of the bankruptcy code.

____ 3. Main St. Corporation has not paid any of its fifteen creditors, six of whom have unsecured claims of more than $8,000. The creditors can force Main St. into bankruptcy under

a. Chapter 7 (liquidation) only.
b. Chapter 7 (liquidation) or Chapter 11 (reorganization).
c. Chapter 11 (reorganization) only.
d. no chapter of the bankruptcy code.

____ 4. Vance files a bankruptcy petition under Chapter 7 to have his debts discharged. Assuming Vance passes the appropriate test, the debts most likely to be discharged include claims for

a. back taxes accruing within three years before the petition was filed.
b. certain fines and penalties payable to the government.
c. domestic support.
d. student loans, if the payment would impose undue hardship on Bob.

____ 5. Rochelle's monthly income is $2,000, her monthly expenses are $2,800, and her debts are nearly $40,000. A debtor in Rochelle's position would most likely find relief under

a. Chapter 7 (liquidation).
b. Chapter 11 (reorganization).
c. Chapter 12 (family farmers or fishermen).
d. Chapter 13 (adjustment).

____ 6. Dixie and Elbert make down payments on goods to be received from Fresh Wood Furniture Store. Before the goods are delivered, Fresh Wood files for bankruptcy. Besides consumers like Dixie and Elbert, Fresh Wood owes wages to its employees and taxes to the government. The order in which these debts will be paid is most likely

a. consumer deposits, unpaid wages, and taxes.
b. taxes, consumer deposits, and unpaid wages.
c. unpaid wages, consumer deposits, and taxes.
d. unpaid wages, taxes, and consumer deposits.

___ **7.** **Based on a Sample CPA Exam Question.** Carlotta files a Chapter 7 petition for a discharge in bankruptcy. She may be denied a discharge if she

    a. fails to explain a loss of assets.
    b. fails to list a debt.
    c. owes back taxes.
    d. owes domestic support payments.

___ **8.** Ophelia is appointed trustee of Pollyanna's estate in bankruptcy. To collect the property of the estate, Ophelia can set aside

    a. a payment within the course of business and a transfer within ninety days to one creditor.
    b. a payment within the course of business only.
    c. a transfer within ninety days prior to the petition's filing in preference to one creditor.
    d. neither a payment within the course of business nor a transfer within ninety days to one creditor.

___ **9.** Riche Niche Stores, Inc., files for bankruptcy. A corporation can file a petition for bankruptcy under

    a. Chapter 7 (liquidation) only.
    b. Chapter 7 (liquidation) or Chapter 11 (reorganization).
    c. Chapter 11 (reorganization) only.
    d. no chapter of the bankruptcy code.

___ **10.** As a bankruptcy trustee, Milton has the power to avoid

    a. domestic-support obligations, child support, and alimony.
    b. fraudulent transfers, preferences, and transactions the debtor could rightfully avoid.
    c. claims by creditors who were not notified of the bankruptcy.
    d. property taxes, income taxes, and amounts borrowed by the debtor to pay taxes.

SHORT ESSAY QUESTIONS

1. Compare Chapters 7, 11, 12, and 13, discussing, for each chapter, the purpose or function, who is eligible for relief, whether proceedings can be initiated voluntarily or involuntarily, procedures leading to discharge, and the advantages.

2. How are secured creditors protected from losing the value of their security as a result of an automatic stay?

GAMEPOINTS

(Answers at the Back of the Book)

1. You download apps to play a variety of video games on your cell phone. You find these games so addictive that despite increasingly negative consequences—a car accident, a divorce, and the loss of your job—you continue to play incessantly. As your debts mount, including unpaid alimony and support, you attend a credit-counseling briefing before filing a bankruptcy petition. Your estate in property is practically nothing but you are unable to satisfactorily explain the lack of assets. Are any of these facts grounds for denying you a discharge under Chapter 7?

2. You start an enterprise to create, develop, and sell video games. But you have an inadequate business plan and lack sufficient financing. Your attempt to cover these mistakes by maxing out credit cards and failing to pay bills only leads to more debt. You have a total of ten unsecured creditors, including Grouper & Halibut, Accountants, whom you owe $15,000. Can Grouper & Halibut file an involuntary Chapter 11 bankruptcy petition against you? Why or why not?

SPECIAL INFORMATION FOR CPA CANDIDATES

On the CPA examination, bankruptcy is tested as part of the section on creditors and debtors, which also tests on the material in the previous chapter. Topics that have been tested in the past include the requirements for filing for bankruptcy under Chapter 7, the basic steps of a bankruptcy, a general knowledge of Chapter 11 and Chapter 13, and specific coverage of preferential transfers, discharge, and debts that are not discharged in a bankruptcy proceeding. The priority of those with competing claims to the collateral is also usually included in questions on the exam.

Chapter 31
Mortgages and Foreclosures after the Recession

WHAT THIS CHAPTER IS ABOUT

The focus of this chapter is on the terms of a mortgage, the different types of mortgage loans available, the characteristics of mortgage fraud, and the law's requirements, prohibitions, penalties, and rewards for each.

CHAPTER OUTLINE

I. MORTGAGES

An individual who buys real property typically borrows the funds from a financial institution to pay for it. A mortgage is a written instrument that gives the creditor an interest in, or a line on, the property as security for the payment.

A. TYPES OF MORTGAGES

A mortgage loan is a contract. A down payment is a part of the purchase price paid in cash. In many cases, borrowers under adjustable-rate mortgages, interest-only mortgages, and balloon mortgages hope to refinance (pay off the original mortgage and obtain a new one on better terms).

1. Fixed-Rate Mortgages

A fixed-rate mortgage is a standard mortgage with a fixed rate of interest. Payments are the same for its duration. The interest rate may be based on the borrower's credit history, credit score, income, and debts.

2. Adjustable-Rate Mortgages (ARMs)

The interest rate on an adjustable-rate mortgage changes periodically. The rate may begin low and fixed. After a certain time, and at certain intervals, the rate adjusts. The adjustment consists of a specified number of points added to an index rate. Most ARMs limit the amount that the rate can increase over the duration of the loan.

3. Interest-Only (IO) Mortgages

An interest-only mortgage gives a borrower the option to pay only the interest portion of the monthly payments for an initial, limited time. The size of the payments then increases to include the principal. The interest on an IO mortgage may be fixed-rate or adjustable.

4. Subprime Mortgages

A subprime mortgage is a loan to a borrower who does not qualify for a standard mortgage. Because subprime borrowers default at a higher rate, subprime mortgages carry higher rates of interest. A subprime mortgage may be a fixed-rate, adjustable-rate, or interest-only loan.

5. Construction Loans

A borrower uses the funds from a construction loan to build a new house. The loan may feature a schedule of draws, with payouts timed to phases of construction.

241

6. **Participation Loans**
   A participation loan gives the lender a percentage of revenue, rental income, or resale income from the property that the loan finances. This may be in exchange for a lower interest rate or a lower down payment requirement.

7. **Balloon Mortgages**
   A balloon mortgage starts with low payments for a specified period, with the balance of the loan due at the end. Borrowers often refinance balloon mortgages on their due dates.

8. **Hybrid and Reverse Mortgages**
   A hybrid mortgage starts as a fixed-rate mortgage and converts into an ARM. A reverse mortgage pays an existing homeowner for the equity in a home. The reverse mortgage is repaid when the home is sold.

B. **HOME EQUITY LOANS**
   Home equity is the portion of a home's value that is not subject to a mortgage. As a loan is paid, equity accrues. A home equity loan is secured by this amount, which can be seized if the loan is not repaid. A home equity is subordinate to a mortgage loan.

C. **CREDITOR PROTECTION**

1. **Insurance and Perfection**
   Creditors can protect their interests through—

   a. *Private mortgage insurance.* If the debtor defaults, the insurer reimburses the creditor for a portion of the loan.

   b. *Recording a mortgage in the appropriate county office.* This perfects the creditor's interest in the property. On the debtor's default, a creditor who has not perfected his or her interest may have the priority of an unsecured creditor.

2. **Statute of Frauds**
   A mortgage must be in writing to be enforceable, but it is not otherwise required to follow a particular form.

3. **Important Mortgage Provisions**
   Terms may include—

   a. Loan terms—the amount, the interest rate, the period of repayment, and others.
   b. Provisions for the maintenance of the property.
   c. A statement obligating the borrower to maintain homeowners' insurance.
   d. A list of the borrower's non-loan financial obligations—property taxes and so on.
   e. A provision for the borrower's payment of regular and ordinary expenses associated with the property—taxes, insurance, and other assessments—through the lender.

II. REAL ESTATE FINANCING LAW
Congress and the Federal Reserve Board impose disclosure requirements and certain prohibitions on lenders to protect borrowers from improper lending practices.

A. **PREDATORY LENDING AND OTHER IMPROPER PRACTICES**

1. **Fraud**
   Predatory lending practices that occur during the loan origination process include failing to disclose terms, providing misleading information, and lying.

2. **Steering and Targeting**
   A lender manipulates a borrower into a loan that benefits the lender but is not the best loan for the borrower.

3. **Loan Flipping**
   A lender convinces a borrower to refinance soon after a mortgage term begins.

B. THE TRUTH-IN-LENDING ACT (TILA)

The Truth-in-Lending Act (TILA) of 1968 requires lenders to disclose the terms of a loan in clear, readily understandable language so that borrowers can make rational choices. In real estate transactions, TILA applies only to residential loans.

1. Required Disclosures

Disclosure must be made on standardized forms and based on uniform formulas. Certain loans—ARMs, reverse mortgages, open-ended home equity loans, and high-interest loans—have special requirements. For all loans, terms that must be disclosed include—

a. Loan principal.
b. Interest rate at which the loan is made.
c. Annual percentage rate (APR), which is the actual cost of the loan on a yearly basis.
d. All fees and costs associated with the loan.

2. Prohibitions and Requirements

Prepayment penalties cannot be charged on most subprime mortgages and home equity loans. A lender cannot coerce an appraiser into misstating the value of property on which a loan is to be issued. A loan cannot be advertised as fixed-rate if its rate or payment amounts fluctuate.

a. Right to Rescind

A mortgage cannot be finalized until seven or more days after a borrower receives TILA paperwork. A borrower has the right to rescind a mortgage within three business days (Sunday is the only non-business day). If a lender does not provide the required disclosures, the rescission period runs for three years.

b. Written Representations

The disclosure requirements apply to written materials but not oral representations.

C. PROTECTION FOR HIGH-COST MORTGAGE LOAN RECIPIENTS

The Home Ownership and Equity Protection Act (HOEPA) of 1994 amended TILA to create a special category of high-cost and high-fee mortgage products. Rules for the loans are in Regulation Z (enacted by the Federal Reserve Board to implement TILA).

1. Which Loans Are Covered?

The rules apply to loans for which—

a. The APR exceeds the interest rate on Treasury securities of comparable maturity by more than 8 percentage points for a first mortgage and 10 points for a second mortgage.
b. The total fees exceed 8 percent of the loan amount or a dollar amount based on the consumer price index, whichever is larger.

2. Special Consumer Protections

a. Disclosures

In addition to the TILA disclosures, HOEPA requires lenders to disclose—

1) The APR, the regular payment amount, and any balloon payments.
2) For a loan with a variable interest rate, the possibility that the rate and payment amounts may increase and to what potential maximum the increase may be.
3) The borrower's option not to complete the loan simply because of the disclosures or the signing of a loan application.
4) The possible loss of the home financed by the loan if the borrower defaults.

b. Prohibitions

HOEPA prohibits lenders from—

1) Requiring a balloon payment on a loan with a term of five years or less.

2) Issuing a loan that results in negative amortization (this occurs when payments do not cover the interest due and the difference is added to the principal, thus increasing the balance).

3) Assuming the status of a holder in due course as a mortgage assignee, thus subjecting an assignee to all claims and defenses the borrower could have asserted against the original lender.

3. Remedies and Liabilities

On a lender's material failure to disclose, a consumer may receive damages in an amount equal to all finance charges and fees paid. On a lender's failure to comply with HOEPA, the borrower's right to rescind is extended to three years.

D. PROTECTION FOR HIGHER-PRICED MORTGAGE LOANS

Higher-Priced Mortgage Loans (HPMLs) are a second category of expensive loans under Regulation Z.

1. Requirements to Qualify

To qualify as an HPML, a mortgage must—

a. Secure a borrower's principal home.
b. Have, if the loan is a *first lien*, an APR that exceeds the average prime offer rate for a comparable transaction by 1.5 percentage points or more.
c. Have, if the loan is a *subordinate lien*, an APR that exceeds the average prime offer rate for a comparable transaction by 3.5 percentage points or more.
d. Not be a mortgage for initial construction, a bridge loan (a temporary loan with a term of one year or less), a home equity line of credit, and a reverse mortgage.

2. Special Protections for Consumers

For an HPML loan, a lender—

a. Cannot base a loan on the value of a borrower's home without verifying the borrower's ability to repay it. This can be done through a review of the borrower's financial records—tax returns, bank account statements, payroll records, and credit obligations.
b. Cannot impose prepayment penalties on a loan for longer than two years.
c. Cannot impose any prepayment penalties on a loan if the source to pay them is a refinancing by the lender.
d. Must establish an escrow account for a borrower's insurance and tax payments for a first mortgage.
e. Cannot structure a loan to evade these protections.

III. FORECLOSURES

If a borrower defaults, or fails to pay a loan, the lender can foreclose on the mortgaged property. The foreclosure process allows a lender to repossess and auction the property. A foreclosure can be expensive and remains on a borrower's credit report for seven years.

A. HOW TO AVOID FORECLOSURE

1. Forbearance and Workout Agreements

a. *Forbearance*—the postponement of part or all of the payments of a loan in danger of foreclosure. This may be based on a borrower's securing a new job, selling the property, or some other factor.

b. *Workout*—a voluntary attempt to cure a default. A workout agreement sets out the parties' rights and responsibilities (for example, a lender may agree to delay foreclosure in exchange for a borrower's financial information).

2. Housing and Urban Development Assistance

An interest-free loan may be obtained from the U.S. Department of Housing and Urban Development (HUD) to bring the mortgage current. A loan must be between four and twelve months delinquent, and the borrower must be able to make full payments. A HUD loan is a subordinate lien that comes due when the property is sold.

3. **Short Sales**
    A short sale is a sale of the property for less than the balance due on a mortgage loan. A borrower—who typically must show some hardship—sells the property with the lender's consent. The lender gets the proceeds. If the lender does not forgive the balance, the borrower owes the deficiency. A short sale mitigates some costs but can affect a borrower's credit rating.

4. **Sale and Leaseback**
    An investor may buy a property and lease it back to its former owner for less than the mortgage payments. The seller-owner pays off the mortgage with the sale proceeds.

5. **Home Affordable Modification Program**
    The U.S. Treasury Department's Home Affordable Modification Program (HAMP) encourages private lenders to modify mortgages to lower the monthly payments of borrowers in default (to 31 percent of the debtor's gross monthly income). HAMP may share a lender's costs to modify a loan and provides other incentives.

    a. **Determination If a Homeowner Qualifies**
        To qualify for a HAMP modification—

        1) A loan must have originated on or before January 1, 2009.
        2) A home must be its owner's primary residence and must be occupied by its owner.
        3) A loan's unpaid balance must not exceed $729,750 for a single-unit property.
        4) A homeowner must be facing verifiable financial hardship.
        5) Mortgage payments must be more than sixty days late or a homeowner must be at risk of imminent default.

    b. **Steps Taken to Alleviate the Mortgage Burden**
        A loan is restructured by adding delinquencies—unpaid interest, taxes, or insurance premiums—to the principal and cutting the interest rate so that a borrower's payments are 31 percent of his or her gross monthly income. If the rate would be less than 2 percent, a lender can re-amortize the loan, extending the payments for up to forty years.

6. **Voluntary Conveyance**
    A deed in lieu of foreclosure conveys property to a lender in satisfaction of a mortgage. The lender thereby avoids the time, risk, and expense of foreclosure. The borrower avoids foreclosure's negative effects. This option works best when the property's value is close to the outstanding loan principal and there are no other loans on it.

7. **Friendly Foreclosure**
    This occurs when a homeowner agrees to submit to a court's jurisdiction, waive any defenses and the right to appeal, and cooperate with the lender. This can create certainty as to the finality of the transaction with respect to others with a financial interest in the property.

8. **Prepackaged Bankruptcy**
    A prepackaged bankruptcy allows a borrower to negotiate the terms with his or her creditors in advance. This effort can save all of the parties' time and expense.

B. **THE FORECLOSURE PROCEDURE**
    A formal foreclosure extinguishes a borrower's equitable right of redemption. The two most common types of foreclosure are judicial foreclosure and power of sale foreclosure. In the former—available in all states—a court supervises the process. In the latter—available in only a few states—a lender forecloses on and sells the property without court supervision.

1. **Acceleration Clauses**

   An acceleration clause allows a lender to call an entire loan due, even if only one payment is missed. Without this clause in a mortgage contract, a lender might have to foreclose on smaller amounts over a period of time as individual payments are missed.

2. **Notice of Default (NOD) and of Sale**

   Filing a notice of default with the appropriate state office initiates a foreclosure. The borrower is put on notice to take steps to pay the loan and cure the default. If this does not occur, the lender gives a notice of sale to the borrower, posts it on the property, files it with the county, and announces it in a newspaper. The property is then sold at auction on the courthouse steps.

3. **Deficiency Judgments**

   If sale proceeds do not cover the amount of the loan, the lender can ask a court for a deficiency judgment. Some states do not permit deficiency judgments for mortgaged residential property.

C. **REDEMPTION RIGHTS**

1. **Equitable Right of Redemption**

   In all states, a borrower can buy the property after default by paying the amount of the debt, plus interest and costs, *before* the foreclosure sale.

2. **Statutory Right of Redemption**

   In some sates, a borrower can buy the property *after* a judicial foreclosure and sale of the property at auction to a third party. The borrower pays the redemption price, plus taxes, interest, and assessments. This right may exist for up to a year after the sale. Some states allow the borrower to retain possession of the property until the redemption period ends.

TRUE-FALSE QUESTIONS

(Answers at the Back of the Book)

____ 1. Steering and targeting occur when a lender convinces a homeowner to refinance soon after obtaining a mortgage.

____ 2. The loan that a lender provides to enable a borrower to purchase real property is a recession.

____ 3. In any case, a borrower has up to seven business days to rescind a mortgage.

____ 4. Federal disclosure requirements apply only to written materials that a mortgage lender provides.

____ 5. Foreclosure allows a lender to legally repossess and auction off the property securing a loan.

____ 6. The annual percentage rate is the mortgage interest rate offered to the least qualified borrowers as established by a survey of potential borrowers.

____ 7. There are additional disclosure requirements for a loan that carries a high rate of interest or entails high fees for the borrower.

____ 8. A lender can make a higher-priced mortgage loan based on the value of the consumer's home without verifying the consumer's ability to repay the loan.

____ 9. On foreclosure, if a mortgage is not paid within a reasonable time after a notice of default, the property securing the loan can be sold without notice to the buyer.

____ 10. A deficiency judgment requires a borrower to pay the debt remaining after collateral is sold.

FILL-IN QUESTIONS

(Answers at the Back of the Book)

A standard mortgage with an unchanging rate of interest is _____ (a fixed-rate/an adjustable-rate/an interest-only) mortgage. A mortgage in which the rate of interest paid by the borrower changes periodically is _____ (a fixed-rate/an adjustable-rate/an interest-only) mortgage. A mortgage under which the borrower can choose to pay only the interest portion of the monthly payment for a specified period of time is _____ (a fixed-rate/an adjustable-rate/an interest-only) mortgage.

A loan made to a borrower who does not qualify for a standard mortgage is a _____ (home equity loan/hybrid mortgage/subprime mortgage). A loan that starts as a fixed-rate mortgage and then converts into an adjustable-rate mortgage is a _____ (home equity loan/hybrid mortgage/subprime mortgage). A loan for which the lender accepts the borrower's equity in his or her home as collateral, which can be seized if the loan is not repaid on time, is a _____ (home equity loan/hybrid mortgage/subprime mortgage).

MULTIPLE-CHOICE QUESTIONS

(Answers at the Back of the Book)

____ **1.** New England Bank provides a loan to enable Martine to buy real property. This loan is

   a. a down payment
   b. a mortgage.
   c. a short sale.
   d. a workout agreement.

____ **2.** Pacific Bank provides Ogden with a standard mortgage with an unchanging rate of interest to buy a home. Payments on the loan remain the same for the duration of the mortgage. This is

   a. a fixed-rate mortgage.
   b. an adjustable-rate mortgage.
   c. an interest-only mortgage.
   d. a violation of the law.

____ **3.** Selma borrows $125,000 from Riverview Credit Union to buy a home. Among the terms that must be disclosed under federal law is the annual percentage rate. This is

   a. the actual cost of the loan on a yearly basis.
   b. the average prime offer rate.
   c. the interest rate at which the loan is made.
   d. the loan principal.

____ **4.** Igor applies to Hometown Mortgage Company for $80,000 to buy a home. Hometown steers Igor toward an adjustable-rate mortgage even though he qualifies for a fixed-rate mortgage. This is

   a. a short sale.
   b a subprime mortgage.
   c. loan flipping.
   d. steering and targeting.

___ 5. Lizette borrows $110,000 from Main Street Bank to buy a home. Federal law regulates primarily

   a. mortgage terms that must be disclosed in writing.
   b. oral representations with respect to the terms of a loan.
   c. the lowest prices for which real property can be sold.
   d. who can buy real property, where they can buy it, and why.

___ 6. **Based on a Sample CPA Exam Question.** Dylan borrows $150,000 from Countywide Credit Union to buy a home. By recording the mortgage, Countywide protects its

   a. priority against a previously filed lien on the property.
   b. priority against any party with an earlier claim to the property.
   c. rights against Dylan.
   d. rights against the claims of later buyers of the property.

___ 7. Bayside Credit Corporation makes mortgage loans to consumers secured by their principal homes. For a Bayside loan to qualify as a Higher-Priced Mortgage Loan (HPML), its annual percentage rate must exceed, by a certain amount,

   a. the average prime offer rate for a comparable transaction.
   b. the consumer's income-to-debt ratio.
   c. the percentage of income that a consumer can devote to its payment.
   d. the projected increase in market value of the consumer's home.

___ 8. Upstate Bank has made mortgage loans to consumers that qualify for the Home Affordable Modification Program (HAMP), which offers incentives to lenders to change the terms of certain loans. The purpose of HAMP is to

   a. convey property through lenders to consumers who can afford it.
   b. force lenders to forgive all high-risk mortgages.
   c. reduce monthly payments to levels that homeowners can pay.
   d. transfer affordable property to investors to lease to consumers.

___ 9. Duke borrows $150,000 from Community Bank to buy a home. If he fails to make payments on the mortgage, the bank has the right to repossess and auction off the property securing the loan. This is

   a. a short sale.
   b. forbearance.
   c. foreclosure.
   d. the equitable right of redemption.

___ 10. Shirley borrows $100,000 from Ridgetop Credit Union to buy a home, which secures the loan. Three years into the term, she stops making payments on it. Ridgetop repossesses and auctions off the property to Toby. The sale proceeds are not enough to cover the unpaid amount of the loan. In most states, Ridgetop can ask a court for

   a. a deficiency judgment.
   b. a reverse mortgage.
   c. a short sale.
   d. nothing.

SHORT ESSAY QUESTIONS

1. How does the law protect borrowers from the lending practices that led to the recent recession?

2. What protection exists for borrowers who take out high-cost, high-fee, or higher-priced mortgages from the lending practices that led to the recession?

GAMEPOINTS

(Answers at the Back of the Book)

1. In the video game "Block x Block," your avatar Blockhead is the executive loan officer for Alpha Mortgage & Credit Company. At this point in the game, Carlotta asks to borrow funds from Alpha to start a new business. She has $100,000 equity in her home. You offer her a $75,000 loan for ten years at an interest rate of 4.25. She accepts. On the day of the closing, a fifteen-year Treasury bond is yielding 2.25 percent. Carlotta pays $4,000 in fees to Alpha. Six weeks later, she sells her interest in the new business to Darwin and wants to rescind the Alpha loan. Which federal law covers this loan? On what basis—if any—might she be able to rescind it?

2. Still playing "Block x Block" your avatar is approached by Edgar. Earlier, Blockhead approved a loan to Edgar to buy a home. The amount was $110,000 at a fixed rate of 5.25 percent with a thirty-tear term secured by the home. Now, having paid $7,500 of the mortgage, Edgar says that he lost his job and wants to defer the payments on the mortgage for six months when he will start a new job. In the current market, the value of Edgar's home has decreased to $85,000. What are methods by which Blockhead could recover the outstanding amount of the mortgage for Alpha?

SPECIAL INFORMATION FOR CPA CANDIDATES

On the CPA examination, mortgages and foreclosure is tested as part of the section on property, which also covers the material on estates, real property, and landlord-tenant law (see Chapter 50) and insurance (see Chapter 51). Topics that have been tested in the past include the formalities in the execution of mortgage agreements—a mortgage is considered an interest in real property and thus must be in writing and signed by the party to be charged. A mortgage must meet the requirements of a deed, and it must be recorded to be enforceable against later parties with a bona fide interest.

The exam may also ask about the rights of the parties to a mortgage. For example, the borrower has the right to possess, lease, and sell the property. The lender has the right to exercise a lien or foreclose on the loan, and to assign it to a third party. The borrower, of course, has a right of redemption. There may also be questions that involve what happens to a mortgage on a sale of the property.

CUMULATIVE HYPOTHETICAL PROBLEM FOR UNIT SIX—INCLUDING CHAPTERS 28–31

(Answers at the Back of the Book)

Clearview 3D, Inc., sells 3D technology to television-set and other viewing-monitor makers.

____ **1.** Dylan fixes the roof of Clearview's warehouse, but Clearview does not pay. Everly repairs one of Clearview's trucks, but Clearview does not pay. Everly keeps the truck. Dylan and Everly place a mechanic's lien and an artisan's lien on Clearview's property. Before foreclosure, notice must be given to Clearview by

   a. Dylan and Everly.
   b. Dylan only.
   c. Everly only.
   d. neither Dylan nor Everly.

____ **2.** In the course of business, Clearview borrows money from Fidelity Bank. Grant co-signs the loan as a surety. Clearview defaults on the loan, and Grant pays the entire amount. To collect from Clearview, Grant has the right of

    a. contribution.
    b. exemption.
    c. exoneration.
    d. subrogation.

____ **3.** Clearview buys office supplies from Home & Business Office Products. Home & Business finances the purchase, accepts the supplies as security, and perfects its interest. Under UCC Article 9, the perfection of a security interest will *not* affect the rights of

    a. a buyer in the ordinary course of business.
    b. a debtor.
    c. a subsequent secured creditor.
    d. a trustee in a debtor's bankruptcy.

____ **4.** Clearview files a voluntary petition in bankruptcy under Chapter 11. A reorganization plan is filed with the court. Normally, the court will confirm a Chapter 11 plan if it is accepted by

    a. Clearview.
    b. Clearview's secured creditors.
    c. Clearview's shareholders.
    d. Clearview's unsecured creditors.

____ **5.** Clearview's Chapter 11 plan is confirmed, and a final decree is entered. Clearview will be

    a. discharged from all debts except as otherwise provided by the law.
    b. liquidated.
    c. operated in business by the bankruptcy trustee.
    d. required to change its business purpose.

QUESTIONS ON THE FOCUS ON ETHICS FOR UNIT SIX— CREDITORS' RIGHTS AND BANKRUPTCY

(Answers at the Back of the Book)

____ **1.** Evermore Credit Agency, Inc., utilizes "self-help" repossession on its debtors' defaults. This remedy simplifies the process of repossession because

    a. it can be done without judicial process.
    b. it is less stressful for debtors.
    c. it provides an incentive for confrontations with debtors.
    d. the UCC clearly defines what constitutes "breach of the peace."

____ **2.** Farmers & Ranchers Bank lends money to Eldon, a vintner (a grape cultivator and winemaker), and the owners of other agricultural enterprises within its region. To compensate for the higher risk of bankruptcy among its debtors when the prices of agricultural products decrease, the bank can

    a. become less selective in granting credit.
    b. increase the interest rate charged to a few borrowers.
    c. increase the interest rate charged to everyone.
    d. require less security (collateral).

____ **3.** Creekside Credit Union lends money to Barton, taking a security interest in his assets. Later, Barton files a bankruptcy petition. From the bank's point of view, once Barton is in bankruptcy, his assets have

    a. diminished value, or no value.
    b. enhanced, or greater, value.
    c. the same value as before the petition.
    d. unique value.

Chapter 32
Agency Formation and Duties

WHAT THIS CHAPTER IS ABOUT

This chapter covers some of the aspects of agency relationships, including how they are formed and the duties involved. An agency relationship involves two parties: the principal and the agent. Agency relationships are essential to a corporation, which can function and enter into contracts only through its agents.

CHAPTER OUTLINE

I. AGENCY RELATIONSHIPS

In an agency relationship, the parties agree that the agent will act on behalf and instead of the principal in negotiating and transacting business with third persons.

A. EMPLOYER-EMPLOYEE RELATIONSHIPS

Normally, all employees who deal with third parties are deemed to be agents. Statutes covering workers' compensation and so on apply only to employer-employee relationships.

B. EMPLOYER–INDEPENDENT CONTRACTOR RELATIONSHIPS

Those who hire independent contractors have no control over the details of their physical performance. Independent contractors can be agents.

C. DETERMINATION OF EMPLOYEE STATUS

The greater an employer's control over the work, the more likely it is that the worker is an employee. Another key factor is whether the employer withholds taxes from payments to the worker and pays unemployment and Social Security taxes covering the worker.

II. FORMATION OF THE AGENCY RELATIONSHIP

Consideration is not required. In most states, a principal must have the capacity to contract, but anyone—including a minor—can be an agent. An agency can be created for any legal purpose.

A. AGENCY BY AGREEMENT

Normally, an agency must be based on an agreement that the agent will act for the principal. Such an agreement can be an express written contract or can be implied by conduct.

B. AGENCY BY RATIFICATION

A person who is not an agent (or who is an agent acting outside the scope of his or her authority) may make a contract on behalf of another (a principal). If the principal approves or affirms that contract by word or by action, an agency relationship is created by ratification (see Chapter 33).

C. AGENCY BY ESTOPPEL

1. The Principal's Actions

When a principal causes a third person to believe that another person is his or her agent, and the third person deals with the supposed agent, the principal is estopped to deny the agency relation.

2. The Third Party's Reasonable Belief

The third person must prove that he or she reasonably believed that an agency relationship existed and that the agent had authority—that an ordinary, prudent person familiar with business practice and custom would have been justified in concluding that the agent had authority.

D. AGENCY BY OPERATION OF LAW

A court may find an agency relationship in the absence of a formal agreement. This may occur in family relationships or in an emergency, when the agent's failure to act outside the scope of his or her authority would cause the principal substantial loss.

III. DUTIES OF AGENTS AND PRINCIPALS

The principal-agent relationship is fiduciary.

A. AGENT'S DUTIES TO THE PRINCIPAL

1. Performance

An agent must use reasonable diligence and skill (the degree of skill of a reasonable person under similar circumstances), unless an agent claims special skills (such as those of an accountant), in which case the agent is expected to use those skills.

2. Notification

An agent must notify the principal of all matters concerning the agency. Notice to the agent is considered to be notice to the principal.

3. Loyalty

An agent must act solely for the principal's benefit (not in the interest of the agent or a third party).

a. Confidentiality

Any information or knowledge acquired through the agency relationship is confidential. It cannot be disclosed during the agency or after its termination.

b. Agent's Loyalty Must Be Undivided

An agent employed by a principal to buy cannot buy from himself or herself, and an agent employed to sell cannot become the purchaser, without the principal's consent.

4. Obedience

When an agent acts on behalf of the principal, the agent must follow all lawful instructions of the principal. Exceptions include emergencies and instances in which instructions are not clearly stated.

5. Accounting

An agent must keep and make available to the principal an account of everything received and paid out on behalf of the principal. An agent must keep separate accounts for the principal's funds.

B. PRINCIPAL'S DUTIES TO THE AGENT

1. Compensation

A principal must pay an agent for services rendered (unless the agent does not act for money). Payment must be timely. If no amount has been agreed to, the principal owes the customary amount for such services.

2. Reimbursement and Indemnification

A principal must (1) reimburse the agent for money paid at the principal's request or for necessary expenses and (2) indemnify an agent for liability incurred because of authorized acts.

3. Cooperation

A principal must cooperate with and assist an agent in performing his or her duties. The principal must do nothing to prevent performance.

4. Safe Working Conditions
A principal must provide safe working conditions.

IV. RIGHTS AND REMEDIES OF AGENTS AND PRINCIPALS
If one party violates his or her duty to the other, remedies available to the party not in breach arise out of contract and tort law, and include damages, termination of the agency, injunction, and accounting.

A. AGENT'S RIGHTS AND REMEDIES AGAINST THE PRINCIPAL
For every duty of the principal, an agent has a corresponding right.

1. Tort and Contract Remedies
Breach of a duty by the principal follows normal contract and tort remedies.

2. Demand for an Accounting
An agent may also withhold performance and demand an accounting.

3. No Right to Specific Performance
If the relation is not contractual, an agent has no right to specific performance (but can recover for past services and future damages).

B. PRINCIPAL'S RIGHTS AND REMEDIES AGAINST THE AGENT
Breach of a duty by the agent follows normal contract and tort remedies. A breach of fiduciary duty may justify the termination of the agency.

1. Constructive Trust
A court imposes a constructive trust if an agent retains benefits or profits that belong to the principal or takes advantage of the agency to obtain property the principal wants to buy. The court declares that the agent holds money or property on behalf of the principal.

2. Avoidance
If an agent breaches an agency agreement under a contract, the principal has a right to avoid any contract entered into with the agent.

3. Indemnification
A third party can sue a principal for an agent's negligence, and in certain situations the principal can sue the agent. The same is true if the agent violates the principal's instructions.

TRUE-FALSE QUESTIONS
(Answers at the Back of the Book)

____ 1. An agent can perform legal acts that bind his or her principal.

____ 2. Employees who deal with third parties are agents of their employers.

____ 3. An agent owes his or her principal a duty to act in good faith.

____ 4. An agent must act solely in his or her own interest.

____ 5. A minor can be a principal but not an agent.

____ 6. Unless the parties agree otherwise, a principal must pay for an agent's services.

____ 7. A principal cannot avoid a contract that a third party enters into with an agent.

____ 8. A third party cannot sue a principal for an agent's negligence.

____ 9. An agent must keep separate accounts for the principal's funds.

____ 10. Information obtained through an agency relationship is confidential.

FILL-IN QUESTIONS

(Answers at the Back of the Book)

An agent's use of reasonable diligence and skill is part of the agent's duty of _____ (obedience/performance). Informing a principal of all material matters that come to the agent's attention concerning the subject matter of the agency is an aspect of the agent's duty of _____ (accounting/notification). Acting solely for the benefit of the principal and not in the interest of the agent or a third party is part of the agent's duty of _____ (loyalty/performance). Following all lawful and clearly stated instructions of the principal is an aspect of the agent's duty of _____ (loyalty/obedience). If an agent is required to keep and make available to the principal a record of all property and money received and paid out on behalf of the principal, this is part of the agent's duty of _____ (accounting/notification).

MULTIPLE-CHOICE QUESTIONS

(Answers at the Back of the Book)

____ 1. Seaway Shipbuilders, Inc., hires Rowena and Querida as employees to deal with third-party purchasers and suppliers. Rowena and Querida are

a. agents and principals.
b. agents only.
c. neither agents nor principals.
d. principals only.

____ 2. NY Cupcakes, Inc. (NYC), tells Milena, whose business is purchasing for others, to select and buy $2,000 worth of fresh fruit ship it to NYC's bakery. Milena buys the goods from Fresh Express and ships the fruit as directed, keeping an account for the expense in NYC's name. NYC and Milena

a. do not have an agency relationship, because Milena's business is buying for others.
b. do not have an agency relationship, because Milena did not indicate that she was acting for NYC.
c. do not have an agency relationship, because their agreement is not in writing.
d. have an agency relationship.

____ 3. **Based on a Sample CPA Question.** Doug agrees to act as an agent for Carpet & More Corporation (CMC) on a commission basis. The agreement does not call for Doug to pay expenses out of his commission. CMC is required to

a. keep records, account to Doug, and pay Doug according to the agreement only.
b. reimburse Doug for all authorized expenses only.
c. keep records, account to Doug, pay him according to the agreement, and reimburse him for authorized expenses.
d. none of the choices.

____ 4. Stetson asks Toni, a real estate broker, to sell his land. Toni learns that Rancho Grande LLC is willing to pay a high price for the land. Without telling Stetson about Rancho Grande, Toni says that she will buy the land. Instead, however, Stetson sells the land to United Cattle Corporation. Toni sues Stetson. Toni will

a. lose, because Stetson was not Toni's principal.
b. lose, because Toni breached her duty to Stetson.
c. win, because Stetson breached his duty to Toni.
d. win, because Toni was never Stetson's agent.

___ **5.** Campbell is a salesperson for DownRiver Enterprises, Inc. In determining whether Campbell is DownRiver's employee or an independent contractor, the most important factor is

  a. the degree of control that DownRiver exercises over Campbell.
  b. the distinction between DownRiver's business and Campbell's occupation.
  c. the length of the working relationship between DownRiver and Campbell.
  d. the method of payment.

___ **6.** Sympatico Symphonic Instruments, Inc., and Rudy wish to enter into an agency relationship for the purpose of buying musical instruments for Sympatico's inventory. This relationship requires

  a. a written agreement and consideration.
  b. a written agreement only.
  c. consideration only.
  d. neither a written agreement nor consideration.

___ **7.** Gifford, a salesperson at Hubris Electronics store, tells Irma, a customer, "Buy your home theatre system here, and I'll set it up for less than what Hubris would charge." Irma buys the system, Gifford sets it up, and Irma pays Giffors, who keeps the money. Gifford has breached the duty of

  a. loyalty.
  b. notification.
  c. obedience.
  d. performance.

___ **8.** Estimable Finance Company hires Flotilda, who holds herself out as possessing special accounting skills, to act as its agent. As an agent, Flotilda must use the degree of skill or care expected of

  a. an average, unskilled person.
  b. a person having those special skills.
  c. a reasonable person.
  d. Estimable Company.

___ **9.** Myra gives Noel the impression that Opal is Myra's agent, when in fact she is not. Noel deals with Opal as Myra's agent. Regarding any agency relationship, Myra

  a. can deny it to the extent of any activity in which Opal might engage.
  b. can deny it to the extent of any injury suffered by Noel.
  c. can deny it to the extent of any liability that might be imposed on Myra.
  d. cannot deny it.

___ **10.** Elman is an officer for Fizzy Frothy Confections Concession Corporation. When acting for Fizzy in ordinary business situations, Elman is

  a. an agent only.
  b. an agent and a principal.
  c. a principal only.
  d. neither an agent nor a principal.

SHORT ESSAY QUESTIONS

1. What are the chief differences among the relationships of principal and agent, employer and employee, and employer and independent contractor? What are the factors that indicate whether an individual is an employee or an independent contractor?

2. What are the ways in which a principal–agent relationship can be formed?

GAMEPOINTS

(Answers at the Back of the Book)

You are the chief executive officer for Game Sportz Corporation with the duty to determine the firm's business goals, strategies, and tactics. Felicity manages the daily operations of the firm. Ethan is its marketing executive. Desiree is your creative resource, sometimes sparkling with new game ideas, sometimes fulfilling those of others. Cody writes and edits the games' manuals on a per-project basis. In light of the principles set out in this chapter, how would you answer the following questions?

1.   As a chief executive officer, you are responsible only to the board of directors. Felicity, Ethan, Desiree, and Cody do your bidding to varying degrees. Felicity, Ethan, and Desiree—and you of course—deal with third parties on the firm's behalf. Who is a principal? Who is an agent? Who is an employee? Who is an independent contractor?

2.   Ethan negotiates on Games Sportz's behalf a marketing campaign that includes rebates to the firm based on the number of hits to links on the company's Web site and its games. Ethan arranges for the payments to be made to his own account, however. When the company learns of this shenanigan, it files a suit against Ethan. What remedies are possible?

SPECIAL INFORMATION FOR CPA CANDIDATES

The material covered in this and the next chapter is always included in the CPA examination. Thus, while the concepts are basic and relatively simple, they are nevertheless essential. Agency concepts are applied in questions in the context of principal-agent relationships, partnership law, and corporation law.

Among the points to keep in mind are the rights and duties of the principal and agent, the fiduciary nature of the relationship, and how an agency relationship is formed. Its formation does not need to be contractual, but if it is, it must meet the requirements of a contract.

Chapter 33
Agency Liability and Termination

WHAT THIS CHAPTER IS ABOUT

This chapter deals with the liability of principals and agents to third parties in contract and tort and principals' liability to third parties for agents' torts. The chapter concludes with a section on the termination of agency relationships.

CHAPTER OUTLINE

Clothe w/ indicia of authority

I. **SCOPE OF AGENT'S AUTHORITY**
A principal's liability in a contract with a third party arises from the authority given the agent to enter contracts on the principal's behalf.

A. EXPRESS AUTHORITY

1. **Equal Dignity Rule**
   In most states, if the contract being executed is or must be in writing, the agent's authority must also be in writing.

   a. **Exception—Executive Officer Doing Ordinary Business**
      A corporate executive doing ordinary business does not need written authority from the corporation.

   b. **Exception—Agent Acting in the Presence of the Principal**
      In this case, the agent does not need written authority.

2. **Power of Attorney**
   A power of attorney can be special or general. An ordinary power terminates on the incapacity or death of the person giving it. A durable power is not affected by the principal's incapacity.

B. IMPLIED AUTHORITY
Conferred by custom, can be inferred from the position an agent occupies, or is implied as reasonably necessary to carry out express authority.

C. APPARENT AUTHORITY

1. **Pattern of Conduct**
   Apparent authority exists when a principal causes a third party reasonably to believe that an agent has authority. This can occur through a pattern of conduct.

2. **Estoppel**
   If the third party changes position in reliance on the principal's representations, the principal may be estopped from denying that the agent had authority.

D. EMERGENCY POWERS
If an emergency demands action by the agent, but the agent is unable to communicate with the principal, the agent has emergency power.

259

E. RATIFICATION

A principal can ratify an unauthorized contract or act, if he or she has the capacity and is aware of all material facts. Ratification can be done expressly or impliedly (by accepting the benefits of a transaction). An entire transaction must be ratified; a principal cannot affirm only part.

1. Effect of Ratification

The principal is bound to the agent's act as if it had been authorized from the outset.

2. Effect of Ratification Without Knowing All the Facts

If the third party acts in reliance to his or her detriment on the apparent ratification, the principal can repudiate but must reimburse the third party's costs.

3. Effect of No Ratification

There is no contract binding the principal. The third party's agreement with the agent is an unaccepted offer. The agent may be liable to the third party for misrepresenting authority.

II. LIABILITY FOR CONTRACTS

Who is liable to third parties for contracts formed by an agent?

A. DEFINITIONS

1. Disclosed Principal

This is a principal whose identity is known by the third party when the contract is made.

2. Partially Disclosed Principal

This is a principal whose identity is not known by the third party, but the third party knows the agent is or may be acting for a principal when the contract is made.

3. Undisclosed Principal

This is a principal whose identity is totally unknown by the third party, who also does not know that the agent is acting in an agency capacity at the time of the contract.

B. IF AN AGENT ACTS WITHIN THE SCOPE OF HIS OR HER AUTHORITY (AUTHORIZED ACTS)

1. Disclosed Principal

If a principal's identity is known to a third party when an agent makes a contract, the principal is liable. The agent is not liable.

2. Partially Disclosed Principal

The principal is liable. In most states, the agent is also liable (but is entitled to indemnification by the principal).

3. Undisclosed Principal

The principal *and* the agent are liable. Exceptions—

    a. The principal was expressly excluded as a party in the contract.
    b. The contract is a negotiable instrument (check or note).
    c. The performance of the agent is personal to the contract.

C. IF THE AGENT HAS NO AUTHORITY (UNAUTHORIZED ACTS)

The principal is not liable in contract to a third party. The agent is liable, for breach of the implied warranty of authority (not on breach of the contract), unless the third party knew the agent did not have authority.

D. ACTIONS BY E-AGENTS

E-agents include semi-autonomous computer programs capable of executing specific tasks. How much authority do e-agents have? Generally, any party who uses an e-agent is bound by the e-agent's operations whether or not the principal was aware of them. In some circumstances, the third party with whom the e-agent deals can avoid the transaction.

III. LIABILITY FOR TORTS AND CRIMES

An agent is liable to third parties for his or her torts. Is the principal also liable?

A. PRINCIPAL'S TORTIOUS CONDUCT

A principal may be liable for harm resulting from the principal's negligence or recklessness (giving improper instructions; authorizing the use of improper materials or tools; establishing improper rules; or failing to prevent others' tortious conduct while they are on the principal's property or using the principal's equipment, materials, or tools).

B. PRINCIPAL'S AUTHORIZATION OF AGENT'S TORTIOUS CONDUCT

A principal who authorizes an agent to commit a tortious act may be liable.

C. LIABILITY FOR AGENT'S MISREPRESENTATION

1. Fraudulent Misrepresentation

If a principal has given an agent authority to make statements and the agent makes false claims, the principal is liable. If an agent appears to be acting within the scope of authority in taking advantage of a third party, the principal who placed the agent in the position of apparent implied authority is liable.

2. Innocent Misrepresentation

When a principal knows that an agent does not have all the facts but does not correct the agent's or the third party's impressions, the principal is liable.

D. LIABILITY FOR AGENT'S NEGLIGENCE

Under the doctrine of *respondeat superior*, an employer is liable for harm caused (negligently or intentionally) to a third party by an employee acting within the scope of employment, without regard to the personal fault of the employer. This is known as *vicarious liability*.

1. Rationale Underlying the Doctrine of *Respondeat Superior*

The basis is the social duty that requires every person to manage his or her affairs, whether accomplished by the person or through agents, so as not to injure another. Liability is imposed on employers in part because they are deemed to be in a better financial position to bear the expense. Insurance can cover the cost. Its risk can be spread among business customers.

2. Determining the Scope of Employment

In determining whether an act is within the scope of employment, a court considers—

a. the time, place, and purpose of the act.
b. whether the act was authorized by the employer.
c. whether the act is one commonly performed by employees on behalf of their employers.
d. whether the employer's interest was advanced by the act.
e. whether the private interests of the employee were involved.
f. whether the employer furnished the means by which an injury was inflicted.
g. whether the employer had reason to know that the employee would do the act in question.
h. whether the act involved the commission of a serious crime.

3. "Detours" and "Frolics"

If a servant takes a detour from his master's business, the master is liable for any ensuing tort. If the servant is on a frolic of his or her own, however, the master is not responsible.

4. Employee Travel Time

The travel of those whose jobs require it is considered within the scope of employment for the duration of the trip, including the return. An employee going to and from work or meals is usually considered outside the scope of employment.

5. Notice of Dangerous Conditions

An employer is charged with knowledge of dangerous conditions that concern the employment situation and that an employee discovers.

6. Borrowed Servants
An employer who lends the services of an employee to a third party may be liable for the employee's negligence, depending on who had the right to control the employee at the time.

E. LIABILITY FOR AGENT'S INTENTIONAL TORTS
Generally, an employer is not liable for an agent's intentional tort because a tort normally has no connection to the agency relation.

1. Employer's Liability for Agent's Torts outside the Scope of Employment
An employer who knows or should know that an employee has a propensity for committing tortious acts is liable for the acts even if they are outside the scope of employment. Also, an employer is liable for permitting an employee to engage in reckless acts that can injure others.

2. Agent's Liability for His or Her Own Torts
An employee is liable for his or her own torts. An employee who commits a tort at the employer's direction can be liable with the employer, even if he or she was unaware of the act's wrongfulness.

F. LIABILITY FOR INDEPENDENT CONTRACTOR'S TORTS
An employer is not liable for harm caused to a third person by the tortious act of an independent contractor (except in cases of hazardous activities such as blasting operations, the transportation of highly volatile chemicals, and the use of poisonous gases, in which strict liability is imposed).

G. LIABILITY FOR AGENT'S CRIMES
A principal is not liable for an agent's crime, unless the principal participated. In some jurisdictions, a principal may be liable for an agent's violating, in the course and scope of employment, such regulations as those governing sanitation, prices, weights, and the sale of liquor.

IV. TERMINATION OF AN AGENCY

A. TERMINATION BY ACT OF THE PARTIES

1. Lapse of Time
An agency agreement may specify the time period during which the agency relationship will exist. If so, the agency ends when that time expires. If no definite time is stated, an agency continues for a reasonable time and can be terminated at will by either party.

2. Purpose Achieved
An agent can be employed to accomplish a particular objective. If so, the agency automatically ends when the objective is accomplished.

3. Occurrence of a Specific Event
An agency can be created to terminate on the occurrence of a certain event. If so, the agency automatically ends when the event occurs.

4. Mutual Agreement
Parties can cancel their agency by mutually agreeing to do so.

5. At the Option of One Party
Both parties have the *power* to terminate an agency, but they may not have the *right* and may therefore be liable for breach of contract.

a. Agency at Will—Principal Must Give Reasonable Notice
To allow the agent to recoup expenses and, in some cases, to make a normal profit.

b. Agency Coupled with an Interest—Irrevocable
This agency is created for the benefit of the agent, who acquires a beneficial interest in the subject matter, and thus it is not equitable to permit a principal to terminate at will. Also, it is not terminated by the death of either the principal or the agent.

    c. Not an Agency Coupled with an Interest—May Be Revocable

       An agency coupled with an interest should not be confused with an agency in which the agent derives only proceeds or profits (such as a commission) from the sale of the subject matter. This is revocable by the principal, subject to any contract between the parties.

B. TERMINATION BY OPERATION OF LAW

  1. Death or Insanity

     Death or insanity of either party automatically and immediately ends an agency. Knowledge of the death is not required.

  2. Impossibility

     When the specific subject matter of an agency is destroyed or lost, the agency terminates. When it is impossible for the agent to perform the agency lawfully because of a change in the law, the agency terminates.

  3. Changed Circumstances

     When an event occurs that has such an unusual effect on the subject matter of the agency that the agent can reasonably infer that the principal will not want the agency to continue, the agency terminates.

  4. Bankruptcy

     Bankruptcy of the principal or the agent usually terminates an agency. In some circumstances, as when the agent's financial status is irrelevant to the purpose of the agency, the agency relationship may continue.

  5. War

     When the principal's country and the agent's country are at war with each other, the agency is terminated.

C. NOTICE REQUIRED FOR TERMINATION

  1. Notice Required

     If the parties themselves terminate the agency, the principal must inform any third parties who know of the agency that it has ended.

    a. Agent's Authority Continues

       An agent's actual authority continues until the agent receives notice of termination. An agent's apparent authority continues until the third person is notified (from any source).

    b. What the Principal Must Do

       The principal is expected to notify directly any third person the principal knows has dealt with the agent. For third persons aware of the agency but who have not dealt with the agent, constructive notice is sufficient.

    c. Form of the Notice

       No particular form of notice is required unless the agent's authority is written, in which case it must be revoked in writing, and the writing must be shown to all who saw the written authority.

  2. No Notice Required

     If an agency terminates by operation of law, there is no duty to notify third persons, unless the agent's authority is coupled with an interest.

TRUE-FALSE QUESTIONS

(Answers at the Back of the Book)

____ 1. A disclosed principal is liable to a third party for a contract by an agent within the scope of authority.

____ 2. A principal is not liable for an agent's torts committed within the scope of his or her employment.

____ 3. A principal is not bound to an unauthorized contract that he or she does not ratify.

____ 4. An undisclosed principal is liable to a third party for a contract by an agent within the scope of authority.

____ 5. In an ordinary agency relationship, the agency terminates automatically on the death of the principal.

____ 6. An employer is liable for *any* harm caused to a third party by an employee acting within the scope of employment.

____ 7. Both parties to an agency have the right to terminate the agency at any time.

____ 8. When an agent enters into an authorized contract on behalf of a principal, the principal must ratify the contract to be bound.

____ 9. When the specific subject matter of an agency is destroyed or lost, the agency terminates.

____ 10. An e-agent is a person.

FILL-IN QUESTIONS

(Answers at the Back of the Book)

If an agent is authorized to hire subagents, the principal _____ (is/is not) liable for the subagents' acts. An agent who hires for _____ (a disclosed/an undisclosed) principal is responsible to the subagent in contract for such things as wages, but the _____ (disclosed/undisclosed) principal is generally liable for _____ (the subagent's crimes/tort injuries) under the doctrine of *respondeat superior*. An agent's unauthorized hiring of a subagent _____ (also results/generally does not result) in a legal relationship between principal and subagent.

MULTIPLE-CHOICE QUESTIONS

(Answers at the Back of the Book)

____ 1. Java Company hires Keith to manage one of its kiosks. Their employment agreement says nothing about Keith being able to hire employees to work in the kiosk, but Keith has this authority. This is

a. apparent authority.
b. express authority.
c. imaginary authority.
d. implied authority.

____ 2. Macro Company employs Nero as an agent. To terminate Nero's authority, Macro must notify

a. Nero and third parties who know of the agency relationship.
b. only Nero.
c. only third parties who know of the agency relationship.
d. the public generally.

____ 3. Security Guns & Ammo, Inc., directs its salespersons never to load a gun during a sale. Bert, a salesperson, loads a gun during a sale. The gun fires, negligently injuring Kathy, who is in the store. Security is

   a. not liable, because Bert was not acting within the scope of employment.
   b. not liable, because employers are not responsible for their employees' torts.
   c. liable under the doctrine of *respondeat superior*.
   d. liable under the doctrine of *res ipsa loquitur*.

____ 4. Ron orally engages Dian to act as his agent. During the agency, Ron knows that Dian deals with Mary. Ron also knows that Pete and Brad are aware of the agency but have not dealt with Dian. Ron decides to terminate the agency. Regarding notice of termination

   a. Dian need not be notified in writing.
   b. Dian's actual authority terminates without notice to her of Ron's decision.
   c. Dian's apparent authority terminates without notice to Mary.
   d. Pete and Brad must be directly notified.

____ 5. Smith Petroleum, Inc., contracts to sell oil to Jones Petrochemicals, telling Jones that it is acting on behalf of "a rich Saudi Arabian who doesn't want his identity known." Smith signs the contract, "Smith, as agent only." In fact, Smith is acting on its own. If the contract is breached, Smith may

   a. not be liable, because Smith signed the contract as an agent.
   b. not be liable, unless Jones knew Smith did not have authority to act.
   c. be liable, unless Jones knew Smith did not have authority to act.
   d. be liable, because Smith signed the contract as an agent.

____ 6. Quality Products Company requires its customers to pay by check. Ray, a Quality agent, tells customers that they can pay him with cash. Quality learns of Ray's collections, but takes no action to stop them. Ray steals some of the cash. Quality may be liable for the loss under the doctrine of

   a. apparent authority.
   b. express authority.
   c. imagined authority.
   d. implied authority.

____ 7. **Based on a Sample CPA Exam Question.** Kay acts within the scope of her authority to enter into a contract with First National Bank on behalf of Kay's undisclosed principal, Digital Engineering, Inc. Digital is

   a. liable on the contract only if Digital ratifies the contract.
   b. liable on the contract only if Digital's identity is later disclosed.
   c. liable on the contract under the stated circumstances.
   d. not liable on the contract.

____ 8. Gurney Makers, Inc., employs Hap as an assembly worker. While attempting, without Gurney's knowledge, to steal a forklift from its property, Hap has an accident, negligently injuring Irene. Irene can recover from

   a. Gurney Makers only.
   b. Hap only.
   c. Gurney Makers and Hap.
   d. neither Gurney Makers nor Hap.

_____ 9. Swifty Delivery Company employs Taesha as a driver. While acting within the scope of employment, Taesha causes an accident in which Vaughn is injured. Vaughn can recover from

    a. neither Swifty nor Taesha.
    b. Swifty only.
    c. Swifty or Taesha.
    d. Taesha only

_____ 10. Green Grocers, Inc., employs Francesca to buy and install a computer system for Green's distribution network. When the system is set up and running, the agency

    a. terminates automatically.
    b. terminates after fourteen days.
    c. continues for one year.
    d. continues indefinitely.

SHORT ESSAY QUESTIONS

1. Identify and describe the categories of authority by which an agent can bind a principal and a third party in contract.

2. What are some of the situations in which a principal is liable for an agent's torts?

GAMEPOINTS

(Answers at the Back of the Book)

From the throne room in your base station on Alpha Centauri—in the video game "Galactic Empire"—you dispatch your loyal, obedient minions to use their diligence and skill to loot the universe on your behalf and return with the treasure for its accounting and their compensation. Applying the agency principles outlined in this chapter, answer the following questions.

1. One minion, Delilah, does not return with gems and gold, but brings back three contracts. Acting within the scope of her authority, she contracted with Evon, who knew your identity at the time; Felipe, who knew that Delilah was acting on behalf of someone but not whom; and Giorgio, who did not know that Delilah was acting on anyone's behalf. For which contracts, if any, are you liable? For which contracts, if any, is Delilah liable?

2. A different minion, Hotspur, steals the treasure chest of a giant Cyclops from an asteroid orbiting a distant star. Launching quickly to escape from the celestial body, Hotspur's space pod negligently bangs into the Cyclops, who is injured. If the Cyclops files a suit against you, can there be a recovery for the injury?

SPECIAL INFORMATION FOR CPA CANDIDATES

The CPA examination covers agency principles in three contexts: agency law, partnership law, and corporation law. The scope of an agent's authority is virtually certain to be part of the exam. In particular, an agent's implied authority and an agent's apparent authority are among the most common topics on the test. It is thus important to be clear about the differences between these two concepts of authority. Implied authority is derived from express authority. Apparent authority arises from what a principal tells or shows a third party. Apparent authority can result from as little as the title or position that a principal gives an agent.

Another important point to keep in mind when applying these principles to questions on the exam is the size and type of the business at issue—the manager of a large store normally has more authority than the employee of a small store. Also, while a principal is ordinarily liable for the unintentional torts of his or her employees, the principal is not ordinarily liable for an employee's crimes.

On the termination of an agency relationship—as on the termination of a partnership—remember that actual notice must be given to creditors, but constructive notice is sufficient for others.

Exeptions to At-will

Contract theory – Implied contract
- Something employer said
- Something on employee handbook or in writing

Tort theories – Promissary Estoppel
- If something is promised and not delivered
  ee. someone promised a position if they stick around
  then not given it

- Public policy –
  - excercised a right or refusal to
    violate a law

Chapter 34
Employment, Immigration, and Labor Law

WHAT THIS CHAPTER IS ABOUT

This chapter outlines the most significant laws regulating employment relationships. Other significant laws regulating the workplace—those prohibiting employment discrimination—are dealt with in Chapter 25.

CHAPTER OUTLINE

I. EMPLOYMENT AT WILL *49 out of 50 states*

Under this doctrine, either the employer or the employee may terminate an employment relationship at any time and for any reason (unless a contract or the law provides to the contrary).

A. EXCEPTIONS TO THE EMPLOYMENT-AT-WILL DOCTRINE

1. Exceptions Based on Contract Theory

Some courts have held that an implied contract exists between an employer and an employee (if, for example, a personnel manual states that no employee will be fired without good cause). A few states have held all employment contracts contain an implied covenant of good faith.

2. Exceptions Based on Tort Theory

Discharge may give rise to a tort action (based on fraud, for example) for wrongful discharge.

3. Exceptions Based on Public Policy

An employer may not fire a worker for reasons that violate a public policy of the jurisdiction (for example, for refusing to violate the law). This policy must be expressed clearly in statutory law. Some state and federal statutes protect whistleblowers from retaliation.

B. WRONGFUL DISCHARGE

An employer cannot fire an employee in violation of an employment contract or a federal or state statute. If so, the employee may bring an action for wrongful discharge.

II. WAGE AND HOUR LAWS

Davis-Bacon Act of 1931 requires "prevailing wages" for employees of some government contractors. Walsh-Healey Act of 1936 requires minimum wage and overtime for employees of some government contractors. Fair Labor Standards Act of 1938 (FLSA) covers all employees and regulates—

Can't work in oppressive job

A. CHILD LABOR *— age, hours, nature of work*

Children under fourteen can deliver newspapers, work for their parents, and work in entertainment and agriculture. Children fourteen and older cannot work in hazardous occupations. *14-16 can work, need permission, hours restricted* *16-18 type of work regulated, hours unrestricted*

B. MINIMUM WAGES

A specified amount (periodically revised) must be paid to employees in covered industries. Wages include the reasonable cost to furnish employees with board, lodging, and other facilities.

Federal statute with state counterparts

269

C. OVERTIME PROVISIONS AND EXEMPTIONS

Employees who work more than forty hours per week must be paid no less than one and a half times their regular pay for all hours over forty. Executives, administrative employees, professional employees, outside salespersons, and computer employees are exempt if their pay exceeds a certain amount, their duties do not include certain types of work, and they meet other requirements.

III. LAYOFFS

Restructuring an operation or downsizing a workforce means a layoff.

A. THE WORKER ADJUSTMENT AND RETRAINING NOTIFICATION (WARN) ACT OF 1988

Employers with at least one hundred full-time workers must provide sixty-days' notice before imposing a mass layoff or closing a plant that employs more than fifty full-time workers.

1. Mass Layoff

This is a reduction in force that, during any thirty-day period, results in an employment loss of at least 33 percent of the full-time employees at a single job site and at least fifty employees, or at least five hundred full-time employees. An employment loss is a layoff that exceeds six months or a reduction in hours of more than 50 percent in each month of any six-month period.

2. Notification Requirements

Workers, including part-time and seasonal workers, or their union representative must be notified. State and local agencies must also be notified. This gives workers time to look for new jobs and state agencies time to provide retraining and other resources. Employers can avoid giving notice by staggering layoffs over many months or many job sites.

3. Remedies for Violations

These include fines of up to $500 per day. Employees can recover up to sixty-days' back pay and job benefits, plus attorneys' fees. Discrimination claims are possible (see Chapter 25).

B. STATE LAWS MAY ALSO REQUIRE LAYOFF NOTICES

Many states have similar or stricter notice requirements that cover more employers and employees.

IV. FAMILY AND MEDICAL LEAVE ACT (FMLA) OF 1993

Employers with fifty or more employees must provide them with up to twelve weeks of family or medical leave during any twelve-month period.

A. COVERAGE AND APPLICATION

Public and private employers are covered. Key employees, part-time employees, and those who have worked less than twelve months during the previous seven years are not covered. The purposes of the leave must be to care for new children (family leave), or close relatives or themselves with a serious health condition (medical leave). The leave can be extended in military-related situations.

B. BENEFITS AND PROTECTIONS

Employers must continue health-care coverage for an employee during the leave, and guarantee employment in the same, or a comparable, position when the employee returns to work.

C. VIOLATIONS

Remedies for violations include damages, job reinstatement, promotion, costs, and fees.

V. WORKER HEALTH AND SAFETY

A. THE OCCUPATIONAL SAFETY AND HEALTH ACT OF 1970

This act provides for workplace safety standards—employers have a general duty to keep workplaces safe—with record-keeping, reporting, notice, and inspection requirements. The Occupational Safety and Health Administration (OSHA) administers the act. Penalties are limited, but an employer may also be prosecuted under state law.

required to keep workplace free from hazards

B. STATE WORKERS' COMPENSATION LAWS

State laws establish procedure for compensating workers injured on the job. Often excluded are domestic workers, agricultural workers, temporary employees, and employees of common carriers.

1. Workers' Compensation Requirements

There must be an employment relationship, and the injury must be accidental and occur on the job or in the course of employment. An employee must notify the employer of an injury (usually within thirty days), and file a claim with a state agency within a certain period (sixty days to two years) from the time the injury is first noticed.

2. Workers' Compensation versus Litigation

An employee's acceptance of benefits bars the employee from suing for injuries caused by the employer's negligence.

VI. INCOME SECURITY

A. SOCIAL SECURITY   *15.3% of paycheck*

The Social Security Act of 1935 provides for payments to persons who are retired, widowed, disabled, etc. Employers and employees must contribute under the Federal Insurance Contributions Act (FICA).

B. MEDICARE

A health insurance program administered by the Social Security Administration for people sixty-five years of age and older and for some under sixty-five who are disabled.

C. PRIVATE PENSION PLANS

The Employee Retirement Income Security Act (ERISA) of 1974 empowers the U.S. Department of Labor to oversee operators of private pension funds. The Pension Benefit Guaranty Corporation (PBGC) pays benefits to participants if their plans cannot.

1. Vesting

Generally, employee contributions to pension plans vest immediately; employee rights to employer contributions vest after five years.

2. Investing

Pension-fund managers must be cautious in investing and must diversify investments to minimize the risk of large losses.

D. UNEMPLOYMENT COMPENSATION

The Federal Unemployment Tax Act of 1935 created a state system that provides unemployment compensation to eligible individuals. A worker must have left his or her job for good cause—not misconduct—be willing and able to work, and be actively seeking employment

E. COBRA

The Consolidated Omnibus Budget Reconciliation Act (COBRA) of 1985 prohibits the elimination of a worker's medical, optical, or dental insurance coverage on the voluntary or involuntary termination or reduction in hours of the worker's employment.

1. Procedures

Except for those fired for gross misconduct, a worker can decide whether to continue coverage. Coverage must be continued for up to eighteen months (twenty-nine, if the worker is disabled).

2. Payment

A worker who opts to continue coverage must pay a premium plus an administrative fee. Penalties for violations include up to 10 percent of the annual cost of the group plan or $500,000, whichever is less.

F. EMPLOYER-SPONSORED GROUP HEALTH PLANS
Under the Health Insurance Portability and Accountability Act (HIPAA), employers who provide health insurance cannot exclude persons with certain preexisting conditions and are restricted in their collection and use of employees' health information.

VII. EMPLOYEE PRIVACY RIGHTS
A right to privacy has been inferred from constitutional guarantees provided by the First, Third, Fourth, Fifth, and Ninth Amendments to the Constitution. Tort law, state constitutions, and some federal and state statutes also provide some privacy rights.

A. ELECTRONIC MONITORING

1. Employee Privacy Protection
Privacy rights are protected at common law (invasion of privacy) and under the U.S. Constitution and state constitutions. The courts generally weigh an employer's interests against an employee's reasonable expectation of privacy, which may depend on whether the employee knows of the monitoring.

2. The Electronic Communications Privacy Act (ECPA) of 1986
Electronic monitoring may violate this act, which prohibits the intentional interception of any electronic communication or the intentional disclosure or use of the information obtained by the interception. A "business-extension exception" permits employers to monitor communications in the ordinary course of business (though not personal communications without consent).

3. Stored Communications
Intentional, unauthorized access to stored electronic communications is prohibited.

B. OTHER TYPES OF MONITORING

1. Lie-Detector Tests
Under the Employee Polygraph Protection Act of 1988, most employers cannot, among other things, require, request, or suggest that employees or applicants take lie-detector tests, except when investigating theft, including theft of trade secrets.

2. Drug Testing

a. Protection for the Privacy Rights of Private Employees
Some state constitutions may prohibit private employers from testing for drugs. State statutes may restrict drug testing by private employers. Other sources of protection include collective bargaining agreements and tort actions for invasion of privacy (see Chapter 4).

b. Protection for Government Employees
Constitutional limitations (the Fourth Amendment) apply. Drug tests have been upheld when there was a reasonable basis for suspecting employees of using drugs, or when drug use could threaten public safety.

3. Genetic Testing
Employers cannot use the results of genetic tests of employees and applicants to make decisions about hiring, firing, placement, or promotion under the Genetic Information Nondiscrimination Act of 2008.

VIII. IMMIGRATION LAW
Federal law sets standards for legal immigration, including preferences for persons with certain skills, and imposes sanctions on employers who hire illegal immigrants.

A. THE IMMIGRATION REFORM AND CONTROL ACT (IRCA) OF 1986
It is illegal to hire, recruit, or refer for a fee for work in the United States a person who is not authorized to work here.

1. **I-9 Employment Verification**

   The U.S. Citizenship and Immigration Services (CIS) supplies Form I-9, Employment Eligibility Verification, which an employer must complete within three days of each employee's hiring (and retain for three years). The employer must verify an individual's identity and eligibility to work.

2. **Enforcement**

   U.S. Immigration and Customs Enforcement (ICE) officers conduct random audits and act on written complaints. A determination of a violation is subject to administrative review at an employer's request. Employers' defenses include good faith and substantial compliance with documentation requirements.

3. **Penalties**

   Possibilities include civil fines of up to $11,000 for each unauthorized employee and criminal penalties of increased fines and imprisonment. An employer may also be barred from future government contracts.

B. **THE IMMIGRATION ACT OF 1990**

Persons who immigrate to the United States to work include those with special skills. To hire such individuals, an employer must petition the CIS. An immigrant employee's ability to stay in the United States and to switch jobs here is limited.

1. **I-551 Alien Registration Receipts**

   An employer may hire a noncitizen who is (a) a lawful permanent resident (as proved by an I-551 Alien Registration Receipt, or "green card") or (b) has a temporary Employment Authorization Document.

2. **How an Employer Can Obtain a "Green Card"**

   To obtain a "green card" for an immigrant, an employer must show that no American worker is qualified, willing, and able to take the job. The job must be advertised, and its qualifications must be a business necessity.

3. **The H-1B Visa Program**

   A sponsoring employer may obtain a visa for a person to work in the United States for three to six years in a specialty occupation that requires highly specialized knowledge and a college degree.

4. **Labor Certification**

   Before submitting an H-1B application, an employer must obtain a Labor Certification form from the U.S. Department of Labor. To obtain the form, the employer must agree to pay a competitive wage and attest that the hiring will not adversely affect other similarly employed workers. The form must be posted.

5. **H-2, O, L, and E Visas**

   Temporary nonimmigrant visas are also available for agricultural seasonal workers, a company's managers and executives, certain investors and entrepreneurs, and performers, athletes, and other acclaimed individuals.

IX. LABOR UNIONS

A. **FEDERAL LABOR LAWS**

1. **Norris-LaGuardia Act of 1932**

   Enacted in 1932. Restricts federal courts' power to issue injunctions against unions engaged in peaceful strikes, picketing, and boycotts.

2. **National Labor Relations Act (NLRA) of 1935**

   Established rights to bargain collectively and to strike, and—

[handwritten margin notes: "Labor law? think 'collective'" with arrow pointing to b; "Employment law 'Individual' EEOC"]

a. Unfair Employer Practices

Prohibits interfering with union activities, discriminating against union employees, refusing to bargain with union, other practices.

b. The National Labor Relations Board (NLRB)

Created to oversee union elections, prevent employers from engaging in unfair practices, investigate employers in response to employee charges of unfair labor practices, issue cease-and-desist orders.

c. Workers Protected by the NLRA

Protected employees include job applicants, including those paid by a union to unionize the employer's work force.

3. Labor-Management Relations Act (LMRA) of 1947

Prohibits unions from refusing to bargain with employers, engaging in certain types of picketing, featherbedding, and other unfair practices. Preserves union shops, but allows states to pass right-to-work laws, which make it illegal to require union membership for employment.

4. Labor-Management Reporting and Disclosure Act (LMRDA) of 1959

a. Union Business

Requires elections of union officers under secret ballot; prohibits ex-convicts and Communists from holding union office; makes officials accountable for union property; allows members to participate in union meetings, nominate officers, vote in proceedings.

b. Hot-Cargo Agreements

Outlaws hot-cargo agreements (or secondary boycotts, in which employers agree not to handle, use, or deal in non-union goods of other employers).

B. UNION ORGANIZATION

If a majority of workers sign authorization cards and the employer refuses to recognize the union, unionizers can petition the NLRB for an election.

1. Union Elections

For an election to be held, there must be support for the union by at least 30 percent of the workers. NLRB ensures secret voting.

2. Union Election Campaigns

Employers may limit campaign activities (fairly) and may campaign against union.

C. COLLECTIVE BARGAINING

This is the process by which labor and management negotiate terms and conditions of employment. Each side must bargain in good faith (be willing to meet and to consider the other's offers and proposals). Refusing to bargain in good faith without justification is an unfair labor practice.

[handwritten margin notes: "Types of strikes"; "ULP unfair labor practice (workers protected)"; "- Economic strike (no worker protections)"]

D. STRIKES

A strike occurs when workers leave their jobs and refuse to work.

1. The Right to Strike

The NLRA guarantees this right, within limits. Strike activities, such as picketing, are protected by the First Amendment. Nonworkers have a right to participate in picketing. Workers can also refuse to cross a picket line of fellow workers who are engaged in a lawful strike.

2. Striker Rights after a Strike Ends

An employer may hire replacement workers. After an economic strike over working conditions, strikers have no right to return to their jobs, but must be given preference to any vacancies and retain their seniority rights. After an unfair labor practice strike, strikers must be given their jobs back.

TRUE-FALSE QUESTIONS

(Answers at the Back of the Book)

____ **1.** Drug testing by private employers is permitted.

____ **2.** There are no exceptions to the employment "at will" doctrine.

____ **3.** Employers are required to establish retirement plans for their employees.

____ **4.** Federal wage-hour laws cover all employers engaged in interstate commerce.

____ **5.** Whistleblower statutes protect employers from workers' disclosure of the employer's wrongdoing.

____ **6.** Under federal law, employers can monitor employees' personal communications.

____ **7.** Management serves as the representative of workers in bargaining with a union.

____ **8.** An employer must consider all job applicants—citizen and noncitizen—in deciding whom to hire.

____ **9.** Similarity of workers' jobs is a factor in determining which workers are to be represented by a union.

____ **10.** An immigrant employee's ability to stay in the United States and to switch jobs here is limited.

FILL-IN QUESTIONS

(Answers at the Back of the Book)

Under the employment-at-will doctrine, _____ (either/neither) party may terminate an employment relationship at any time and for any reason _____ (unless/even if) a contract provides to the contrary. An employee who is fired in violation of a federal or state statute _____ (may/may not) bring an action for wrongful discharge. _____ (Some/No) courts have held that an implied contract exists between an employer and an employee. _____ (All/A few states) have held that all employment contracts contain an implied covenant of good faith. An employer _____ (may/may not) fire a worker for reasons that violate a public policy of the jurisdiction.

MULTIPLE-CHOICE QUESTIONS

(Answers at the Back of the Book)

____ **1. Based on a Sample CPA Exam Question.** Fast Jack is a fast-food restaurant. To verify Fast Jack's compliance with statutes governing employees' wages and hours, personnel records should be checked against the provisions of

    a. the Fair Labor Standards Act.
    b. the Family and Medical Leave Act.
    c. the National Labor Relations Act.
    d. the Taft-Hartley Act.

____ **2.** National Workers Union (NWU) represents the employees of Office Supplies Company, Inc. NWU calls an economic strike, and Office hires replacement workers. After the strike, the replacement workers

    a. must be retained and the former strikers must be rehired.
    b. must be terminated and the former strikers must be rehired.
    c. must be terminated whether or not the former strikers are rehired.
    d. may be retained or terminated whether or not the former strikers are rehired.

____ 3. Reddy Power Corporation provides health insurance for its employees. When Reddy closes one of its offices and terminates the employees, the employees

a. can collect "severance pay" equal to twelve weeks' of health insurance coverage.
b. can continue their heath insurance at Reddy's expense.
c. can continue their heath insurance at their expense.
d. lose their heath insurance immediately on termination of employment.

____ 4. Reba works for Silo Storage Company as an at-will employee. This employment may be termi-nated at any time for any reason by

a. neither Reba nor Silo Storage.
b. Reba only.
c. Reba or Silo Storage.
d. Silo Storage only.

____ 5. Millions Mining Company is a private employer that wants to test its employees for drug use. This testing may

a. be limited or prohibited at the sole discretion of the employer.
b. be limited or prohibited under a state constitution, statute, or court decision.
c. not be permitted under any circumstances.
d. not be prohibited under any circumstances.

____ 6. Mosul, Natomi, and Omar apply to work for Precision Engineering, Inc. These individuals' identi-ties and eligibility to work must be verified by

a. the employer.
b. the individuals.
c. the individuals' country of origin.
d. the U.S. Citizenship and Immigration Services.

____ 7. Delta Aircraft Company, a U.S. employer, may hire Ewan, a noncitizen, if Ewan is

a. a lawful permanent resident of the United States.
b. an unlawful but currently employed visitor to the United States.
c. an unlawful but only temporary and unemployed resident in the United States.
d. all of the choices.

____ 8. Omega Oil Refining Corporation wants to hire Parfez, who has certain special skills to fill a tech-nical position. To hire Parfez, Omega must petition

a. CIS.
b. OSHA.
c. ICE.
d. NLRB

____ 9. During a union election campaign at Wayward Shipping Corporation, Wayward may not

a. designate where and when campaigning may occur.
b. prohibit all solicitation during work time.
c. promise to hire more workers if the union loses the election.
d. threaten employees with the loss of their jobs if the union wins the election.

____ 10. Fruit Packaging Corporation provides health insurance for its 150 employees, including Gladys. When Gladys takes twelve weeks' leave to care for her child, she

a. can collect "leave pay" equal to twelve weeks' of health insurance coverage.
b. can continue her heath insurance at Fruit Packaging's expense.
c. can continue her heath insurance at her expense.
d. loses her heath insurance immediately on taking leave.

SHORT ESSAY QUESTIONS

1. What is the employment-at-will doctrine? What are its exceptions?

2. What are important federal laws concerning labor unions? What specifically does each law provide?

GAMEPOINTS

(Answers at the Back of the Book)

1. You are playing "Brain Drain," a video game that involves a quest through the unexplored realms of the imagination, attempting to reach Level 14. It is difficult to advance from level to level because the obstacles that must be overcome and the objectives that must be attained are different, complex, and puzzling. For four consecutive weeks, you play 45, 42, 39, and 31 hours. If this play were work, and you were a nonexempt employee covered by the Fair Labor Standards Act, how many hours of overtime pay, if any, would you be entitled to? What would be the rate?

2. In the video game, "Invasive Species," Earth is invaded by huge, insect-like aliens with superior intelligence. Your avatar Derek works for Invasion Extermination Service, Inc. Following the service's prescribed procedures, Derek sprays the invaders with "Eradicate," a chemical supplied by the service. Eradicate effectively wipes out the invaders—one at a time with a short delay, which allows for plenty of game action—but also injures your avatar. According to the principles set out in this chapter, is Derek eligible for workers' compensation? Could Derek successfully sue his employer for negligence?

OHSA
- requires workplace to be
free from standards

*BFOQ
Bona fied Occupational Qualification

Chapter 35
Employment Discrimination

WHAT THIS CHAPTER IS ABOUT

The law restricts employers and unions from discriminating against workers on the basis of race, color, religion, national origin, gender, age, or handicap. A class of persons defined by one or more of these criteria is a *protected class*. This chapter outlines these laws.

CHAPTER OUTLINE

I. TITLE VII OF THE CIVIL RIGHTS ACT OF 1964
Prohibits employment discrimination against employees, applicants, and union members on the basis of race, color, national origin, religion, and gender. —except for BFOQ

A. WHO IS SUBJECT TO TITLE VII?
Employers with fifteen or more employees, labor unions with fifteen or more members, labor unions that operate hiring halls, employment agencies, and federal, state, and local agencies.

B. THE EQUAL EMPLOYMENT OPPORTUNITY COMMISSION
(1) A victim files a claim with the Equal Employment Opportunity Commission (EEOC); (2) the EEOC investigates and seeks a voluntary settlement; (3) if no settlement is reached, the EEOC may sue the employer; (4) if the EEOC chooses not to sue, the victim may file a lawsuit.

C. INTENTIONAL AND UNINTENTIONAL DISCRIMINATION
Title VII prohibits both intentional and unintentional discrimination.

1. Disparate-Treatment Discrimination
This is intentional discrimination by an employer against an employee.

  a. *Prima Facie* Case—Plaintiff's Side of the Case
  A plaintiff must show (1) he or she is a member of a protected class, (2) he or she applied and was qualified for the job, (3) he or she was rejected by the employer, (4) the employer continued to seek applicants or filled the job with a person not in a protected class.

  b. Defense—Employer's Side of the Case
  An employer must articulate a legal reason for not hiring the plaintiff. To prevail, the plaintiff must show that the employer's reason is a pretext and that discriminatory intent motivated the decision.

2. Disparate-Impact Discrimination

  a. Types of Disparate-Impact Discrimination
  Disparate-impact discrimination results if, because of a requirement or hiring practice—

    1) an employer's work force does not reflect the percentage of members of protected classes that characterizes qualified individuals in the local labor market, or

279

      2) members of protected class are excluded from employer's work force at substantially higher rate than nonmembers (under EEOC's "four-fifths rule," selection rate for protected class must be at least 80 percent of rate for group with the highest rate).

    b. *Prima Facie* **Case—Plaintiff's Side of the Case**
    Plaintiff must show a connection between a requirement or practice and a disparity; no evidence of discriminatory intent is needed.

D. DISCRIMINATION BASED ON RACE, COLOR, AND NATIONAL ORIGIN
Employers cannot effectively discriminate against employees on the basis of race, color, national origin, or religion (absent a substantial, demonstrable relationship between the trait and the job, etc.).

1. Reverse Discrimination
Discrimination against majority individuals is reverse discrimination.

2. Potential Section 1981 Claims
This statute (42 U.S.C. Section 1981) protects against discrimination on the basis of race or ethnicity in the formation or enforcement of contracts, including employment contracts, with no limit on the amount of damages.

E. DISCRIMINATION BASED ON RELIGION
Title VII prohibits employers and unions from discriminating against persons because of their religions.

F. DISCRIMINATION BASED ON GENDER
Employers cannot discriminate against employees on the basis of gender (unless gender is essential to a job, etc.). The Pregnancy Discrimination Act of 1978 amended Title VII: employees affected by pregnancy or related conditions must be treated the same as persons not so affected but similar in ability to work.

1. Equal Pay Act
The Equal Pay Act of 1963 prohibits gender-based discrimination in wages paid for equal work when a job requires equal skill, effort, and responsibility under similar conditions.

2. 2009 Equal Pay Legislation
The Paycheck Fairness Act of 2009 prohibits gender-based discrimination in assessing an employee's education, training, or experience. Under the Lily Ledbetter Fair Pay Act of 2009, each time a person is paid discriminatory wages, benefits, or compensation, a cause of action arises and the victim has 180 days to file a complaint.

G. CONSTRUCTIVE DISCHARGE
Constructive discharge occurs when an employer causes working conditions to be so intolerable that a reasonable person in an employee's position would feel compelled to quit.

1. Proving Constructive Discharge
An employee must show that the employer caused the intolerable conditions, and knew, or had reason to know, of the intolerable conditions and failed to correct them within a reasonable time.

2. Applies to All Title VII Discrimination
An employee can seek damages for loss of income, including back pay.

H. SEXUAL HARASSMENT

1. Forms of Harassment
(1) *Quid pro quo* harassment: when promotions, etc., are doled out on the basis of sexual favors; (2) hostile-environment harassment: when an employee is subjected to offensive sexual comments, etc.

2. Harassment by Supervisors, Co-Workers, or Others

a. When an Employer May Be Liable
If anyone (employee or nonemployee) harasses an employee, and the employer knew, or should have known, and failed to take immediate corrective action, the employer may be liable. To be liable for a supervisor's harassment, the supervisor must have taken a tangible employment action against the employee.

b. Employer's Defense
(1) Employer took "reasonable care to prevent and correct promptly any sexually harassing behavior," and (2) employee suing for harassment failed to follow employer's policies and procedures.

3. Same-Gender Harassment
Title VII protects persons who are harassed by members of the same gender.

I. ONLINE HARASSMENT
Employers may avoid liability if they take prompt remedial action. Privacy rights must be considered if the action includes electronic monitoring of employees.

J. REMEDIES UNDER TITLE VII
Reinstatement, back pay, retroactive promotions, and damages.

1. Damages
Compensatory damages are available only in cases of intentional discrimination. Punitive damages are available only if an employer acted with malice or reckless indifference

2. Limits
Total damages are limited to specific amounts against specific employers (from $50,000 against those with 100 or fewer employees to $300,000 against those with more than 500 employees).

II. DISCRIMINATION BASED ON AGE

A. AGE DISCRIMINATION IN EMPLOYMENT ACT (ADEA) OF 1967
Prohibits employment discrimination on the basis of age (including mandatory retirement), by employers with twenty or more employees, against individuals forty years of age or older. Administered by the EEOC, but private causes of action are also possible.

B. PRINCIPLES ARE SIMILAR TO TITLE VII
To establish a *prima facie* case, a plaintiff must show that he or she was (1) forty or older, (2) qualified for a position, and (3) rejected in circumstances that prove age discrimination. The employer must articulate a legal reason for the action. The plaintiff may show it is a pretext.

C. STATE EMPLOYEES NOT COVERED BY THE ADEA
Under the Eleventh Amendment to the Constitution, a state is immune from suits brought by private individuals in federal court unless the state consents to the suit. A state agency sued by a state employee for age discrimination may have the suit dismissed on this ground.

III. DISCRIMINATION BASED ON DISABILITY
Under the Americans with Disabilities Act (ADA) of 1990, an employer cannot refuse to hire a person who is qualified but disabled. Covered are all employers (except the states) with fifteen or more employees.

A. PROCEDURES AND REMEDIES UNDER THE ADA

1. Procedures

A plaintiff must show he or she (1) has a disability, (2) is otherwise qualified for a job and (3) was excluded solely because of the disability. A suit may be filed only after a claim is pursued through the EEOC (which may file a suit even if the employee agrees to arbitration).

2. Remedies

Job reinstatement, back pay, some compensatory and punitive damages (for intentional discrimination), and certain other relief. Repeat violators may be fined up to $100,000.

B. WHAT IS A DISABILITY?

"(1) A physical or mental impairment that substantially limits one or more of the major life activities . . . ; (2) a record of such impairment; or (3) being regarded as having such an impairment." Includes AIDS, blindness, cancer etc., but not kleptomania and others. Employers cannot consider mitigating measures (such as glasses) or medication when determining whether an individual has a disability.

C. REASONABLE ACCOMMODATION

For a person with a disability, an employer may have to make a reasonable accommodation (more flexible working hours, new job assignment, different training materials or procedures)—but not an accommodation that will cause *undue hardship* ("significant difficulty or expense").

1. Job Applications and Physical Exams

The application process must be accessible to those with disabilities. Employers cannot require a disabled person to take a preemployment physical (unless all applicants do). Disqualification must be from problems that render a person unable to perform the job.

2. Substance Abusers

The ADA protects addicts who have completed or are in supervised rehabilitation, and alcoholics to the extent of equal treatment.

3. Health-Insurance Plans

Workers with disabilities must be given the same access as other workers to employer-provided insurance plans. If a plan includes a disability-based distinction, it violates the ADA unless proved to be a business necessity.

4. Association Discrimination

An employer cannot take an adverse employment action based on the disability of a person with whom an applicant or employee is known to have a relationship or association (a disabled spouse, for example).

IV. DEFENSES TO EMPLOYMENT DISCRIMINATION

The first defense is to assert that the plaintiff did not prove discrimination. If discrimination is proved, an employer may attempt to justify it as—

A. BUSINESS NECESSITY

An employer may show that there is a legitimate connection between a job requirement that discriminates and job performance.

B. BONA FIDE OCCUPATIONAL QUALIFICATION (BFOQ)

Another defense applies when discrimination against a protected class is essential to a job—that is, when a particular trait is a BFOQ. Generally restricted to cases in which gender is essential. Race can never be a BFOQ.

C. SENIORITY SYSTEMS

An employer with a history of discrimination may have no members of protected classes or disabled workers in upper-level positions. If no present intent to discriminate is shown, and promotions, etc., are distributed according to a fair seniority system, the employer has a good defense.

D. AFTER-ACQUIRED EVIDENCE OF EMPLOYEE MISCONDUCT

Evidence of an employee's prior misconduct acquired after a lawsuit is filed may limit damages but is not otherwise a defense.

V. **AFFIRMATIVE ACTION** — *court created, not legislative*

"temporary" reverse discrimination

An affirmative action program attempts to make up for past discrimination by giving members of protected classes preferential treatment in hiring or promotion.

A. CONSTITUTIONALITY OF AFFIRMATIVE ACTION PROGRAMS
An employment program cannot use quotas or preferences for unqualified persons. Once it succeeds, it must be changed or dropped. Some states have ended government-sponsored programs.

B. AFFIRMATIVE ACTION IN SCHOOLS
Automatic preference on the basis of a protected characteristic violates the equal protection clause.

TRUE-FALSE QUESTIONS

(Answers at the Back of the Book)

____ 1. Once an affirmative action program has succeeded, it must be changed or dropped.

____ 2. In a sexual harassment case, an employer cannot be held liable for the actions of an employee.

____ 3. In a sexual harassment case, an employer cannot be held liable for the actions of a nonemployee.

____ 4. Women affected by pregnancy must be treated for all job-related purposes the same as persons not so affected but similar in ability to work.

____ 5. Employment discrimination against persons with a physical or mental impairment that substantially limits their everyday activities is prohibited.

____ 6. Discrimination complaints brought under federal law must be filed with the Equal Opportunity Employment Commission.

____ 7. If the Equal Employment Opportunity Commission decides not to investigate a claim, the victim has no other option.

____ 8. All employers are subject to Title VII of the Civil Rights Act of 1964.

____ 9. Disparate-treatment discrimination occurs when an employer intentionally discriminates against an employee.

____ 10. Title VII prohibits employers and unions from discriminating against persons because of their religions.

FILL-IN QUESTIONS

(Answers at the Back of the Book)

The Equal Employment Opportunity Commission (EEOC) monitors compliance with the federal antidiscrimination laws. The EEOC _____ (can/cannot) sue organizations that violate these laws. A victim files a claim with the EEOC, which investigates and _____ _____ (must sue/may sue if a settlement between the parties is not reached). If the EEOC does not sue, the victim may sue. On proof of discrimination, a victim may be awarded _____ _____ (reinstatement and back pay/reinstatement, back pay, and retroactive promotions).

MULTIPLE-CHOICE QUESTIONS

(Answers at the Back of the Book)

____ 1. Dona applies to Estuary Management Corporation for an administrative assistant's job, which requires certain typing skills. Dona cannot type but tells Estuary that she is willing to learn. Estuary does not hire her, and she later sues. To successfully defend against the suit under Title VII, Estuary must show that

a. being a member of the majority is a BFOQ.
b. Dona was not willing to learn to type.
c. Estuary has a valid business necessity defense.
d. Estuary's work force reflects the same percentage of members of a protected class that characterizes qualified individuals in the local labor market.

____ 2. Greg and Holly work for Interstate Services, Inc. (ISI), as electrical engineers. Greg is paid more than Holly because, according to ISI, he is a man with a family to support. This is prohibited by

a. the Age Discrimination in Employment Act of 1967.
b. the Americans with Disabilities Act of 1990.
c. the Equal Pay Act of 1963.
d. none of the choices.

____ 3. **Based on a Sample CPA Exam Question.** Under the Age Discrimination in Employment Act of 1967, Turnover Business Corporation is prohibited from

a. committing unintentional age discrimination.
b. forcing an employee to retire.
c. terminating an employee between the ages of sixty-five and seventy for cause.
d. terminating an employee as part of a rational business decision.

____ 4. Neville, who is hearing impaired, applies for a position with Mold Casters Company. Neville is qualified but is refused the job and sues Mold Casters. To succeed under the Americans with Disabilities Act, Neville must show that

a. Neville was willing to make a "reasonable accommodation" for Mold Casters.
b. Neville would not have to accept "significant additional costs" to work for Mold Casters.
c. Mold Casters refused to make a "reasonable accommodation" for Neville.
d. Mold Casters would not have to accept "significant additional costs" to hire Neville.

____ 5. Insurance Sales, Inc., promotes employees on the basis of color. Employees with darker skin color are passed over in favor of those with lighter skin color, regardless of their race. This is prohibited by

a. the Americans with Disabilities Act of 1990.
b. the Equal Pay Act of 1963.
c. Title VII of the Civil Rights Act of 1964.
d. none of the choices.

____ 6. Mina is an employee of Widebody Trucking Corporation. Mina attempts to resolve a gender-based discrimination claim with Widebody, whose representative denies the claim. Mina's next best step is to

a. ask the Equal Opportunity Employment Commission whether a claim is justified.
b. file a lawsuit.
c. forget about the matter.
d. secretly sabotage company operations for revenge.

_____ 7. Curt, personnel director for Digital Products, Inc., prefers to hire Asian Americans, because "they're smarter and work harder" than other minorities. This is prohibited by

    a. the Age Discrimination in Employment Act of 1967.
    b. the Americans with Disabilities Act of 1990.
    c. Title VII of the Civil Rights Act of 1964.
    d. none of the choices.

_____ 8. Simplex Corporation terminates Tom, who sues on the basis of age discrimination. To succeed under the Age Discrimination in Employment Act, Tom must show that at the time of the discharge, he was

    a. forty or older.
    b. forty or younger.
    c. replaced with someone forty or older.
    d. replaced with someone forty or younger.

_____ 9. Heavy Equipment Company requires job applicants to pass certain physical tests. Only a few female applicants can pass the tests, but if they pass, they are hired. To successfully defend against a suit on this basis under Title VII, the employer must show that

    a. any discrimination is not intentional.
    b. being a male is a BFOQ.
    c. passing the tests is a business necessity.
    d. some men cannot pass the tests.

_____ 10. Dex and Erin work for Citycore Promotions Company. Dex is Erin's supervisor. During work, he touches her in ways that she perceives as sexually offensive. She resists the advances. He cuts her pay. Citycore is

    a. liable, because Dex's conduct constituted sexual harassment.
    b. liable, because Erin resisted Dex's advances.
    c. not liable, because Dex's conduct was not job-related.
    d. not liable, because Erin resisted Dex's advances.

SHORT ESSAY QUESTIONS

1. Compare and contrast disparate-treatment discrimination and disparate-impact discrimination, and Title VII's response to each in the context of employment.

2. What does the Americans with Disabilities Act require employers to do?

GAMEPOINTS

(Answers at the Back of the Book)

1. You are playing the video game "Discrimination!" in which a player accrues points by correctly spotting, reporting, and resolving instances of discrimination in various workplaces. In one scenario, set in a packing plant owned and operated by Savory Treats, Inc., a gourmet-food packaging and shipping firm, Tanner, the company's owner, tells Vera, its human resources director, not to hire Willis, a disabled applicant. In Tanner's words, "we don't want to make changes to accommodate this guy—it'll give the other employees ideas." Is this discrimination? Why or why not?

2. Sam works as a driver for Toxic Games Warehouse, a wholesale distributor and online retailer of video games and accessories. Over a ten-year period, Sam repeatedly applies for—and is denied—a promotion to the position of dispatcher. Sam meets the requirements for the job, which are a year's driving experience and a specific license. After one interview, Sam overhears the interviewer tell a co-worker that Sam, who is white, didn't get the job because "whites are lazy." Is this employment discrimination? Explain.

SPECIAL INFORMATION FOR CPA CANDIDATES

The CPA examination has included an occasional question on discrimination—what is prohibited and what individuals are protected. These questions have concerned the broad coverage of the law, rather than specific details.

CUMULATIVE HYPOTHETICAL PROBLEM
FOR UNIT SEVEN—INCLUDING CHAPTERS 32–35

(Answers at the Back of the Book)

Dot, Earl, Frank, Gail, Hal, Ira, Jane, Karen, Larry, and Mike work for International Sales Corporation (ISC).

____ 1. Earl retires from ISC at the age of sixty-five. Frank retires at sixty-seven. Because of a disability, Gail, after fifteen years, is unable to continue working for ISC. Hal is discharged from ISC as part of a reduction in force. All of the following benefits are part of Social Security EXCEPT

a. Earl's government retirement payments.
b. Frank's Medicare payments.
c. Gail's government disability payments.
d. Hal's unemployment benefits.

____ 2. Dot, who works in ISC's warehouse, is injured on the job. Dot may NOT collect workers' compensation benefits if she

a. files a civil suit against a third party based on the injury.
b. intentionally caused her own injury.
c. was injured as a result of a co-worker's act.
d. worked for ISC for less than sixty days.

____ 3. Ira works for ISC as a sales representative at a salary of $3,000 per month, plus a 10 percent commission. As ISC's agent, Ira

a. cannot be dismissed during the six-month period without cause.
b. cannot enforce the agency unless it is in writing and signed by Delta.
c. is an agent coupled with an interest.
d. must act solely in Delta's interest in matters concerning Delta's business.

____ 4. Four employees file suits against ISC, alleging discrimination. Title VII of the Civil Rights Act of 1964 covers all of the following EXCEPT Jane's suit alleging discrimination on the basis of

a. age.
b. gender.
c. race.
d. religion.

____ 5. Karen, an ISC manager, wants to institute a policy of mandatory retirement for all employees at age sixty-four. Larry, an ISC manager, wants to discharge Mike, who is age sixty-seven, for cause. Under federal anti-discrimination law

a. Karen's and Larry's wishes can be granted.
b. neither Karen's and Larry's wishes can be granted.
c. only Karen's wish can be granted.
d. only Larry's wish can be granted.

QUESTIONS ON THE FOCUS ON ETHICS FOR UNIT SEVEN—
AGENCY AND EMPLOYMENT

(Answers at the Back of the Book)

_____ **1.** Eve is Fred's agent. Ethics would prevent Eve from

a. being loyal to Fred.
b. disclosing Eve's interest in property being bought by Fred.
c. profiting from the agency relation with Fred's consent
d. representing Gary in a transaction with Fred.

_____ **2.** Harry is Irma's agent. Ethics might prescribe otherwise, but Harry's legal duties to Irma do not include

a. compensation.
b. cooperation.
c. loyalty.
d. reimbursement.

_____ **3.** Dave works for Executive Sales Corporation. Reasons for holding Executive liable under the doctrine of _respondeat superior_ for Dave's tort injuring Flo do _not_ include the employer's

a. ability to afford Flo more effective relief.
b. ability to pay for Flo's injury.
c. control over Dave.
d. guilt or innocence.

Sole prop.

- growth limited
- cant bring on partner
- can't issue stock

Chapter 36
Sole Proprietorships and Franchises

WHAT THIS CHAPTER IS ABOUT

This chapter briefly outlines the features of a sole proprietorship, the most common form of business, and discusses private franchises, which are widely used by entrepreneurs to seek profits.

CHAPTER OUTLINE

I. **SOLE PROPRIETORSHIPS** *2/3 of all businesses in US.*
   The simplest form of business—the owner is the business. *tend to be very small*

   A. **ADVANTAGES OF THE SOLE PROPRIETORSHIP**
   These include that the proprietor takes all the profits; this organization is easier to start than others (few legal forms involved); the form has more flexibility (the proprietor is free to make all decisions); and the owner pays only personal income tax on profits.

   B. **DISADVANTAGES OF THE SOLE PROPRIETORSHIP**
   can't issue stocks These include that the proprietor has all the risk (unlimited liability for all debts); there is limited opportunity to raise capital; and the business dissolves when the owner dies.

II. **FRANCHISES**
   A franchise is any arrangement in which the owner of a trademark, a trade name, or a copyright has licensed others to use it in selling goods or services.

   A. **TYPES OF FRANCHISES**

      1. **Distributorship**
      This is when a manufacturer licenses a dealer to sell its product (such as an automobile dealer). Often covers an exclusive territory.

      2. **Chain-Style Business Operation**
      This occurs when a franchise operates under a franchisor's trade name and is identified as a member of a group of dealers engaged in the franchisor's business (such as most fast-food chains). The franchisee must follow standardized or prescribed methods of operations, and may be obligated to obtain supplies exclusively from the franchisor.

      3. **Manufacturing Arrangement**
      This type exists when a franchisor transmits to the franchisee the essential ingredients or formula to make a product (such as Coca-Cola), which the franchisee makes and markets according to the franchisor's standards.

   B. **LAWS GOVERNING FRANCHISING**

      1. **Federal Protection of Franchises**

289

a. Automobile Dealers' Franchise Act of 1965
The Automobile Dealers' Franchise Act protects dealership franchisees from manufacturers' bad faith termination of their franchises.

b. Petroleum Marketing Practices Act (PMPA) of 1979
The PMPA prescribes the grounds and conditions under which a gasoline station franchisor may terminate or decline to renew a franchise.

c. Antitrust Laws
These laws may apply if there is an anticompetitive agreement (see Chapter 47).

d. Federal Trade Commission (FTC) Franchise Rule
Franchisors must disclose material facts necessary to a prospective franchisee's making an informed decision concerning a franchise. This must be in writing, but it may be made available online.

2. State Protection for Franchisees
State law is similar to federal law. State deceptive practices acts may apply, as may Article 2 of the Uniform Commercial Code.

C. THE FRANCHISE CONTRACT
A franchise relationship is created by a contract between the franchisor and the franchisee.

1. Payment for the Franchise
A franchisee pays (1) a fee for the franchise license, (2) fees for products bought from or through the franchisor, (3) a percentage of sales, and (4) a percentage of advertising and administrative costs.

2. Business Premises
The agreement may specify whether the premises for the business are leased or purchased and who is to supply equipment and furnishings.

3. Location of the Franchise
The franchisor determines the territory to be served and its exclusivity. The implied covenant of good faith and fair dealing may apply to a dispute over territorial rights.

4. Business Organization
A franchisor may specify requirements for the form and capital structure of the franchisee's business.

5. Quality Control
A franchisor may specify standards of operation (such as quality standards) and personnel training methods. Too much control may result in a franchisor's liability for torts of a franchisee's employees.

6. Pricing Arrangements
A franchisor may require a franchisee to buy certain supplies from the franchisor at an established price. A franchisor may also suggest retail prices for the goods that the franchisee sells.

III. FRANCHISE TERMINATION
Determined by the parties. Usually, termination must be "for cause" (such as breach of the agreement, etc.) and notice must be given. A franchisee must be given reasonable time to wind up the business.

A. WRONGFUL TERMINATION
Important in determining whether termination is wrongful is whether it occurred in bad faith, whether the contract's relevant provisions are unconscionable, and so on.

B. THE IMPORTANCE OF GOOD FAITH AND FAIR DEALING
Courts generally try to balance the rights of both parties and provide a remedy if the franchisor acted unfairly. If termination occurred in the normal course of business and reasonable notice was given, however, termination was not likely wrongful.

TRUE-FALSE QUESTIONS

(Answers at the Back of the Book)

____ 1. In a sole proprietorship, the owner and the business are entirely separate.

____ 2. In a sole proprietorship, the owner receives all of the profits.

____ 3. The income of a sole proprietorship is taxed to the owner as personal income.

____ 4. The death of the owner automatically dissolves a sole proprietorship.

____ 5. A court always determines the termination of a franchise.

____ 6. A franchise is an arrangement in which the owner of a trademark, a trade name, or a copyright has licensed others to use it in selling goods or services.

____ 7. A franchisee is not subject to the franchisor's control in the area of product quality.

____ 8. There is no state law covering franchises.

____ 9. There are no federal laws covering franchises.

____ 10. A franchisor may specify the form and capital structure of the franchisee's business.

FILL-IN QUESTIONS

(Answers at the Back of the Book)

An automobile dealership is an example of a _____ (chain-style/distributorship/manufacturing) franchise. McDonald's is an example of a _____ _____ (chain-style/distributorship/manufacturing) franchise. Coca-Cola is an example of a _____ (chain-style/distributorship/manufacturing) franchise.

MULTIPLE-CHOICE QUESTIONS

(Answers at the Back of the Book)

____ 1. Rae owns Solo Enterprises, a sole proprietorship. Rae's liability for the obligations of the business is

a. limited by state statute.
b. limited to the amount of his original investment.
c. limited to the total amount of capital Ann invests in the business.
d. unlimited.

____ **2.** Violet invests in a franchise with Whiz Gas Stations, Inc. Whiz requires Violet to buy Whiz products for every phase of the operation. Violet's best argument to challenge this requirement is that it violates

    a. an implied covenant of good faith and fair dealing.
    b. antitrust laws.
    c. the Federal Trade Commission's Franchise Rule.
    d. the U.S. Franchise Agency's Purchase and Sale Regulations.

____ **3.** Bing invests in a franchise with Copy Centers, Inc. The franchise agreement may require Bing to pay a percentage of Copy's

    a. administrative and advertising expenses.
    b. administrative expenses only.
    c. advertising expenses only.
    d. neither administrative nor advertising expenses.

____ **4.** Dryden wants the exclusive right to sell Elan Corporation software in a specific area. If Elan agrees, it may require Dryden to pay

    a. a fee for a license and a percentage of the receipts.
    b. neither a fee for a license nor a percentage of the receipts.
    c. only a fee for a license to sell the software.
    d. only a percentage of the receipts from sales of the software.

____ **5.** Fridley buys a franchise from Global Services, Inc. In their agreement, Global may specify

    a. neither requirements for the form of business nor standards of operation.
    b. requirements for the form of business and standards of operation.
    c. requirements for the form of business only.
    d. standards of operation only.

____ **6.** Rhett buys a franchise from Sports Club Corporation. If their agreement is like most franchise agreements, it will allow Sports Club to terminate the franchise

    a. for any reason only with notice.
    b. for any reason without notice.
    c. for cause only.
    d. under no circumstances.

____ **7.** Salvador invests in a franchise with Thai Foods Corporation. With respect to the franchise, Salvador may have legal protection under

    a. federal and state law.
    b. federal law only.
    c. neither federal nor state law.
    d. state law only.

____ **8.** Devonna, the owner of Evangelina Sales, a sole proprietorship, wants to increase the business's capital without sacrificing control. This can be attained most successfully by

    a. borrowing funds.
    b. bringing in partners.
    c. issuing stock.
    d. selling the business.

___ **9.** Perry considers buying a franchise instead of developing and marketing his own products. A franchise could involve the licensing to Perry of

    a. a copyright only.
    b. a trademark or a trade name only.
    c. a copyright, a trademark, or a trade name.
    d. not a copyright, a trademark, or a trade name.

___ **10.** Lasso Farm & Ranch Outfitters, Inc., grants a franchise to Mort. Mort is Lasso's

    a. agent.
    b. franchisee.
    c. franchisor.
    d. principal.

SHORT ESSAY QUESTIONS

1. What do franchise agreements generally provide with respect to a franchisee's location and form of doing business?

2. How do franchise agreements generally delegate price and quality controls over the franchisee's business?

GAMEPOINTS

(Answers at the Back of the Book)

1. You're playing "Solo," a video game in which the goal is to amass as much personal profit from the investment of your time and money in your business enterprise as possible. At the start of the game, your business is small—your avatar is your only "employee"—and you expect to make little or no profit for at least a couple of "years." Your competitors include seemingly heartless corporate money mongers and faceless government bureaucrats, whose only reason for existence appears to be to prevent your success. Which form of business organization are you most likely to choose at the start? Why? What are its disadvantages? How can you raise additional capital without losing control of your outfit?

2. "Burgers & Fries" is a video game in which you operate fast food franchise restaurants. You start with a single, small outlet that grows with its success. You expand your operation with your profits, adding as many outlets as you can, balancing your franchisor's requirements, your customers' requests, your business costs, and your desire to increase your wealth. Your agreement with your franchisor includes sales quotas. The agreement also states that your franchise can be terminated at any time for "cause." Would a failure to meet those quotas constitute "cause"? Explain.

SPECIAL INFORMATION FOR CPA CANDIDATES

For the CPA exam, it is most important to know the differences among the types of business organizations. Not traditionally tested on the exam are franchises. Of course, they may some day appear in a question on the test.

— way for sole propieters to grow business

Chapter 37
Partnerships and Limited Liability Partnerships

WHAT THIS CHAPTER IS ABOUT

This chapter outlines the law of different types of partnerships. These include general partnerships, limited partnerships, limited liability partnerships, and limited liability limited partnerships.

CHAPTER OUTLINE

I. **BASIC PARTNERSHIP CONCEPTS** *General Partnership*

A partnership arises from an agreement between two or more persons to carry on a business for profit. *— must have the intent to make profit (can't have non-profit partnership)*

A. AGENCY CONCEPTS AND PARTNERSHIP LAW
Agency principles (see Chapters 31 and 32) apply to all partnerships.

B. THE UNIFORM PARTNERSHIP ACT
The Uniform Partnership Act (UPA) governs partnerships.

C. DEFINITION OF A PARTNERSHIP
A partnership is "an association of two or more persons to carry on as co-owners a business for profit" [UPA 101(6)]. The intent to associate is a key element. A corporation can be a partner [UPA 101(10)].

D. WHEN DOES A PARTNERSHIP EXIST?
There are three essential elements:

1. A sharing of profits or losses.
2. A joint ownership of the business.
3. An equal right in the management of the business.

E. RECEIPT OF PROFITS AND PARTNERSHIP STATUS
A partnership does not exist if profits are received as payment of—[UPA 202(c)(3)]

1. A debt by installments or interest on a loan.
2. Wages of an employer or for the services of an independent contractor.
3. Rent to a landlord.
4. An annuity to a surviving spouse or representative of a deceased partner.
5. A sale of the goodwill of a business or property.

F. JOINT PROPERTY OWNERSHIP AND PARTNERSHIP STATUS
The joint ownership of property is not enough to create a partnership. Sharing profits from the ownership does not by itself establish a partnership (although sharing profits *and* losses does).

295

G. ENTITY VERSUS AGGREGATE
Under the UPA, a partnership is treated as an entity [UPA 201, 307(a). A partnership can own property as an entity, and sue and be sued in the firm name.

H. TAX TREATMENT OF PARTNERSHIPS
For federal income tax purposes, a partnership is regarded as an aggregate of individual partners.

II. PARTNERSHIP FORMATION
A partnership agreement generally states the intention to create a partnership, contribute capital, share profits and losses, and participate in management.

A. THE PARTNERSHIP AGREEMENT
The agreement can be oral, written, or implied by conduct. Some must be in writing under the Statute of Frauds (see Chapter 15). Partners can agree to any term that is not illegal or contrary to public policy.

B. DURATION OF THE PARTNERSHIP
A partnership for a term ends on a specific date or the completion of a particular project. Dissolution without consent of all partners before the end of the term is a breach of the agreement. If there is no fixed term, a partnership is at will, and any partner can dissolve the firm at any time.

C. PARTNERSHIP BY ESTOPPEL
When parties who are not partners hold themselves out as partners and make representations that third persons rely on in dealing with them, liability is imposed. A partner who misrepresents a non-partner's status is also liable (and the non-partner's acts may bind the partnership).

III. PARTNERSHIP OPERATION

A. RIGHTS OF PARTNERS

1. Management

a. In Ordinary Matters, the Majority Rules
All partners have equal rights to manage the firm [UPA 401(e)]. Each partner has one vote.

b. When Unanimous Consent Is Required
Unanimous consent is required to [UPA 301(2), 401(j)]—

1) Alter the essential nature of the firm's business or capital structure.
2) Admit new partners or enter a new business.
3) Assign property into a trust for the benefit of creditors.
4) Dispose of the firm's goodwill.
5) Confess judgment against the firm or submit firm claims to arbitration.
6) Undertake any act that would make conduct of partnership business impossible.
7) Amend partnership articles.

2. Interest in the Partnership
Unless the partners agree otherwise, profits and losses are shared equally [UPA 401(b)].

3. Compensation
Doing partnership business is a partner's duty and not compensable.

4. Inspection of the Books
A partner has a right to complete information concerning the conduct of partnership business [UPA 403]. Partnership books must be kept at the principal business office.

5. **Accounting of Partnership Assets or Profits**
An accounting can be called for voluntarily or compelled by a court. Formal accounting occurs by right in connection with dissolution. A partner also has the right to an accounting to resolve claims among the partners or with the partnership.

6. **Property Rights**
Property acquired by a partnership is normally partnership property [UPA 203, 204]. A partner can use this property only on the firm's behalf [UPA 401(g)]. A partner is not a co-owner of this property and has no interest in it that can be transferred (although a partner can assign his or her right to a share of the profits) [UPA 501]. A partner's interest is subject to a judgment creditor's lien, attachable through a charging order [UPA 504].

B. DUTIES AND LIABILITIES OF PARTNERS

1. **Fiduciary Duties**
A partner owes the firm and its partners duties of loyalty and care [UPA 404].

   a. **Duty of Care**
   A partner must refrain from "grossly negligent or reckless conduct, intentional misconduct, or a knowing violation of law" [UPA 404(c)].

   b. **Duty of Loyalty**
   A partner must account to the firm for "any property, profit, or benefit" in the conduct of its business or from a use of its property, and refrain from dealing with the firm as an adverse party or competing with it [UPA 404(b)].

   c. **Breach and Waiver of Fiduciary Duties**
   These duties cannot be waived and partners must comply with the obligations of good faith and fair dealing, but a partner may pursue his or her own interests without automatically violating these duties. [UPA 103(b). 404(d)].

2. **Authority of Partners**
Each partner is an agent of the partnership in carrying out its business, unless designated otherwise.

   a. **The Scope of Implied Powers**
   Partners exercise all implied powers necessary and customary to carry on the business.

   b. **Authorized versus Unauthorized Actions**
   A partner cannot act purportedly on behalf of the partnership outside the scope of the business (by, for example, selling partnership assets without consent).

3. **Liability of Partners**

   a. **Joint Liability**
   In some states, partners are only jointly liable for partnership obligations, including contracts [UPA 306(a)]. This does not include debts arising from torts, and a creditor must sue all of the partners together (though each may be held liable individually).

   b. **Joint and Several Liability**
   In most states, partners are jointly and severally liable for all partnership obligations, including contracts, torts, and breaches of trust [UPA 306(a)] (though a creditor must first try to collect a partnership debt from the firm). A partner who commits a tort must reimburse the partnership for any damages it pays.

   c. **Liability of Incoming Partners**
   A newly admitted partner is liable for partnership debts incurred before his or her admission only to the extent of his or her interest in the partnership [UPA 306(b)].

IV.   DISSOCIATION OF A PARTNER

Dissociation occurs when a partner ceases to be associated in the carrying on of the partnership business. The partner can have his or her interest bought by the firm, which otherwise continues in business.

A.   EVENTS CAUSING DISSOCIATION

Dissociation occurs when a partner give notices and withdraws, declares bankruptcy, assigns his or her interest, dies, becomes incompetent, or is expelled by the firm or by a court. Other events can be specified in the partnership agreement [UPA 601].

B.   WRONGFUL DISSOCIATION

Dissociation is wrongful if it is in breach of the partnership agreement, or occurs before the expiration of its term or completion of its undertaking [UPA 602]. A partner who wrongfully dissociates is liable to the partnership and to the other partners for damages caused by the dissociation.

C.   EFFECTS OF DISSOCIATION

1.   The Partner

A partner's right to participate in the firm's business ends [UPA 603]. The duty of loyalty ends. The duty of care continues only with respect to events that occurred before dissociation, unless the partner participates in winding up the firm's business.

2.   The Partnership

The partner's interest in the firm must be purchased according to the rules in UPA 701. To avoid liability for obligations under a theory of apparent authority, a partnership should notify its creditors of a partner's dissociation and file a statement of dissociation in the appropriate state office [UPA 704].

V.   PARTNERSHIP TERMINATION

Caused by any change in the relations of the partners that shows unwillingness or inability to carry on partnership business [UPA 801]. To continue the business, a partner can organize a new partnership.

A.   DISSOLUTION

Dissolution terminates the right of the partnership to exist as a going concern, but the firm remains long enough to wind up its affairs.

1.   Dissolution by Agreement

Partners can agree to dissolve the partnership at any time. A partnership dissolves on the occurrence of an event specified in the partnership agreement for its dissolution.

2.   Dissolution by Operation of Law

A partnership for a definite term or undertaking is dissolved when the term expires or the undertaking is accomplished. A partnership is dissolved if an event occurs that makes it impossible to continue lawfully, although the partners can continue if they change the nature of the business [UPA 801(4)].

3.   Dissolution by Judicial Decree

A court can dissolve a partnership for commercial impracticality, a partner's improper conduct, or other circumstances [UPA 801(5)].

B.   WINDING UP AND DISTRIBUTION OF ASSETS

This involves collecting and preserving partnership assets, paying debts, and accounting to each partner for the value of his or her interest. No new obligations can be created on behalf of the firm.

1. Distribution of Assets
Priorities for a partnership's assets are (1) payment of debts, including those owed to partner and non-partner creditors, and (2) return of capital contributions and distribution of profits to partners.

2. If the Partnership's Liabilities Are Greater Than Its Assets
The general partners bear the losses in the same proportion in which they shared the profits.

C. PARTNERSHIP BUY-SELL AGREEMENTS
Partners may agree that one or more partners may buy out the others—who buys what, under what circumstances, and at what price. If a partner's dissociation does not result in dissolution, a buy-out of his or her interest is mandatory [UPA 701] at basically the price as he or she would get on dissolution.

VI. LIMITED LIABILITY PARTNERSHIPS — *not a limited partnership — special type of general partnership*
A limited liability partnership (LLP) enjoys the tax advantages of a partnership, while partners avoid personal liability for the wrongdoing of other partners. *when something bad happens only liable partner faces unlimited liability*

A. FORMATION OF AN LLP *as well as possibly the managing partner*
The appropriate form must be filed with a central state agency. The business's name must include "Limited Liability Partnership" or "LLP." Annual reports must be filed with the state [UPA 1001, 1002, 1003].

B. LIABILITY IN AN LLP
The UPA exempts partners in an LLP from personal liability for any partnership obligation, "whether arising in contract, tort, or otherwise" [UPA 306(c)].

1. Liability outside the State of Formation
Most states apply the law of the state in which the LLP was formed [UPA 1101].

2. Sharing Liability among Partner
A partner who commits a wrongful act is liable for the results, as is any other partner who committed the act. Some states provide that each partner is liable only up to the proportion of his or her responsibility for the result.

C. FAMILY LIMITED LIABILITY PARTNERSHIPS
disappearing in many states This is a limited liability partnership (LLP) in which most of the partners are related. All partners must be natural persons or persons acting in a fiduciary capacity for natural persons. Family-owned farms may benefit from this form.

VII. LIMITED PARTNERSHIPS — *Limited partners cannot be part of managing*
Limited partnerships must include at least one general partner and one or more limited partners. General partners assume management responsibility and liability for all partnership debts.

A. FORMATION OF A LIMITED PARTNERSHIP
Formation of a limited partnership is a public, formal proceeding: there must be two or more partners (at least one of whom is a general partner), and a certificate of limited partnership must be signed and filed with a designated state official (typically the secretary of state).
liability limited to amount of partners investment

B. LIABILITIES OF PARTNERS IN A LIMITED PARTNERSHIP
General partners assume liability for all partnership debts. A limited partner is liable only to the extent of any contribution that is promised to the firm or any part of a contribution that was withdrawn [RULPA 502]. But participating in management results in a limited partner's personal liability for partnership debt, if creditors knew of participation [RULPA 303].
become general partners

C. RIGHTS AND DUTIES IN A LIMITED PARTNERSHIP
Limited partners have essentially the same rights as general partners—a right of access to the partnership books and other information regarding partnership business.

D. DISSOCIATION AND DISSOLUTION
Lawyers and doctors cannot be limited partners because they must work, have license, contribute, etc.

1. **General Partners—Dissolution**
   Dissociation in any form—retirement, death, or mental incompetence—of a general partner dissolves the firm, unless continued by all other partners [RULPA 801]. Illegality, expulsion, or bankruptcy of a general partner dissolves a firm.

2. **Limited Partners—No Dissolution**
   Death or assignment of interest of a limited partner does not dissolve the firm [RULPA 702, 704, 705], nor does personal bankruptcy.

3. **Court Decree—Dissolution**
   A limited partnership can be dissolved by court decree [RULPA 802].

4. **Priority to Assets on Dissolution**
   (1) Creditors, including partners who are creditors; (2) partners and former partners receive unpaid distributions of partnership assets and, except as otherwise agreed, a return on their contributions and amounts proportionate to their share of distributions [RULPA 804].

E. **LIMITED LIABILITY/LIMITED PARTNERSHIPS** *LLLP*
   This form is similar to a limited partnership, except that the liability of all partners in a limited liability limited partnership (LLLP) is limited to the amount of their investment in the firm.

[handwritten: not recognized by all states]

[handwritten: ① people wont use LP if state recognized these]

[handwritten: no one has unlimited liability]

TRUE-FALSE QUESTIONS

(Answers at the Back of the Book)

_____ 1. A partnership is an association of two or more persons to carry on, as co-owners, a business for profit.

_____ 2. In most states, no partnership can exist unless a certificate of partnership is filed with a state.

_____ 3. A general partner is not personally liable for partnership debts if its assets are insufficient to pay its creditors.

_____ 4. Unless the partnership agreement states otherwise, a general partner has one vote in management matters.

_____ 5. A partnership is usually considered a legal entity apart from its owners.

_____ 6. Unless a partnership agreement specifies otherwise, profits are shared in the same ratio as capital contributions.

_____ 7. The death of a *limited* partner dissolves a limited partnership.

_____ 8. In a limited liability partnership, no partner is exempt from personal liability for partnership obligations.

_____ 9. In a limited partnership, the liability of a *limited* partner is limited to the amount of capital he or she invests in the partnership.

_____ 10. In a limited liability limited partnership, the liability of a *general* partner is limited to the amount of capital he or she invests in the partnership.

FILL-IN QUESTIONS

(Answers at the Back of the Book)

In most states, partners _____ (are/are not) subject to joint and several liability on partnership debts, contracts, and torts. This means that a third party may sue _____ (one or more/only all) of the partners on a partnership _____ (obligation/tort). If the third party does not sue all of the partners, the liability of those partners who are not sued _____ (is/is not) extinguished. The third party's release of one partner _____ (does not release/releases) the other partners.

MULTIPLE-CHOICE QUESTIONS

(Answers at the Back of the Book)

____ 1. Cosmo holds himself out as a partner of Dayton Associates, a partnership, even though he has no connection to the firm. Cosmo obtains a loan based on the misrepresentation. Cosmo's default on the loan results in

a. Cosmo and Dayton's joint liability for the amount.
b. Cosmo's sole liability for the amount.
c. Delta's sole liability for the amount.
d. neither Cosmo's nor Dayton's liability.

____ 2. Holly owns International Imports. She hires Jordan as a salesperson, agreeing to pay $10.00 per hour, plus a commission of 10 percent of his sales. The term is one year. Holly and Jordan are

a. not partners, because Jay does not have an ownership interest or management rights in the business.
b. not partners, because the pay includes an hourly wage.
c. not partners, because the pay includes only a 10-percent commission.
d. partners for one year.

____ 3. Kris is admitted to an existing partnership. A partnership debt incurred before the date of her admission comes due. Kris is

a. not liable for the debt.
b. only liable for the debt to the amount of her capital contribution.
c. personally liable only to the extent that the other partners do not pay the debt.
d. personally liable to the full extent of the debt.

____ 4. Delilah is a partner in Estelinda Technical Group. Delilah's dissociation from the partnership will cause

a. the automatic termination of the firm's legal existence.
b. the immediate maturity of all partnership debts.
c. the partnership's buyout of Delilah's interest in the firm.
d. the temporary suspension of all partnership business.

____ 5. Owen and Page are partners in Quality Investments, a partnership. Owen convinces Roy, a customer, to invest in a nonexistent gold mine. Owen absconds with Roy's money. If Roy sues Page, Roy will

a. lose, because partners are not jointly and severally liable.
b. lose, because only partnership assets are available to pay the judgment.
c. win, because partners are jointly and severally liable.
d. win, because partnership assets are available to pay the judgment.

____ 6. Bobbi owns Bobbi's Salon, which owes back rent to Capital Properties, a landlord. Bobbi agrees to pay a percentage of her profit each month until the debt is paid. Capital Properties is

a. Bobbi's creditor and partner.
b. Bobbi's creditor only.
c. Bobbi's partner only.
d. neither Bobbi's creditor nor partner.

___ **7.** **Based on a Sample CPA Question.** Elton is a limited partner in Destiny Tours, a limited partnership. Collection Credit Company, a Destiny creditor, claims that Eton is subject to personal liability for Destiny's debts because Elton has the right, as a limited partner to take control of the firm. Collection Credit is correct about

    a. Elton's liability only.
    b. Elton's right to control the firm only.
    c. Elton's liability and Elton's right to control the firm.
    d. none of the choices.

___ **8.** Jack and Kiley form J&K, a limited partnership. Jack is a general partner. Kiley is a limited partner. Dissolution of the firm would result from Kiley's

    a. assignment of her interest in the firm to a third party only.
    b. assignment of her interest, bankruptcy, or death.
    c. bankruptcy or death only.
    d. none of the choices.

___ **9.** Myra, Nico, and Odel are partners in Payroll Accounting Services (PAS). Myra quits the firm, with Nico and Odel's knowledge. Later, Nico and Odel sign a contract with a supplier. The contract is binding on

    a. Nico and Odel only.
    b. Nico, Odel, and PAS only.
    c. PAS only.
    d. no one.

___ **10.** Drs. Lucas and Mikayla are partners in a medical clinic, which is organized as a limited liability partnership. Lucas manages the clinic. A court holds Mikayla liable in a malpractice suit. Lucas is liable

    a. in no way.
    b. in proportion to the total number of partners in the firm.
    c. to the extent of her capital contribution.
    d. to the full extent of the liability.

SHORT ESSAY QUESTIONS

1. What are the rights held by partners in terms of management, interest in the partnership, compensation, inspection of books, accounting, and property rights?

2. How does the concept of joint and several liability, relate to partnerships?

GAMEPOINTS

(Answers at the Back of the Book)

1. The video game "Phantasm" requires two or more players who confront malicious phenomena—ghosts, zombies, and so on—and combine their abilities to capture the bad guys for delivery to university research centers. In the game, you orally agree with your partner to pursue this adventure for five years, with the profits to be split 60/40. If this were a real partnership, would the agreement be enforceable? Should the terms be in writing? Explain.

2. You are playing "Business Buddy," a video game in which the play consists of two or more players who operate as partners to buy, sell, and trade commodities—oil, corn, swine, and other animals, vegetables, and minerals—in global markets. One of your "buddies" is your cousin Melvin. Your agreement states that only you have the authority to bind the partnership to contracts with others. Without your knowledge, however,

Melvin tells the Greater Asian Goatherds Association that he represents your firm and contracts to buy a large herd of goats. What factor determines whether your partnership is bound to this contract? If the contract is binding on the firm, to what extent are you personally liable?

SPECIAL INFORMATION FOR CPA CANDIDATES

For the CPA exam, it is important to know the differences among the types of business organizations, including sole proprietorships and partnerships.

The UPA definition of *partnership* has frequently been on the exam. Keep in mind that unless partners agree otherwise, they share profits, losses, and management rights equally, and that only surviving partners are entitled to a salary. Other important points include that partners are jointly and severally liable for torts committed by copartners carrying on the business and for all partnership contracts.

For the CPA examination, an important point in the material in this chapter is the liability of partners to each other and to third parties—remember that every partner is an agent of the partnership and of the other partners. Review the liability of withdrawing partners and new partners.

* C - corp — owners and managers separated
board elected by shareholders
board appoints officers of company

Disadvantages → — Double taxation
      ↳ corporation pays taxes
       ↳ after taxes corporation pays
        dividends which are taxed

    — very regulated

* Sub - S corporation — only 1 class of stock
       = limited shareholders
       = no foreign investment
       — retained earnings limited

—

— no double taxation

        in response states
        developed →

Chapter 38
Limited Liability Companies and Special Business Forms

WHAT THIS CHAPTER IS ABOUT

This chapter sets out the law relating to a relatively new form of business organization—the limited liability company (LLC). The chief features of this form are its limited liability and tax advantages. The chapter also looks at the features of other forms—joint ventures, business trusts, cooperatives, and so on.

CHAPTER OUTLINE

I. THE LIMITED LIABILITY COMPANY

A limited liability company (LLC) is a hybrid form of business enterprise. State statutes govern LLCs. Despite some similarities among these state laws, less than one-fifth of the states have adopted the Uniform Limited Liability Company Act (ULLCA).

A. TAXATION OF THE LLC
An LLC is taxed as a partnership unless it chooses to be taxed as a corporation.

B. THE NATURE OF THE LLC
An LLC offers the limited liability of a corporation [ULLCA 303]. Courts may pierce the LLC veil to hold members liable for the firm's obligations.

C. THE FORMATION OF THE LLC
Articles of organization must be filed with the state. Certain information is required. The business's name must include and LLC designation.

D. JURISDICTIONAL REQUIREMENTS
An LLC is a citizen of every state of which its members are citizens.

E. ADVANTAGES OF THE LLC

1. Limited Liability
An LLC offers the limited liability of the corporation—the liability of its members is limited to the amount of their investments.

2. Flexibility in Taxation
An LLC offers the tax advantages of a partnership. LLCs with two or more members can elect to be taxed as either a partnership or a corporation. If no choice is made, an LLC is taxed as a partnership. One-member LLCs are taxed as sole proprietorships unless they elect to be taxed as corporations.

3. Management and Foreign Investors
An LLC has flexibility in terms of its management and operations (see below). Foreign investors may become LLC members, which encourages investment.

305

F. DISADVANTAGES OF AN LLC

Until uniform statutes are adopted by most states, an LLC with multistate operations may face difficulties. To be treated as a partnership for tax purposes, an LLC must have at least two members.

II.   OPERATION AND MANAGEMENT OF AN LLC

A. THE LLC OPERATING AGREEMENT

Members decide how to operate the business. Provisions relate to management, division of profits, transfer of membership, what events trigger dissolution, and so on. In the absence of an agreement, LLC statutes govern.

1. A Writing Is Preferred

An operating agreement is not required in all states and if required may not need to be in writing. But a written agreement protects members' interests if there is a dispute or if an LLC statute is contrary to their intent.

2. Partnership Law May Apply

If there is no operating agreement or LLC statute, the principles of partnership law apply. This may give the members broad authority to bind the LLC.

B. MANAGEMENT OF AN LLC

In a member-managed LLC, all members participate in management [ULLCA 404(a)]. In a manager-managed LLC, the members designate a group of persons (member or not) to manage the firm. These managers owe the fiduciary duties of loyalty and care to the LLC and in some states to its members [ULLCA 409(a), (h)].

C. OPERATING PROCEDURES

The operating agreement may specify procedures for making decisions. If it does not, choosing and removing managers is done by majority vote [ULLCA 404(b)(3)]. Details concerning meetings and voting rights may also be included. If not, in some states, each member has one vote.

III.   DISSOCIATION AND DISSOLUTION OF AN LLC

A member has the power to dissociate from an LLC but may not have the right to do so. Events that trigger dissociation include withdrawal, expulsion by other members or a court, bankruptcy, incompetence, and death.

A. EFFECT OF DISSOCIATION

The dissociating member loses the right to participate in management and to act as agent for the LLC. The other members can buy his or her interest for a fair value (within 120 days under the ULLCA).

B. DISSOLUTION

The remaining members can continue or dissolve the LLC, unless the operating agreement provides otherwise. A court can order dissolution if, for example, the members have acted illegally. An LLC is bound by the reasonable acts of its members during the winding up process. Proceeds are distributed to LLC creditors (including members) first, to capital contributors second, and to members third.

IV.   SPECIAL BUSINESS FORMS

A. JOINT VENTURE — *normally for single thing (partner on a car project)*

A joint venture is an enterprise in which two or more persons combine their efforts or property for a single transaction or project, or a related series of transactions or projects. Unless otherwise agreed, joint venturers share profits and losses equally.

1. Similarities to Partnerships

The characteristics of a joint venture are similar to those of a partnership.

FSIA — Foreign Sovereign Immunity Act

if other partner is a government shell — cannot go forward with a lawsuit

2. Differences from Partnerships
Members in a joint venture have less implied and apparent authority than partners.

B. SYNDICATE — *like a mutual fund in organization*
A group of individuals getting together to finance a particular project, such as the building of a shopping center or the purchase of a professional basketball franchise, is a syndicate. It may exist as a corporation or a partnership. In some cases, the members merely own property jointly and have no legally recognized business arrangement.

C. JOINT STOCK COMPANY
Usually treated like a partnership (formed by agreement, members have personal liability, etc.), but members are not agents of one another, and has many characteristics of a corporation: (1) ownership by shares of stock, (2) managed by directors and officers, and (3) perpetual existence.

D. BUSINESS TRUST
A business trust is created by a written trust agreement. Legal ownership and management of the property of the business is in one or more trustees; profits are distributed to beneficiaries, who are not personally responsible for the debts of the trust. A business trust resembles a corporation. *trustee owns property, but can only do that equitable act to owners benefit /*

E. COOPERATIVE
A cooperative is an association organized to provide an economic service without profit to its members (or shareholders).

1. Incorporated Cooperative
Subject to state laws governing nonprofit corporations. Distributes profits to owners on the basis of their transactions with the cooperative rather than on the basis of the amount of capital they contributed.

2. Unincorporated Cooperatives
Often treated like partnerships. The members have joint liability for the cooperative's acts.

TRUE-FALSE QUESTIONS
(Answers at the Back of the Book)

____ **1.** Forming a limited liability company does not require the filing of any documents in a state office.

____ **2.** A limited liability company is a citizen of every state of which its members are citizens.

____ **3.** A limited liability company does not offer the limited liability of a corporation.

____ **4.** In a limited liability company, members do not have to participate in its management.

____ **5.** Most limited liability company (LLC) statutes provide that unless the members agree otherwise, all profits of the LLC will be divided equally.

____ **6.** A syndicate may exist in the form of a corporation.

____ **7.** A joint venture is similar to a sole proprietorship.

____ **8.** A cooperative may take the form of a partnership or a corporation, but its distinguishing feature is that it is organized to provide an economic service without profit.

____ **9.** A joint stock company has many characteristics of a corporation.

____ **10.** A business trust resembles a partnership.

FILL-IN QUESTIONS

(Answers at the Back of the Book)

Unless the participants agree otherwise, all of the _____ (members/shareholders) of a _____ (limited liability company/joint stock company) may participate in management without assuming liability for the obligations of the firm. In contrast, the _____ (members/shareholders) of a _____ (limited liability company/joint stock company) may be personally liable for the debts of the firm whether or not they participate in the firm's management.

MULTIPLE-CHOICE QUESTIONS

(Answers at the Back of the Book)

____ 1. Ebsen and Flossy form Eb & Flo, LLC, a limited liability company (LLC), to contract for the installation of custom plumbing and piping. One advantage of an LLC is that it may be taxed as

    a. a corporation.
    b. a partnership.
    c. a sole proprietorship.
    d. a syndicate.

____ 2. Lonny is a member of Magna Management, a limited liability company that manages commercial properties for their owners. Lonny is liable for the firm's debts

    a. in proportion to the total number of members.
    b. to the extent of his capital contribution.
    c. to the extent that the other members do not pay the debts.
    d. to the full extent of the debts.

____ 3. Cal and Dyson form Elemeno Construction, a limited liability company, to design and make prefabricated housing. They can participate in its management

    a. only to the extent that they assume personal liability for the firm's debts.
    b. only to the extent of the amount of their investment in the firm.
    c. to any extent.
    d. to no extent.

____ 4. Rhianna and Stuart form Toons, LLC, a limited liability company (LLC), to market anime-related merchandise. A disadvantage of an LLC is that

    a. its income is double taxed.
    b. its members are subject to personal liability for the firm's debts.
    c. its members cannot participate in its management.
    d. state laws concerning limited liability companies are not yet uniform.

____ 5. **Based on a Sample CPA Exam Question.** Tropical Traders, Inc., and US Outlet Stores, Inc., form a joint venture to develop and market business software. A joint venture is

    a. a corporate enterprise for a single undertaking of limited duration.
    b. an association limited to no more than two persons in business for profit.
    c. an association of persons engaged as co-owners in a single undertaking for profit.
    d. an enterprise of numerous co-owners in a nonprofit undertaking.

___ **6.** Mole Corporation and Nano, Inc., form a joint venture to develop and market molecular-based computer chips. A joint venture is similar to

    a. a corporation.
    b. a partnership.
    c. a sole proprietorship.
    d. a syndicate.

___ **7.** Evan and Freebo form a syndicate to finance Grande Vista, a real estate project. A syndicate

    a. is similar to a corporation.
    b. is similar to a partnership.
    c. is a hybrid of a corporation and a partnership.
    d. may exist as a partnership or a corporation.

___ **8.** Leza and Mike form a joint stock company to manage investments. A joint stock company is a hybrid of

    a. a corporation and a joint venture.
    b. a corporation and a partnership.
    c. a joint venture and a partnership.
    d. a limited liability company and a sole proprietorship.

___ **9.** Coastline Railway, Inc., and Drinkwater Transport Corporation pool their assets to form a business trust. This is similar to

    a. a corporation.
    b. a joint venture.
    c. a partnership.
    d. a sole proprietorship.

___ **10.** Organic Farms, LLC, is a limited liability company. Its members hire outside managers to operate the LLC. These managers owe Organic Farms

    a. a duty of care only.
    b. a duty of loyalty only.
    c. fiduciary duties of care and loyalty.
    d. neither a duty of care nor a duty loyalty.

SHORT ESSAY QUESTIONS

1. What are the advantages of doing business as a limited liability company?

2. What are the principal characteristics of a cooperative?

GAMEPOINTS

(Answers at the Back of the Book)

1. In the video game "Hamster Hotel," your avatar is a hotelier who joins efforts with an investment firm—specialists in vacation destination funding—to design, build, outfit, and operate a resort with rooms and activities modeled on pet-hamster paraphernalia and preoccupations. Features include human-scaled wheels, water bottles, and pet toys. Which form of business organization outlined in this chapter are you and the investment firm most likely to use to engage in this endeavor? How will the profits and losses be shared?

2. You are playing "Team Up," a video game in which the play consists of choosing athletes for a fantasy sports team to compete with other teams for a championship title. Before selecting your team's players, you form the team's organization, Super Sport LLC. You are Super Sport's sole member. According to the principles discussed in this chapter, how would the firm's profits be taxed? Can a "non-member" manage the day-to-day business of the firm? If one of your players assaults a fan during a game, could you be held fully liable?

SPECIAL INFORMATION FOR CPA CANDIDATES

For the CPA exam, it is most important to know the differences among the types of business organizations, including limited liability companies and other special forms of business firms.

Chapter 39
Corporate Formation and Financing

See p. 304 in this guide

pg 762
pg. 769-770

Pg. 760 Concept summary

WHAT THIS CHAPTER IS ABOUT

This chapter covers corporate rights, powers, classifications, formation, and financing. Most corporations are formed under state law, and a majority of states follow some version of the Revised Model Business Corporation Act (RMBCA).

Seperate ownership from managment

CHAPTER OUTLINE

I. THE NATURE AND CLASSIFICATION OF CORPORATIONS

A corporation is recognized as a "legal person" and has the same rights as a natural person (see Chapter 4)—access to the courts, due process, freedom from unreasonable searches and seizures, and free speech.

A. CORPORATE PERSONNEL
Shareholders elect a board of directors, which is responsible for overall management and hires corporate officers to run daily operations.

B. THE LIMITED LIABILITY OF SHAREHOLDERS
The key feature of a corporation is the limit of its owners' liability, for corporate obligations, to the amounts of their investments in the firm. Of course, a lender may require otherwise or a court may "pierce the corporate veil" (see below).

C. CORPORATE EARNINGS AND TAXATION
Corporations can retain corporate profits or pass them on to shareholders in the form of dividends. Profits that are not distributed are retained earnings and can be invested for higher profits, which may cause the price of the stock to rise, benefiting shareholders.

1. Corporate Taxation
Corporate profits are taxed twice—as income to the corporation and, when distributed as dividends, as income to the shareholders.

2. Holding Companies
A holding company (or parent company) holds the shares of another company. Such firms are often established in offshore no-tax or low-tax jurisdictions. A corporation whose shares are held in a holding company may transfer cash and other investments to be taxed in that jurisdiction.

D. TORTS AND CRIMINAL ACTS
A corporation is liable for the torts committed by its agents within the course and scope of employment. A corporation may be held liable for the crimes of its employees and agents if the punishment for the crimes can be applied to a corporation.

E. CLASSIFICATION OF CORPORATIONS

311

1. **Domestic, Foreign, and Alien Corporations**

   A corporation is a *domestic* corporation in the state in which it incorporated, a *foreign* corporation in other states, and an *alien* corporation in other countries. A foreign corporation normally must obtain a certificate of authority to do business in any state except its home state.

2. **Public and Private Corporations**

   A *public* corporation is formed by the government to meet a political or governmental purpose (the U.S. Postal Service, AMTRAK). A *private* corporation is created for private benefit and is owned by private persons.

3. **Nonprofit Corporations**

   These are corporations formed without a profit-making purpose (private hospitals, educational institutions, charities, and religious organizations).

4. **Closely Held Corporations**

   A close corporation is exempt from most of the nonessential formalities of corporate operation (bylaws, annual meetings, etc. [RMBCA 7.32]). To qualify, a firm must have a limited number of shareholders, and restrict its issue and transfer of stock.

   a. **Management of a Closely Held Corporation**

   Resembles that of a sole proprietorship or a partnership—one or a few shareholders usually hold the positions of directors and officers.

   b. **Transfer of Shares in Closely Held Corporations**

   Shareholders may be required to offer their shares to the closely held corporation or the other shareholders before selling them to outside buyers.

   c. **Shareholder Agreement to Restrict Stock Transfer**

   Under a shareholder agreement, there is often a restriction on transfer of the shares, which may also limit their market.

   d. **Misappropriation of Closely Held Corporation Funds**

   The remedy for minority shareholders on a majority shareholder's misappropriation of company funds is to have their shares appraised and be paid their fair market value.

5. **S Corporations**

   a. **Requirements**

   Must be a domestic corporation; must not be a member of an affiliated group of corporations; shareholders must be individuals, estates, or certain trusts; must have 100 or fewer shareholders; can have only one class of stock; no shareholder can be a nonresident alien.

   b. **Benefits**

   Shareholders can use corporate losses to offset other income; only a single tax on corporate income is imposed at individual income tax rates at the shareholder level (even if it is not distributed).

6. **Professional Corporations**

   Generally subject to the law governing ordinary corporations.

   a. **Limited Liability**

   A shareholder in a professional corporation is protected from liability for torts (except malpractice) committed by other members.

   b. **Unlimited Liability**

   A court might regard a professional corporation as a partnership, in which each partner may be liable for the malpractice of the others.

II.   CORPORATE FORMATION

A. PROMOTIONAL ACTIVITIES

Promoters take the first steps in organizing a corporation—issue a prospectus (see Chapter 42) and secure the corporate charter (see below). Promoters are personally liable on preincorporation contracts until the corporation assumes the contract by novation (see Chapter 17).

B. INCORPORATION PROCEDURES

1. Select the State of Incorporation

Some states offer more advantageous tax or incorporation provisions.

2. Secure the Corporate Name

a. Must Include Words That Disclose Corporate Status

All state require that a name include Corporation, Incorporated, Limited, Company, or and abbreviation of one of these terms.

b. Cannot Infringe on Another's Trademark Rights

States review corporate names to avoid duplication and deception. A name should also be able to serve as a domain name.

3. Prepare the Articles of Incorporation

The articles include basic information about the corporation and serve as a primary source of authority for its organization and functions.

a. Shares of the Corporation

The amount of stock authorized for issuance; its valuation; and other information as to equity, capital, and credit must be outlined.

b. Registered Office and Agent

Usually, the registered office is the principal office of the corporation; the agent is a person designated to receive legal documents on behalf of the corporation.

c. Incorporators

Incorporators (some states require only one) must sign the articles when they are submitted to the state; often this is their only duty, and they need have no other interest in the corporation.

d. Duration and Purpose

A corporation can have perpetual existence in most states. The intended business activities of the corporation must be specified. Stating a general corporate purpose is usually sufficient.

e. Internal Organization

Management structure can be described in bylaws later.

4. File the Articles with the State

The articles of incorporation are sent to the appropriate state official (usually the secretary of state). Many states issue a certificate of incorporation authorizing the corporation to conduct business.

C. FIRST ORGANIZATIONAL MEETING TO ADOPT BYLAWS

The incorporators or the board; the business conducted depends on state law, the nature of the corporation's business, the provisions of the articles, and the wishes of the promoters. Adoption of the bylaws is the most important function of the first organizational meeting.

D. IMPROPER INCORPORATION

On the basis of improper incorporation, a person attempting to enforce a contract or bring a tort suit against the corporation could seek to make the shareholders personally liable. If a corporation seeks to enforce a contract, the defaulting party who learns of a defect in incorporation may be able to avoid liability.

1. *De Jure* Corporations

Occurs if there is substantial compliance with all requirements for incorporation. In most states, the certificate of incorporation is evidence that all requirements have been met, and neither the state nor a third party can attack the corporation's existence.

2. *De Facto* Corporations

The existence of a corporation cannot be challenged by third persons (except the state) if (1) there is a statute under which the firm can be incorporated, (2) the parties made a good faith attempt to comply with it, and (3) the firm has attempted to do business as a corporation. Some states do not apply this doctrine.

E. CORPORATION BY ESTOPPEL

If an association that is neither an actual corporation nor a *de facto* or *de jure* corporation holds itself out as being a corporation, it will be estopped from denying corporate status in a suit by a third party.

III. CORPORATE POWERS

A. EXPRESS POWERS

Express powers are in (in order of priority) the U.S. Constitution, state constitution, state statutes, articles of incorporation, bylaws, and board resolutions.

B. IMPLIED POWERS

A corporation has the *implied* power to perform all acts reasonably appropriate and necessary to accomplish its purposes.

C. *ULTRA VIRES* DOCTRINE

Ultra vires acts are beyond the purposes stated in the articles. Earlier cases involved contracts (which generally were enforced [RMBCA 3.04]). Now, courts usually allow any legal action a firm takes to profit shareholders, and a declining number of cases are brought mostly against nonprofit or municipal corporations.

IV. PIERCING THE CORPORATE VEIL

When a corporate owners use the entity to perpetuate a fraud, circumvent the law, or in some other way accomplish an illegitimate objective, a court will pierce the corporate veil.

A. FACTORS THAT LEAD COURTS TO PIERCE THE CORPORATE VEIL

Situations that may cause a court to disregard the corporate veil include—

1. A party is tricked or misled into dealing with the corporation rather than the individual.
2. The corporation is set up never to make a profit or always to be insolvent, or it is too thinly capitalized.
3. The corporation is formed to evade an existing legal obligation.
4. Statutory corporate formalities are not followed.
5. Personal and corporate interests are commingled to the extent that the corporation has no separate identity. Loans to the firm, for example, must be in good faith and for fair value.

B. A POTENTIAL PROBLEM FOR CLOSELY HELD CORPORATIONS

The potential for corporate formalities to be overlooked, or for other circumstances to occur that may lead a court to pierce the corporate veil, is especially great in a closely held corporation.

V. CORPORATE FINANCING

A. BONDS

Bonds are issued as evidence of funds that business firms borrow from investors. A lending agreement called a *bond indenture* specifies the terms (maturity date, interest). A trustee ensures that terms are met.

B. STOCKS

The most important characteristics of stocks are: (1) investors need not be repaid, (2) stockholders receive dividends only when voted by the directors, (3) stockholders are the last investors to be paid on dissolution, and (4) stockholders vote for management and on major issues.

C. VENTURE CAPITAL AND PRIVATE EQUITY CAPITAL

1. Venture Capital

Start-up businesses and high-risk enterprises may obtain venture capital financing (capital from professional investors), as well as managerial or technical expertise, in exchange for a share of ownership in the firm or control over its decisions.

2. Private Equity Capital

Private equity investors pool their funds to buy an existing corporation to reorganize or sell.

TRUE-FALSE QUESTIONS

(Answers at the Back of the Book)

____ 1. A shareholder can sue a corporation, and a corporation can sue a shareholder.

____ 2. Generally, a promoter is personally liable on a preincorporation contract.

____ 3. A foreign corporation is formed in another country but does business in the United States.

____ 4. Any power set out in a corporation's charter or bylaws is *ultra vires*.

____ 5. To a corporation, stocks represent corporate ownership.

____ 6. To a corporation, bonds represent corporate debt.

____ 7. S corporations cannot avoid federal taxes at the corporate level.

____ 8. In some states, a close corporation can operate without formal shareholders' or directors' meetings.

____ 9. State corporation laws are completely uniform.

____ 10. A corporation is liable for torts of its officers committed within the course and scope of employment.

FILL-IN QUESTIONS

(Answers at the Back of the Book)

Those who, for themselves or others, take the preliminary steps in organizing a corporation are _____ (promoters/incorporators). These persons enter into contracts with professionals, whose services are needed in planning the corporation, and are personally liable on these contracts, _____ (unless/even if) the third party issues a release or the corporation assumes the contract. A person who applies to the state on behalf of the corporation to obtain its certificate of incorporation is _____ (a promoter/an incorporator). This person _____ (must/need not) have any interest in the corporation.

MULTIPLE-CHOICE QUESTIONS

(Answers at the Back of the Book)

____ 1. Blaine and Cory want to incorporate to buy, play, sell, and trade video games. The first step in the incorporation procedure is to

a. file the articles of incorporation.
b. hold the first organizational meeting.
c. obtain a corporate charter.
d. select a state in which to incorporate.

____ 2. Metal Fasteners Company (MFC) is a corporation. MFC has the implied power to

a. amend the corporate charter.
b. declare dividends.
c. file a derivative suit.
d. perform all acts reasonably appropriate and necessary to accomplish its corporate purposes.

____ 3. Responsibility for the overall management of Fashionista Stores, Inc., a corporation, is entrusted to

a. the board of directors.
b. the corporate officers and managers.
c. the owners of the corporation.
d. the promoters of the corporation.

____ 4. Daystar Company is a private, for-profit corporation that (1) was formed to market business office software, (2) is owned by ten shareholders, (3) is subject to double taxation, and (4) has made no public offering of its shares. Daystar is

a. a closely held corporation.
b. a nonprofit corporation.
c. an S corporation.
d. a professional corporation.

____ 5. Fillmore Pharmaceutical, Inc., issues bonds. Bonds

a. are issued by S corporations only.
b. are sometime referred to as "stock with preferences."
c. have fixed maturity dates.
d. require periodic interest payments from their owners.

____ 6. Like other corporations, Distribution Services, Inc., issues securities most likely to

a. increase its market share.
b. increase its visibility.
c. obtain financing.
d. reduce its distribution costs.

____ 7. Tasty Pastries, Inc., is a consumer products firm. As a source of authority for its organization and functions, its articles of incorporation are

a. a primary source.
b. a secondary source.
c. a source of final resort.
d. not a reliable source.

____ **8.** Medical Supplies Company issues common stock for sale to the public. If Nero buys ten shares of the stock, he has a proportionate interest with regard to

    a. control, earnings, and net assets.
    b. control only.
    c. earnings and net assets only.
    d. none of the choices.

____ **9.** Simplex Corporation substantially complies with all conditions precedent to incorporation. Simplex

    a. is a corporation by estoppel.
    b. has *de facto* existence.
    c. has *de jure* existence.
    d. none of the choices.

____ **10.** Koz is a shareholder of Lil' Biz Company, Inc. A court might "pierce the corporate veil" and hold Koz personally liable for Lil's debts

    a. if Koz's personal interests commingle with Lil's interests to the extent it has no separate identity.
    b. if Little calls too many shareholders' meetings.
    c. if Little is overcapitalized.
    d. under no circumstances.

SHORT ESSAY QUESTIONS

1. What is the significance of the following items as they relate to a company's articles of incorporation: (1) corporate name, (2) nature and purpose, (3) duration, (4) capital structure, (5) internal organization, (6) registered office and agent, and (7) incorporators?

2. What are the features of nonprofit, close, S, and professional corporations?

GAMEPOINTS

(Answers at the Back of the Book)

1. You are playing the video game "Captains of Industry" in which the objective is to attain a dominant position in an industry without violating, or creating the appearance of violating, the law. To begin play, you make a good faith effort to incorporate Platinum, Inc., without realizing that you have not followed all of the prescribed procedures. As the game continues, you contract in good faith with Silver Corporation on Platinum's behalf. What type of entity is Platinum? Can Silver avoid its contract with Platinum on the basis of the defect in incorporation? Discuss.

2. "Money2Burn" is a video game of finance in which each player's goal is to become the wealthiest person in the world. You are the chief executive officer of Gold, Inc. The articles of incorporation state that Gold may engage in any activity for "any lawful purpose." On the firm's behalf, you enter into a contract to sell substantially all of its assets to Diamond Holdings. Is this an *ultra vires* act? Can the sale proceed without more? If not, what "more" is required? Explain.

SPECIAL INFORMATION FOR CPA CANDIDATES

Over time, the CPA examination has come to emphasize statutory principles (such as the MBCA and the RMBCA) and deemphasize common law principles (such as *de jure* and *de facto* corporations and the *ultra vires* doctrine—the most likely application of the latter is in a question that involves an executory contract).

Other important points to keep in mind include the liability of a promoter who organizes a new corporation (and how a promoter can avoid liability), the liability of the corporation in regard to preincorporation contracts, the relationship of the promoters to shareholders and the corporation, and the circumstances under which a shareholder may be liable for the debts of a corporation.

Chapter 40
Corporate Directors, Officers, and Shareholders

WHAT THIS CHAPTER IS ABOUT

This chapter outlines the rights and responsibilities of all participants—directors, officers, and shareholders—in a corporate enterprise. Also noted are the ways in which conflicts among these participants are resolved.

CHAPTER OUTLINE

I. **ROLES OF DIRECTORS AND OFFICERS**
The board of directors governs a corporation. Officers handle daily business.

   A. **DIRECTORS' MANAGEMENT RESPONSIBILITIES**
These include major policy and financial decisions; appointment, supervision, pay, and removal of officers and other managerial employees.

   B. **ELECTION OF DIRECTORS**

     1. **Number of Directors**
This is set in a corporation's articles or bylaws.

     2. **How Directors Are Chosen**
The first board (appointed by the incorporators or named in the articles) serves until the first shareholders' meeting. Shareholders by majority vote (see below) elect subsequent directors.

     3. **Removal of Directors**
Shareholder action can remove a director for cause (or the board may have the power). In most states, a director cannot be removed without cause, unless shareholders have reserved the right.

   C. **COMPENSATION OF DIRECTORS**
Nominal sums may be paid to directors, and there is a trend to provide more. Directors may set their own compensation [RMBCA 8.11]. A director who is also a corporate officer is an inside director. A director who does not hold a management position is an outside director.

   D. **BOARD OF DIRECTORS' MEETINGS**

     1. **Formal Minutes and Notice**
A board conducts business by holding formal meetings with recorded minutes. The dates for regular meetings are usually set in the articles and bylaws or by board resolution, and no other notice is required. Telephone or e-conferencing is possible [RMBCA 8.20].

     2. **Quorum Requirements and Voting**
Quorum requirements vary. If the firm specifies none, in most states a quorum is a majority of the number of directors authorized in the articles or bylaws [RMBCA 8.24]. Voting is done in person, one vote per director.

319

E. RIGHTS OF DIRECTORS

1. **Participation**
   A director has a right to participate in corporate business. Special meetings require notice to all directors [RMBCA 8.23].

2. **Inspection**
   A director has a right of inspection, which means access to all corporate books and records to make decisions.

3. **Indemnification**
   Most states permit a corporation to indemnify a director for costs and fees in defending against corporate-related lawsuits. Many firms buy insurance to cover indemnification [RMBCA 8.51].

F. COMMITTEES OF THE BOARD OF DIRECTORS

1. **Executive Committee**
   Most states permit a board to elect an executive committee from among the directors to handle management between board meetings. The committee is limited to ordinary business matters.

2. **Audit Committee**
   Selects, compensates, and oversees independent public accountants who audit the firm's financial records under the Sarbanes-Oxley Act of 2002.

3. **Nominating Committee**
   Chooses candidates on which shareholders vote for the board of directors [RMBCA 8.25].

4. **Compensation Committee**
   Sets salaries and benefits for corporate executives and may determine directors' compensation.

5. **Litigation Committee**
   Decides whether to pursue litigation on behalf of the corporation.

G. CORPORATE OFFICERS AND EXECUTIVES

The board hires officers and other executive employees. Officers act as corporate agents (see Chapters 32 and 33). The rights of corporate officers and other high-level managers are defined by employment contracts. Normally, the board can remove officers at any time (but the corporation could be liable for breach of contract). Officers' duties are the same as those of directors.

II. DUTIES AND LIABILITIES OF DIRECTORS AND OFFICERS

Directors and officers are fiduciaries of the corporation.

A. DUTY OF CARE

Directors and officers must act in good faith, in what they consider to be the best interests of the corporation, and with the care that an ordinarily prudent person would exercise in similar circumstances.

1. **Duty to Make Informed and Reasonable Decisions**
   Directors must be informed on corporate matters and act in accord with their knowledge and training. A director can rely on information furnished by competent officers, or others, without being accused of acting in bad faith or failing to exercise due care [RMBCA 8.30].

2. **Duty to Exercise Reasonable Supervision**
   Directors must exercise reasonable supervision when work is delegated.

    3. Dissenting Directors
    Directors must attend board meetings; if not, he or she should register a dissent to actions taken (to avoid liability for mismanagement).

B. THE BUSINESS JUDGMENT RULE
Honest mistakes of judgment and poor business decisions do not make directors and officers liable to the firm for poor results. There can be no bad faith, fraud, or breach of fiduciary duties. The decision must be within the director's managerial authority and the power of the corporation. The director or officer must—

1. Take reasonable steps to become informed.
2. Have a reasonable basis for a decision.
3. Have no personal conflict of interest with the corporation on the matter.

C. DUTY OF LOYALTY
Directors and officers cannot use corporate funds or confidential information for personal advantage. Specifically, they cannot—

1. Compete with the corporation.
2. Usurp a corporate opportunity.
3. Have an interest that conflicts with the interest of the corporation.
4. Engage in insider trading (see Chapter 41).
5. Authorize a corporate transaction that is detrimental to minority shareholders.
6. Sell control over the corporation.

D. DISCLOSURE OF POTENTIAL CONFLICTS OF INTEREST
Directors and officers must disclose fully any conflict of interest that might occur in a deal involving the corporation. A contract may be upheld if it was fair and reasonable to the firm when it was made, there was full disclosure of the interest of the officers or directors involved, and it was approved by a majority of disinterested directors or shareholders.

E. LIABILITY OF DIRECTORS AND OFFICERS
Directors and officers are personally liable for their torts and crimes, and may be liable for those of subordinates (under the "responsible corporate officer" doctrine or the "pervasiveness of control" theory). The corporation is liable for such acts when committed within the scope of employment.

III. THE ROLE OF SHAREHOLDERS

A. SHAREHOLDERS' POWERS
Shareholders own the corporation, approve fundamental corporate changes, and elect and remove directors.

B. SHAREHOLDERS' MEETINGS
Regular meetings must occur annually; special meetings can be called to handle urgent matters.

    1. Notice of Meetings
    Notice must occur at least ten days and not more than sixty days before a meeting [RMBCA 7.05]. Notice of a special meeting must state the purpose.

    2. Proxies
    Rather than attend a meeting, shareholders normally authorize third parties to vote their shares. A proxy may be revocable and may have a time limit.

    3. Shareholder Proposals
    When a firm submits proxy materials to its shareholders (via mail or Web site posting), it must allow them to vote on pending policy proposals.

C. SHAREHOLDER VOTING

1. Quorum Requirements

At the meeting, a quorum must be present. A majority vote of the shares present is required to pass resolutions. Fundamental changes require a higher percentage.

2. Voting Techniques

Each common shareholder has one vote per share. The articles can exclude or limit voting rights.

a. Cumulative Voting

The number of members of the board to be elected multiplied by the total number of voting shares is the number of votes a shareholder has and can be cast for one or more nominees.

b. Shareholder Voting Agreements

A group of shareholders can agree to vote their shares together. A shareholder can vote by proxy. Any person can solicit proxies.

c. Voting Trust

Exists when legal title (recorded ownership on the corporate books) is transferred to a trustee who is responsible for voting the shares. The shareholder retains all other ownership rights.

IV. RIGHTS OF SHAREHOLDERS

A. STOCK CERTIFICATES

Notice of shareholder meetings, dividends, and corporate reports are distributed to owners listed in the corporate books, not on the basis of possession of stock certificates (which most states do not require).

B. PREEMPTIVE RIGHTS

These rights usually apply only to additional, newly issued stock sold for cash (not treasury shares) and must be exercised within a specified time (usually thirty days). When new shares are issued, each shareholder is given *stock warrants* (transferable options to acquire a certain number of shares at a stated price) [RMBCA 6.30].

C. DIVIDENDS

Dividends can be paid in cash, property, or stock. Once declared, a cash dividend is a corporate debt. Dividends are payable only from (1) retained earnings, (2) current net profits, or (3) any surplus.

1. Illegal Dividends

A dividend paid when a corporation is insolvent is illegal and must be repaid. A dividend paid from an unauthorized account or causing a corporation to become insolvent may have to be repaid. In any case, the directors can be held personally liable.

2. The Directors' Failure to Declare a Dividend

Shareholders can ask a court to compel a declaration of a dividend, but for the court to grant the request, the directors' failure to do so must have been an abuse of discretion.

D. INSPECTION RIGHTS

Shareholders (or their attorney, accountant, or agent) can inspect and copy corporate books and records for a proper purpose, if the request is made in advance [RMBCA 16.02]. This right can be denied to prevent harassment or to protect confidential corporate information.

E. TRANSFER OF SHARES

Restrictions on transferability must be noted on the face of stock certificates, and must be reasonable.

F. SHAREHOLDER'S DERIVATIVE SUIT

If directors fail to sue in the corporate name to redress a wrong suffered by the firm—ninety days after a shareholders' demand in writing that the directors act—shareholders can bring the suit. Any recovery normally goes into the corporate treasury.

V.   LIABILITY OF SHAREHOLDERS

In most cases, if a corporation fails, shareholders lose only their investment. Exceptions include (see also Chapter 39)—

A. WATERED STOCK

In most cases, a shareholder who receives watered stock (stock sold by a corporation for less than par value) must pay the difference to the corporation. In some states, such shareholders may be liable to creditors of the corporation for unpaid corporate debts.

B. DUTIES OF MAJORITY SHAREHOLDERS

A single shareholder (or a few acting together) who owns enough shares to control the corporation owes a fiduciary duty to the minority shareholders and creditors when they sell their shares.

TRUE-FALSE QUESTIONS

(Answers at the Back of the Book)

____ 1. The business judgment rule immunizes officers from liability for poor decisions made in good faith.

____ 2. An officer is a fiduciary of a corporation.

____ 3. Preemptive rights entitle shareholders to bring a derivative suit against the corporation.

____ 4. Only certain funds are legally available for paying dividends.

____ 5. Damages recovered in a shareholder's derivative suit are paid to the shareholder who filed the suit.

____ 6. Generally, shareholders are not personally responsible for the debts of the corporation.

____ 7. Directors, but not officers, owe a duty of loyalty to the corporation.

____ 8. The business judgment rule makes a director liable for losses to the firm in most cases.

____ 9. Shareholders may vote to remove members of the board of directors.

____ 10. At a shareholders' meeting, a quorum must be present to vote on resolutions.

FILL-IN QUESTIONS

(Answers at the Back of the Book)

A stock certificate may be lost or destroyed, _____(and ownership is/but ownership is not) destroyed with it. A new certificate _____ (can/cannot) be issued to replace one that has been lost or destroyed. Notice of meetings, dividends, and operational and financial reports are all distributed according to the individual _____ _____ (in possession of the certificate/recorded as the owner in the corporation's books).

MULTIPLE-CHOICE QUESTIONS

(Answers at the Back of the Book)

____ 1. The board of directors of Orion, Inc., announces a cash dividend. A cash dividend may *not* be paid from

a. accumulated surplus.
b. gross profits.
c. net profits.
d. retained earnings.

____ 2. Joeli is a shareholder of Agro Implement Company. As a shareholder, Joeli does *not* have a right to

a. compensation.
b. dividends.
c. inspect corporate books and records.
d. transfer shares.

____ 3. Dylan and Evette are officers of Fullfit Clothing Corporation. As officers, their rights are set out in

a. international agreements.
b. state corporation statutes.
c. the firm's certificate of authority.
d. the officers' employment contracts.

____ 4. Federico is a director of Green Energy Corporation. As a director, Federico owes Green a duty of

a. care and loyalty.
b. care only.
c. loyalty only.
d. neither care nor loyalty.

____ 5. **Based on a Sample CPA Exam Question.** The management of Orchards & Vines, Inc., is at odds with the shareholders over some recent decisions. The shareholders may file a shareholders' derivative suit to

a. compel dissolution of Orchards & Vines.
b. compel payment of a properly declared dividend.
c. enforce a right to inspect corporate records.
d. recover damages from the management for an *ultra vires* act.

____ 6. Jeans & Sweats Corporation uses cumulative voting in its elections of directors. Kyla owns 3,000 shares. At an annual meeting at which three directors are to be elected, Kyla may cast for any one candidate

a. 1,000 votes.
b. 3,000 votes.
c. 9,000 votes.
d. 27,000 votes.

____ 7. HomeBase Corporation invests in intrastate businesses. In HomeBase's state, as in most states, the minimum number of directors that must be present before its board can transact business is

a. all of the directors authorized in the articles.
b. a majority of the number authorized in the articles or bylaws.
c. any odd number.
d. one.

___   8.   Nanobyte Company makes and sells computer chips. Like most corporations, Nanobyte's officers are hired by its

   a.   directors.
   b.   incorporators.
   c.   officers.
   d.   shareholders.

___   9.   Robin is a director of Sherwood Forest Company. Robin has a right to

   a.   compensation.
   b.   first refusal.
   c.   participation.
   d.   preemption.

___   10.   Perla is a director of Quik Purchasing Corporation. Without informing Quik, Perla goes into business with Rapid Buys, Inc., to compete with Quik. This violates

   a.   the business judgment rule.
   b.   the duty of care.
   c.   the duty of loyalty.
   d.   none of the choices.

SHORT ESSAY QUESTIONS

1.   How do the duty of care and the duty of loyalty govern the conduct of directors and officers in a corporation?

2.   What are the rights of the shareholders of a corporation?

GAMEPOINTS

(Answers at the Back of the Book)

1.   In the video game "Corporate Cowboy," your task is to investigate complaints of wrongdoing on the part of corporate directors and officers, decide whether there is a violation of the law, and deal with the wrongdoers accordingly. Jane, a shareholder of Goodly Corporation, alleges that its directors decided to invest heavily in the firm's growth in negligent reliance on its officers' faulty financial reports. This caused Goodly to borrow to meet its obligations, resulting in a drop in its stock price. Are the directors liable? Why or why not?

2.   You are playing the video game "Conflict of Interest" in which you accrue points by correctly spotting corporate misconduct, skillfully battling against it, and successfully righting the wrong. Your chief opponent is the game's avatar. Ellen, a shareholder of Finagle, Inc., asks you to help her right a wrong suffered by the firm as a result of an act by Bernie, one of the firm's directors and officers. Can Ellen sue Bernie on Finagle's behalf? If so, and Bernie is held liable, who recovers the damages? What defense is the game's avatar likely to assert on Bernie's behalf?

SPECIAL INFORMATION FOR CPA CANDIDATES

   For the CPA examination, be sure that you understand the relationship of directors and officers to the corporation. These individuals have fiduciary duties and agency authority that shareholders do not have. Officers and directors must exercise reasonable care, subject to the business judgment rule (which absolves those who act in good faith).

Note that this is not the same as the due diligence standard of the Securities Exchange Commission (SEC) (see Chapter 42). For that reason, pay close attention to which standard a question involves. Regarding shareholders, you should know their rights, and in what circumstances a shareholder may be personally liable for the obligations of a corporation.

Chapter 41
Corporate Merger, Consolidation, and Termination

WHAT THIS CHAPTER IS ABOUT

This chapter covers corporate mergers, consolidations, purchase of another corporation's assets, and purchase of a controlling interest in another corporation. The chapter also touches on the reasons for, and methods used in, terminating a corporation.

CHAPTER OUTLINE

I. **MERGER, CONSOLIDATION, AND SHARE EXCHANGE**
    Whether a combination is a merger or a consolidation, the rights and liabilities of shareholders, the corporation, and its creditors are the same.

    A. **MERGER**

    Merger → A + B + C = New A

    1. **What a Merger Is**
        A merger is the combination of two or more corporations, often by one absorbing the other. After a merger, only one of the corporations exists.

    2. **The Results of a Merger**
        The surviving corporation has all of the rights, assets, liabilities, and debts of itself and the other corporation. Its articles of incorporation are deemed amended to include changes stated in the articles of merger.

    B. **CONSOLIDATION**

    A + B + C = D (new entity)

    In a consolidation, two or more corporations combine so that each corporation ceases to exist and a new one emerges. The results of a consolidation are essentially the same as the results of a merger.

    C. **SHARE EXCHANGE**
    In a share exchange, some or all of the stock of a company are exchanged for some or all of the stock of another. A company that holds all of the shares of another is the other's parent corporation of which the wholly owned firm is a subsidiary corporation.

    D. **MERGER, CONSOLIDATION, AND SHARE EXCHANGE PROCEDURES**
    The basic steps are—

    1. Each board approves the plan (which must specify the terms and conditions of the merger and how the value of the shares will be determined).
    2. Each firm's shareholders vote on the plan at a shareholders' meeting.
    3. The plan is filed, usually with the secretary of state.
    4. The state issues a certificate of merger or consolidation.

    E. **SHORT-FORM MERGERS**
    A substantially owned subsidiary corporation can merge into its parent corporation without shareholder approval, if the parent owns at least 90 percent of the subsidiary's outstanding stock.

327

F. SHAREHOLDER APPROVAL

The board of directors and the shareholders must authorize actions taken on extraordinary matters (sale, lease, or exchange of all or substantially all corporate assets; amendment to the articles of incorporation; merger; consolidation; dissolution).

G. APPRAISAL RIGHTS

If provided by statute, a shareholder can dissent from a merger, consolidation, share exchange, sale of substantially all the corporate assets not in the ordinary course of business, and (in some states) amendments to articles.

1. Appraisal Rights Procedures

A shareholder must be notified if he or she has these rights, and must then file written notice of dissent before the shareholders vote on the proposed transaction. If the transaction is approved, the shareholder must make a written demand for payment of "fair value" for his or her shares.

2. Appraisal Rights and Shareholder Status

Once the right has been exercised, the shareholder loses his or her shareholder status.

3. Fair Value

The "fair value" of shares is their value on the day before the date the vote is taken [RMBCA 13.01]. The corporation must make a written offer to buy the shareholder's stock. If fair value cannot be agreed to, a court will set it.

II. PURCHASE OF ASSETS

A. SALES OF CORPORATE ASSETS

A corporation that buys all or substantially all of the assets of another corporation does not need shareholder approval. The corporation whose assets are acquired must obtain approval of its board and shareholders (and see the antitrust guidelines in Chapter 47).

B. SUCCESSOR LIABILITY IN PURCHASES OF ASSETS

An acquiring corporation is not responsible for the seller's liabilities, unless there is—

1. An implied or express assumption.
2. A sale amounting to a merger or consolidation.
3. A buyer retaining the seller's personnel and continuing the business.
4. A sale executed in fraud to avoid liability.

III. PURCHASE OF STOCK

A purchase of a substantial number of voting shares of a corporation's stock enables an acquiring corporation to control a target corporation. The acquiring corporation deals directly with shareholders to buy shares.

A. TENDER OFFERS

A tender offer is a public offer. The offer can turn on the receipt of a specified number of shares by a specified date.

1. The Price Offered for the Target's Stock

This price is generally higher than the stock's market price before the tender offer. It may involve an exchange of stock or cash for stock in the target.

2. Federal and State Laws

Federal securities laws control the terms, duration, and circumstances in which most tender offers are made. Most states also impose regulations.

B. RESPONSES TO TENDER OFFERS

Among other tactics, a target may make a self-tender (offer to buy its own stock), issue more stock, or engage in a media campaign against the offer. A target may sell its most desirable assets or take other defensive measures (such as a poison pill: allow its shareholders to buy additional shares at low prices). It may seek an injunction on the ground that a takeover will violate antitrust laws.

C. TAKEOVER DEFENSES AND DIRECTORS' FIDUCIARY DUTIES

The directors of the target firm must act in the best interest of their company in deciding whether the shareholders' acceptance or rejection of the offer would be most beneficial. The directors must fully disclose all material facts.

D. TAKEOVERS AND ANTITRUST LAW

A target may seek an injunction on the ground that a takeover will violate antitrust laws..

IV. TERMINATION

A. VOLUNTARY DISSOLUTION

Shareholders can initiate dissolution by a unanimous vote or directors may propose dissolution to the shareholders for a vote. The corporation files articles of dissolution with the secretary of state. The corporation notifies its creditors and sets a date (at least 120 days following the date of dissolution) by which all claims against the corporation must be received [RMBCA 14.06].

B. INVOLUNTARY DISSOLUTION

1. By the State

In an action brought by the secretary of state or the state attorney general, a corporation may be dissolved for—

a. Failing to comply with corporate formalities or other statutory requirements.
b. Incorporating through fraud or misrepresentation.
c. Abusing corporate powers (*ultra vires* acts).

2. By a Shareholder

The articles of a close corporation may empower any shareholder to dissolve the corporation at will or on the occurrence of a certain event (such as the death of another shareholder).

3. By a Court

A court can dissolve a corporation when a board is deadlocked or for mismanagement.

C. WINDING UP

If dissolution is by voluntary action, the members of the board act as trustees of the assets, and wind up the affairs of the corporation for the benefit of corporate creditors and shareholders. If dissolution is involuntary, the board does not wish to act as trustee, or shareholders or creditors can show why the board should not act as trustee, a court will appoint a receiver to wind up the corporate affairs.

V. MAJOR BUSINESS FORMS COMPARED

The appropriate form for doing business depends on an enterprise's characteristics, tax status, and goals.

TRUE-FALSE QUESTIONS

(Answers at the Back of the Book)

____ 1. In a short-form merger, the merging corporation's shareholders do not need to approve the merger.

____ **2.** Appraisal rights are always available to shareholders.

____ **3.** Shareholder approval is not required to amend articles of incorporation.

____ **4.** Shareholder approval is not required when a corporation sells all of its assets to another company.

____ **5.** A self-tender is a corporation's offer to buy stock from its own shareholders.

____ **6.** Dissolution of a corporation cannot occur without the unanimous approval of its shareholders.

____ **7.** In a consolidation, the new corporation inherits all of the rights of the consolidating corporations.

____ **8.** A corporation that buys the assets of another corporation always assumes the debts of the selling corporation.

____ **9.** In a merger, the surviving corporation inherits the disappearing corporation's preexisting rights.

____ **10.** Appraisal rights are not normally available in sales of substantially all the corporate assets not in the ordinary course of business.

FILL-IN QUESTIONS

(Answers at the Back of the Book)

If provided by statute, a shareholder can dissent from any _____ (extraordinary/ordinary) fundamental changes in a corporation. To do so, the _____ (corporation/shareholder) must file a written notice of dissent _____ (after/before) the shareholders vote on the proposed change. If the change is approved, the shareholder must make a written demand for payment. The fair value of shares is usually their value on the day _____ (after/before) the date on which _____ (the change is made/the vote is taken).

MULTIPLE-CHOICE QUESTIONS

(Answers at the Back of the Book)

____ **1.** Mortar & Brick, Inc., merges with Net Online Corporation. Only Net Online remains. After the merger, Net Online acquires Mortar & Brick's assets

a. automatically.
b. only after completing certain additional statutory procedures.
c. only if Mortar & Brick's former shareholders expressly approve.
d. only if the acquisition is a specified result of the merger.

____ **2.** Farsight Software, Inc., plans to consolidate with Games Unlimited, Inc., to form Farsight Games Corporation. This requires the approval of

a. neither their boards of directors nor their shareholders.
b. their boards *and* their shareholders.
c. their boards only.
d. their shareholders only.

____ **3.** Precision Corporation and Quotient Company consolidate to form PQ, Inc. PQ assumes Precision's and Quotient's

    a. assets and liabilities.
    b. assets only.
    c. liabilities only.
    d. neither assets nor liabilities.

____ **4. Based on a Sample CPA Exam Question.** Digital Equipment, Inc., sells computer products. Which of the following may Digital's board of directors do without shareholder approval?

    a. Amend the articles of incorporation
    b. Buy substantially all of the assets of another corporation
    c. Dissolve the corporation
    d. Sell substantially all of the assets of Digital

____ **5.** Oldway, Inc., is unprofitable. In a suit against Oldway, a court might order dissolution if the firm does *not*

    a. buy its stock from its shareholders.
    b. declare a dividend.
    c. make a profit this year.
    d. pay its taxes.

____ **6.** Spice Corporation and Sugar, Inc., combine so that only Spice remains, as the surviving corporation. This is

    a. a consolidation.
    b. a merger.
    c. a purchase of assets.
    d. a purchase of stock.

____ **7.** Chewy files a suit against Dinner Café Company. While the suit is pending, Eateries, Inc., merges with Dinner Café. Eateries absorbs Dinner Café. After the merger, liability in the suit rests with

    a. Chewy.
    b. Dinner Café.
    c. Eateries.
    d. the court.

____ **8.** Macro Corporation and Micro Company combine and a new organization, MM, Inc., takes their place. This is

    a. a consolidation.
    b. a merger.
    c. a purchase of assets.
    d. a purchase of stock.

____ **9.** DozeNot Corporation and Eversleep, Inc., plan to merge. Most likely, the articles of merger will be filed with

    a. a county recording office.
    b. the Securities and Exchange Commission.
    c. the state secretary of state.
    d. the U.S. Treasury Department.

____ **10.** Vaughn is a shareholder in Whirly Gigs, Inc. Vaughn could typically exercise appraisal rights if Whirly Gigs was involved in

a. a consolidation only.
b. a merger only.
c. a consolidation or a merger.
d. neither a consolidation nor a merger.

SHORT ESSAY QUESTIONS

1. Discuss the following takeover defense terms: greenmail; Pac-man; poison pill; and white knight.

2. Describe the procedure for a merger or a consolidation.

GAMEPOINTS

(Answers at the Back of the Book)

1. "Geode Inc." is a video game in which you engage in corporate combinations to expand your business empire. The play involves making better deals than your opponents, who are also are poised to crystallize their interests, because whoever ends the game with the wealthiest enterprise wins. In Level Three—"Acquisition Action"—you must merge, consolidate, or exchange shares with three firms—Igneous Inc., Metamorphix Inc., and Obsidian Corporation. Is there a single procedure that all of these actions follow? If so, what are the steps? Explain quickly—before your opponents cut out of any deals.

2. The play in "Geode Inc." progresses and you're making some good deals, getting the better of your opponents. Your empire has acquired Igneous and Metamorphix. Before the shareholder vote on your proposal to acquire Obsidian, however, Rocko, an Obsidian shareholder, presents your avatar with a written notice of dissent from the transaction. Rocko demands money for his Obsidian shares. Does Rocko have a right to make this demand? If so, to what is he entitled?

SPECIAL INFORMATION FOR CPA CANDIDATES

One of the most important aspects of the material in this chapter, to remember for the CPA examination, is the role of shareholders. Note particularly the events that require shareholder approval (and those that don't). Also, review the section on appraisal rights: they are available *only* when specifically provided by statute.

Chapter 42
Securities Law and Corporate Governance

WHAT THIS CHAPTER IS ABOUT

The general purpose of securities laws is to provide sufficient, accurate information to investors to enable them to make informed buying and selling decisions about securities. This chapter provides an outline of federal securities laws. This chapter also discusses issues of corporate governance.

CHAPTER OUTLINE

I. THE SECURITIES AND EXCHANGE COMMISSION (SEC)
The SEC administers the federal securities laws and regulates the sale and purchase of securities.

A. THE SEC'S MAJOR RESPONSIBILITIES

1. Interpret federal securities laws and investigate violations.
2. Issue new rules and amend existing rules.
3. Oversee the inspection of securities firms, brokers, investment advisers, and ratings agencies.
4. Oversee private regulatory organizations in the securities, accounting, and auditing fields.
5. Coordinate U.S. securities regulation with federal, state, and foreign authorities.

B. UPDATING THE REGULATORY PROCESS
The SEC requires companies to file certain information electronically so that it may be made available online in the SEC's EDGAR (Electronic Data Gathering, Analysis, and Retrieval) database.

C. THE SEC'S EXPANDING REGULATORY POWERS
The SEC's powers include the power to seek sanctions against those who violate foreign securities laws; to suspend trading if prices rise and fall in short periods of time; to exempt persons, securities, and transactions from securities law requirements; and to require more corporate disclosure.

II. THE SECURITIES ACT OF 1933
Requires all essential information concerning the issuance (sales) of new securities to be disclosed to investors.

A. WHAT IS A SECURITY?

1. **A Security Is an Investment** _[handwritten: Investment in common enterprise in which you expect to make a profit off other peoples work]_
   Examples: stocks, bonds, stock options, and investment contracts in condominiums, franchises, limited partnerships, and oil or gas or other mineral rights.

2. **Courts' Interpretation of the Securities Act**
   A security exists in any transaction in which a person (1) invests (2) in a common enterprise (3) reasonably expecting profits (4) derived *primarily* or *substantially* from others' managerial or entrepreneurial efforts.

333

B. REGISTRATION STATEMENT

Before offering securities for sale, issuing corporations must (1) file a registration statement with the Securities and Exchange Commission (SEC) and (2) provide investors with a prospectus that describes the security being sold, the issuing corporation, and the investment or risk.

1. **Contents of the Registration Statement**

   The statement must be in plain English, must be filed electronically, and must describe—

   a. The security being offered and its relationship to the registrant's other securities.
   b. The registrant's properties and business, including a financial statement certified by an independent public accountant.
   c. The registrant's management; its compensation and other benefits, including pensions and stock options, and any interests of directors or officers in material transactions with the corporation.
   d. How the registrant intends to use the proceeds of the sale.
   e. Pending lawsuits.

2. **Registration Process**

   Securities cannot be sold or advertised until after the SEC reviews the registration statement for completeness (unless it was issued by a well-known seasoned investor).

   a. **Waiting Period**

      After a statement is filed, there is a waiting period of at least twenty days. During this time, only certain types of offers—and no sales—are allowed. A preliminary (red herring) prospectus may be issued, often without stating a price. A free-writing prospectus (any type of offer that describes the issuer or the security) tells investors to obtain a prospectus at the SEC's Web site.

   b. **Posteffective Period**

      An issuer can now offer and sell the securities without restrictions (except that investors who were given a preliminary or free-writing prospectus must be given a final prospectus).

   c. **Restrictions Relaxed for Well-Known Seasoned Issuers**

      A well-known seasoned issuer is a firm that has issued at least $1 billion in securities in the previous three years or has at least $700 million of value of outstanding stock in the public's hands. This issuer can offer securities for sale without waiting for SEC review and approval of the registration statement.

C. EXEMPT SECURITIES

Securities that can be sold (and resold) without being registered include—

1. Government-issued securities.
2. Bank and financial institution securities.
3. Short-term notes and drafts (maturity does not exceed nine months.)
4. Securities of nonprofit, educational, and charitable organizations.
5. Securities issued by common carriers (trucking companies and railroads).
6. Any insurance, endowment, or annuity contract issued by a state-regulated insurance company.
7. Securities issued in a corporate reorganization in which one security is exchanged for another or in a bankruptcy proceeding.
8. Securities issued in stock dividends and stock splits.

D. EXEMPT TRANSACTIONS

Securities that can be sold without being registered include those sold in the following transactions.

1. **Regulation A Offerings**

   An issuer's offer of up to $5 million in securities in any twelve-month period is exempt. The issuer must file with the SEC a notice of the issue and an offering circular (also provided to investors before the sale) but this is a simpler and less expensive process than full registration. A company can "test the waters" (determine potential interest) before preparing the circular.

2. **Regulation D Offerings**

   Private, noninvestment company offers may be exempt. (A *noninvestment company* is a firm that is not engaged primarily in the business of investing or trading in securities.)

   a. **Offerings Up to $1 Million**

      Private, noninvestment company offerings up to $1 million in a twelve-month period are exempt [Rule 504]. This is the exemption used by most small businesses.

   b. **Offerings Up to $5 Million**

      Private, noninvestment company offerings up to $5 million in a twelve-month period if (1) no general solicitation or advertising is used; (2) the SEC is notified of the sales; (3) precaution is taken against nonexempt, unregistered resales; and (4) there are no more than thirty-five unaccredited investors. If the sale involves any unaccredited investors, all investors must be given material information about the company, its business, and the securities. The buyer cannot sell the securities for at least a year [Rule 505].

   c. **Offerings in Unlimited Amounts**

      Nonpublic and not generally advertised offerings in unlimited amounts are subject to essentially the same requirements as Rule 505, except (1) there is no limit on the amount of the offering and (2) the issuer must believe that each unaccredited investor has sufficient knowledge or experience to evaluate the investment [Rule 506].

3. **Resales and Safe Harbor Rules**

   Most securities can be resold without registration. Resales of small offerings [Rule 505] and private offerings [Rule 506] are exempt from registration under the following rules.

   a. **Rule 144**

      There must be adequate public information about the issuer, the securities must be sold in limited amounts in unsolicited brokers' transactions, the SEC must be notified of the resale, and—

      1) **The Securities Must Have Been Owned for at Least Six Months**

         If the issuer is subject to the 1934 act's reporting requirements.

      2) **The Securities Must Have Been Owned for at Least One Year**

         If the issuer is *not* subject to the 1934 act's reporting requirements.

   b. **Rule 144A**

      The securities, on issue, must not have been of the same class as securities listed on a national securities exchange or a U.S. automated interdealer quotation system. The securities are sold only to an institutional investor. The seller on resale must take steps to tell the buyer they are exempt.

E. **VIOLATIONS OF THE 1933 ACT**

   If registration statement or prospectus contains material false statements or omissions, liable parties include anyone who signed the statement.

1. **Penalties**

   Fines up to $10,000; imprisonment up to five years; injunction against selling securities; order to refund profits; damages in civil suits.

2. **Defenses**

Statement or omission was not material; plaintiff knew of misrepresentation and bought stock anyway; Most important is the *due diligence* defense, under which any defendant, except the issuer, can assert that he or she reasonably believed at the time of the registration statement the information was true and there were no material omissions.

III.   THE SECURITIES EXCHANGE ACT OF 1934

This act regulates the markets in which securities are traded by requiring continuous periodic disclosure by Section 12 companies (corporations with securities on the exchanges and firms with assets in excess of $10 million and five hundred or more shareholders).

A.   INSIDER TRADING—SECTION 10(b) AND SEC RULE 10b-5

Section 10(b) proscribes the use of "any manipulative or deceptive device or contrivance in contravention of such rules and regulations as the [SEC] may prescribe." SEC Rule 10b-5 prohibits the commission of fraud in connection with the purchase or sale of any security (registered or unregistered) when the requisites of federal jurisdiction are met. States have securities laws that may apply if federal law does not.

1. **What Triggers Liability**

Any material omission or misrepresentation of material facts in connection with the purchase or sale of a security can trigger liability. Fraud includes the failure to disclose inside information.

2. **What Does Not Trigger Liability**

Under the Private Securities Litigation Reform Act of 1995, financial forecasts and other forward-looking statements do not trigger liability if they include "meaningful cautionary statements identifying factors that could cause actual results to differ materially."

3. **Who Can Be Liable**

Those who take advantage of inside information when they know that it is unavailable to the person with whom they are dealing can be liable.

   a. **Insiders**

   Officers, directors, majority shareholders, and persons having access to or receiving information of a nonpublic nature on which trading is based (accountants, attorneys).

   b. **Outsiders**

   1) **Tipper/Tippee Theory**

   One who acquires inside information as a result of an insider's breach of fiduciary duty to the firm whose shares are traded can be liable, if (1) there is a breach of duty not to disclose the information, (2) the disclosure is for personal benefit, and (3) the tippee knows or should know of the breach and benefits from it.

   2) **Misappropriation Theory**

   One who wrongfully misappropriates inside information and trades on it to his or her gain can be liable, if a duty to the lawful possessor of the information was breached and harm to another results. Liability is based on a fiduciary's deception of those who entrusted him or her with access to confidential information.

B.   INSIDER REPORTING AND TRADING—SECTION 16(b)

Officers, directors, and shareholders owning 10 percent of the securities registered under Section 12 are required to file reports with the SEC concerning their ownership and trading of the securities.

1. **Corporation Is Entitled to All Profits**

A firm can recapture *all* profits realized by an insider on *any* purchase and sale or sale and purchase of its stock in any six-month period.

2. Applicability of Section 16(b)

Section 16(b) applies to stock, warrants, options, and securities convertible into stock.

C. REGULATION OF PROXY STATEMENTS

Section 14(a) regulates the solicitation of proxies from shareholders of Section 12 companies. Whoever solicits a proxy must disclose, in the proxy statement, all of the pertinent facts.

D. VIOLATIONS OF THE 1934 ACT

Violations of Section 10(b) and Rule 10b-5 include insider trading (a crime). Section 10(b) and Rule 10b-5 require proof of *scienter* (intent to defraud or knowledge of misconduct). Violations of Section 16(b) include sales by insiders of stock acquired less than six months before.

1. Criminal Penalties

Maximum jail term is twenty-five years; fines up to $5 million for individuals and $2.5 million for partnerships and corporations. The standard of proof is beyond a reasonable doubt.

2. Civil Sanctions

a. The SEC

The SEC can bring suit in federal court against anyone violating or aiding in a violation of the 1934 act or SEC rules. Penalties include triple the profits gained or loss avoided by the guilty party.

b. Private Parties

A corporation can sue under Section 16(b) to recover short-swing profits. A private party can sue under Section 10(b) and Rule 10b-5 to rescind a contract to buy or sell securities or to obtain damages to the extent of a violator's illegal profits. Those found liable have a right of contribution.

IV. STATE SECURITIES LAWS

A. REQUIREMENTS

All states regulate the offer and sale of securities within individual state borders. Exemptions from federal law are not exemptions from state laws, which have their own exemptions. Disclosure requirements and antifraud regulations are often patterned on federal provisions.

B. CONCURRENT REGULATION

Under the National Market Securities Improvement Act of 1996, the SEC regulates most national securities activities. The Uniform Securities Act, issued by the National Conference of Commissioners on Uniform State Laws and adopted in seventeen states, is designed to coordinate state and federal securities regulation and enforcement efforts.

V. CORPORATE GOVERNANCE

Corporate governance is the system by which corporations are governed and controlled, according to the Organization of Economic Cooperation and Development. Effective governance requires more than compliance with the law. Because corporate ownership is separated from corporate control, conflicts of interest can arise.

A. ATTEMPTS AT ALIGNING THE INTERESTS OF OFFICERS WITH SHAREHOLDERS

Providing stock options to align the financial interests of shareholders and officers has proved to be an imperfect control device. Officers have manipulated circumstances to artificially inflate stock prices to keep the value of options high, or the options have been "repriced" to avoid losses when stock prices dropped.

B. THE GOAL IS TO PROMOTE ACCOUNTABILITY

Corporate oversight involves (1) the audited reporting of corporate financial progress so that managers can be evaluated and (2) legal protection for shareholders.

C. GOVERNANCE AND CORPORATE LAW

Under the law, a corporation must have a board of directors elected by the shareholders. Thus, the key element of corporate structure is the board, which makes important decisions about the firm.

1. The Board of Directors

Directors, who must operate for the shareholders' benefit, are responsible for monitoring officers and can be sued for failing to do their jobs effectively.

2. The Compensation Committee

This committee determines the amount of compensation to be paid to the officers and is responsible for assessing those officers' performance.

D. THE SARBANES=OXLEY ACT OF 2002

This act imposes strict disclosure requirements and harsh penalties for violations of securities laws.

1. Reporting on Effectiveness of Internal Controls

An independent audit of management's assessment of internal controls must be filed with the SEC. Public companies with a market capitalization of less than $75 million are exempt.

2. Other Provisions

Certain reports must be filed with the SEC earlier than under previous law. Other provisions create new private civil actions and expand the SEC's remedies.

3. Internal Controls and Accountability

The act introduces federal corporate governance requirements for public companies' boards and auditors to monitor company officers and ensure that corporate financial reports filed with the SEC are accurate and timely.

4. Certification and Monitoring

Chief executive officers and chief financial officers must certify that these documents are accurate and complete. These officers are directly accountable for the accuracy of the reports, and may be subject to civil and criminal penalties for violations.

VI. ONLINE SECURITIES FRAUD

A. INVESTMENT SCAMS

There are infinite variations of investment scams, but most promise spectacular returns for small investments. Many are pyramid ("Ponzi") schemes, in which initial "investors" are paid with funds provided by later participants. Scams may be propagated via spam, fraudulent Web pages, online newsletters and bulletin boards, chat rooms, blogs, and tweets.

B. ONLINE INVESTMENT NEWSLETTERS AND FORUMS

To inflate the price of a stock and profit from its sale, its holders may pay others to tout the stock online. Potential investors may be duped if the identities of those who pay for this service are not disclosed when the law requires it. The same tactic may be employed in other online venues such as forums, using any number of aliases to falsify interest in the stock.

C. PONZI SCHEMES

These schemes often claim to consist of risk-free or low-risk investments. They sometimes fool U.S. residents into investing in offshore companies.

TRUE-FALSE QUESTIONS

(Answers at the Back of the Book)

____ 1. A security that does not qualify for an exemption must be registered before it is offered to the public.

____ **2.** Before a security can be sold to the public, prospective investors must be provided with a prospectus.

____ **3.** Stock splits are generally exempt from the registration requirements of the Securities Act of 1933.

____ **4.** Sales of securities may not occur until twenty days after registration.

____ **5.** Private offerings of securities in unlimited amounts that are not generally solicited or advertised must be registered before they can be sold.

____ **6.** A proxy statement must fully and accurately disclose all of the facts that are pertinent to the matter on which shareholders are being asked to vote.

____ **7.** All states have disclosure requirements and antifraud provisions that cover securities.

____ **8.** *Scienter* is not a requirement for liability under Section 10(b) of the Securities Exchange Act of 1934.

____ **9.** No one who receives inside information as a result of another's breach of his or her fiduciary duty can be liable under SEC Rule 10b-5.

____ **10.** No security can be resold without registration.

FILL-IN QUESTIONS

(Answers at the Back of the Book)

The SEC can award "bounty" payments to persons providing information leading to the _____ (conviction/prosecution) of insider-trading violations. Civil penalties include _____ (double/triple) the profits gained or the loss avoided. Criminal penalties include maximum jail terms of _____ (ten/ twenty-five) years. Violators _____ (may/may not) also be subject to multi-million-dollar fines.

MULTIPLE-CHOICE QUESTIONS

(Answers at the Back of the Book)

____ **1.** Frank, an officer of Gyra Gizmo, Inc., learns that Gyra has developed a new source of energy. Frank tells Huey, an outsider. They each buy Gyra stock. When the development is announced, the stock price increases, and they each immediately sell their stock. Subject to liability for insider trading

    a. are Frank and Huey.
    b. is Frank only.
    c. is Huey only
    d. is Gyra, but neither Frank nor Huey.

____ **2.** Elmo, a director of Far East Development Company, learns that a Far East engineer has developed a new, improved product. Over the next six months, Elmo buys and sells Far East stock for a profit. Of Elmo's profit, Far East may recapture

    a. all.
    b. half.
    c. 10 percent.
    d. none.

____ **3.** Centro Associates sells securities. The definition of a security does *not* include, as an element,

   a. an investment.
   b. a common enterprise.
   c. a reasonable expectation of profits.
   d. profits derived entirely from the efforts of the investor.

____ **4.** Superior, Inc., is a private, noninvestment company. In one year, Superior advertises a $300,000 offering. Concerning registration, this offering is

   a. exempt because of the low amount of the issue.
   b. exempt because it was advertised.
   c. exempt because the issuer is a private company.
   d. not exempt.

____ **5.** Huron, Inc., makes a $6 million private offering to twenty accredited investors and less than thirty unaccredited investors. Huron advertises the offering and believes that the unaccredited investors are sophisticated enough to evaluate the investment. Huron gives material information about itself, its business, and the securities to all investors. Concerning registration, this offering is

   a. exempt because of the low amount of the issue.
   b. exempt because it was advertised.
   c. exempt because the issuer believed that the unaccredited investors were sophisticated enough to evaluate the investment.
   d. not exempt.

____ **6.** Ontario, Inc., in one year, advertises two $2.25 million offerings. Buying the stock are twelve accredited investors. Concerning registration, this offering is

   a. exempt because of the low amount of the issue.
   b. exempt because it was advertised.
   c. exempt because only accredited investors bought stock.
   d. not exempt.

____ **7.** Fat City Games, Inc.'s registration statement must include

   a. a description of the accounting firm that audits Fat City.
   b. a description of the security being offered for sale.
   c. a financial forecast for Fat City's next five years.
   d. a marketing and management plan to ensure Fat City's success.

____ **8.** Natural Soy, Inc., wants to make an offering of securities to the public. The offer is not exempt from registration. Before Natural Soy sells these securities, it must provide *investors* with

   a. a marketing and management plan.
   b. a prospectus.
   c. a registration statement.
   d. samples of its products.

____ **9. Based a Sample CPA Question.** Under the Securities Exchange Act of 1934, the Securities and Exchange Commission is responsible for all of the following activities EXCEPT

   a. investigating securities fraud.
   b. prosecuting criminal violations of federal securities laws.
   c. regulating the activities of securities brokers.
   d. requiring disclosure of facts concerning offerings of securities listed on national securities exchanges.

___ **10.** Great Lakes Company is a private, noninvestment company. Last year, as part of a $250,000 advertised offering, Great Lakes sold stock to Jon, a private investor. Jon would now like to sell the shares. Concerning registration, this resale is

    a. exempt because of the low amount of the original issue.
    b. exempt because the offering was advertised.
    c. exempt because all resales are exempt.
    d. not exempt.

SHORT ESSAY QUESTIONS

1. What is the process by which a company sells securities to the public?

2. How is insider trading regulated by Section 10(b), SEC Rule 10b-5, and Section 16(b)?

GAMEPOINTS

(Answers at the Back of the Book)

1. The video game "High End High" is set in the world of finance. Your avatar has the opportunity to invest in a variety of enterprises in different scenarios, mostly involving exotic or cutting edge products or services. In the game, NanoGene, Inc., advertises online that it will make a $4.5 million offering of stock on within thirty days. The firm makes the offer and less than a week after the first sale notifies the Securities and Exchange Commission (SEC). All buyers—including you and fifty-two other unaccredited investors, as well as more sophisticated individuals and institutions—are given material information about the company, its business, its possible future, and its stock. You invest heavily in NanoGene, and the offering, which the firm does not register, is sold out within six months. Did you invest in a company that will soon be leveled with sanctions by the SEC? Discuss.

2. Still playing "High End High," which you can lose only by losing everything, you decide that, unlike your precipitous invest mention NanoGene, you will now act only on "material information." What information do you think meets this qualification?

SPECIAL INFORMATION FOR CPA CANDIDATES

Securities law is an important part of the CPA examination. Among the significant details you should pick up from your study of this chapter are the basic differences between the two federal securities acts, the definition of a security, and the requirements for selling securities that are not exempt—registration statement, prospectus, and the twenty-day waiting period. Among the regulations that exempt certain securities and transactions from the registration requirements, the most important for purposes of the CPA exam are Regulation A and Regulation D. These rules are consistently tested. In your study of the Securities Exchange Act of 1934, emphasize insider trading but be aware that other aspects of the act may be tested.

Chapter 43
Law for Small Business

WHAT THIS CHAPTER IS ABOUT

For small businesses, business law takes on special significance, in part because of the small size of those businesses. This chapter covers some aspects of the law as it applies in that context.

CHAPTER OUTLINE

I. THE IMPORTANCE OF LEGAL COUNSEL

A. FIND AN ATTORNEY
Sources include friends, business associates, other small business owners, business networks (chambers of commerce or bar organizations), Yellow Pages, *Martindale-Hubbell Law Directory* (available in libraries or at www.martindale.com).

B. RETAIN AN ATTORNEY
Benefits of retaining an attorney include the lawyer's contacts (such as potential investors), business expertise, confidentiality of attorney-client communications, and flexibility of payment plans (for example, regular monthly billing, as opposed to one-time lump sum).

C. HIRE AN ACCOUNTANT
A professional accountant is more expensive than bookkeeping software, but may be more accurate and adds to credibility with investors.

II. SELECTION OF THE BUSINESS ORGANIZATION
Factors to consider when choosing a business form include:

A. LIMITATIONS ON LIABILITY
Some business forms limit liability if, for example, a court awards damages to a customer injured on the premises (the owner is not personally liable). Corporations, limited partnerships, limited liability corporations (LLCs), and limited liability partnerships (LLPs) limit personal liability. Despite these limits, insurance should be obtained to cover losses that might otherwise bankrupt a small business.

B. TAX CONSIDERATIONS

1. Sole Proprietorships
A sole proprietor pays taxes on business income as an individual.

2. Partnerships
Partnerships do not pay tax, but the partners pay income tax on the firm's profits.

3. Corporations
Most corporations pay double taxes (the corporation pays tax on profits, and the shareholders pay tax on distributions). S corporations and LLCs are taxed like partnerships.

C. CONTINUITY OF LIFE
In most cases, corporations survive their owners. In a partnership, the death or withdrawal of a partner may terminate the partnership unless the partners have expressly provided otherwise. A sole proprietorship ends with the death of the sole proprietor.

343

D. LEGAL FORMALITY AND EXPENSE

1. Benefits of Formal Business Arrangements
These include an agreement setting out ownership rights if a dispute arises, and the advantages (or disadvantages) provided by statutes and case law relating to particular business forms.

2. Forms That Avoid Formality and Expense
Sole proprietorships and general partnerships avoid the formalities and costs of incorporating or creating a limited partnership.

3. All Businesses
Any business must meet such legal requirements as business name registration, occupational licensing, state tax registration, health and environmental permits, zoning and building codes, import/export regulations, and laws governing the workplace.

III. THE LIMITED LIABILITY COMPANY
The limited liability company (LLC) has become the preferred choice of business organization. Benefits include the limited liability of the corporation without its double taxation.

A. THE BASIC STRUCTURE
An operating agreement serves as the firm's charter. The owners are called members (and may be persons or entities such as corporations). Its operators are known as managers.

1. Flexibility in Determining Members' Rights
States allow LLCs much flexibility—for example, formal annual meetings are not required—but each states provides rules that apply unless an operating agreement provides otherwise.

2. Extent of Fiduciary Duties
States impose requirements of fair and honest dealing among members an managers.

B. CONVERTING AN LLC INTO A CORPORATION
By incorporating, an LLC can attract more outside investment capital. By retaining earnings to invest in future growth, the firm can avoid double taxation. Conversion may require the members' unanimous consent, filing LLC articles of dissolution with the state, and forming the new firm (discussed below).

IV. HOW TO FORM A BUSINESS ENTITY
There are no special requirements for creating a sole proprietorship. A general partnership requires only an agreement between the partners. Forming a limited partnership or corporation (see Chapter 37) is more complicated.

A. CORPORATE NAME
The name must be different from those of existing businesses (even unincorporated businesses) and should include the word *corporation, company,* or *incorporated*. It should be filed with the appropriate state office (usually secretary of state) to protect it as a trade name in the state.

B. ARTICLES OF INCORPORATION, BYLAWS, AND INITIAL MEETING

1. Articles of Incorporation
States vary with respect to what provisions must be included in the articles. S corporations must file additional forms with the IRS and (in most states) with the appropriate state agency.

2. Bylaws
Include provisions for the dates on which annual meetings will be held, terms for voting quorums, and other rules.

3. **Initial Board of Directors' Meeting**
    Directors adopt bylaws, appoint corporate officers and define their authority, issue stock, open bank accounts, take other necessary steps.

C. **CORPORATE RECORDS BOOK**
    Organizes important documents, such as articles of incorporation and minutes of director and shareholder meetings. Stock certificates may need to be created and a corporate seal may need to be obtained.

V.   INTELLECTUAL PROPERTY

Protecting rights in intellectual property (see Chapter 8) is a central concern to some new businesses, such as software companies.

A. **TRADEMARKS**
    A trademark cannot be too similar to another mark or mislead customers to think that someone else made a product. Generally, the first to use a trademark owns it.

    1. **Trademark Selection**
        A mark should be distinctive (for example, a made-up word such as Exxon). Name-consulting companies help in selecting marks, but may be too expensive for small business entrepreneurs.

    2. **Trademark Search**
        To ensure that a mark is not too similar to existing marks, check the Yellow Pages in the relevant area, consult *Gale's List of Tradenames*, look at the federal and state trademark registers, etc.

    3. **Trademark Registration**
        A trademark can be registered with the U.S. Patent and Trademark Office (PTO). This provides nationwide protection for a mark that is in use or will be within six months. If a logo consists of a distinctive name as well as a graphic, each can be registered independently.

    4. **Trademark Protection**

        a. **Symbols to Put Others on Notice**
            If a mark is federally registered, the symbol ® may be used. If a mark is not registered, the symbol ™ can be used.

        b. **Renewal of Registration**
            Five years after the initial registration, registration may be renewed, and every ten years thereafter.

        c. **Abandonment**
            Allowing others to use a mark without restrictions or without protest can constitute abandonment. Abandonment is presumed if a mark registered with the PTO is not used for two years.

B. **TRADE SECRETS**

    1. **What a Trade Secret Is**
        Trade secrets (see Chapter 8) are anything that makes an individual company unique and that would have value to a competitor.

    2. **What a Firm Can Do to Protect Its Trade Secrets**
        Require employees to agree not to (1) divulge trade secrets, and (2) work for a competitor, or set up a competing business, in which the company's trade secrets will likely be disclosed. A company can sue an individual or firm that misappropriates trade secrets.

VI. FINANCIAL CAPITAL

Raising capital is critical to business growth.

A. LOANS

Capital can be raised through a bank loan, but this may not be possible for many entrepreneurs. Loans may be available from the Small Business Administration (SBA).

B. VENTURE CAPITAL

Most new businesses raise capital by exchanging ownership rights (equity) in the firm for capital (the investor may be called a venture capitalist).

1. Procedure

To attract outside capital requires a business plan that describes the company, its products, and its anticipated performance. The investor examines the firm's books and assets (he or she should sign a confidentiality agreement not to disclose trade secrets). The parties negotiate a deal.

2. Points for Negotiation

These include the terms of financing, how much ownership and control the venture capitalist will receive, type and quantity of stock, and related issues.

C. SECURITIES REGULATION

When an investor exchanges capital for an interest in an enterprise and the interest consists of shares of stock (or otherwise qualifies as a security—see Chapter 41), it is subject to securities laws.

1. Private Offering

A limited amount of money can be raised from a limited number of investors without registering shares as securities with the Securities and Exchange Commission.

2. Public Offering

Making shares available for purchase by members of the public is highly regulated (but may raise a lot of capital). The securities must be registered. A simplified registration form for small businesses is the Small Corporate Offering Registration (SCOR).

VII. SHAREHOLDER AGREEMENTS AND KEY-PERSON INSURANCE

For any enterprise, a written agreement establishes what happens if partners or shareholders die, go bankrupt, get divorced, have their ownership interest attached, become disabled, or are so at odds that they cannot work together.

A. BUY-SELL AGREEMENT (KEY TERM OF SHAREHOLDER AGREEMENT)

Enables buy-out of a shareholder and provides for the price to be paid. Might include (1) a right of first refusal (prevents sale to a third party without first giving the other owners a right to buy), or (2) a "take-along" right (allows an investor to participate in sale of shares to a third party).

B. KEY-PERSON INSURANCE

This protects against the risk that a key person (manager, for example) may become disabled or die and (see Chapter 49) helps to cover losses caused by the death or disability.

VIII. CONTRACT LAW AND SMALL BUSINESS

A. BASIC CONTRACT PRINCIPLES APPLY

Basic contract law (see Chapters 10 through 18) applies to leases and sales of real property and equipment. A contract should be in writing in case of a dispute, or in some cases (see Chapter 15) so it can be enforced.

B. AGENCY PRINCIPLES AND PERSONAL LIABILITY

If a firm is organized in a form other than a sole proprietorship, persons who sign contracts or negotiable instruments (Chapter 26) on its behalf will want to do so as agents to avoid personal liability.

IX.   EMPLOYMENT ISSUES

A. HIRING EMPLOYEES

Some important considerations are:

1. Disclosing Trade Secrets

Employees should not disclose trade secrets of former (or current) employers.

2. Promising Job Security

Employees should not unintentionally be promised job security. (Such promises can be implied from statements in employment manuals.) All terms could be put in writing (for example, that employment is at-will—see Chapter 34), including grounds for termination.

3. Screening Applicants

If appropriate, an applicant may be required to take a drug test. Credentials and job experience should be verified (to avoid a negligent-hiring lawsuit—for example, hiring someone as a driver who has no driver's license).

4. Verifying Applicants' Credentials

Applicants' credentials and job experience should be verified. Federal law has certain requirements with respect to employing noncitizens.

B. WORKERS' COMPENSATION

In most states, an employee injured in the course of employment receives workers' compensation (and cannot sue the employer for more). Employers pay premiums for this insurance based in part on their safety records.

C. FIRING EMPLOYEES

1. Employee Files

Good cause for terminating a worker should be documented to succeed in suits against you for unlawful discrimination or some other legal violation. (Half the states allow employees access to their personnel records.)

2. Severance Pay

A law may govern the timing of a final paycheck, but severance pay is not required.

3. Wrongful Discharge

An action for wrongful discharge may follow a termination in bad faith (such as in violation of an employment contract).

D. INDEPENDENT CONTRACTORS

Independent contractors are not employees (see Chapter 31) and an employer cannot control how they do their work.

1. Taxes

Income taxes and Social Security/Medicare taxes do not have to be withheld or paid. Employers need not pay premiums for workers' compensation insurance or unemployment insurance.

2. Antidiscrimination Laws

An independent contractor cannot sue an employer for discrimination.

3. Misclassification of Employees as Independent Contractors

If a government agency determines that workers are employees, not independent contractors, there may be tax liability and penalties.

TRUE-FALSE QUESTIONS

(Answers at the Back of the Book)

____ 1. The most important factor is choosing an attorney is the price.

____ 2. In most cases, corporations survive their owners.

____ 3. A corporation's name can be the same as that of another existing business.

____ 4. Allowing others to use a trademark without protesting that use can be deemed abandonment.

____ 5. No money can be raised through an offering of stock without registering the shares as securities with the Securities and Exchange Commission.

____ 6. Key-person insurance helps to cover business losses caused by the death or disability of an essential employee.

____ 7. No contract needs to be in writing to be enforceable.

____ 8. Factors to consider when choosing a business organization include continuity of life.

____ 9. An employer's promises of job security are never binding.

____ 10. If appropriate, a job applicant can be required to take a drug test.

FILL-IN QUESTIONS

(Answers at the Back of the Book)

An employer must withhold and pay federal and state income taxes and Social Security/Medicare taxes for _____ (employees/independent contractors/employees and independent contractors). An employer must pay premiums for workers' compensation insurance and unemployment insurance to cover _____ (employees/independent contractors/employees and independent contractors). An employer can be sued for discrimination by _____ (employees/independent contractors/employees and independent contractors).

MULTIPLE-CHOICE QUESTIONS

(Answers at the Back of the Book)

____ 1. Suzu is starting Yin Yang Mats, a business to make and market different-shaped yoga mats. She hires Tristan, an attorney, to handle the initial paperwork. The advantages of retaining an attorney at this point in a business include the lawyer's

a. business contacts.
b. professional image.
c. social skills.
d. extralegal credentials.

____ **2.** Dre is starting Eden Garden, a salon and spa for select clients. Dre can avoid *all* business-related legal requirements if he organizes the business as

a. a limited liability company.
b. a partnership.
c. a sole proprietorship.
d. none of the choices.

____ **3.** Irving and Jewel design a fish-cleaning device that they call Heads & Tails. To market the device, they form a corporation. At the directors' initial meeting, the directors are most likely to

a. adopt bylaws only.
b. choose a corporate name.
c. distribute stock certificates.
d. draft articles of incorporation.

____ **4.** Farah starts a business to market nationally a countertop grill called Grill Bites. Registering her trademark with the U.S. Patent and Trademark Office provides nationwide protection for the mark

a. if the mark is currently in use.
b. only if the mark has not yet been used.
c. only if the mark will not be used for at least six months.
d. only if the mark is currently in *national* use.

____ **5.** Sherman is starting Tight Spaces, a business to make and market compact travel accessories. He hires Una, an accountant, to manage the new firm's bookkeeping. The advantages of retaining an accountant include

a. the addition to Sherman's credibility with potential investors.
b. the errors by the accountant that can provoke litigation.
c. the expense that the cost of an accountant adds to Sherman's liabilities.
d. the software that Sherman can appropriate to manage his own accounts.

____ **6.** Dharla operates Breakfast Café as a corporation. Farmland Foods supplies the café with eggs and other staples. Elvin, a customer, slips and breaks his arm in the café and is awarded damages by a court. Most likely, those damages must be paid by

a. Breakfast Café.
b. Dharla.
c. Elvin.
d. Farmland Foods.

____ **7.** Birdie is a plant manager for Cog Notch Corporation. To avoid personal liability for contracts signed on Cog Notch's behalf, Birdie should sign

a. as an agent for the corporation.
b. in her individual capacity.
c. as a machined parts specialist.
d. under a false name.

____ **8.** Sara and Tonya operate Ride Right, an auto repair shop, as a partnership. Taxes on the business's income are paid by

a. Sara and Tonya.
b. no one.
c. the business.
d. the state and the federal government.

___ 9. Fertile Meadow Organic Farm Company's attempt to raise $2 million from a few select investors is

a. a private offering.
b. a public offering.
c. a shareholder agreement.
d. key-person insurance.

___ 10. The six shareholders of Slim n' Trim Fitness Clubs, Inc., want to prevent each other from selling the shares to third parties without first being given the opportunity to buy the shares. They can provide for this in

a. a private offering.
b. a public offering.
c. a shareholder agreement.
d. key-person insurance.

SHORT ESSAY QUESTIONS

1. What are the primary factors to consider when choosing a business form?

2. What are some of the important considerations in discharging an employee?

GAMEPOINTS

(Answers at the Back of the Book)

1. With an espresso machine, a high-speed Internet connection, and a fertile imagination, you create "Biz Wiz," which promises to be one of most successful video game lines in history. The game opens with an extensive array of life and style choices for a player's avatar. Once begun, the play of the game responds to a player's choices of means and methods to acquire business wealth, subtly rewarding and punishing impulses of altruism and avarice with irony. To get the first game off the ground, you need capital. How can you get it?

2. Charles is interested in investing in your enterprise but insists on learning more about "Biz Wiz" than a thirty-second summary of the game and its prospects. Meanwhile, you've hired Dory, a video game designer, to write some of the code for "Biz Wiz's" sequel. How can you prevent Charles and Dory from revealing to others what they learn about your games?

SPECIAL INFORMATION FOR CPA CANDIDATES

The CPA requires knowledge of some of the concepts discussed in this chapter. Many of these topics are discussed in more detail in other chapters. For example, for the exam, it is important to understand the differences among the basic forms of business organizations. These forms and their differences are discussed in more detail in Chapters 36 through 41. Securities law is an important part of the exam and is covered in detail in Chapter 42. Employment topics that may be part of the exam include workers' compensation (see Chapter 34). For specific information about the relevance, as regards the CPA exam, of other topics discussed in other chapters, see those chapters.

CUMULATIVE HYPOTHETICAL PROBLEM
FOR UNIT EIGHT—INCLUDING CHAPTERS 36–43

(Answers at the Back of the Book)

Fern, Gigi, and Ho are sole proprietors who decide to pool their resources to produce and maintain an Internet game site, "we-World."

____ 1. Fern, Gigi, and Ho decide to form a partnership. They transfer their business assets and liabilities to the firm and start business on May 1, 2010. The parties execute a formal partnership agreement on July 1. The partnership began its existence

  a. on May 1.
  b. on July 1.
  c. when each partner's individual creditors consented to the asset transfer.
  d. when the parties initially decided to form a partnership.

____ 2. After six months in operation, Fern, Gigi, and Ho decide to change the form of their partnership to a limited partnership. To form a limited partnership, they must

  a. accept limited liability for all of the partners.
  b. create the firm according to specific statutory requirements.
  c. designate one general partner to be a limited partner.
  d. each make a capital contribution.

____ 3. Fern, Gigi, and Ho's we-World is very successful. In March 2012, they decide to incorporate. The articles of incorporation must include all of the following except

  a. the name of a registered agent.
  b. the name of the corporation.
  c. the names of the incorporators.
  d. the names of the initial officers.

____ 4. In January 2013, Fern, Gigi, and Ho decide to issue additional stock in we-World, Inc. The registration statement must include

  a. a copy of the corporation's most recent proxy statement.
  b. the names of prospective accredited investors.
  c. the names of the current shareholders.
  d. the principal purposes for which the proceeds from the offering will be used.

____ 5. The issue of shares that we-World, Inc., plans to make qualifies under Rule 504 of Regulation D of the Securities Act of 1933. Under this rule, we-World

  a. may not make the offering through general advertising.
  b. may sell the shares to an unlimited number of investors.
  c. must offer the shares for sale for more than twelve months.
  d. must provide all prospective investors with a prospectus.

QUESTIONS ON THE FOCUS ON ETHICS FOR UNIT EIGHT— BUSINESS ORGANIZATIONS

(Answers at the Back of the Book)

____ **1.** Hollis is an officer with Imprints, Inc., a screen-printing service Hollis finds herself in a position to acquire assets that would benefit Imprints if acquired in its name. If Hollis usurps this opportunity, she may violate the duty of

    a. acting in one's own interest.
    b. agency.
    c. care.
    d. loyalty.

____ **2.** Chico is a director of Blammo Motorbikes Corporation. Normally, Chico owes fiduciary duties only to

    a. himself.
    b. Blammo's creditors.
    c. Blammo's personnel.
    d. Blammo's shareholders.

____ **3.** HVAC Insulate Company sends its employees, including Jen, an e-mail announcement of certain positive, non-public information. Jen buys and sells HVAC stock within ten days for a substantial profit. Kyoko, HVAC's attorney, learns of the trades. Kyoko has a legal duty to report the trades to

    a. HVAC's highest authority.
    b. the parties with whom Jen bought and sold shares.
    c. the Securities and Exchange Commission.
    d. no one.

Chapter 44
Administrative Law

WHAT THIS CHAPTER IS ABOUT

Administrative agencies regulate virtually every aspect of a business's operation. Agencies' rules, orders, and decisions make up the body of administrative law. How agencies function is the subject of this chapter.

CHAPTER OUTLINE

I. THE PRACTICAL SIGNIFICANCE OF ADMINISTRATIVE LAW

Congress delegates some of its authority to make and implement laws, particularly in highly technical areas, to administrative agencies.

A. ADMINISTRATIVE AGENCIES EXIST AT ALL LEVELS OF GOVERNMENT

Administrative agencies at all levels of government—federal, state, and local—affect all aspects of business—capital structure and financing, employer-employee relations, production and marketing, and more.

B. AGENCIES PROVIDE A COMPREHENSIVE REGULATORY SCHEME

Agencies at different levels of government may cooperate to create and enforce regulations.

II. AGENCY CREATION AND POWERS

A. ENABLING LEGISLATION

To create an agency, Congress passes enabling legislation, which specifies the powers of the agency.

B. TYPES OF AGENCIES

1. Executive Agencies

Includes cabinet departments and their subagencies. Subject to the authority of the president, who can appoint and remove their officers.

2. Independent Regulatory Agencies

Includes agencies outside the major executive departments. Their officers serve for fixed terms and cannot be removed without just cause.

C. AGENCY POWERS AND THE CONSTITUTION

Agency powers include functions associated with the legislature (rulemaking), executive branch (enforcement), and courts (adjudication). Under Article I of the Constitution and the delegation doctrine, Congress has the power to establish agencies, which create *legislative rules* to implement laws and *interpretive rules* to declare policy.

1. Executive Controls

The executive branch exercises control over agencies through the president's powers to appoint federal officers and to veto enabling legislation or congressional attempts to modify an existing agency's authority.

2. Legislative Controls

Congress exercises authority over agency power through enabling legislation and subsequent legislation. Congress can restrict or expand agency power substantively, limit or increase it through funding, or set time limits. Congress can investigate an agency. Individual legislators may affect agency policy through attempts to help their constituents deal with agencies. The Administrative Procedure Act (APA) of 1946 and other laws also act as a check on agency power.

3. Judicial Controls

The APA provides for judicial review of most agency decisions. According to the exhaustion doctrine, a party must have used all potential administrative remedies before filing a suit.

III. THE ADMINISTRATIVE PROCEDURE ACT

Rulemaking, investigation, and adjudication make up the administrative process. The APA imposes procedural requirements that agencies must follow.

A. THE ARBITRARY AND CAPRICIOUS TEST

The APA provides that courts should set aside agency decisions that are "arbitrary, capricious, an abuse of discretion, or otherwise not in accordance with the law." This includes such factors as the following.

1. Failure to provide a rational explanation for a decision.
2. Change in prior policy without an explanation.
3. Consideration of legally inappropriate factors.
4. Failure to consider a relevant factor.
5. Render of a decision plainly contrary to the evidence.

B. RULEMAKING

Rulemaking is the formulation of new regulations. Legislative rules, or substantive rules, are as legally binding as the laws that Congress makes. Interpretive rules are not binding but indicate how an agency will apply a certain statute.

1. Notice of the Proposed Rulemaking

An agency begins by publishing, in the *Federal Register,* a notice that states where and when proceedings will be held, terms or subject matter of the proposed rule, the agency's authority for making the rule, and key information underlying the proposed rule.

2. Comment Period

Interested parties can express their views. An agency must respond to significant comments by modifying the final rule or explaining, in a statement accompanying the final rule, why it did not.

3. The Final Rule

The agency publishes the final rule—the terms of which may differ from the proposed rule—in the *Federal Register*. This final "legislative rule" has binding legal effect unless overturned by a court. The period must be at least thirty days and is often sixty days or more.

C. INFORMAL AGENCY ACTIONS

A rule that only states an agency's interpretation of its enabling statute's meaning is an "interpretative rule" and may be issued without formal rulemaking. These rules impose no direct or binding effect.

IV. JUDICIAL DEFERENCE TO AGENCY DECISIONS

Courts generally defer to an agency's factual judgment on a subject within the area of its expertise and its interpretation of its legal authority.

A. THE HOLDING OF THE *CHEVRON* CASE

When reviewing an agency's interpretation of law, a court should ask (1) whether the enabling statute directly addresses the issue and if not (2) whether the agency's interpretation is reasonable.

B. WHEN COURTS WILL GIVE *CHEVRON* DEFERENCE TO AGENCY INTERPRETATION

The extent of this deference has been much debated. If an agency's decision has resulted from formal rulemaking, it is more likely to be subject to deference.

V. ENFORCEMENT AND ADJUDICATION

A. INVESTIGATION

Agencies must have knowledge of facts and circumstances pertinent to proposed rules. Agencies must also obtain information and investigate conduct to ascertain whether its rules are being violated.

1. Inspections and Tests

Through on-site inspections and testing, agencies gather information to prove a regulatory violation or to correct or prevent a bad condition.

2. Subpoenas

A subpoena *ad testificandum* is an order to a witness to appear at a hearing. A subpoena *duces tecum* is an order to a party to hand over records or other documents. Limits on agency demands for information through these subpoenas, and otherwise, include—

   a. An investigation must have a legitimate purpose.
   b. The information that is sought must be relevant.
   c. Demands must be specific.
   d. The party from whom the information is sought must not be unduly burdened by the request.

3. Search Warrants

A search warrant directs an officer to search a specific place for a specific item and present it to the agency.

   a. **Search Warrants Usually Required**
   The Fourth Amendment protects against unreasonable searches and seizures by requiring that in most instances a physical search must be conducted under the authority of a search warrant.

   b. **Some Warrantless Searches Legal**
   Warrants are not required to conduct searches in businesses in highly regulated industries, in certain hazardous operations, and in emergencies.

B. ADJUDICATION

Adjudication involves the resolution of disputes by an agency.

1. Negotiated Settlements

The purpose of negotiation is (1) for agencies: to eliminate the need for further proceedings and (2) for parties subject to regulation: to avoid publicity and the expense of litigation.

2. Formal Complaints

If there is no settlement, the agency may issue a formal complaint. The party charged in the complaint may respond with an answer. The case may go before an administrative law judge (ALJ).

3. The Role of an Administrative Law Judge (ALJ)

The ALJ presides over the hearing. The ALJ has the power to administer oaths, take testimony, rule on questions of evidence, and make determinations of fact. An ALJ works for the agency, but must be unbiased. Certain safeguards in the APA prevent bias and promote fairness.

4. Hearing Procedures
Procedures vary widely from agency to agency. Agencies exercise substantial discretion over the type of procedures used. A formal hearing resembles a trial, but more items and testimony are admissible in an administrative hearing.

5. Agency Orders
After a hearing, the ALJ issues an initial order. Either side may appeal to the commission that governs the agency and ultimately to a federal appeals court. If there is no appeal or review, the initial order becomes final.

VI. PUBLIC ACCOUNTABILITY

A. FREEDOM OF INFORMATION ACT (FOIA) OF 1966
The federal government must disclose certain records to any person on request. A failure to comply may be challenged in federal district court.

B. GOVERNMENT-IN-THE-SUNSHINE ACT OF 1976
Requires (1) that "every portion of every meeting of an agency" that is headed by a "collegial body" is open to "public observation" and (2) procedures to ensure that the public is provided with adequate advance notice of meetings and agendas (with exceptions).

C. REGULATORY FLEXIBILITY ACT OF 1980
Whenever a new regulation will have a "significant impact upon a substantial number of small entities," the agency must conduct a regulatory flexibility analysis. The analysis must measure the cost imposed by the rule on small businesses and must consider less burdensome alternatives.

D. SMALL BUSINESS REGULATORY ENFORCEMENT FAIRNESS ACT
Under this act, passed in 1996—

1. Congress Reviews New Federal Regulations
Congress reviews new regulations for at least sixty days before they take effect. Opponents have time to present arguments to Congress.

2. Agencies Must Issue "Plain English" Guides
Agencies must prepare guides that explain how small businesses can comply with their regulations.

3. Regional Boards Rate Federal Agencies
The National Enforcement Ombudsman receives comments from small businesses about agencies. Based on the comments, Regional Small Business Fairness Boards rate the agencies.

TRUE-FALSE QUESTIONS

(Answers at the Back of the Book)

____ 1. Enabling legislation specifies the powers of an agency.

____ 2. Most federal agencies are part of the executive branch of government.

____ 3. To create an agency, Congress enacts enabling legislation.

____ 4. Agency rules are not as legally binding as the laws that Congress enacts.

____ 5. After an agency adjudication, the administrative law judge's order must be appealed to become final.

____ 6. Congress has no power to influence agency policy.

____ 7. The Administrative Procedure Act provides for judicial review of most agency actions.

____ 8. When a new regulation will have a significant impact on a substantial number of small entities, an analysis must be conducted to measure the cost imposed on small businesses.

____ 9. Courts generally defer to an agency's findings on facts within the area of its expertise.

____ 10. An agency cannot conduct a search without a warrant.

FILL-IN QUESTIONS
(Answers at the Back of the Book)

The rulemaking process begins with the publication in the _____ (*Congressional Record/Federal Register*) of a notice of the proposed rulemaking. The agency may conduct a public hearing at which it presents evidence to justify the proposed rule, and _____ (anyone/no one) may present opposing evidence. The agency _____ (must/need not) respond to significant comments. After the hearing, the agency publishes the final draft of the rule in the _____ (*Congressional Record/Federal Register*).

MULTIPLE-CHOICE QUESTIONS
(Answers at the Back of the Book)

____ 1. Paige, a congressperson, believes a new federal agency is needed to oversee the consumer lending industry. Congress has the power to establish an agency with functions that include

   a. adjudication.
   b. prevarication.
   c. qualification.
   d. regurgitation.

____ 2. Like other federal agencies, the Environmental Protection Agency may obtain information concerning activities and organizations that it oversees by issuing

   a. a complaint.
   b. a rule.
   c. a subpoena.
   d. a judgment.

____ 3. In making rules, the procedures of the Equal Employment Opportunity Commission and other federal agencies normally includes a period during which

   a. judges are asked about a proposed rule.
   b. probable violators of a proposed rule are notified and publicized.
   c. the administrators "notice" a problem and "comment" on it.
   d. the public is asked to comment on a proposed rule.

____ **4.** The Occupational Safety and Health Administration (OSHA) issues a subpoena for Precision Systems Corporation to hand over its files. Precision's possible defenses against the subpoena include

    a. OSHA cannot issue a subpoena.
    b. OSHA is a federal agency, but Precision only does business locally.
    c. OSHA's request is not specific enough.
    d. OSHA's request violates Precision's right to privacy.

____ **5.** The Federal Trade Commission (FTC) issues an order relating to the advertising of Discount Mart, Inc. Discount appeals the order to a court. The court may review whether the FTC's action is

    a. arbitrary, capricious, or an abuse of discretion.
    b. discourteous, disrespectful, or dissatisfying to one or more parties.
    c. flippant, wanton, or in disregard of social norms.
    d. impious, non-utilitarian, or in violation of ethical precepts.

____ **6.** The Federal Energy Regulatory Commission (FERC) wants to close a series of its meetings to the public. To open the meetings, Jennifer or any citizen could sue the FERC under

    a. the Freedom of Information Act.
    b. the Government-in-the-Sunshine Act.
    c. the Regulatory Flexibility Act.
    d. no federal or state law.

____ **7.** The U.S. Fish and Wildlife Service orders Elin to stop using a certain type of fishing net from her boat. To appeal this order to a court, Elin must

    a. appeal simultaneously to the agency and the court.
    b. bypass all administrative remedies and appeal directly to the court.
    c. exhaust all administrative remedies.
    d. ignore the agency and continue using the net.

____ **8.** The National Oceanic and Atmospheric Administration (NOAA) is a federal agency. To limit the authority of NOAA, the president can

    a. abolish NOAA.
    b. take away NOAA's power.
    c. refuse to appropriate funds to NOAA.
    d. veto legislative modifications to NOAA's authority.

____ **9.** The Federal Communications Commission (FCC) publishes notice of a proposed rule. When comments are received about the rule, the FCC must respond to

    a. all of the comments.
    b. any significant comments that bear directly on the proposed rule.
    c. only comments by businesses engaged in interstate commerce.
    d. only comments by businesses that will be affected by the rule.

____ **10.** Sol is an administrative law judge (ALJ) for the National Labor Relations Board. In hearing a case, Sol has the authority to make

    a. decisions binding on the federal courts.
    b. determinations of fact.
    c. new laws.
    d. new rules.

SHORT ESSAY QUESTIONS

1. What are the conditions to judicial review of an agency enforcement action?

2. How does Congress hold agency authority in check?

GAMEPOINTS

(Answers at the Back of the Book)

1. You are playing the video game "Risky Hazards," in which your character is an inspector for the Occupational Safety and Health Administration. In one scenario, you enter what appears to be a deserted warehouse to find a small group working in a dimly lit corner. The premises are fraught with hazards—loose wires, dangling ceiling tiles, dripping liquids, locked exit doors. A figure claiming to be a supervisor argues, "You can't come in here during working hours, this is private property, and you didn't give twenty-four-hours notice. Besides, there's no emergency—you need a warrant to come in here." Are any of these points valid? Explain.

2. In the video game "Magic Coffee Beans," your character is the owner of the Tasty Pastry Café. Your objective is to do brisk business profitably and expand to other locations. An inspector for the state equal opportunity agency cites your café for failing to provide access for disabled persons. The cost to comply would undercut your profit. Unable to negotiate a solution to all of the parties' satisfaction, the agency files a formal complaint against the Tasty Pastry. What's next?

SPECIAL INFORMATION FOR CPA CANDIDATES

The material in this chapter has not been part of the CPA examination in the past. Regarding specific administrative agencies, however, you will be expected to know that the commerce clause supports the Securities Exchange Commission's regulation of interstate buying and selling of securities.

Although you should plan on taking the CPA examination as soon as possible after completing your undergraduate education (because the exam is an academic test, covering material that is part of the curriculum in the accounting programs in business schools), you should find some relief in the fact that the exam does not cover new law for at least one year after the law is enacted. If a question is posed on the test on a topic on which a new law has been enacted within the twelve months preceding the test, you will be given credit for answering the question in accord with the old law or the new law.

Chapter 45
Consumer Law

WHAT THIS CHAPTER IS ABOUT

Federal and state laws protect consumers from unfair trade practices, unsafe products, discriminatory or unreasonable credit requirements, and other problems related to consumer transactions. This chapter focuses on *federal* consumer law.

CHAPTER OUTLINE

I. DECEPTIVE ADVERTISING

The Federal Trade Commission Act of 1914 created the Federal Trade Commission (FTC) to prevent unfair and deceptive trade practices. *Deceptive advertising* is advertising that would mislead a consumer—scientifically untrue claims and misleading half-truths, for example. Puffing (vague generalities, obvious exaggeration) is not deceptive.

A. BAIT-AND-SWITCH ADVERTISING

This occurs when a seller refuses to show an advertised item, fails to have adequate quantities on hand, fails to promise to deliver within a reasonable time, or discourages employees from selling the item. The FTC has issued rules to prevent this practice.

B. ONLINE DECEPTIVE ADVERTISING

The same laws that apply to other forms of advertising apply to online ads, under FTC guidelines—

1. Ads must be truthful and no misleading.
2. Any claims in an ad must be substantiated.
3. Ads cannot be unfair (likely to cause substantial, reasonably unavoidable consumer injury not outweighed by any benefit to the consumer or competition).
4. Disclosure of qualifying or limiting information must be "clear and conspicuous." Burying this information on an internal Web page is not recommended except in certain circumstances.

C. FTC ACTIONS AGAINST DECEPTIVE ADVERTISING

1. The Complaint Order

An FTC action against those who are accused of deceptive advertising begins with an investigation, often after a consumer complaint. The investigation may lead to a formal complaint. If the alleged offender does not agree to settle, a hearing is held before an administrative law judge.

2. The Cease-and-Desist Order

A cease-and-desist order or an order that requires counteradvertising may be issued. FTC orders may be appealed, but courts generally defer to the FTC's judgment.

D. TELEMARKETING AND FAX ADVERTISING

1. Telephone Consumer Protection Act (TCPA) of 1991

The TCPA prohibits (1) phone solicitation using an automatic dialing system or a prerecorded voice and (2) transmission of ads via fax without the recipient's permission. The Federal

361

Communications Commission can impose fines of up to $11,000 per day for junk fax violations. Consumers can recover actual losses or $500, whichever is greater, for each violation. If a defendant willfully or knowingly violated the act, a court can award treble damages.

2. Telemarketing and Consumer Fraud and Abuse Prevention Act of 1994
This act authorized the FTC to set rules for telemarketing and bring actions against fraudulent telemarketers. The FTC's Telemarketing Sales Rule of 1995 makes it illegal to misrepresent information and requires disclosure. The FTC also set up the national Do Not Call Registry.

II.   LABELING AND PACKAGING

A. FEDERAL STATUTES
Federal statutes included the Fur Products Labeling Act of 1951, the Wool Products Labeling Act of 1939, the Flammable Fabrics Act of 1953, the Comprehensive Smokeless Tobacco Health Education Act of 1986, and the Energy Policy and Conservation Act of 1975.

B. FAIR PACKAGING AND LABELING ACT OF 1966
This act requires that product labels identify (1) the product, (2) the net quantity of contents; and the size of a serving if the number of servings is stated, (3) the manufacturer, and (4) the packager or distributor. The U.S. Food and Drug Administration and the U.S. Department of Agriculture are the chief agencies that issue regulations on food labeling.

III.   SALES
Federal agencies that regulate sales include the FTC and the Federal Reserve Board of Governors (Regulation Z governs credit provisions in sales contracts)..

A. COOLING-OFF LAWS
Some states' "cooling-off" laws permit a buyer to rescind a door-to-door purchase within a certain time. The FTC has a three-day period. Other state laws, including the Uniform Commercial Code's warranty sections, also apply.

B. TELEPHONE AND MAIL-ORDER SALES

1. FTC "Mail or Telephone Order Merchandise Rule" of 1993
For goods bought via phone lines or through the mail, merchants must ship orders within the time promised in their ads, notify consumers when orders cannot be shipped on time, and issue a refund within a specified time if a consumer cancels an order.

2. Postal Reorganization Act of 1970
Unsolicited merchandise sent by the mail may be retained, used, discarded, or disposed of, without obligation to the sender.

C. ONLINE SALES
The same federal and state laws that apply to other media generally protect consumers online.

IV.   CREDIT PROTECTION

A. TRUTH-IN-LENDING ACT (TILA) OF 1968
The TILA, administered by the Federal Reserve Board, requires the disclosure of credit terms.

1. Who Is Subject to the TILA?
Creditors who, in the ordinary course of business, lend money or sell goods on credit to consumers, or arrange for credit for consumers, are subject to the TILA.

2. **Disclosure Requirements**
   Under Regulation Z, in any transaction involving a sales contract in which payment is to be made in more than four installments, a lender must disclose all the credit terms clearly and conspicuously.

3. **Equal Credit Opportunity Act of 1974**
   This act prohibits (1) denial of credit on the basis of race, religion, national origin, color, sex, marital status, age and (2) credit discrimination based on whether an individual receives certain forms of income.

4. **Credit-Card Protection**
   Liability of a cardholder is $50 per card for unauthorized charges made before the issuer is notified the card is lost. An issuer cannot bill for unauthorized charges if a card was improperly issued. To withhold payment for a faulty product, a cardholder must use specific procedures. Other rules—

   a. Protect consumers from retroactive increases in interest rates on existing balances unless an account is sixty days delinquent.
   b. Require forty-five days advance notice to consumers before changing credit terms.
   c. Require monthly bills to be sent twenty-one days before their due date.
   d. Limit interest-rate increases to specific situations.
   e. Prohibit over-limit fees except in specific situations.
   f. Require the application of payments for more than the minimum amount due to the highest-interest balances (such as cash advances).
   g. Prevent computing finance charges based on the previous billing cycle.

5. **Consumer Leasing Act of 1988**
   Those who lease consumer goods in the ordinary course of their business, if the goods are priced at $25,000 or less and the lease term exceeds four months, must disclose all material terms in writing.

B. **FAIR CREDIT REPORTING ACT (FCRA) OF 1970**

1. **What the FCRA Provides**
   Consumer credit reporting agencies may issue credit reports only for certain purposes (extension of credit, etc.); a consumer who is denied credit, or is charged more than others would be, on the basis of a report must be notified of the fact and of the agency that issued the report, and be allowed to correct any misinformation.

2. **Consumers Can Have Inaccurate Information Deleted**
   If a consumer discovers that the report contains inaccurate information, the agency must delete it within a reasonable period of time.

3. **Remedies for Violations**
   A credit agency may be liable for actual damages and additional damages up to $1,000, plus attorneys' fees. Creditors and others, including insurance companies, that use credit information may also be liable.

C. **FAIR AND ACCURATE CREDIT TRANSACTIONS ACT (FACT ACT) OF 2003**
   The FACT Act established a national "fraud alert" system so that consumers who suspect ID theft can place an alert on their credit files. Also—

1. **Credit-Reporting Agencies' Responsibilities**
   Consumer credit-reporting agencies must provide consumers with free copies of their reports and stop reporting allegedly fraudulent information once a consumer shows that ID theft occurred.

2. Other Businesses' Responsibilities

Businesses must include shortened ("truncated") account numbers on credit card receipts and provide consumers with copies of records to help prove an account or transaction was fraudulent.

D. FAIR DEBT COLLECTION PRACTICES ACT (FDCPA) OF 1977

The FDCPA applies only to debt-collection agencies that, usually for a percentage of the amount owed, attempt to collect debts on behalf of someone else.

1. What the FDCPA Prohibits

a. Contacting the debtor at the debtor's place of employment if the employer objects.
b. Contacting the debtor during inconvenient times or at any time if an attorney represents the debtor.
c. Contacting third parties other than the debtor's parents, spouse, or financial advisor about payment unless a court agrees.
d. Using harassment, or false and misleading information.
e. Contacting the debtor any time after the debtor refuses to pay the debt, except to advise the debtor of further action to be taken.

2. Notification and Bona Fide Errors

Collection agencies must give a debtor a validation notice that states he or she has thirty days to dispute the debt and request written verification of it. Debt collectors are not liable if they can show that a violation was unintentional and the result of a "bona fide error" despite following procedures designed to avoid such errors.

3. Remedies

A debt collector may be liable for actual damages, plus additional damages not to exceed $1,000 and attorneys' fees.

E. GARNISHMENT OF WAGES

To collect a debt, a creditor may use garnishment, which involves attaching a debtor's assets that are in the possession of a third party (employer, bank). The debtor must be notified and have an opportunity to respond. The amount that may be garnished is limited.

V. CONSUMER HEALTH AND SAFETY

A. FOOD AND DRUGS

The Federal Food, Drug, and Cosmetic Act (FFDCA) of 1938 sets food standards, levels of additives, classifications of food and food ads; regulates medical devices. Drugs must be shown to be effective and safe. Enforced by the Food and Drug Administration (FDA).

B. CONSUMER PRODUCT SAFETY

The Consumer Product Safety Act of 1972 requires manufacturers to report on any products already sold or intended for sale if the products have proved to be hazardous. The act includes a scheme for the regulation of products and safety by the Consumer Product Safety Commission (CPSC). The CPSC—

1. Conducts research on product safety.
2. Maintains a clearinghouse on the risks associated with some products.
3. Sets standards for consumer products.
4. Bans the manufacture or importation and sale of products that are potentially hazardous to consumers.
5. Removes from the market any products imminently hazardous.
6. Requires manufacturers to report on any products already sold or intended for sale if the products have proved to be hazardous.
7. Administers other product safety legislation.

TRUE-FALSE QUESTIONS

(Answers at the Back of the Book)

____ 1. Advertising will be deemed deceptive if a consumer would be misled by the advertising claim.

____ 2. Labels must be accurate.

____ 3. A consumer cannot rescind a contract freely entered into.

____ 4. The TILA applies to creditors who, in the ordinary course of business, sell goods on credit to consumers.

____ 5. A consumer can include a note in his or her credit file to explain any misinformation in the file, but the misinformation cannot be deleted.

____ 6. The same laws that apply to other media generally protect consumers online.

____ 7. The Fair Debt Collection Practices Act applies to anyone who attempts to collect a debt.

____ 8. There are no federal agencies that regulate sales.

____ 9. One who leases consumer goods in the ordinary course of business does not have to disclose any material terms in writing.

____ 10. An advertiser cannot fax ads to consumers without their permission.

FILL-IN QUESTIONS

(Answers at the Back of the Book)

The Truth-in-Lending Act contains provisions regarding credit cards. One provision limits the liability of the cardholder to _____ ($50/$500) per card for unauthorized charges made _____ (after/before) the credit card issuer is notified that the card has been lost. Another provision _____ (allows/prohibits) a credit card company _____ (from billing/to bill) a consumer for any unauthorized charges _____ (unless/if) the credit card was improperly issued by the company.

MULTIPLE-CHOICE QUESTIONS

(Answers at the Back of the Book)

____ 1. Ed takes out a student loan from First National Bank. After graduation, Ed goes to work, but he does not make payments on the loan. The bank agrees with Good Collection Agency (GCA) that if GCA collects the debt, it can keep a percentage of the amount. To collect the debt, GCA can contact

a. Ed at his place of employment, even if his employer objects.
b. Ed at unusual or inconvenient times or any time if he retains an attorney.
c. Ed only to advise him of further action that GCA will take.
d. third parties, including Ed's parents, unless ordered otherwise by a court.

____ **2.** Tasty Treat Company advertises that its cereal, "Fiber Rich," reduces cholesterol. After an investigation and a hearing, the FTC finds no evidence to support the claim. To correct the public's impression of Fiber Rich, the most appropriate action would be

    a. a cease-and-desist order.
    b. a civil fine.
    c. a criminal fine.
    d. counteradvertising.

____ **3.** Snarky Bling Corporation sells consumer products. Generally, the labels must use words as they are

    a. normally used in the scientific community.
    b. ordinarily understood by consumers.
    c. reasonably approved by ABC's officers.
    d. typically explained by the marketing department.

____ **4.** Nick comes to Maria's home and, after a long presentation, sells her a vacuum cleaner. Maria has

    a. no right to rescind this transaction.
    b. three days to exercise any "lowest" price guaranty.
    c. three days to rescind this transaction.
    d. three days to substitute a neighbor as the customer in this transaction.

____ **5.** The ordinary business of Homeowner Credit Company is to lend money to consumers. Homeowner must disclose all credit terms clearly and conspicuously in

    a. all credit transactions.
    b. any credit transaction in which payments are to be made in more than four installments.
    c. any credit transaction in which payments are to be made in more than one installment.
    d. no credit transaction.

____ **6.** Eve borrows money to buy a car and to pay for repairs to the roof of her house. She also buys furniture in a transaction financed by the seller whom she will repay in installments. If all of the parties are subject to the Truth-in-Lending Act, Regulation Z applies to

    a. the car loan only.
    b. the home improvement loan only.
    c. the retail installment sale only.
    d. the car loan, the home improvement loan, and the retail installment sale.

____ **7.** Krunchies, Inc., sells snack foods. Krunchies must include on the packages

    a. no nutrition information.
    b. the identity of the product only.
    c. the identity of the product, the net quantity of the contents, and the number of servings.
    d. the net quantity of the contents and the number of servings only.

____ **8.** US Tobacco Corporation (USTC) sells tobacco products. On the packages of its *smokeless* tobacco products, USTC must include warnings about health hazards associated with

    a. cigarettes.
    b. smokeless products.
    c. tobacco products generally.
    d. none of the choices.

____ 9. Slick Toy Company begins marketing a new toy that is highly flammable. The Consumer Product Safety Commission may

    a. ban the toy's future manufacture and sale, and order that the toy be removed from the market.
    b. ban the toy's future manufacture and sale only.
    c. do nothing until there is an injury or damage on which to base an action.
    d. order that the toy be removed from the market only.

____ 10. Jada receives an unsolicited credit card in the mail and tosses it on her desk. Without Jada's permission, her roommate Loni uses the card to buy new clothes for $1,000. Jada is liable for

    a. $1,000.
    b. $500.
    c. $50.
    d. $0.

SHORT ESSAY QUESTIONS

1. What are some of the more common deceptive advertising techniques and the ways in which the FTC may deal with such conduct?

2. What are the primary provisions of the Truth-In-Lending Act?

GAMEPOINTS

(Answers at the Back of the Book)

1. You are an extraordinarily successful video game designer with six multi-million sellers, including "Fireball" and its sequels "Infernal Inferno" and "Flaming Skull." You visit your local Car Sales Showroom and choose a couple of rides. To pay for the vehicles and their customizing, you contact Gamesters Credit Union. In the course of the loan transaction, the Gamester's representative tells you the interest rate but not all of the lender's terms because "it would take too long." Does this comply with the law?

2. To increase the sales of your most recent video game release and profit from related merchandise, you begin your "Life Is Hot" North American tour of video game outlets and competitive venues. In your contract with Midwest Promotions, Inc., covering twenty-two dates, you demand a buffet of specific foods to be available at each location. What is the general legal standard with respect to food? Which federal agencies monitor and enforce statutes involving food?

SPECIAL INFORMATION FOR CPA CANDIDATES

The CPA examination generally does not test on the material covered in this chapter.

When studying for the CPA exam, many students integrate their review of business law topics with their review of other topics that make up distinct subject matter on the exam. For example, when reviewing the law behind business organizations, it can be most helpful to review the accounting and reporting details behind businesses' financial statements. Which topics to integrate and how much time to spend on each depends in part on each student's knowledge and understanding of the individual topics, as well as the emphasis that should be placed on a topic because of its importance for the exam.

Chapter 46
Environmental Law

WHAT THIS CHAPTER IS ABOUT

This chapter covers environmental law, which is the law that relates to environmental protection—common law actions and federal statutes and regulations.

CHAPTER OUTLINE

I. COMMON LAW ACTIONS

A. NUISANCE
Persons cannot use their property in a way that unreasonably interferes with others' rights to use or enjoy their own property. An injured party may be awarded damages or an injunction.

1. Private Nuisance
A private nuisance occurs when an individual suffers distinct harm separate from that affecting the general public. Some states require this for an individual plaintiff.

2. Public Nuisance
A public authority can maintain an action to stop a public nuisance.

B. NEGLIGENCE AND STRICT LIABILITY
A business that fails to use reasonable care may be liable to a party whose injury was foreseeable. Businesses that engage in ultrahazardous activities are strictly liable for whatever injuries the activities cause.

II. FEDERAL, STATE, AND LOCAL REGULATION

A. STATE AND LOCAL REGULATIONS
States regulate the environment through zoning or more direct regulation. City, county, and other local governments control some aspects through zoning laws, waste removal and disposal regulations, aesthetic ordinances, and so on.

B. FEDERAL REGULATION

1. Environmental Regulatory Agencies
The Environmental Protection Agency (EPA) coordinates federal environmental responsibilities and administers most federal environmental policies and statutes. State and local agencies implement environmental statutes and regulations. Citizens can sue to enforce the regulations.

2. Environmental Impact Statements
The National Environmental Policy Act (NEPA) of 1969 requires all federal agencies to consider environmental factors in making significant decisions.

a. When an Environmental Impact Statement Must Be Prepared
Whenever a major federal action significantly affects the quality of the environment. An action qualifies as *major* if it involves a substantial commitment of resources (monetary or otherwise). An action is *federal* if a federal agency has the power to control it.

369

  b. What an EIS Must Analyze
  (1) The impact on the environment that the action will have, (2) any adverse effects to the environment and alternative actions that might be taken, and (3) irreversible effects the action might generate.

  c. When an Agency Decides That an EIS Is Unnecessary
  It must issue a statement supporting this conclusion.

III. AIR POLLUTION

The Clean Air Act of 1963 (and amendments) is the basis for regulation.

A. MOBILE SOURCES

Regulations governing air pollution from automobiles and other mobile sources specify standards and time schedules. For example, under the 1990 amendments to the Clean Air Act—

1. New Automobiles' Exhaust
Manufacturers had to cut emission of nitrogen oxide by 60 percent and emission of other pollutants by 35 percent. Other sets of emission controls became effective in 2004.

2. Sport Utility Vehicles and Light Trucks
These vehicles are now subject to the same standards as cars.

3. New Standards
The EPA updates these and other standards when new scientific evidence is available. In 2009, the EPA concluded that greenhouse gases, including carbon dioxide, are a public danger.

B. STATIONARY SOURCES

The primary responsibility for controlling and preventing pollution from stationary sources (such as industrial plants) rests with the states. The EPA sets air quality standards for stationary sources (such as industrial plants), and the states formulate plans to achieve them.

1. Listing of Hazardous Air Pollutants
The focus is on hazardous air pollutants (HAPs), which are likely to cause death or serious illnesses (such as cancer). The EPA lists about 200 HAPs.

2. Air Pollution Control Standards
Different standards apply to sources in clean areas and sources in polluted areas, and to existing sources and major new sources. Performance standards for major sources require the use of maximum achievable control technology (MACT), which is subject to EPA guidelines.

C. PENALTIES

Civil penalties include assessments of up to $25,000 per day, or an amount equal to a violator's economic benefits from noncompliance, plus up to $5,000 per day for other violations. Criminal penalties include fines of up to $1 million and imprisonment of up to two years. Private citizens can also sue.

IV. WATER POLLUTION

A. NAVIGABLE WATERS

The Clean Water Act of 1972 amended the Federal Water Pollution Control Act (FWPCA) of 1948 to provide—

1. Goals
The goals of the statutes are to (1) make waters safe for swimming, (2) protect fish and wildlife, and (3) eliminate the discharge of pollutants into the water.

2. **Focus on Point-Source Emissions**
    Under a National Pollutant Discharge Elimination System (NPDES), a point source of pollution emitted into water must have a permit. Permits can be obtained from the EPA and authorized state agencies and Indian tribes, and must be reissued every five years. The NPDES includes—

    a. National effluent standards set by the EPA for each industry.
    b. Water-quality standards set by the states under EPA supervision.
    c. A discharge-permit program that sets water-quality standards to limit pollution.
    d. Provisions for toxic chemicals and oil spills.
    e. Construction grants and loans for publicly owned treatment works (chiefly sewage plants).

3. **Standards for Equipment**
    Regulations specify the use of the best available control technology (BACT) for new sources. Existing sources must first install the best practical control technology (BPCT).

4. **Wetlands**
    Wetlands include "those areas that are inundated or saturated by surface or ground water at a frequency and duration sufficient to support, and that under normal circumstances do support, a prevalence off vegetation typically adapted for life in saturated soil conditions."

5. **Violations, Penalties, and Remedies**
    Lying about a discharge is more serious than admitting to an improper discharge. Civil penalties range from $10,000 (up to $25,000 per violation) to $25,000 per day. Criminal penalties (for intentional violations only) include substantial fines and imprisonment. Injunctions, damages, and clean-up costs can be imposed. And citizens can sue.

B. **DRINKING WATER**
    The Safe Drinking Water Act of 1974 requires the EPA to set maximum levels for pollutants in public water systems. Operators must come as close to these as possible using the best available technology. Suppliers must inform the public of the source of the water, the level of contaminants, and possible health concerns.

C. **OCEAN DUMPING**
    The Marine Protection, Research, and Sanctuaries Act of 1972—

    1. **Radiological Waste and Other Materials**
        Dumping of radiological, chemical, and biological warfare agents, and high-level radioactive waste is prohibited. Transporting and dumping other materials requires a permit.

    2. **Penalties**
        Civil penalties include assessments of not more than $50,000 or revocation or suspension of a permit. Criminal penalties include fines of up to $50,000, imprisonment for not more than a year, or both. Injunctions can be imposed.

D. **OIL POLLUTION**
    The Oil Pollution Act of 1990 provides that any oil facility, shipper, vessel owner, or vessel operator that discharges oil may be liable for clean-up costs, and damages for harm to natural resources, private property, and local economies. Fines of $2 million to $350 million are possible.

V. TOXIC CHEMICALS

A. **PESTICIDES AND HERBICIDES**

    1. **Federal Insecticide, Fungicide, and Rodenticide Act (FIFRA) of 1947**

a. Registration, Certification, and Use
Products must be (1) registered before they can be sold, (2) certified and used only for approved applications, and (3) used in limited quantities when applied to food crops.

b. Labels
Labels must not be false or misleading. A product cannot be sold with a destroyed or defaced label.

c. Penalties
For producers: suspension or cancellation of registration, up to a $50,000 fine, imprisonment up to one year. For commercial dealers: up to a $25,000 fine, imprisonment up to one year. For farmers and other private users: a $1,000 fine, imprisonment up to thirty days.

2. Acceptable Risks
To remain on the market, a product must have no more than a one-in-a-million risk to people of cancer from exposure, which includes eating food with pesticide residue.

B. TOXIC SUBSTANCES
Under the Toxic Substances Control Act of 1976, for substances that potentially pose an imminent hazard or an unreasonable risk of injury to health or the environment, the EPA may require special labeling, set production quotas, or limit or prohibit the use of a substance.

VI.   HAZARDOUS WASTES

A. RESOURCE CONSERVATION AND RECOVERY ACT (RCRA) OF 1976
Under the RCRA, the EPA determines which forms of solid waste are hazardous, and sets requirements for disposal, storage, and treatment. Penalties include up to $25,000 (civil) per violation, $50,000 (criminal) per day, imprisonment up to two years (may be doubled for repeaters).

B. SUPERFUND
The Comprehensive Environmental Response, Compensation, and Liability Act (CERCLA) of 1980 regulates the clean-up of leaking hazardous waste disposal sites.

1. Potentially Responsible Parties
If a release or a threatened release occurs, the EPA can clean up a site and recover the cost from (1) the person who generated the wastes disposed of at the site, (2) the person who transported the wastes to the site, (3) the person who owned or operated the site at the time of the disposal, or (4) the current owner or operator.

2. Joint and Several Liability
One party can be charged with the entire cost (which that party may recover in a contribution action against others).

3. Minimizing Liability
Businesses that conduct self-audits and promptly detect, disclose, and correct wrongdoing are subject to lighter penalties. There may be no fines for small companies that correct violations within 180 days (360 days if pollution-prevention techniques are involved).

4. Defenses to Liability
An innocent property owner may avoid liability by showing the lack of a contractual or employment relation to the party who released the hazardous substance. In effect, this requires a buyer to investigate possible hazards at the time property is bought.

TRUE-FALSE QUESTIONS

(Answers at the Back of the Book)

____   1.   No common law doctrines apply against polluters today.

____   2.   Local governments can control some aspects of the environment through zoning laws.

____   3.   Under federal environmental laws, there is a single standard for all polluters and all pollutants.

____   4.   The Toxic Substances Control Act of 1976 regulates clean-ups of leaking hazardous waste disposal sites.

____   5.   The Environmental Protection Agency (EPA) can clean up a release of hazardous waste at a hazardous waste disposal site and recover the entire cost from the site's owner or operator.

____   6.   States may restrict discharge of chemicals into the water or air.

____   7.   A party who violates the Clean Air Act may realize economic benefits from the noncompliance.

____   8.   The Environmental Protection Agency sets limits on discharges of pollutants into water.

____   9.   A party who only transports hazardous waste to a disposal site cannot be held liable for any costs to clean up the site.

____   10.   The Environmental Protection Agency sets maximum levels for noise.

FILL-IN QUESTIONS

(Answers at the Back of the Book)

The National Environmental Policy Act requires _____ (federal/state and local) agencies to prepare environmental impact statements (EIS) when major _____ (federal/state and local) actions significantly affect the quality of the environment. An EIS analyzes (1) the _____ (environmental impact that an action will have/environment's impact on a project), (2) any adverse effects to the _____ (environment/project) and alternative courses of action, and (3) irreversible effects that _____ (an action might cause to the environment/the environment might cause to the project). If an agency decides that an EIS is unnecessary, it must issue a statement announcing that decision _____ (and reasons/but it need not provide reasons) supporting the conclusion.

MULTIPLE-CHOICE QUESTIONS

(Answers at the Back of the Book)

____   1.   The U.S. Department of the Interior's approval of coal mining operations in several eastern states requires an environmental impact statement

a.   because it affects the quality of the environment, is "federal," and is "major."
b.   only because it affects the quality of the environment.
c.   only because it is "federal."
d.   only because it is "major."

___ 2. Red Glow Power Plant burns fossil fuels. Under the Clean Air Act and EPA regulations, as a major new source of possible pollution, to reduce emissions the plant must use

    a. the best available technology (BAT).
    b. the lowest common denominator (LCD).
    c. the maximum achievable control technology (MACT).
    d. the minimum allowable technology (MAT).

___ 3. National Motors Corporation (NMC) makes sport utility vehicles (SUVs). Under the Clean Air Act, NMC is required to makes its SUVs comply with standards that, with respect to automobile exhaust emissions, are

    a. different but neither more nor less strict.
    b. less strict.
    c. more strict.
    d. the same.

___ 4. Mills Industries, Inc., fails to obtain a permit before discharging waste into navigable waters. Under the Clean Water Act, Eagle can be required

    a. only to clean up the pollution.
    b. only to pay for the cost of cleaning up the pollution.
    c. to clean up the pollution or pay for the cost of doing so.
    d. to do nothing.

___ 5. Petro, Inc., ships unlabeled containers of hazardous waste to off-site facilities for disposal. If the containers later leak, Petro could be found to have violated

    a. neither the Comprehensive Environmental Response, Compensation, and Liability Act (CERCLA) nor the Resource Conservation and Recovery Act (RCRA).
    b. the CERCLA and the RCRA.
    c. the CERCLA only.
    d. the RCRA only.

___ 6. HazMat Company operates a hazardous waste storage facility. If HazMat buries unlabeled containers without determining their contents and the containers leak, HazMat could be found to have violated

    a. neither the Comprehensive Environmental Response, Compensation, and Liability Act (CERCLA) nor the Resource Conservation and Recovery Act (RCRA).
    b. the CERCLA and the RCRA.
    c. the CERCLA only.
    d. the RCRA only.

___ 7. The U.S. Department of the Interior approves minor landscaping around a federal courthouse in St. Louis. This does *not* require an environmental impact statement

    a. only because it does not affect the quality of the environment.
    b. only because it is not "major."
    c. only because it is not "federal."
    d. because it does not affect the quality of the environment, is not "major," and is not "federal."

___ 8. Evolve Industries' factories emit toxic air pollutants. Under the Clean Air Act and EPA regulations, Evolve is required to

    a. eliminate all air polluting emissions.
    b. install emission control equipment on its products.
    c. reduce emissions by installing the maximum achievable control technology.
    d. remove all pollutants from its factories.

___ **9.** Suburban Development Company (SDC) owns wetlands that it wants to fill in and develop as a site for homes. Under the Clean Water Act, before filling and dredging, SDC must obtain a permit from

    a. no one.
    b. the Army Corps of Engineers.
    c. the EPA.
    d. the U.S. Department of the Navy.

___ **10.** Nimby Company owns a hazardous waste disposal site that it sells to Omega Properties, Inc. Later, the EPA discovers a leak at the site and cleans it up. The EPA can recover the cost from

    a. Nimby only.
    b. Nimby or Omega.
    c. neither Nimby nor Omega.
    d. Omega only.

SHORT ESSAY QUESTIONS

1. What does the National Environmental Policy Act require?

2. What federal laws regulate toxic chemicals?

GAMEPOINTS

(Answers at the Back of the Book)

1. In the video game "eMission Impossible," your avatar's name is "Felps" and your objective—should you decide to accept it—is to expose Sludge, your nemesis, to the punishment that can be meted out with the Sword of Clean Sweep. Your avatar sails through a galaxy of pollutants before landing on the planet Toxin. There, on the shore of a bay that empties into the vast Toxin Sea, waste is spewing into the water from a variety of sources—a trash removal outfit, a radioactive materials storage unit, a military base, and an oil refinery. Which laws discussed in this chapter apply to this dumping? What are the penalties?

2. In the play of "eMission Impossible," Felps accuses Sludge—the odious reprobate—of leaking hazardous waste from Toxin into the vastness of space. Sludge doesn't deny a role, but claims that Toxin is no longer his. Felps can draw the Sword of Clean Sweep if you can successfully argue, under the principles set out in this chapter, that Sludge is liable. What do you say?

SPECIAL INFORMATION FOR CPA CANDIDATES

The CPA examination does not currently test concepts of environmental law.

Chapter 47
Antitrust Law

WHAT THIS CHAPTER IS ABOUT

This chapter outlines aspects of the major antitrust statutes—the Sherman Act, the Clayton Act, and the Federal Trade Commission Act. The basis of the antitrust laws is a desire to foster competition (to result in lower prices and so on) by limiting restraints on trade (agreements between firms that have the effect of reducing competition in the marketplace).

CHAPTER OUTLINE

I. THE SHERMAN ANTITRUST ACT

The Sherman Antitrust Act of 1890 is one of the government's most powerful weapons to maintain a competitive economy.

A. MAJOR PROVISIONS OF THE SHERMAN ACT

Section 1 requires two or more persons; cases often concern agreements (written or oral) that have a wrongful purpose and lead to a restraint of trade. Section 2 cases deal with existing monopolies.

B. JURISDICTIONAL REQUIREMENTS

The Sherman Act applies to restraints that substantially affect interstate commerce. The act also covers activities by U.S. nationals abroad that have an effect on U.S. foreign commerce.

II. SECTION 1 OF THE SHERMAN ACT

Section 1 prohibits horizontal restraints and vertical restraints.

A. *PER SE* VIOLATIONS VERSUS THE RULE OF REASON

Some restraints are deemed *per se* violations. Others are subject to analysis under the rule of reason.

1. *Per Se* Violations

Agreements that are blatantly anticompetitive are illegal *per se*.

2. Rule of Reason

A court considers the purpose of an agreement, the power of the parties, the effect of the action on trade, and in some cases, whether there are less restrictive alternatives to achieve the same goals. If the competitive benefits outweigh the anticompetitive effects, the agreement is held lawful.

B. HORIZONTAL RESTRAINTS

Horizontal restraints are agreements that restrain competition between rivals in the same market.

1. Price Fixing

Any agreement among competitors to fix prices is a *per se* violation.

2. Group Boycotts
An agreement by two or more sellers to refuse to deal with a particular person or firm is a *per se* violation, if it is intended to eliminate competition or prevent entry into a given market.

3. Horizontal Market Division
An agreement between competitors to divide up territories or customers is a *per se* violation.

4. Trade Associations
Trade associations are businesses within the same industry or profession organized to pursue common interests. The rule of reason is applied.

5. Joint Ventures
A joint venture is an undertaking by two or more individuals or firms for a specific purpose. If price fixing or a market division is not involved, the agreement will be analyzed under the rule of reason.

C. VERTICAL RESTRAINTS
A restraint of trade that results from an agreement between firms at different levels in the manufacturing and distribution process.

1. Territorial or Customer Restrictions
This restriction consists of an agreement between a manufacturer and a distributor or retailer to restrict sales to certain areas or customers. It is judged under a rule of reason.

2. Resale Price Maintenance Agreements
In a resale price maintenance agreement between a manufacturer and a distributor or retailer, the manufacturer specifies the retail prices of its products. This is subject to the rule of reason.

III. SECTION 2 OF THE SHERMAN ACT
Section 2 applies to individuals and to several people; cases concern the structure of a monopoly in the marketplace and the misuse of monopoly power. Section 2 covers two distinct types of behavior: monopolization and attempts to monopolize.

A. MONOPOLIZATION
This offense has two elements: (1) the possession of monopoly power in the relevant market and (2) the willful acquisition or maintenance of that power.

1. Monopoly Power
Monopoly power is sufficient market power to affect prices and output.

a. Market-Share Test
A firm has monopoly power if it has a dominant share of the relevant market and there are significant barriers for new competition entering the market.

b. The Relevant Market Has Two Elements—

1) Relevant Product Market
This market includes all products with identical attributes and those that are reasonably interchangeable (acceptable substitutes for each other).

2) Relevant Geographical Market
If competitors sell in only a limited area, the geographical market is limited to that area.

2. The Intent Requirement
If a firm has market power as a result of a purposeful act to acquire or maintain that power through anticompetitive means, it is a violation of Section 2. Intent may be inferred from evidence that the firm had monopoly power and engaged in anticompetitive behavior.

3. Unilateral Refusals to Deal
A firm is free to deal, or not, unilaterally, with whomever it wishes unless it has or is likely to acquire monopoly power and the refusal is likely to have an anticompetitive effect.

B. ATTEMPTS TO MONOPOLIZE
Any action (such as predatory pricing or bidding) challenged as an attempt to monopolize (1) must be intended to exclude competitors and garner monopoly power and (2) must have a dangerous probability of success.

IV. THE CLAYTON ACT
Enacted in 1914, the Clayton Act is aimed at practices not covered by the Sherman Act. Conduct is illegal only if it substantially tends to lessen competition or create monopoly power.

A. SECTION 2—PRICE DISCRIMINATION
Price discrimination occurs when a seller charges different prices to competitive buyers for identical goods.

1. Required Elements
(1) The seller must be engaged in interstate commerce, (2) the goods must be of like grade or quality, (3) the goods must have been sold to two or more buyers, and (4) the effect of the price discrimination must be to substantially lessen competition or create a competitive injury.

2. Defenses
(1) A buyer's purchases saved the seller costs in producing and selling goods, (2) when a lower price is charged temporarily and in good faith to meet another seller's equally low price to the buyer's competitor, or (3) changing conditions affected the market for or marketability of the goods.

B. SECTION 3—EXCLUSIONARY PRACTICES

1. Exclusive-Dealing Contracts
This is a contract under which a seller forbids a buyer to buy products from the seller's competitors. Prohibited if the effect is "to substantially lessen competition or tend to create a monopoly."

2. Tying Arrangements
This occurs when a seller conditions the sale of a product on the buyer's agreement to buy another product produced or distributed by the same seller. Legality depends on the agreement's purpose and its likely effect on competition in the relevant markets. Subject to the rule of reason.

C. SECTION 7—MERGERS
A person or firm cannot hold stock or assets in another firm if the effect may be to substantially lessen competition. A crucial consideration in most cases is market concentration (percentage of market shares of firms in the relevant market).

1. Horizontal Mergers
These are mergers between firms competing with each other in the same market. If a merger creates an entity with a resulting significant market share, it may be presumed illegal.

a. Factors
These include—

1) The degree of concentration in the relevant market.
2) The ease of entry into the relevant market.
3) Economic efficiency.
4) The financial condition of the merging firms.
5) The nature and prices of the products.

     b. **Market Concentration—FTC/DOJ Guidelines**
     The Herfindahl-Hirschman Index (HHI) is computed by adding the squares of each of the percentage market shares of firms in the relevant market.

      1) **Pre-merger HHI Between 1,000 and 1,800**
      The industry is moderately concentrated, and the merger will be challenged only if it increases the HHI by 100 points or more.

      2) **Pre-merger HHI Greater than 1,800**
      The market is highly concentrated; if a merger produces an increase in the HHI between 50 and 100 points, it raises concerns; if more than 100 points, it is likely to enhance market power.

   2. **Vertical Mergers**
   This occurs when a company at one stage of production acquires a company at a higher or lower stage of production. Legality depends on whether the merger creates a single firm that controls an undue percentage of the market, barriers to entry into that market, and the parties' intent.

D. SECTION 8—INTERLOCKING DIRECTORATES
No person may be a director in two or more corporations at the same time if either firm has capital, surplus, or undivided profits of more than $24,001,000 or competitive sales of $2,400,100 or more (as of 2007).

V.   ENFORCEMENT AND EXEMPTIONS

A. U.S. DEPARTMENT OF JUSTICE (DOJ)
The DOJ prosecutes violations of the Sherman Act as criminal or civil violations. Violations of the Clayton Act are not crimes; the DOJ can enforce it only through civil proceedings. Remedies include divestiture and dissolution.

B. FEDERAL TRADE COMMISSION (FTC)
The FTC enforces the Clayton Act; has the sole authority to enforce the Federal Trade Commission Act of 1914 (Section 5 condemns all forms of anticompetitive behavior that are not covered by other federal antitrust laws); issues administrative orders; can seek court sanctions.

C. PRIVATE PARTIES

   1. **Treble Damages and Attorneys' Fees**
   Private parties can sue for treble damages and attorneys' fees under the Clayton Act if they are injured by a violation of any federal antitrust law (except the FTC Act).

   2. **Injunctions**
   Private parties may seek an injunction to prevent an antitrust violation if it will injure business activities protected by the antitrust laws.

D. EXEMPTIONS FROM ANTITRUST LAWS

   1. **Labor Activities**
   A labor union can lose its exemption if it combines with a non-labor group.

   2. **Agricultural Associations and Fisheries**
   Except exclusionary practices or restraints of trade against competitors.

   3. **Insurance Companies**
   Exempt in most cases when state regulation exists.

4. **Foreign Trade**
   U.S. exporters may cooperate to compete with similar foreign associations (if it does not restrain trade in the United States or injure other U.S. exporters).

5. **Professional Baseball**
   Players may sue team owners for anticompetitive practices. Other professional sports are not exempt.

6. **Oil Marketing**
   States set quotas on oil to be marketed in interstate commerce.

7. **Cooperative Research and Production**
   Cooperative research among small business firms is exempt.

8. **Joint Efforts to Obtain Legislative or Executive Action**
   Joint efforts by businesspersons to obtain executive or legislative action are exempt (*Noerr-Pennington* doctrine). Exception: an action is not protected if "no reasonable [person] could reasonably expect success on the merits" and it is an attempt to make anticompetitive use of government processes.

9. **Other Exemptions**

   a. Activities approved by the president in furtherance of defense.
   b. State actions, when the state policy is clearly articulated and the policy is actively supervised by the state.
   c. Activities of regulated industries when federal commissions, boards, or agencies have primary regulatory authority.

VI. U.S. ANTITRUST LAWS IN THE GLOBAL CONTEXT

A. THE EXTRATERRITORIAL APPLICATION OF U.S. ANTITRUST LAWS
For U.S. courts to exercise jurisdiction over a foreign entity under U.S. antitrust laws, a violation must (1) have a substantial effect on U.S. commerce or (2) constitute a *per se* violation. Foreign governments and persons can also sue U.S. firms and persons for antitrust violations.

B. THE APPLICATION OF FOREIGN ANTITRUST LAWS
Foreign antitrust laws may apply to U.S. firms in some cases. The European Union's antitrust provisions are stricter in some ways than U.S. antitrust laws.

TRUE-FALSE QUESTIONS

(Answers at the Back of the Book)

____ 1. A horizontal restraint results from an agreement between firms at different levels in the manufacturing and distribution process.

____ 2. An agreement that restrains competition between rivals in the same market is a vertical restraint.

____ 3. Power sufficient to control prices and exclude competition in a market is monopoly power.

____ 4. An exclusive dealing contract is a contract under which competitors agree to divide up customers.

____ 5. Price discrimination occurs when a seller forbids a buyer to buy products from the seller's competitors.

____ 6. A horizontal merger results when a company at one stage of production acquires another company at a higher or lower stage in the chain of production and distribution.

____   **7.**   A merger between firms that compete with each other in the same market is a vertical merger.

____   **8.**   A relevant product market includes products that are sufficient substitutes for each other.

____   **9.**   An agreement that is inherently anticompetitive is illegal *per se*.

____   **10.** An agreement between competitors to fix prices is a *per se* violation.

FILL-IN QUESTIONS

(Answers at the Back of the Book)

_____ (Monopoly power/A restraint of trade) is any agreement that has the effect of reducing competition in the marketplace. _____ (Monopoly power/ Restraint of trade) is an extreme amount of market power. A firm that can raise its prices somewhat without too much concern for its competitors' response has some degree of market power. Determining whether such power is sufficient to call it _____ (monopoly power/ a restraint of trade) is one of the most difficult tasks in antitrust law.

MULTIPLE-CHOICE QUESTIONS

(Answers at the Back of the Book)

____   **1.**   National Coal Association (NCA) is a group of independent coal mining companies. Demand for coal falls. The price drops. Coal Refiners Association, a group of coal refining companies, agrees to buy NCA's coal and sell it according to a schedule that will increase the price. This agreement is

   a. a *per se* violation of the Sherman Act.
   b. exempt from the antitrust laws.
   c. subject to continuing review by the appropriate federal agency.
   d. subject to the rule of reason.

____   **2.**   Interstate Sales, Inc. (ISI), is charged with violating antitrust law. ISI's conduct is a *per se* violation

   a. if the anticompetitive harm outweighs the competitive benefits.
   b. if the competitive benefits outweigh the anticompetitive harm.
   c. if the conduct is blatantly anticompetitive.
   d. only if it does not qualify for an exemption.

____   **3.**   Tech, Inc., sells its brand-name computer equipment directly to its franchised retailers. Depending on how existing franchisees do, Tech may limit the number of franchisees in a given area to reduce intrabrand competition. Tech's restrictions on the number of dealers is

   a. a *per se* violation of the Sherman Act.
   b. exempt from the antitrust laws.
   c. subject to continuing review by the appropriate federal agency.
   d. subject to the rule of reason.

____   **4.**   Platinum Corporation is charged with a violation of antitrust law that requires evaluation under the rule of reason. The court will consider

   a. only the effect of the conduct on trade.
   b. only the power of the parties to accomplish what they intend.
   c. only the purpose of the conduct.
   d. the effect of the conduct, the power of the parties, and the purpose of the conduct.

_____ **5.** Ridgetop, Inc., controls 80 percent of the market for telecommunications equipment in the southeastern United States. To show that Ridgetop is monopolizing that market in violation of the Sherman Act requires proof of

    a. only the possession of monopoly power in the relevant market.
    b. only the willful acquisition or maintenance of monopoly power.
    c. the possession of monopoly power in the relevant market _and_ its willful acquisition or maintenance.
    d. none of the choices.

_____ **6.** Handy Tools, Inc., charges Jake's Valu Tools Store five cents per item and Kitchener's Home Store ten cents per item for the same product. The two stores are competitors. If this substantially lessens competition, it constitutes

    a. a market division.
    b. an exclusionary practice.
    c. a tying arrangement.
    d. price discrimination.

_____ **7.** A group of foreign manufacturers organize to control the price for replacement auto parts in the United States. Drivers Choice Company, a U.S. firm, joins the group. If their actions have a substantial effect on U.S. commerce, a suit for violations of U.S. antitrust laws may be brought against

    a. Drivers Choice and the foreign manufacturers.
    b. neither Drivers Choice nor the foreign manufacturers.
    c. only Drivers Choice.
    d. only the foreign manufacturers.

_____ **8.** Medico Pharma Company is charged with violating antitrust law, subject to evaluation under the rule of reason. Medico's conduct is unlawful

    a. if the anticompetitive harm outweighs the competitive benefits.
    b. if the competitive benefits outweigh the anticompetitive harm.
    c. if the conduct is blatantly anticompetitive.
    d. only if it does not qualify for an exemption.

_____ **9.** Price Data Corporation and Consumer Marketing, Inc., are competitors. They form a joint venture to research, develop, and produce new software for a particular line of research and reporting. This joint venture is

    a. a _per se_ violation of the Sherman Act.
    b. exempt from the antitrust laws.
    c. subject to continuing review by the appropriate federal agency.
    d. subject to the rule of reason.

_____ **10.** Richer Resources, Inc., and Sellers Supply Corporation are competitors. They merge, and after the merger, Richer Resources is the surviving firm. To assess whether this is in violation of the Clayton Act requires a look at

    a. concentration.
    b. discrimination.
    c. division.
    d. power.

SHORT ESSAY QUESTIONS

1. How does Section 1 of the Sherman Act deal with horizontal restraints?

2. How does the Clayton Act deal with exclusionary practices?

GAMEPOINTS

(Answers at the Back of the Book)

1. You go to Games Galore Store to buy a copy of the latest installment in the "Furious Finale" video game series. It is available only at the manufacturer's price, which is the same price at all local outlets, and not otherwise available. Previous installments were nearly half the price and could be bought directly from the maker, who has agreed with the merchants that it will not compete in their market if they sell at the "suggested" price. Is this legal? Explain.

2. Over time, Super Joystick, Inc., acquires the power to affect the market price of its products, which consist of popular video game titles. Enticed by the prospect of greater profits, Super Joystick begins to refuse to do business with those who do not contract with the company exclusively. Some retail firms fearfully agree to the deal. Prices for Super Joystick's products rise and its competitors' shares of the market drop. Is this a violation of antitrust laws? If so, why?

SPECIAL INFORMATION FOR CPA CANDIDATES

Some of the material in this chapter is tested on the CPA examination. In particular, for the purposes of the exam, restraints of trade are acceptable in only two situations, both involving covenants not to compete (discussed in Chapter 13).

Chapter 48
Professional Liability and Accountability

WHAT THIS CHAPTER IS ABOUT

This chapter outlines the potential common law liability of professionals, the potential liability of accountants under securities laws and the Internal Revenue Code, and the duty of professionals to keep their clients' communications confidential.

CHAPTER OUTLINE

I. POTENTIAL LIABILITY TO CLIENTS

A. LIABILITY FOR BREACH OF CONTRACT
For a professional's breach of contract, a client can recover damages, including expenses incurred to secure another professional to provide the services and other reasonable and foreseeable losses.

B. LIABILITY FOR NEGLIGENCE
Professionals must exercise the standard of care, knowledge, and judgment generally accepted by members of their professional group.

1. Accountant's Duty of Care

a. Comply with Accounting Principles and Standards
Accountants must comply with generally accepted accounting principles (GAAP) and generally accepted auditing standards (GAAS) (though compliance does not guarantee relief from liability). Violation of either is *prima facie* evidence of negligence. There may be a higher state law standard. (Note: By 2016, these standards will have been replaced by the International Financial Reporting Standards (IFRS) established by the International Accounting Standards Board.)

b. Act in Good Faith
If an accountant conforms to GAAP and acts in good faith, he or she will not be liable to a client for incorrect judgment.

c. Investigate Suspicious Financial Transactions
An accountant who uncovers suspicious financial transactions and fails to investigate the matter fully or to inform his or her client of the discovery can be held liable to the client for the resulting loss.

d. Qualify or Disclaim Opinions
An accountant is not liable for damages resulting from whatever is qualified or disclaimed.

e. Designate Financial Statements as Unaudited
An accountant may be liable for failing to designate a balance sheet as "unaudited." An accountant may also be liable for failing to disclose to a client facts that give reason to believe misstatements have been made or fraud has been committed.

385

f. Defenses to Negligence

1) The accountant was not negligent.
2) The accountant's negligence, if any, was not the proximate cause of the client's loss.
3) The client was also negligent.

2. Attorney's Duty of Care

a. General Duty
Attorneys owe a duty to provide competent and diligent representation. The standard is that of a reasonably competent general practitioner of ordinary skill, experience, and capacity.

b. Specific Responsibilities
Attorneys must be familiar with well-settled principles of law applicable to a case, discover law that can be found through a reasonable amount of research, and investigate and discover facts that could materially affect the client's legal rights.

c. Misconduct and Malpractice
A criminal act may constitute professional misconduct. A failure to exercise reasonable care and professional judgment can result in liability for malpractice (if a plaintiff is injured).

C. LIABILITY FOR FRAUD

1. Actual Fraud
A professional may be liable if he or she intentionally misstates a material fact to mislead his or her client and the client justifiably relies on the misstated fact to his or her injury.

2. Constructive Fraud
A professional may be liable for constructive fraud whether or not he or she acted with fraudulent intent (for example, an accountant who is grossly negligent; gross negligence includes the intentional failure to perform a duty in reckless disregard of the consequences).

D. LIMITING PROFESSIONALS' LIABILITY
Professionals can limit their liability for the misconduct of other professionals with whom they work by organizing as a professional corporation (see Chapter 39) or a limited liability partnership (see Chapter 37).

II. POTENTIAL LIABILITY TO THIRD PARTIES
Most courts hold that auditors can be held liable to third parties for negligence.

A. THE *ULTRAMARES* RULE

1. The Privity Requirement
An accountant owes a duty only to a third person with whom he or she has a direct contractual relationship (privity) or a relationship "so close as to approach that of privity."

2. The "Near Privity" Rule
In a few states, if a third party has a sufficiently close relationship or nexus with an accountant, the *Ultramares* privity requirement may be satisfied without establishing an accountant-client relationship.

B. THE *RESTATEMENT* RULE
Most courts hold accountants liable for negligence to persons whom the accountant "intends to supply the information or knows that the recipient intends to supply it" and persons whom the accountant "intends the information to influence or knows that the recipient so intends" [*Restatement (Second) of Torts*, Section 552].

C. LIABILITY OF ATTORNEYS TO THIRD PARTIES

In some cases, attorneys may be liable to third parties who rely on legal opinions to their detriment.

III. THE SARBANES-OXLEY ACT OF 2002

This act imposes requirements on a public accounting firm that provides auditing services to an *issuer* (a company that has securities registered under Section 12 of the Securities Exchange Act of 1934; that is required to file reports under Section 15(d) of the 1934 act; or that files—or has filed—a registration statement not yet effective under the Securities Act of 1933).

A. THE PUBLIC COMPANY ACCOUNTING OVERSIGHT BOARD

This board, which reports to the Securities and Exchange Commission, oversees the audit of public companies subject to securities laws to protect public investors and ensure that public accounting firms comply with the provisions of the Sarbanes-Oxley Act.

B. APPLICABILITY TO PUBLIC ACCOUNTING FIRMS

Public accounting firms are firms and associated persons that are "engaged in the practice of public accounting or preparing or issuing audit reports."

1. **Nonaudit Services**

   It is unlawful to perform for an issuer both audit and nonaudit services, which include bookkeeping for an audit client, financial systems design and implementation, appraisal services, fairness opinions, management functions, and investment services.

2. **Audit Services**

   A public accounting firm cannot provide audit services to an issuer if the lead audit partner or the reviewing partner provided those services to the issuer in each of the prior five years, or if the issuer's chief executive officer, chief financial officer, chief accounting officer, or controller worked for the auditor and participated in an audit of the issuer within the preceding year.

3. **Reports to an Issuer's Audit Committee**

   These reports must be timely and indicate critical accounting policies and practices, as well as alternatives discussed, and other communications, with the issuer's management.

C. DOCUMENT DESTRUCTION

The act prohibits destroying or falsifying records to obstruct or influence a federal investigation or in relation to a bankruptcy. Penalties include fines and imprisonment up to twenty years.

D. REQUIREMENTS FOR MAINTAINING WORKING PAPERS

In some states, working papers are the accountant's property. The client has a right of access to them. They cannot be transferred to another accountant or otherwise disclosed without the client's permission (or a court order). Unauthorized disclosure is a ground for a malpractice suit. Under the Sarbanes-Oxley Act, accountants are required, in some circumstances, to maintain working papers relating to an audit or review for five years. A knowing violation may result in a fine and imprisonment for up to ten years.

IV. POTENTIAL LIABILITY OF ACCOUNTANTS UNDER SECURITIES LAWS

A. LIABILITY UNDER THE SECURITIES ACT OF 1933

1. **Section 11—Misstatements or Omissions in Registration Statements**

   An accountant may be liable for misstatements and omissions of material facts in registration statements (which they often prepare for filing with the Securities and Exchange Commission (SEC) before an offering of securities—see Chapter 41).

a. To Whom an Accountant May Be Liable

An accountant may be liable to anyone who acquires a security covered by the statement. A plaintiff must show that he or she suffered a loss on the security. There is no requirement of privity or proof of reliance.

b. Due Diligence Defense

An accountant may avoid liability by showing that, in preparing the financial statements, he or she had—

1) Reasonable Grounds to Believe that the Statements Were True

After a reasonable investigation, the accountant believed that the statements were true and omitted no material facts.

2) Followed GAAP and GAAS

Failure to follow GAAP and GAAS is proof of a lack of due diligence.

3) Verified Information Furnished by Officers and Directors

This defense requires that accountants verify information furnished by the offering firm's officers and directors.

c. Other Defenses to Liability

1) There were no misstatements or omissions.
2) The misstatements or omissions were not of material facts.
3) The misstatements or omissions had no causal connection to the purchaser's loss.
4) The purchaser invested in the securities knowing of the misstatements or omissions.

2. Section 12(2)—Misstatements or Omissions in Other Communications in an Offer

Anyone offering or selling a security may be liable for fraud on the basis of communication to an investor of a misstatement or omission [Section 12(2)].

3. Penalties and Sanctions for Violations

The U.S. Department of Justice brings criminal actions against willful violators. Penalties: fines up to $10,000; imprisonment up to five years. The SEC can seek an injunction and other relief (such as an order to refund profits).

B. LIABILITY UNDER THE SECURITIES EXCHANGE ACT OF 1934

1. Section 18—False or Misleading Statements in Certain SEC Documents

An accountant may be liable for making or causing to be made in an application, report, document, or registration statement filed with the SEC a statement that at the time and in light of the circumstances was false or misleading with respect to any material fact.

a. To Whom an Accountant May Be Liable

Only sellers and purchasers who can prove (1) the statement affected the price of the security and (2) they relied on the statement and were unaware of its inaccuracy.

b. Defenses

1) Proof of Good Faith

Proof that the accountant did not know the statement was false or misleading. This can be refuted by showing the accountant's (1) intent to deceive or (2) reckless conduct and gross negligence.

2) Buyer or Seller Knew the Statement Was False or Misleading

3) Statute of Limitations Tolled

An action must be brought within one year after the discovery of facts constituting the cause and within three years after the cause accrues.

2. Section 10(b) and Rule 10b-5—Misstatements or Omissions
These laws cover written and oral statements.

   a. Section 10(b)
   Makes it unlawful for any person to use, in connection with the purchase or sale of any security, any manipulative or deceptive device or contrivance in contravention of SEC rules and regulations.

   b. Rule 10b-5
   Makes it unlawful for any person, by use of any means or instrumentality of interstate commerce, to—

      1) Employ any device, scheme, or artifice to defraud.

      2) Make any untrue statement of a material fact or to omit to state a material fact necessary to make the statements made, in light of the circumstances, not misleading.

      3) Engage in any act, practice, or course of business that operates or would operate as a fraud or deceit on any person, in connection with the purchase or sale of any security.

   c. To Whom An Accountant May Be Liable
   Only to sellers or purchasers. Privity is not required. To recover, a plaintiff must prove (1) *scienter*, (2) a fraudulent action or deception, (3) reliance, (4) materiality, and (5) causation.

C. THE PRIVATE SECURITIES LITIGATION REFORM ACT OF 1995

   1. Adequate Procedures and Disclosure
   An auditor must use adequate procedures in an audit to detect any illegal acts. If something is detected, the auditor must disclose it to the board, audit committee, or SEC, depending on the circumstances.

   2. Proportionate Liability
   A party is liable only for the proportion of damages for which he or she is responsible.

   3. Aiding and Abetting
   An accountant who knows that he or she is participating in an improper activity and knowingly aids the activity (even by silence) is guilty of aiding and abetting. The SEC may obtain an injunction or damages.

V. POTENTIAL CRIMINAL LIABILITY OF ACCOUNTANTS

A. CRIMINAL VIOLATIONS OF SECURITIES LAWS
An accountant may be subject to imprisonment of up to five years and a fine of up to $10,000 under the 1933 act and up to $100,000 under the 1934 act. Under the Sarbanes-Oxley Act, for a securities filing accompanied by an accountant's false or misleading certified audit statement, the accountant may be fined up to $5 million and imprisoned up to twenty years.

B. CRIMINAL VIOLATIONS OF TAX LAWS

   1. Aiding or Assisting in the Preparation of a False Tax Return
   Under the Internal Revenue Code, this is a felony punishable by a fine of $100,000 ($500,000 in the case of a corporation) and imprisonment for up to three years [Section 7206(2)]. (This applies to anyone, not only accountants.)

   2. Understatement of a Client's Tax Liability
   Liability is limited to one penalty per taxpayer per tax year.

      a. Negligent or Willful Understatement

      A tax preparer is subject to a penalty of $250 per return for negligent understatement and $1,000 for willful understatement or reckless or intentional disregard of rules or regulations [Section 6694].

      b. Aiding and Abetting an Individual's Understatement

      $1,000 per document ($10,000 in corporate cases) [Section 6701].

   3. Other Liability Related to Tax Returns

   A tax preparer may be subject to penalties for failing to furnish the taxpayer with a copy of the return, failing to sign the return, or failing to furnish the appropriate tax identification numbers [Section 6695].

VI. CONFIDENTIALITY AND PRIVILEGE

A. ATTORNEY-CLIENT RELATIONSHIPS

The law protects the confidentiality of attorney-client communications. The client holds the privilege, and only the client may waive it.

B. ACCOUNTANT-CLIENT RELATIONSHIPS

In response to a federal court order, an accountant must provide the information sought; there is no privilege. In most states, on a court order, an accountant must disclose information about his or her client. In a few states, no disclosure is allowed (even in a court) without the client's permission.

TRUE-FALSE QUESTIONS

(Answers at the Back of the Book)

____   **1.** Professionals must exercise the standard of care, knowledge, and judgment observed by their peers.

____   **2.** A violation of GAAP and GAAS is *prima facie* evidence of negligence.

____   **3.** Compliance with GAAP and GAAS will relieve an accountant of liability.

____   **4.** In all states, an accountant is liable to anyone who relies on the accountant's negligently prepared reports.

____   **5.** Accountants are not subject to criminal penalties under federal securities laws.

____   **6.** A tax preparer may be subject to penalties under the Internal Revenue Code for assisting in filing a false tax return.

____   **7.** There is no penalty under the Internal Revenue Code for failing to give the taxpayer a copy of the return.

____   **8.** State-provided rights to confidentiality of accountant-client communications are not recognized in federal cases.

____   **9.** Under the Private Securities Litigation Reform Act of 1995, a party is liable only for the proportion of damages for which he or she is responsible.

____ **10.** For an accountant to be liable to a seller or purchaser for misstatements or omissions under SEC Rule 10b-5, there must be privity.

FILL-IN QUESTIONS

(Answers at the Back of the Book)

Accountants must comply with generally accepted accounting principles (GAAP) and generally accepted auditing standards (GAAS). An accountant who conforms to GAAP and acts in good faith _____ (may/will not) be liable to a client for incorrect judgment. An accountant who uncovers suspicious financial transactions but fails to investigate fully or to inform the client _____ (may/will not) be liable. If a client suffers a loss due to fraud that an accountant negligently fails to discover, the accountant _____ (may/will not) be liable.

MULTIPLE-CHOICE QUESTIONS

(Answers at the Back of the Book)

____   1. Kirsten, an accountant, accumulates working papers in performing an audit for her client, Limousine Service Corporation. Kirsten can release those papers

  a. only on the request of another accountant.
  b. only with Limousine's permission.
  c. under any circumstances.
  d. under no circumstances.

____   2. **Based on a Sample CPA Exam Question.** Digital, Inc., asks Eton, an accountant, to prepare its financial statements. Eton conducts the audit negligently. The firm uses the statements to obtain a loan from First Credit Bank. The loan is not repaid. In most states, Eton is

  a. liable only to Digital for the negligent audit.
  b. liable to any possible foreseeable user of the statements.
  c. liable to First Credit if Eton knew the bank would rely on the statements.
  d. liable to First Credit only if it was in privity of contract with Eton.

____   3. Xtra, Inc., includes financial statements prepared by Yvon, an accountant, in a registration statement filed with the SEC as part of a public stock offer. Zach buys 100 shares and later suffers losses due to misstatements of fact in the statements. Zach sues Yvon under the Securities Act of 1933. Zach will

  a. lose, because Zach relied on the statements.
  b. lose, if Yvon and Zach were not in privity.
  c. win, if Yvon prepared the statements with knowledge of the misstatements.
  d. win, if the misstatements were material.

____   4. Dirk, an accountant, audits financial statements for Eventide Corporation and issues an unqualified opinion on them. Fran buys 100 shares of Eventide stock and later suffers losses due to misrepresentations in the statements. Fran sues Dirk under the Securities Exchange Act of 1934. Fran will

  a. lose, because Fran relied on the statements.
  b. lose, if Dirk and Fran were not in privity.
  c. win, if Dirk prepared the statements with knowledge of the misstatements.
  d. win, if the misstatements were material.

____   5. Jack is an accountant. In most states, Jack can be compelled to disclose a client's communication

  a. only on a court order.
  b. only with the client's permission.
  c. under any circumstances.
  d. under no circumstances.

____ **6.** In auditing Great Mart Corporation's books, Hal is assisted by Ira, a Great Mart employee. Hal does not discover Ira's theft of Great Mart money because Ira hides records that would reveal it. When Ira absconds with the money, Great Mart sues Hal. Great Mart will

   a. lose, because Hal could not reasonably have been expected to discover the theft.
   b. lose, because Hal is not liable for the results once she has performed.
   c. win, because Hal did not discover the theft.
   d. win, because Hal did not inform Great Mart of the theft.

____ **7.** Carol, an accountant, breaches her contract with Diners Café, a local restaurant. Damages that Diners may recover include

   a. only penalties imposed for failing to meet deadlines.
   b. only the cost to secure the contracted-for services elsewhere.
   c. penalties for missing deadlines and the cost to secure services elsewhere.
   d. none of the choices.

____ **8.** Lily is injured in an auto accident, but Mega Insurance, Inc., refuses to pay her claim. She hires Nick, an attorney, who fails to file a suit against Mega before the time for filing runs out. Lily sues Nick. She will

   a. lose, because clients are ultimately responsible for such deadlines.
   b. lose, because Nick could not reasonably have been expected to file on time.
   c. win, because Nick committed malpractice.
   d. win, because the insurance company refused to pay her claim.

____ **9.** Fix-It Auto Repairs hires Gina, an accountant, to perform an audit, in the course of which she accumulates several hundred pages of notes, computations, and other memoranda. After the audit

   a. Fix-It has the right to retain all working papers.
   b. Gina has the right to retain all working papers.
   c. the working papers are filed with the SEC.
   d. the working papers must be destroyed.

____ **10.** Jane is an accountant whom Kary, a former client, charges with negligence. Jane's defenses include

   a. only that she was not negligent.
   b. only that if she was negligent, it was not the proximate cause of Kary's loss.
   c. that she was not negligent, and if she was negligent, it was not the proximate cause of Kary's loss.
   d. none of the choices.

SHORT ESSAY QUESTIONS

1. Contrast an accountant's past and present potential common law liability to third persons.

2. What is the difference between the attorney-client privilege and the accountant-client privilege?

GAMEPOINTS

(Answers at the Back of the Book)

1. One of the top-selling video games is "Accountant & Attorney." The play features selections of consequence—your choices affect your avatar and the environment of the game. For example, your character is asked to review a credit-card agreement for one of your clients, the Bank of Moolah, to present to its customers. You can rewrite the agreement to be more—or less—understandable to the average consumer. Your choice can lead to more profit for your client or to lawsuits, or both. What professional ethical arguments can you make for drafting the agreement to be denser?

2. As the play advances in the game of "Accountant & Attorney," your avatar, a successful accountant, buys every house, business, and other accoutrement available. Looking forward to new conquests, your avatar prepares a financial statement for Precarious Corporation, aware that its management will use the statement to obtain a loan from Lucre Bank. If you make negligent omissions in the statement that cause Lucre to lose the amount of its loan, can the bank successfully sue you?

SPECIAL INFORMATION FOR CPA CANDIDATES

Of course, the material in this chapter is part of the CPA examination. Among the most important points for you to know for the test are the accountant's potential tort liability to third parties—of the three basic approaches to liability, the CPA exam has in the past followed the *Ultramares* rule. With respect to liability under the Securities Acts, "mere" negligence is a defense under the 1934 act (which, as you may recall, requires "gross" negligence for liability). With respect to the possible criminal penalties, the CPA exam expects you to know them. Also keep in mind that unless a state provides for an accountant-client privilege, there is none. Related material on professional responsibility tested in the business law portion of the exam is covered in your auditing course.

CUMULATIVE HYPOTHETICAL PROBLEM FOR UNIT NINE—INCLUDING CHAPTERS 44–48

(Answers at the Back of the Book)

Benzate Chemical Corporation makes and sells chemical products to industrial customers and individual consumers.

____ **1.** Benzate's manufacturing process generates hazardous waste that is transported to Clean Drop Company's disposal site by Dump Trucking, Inc. If the EPA cleans up Clean Drop's site, liability for the cost may be assessed against

   a. Benzate or Clean Drop only.
   b. Clean Drop or Dump Trucking only.
   c. Benzate or Dump Trucking only.
   d. Benzate, Clean Drop, or Dump Trucking.

____ **2.** Benzate advertises its products with slogans that consist of vague generalities. Because of this advertising, the Federal Trade Commission may

   a. issue a cease-and-desist order only.
   b. require counteradvertising only.
   c. issue a cease-and-desist order or require counteradvertising.
   d. none of the choices.

____ **3.** Benzate charges Ersatz Refining, Inc., less per item than Benzate charges Faraway Export Corporation for the same product. The two industrial buyers are competitors. This pricing difference violates antitrust law

   a. if both buyers' customers pay the same price for the buyers' products.
   b. if Ersatz and Faraway know what each other pays.
   c. if the pricing substantially lessens competition.
   d. under no circumstances.

___ **4.** Seymour, an accountant, audits Benzate's financial statements. Later, Benzate obtains a loan from Chemical Manufacturers Bank. When Benzate defaults on the loan, the bank files a suit against Seymour based on fraud. The accountant's best defense is

    a. a disclaimer included with the financial statements.
    b. contributory negligence on the part of Benzate.
    c. lack of privity between Seymour and the trust.
    d. lack of reliance on the financial statements on the part of Chemical Manufacturers Bank.

___ **5.** Zoey, an accountant, prepares financial statements for a registration statement for Benzate. To be successful against Zoey in a civil action under the Securities Act of 1933 for misleading statements in the registration statement, an investor must prove

    a. the accountant's intent to deceive.
    b. the investor's reliance on the statements.
    c. privity between the accountant and the investor.
    d. none of the choices.

QUESTIONS ON THE FOCUS ON ETHICS FOR UNIT NINE— GOVERNMENT REGULATION

(Answers at the Back of the Book)

___ **1.** Prime Sales, Inc., a telemarketing firm, files a suit to block the enforcement of the Federal Trade Commission's (FTC) amendment to the Telemarketing Sales Rule establishing a national "do not call" list, on the ground that it violates the First Amendment to the U.S. Constitution. The court will most likely hold that

    a. Prime Sales is engaged in an illegal suit.
    b. the "do not call" list is constitutional.
    c. the FTC exceeded its authority.
    d. the Telemarketing Sales Rule should be suspended pending review.

___ **2.** Equity Corporation, a credit-reporting agency, sells information about consumers to merchants and others. Under the Fair Credit Reporting Act, Equity must

    a. not allow consumers, creditors, or others to challenge the information.
    b. notify consumers when the information is sold.
    c. not sell information about consumers who request to be "blacklisted."
    d. report the information accurately.

___ **3.** Among other global enterprises, Yang Ltd. in China, Rio de Angel S.A. in South America, and Clear Creek Corporation in the United States emit pollutants in to the air and water. The chief difficulty in applying a single standard to each of these polluters is that pollutants

    a. are not persons or entities.
    b. are too costly to clean up in proportion to the benefit gained.
    c. do not stop at a nation's borders.
    d. increase in output the more economic growth a nation experiences.

Chapter 49
Personal Property and Bailments

WHAT THIS CHAPTER IS ABOUT

Real property consists of land and everything permanently attached to it. This chapter covers the nature of personal property, forms of property ownership, the acquisition of personal property, and bailments. Personal property can be tangible (such as a car) or intangible (such as stocks, bonds, patents, or copyrights).

CHAPTER OUTLINE

I. PERSONAL PROPERTY VERSUS REAL PROPERTY

Personal property is moveable. (Real property is immoveable.) When two or more persons own property, concurrent ownership exists.

A. WHY THE DISTINCTION IS IMPORTANT

Taxation of types of property differs—businesses may be taxed on personal property (when non-business owners often are not). Transfer of personal property can be less formal. Ownership of personal property can often be proved by simple possession.

B. CONVERTING REAL TO PERSONAL PROPERTY

Tress and other vegetation severed, and minerals mined, from real property is personal property.

II. FIXTURES

Personal property so closely associated with certain real property that it is viewed as part of it (such as plumbing in a building). Fixtures are included in a sale of land if the contract does not provide otherwise.

A. FACTORS IN DETERMINING THAT AN ITEM IS A FIXTURE

The intent of the parties, whether the item can be removed without damaging the real property, and whether the item is sufficiently adapted so as to have become a part of the real property.

B. TRADE FIXTURES

Installed for a commercial purpose by a tenant, whose property it remains, unless removal would irreparably damage the real property.

III. ACQUIRING OWNERSHIP OF PERSONAL PROPERTY

PP. 959 - 962

A. PURCHASE

Outlined in Chapters 19 through 22.

B. POSSESSION

An example of acquiring ownership by possession is the capture of wild animals. (Exceptions: (1) wild animals captured by a trespasser are the property of the landowner, and (2) wild animals captured or killed in violation of statutes are the property of the state.)

Fee simple absolute

C. PRODUCTION

Those who produce personal property have title to it. (Exception: employees do not own what they produce for their employers.)

D. GIFT

A *gift* is a voluntary transfer of property ownership not supported by consideration.

1. The Three Requirements for an Effective Gift

a. Donative Intent

Determined from the language of the donor and the surrounding circumstances (relationship between the parties and the size of the gift in relation to the donor's other assets).

b. Delivery

1) Constructive Delivery

If a physical object cannot be delivered, an act that the law holds to be equivalent to an act of real delivery is sufficient (a key to a safe-deposit box for its contents, for example).

2) Giving Up Control

Effective delivery requires giving up control over the property.

c. Acceptance

Courts assume a gift is accepted unless shown otherwise.

2. Gifts *Inter Vivos* and Gifts *Causa Mortis*

Gifts *inter vivos* are made during one's lifetime. Gifts *causa mortis* are made in contemplation of imminent death, do not become effective until the donor dies, and are automatically revoked if the donor does not die.

E. ACCESSION

Accession occurs when someone adds value to a item of personal property by labor or materials. Ownership can be at issue if—

1. Accession Occurs without Permission of the Owner

Courts tend to favor the owner over the one who improved the property (and deny the improver any compensation for the value added).

2. Accession Greatly Increases the Value or Changes the Identity

The greater the increase, the more likely that ownership will pass to the improver who must compensate the original owner for the value of the property before the accession.

F. CONFUSION

Commingling property so that one person's cannot be distinguished from another's. Frequently involves fungible goods. If the goods are confused due to a wrongful act, the innocent party acquires all of the goods. If confusion is by agreement, mistake, or a third party's act, the owners share in proportion to the amount each contributed.

IV. MISLAID, LOST, OR ABANDONED PROPERTY   974?

A. MISLAID PROPERTY

Mislaid property is property that has been voluntarily placed somewhere by the owner and then inadvertently forgotten. When the property is found, the owner of the place where it was mislaid (not the finder) becomes the caretaker.

B. LOST PROPERTY

Lost property is property that is involuntarily left. A finder can claim title against the whole world, except the true owner. Many states require the finder to make a reasonably diligent search to locate the true owner. *Estray statutes* allow finders, after passage of a specified time, to acquire title to the property if it remains unclaimed.

C. ABANDONED PROPERTY

Abandoned property is property that has been discarded by the true owner, who has no intention of claiming title to it. A finder acquires title good against the whole world, including the original owner. A trespasser does not acquire title, however; the owner of the real property on which it was found does.

V. BAILMENTS

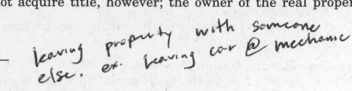

leaving property with someone else. ex. leaving car @ mechanic

The elements of a bailment are—

A. PERSONAL PROPERTY

Only personal property (tangible or intangible) is bailable.

B. DELIVERY OF POSSESSION (WITHOUT TITLE)

A bailee must (1) be given exclusive possession and control of the property and (2) knowingly accept it. Delivery may be actual or constructive. An involuntary bailment can occur accidentally or by mistake.

C. AGREEMENT THAT THE PROPERTY BE RETURNED OR DISPOSED OF

The agreement must provide for the return of the property to the bailor or a third person, or for its disposal by the bailee.

VI. ORDINARY BAILMENTS

The three types of ordinary bailments are: (1) bailment for the sole benefit of the bailor (gratuitous bailment), (2) bailment for the sole benefit of the bailee, and (3) bailment for their mutual benefit (bailment for hire, the most common type of bailment).

A. RIGHTS OF THE BAILEE

1. Right of Possession

This is temporary control and possession of property that ultimately is to be returned to the owner. A bailee can recover damages from any third persons for damage or loss to the property.

2. Right to Use Bailed Property

The extent to which bailees can use the property depends on the contract. If no provision is made, the extent depends on how necessary it is for the goods to be at the bailee's disposal.

3. Right of Compensation

A bailee has a right to be compensated as agreed and to be reimbursed for costs in the keeping of the property. To enforce this right, a bailee can place a lien on the property (see Chapter 28).

4. Right to Limit Liability

A bailee can limit liability as long as the limitation is called to the attention of the bailor (fine print on the back of a ticket stub is not sufficient), and the limitation is not against public policy (if a bailee attempts to exclude liability for his or her negligence, the clause is unenforceable).

B. DUTIES OF THE BAILEE

1. **Duty of Care**
   Bailees must exercise care over the property in their possession (or be liable in tort—see Chapters 6 and 7). The appropriate standard is—

   a. **Slight Care**
   In bailments for the sole benefit of the bailor, the bailee is liable only for gross negligence.

   b. **Great Care**
   In bailments for the sole benefit of the bailee, the bailee is liable for even slight negligence.

   c. **Ordinary Care**
   In bailments for the mutual benefit of both parties, the bailee is liable for a failure to use reasonable care.

2. **Duty to Return Bailed Property**
   When a bailment ends, the bailee must relinquish the property. Failure to do so is a breach of contract and could constitute conversion or negligence.

   a. **Presumption of Negligence**
   If a bailee has the property and damage occurs that normally results only from someone's negligence, the bailee's negligence is presumed. The bailee must prove he or she was not at fault.

   b. **Delivery of Goods to the Wrong Person**
   A bailee may be liable if the property is given to the wrong person.

   c. **Exceptions**
   The property is destroyed, lost, or stolen through no fault of the bailee, or given to a third party with a superior claim.

C. **DUTIES OF THE BAILOR**
   A bailor has a duty to provide the bailee with goods free from defects that could injure the bailee.

1. **Bailor's Duty Has Two Aspects**

   a. In a mutual-benefit bailment, a bailor must notify a bailee of all known defects and any hidden defects that the bailor knows of or could discover with reasonable diligence and proper inspection.
   b. In a bailment for the sole benefit of a bailee, the bailor must notify the bailee of known defects.

2. **To Whom Does Liability Extend?**
   Liability extends to anyone who might be expected to come in contact with the goods. A bailor may also be liable under UCC Article 2A's implied warranties.

VII. SPECIAL TYPES OF BAILMENTS

A. **COMMON CARRIERS**
   Common carriers are publicly licensed to provide transportation services to the general public.

1. **Strict Liability**
   Under UCC 7–309 and the common law, common carriers are strictly liable, regardless of negligence, for all loss or damage to goods in their possession, unless it is caused by an act of God, an act of a public enemy, an order of a public authority, an act of the shipper, or the nature of the goods.

2. Limits to Liability

Common carriers can limit their liability to an amount stated on the shipment contract. The shipper bears any loss occurring through its own fault or improper crating or packaging procedures.

B. WAREHOUSE COMPANIES

Warehouse companies are liable for loss or damage to property resulting from negligence [UCC 7–204(1)]. A warehouse company can limit the dollar amount of liability, but the bailor must be given the option of paying an increased storage rate for an increase in the liability limit [UCC 7–204(2)].

traditional Bailments

C. INNKEEPERS

Those who provide lodging to the public for compensation as a regular business are strictly liable for injuries to guests (not permanent residents).

1. Hotel Safes

In many states, innkeepers can avoid strict liability for loss of guests' valuables by providing a safe. Statutes often limit the liability of innkeepers for articles that are not kept in the safe.

2. Parking Facilities

If an innkeeper provides parking facilities, and the guest's car is entrusted to the innkeeper, the innkeeper will be liable under the rules that pertain to parking lot bailees (ordinary bailments).

TRUE-FALSE QUESTIONS

(Answers at the Back of the Book)

____ 1. Generally, those who produce personal property have title to it.

____ 2. If goods are confused due to a wrongful act and the innocent party cannot prove what percentage is his or hers, the wrongdoer gets title to the whole.

____ 3. To constitute a gift, a voluntary transfer of property must be supported by consideration.

____ 4. If an accession is performed in good faith, the improver keeps the property as improved.

____ 5. One who finds abandoned property acquires title to it good against the true owner.

____ 6. Any delivery of personal property from one person to another creates a bailment.

____ 7. A bailee is not responsible for the loss of bailed property in his or her care.

____ 8. A bailee's only duty is to surrender the property at the end of the bailment.

____ 9. In some ordinary bailments, bailees can limit their liability.

____ 10. Warehouse companies have the same duty of care as ordinary bailees.

FILL-IN QUESTIONS

(Answers at the Back of the Book)

A gift made during the donor's lifetime is a gift _____ (*causa mortis/inter vivos*). A gift _____ (*causa mortis/inter vivos*) is made in contemplation of imminent death. Gifts _____ (*causa mortis/inter vivos*) do not become absolute until the donor dies from the contemplated illness or disease. A gift _____ (*causa mortis/inter vivos*) is revo-

cable at any time up to the death of the donor and is automatically revoked if the donor recovers. A gift
_____ (*causa mortis/inter vivos*) is revocable at any time before the donor's death.

MULTIPLE-CHOICE QUESTIONS

(Answers at the Back of the Book)

____   1. Bryanna designs an Internet Web site to advertise her services as a designer of Web sites. Calvert hires her to design a Web site for his business. Bryanna has title to

a. Bryanna's Web site, Calvert;s Web site, and any other Web site she creates.
b. Bryanna's Web site only.
c. Fred's Web site only.
d. no Web site.

____   2. Equipment Rental, Inc., leases a forklift to Fabulous Warehouse Company for a price. With respect to any defects in the forklift, Equipment Rental has

a. a duty to inform Fabulous Warehouse of hidden defects only.
b. a duty to inform Fabulous Warehouse of known and hidden defects.
c. a duty to inform Fabulous Warehouse of known defects only.
d. no duty to inform Fabulous Warehouse of defects.

____   3. Gala wants to give Hermione a pair of diamond earrings that Gala has in her safe-deposit box at InterCity Bank. Gala gives Hermione the key to the box and tells her to go to the bank and take the earrings from the box. Hermione does so. Two days later, Gala dies. The earrings belong to

a. Gala's heirs.
b. Hermione.
c. InterCity Bank.
d. the state.

____   4. Jordan is employed in remodeling homes bought and sold by Klondike Realty. In one of the homes, Jordan finds an item of jewelry and takes it to Lumino Gems, Inc., to be appraised. Miklos, the appraiser, removes some of the jewels. Title to the jewels that were removed is most likely with

a. Jordan.
b. Klondike Realty.
c. Lumino Gems.
d. Miklos.

____   5. Jan, Ken, and Lee store their grain in three silos. Jan contributes half of the grain, Ken a third, and Lee a sixth. A tornado hits two of the silos and scatters the grain. Of the grain that is left, most likely

a. Jan and Ken split it equally because they lost the most.
b. Jan, Ken, and Lee share it equally.
c. Jan owns half, Ken a third, and Lee a sixth.
d. Ken owns it all because only a third is left.

____   6. Polly parks her car in an unattended lot behind a Whiz Mart store, which is closed. Polly locks the car and takes the keys. This is not a bailment because there is no

a. contract.
b. money.
c. personal property.
d. transfer of possession.

___ **7.** Nichelle wants to give Oglethorpe a notebook computer in a locker at Pleasant Valley Mall. Nichelle gives Oglethorpe the key to the locker and tells him to take the computer. Oglethorpe says that he doesn't want the computer and leaves the key on Nichelle's desk. The next day, Nichelle dies. The computer belongs to

a. Nichelle's heirs.
b. Oglethorpe.
c. Pleasant Valley Mall.
d. the state.

___ **8.** Charmain goes to Don's Salon for a haircut. Behind a plant on a table in the waiting area, Charmain finds a wallet containing $5,000. The party entitled to possession of the wallet is

a. Charmain.
b. Don, the owner of the salon and lessee of the space in the building.
c. the owner of the building in which Don leases the space for the salon.
d. the state.

___ **9.** Cleo checks her coat at Dinnerhouse Restaurant. Hidden in the sleeve is a purse. By accepting the coat, Dinnerhouse is a bailee of

a. neither the coat nor the purse.
b. the coat and the purse.
c. the coat only.
d. the purse only.

___ **10.** Vittorio Corporation ships goods via Worldwide Company. Worldwide will not be liable for the loss of the goods if they are

a. crushed in a warehouse accident that is the fault of Worldwide's crane operator.
b. damaged because Vittorio failed to package the goods properly.
c. destroyed in a traffic accident that is the fault of Worldwide's truck driver.
d. stolen by an unknown person.

SHORT ESSAY QUESTIONS

1. What is the duty of a bailor to inform a bailee of defects with respect to bailed goods? If liability arises, to whom might that liability extend?

2. What are the three elements involved in creating a valid gift?

GAMEPOINTS

(Answers at the Back of the Book)

1. The video game "Myth" is based on the tales of Zeus, Jupiter, and other Greek and Roman gods and goddesses. One of the most popular segments of the game begins with the release of evil from Pandora's box with you, the player, assigned the task of rounding up the wicked spirits and returning them to the box. Taylor, who created the game, owns the copyright. Taylor also owns a house and some shares of stock, in which she invested some of her profits from sales of "Myth." Which of these items is personal property?

2. You're playing the video game "Wreck & Reap," in which your avatar Kosmo, aboard your starship *Lightspeed*, engages in interplanetary combat with one of the ships of Menace, an enemy of your Galaxian Empire. At *Lightspeed*'s helm, Kosmo destroys the enemy vessel, but *Lightspeed* is disabled. Kosmo escapes in a space-to-surface craft, planning to later salvage what can be recovered from your orbiting starship.

Meanwhile, a different marauder from Menace discovers the wreck and strips it. In your suit against Menace in the Court of the Universe, your enemy claims that *Lightspeed* was abandoned. Under the principles discussed in this chapter, does Menace have title to whatever was taken from the starship? Explain.

SPECIAL INFORMATION FOR CPA CANDIDATES

Currently, personal property is not a specific topic tested on the CPA examination. In the past, however, the test has asked questions that involve personal property ownership, including such aspects as the acquisition of ownership (especially gifts) and the types of ownership. Fixtures have been covered (remember that the harder it is to remove an item, the more likely it will be regarded as a fixture, but that trade fixtures are judged differently.

Personal property, its ownership, and its transfer may also be at issue on such parts of the exam as those that test on sales of goods under the Uniform Commercial Code, sales involving the common law of contracts, negotiable instruments, securities law, and secured transactions. You may find it helpful to briefly review those topics from the frame of reference of the principles in this chapter.

Bailments were also previously tested on the CPA examination. You were expected to be familiar with what degree of care (slight, great, or reasonable) is required in which type of bailment (gratuitous for the bailor, gratuitous for the bailee, or mutual).

Chapter 50
Real Property and Landlord-Tenant Relationships

WHAT THIS CHAPTER IS ABOUT

This chapter covers ownership rights in real property, including the nature of those rights and their transfer. The chapter also outlines the right of the government to take private land for public use, zoning laws, and other restrictions on ownership.

CHAPTER OUTLINE

I. THE NATURE OF REAL PROPERTY
Real property consists of land and the buildings, plants, and trees on it.

A. LAND AND STRUCTURES
Includes the soil on the surface of the earth, natural products or artificial structures attached to it, the water on or under it, and the air space above.

B. AIRSPACE AND SUBSURFACE RIGHTS
Limitations on air rights or subsurface rights normally have to be indicated on the deed transferring title at the time of purchase.

1. Airspace Rights
Flights over private land do not normally violate the owners' rights.

2. Subsurface Rights
Ownership of the surface can be separated from ownership of the subsurface. In excavating, if a subsurface owner causes the land to subside, he or she may be liable to the owner of the surface.

C. PLANT LIFE AND VEGETATION
A sale of land with growing crops on it includes the crops, unless otherwise agreed. When crops are sold alone, they are personal property.

II. OWNERSHIP AND OTHER INTERESTS IN REAL PROPERTY   Pg. 982

A. OWNERSHIP IN FEE SIMPLE
A *fee simple absolute* owner has the most rights possible—to give away the property, sell it, transfer it by will, use it for any purpose, and possess it to the exclusion of all the world—potentially forever.

B. LIFE ESTATES
A life estate lasts for the life of a specified individual ("to A for his life"). A life tenant can use the land (but not commit waste), mortgage the life estate, and create liens, easements, and leases (but not longer than the life defining the estate).   *Rule of perpetuities*

C. CONCURRENT OWNERSHIP
Persons who share ownership rights simultaneously are concurrent owners.

403

1. **Tenancy in Common**
   A tenancy in common exists when each of two or more persons owns an *undivided* interest (each has rights in the whole—if each had rights in specific items, the interests would be *divided*). On death, a tenant's interest passes to his or her heirs. Most states presume that a co-tenancy is a tenancy in common unless there is a clear intention to establish a joint tenancy.

2. **Joint Tenancy**
   This occurs when each of two or more persons owns an undivided interest in the property; a deceased joint tenant's interest passes to the surviving joint tenant or tenants. A joint tenancy can be terminated before a joint tenant's death by gift, by sale, or by partition (divided into equal parts).

3. **Tenancy by the Entirety**
   A transfer of real property to a husband and wife can create a tenancy by the entirety; neither spouse can transfer separately his or her interest during his or her life. In some states, this tenancy has been abolished. A divorce, a spouse's death, or mutual agreement will end this tenancy.

4. **Community Property**
   Here, each spouse owns an undivided half interest in property that either spouse acquired during the marriage (except property acquired by gift or inheritance). Recognized in only some states, on divorce the property is divided equally in a few states and at a court's discretion in others.

D. LEASEHOLD ESTATES
A leasehold estate is created when an owner or landlord conveys the right to possess and use property to a tenant for a certain period of time.

1. **Fixed-Term Tenancy or Tenancy for Years**
   This is created by contract (which can sometimes be oral) by which property is leased for a specific period (a month, a year, a period of years). At the end of the period, the lease ends (without notice). If the tenant dies during the lease, the lease interest passes to the tenant's heirs.

2. **Periodic Tenancy**
   A periodic tenancy is created by a lease that specifies the payment of rent at certain intervals and it automatically renews unless it is terminated. It can arise if a landlord allows a tenant for years to hold over. Terminates, at common law, on one period's notice.

3. **Tenancy at Will**
   This tenancy can be terminated by either party without notice ("at will"). It exists, for example, when a tenant for years retains possession after termination with the landlord's consent before payment of the next rent (when it becomes a periodic tenancy). It lasts as long as the landlord and tenant agree, but terminates on the death of either party.

4. **Tenancy at Sufferance**
   A tenancy at sufferance is a possession of land without right (without the owner's permission).

E. NONPOSSESSORY INTERESTS

1. **Easements and Profits**
   Easement: the right of a person to make limited use of another person's land without taking anything from the property. *Profit*: the right to go onto another's land and take away a part or product of the land.

   a. **Easement or Profit Appurtenant**
      This arises when a landowner has a right to go onto (or remove things from) an adjacent owner's land.

b. Easement or Profit in Gross

This exists when a right to use or take things from another's land does not depend on owning the adjacent property.

c. Creation of an Easement or Profit

An easement or profit can be created by deed, will, contract, implication, necessity, or prescription.

d. Termination of an Easement or Profit

An easement of profit terminates when deeded back to owner of the land burdened, its owner becomes owner of the land burdened, contract terminates, or it is abandoned with the intent to relinquish the right to it.

2. Licenses

This is the revocable right of a person to come onto another person's land.

III. TRANSFER OF OWNERSHIP

A. LISTING AGREEMENTS

Under a listing agreement, a real estate seller may employ a real estate agent to find a buyer. This agreement can specify its duration and other terms, including the agent's commission. The agreement may be *exclusive* (only the designated agent can sell) or *open* (any agent can sell).

B. REAL ESTATE SALES CONTRACTS

The steps in a sale of real estate include the formation of a contract, a title search, financing (which may include a *mortgage*), a property inspection, and a closing.

1. Contingencies

A contract may be made contingent on the buyer obtaining financing at or below a certain rate of interest, or selling other property, or obtaining a survey and title insurance. A contract may be contingent on the property passing an inspection for defects and insect infestation.

2. Closing Date and Escrow

The buyer may deposit funds with, and the seller may give a deed to, an escrow agent to transfer when the conditions of sale are met.

3. Implied Warranties in the Sales of New Homes

In a few states, a seller makes no warranties (unless the deed or contract specifies otherwise)—a buyer takes the property "as is." In most states, a seller of a new house impliedly warrants that it is fit for human habitation (in reasonable working order and of reasonably sound construction). In a few states, a later buyer can recover from the original builder under this warranty.

4. Seller's Duty to Disclose Hidden Defects

In most states, sellers must disclose any known defect that materially affects the value of the property and that the buyer could not reasonably discover.

C. DEEDS

Possession and title to land can be passed by deed without consideration.

1. Requirements

(1) Names of the grantor and grantee, (2) words evidencing an intent to convey, (3) legally sufficient description of the land, (4) grantor's (and usually the spouse's) signature, and (5) delivery.

2. Warranty Deed (garantee)

This provides the most protection against defects of title—covenants that the grantor has title to, and the power to convey, the property; that the buyer will not be disturbed in his or her possession of the land; and that transfer is made without unknown adverse claims of third parties.

3. Special Warranty Deed

This warrants only that the grantor held good title during his or her ownership of the property, not that there were no title defects when others owned it. If all liens and encumbrances are disclosed, the seller is not liable if a third person interferes with the buyer's ownership.

4. Quitclaim Deed

This warrants less than any other deed. It conveys to the grantee only the interest the grantor had.

5. Grant Deed

By statute, this may impliedly warrant that the grantor owns the property and has not encumbered it or conveyed it to another.

6. Sheriff's Deed

This gives ownership rights to a buyer at a sheriff's sale. *get debtor to waive redemption rights or they can reclaim property*

D. RECORDING STATUTES

Recording statutes require transfers to be recorded in public records (generally in the county in which the property is located) to give notice to the public that a certain person is the owner. Many states require the grantor's signature and two witnesses' signatures.

1. Marketable Title

A grantor must transfer title that is free from undisclosed encumbrances and defects.

2. Title Search

This is an examination of the title records for all transactions concerning a specific parcel of real property to discover its true owner and other interested parties.

3. Methods of Ensuring Good Title

These include hiring an attorney to provide an opinion based on a reading of an abstract of title; holding a court hearing in those states that use the Torrens system of title registration; and (most commonly) obtaining title insurance, which insures the grantee against losses due to title defects.

E. ADVERSE POSSESSION

A person who possesses another's property acquires title good against the original owner if the possession is (1) actual and exclusive; (2) open, visible, and notorious; (3) continuous and peaceable for a statutorily required period of time; and (4) hostile, as against the whole world.

IV. LIMITATIONS ON THE RIGHTS OF PROPERTY OWNERS

A. EMINENT DOMAIN

The government can take private property for public use (most states limit taking of private property and giving it to private developers). To obtain title, a condemnation proceeding is brought. The U.S. Constitution's Fifth Amendment requires that just compensation be paid for a taking; thus, in a separate proceeding a court determines the land's fair value (usually market value) to pay the owner.

B. RESTRICTIVE COVENANTS

A restrictive covenant is a private restriction on the use of land. It runs with the land if the original parties and their successors are entitled to its benefit or burdened with its obligation. It must be in writing and subsequent owners of the property must know of it.

C. INVERSE CONDEMNATION

Inverse condemnation occurs when a government takes private property without paying for it. This may be accomplished by use or occupation of the land, or through the imposition of regulations that cause land to lose its value. The former owner must sue to obtain compensation.

V. Zoning and Government Regulations

Zoning laws control development within a municipality by regulating the use of property in different zones. This is a constitutional use of a municipality's police powers as long as it is rationally related to the community's health, safety, or welfare.

A. PURPOSE AND SCOPE OF ZONING LAWS

Zoning laws encourage sustainable and organized development, and control growth. Among other things, zoning ordinances classify land by permissible use as part of a comprehensive plan.

1. Permissible Uses of Land

Generally, municipalities divide land into districts for present and future uses. The districts may be divided into subdistricts. Types of permissible uses are—

a. *Residential.* Here, buildings are constructed for human habitation.

b. *Commercial.* This land is designated for business or government activities—stores, offices, hotels, theaters, sports stadiums, and courthouses, for example.

c. *Industrial.* This category includes manufacturing, shipping, and transportation. Because of the potential for these uses to interfere with others' enjoyment of their property, these areas are often farther from residential and commercial districts.

d. *Conservation.* These districts are dedicated to soil and water conservation efforts.

2. Other Zoning Restrictions

Ordinances may dictate details such as the distance a building must be from a property line, visual appearance (for example, height and width), and the location and operation of certain businesses to regulate traffic and for other purposes.

B. EXCEPTIONS TO ZONING LAWS

1. Variances

A variance allows an exception to zoning rules. But the need for a variance cannot be self-created (for example, a party cannot buy property for a purpose that is not permitted and argue that a variance is needed to use the property). To obtain a variance, there must be—

a. *Notice.* Neighbors who might object must be notified.

b. *Public hearing.* The party seeking the variance must show that it is necessary for reasonable development, it is the least intrusive option, and the essential character of the neighborhood will not change.

c. *Decision.* A hearing examiner determines whether the variance will be granted.

2. Special-Use Permits

A special-use, or conditional-use, permit allows an owner to use property for a certain purpose only in compliance with specific requirements (a business that conforms to the style of a neighborhood in a residential district, for example).

3. Special Incentives

Special incentives (tax credits or lower tax rates) can encourage certain uses (new businesses or preservation of historical homes) or support environmental goals (energy efficiency).

VI.   LANDLORD-TENANT RELATIONSHIPS

To ensure the validity of a lease, in most states it should be in writing for a term exceeding a year, describe the property, and indicate the length of term and the amount and due dates of rent. A landlord cannot discriminate against tenants on the basis of race, color, religion, national origin, or sex. A tenant cannot promise to do something against these (or other) laws, including building codes.

A.   PARTIES' RIGHTS AND DUTIES

1.   Possession

a.   Landlord's Duty to Deliver Possession
A landlord must give a tenant possession of the property at the beginning of the term.

b.   Tenant's Right to Retain Possession
The tenant retains possession exclusively until the lease expires.

c.   Covenant of Quiet Enjoyment
The landlord promises that during the lease term no one having superior title to the property will disturb the tenant's use and enjoyment of it. If so, the tenant can sue for damages for breach.

d.   Eviction
If the landlord deprives the tenant of possession of the property or interferes with his or her use or enjoyment of it, an eviction occurs. *Constructive eviction* occurs when this results from a landlord's failure to perform adequately his or her duties under the lease.

2.   Use and Maintenance of the Premises

a.   Tenant's Use
Generally, a tenant may make any legal use of the property, as long as it is reasonably related to the purpose for which the property is ordinarily used and does not harm the landlord's interest. A tenant is not responsible for ordinary wear and tear.

b.   Landlord's Maintenance
A landlord must comply with local building codes.

3.   Implied Warranty of Habitability
In most states, a landlord must furnish residential premises that are habitable. This applies to substantial defects the landlord knows or should know about and has had a reasonable time to repair.

4.   Rent
A tenant must pay rent even if he or she moves out or refuses to move in (if the move is unjustifiable). If the landlord violates the implied warranty of habitability, a tenant may withhold rent, pay for repair and deduct the cost, cancel the lease, or sue for damages.

B.   TRANSFERRING RIGHTS TO LEASED PROPERTY

1.   Transferring the Landlord's Interest
A landlord can sell, give away, or otherwise transfer his or her real property. If complete title is transferred, the tenant becomes the tenant of the new owner, who must also abide by the lease.

2.   Transferring the Tenant's Interest
Before a tenant can assign or sublet an interest, the landlord's consent may be required (it cannot be unreasonably withheld). If an assignee or sublessee later defaults, the tenant must pay the rent.

C. TERMINATION OF THE LEASE

On termination, a tenant is no longer liable for rent and is no longer entitled to possession of the property. A lease terminates when its term ends or by—

1. Notice

A periodic tenancy (see Chapter 47) will renew automatically unless one of the parties gives timely notice of termination.

2. Sale

If a landlord conveys his or her interest in the property to the tenant, the transfer is a release, and the tenant's interest in the property merges into the title to the property (which he or she holds).

3. Agreement

The parties may agree to end a tenancy before it would otherwise terminate.

4. Abandonment

A landlord may treat a tenant's moving out with no intent of returning before the end of the term as an offer of surrender. Retaking possession relieves the tenant of the duty to pay rent.

TRUE-FALSE QUESTIONS

(Answers at the Back of the Book)

____   1.   A fee simple absolute is potentially infinite in duration and can be disposed of by deed or by will.

____   2.   The owner of a life estate has the same rights as a fee simple owner.

____   3.   An easement allows a person to use land and take something from it, but a profit allows a person only to use land.

____   4.   Deeds offer different degrees of protection against defects of title.

____   5.   If the covenant of quiet enjoyment is breached, the tenant can sue the landlord for damages.

____   6.   The government can take private property for *private* uses only.

____   7.   A periodic tenancy is a tenancy for a specified period of time, such as a month, a year, or a period of years.

____   8.   Generally, a tenant must pay rent even if he or she moves out, if the move is unjustifiable.

____   9.   In most states, the seller of a new house impliedly warrants that it will be fit for human habitation.

____   10.   When a landlord sells leased premises to a third party, any existing leases terminate automatically.

FILL-IN QUESTIONS

(Answers at the Back of the Book)

The deed that provides the most protection against defects of title is the _____ (warranty/special warranty/quitclaim) deed. Among other things, it covenants that the transfer is made without any unknown adverse claims of third parties. The deed that warrants only that the grantor has done nothing to lessen the value of the property is the _____ (warranty/special warranty/quitclaim) deed. Under this deed, the seller may not be liable if a third person interferes with the buyer's ownership. The deed that warrants less than any other deed is the _____ (warranty/special warranty/quitclaim) deed. This deed conveys to the grantee only whatever interest the grantor had.

MULTIPLE-CHOICE QUESTIONS

(Answers at the Back of the Book)

____ 1. Ezmé owns two hundred acres next to Floyd's lumber mill. Ezmé sells to Floyd the privilege of removing the timber from her land. This privilege is

    a. a leasehold estate.
    b. a license.
    c. an easement.
    d. a profit.

____ 2. Investors Property, Inc., sells an office building to Jaime with a deed that makes the greatest number of warranties and provides the most extensive protection against defects of title. This deed is

    a. a grant deed.
    b. a quitclaim deed.
    c. a special warranty deed.
    d. a warranty deed.

____ 3. To acquire the ownership of a strip of waterfront property by adverse possession, Glenn must occupy the property exclusively, continuously, and peaceably for a specified period of time

    a. in an open, hostile, and adverse manner.
    b. until the owner files a suit.
    c. without the owner's knowledge.
    d. with the state's permission.

____ 4. Eligio owns an apartment building in fee simple. Eligio can

    a. give the building away only.
    b. give the building away, sell it, or transfer it by will.
    c. not give the building away, sell it, or transfer it by will.
    d. sell the building or transfer it by a will only.

____ 5. Urban City wants to acquire undeveloped land within the city limits to convert into a public park. Urban City brings a judicial proceeding to obtain title to the land. This is

    a. adverse possession.
    b. an easement.
    c. constructive eviction.
    d. the power of eminent domain.

____ 6. **Based on a Sample CPA Exam Question.** Samira Entertainment Company sells an office building to Tivoli Restaurants, Inc. To be valid, the deed that conveys the property must include

    a. a description of the property.
    b. a due date for the payment of the price.
    c. a requirement that the seller perform structural repairs to the building.
    d. a requirement that the buyer carry liability insurance.

_____ 7. Dayton owns a half-acre of land fronting Elsinore Lake. Fritz owns the property behind Dayton's land. No road runs to Dayton's land, but Fritz's driveway runs between a road and Dayton's property, so Dayton uses Fritz's driveway. The right-of-way that Dayton has across Fritz's property is

a. a leasehold estate.
b. a license.
c. an easement.
d. a profit.

_____ 8. Cicero operates The Italian Cafe in space that he leases in Elkland Mall, which is owned by Fidelia Properties Inc. Fidelia sells the mall to Gusto Investments, Inc. For the rest of the lease term, Cicxero owes rent to

a. The Italian Cafe.
b. Fidelia Properties.
c. Gusto Investments.
d. no one.

_____ 9. Jeremy leases an apartment from Kim. Three months later, Jeremy moves out, and arranges with Lucy to move in and pay the rent to Kim for rest of the term. This is

a. an assignment.
b. an easement.
c. an eviction.
d. a sublease.

_____ 10. Kukla signs a lease for an apartment, agreeing to make rental payments before the fifth of each month. The lease does not specify a termination date. This is

a. a fixed-term tenancy, or a tenancy for years.
b. a periodic tenancy.
c. a tenancy at sufferance.
d. a tenancy at will.

SHORT ESSAY QUESTIONS

1. Describe the power of eminent domain and the process by which private property is condemned for a public purpose

2. What does the implied warranty of habitability require, and when does it apply?

GAMEPOINTS

(Answers at the Back of the Book)

1. To develop what you believe is a terrific idea for a video game, you lease 50,000 square feet in an office building from Commercial Property, LLC, under a written five-year lease. Your goal is to put the game on the market within two years. Several months into the term, a competitor unexpectedly releases a new game title featuring play that would make your game appear to be a poorly crafted imitation. Can you assign the lease to another party? Explain.

2. The object of the video game "Gotcha" is to make life difficult for those characters who, through criminal activity, make life difficult for others. Points are scored when a crime is stopped and a criminal is legitimately punished. Bret is a tenant a building under a lease that does not contain any specific restrictions. He makes repairs to the apartment, for which he does not maintain a renters' insurance policy, and where he also keeps a dog and counterfeits copies of video games. Can your avatar Smiley score points by recommending Bret's eviction for any of these acts? If so, which?

SPECIAL INFORMATION FOR CPA CANDIDATES

Real property and property interests are covered on the CPA examination.

Of the material in this chapter, you should know the basic rights and interests of real property ownership, including the different types of tenancies. Regarding deeds, you should know the priorities of competing claims under the recording statutes and the differences among a warranty deed, a special warranty deed, and a quitclaim deed. You should also know the elements of adverse possession.

Life estates are included in questions about trusts (see Chapter 52). Other material to review with this chapter for the real property questions on the exam include the types of property ownership, especially joint tenancy with the right of survivorship; mortgage law (see Chapter 31); and insurance (Chapter 51).

The section of the exam on property law includes questions on landlord-tenant law. It can be important for you to remember that a tenant is entitled to exclusive possession of the premises for the term of the lease. Eviction may result for using the property for illegal or prohibited purposes or for failing to pay the rent. You should know the difference between an assignment and a sublease (the former involves the tenant's entire interest under the lease; the later involves all or part of the premises for a shorter term). Unless the lease prohibits it, a tenant can assign or sublet without the landlord's consent.

Material in other chapters that you may wish to review for the exam includes the types of tenancies covered in Chapter 49.

On the contracts section of the exam, there may be a question about a lease that cannot be completed within a year. Of course, any such lease must be in writing to be enforceable under the Statute of Frauds.

Chapter 51
Insurance

WHAT THIS CHAPTER IS ABOUT

Insurance is a contract in which one party agrees to compensate the other for any future loss on a specified subject by a specified peril. Essentially, insurance is an arrangement for managing—transferring and allocating—risk. This chapter covers the law relating to insurance.

CHAPTER OUTLINE

I. TERMINOLOGY AND CONCEPTS

    A. RISK MANAGEMENT
    Risk management consists of plans to protect personal and financial interests should an event undermine their security. The most common method is to transfer risk from a business or individual to an insurance company.

    B. INSURANCE TERMINOLOGY
    An insurance company is an *underwriter* or an *insurer*; the party covered by insurance is the *insured*; an insurance contract is a *policy*; consideration paid to an insurer is a *premium*; policies are obtained through an *agent* or *broker*.

    C. CLASSIFICATIONS OF INSURANCE
    Insurance is classified according to the nature of the risk involved.

    D. INSURABLE INTEREST
    To obtain insurance, one must have a sufficient interest in what is insured.

        1. Life Insurance
        One must have a reasonable expectation of benefit from the continued life of another. The benefit may be related to money or may be founded on a relationship (by blood or affinity).

        a. Key-Person Insurance
        An organization (partnership, corporation) can insure the life of a person who is important to that organization (partner, officer).

        b. When the Insurable Interest Must Exist
        An interest in someone's life must exist *when the policy is obtained*.

        2. Property Insurance
        One has an insurable interest in property when one would sustain a pecuniary loss from its destruction. An insurable interest in property must exist *when the loss occurs*.

II. THE INSURANCE CONTRACT
Policies generally are standard; in some states, this is required.

    A. APPLICATION FOR INSURANCE
    The application is part of the contract. Misstatements can void a policy, especially if the insurer shows that it would not have issued the policy if it had known the facts.

B. EFFECTIVE DATE OF COVERAGE

A policy is effective when (1) a binder is written, (2) the policy is issued, (3) a certain time elapses, or (4) a specified condition is met.

1. When a Policy Is Obtained from a Broker

A broker is the agent of the applicant. Until the broker obtains a policy, the applicant is normally not insured.

2. When a Policy Is Obtained from an Agent

An agent is the agent of the insurer. One who obtains a policy from an agent can be protected from the moment the application is made (under a binder), or the parties may agree to delay coverage until a policy is issued or some condition is met (such as a physical exam).

C. PROVISIONS AND CLAUSES

Some important clauses include—

1. Provisions Mandated by Statute

A court will deem that a policy contains such a clause even if it is not actually included in the language of the contract.

2. Incontestability Clause

After a life or health policy has been in force for a certain time (two or three years), the insurer cannot cancel the policy or avoid a claim on the basis of statements made in the application.

3. Coinsurance Clause

A standard provision in fire insurance policies; applies only in cases of *partial* loss. If an owner insures property up to a specified percentage (usually 80 percent) of its value, he or she will recover any loss up to the face amount of the policy. If the insurance is for less than this percentage, the owner is responsible for a proportionate share.

4. Appraisal and Arbitration Clauses

If insurer and insured disagree about the value of a loss, they can demand separate appraisals, to be resolved by a third party (*umpire*).

5. Multiple Insurance Coverage

If policies with several companies cover the same risk and the amount of coverage exceeds the loss, the insured collects from each insurer its proportionate share of the liability to the total amount of insurance.

6. Antilapse Clause

Provides grace period for insured to pay an overdue premium.

D. INTERPRETING PROVISIONS OF AN INSURANCE CONTRACT

Words in an insurance contract have their ordinary meanings. If there is an ambiguity or uncertainty, it is interpreted against the insurer.

E. CANCELLATION

A policy may be canceled for nonpayment of premiums, fraud or misrepresentation, conviction for a crime that increases the hazard insured against, or gross negligence that increases the hazard insured against. An insurer may be required to give advance written notice.

F. DUTIES AND OBLIGATIONS OF THE PARTIES

The insured and the insurer have an implied duty to act in good faith.

1. Duties of the Insured

An applicant must disclose all material facts (whatever an insurer would consider in determining a premium amount or deciding whether to issue a policy). An insured must—

    a. Pay the premiums as stated in the policy.

    b. Notify the insurer within a reasonable time if an event occurs that gives rise to a claim.

    c. Cooperate with the insurer during an investigation or litigation.

2. Duties of the Insurer
Regarding a claim, an insurer has a duty to investigate the facts and to make reasonable efforts to settle. If a claim cannot be settled, the insurer has a duty to defend the insured.

3. Bad-Faith Actions
If an insurer's denial of a claim or refusal to settle a claim for a reasonable amount within a policy's limits is in bad faith, the insured may recover damages, including punitive damages, in tort.

G. DEFENSES AGAINST PAYMENT
Fraud, misrepresentation, violation of warranties, and actions that are against public policy or that are otherwise illegal.

III. TYPES OF INSURANCE

A. LIFE INSURANCE
A fixed amount is paid to a beneficiary on an insured's death.

1. Types of Life Insurance
Basic types: *whole life* has cash surrender value that grows at a predetermined rate and can be used as collateral for a loan; *term* provides protection for a specified period; has no cash surrender value.

2. Liability
Unless excluded, any cause of death is the insurer's risk. Typical exclusions: death by suicide, when the insured is a passenger in a commercial vehicle, in military action in war, or execution by the government.

3. Misstatement of Age
This does not void a policy, but premiums or benefits are adjusted.

4. Assignment
An insured can change beneficiaries, with notice to the insurer.

5. Creditors' Rights
Generally, a judgment creditor can reach an insured's interest in life insurance. The creditor cannot compel the insured to obtain cash surrender value or change the beneficiary to the creditor.

6. Termination
Usually occurs only on default in premium payments (policy lapses), payment of benefits, expiration of term, or cancellation by insured.

B. FIRE INSURANCE
Protects the homeowner against fire, lightning, and damage from smoke and water caused by the fire or the fire department.

1. Liability
Usually, recovery is limited to losses resulting from hostile fires. In some cases, the insured must file proof of a loss as a condition for recovery. In most cases, premises must be occupied at the time of loss, unless the parties agree otherwise.

2. Assignment
Not assignable without the insurer's consent (it would materially change the insurer's risk).

C. HOMEOWNERS' INSURANCE

1. Property Coverage
Included are the garage; house; other private buildings; personal possessions at home, in travel, or at work; and expenses for living away from home because of a fire or some other covered peril.

2. Liability Coverage
Covered are injuries occurring on the insured's property; damage or injury by the insured to others or their property, except for professional malpractice.

D. AUTOMOBILE INSURANCE

1. Liability Insurance
Covers bodily injury and property damage.

2. Collision Insurance
Covers damage to the insured's car in any type of collision. Most people agree to pay a deductible before the insurer becomes liable.

3. Comprehensive Insurance
Covers loss, damage, and destruction by fire, hurricane, hail, vandalism, and theft.

4. Uninsured Motorist Insurance
Covers the driver and passengers against injury caused by any driver without insurance or by a hit-and-run driver. Some states require it all automobile policies sold to drivers.

5. Other-Driver Coverage
Protects vehicle owner and anyone who drives the vehicle with owner's permission.

6. No-fault Insurance
Provides that claims arising from an accident are made against the claimant's own insurer, regardless of whose fault the accident was.

E. BUSINESS LIABILITY INSURANCE

1. Key-person Insurance
See above (I, D, 1, a).

2. General Liability Insurance
Covers as many risks as the insurer agrees to cover. Policies can be drafted to meet special needs, such as specific risks of product liability (see Chapter 23).

3. Professional Malpractice Insurance
Protects professionals against malpractice claims.

4. Workers' Compensation Insurance
Covers payments to employees who are injured in accidents occurring on the job or in the course of employment (see Chapter 33).

TRUE-FALSE QUESTIONS

(Answers at the Back of the Book)

_____   1.   An applicant must disclose all material facts to an insurer.

_____   2.   Insurance is classified by the nature of the person or interest protected.

_____   3.   An insurance broker is always an agent of an insurance company.

____ 4. An insurance applicant is usually protected from the time an application is made, if a premium is paid.

____ 5. A person can insure anything in which he or she has an insurable interest.

____ 6. An application for insurance is not part of the insurance contract.

____ 7. An insured can change beneficiaries under a life insurance policy without the insurer's consent.

____ 8. A coinsurance clause in a fire insurance policy always reduces the amount of the insured's recovery.

____ 9. More than one party can have an insurable interest in, for example, the same property.

____ 10. Under an antilapse clause, an insurance policy lapses unless the insured pays a premium on time.

FILL-IN QUESTIONS

(Answers at the Back of the Book)

The words used in an insurance contract have their _____ (ordinary/special) meaning and are interpreted by the courts in light of the _____ (insured's conduct/nature of the coverage) involved. When there is an ambiguity in a policy, a provision is interpreted against the _____ (insurance company/insured). When it is unclear whether an insurance contract actually exists because the written policy has not been delivered, the uncertainty will be determined against the _____ (insurance company/insured). A court presumes the policy _____ (is/is not) in effect unless the _____ (insurance company/insured) can show otherwise.

MULTIPLE-CHOICE QUESTIONS

(Answers at the Back of the Book)

____ 1. Pam states, on her application to Quality Insurance, Inc., for a life insurance policy, that she has not been hospitalized within the last five years, forgetting that two years earlier she was hospitalized briefly. One year later, Pam dies for a cause unrelated to the earlier hospitalization. Quality denies payment. If Pam's beneficiary sues Quality, the beneficiary will

a. lose, because Pam's misstatement concerned a material fact.
b. lose, because an insurer can use any misstatement on an application to avoid payment.
c. win, because an insurer cannot use a misstatement on an application to avoid payment.
d. win, because Pam's misstatement did not concern a material fact.

____ 2. Ollie applies to ProRata Insurance Company for a fire insurance policy for his warehouse. To obtain a lower premium, he misrepresents the age of the property. The policy is granted. After the warehouse is destroyed by fire, ProRata learns the true facts. ProRata can

a. not refuse to pay, because an application is not part of an insurance contract.
b. not refuse to pay, because fire destroyed the warehouse.
c. refuse to pay on the ground of fraud in the application.
d. refuse to pay on the ground that fire destroyed the warehouse.

____   **3.** Kirby is an executive with DigiCom, Inc. Because his death would cause a financial loss to the firm, it insures his life. Later, he resigns to work for a competitor, E-Tech Corporation. Six months later, Kirby dies. Regarding payment for the loss, DigiCom can

a. collect, because the firm's insurable interest existed when the policy was obtained.
b. collect if the firm suffered a financial loss when Kirby resigned.
c. not collect, because the firm's insurable interest did not exist when a loss occurred.
d. not collect, because the firm suffered no financial loss from Kirby's death.

____   **4. Based on a Sample CPA Exam Question.** Tom buys a house and obtains from Union Insurance Company a fire insurance policy on the property. If fire destroys the house, to collect payment under the policy, Tom's insurable interest

a. exists only if the property is owned by Tom or a related individual.
b. exists only if the property is owned in fee simple.
c. must exist when the loss occurs.
d. must exist when Union issues the policy and when the loss occurs.

____   **5.** Satellite Communications, Inc., takes out an insurance policy on its plant with United Insurance, Inc. United could cancel the policy

a. for any reason.
b. if any of Satellite's drivers have their driver's licenses suspended.
c. if Satellite begins using grossly careless manufacturing practices.
d. if Satellite's president appears as a witness in a case against United.

____   **6.** Deb takes out a fire insurance policy with Eagle Insurance Company on her $200,000 warehouse. The policy contains a coinsurance clause with a specified percentage of 80 percent. Deb insures the property for $160,000. In a fire, she suffers a $100,000 loss. She can recover

a. $200,000.
b. $160,000.
c. $100,000.
d. $80,000.

____   **7.** Espresso Company has insurance policies with General Insurance, Inc., and InsurCorp covering the risk of loss of Espresso's building in a fire. Each policy has a multiple insurance clause. If the building is partially destroyed in a fire, Espresso can collect from each insurer

a. each insurer's proportionate share of the loss to the total amount of insurance.
b. half of the amount of the loss.
c. the full amount of the loss.
d. nothing.

____   **8.** Biz Investo, Inc., has property insurance with Coverall Insurance, Inc. Biz Investo suffers a loss in a burglary, but the parties cannot agree on the amount of recovery. Under an appraisal and arbitration clause

a. Biz Investo can demand an appraisal that Coverall must pay.
b. Coverall can demand an appraisal that Biz Investo must accept.
c. each party can demand separate appraisals to be resolved by a third party.
d. the government sets the value of the loss which both parties must accept.

___ 9. Techniqua Corporation makes computers. To insure its products to cover injuries to consumers if the products prove defective, Techniqua should buy

    a. group insurance.
    b. liability insurance.
    c. major medical insurance.
    d. term life insurance.

___ 10. McCoo buys eNet, a company that provides Internet access, and takes out property insurance with InsCo to cover a loss of the equipment. Two years later, McCoo sells eNet. Six months after the sale, eNet's equipment is stolen. Under InsCo's policy, McCoo can recover

    a. InsCo's proportionate share of the loss to the total amount of insurance.
    b. the total amount of the insurance.
    c. the total amount of the loss.
    d. nothing.

SHORT ESSAY QUESTIONS

1. What is the concept of insurable interest, and what is its effect on insurance payments?

2. What are some of the types of insurance policies that businesses carry to protect themselves from risk?

GAMEPOINTS

(Answers at the Back of the Book)

1. You are playing the video game "Fire Fights," in which your character Frank the Firefighter speeds from one fiery inferno to another, answering calls to douse towering flames, rescue trapped inhabitants, and save burning structures from destruction. In one scenario, Bernie occupies an office building as a tenant under a ten-year lease and has a lender's interest in a warehouse owned by Cable Corp. In which of these buildings does Bernie have an insurable interest, and why?

2. Still playing "Fire Fights," your character Frank is called to a blaze in Pasta Café. Donatello, the owner, bought the café for $350,000 and insured it under a $300,000 fire insurance policy with an 80 percent coinsurance clause. The fire causes $60,000 in damage. Why is a coinsurance clause included in an insurance policy?

SPECIAL INFORMATION FOR CPA CANDIDATES

Insurance is part of the property section of the CPA examination. The most important points for your review are the warranties that an insured makes when applying for a policy, the workings of coinsurance clauses, and the concept of insurable interest. When must a party have an insurable interest to obtain insurance? Can more than one party have an insurable interest in, for example, the same property? (Yes.) Does a coinsurance clause apply in a case of total loss? Except for questions concerning insurable interest, the CPA exam does not cover automobile or life insurance.

Chapter 52
Wills and Trusts

WHAT THIS CHAPTER IS ABOUT

This chapter covers some of the laws governing the succession of property. (See also Chapter 47 on joint tenancy and Chapter 49 on insurance.) A person can direct the passage of property after death by will. If no valid will has been executed, state intestacy laws apply. A person can also transfer property with a trust.

CHAPTER OUTLINE

I. WILLS

A *will* is a declaration of how a person wants property disposed of after death; a formal instrument that must follow the statutory requirements to be effective.

A. TERMINOLOGY OF WILLS

A *testator* is a person who makes a will; a *probate court* oversees the administration of a will by an *executor* (appointed by the testator in the will) or by an *administrator* (appointed by the court).

B. LAWS GOVERNING WILLS

Vary from state to state. Some of the law includes the Uniform Probate Code (UPC), which codifies principles and procedures for the resolution of conflicts in settling estates and relaxes some of the requirements for a will.

C. GIFTS BY WILL

A gift of real estate by will is a *devise*; the recipient is a *devisee*. A gift of personal property is a *bequest* or *legacy*; a recipient is a *legatee*. Gifts can be specific, general, or residuary. If there are not enough assets to pay all general bequests, an *abatement* reduces the gifts.

D. REQUIREMENTS FOR A VALID WILL

1. A Testator Must Have Capacity

When a will is made, the testator must be of legal age (in most states, at least eighteen years old) and sound mind (a person can be adjudged mentally incompetent or have delusions about certain subjects and, during lucid moments, still be of sound mind).

2. A Testator Must Have Intent

A testator must (1) intend a document to be his or her will, (2) understand the property being distributed, and (3) remember the "natural objects of his or her bounty" (family members and others for whom the testator has affection).

3. A Will Must Be in Writing

An outside document can be incorporated by reference if it exists when the will is executed and is identified in the will. In a few states, an oral (nuncupative) will is valid to pass personal property below a certain value if made in the expectation of imminent death.

4. A Will Must Be Signed by the Testator

The testator must sign with the intent to validate the will; the signature need not be at the end.

421

5. A Will Must Be Witnessed
The number of witnesses, their qualifications, and the manner in which it must be done vary from state to state.

6. In a Few States, a Will Must Be "Published"
Publication is an oral declaration by the maker to the witnesses that the document they are about to sign is his or her will.

E. REVOCATION OF WILLS
A will is revocable, in whole or in part, by its maker any time during the maker's lifetime by physical act (intentionally obliterating or destroying a will, or directing someone else to do so); by a document (a codicil, a new will); or by operation of law (marriage, divorce, annulment, birth of child).

F. RIGHTS UNDER A WILL
A surviving spouse can renounce the amount given by will and elect a forced share, if the share is larger than the gift. In most states, a forced share is one-third of an estate or an amount equal to a spouse's share under intestacy laws (see below). A beneficiary can renounce his or her share.

G. PROBATE PROCEDURES
Probate: establish the validity of a will and administer the estate. The UPC includes rules and procedures for resolving conflicts in settling estates and relaxes some of the will requirements.

1. Informal Probate
In some states, cars, bank accounts, etc., can pass by filling out forms, or property can be transferred by affidavit. Most states allow heirs to distribute assets themselves after a will is admitted to probate.

2. Formal Probate
For large estates, a probate court supervises distribution.

3. Property Transfers outside the Probate Process
Will substitutes include living trusts (see below), life insurance, and joint tenancies.

II. INTESTACY LAWS
Statutes of descent and distribution regulate how property is distributed when a person dies without a valid will. The rules vary widely from state to state, but typically, the debts of the decedent are satisfied out of his or her estate, and the remaining assets pass to the surviving spouse and children.

A. SURVIVING SPOUSE AND CHILDREN

1. Legitimate Heirs
The spouse usually receives a share of the estate (such as one-half if there is a surviving child); the children receive the rest. If no children or grandchildren survive, the spouse succeeds to the entire estate. In most stares, any child born of a union that has the characteristics of a formal marriage is legitimate.

2. Illegitimate Children
Under the UPC, a child can inherit from a natural parent that has openly acknowledged the child [UPC 2–114]. Inheritance rights may differ from those of legitimate children, however.

B. ORDER OF DISTRIBUTION

1. Lineal Descendants
If there is no surviving spouse or child, grandchildren are next in line, then parents. Generally, title descends (to children, etc.) before it ascends (to parents, etc.).

2. Collateral Heirs
If there are no lineal descendants, brothers, sisters, nieces, nephews, aunts, and uncles inherit. If none survive, property goes to collateral heirs' next of kin (relatives by marriage are not considered kin).

3. Methods of Distribution
Per stirpes: a class or group of distributees take the share that their deceased parent would have been entitled to had that parent lived. *Per capita*: each person takes an equal share of the estate.

III. TRUSTS

Trusts are arrangements by which a grantor (settlor) transfers legal title to the trust property to a trustee, who administers the property as directed by the grantor for the benefit of the beneficiaries.

A. ESSENTIAL ELEMENTS

1. A designated beneficiary.
2. A designated trustee.
3. A fund sufficiently identified to enable title to pass to the trustee.
4. Actual delivery to the trustee with the intention of passing title.

B. EXPRESS TRUSTS

1. Living Trust (or *Inter Vivos* Trust)
Created by trust deed to exist during the settlor's lifetime. May be *revocable*, in which the grantor retains control over the property and must pay taxes on it, or *irrevocable*, in which the grantor gives up control and does not pay the taxes.

2. Testamentary Trust
Created by will to come into existence on the settlor's death (if the will is invalid, the trust is invalid). If not named in the will, a trustee is appointed by a court. Trustee's actions are subject to judicial approval.

3. Charitable Trust
Designed to benefit a segment of the public or the public in general, usually for charitable, educational, religious, or scientific purposes. Identities of the beneficiaries are uncertain.

4. Spendthrift Trust
Prevents a beneficiary's transfer of his or her right to future payments of income or capital by expressly placing restraints on the alienation of trust funds.

5. Totten Trust
Created when one person deposits money in his or her own name as trustee. Revocable at will until the depositor dies or completes the gift (for example, by delivery of the funds to the beneficiary).

C. IMPLIED TRUSTS

1. Constructive Trust
A constructive trust is an equitable remedy that enables plaintiffs to recover property (and sometimes damages) from defendants who would otherwise be unjustly enriched. A court declares the legal owner of the property to be a trustee for parties entitled to the benefit of the property.

2. Resulting Trust
A resulting trust arises when the conduct of the parties raise an inference that the party holding legal title to the property does so for the benefit of another.

D. THE TRUSTEE

Anyone capable of holding title to, and dealing in, property can be a trustee.

1. Trustee's Duties

Preserve the trust property; make the trust property productive; and if required by the terms of the trust agreement, pay income to the beneficiaries.

a. General Duties

Honesty, good faith, and prudence in administering the trust for the exclusive interest of the beneficiary; invest and manage trust assets as a prudent investor would manage his or her assets.

b. Specific Duties

1) Keep Accurate Accounts of the Trust's Administration

Furnish complete information to the beneficiary. Keep trust assets separate from his or her assets. Pay to an income beneficiary the net income of the trust at reasonable intervals.

2) Invest the Trust Property

Distribute the risk of loss from investments by diversification and dispose of assets that do not represent prudent investments.

2. Trustee's Powers

Whatever the settlor prescribes. State law applies only to the extent that it does not conflict with the terms of the trust.

a. If State Law Applies

May restrict the investment of trust funds, confining trustees to investments in conservative debt securities.

b. Discretion to Distribute the Principal or Invest the Income

Subject to trust purposes, a trustee may make adjustments in annual distributions to provide the beneficiary with predictable income.

3. Allocations between Principal and Income

Ordinary receipts and expenses (rent, royalties) are chargeable to income; extraordinary receipts and expenses (proceeds from the sale of property, stock dividends) are allocated to principal.

E. TRUST TERMINATION

Typically, a trust instrument specifies a termination date. If the trust's purpose is fulfilled before that date, a court may order the trust's termination. If no date is specified, a trust terminates when its purpose is fulfilled (or becomes impossible or illegal).

IV. OTHER ESTATE-PLANNING ISSUES

In anticipation of becoming incapacitated or otherwise unable to act, persons sometimes plan for others to manage their affairs.

A. POWER OF ATTORNEY

This authorizes a person to act on another's behalf, sometimes for limited purposes (see Chapter 32).

1. Durarble Power of Attorney

Authorizes a person to act on behalf of an incompetent person when he or she becomes incapacitated.

2. Health-Care Power of Attorney
Designates a person to choose medical treatment for a person who is unable to make such a choice.

B. LIVING WILL
This is an advance health directive that designates whether or not a person wants certain life-saving procedures to be taken if they will not result in a reasonable quality of life.

TRUE-FALSE QUESTIONS

(Answers at the Back of the Book)

____ 1. A will is revocable only after the testator's death.

____ 2. The testator generally must sign a will.

____ 3. If a person dies without a will, all of his or her property automatically passes to the state.

____ 4. An *inter vivos* trust is a trust created by a grantor during his or her lifetime.

____ 5. A testamentary trust is created by will to begin on the settlor's death.

____ 6. A will can only distribute property.

____ 7. If a person marries *after* executing a will, the spouse gets nothing on the person's death.

____ 8. A beneficiary can renounce his or her share of property under a will.

____ 9. A trustee has a duty to dispose of trust assets that do not represent prudent investments.

____ 10. A trust terminates on the trustee's death.

FILL-IN QUESTIONS

(Answers at the Back of the Book)

When a person dies, a personal representative settles the decedent's affairs. A personal representative named in a will is an _____ (administrator/executor). A personal representative appointed by a court for a decedent who dies without a will, who fails to name a personal representative in a will, who names a personal representative lacking the capacity to serve, or who writes a will that the court refuses to admit to probate is an _____ (administrator/executor).

MULTIPLE-CHOICE QUESTIONS

(Answers at the Back of the Book)

____ 1. Serge wants Tonio and Uldric, his sons, to get the benefit of Serge's farm when he dies. Serge can provide for them to get the farm's income, under another party's management, by setting up

a. a constructive trust.
b. an interstate trust.
c. a resulting trust.
d. a testamentary trust.

____ 2. **Based on a Sample CPA Exam Question.** Elaine dies without a will, but is survived by her brother Fester, her child Gavril, and her parents. The party with the first priority to receive Elaine's estate is

    a. her brother Fester.
    b. her child Gavril.
    c. her parents.
    d. the state.

____ 3. Hong executes a will that leaves all of her property to Ivan. Two years later, Hong executes a will that leaves all of her property to Jem. The second will does not expressly revoke the first will. Hong dies. The property passes to

    a. Ivan, because he was given the property in the first will.
    b. Ivan, because the second will did not expressly revoke the first will.
    c. Jem, because the first will was revoked by the second will.
    d. Jem, because two years separated the execution of the wills.

____ 4. Kelly dies intestate, survived by Lisa, her mother; Mike, her spouse; Nick and Owen, their sons; and Pam, the daughter of Ruth, their daughter, who predeceased her mother. Under intestacy laws

    a. Lisa and Mike receive equal portions of Kelly's estate.
    b. Mike receives all of Kelly's estate.
    c. Mike receives one-third of Kelly's estate, and Nick, Owen, and Pam receive equal portions of the rest.
    d. Nick and Owen receive half of Kelly's estate, and Mike receives the rest.

____ 5. Clark's will provides for specific items of property to be given to certain individuals, including employees of his business. The will also provides for certain sums of money to be given to his daughters, Delilah and Eden. Because Clark's assets are insufficient to pay in full all of the bequests

    a. all of the property must be sold and the proceeds distributed to the heirs.
    b. Delilah and Eden get nothing.
    c. the employees, who are not in a blood relationship with Clark, get nothing.
    d. the gifts to Delilah and Eden will be reduced proportionately.

____ 6. Gregor's will provides, "I leave all my computer equipment to my good friend, Hume." When Gregor dies, the personal representative gives Hume the computer equipment. Hume is

    a. a devisee.
    b. a legatee.
    c. a residuary.
    d. none of the choices.

____ 7. Elin believes that probate is too time-consuming and costly, and wants her assets to pass to her heirs as quickly and inexpensively as possible. To avoid probate most successfully, Elin can

    a. create a testamentary trust.
    b. draft a will and not sign it.
    c. have her heirs decide among themselves who will get what on her death.
    d. hold the assets in joint tenancy.

_____ 8. Don is the trustee of a testamentary trust. The trust grants Don discretion to invest the assets. In most states, this means that Don

    a. is entitled to invest the assets as he sees fit.
    b. must confine trust investments to conservative securities.
    c. must invest according to the prudent person rule.
    d. must invest as aggressively as possible.

_____ 9. Kim is the trustee of a testamentary trust. Ordinary trust expenses, such as the rent for Kim's office, are chargeable to

    a. Kim.
    b. the court that oversees Kim's administration.
    c. trust income.
    d. trust principal.

_____ 10. Serena is Thom's adult daughter. Thom decides that he wants Serena to act on his behalf if he becomes incapacitated. Thom should arrange for Serena to have

    a. a living trust.
    b. a durable power of attorney.
    c. a power of trustee.
    d. a Totten trust.

SHORT ESSAY QUESTIONS

1. What requirements must be satisfied to create a valid will?

2. In what ways may a will be revoked?

GAMEPOINTS

(Answers at the Back of the Book)

1. In the video game "Ancient Warriors," your character combats evildoers from the past. Each warrior is more difficult to overcome than its predecessors. By skillfully using the weapons and attributes that accrue to your character after a victory, however, you have been able to defeat each combatant. Then Golgotha and two cohorts emerge from the shadows. Quickly, your character grabs a scrap of paper, writes what appears to be a will, signs it, and has Golgotha and the cohorts sign it as witnesses. If this were not in a video game, would it be a valid will? Discuss.

2. You are playing the video game "Tricks 'n Treats," in which you score by pinpointing the chicanery of opponents, who would otherwise take advantage of your ignorance to divest you and others of property. The scenarios are based in both real-life and fanciful situations. In one segment, you have been designated the beneficiary of a trust. The property consists of a well-managed farm. Your opponent Dreadful claims, however, that because the farm was conveyed to the trustee and not to you, the trust is not valid. You disagree, of course. Who's correct and why?

SPECIAL INFORMATION FOR CPA CANDIDATES

The CPA examination has not traditionally asked questions about the requirements or validity of a will. The exam has covered, however, some details of trust administration, particularly allocations between principal and income, as explained in this chapter, and distributions.

Trusts have also been tested in property questions on the exam.

CUMULATIVE HYPOTHETICAL PROBLEM
FOR UNIT TEN—INCLUDING CHAPTERS 49–52

(Answers at the Back of the Book)

As joint tenants, Dirk and Elena own twenty acres of land, on which there is a warehouse surrounded by a fence.

____ 1. In determining whether the fence is a fixture, the most important factor is

    a. the adaptability of the fence to the land.
    b. the intent of Dirk and Elena.
    c. the manner in which the fence is attached to the land.
    d. the value of the fence.

____ 2. Dirk wants to sell the land and the warehouse. He executes and delivers a deed to Fuller. Elena will

    a. own all of the land and the warehouse because she did not sign the deed.
    b. own exactly twenty acres and half a warehouse.
    c. retain a 1/2 undivided interest in the property.
    d. share ownership of the property with Fuller as a joint tenant.

____ 3. For the deed between Dirk and Fuller to be effective, one of the conditions is that the deed must

    a. be delivered by Dirk with the intent to transfer title.
    b. be recorded within certain statutory time limits.
    c. include the sale price.
    d. include the signatures of both Dirk and Fuller.

____ 4. On the warehouse, the owners obtain a $300,000 fire insurance policy from Garden Variety Insurance Company that includes an 80 percent coinsurance clause. At the time, the warehouse is valued at $400,000. When the warehouse is valued at $500,000, it sustains fire damage of $60,000. Recovery under the policy is

    a. $45,000.
    b. $60,000.
    c. $75,000.
    d. $300,000.

____ 5. Hermes Sales, Inc., rents the warehouse from the owners, under a two-year lease that requires Hermes to pay the property taxes. At the start of the second year, Hermes agrees with Isis Transport to allow it to occupy the warehouse and pay rent to Hermes. No one pays the property taxes for the second year. In a suit to collect, the owners would most likely

    a. lose and have to pay the taxes themselves.
    b. prevail against Hermes because the agreement with Isis was a sublease.
    c. prevail against Hermes and Isis because they are jointly and severally liable.
    d. prevail against Isis because the lease was assigned to Isis.

QUESTIONS ON THE FOCUS ON ETHICS FOR UNIT TEN— PROPERTY AND ITS PROTECTION

(Answers at the Back of the Book)

____ 1. Gamma Company buys forty acres of land to build a corporate complex. After construction begins, the county zones the surrounding, undeveloped area for a nature preserve, in which it includes 75 percent of Gamma's land. The county owes Gamma

   a. just compensation.
   b. land of equivalent value.
   c. private use of the preserve.
   d. nothing.

____ 2. Dale finds a laptop computer. The laptop's true owner is Flo. As a finder, Dale can acquire good title to the laptop against

   a. everyone except Flo.
   b. everyone including Flo.
   c. Flo but no one else.
   d. no one.

____ 3. Ross gives his silver trophies to United Awards, Inc., to hold temporarily. While in United's possession, the trophies are destroyed. United may be liable for the loss if this was a bailment for

   a. no one's benefit.
   b. Ross's sole benefit.
   c. United's sole benefit.
   d. the mutual benefit of both parties.

Business Law for the Uniform CPA Examination

THE UNIFORM CPA EXAMINATION

To obtain a Certified Public Accountant (CPA) certificate or license, accountants must meet certain requirements. State boards of accountancy set these requirements. A general summary of CPA licensure requirements by jurisdiction can be found on the Web site of the National Association of State Boards of Accountancy (NASBA) at www.nasba.org. In every state, one of the requirements is passing the Uniform CPA Examination. The Board of Examiners of the American Institute of Certified Public Accountants (AICPA) is responsible for the preparation and advisory grading of the Uniform CPA Examination. The examination is given in "testing windows" that consist of the first two months of each calendar quarter:

- January 1 through February 28
- April 1 through May 31
- July 1 through August 31
- October 1 through November 30

The test contains four sections: auditing and attestation, business environment and concepts, financial accounting and reporting, and regulation.

The business environment and concepts portion of the exam is allotted two and a half hours, and the regulation portion is given three hours. The format consists chiefly of questions in a multiple-choice format in each of these portions and two additionally case study simulations in the regulation portion. The multiple-choice questions may be similar to some of the multiple-choice questions in this *Study Guide*. They are given in a series of "testlets," which comprise three groups that contain an equal number of between twenty-four and thirty questions each.

Case study simulations test candidates' knowledge of accounting knowledge and skills in real-life work-related situations. Each simulation is expected to take a candidate thirty minutes to fifty minutes to answer, depending on the subject, and is intended to complement the multiple-choice questions. Each case study includes instructions for a writing skills exercise.

Distinctions about subject matter are not always clear-cut. That is, there may be some overlap of subjects within the four sections of the examination and within the seven areas of the business law section of the examination. For instance, the factual situation in a business law question may require knowledge of accounting or auditing, and the answers may involve a response based in part on this knowledge.

THE SUBJECT MATTER OF THE UNIFORM CPA EXAMINATION

The structure of business organizations is covered in the business environment and concepts portion of the test. Knowledge of business law, including federal taxation, and ethics and professional responsibility is tested in the regulation portion of the examination. Detailed information about the subject matter of the examination and the approximate percentage of the examination devoted to each of the broad topics is provided in specifications adopted by the Board of Examiners of the AICPA. The regulation section tests the candidates' knowledge of the legal implications of business transactions, particularly as they relate to accounting and auditing, and candidates' knowledge of the CPA's professional responsibilities to the public and the profession.

As outlined by the Board of Examiners of the AICPA, the regulation portion includes a CPA's professional and legal responsibilities, agency, contracts, debtor-creditor relationships, government regulation of business, the Uniform Commercial Code, and federal taxation of property, income, business organizations, and trusts.   The subjects on the examination normally are covered in standard textbooks on business law, auditing, taxation, and accounting, and in other sources, such as the *AICPA Professional Standards Code of Professional Conduct and Bylaws*.   Candidates are expected to recognize the existence of legal implications and the applicable basic legal principles, and they are usually asked to indicate the probable result of the application of such basic principles.

The regulation section is chiefly conceptual in nature and is broad in scope, as determined by the Board of Examiners of the AICPA.   The examination is not intended to test competence to practice law or expertise in legal matters, but is intended to determine that the candidates' knowledge is sufficient (1) to recognize relevant legal issues, (2) to recognize the legal implications of business situations, (3) to apply the underlying principles of law to accounting and auditing situations, and (4) to seek legal counsel or recommend that it be sought.

The regulation section deals with federal and widely adopted uniform laws.   If there is no federal or applicable uniform law on a subject, the questions ask for knowledge of the majority rules.   Federal tax elements may be covered in the overall context of a question. In responding to the case study simulations in the examination, candidates will use database that include portions of the federal tax code and other specific documents. A database will include all of an item that is needed to complete the simulation. These databases are update annually.

Writing skills are assessed in exercises included in the case study simulations.   Candidates are asked to read a situation description for which they are expected to write an appropriate document. The instructions indicate the form of the document, which may be a memo or a letter. The response is expected to provide the correct information in writing that is clear, complete, and professional. For more information about the required writing skills and the examination's subject matter, go to www.cpa-exam.org.

STUDY TIP Effective Writing Skills

Generally, in responding to the writing skills questions in the case study simulations on the Uniform CPA Examination, responses should be organized in short paragraphs, each limited to the explanation of a single main point, with short sentences.   Short sentences and simple wording also demonstrate the ability to write concisely—that is, the ability to express an important point in as few words as possible.   Clarity involves using words of precise meaning in well-constructed sentences.   These words include terms that are appropriate for the subject being tested.   Correct grammar—including punctuation, capitalization, spelling, and word usage—enhance clarity. In responding to a question, do not broadly discuss general subject matter.   Address a question directly.

THE ETHICS, BUSINESS LAW, AND BUSINESS STRUCTURE CONTENT OF THE EXAMINATION

The specific content of the related portions of the Uniform CPA Examination is as follows:[1]

AUDITING AND ATTESTATION

VI. Professional Responsibilities (16 to 20 percent[2])

---

[1] This and other information pertaining to the CPA examination is available through the Web site of the American Institute of Certified Public Accountants (AICPA) at **www.aicpa.org**.

    A. Ethics and Independence
    B. Other Professional Responsibilities

REGULATION

I. Ethics, Professional, and Legal Responsibilities (15 to 19 percent)

    A. Ethics and Responsibilities in Tax Practice
    B. Licensing and Disciplinary Systems
    C. Legal Duties and Responsibilities

        1. Common Law Duties and Liability to Clients and Third Parties
        2. Federal Statutory Liability
        3. Privileged Communications, Confidentiality, and Privacy Acts

II. Business Law (17 to 21 percent)

    A. Agency

        1. Formation and Termination
        2. Authority of Agents and Principals
        3. Duties and Liabilities of Agents and Principals

    B. Contracts

        1. Formation
        2. Performance
        3. Third-Party Assignments
        4. Discharge, Breach, and Remedies

    C. Uniform Commercial Code

        1. Sales Contracts
        2. Negotiable Instruments
        3. Secured Transactions
        4. Documents of Title and Title Transfer

    D. Debtor-Creditor Relationships

        1. Rights, Duties, and Liabilities of Debtors, Creditors, and Guarantors
        2. Bankruptcy and Insolvency

    E. Government Regulation of Business

        1. Federal Securities Regulation
        2. Other Federal Laws and Regulations (Antitrust, Copyright, Patents, Money-Laundering, Labor, Employment, and ERISA)

    F. Business Structure (Selection of Business Entity)

        1. Advantages, Disadvantages, Implications, and Constraints
        2. Formation, Operation, and Termination
        3. Financial Structure, Capitalization, Profit and Loss Allocation, and Distributions
        4. Rights, Duties, Legal Obligations and Authority of Owners and Management

---

[2] These topics reflect the Content Specification Outlines that became effective in January 2011.

BUSINESS ENVIRONMENT AND CONCEPTS

    I.   Corporate Governance (16 to 20 percent)

        A.   Rights, Duties, Responsibilities, and Authority of the Board of Directors, Officers, and Other Employees

        B.   Control Environment

            1.   Tone at the Top—Establishing Control Environment
            2.   Monitoring Control Effectiveness
            3.   Change Control Process

Cross References:
Business Law and Related Subjects in the Uniform CPA Examination—
Chapters in *Business Law, Twelfth Edition*

SUBJECTS	CHAPTERS
PROFESSIONAL RESPONSIBILITIES	
A. Ethics and Independence	5, 48
B. Other Professional Responsibilities	5, 48
ETHICS, PROFESSIONAL, AND LEGAL RESPONSIBILITIES	
A. Ethics and Responsibilities in Tax Practice	5, 48
B. Licensing and Disciplinary Systems	5, 48
C. Legal Duties and Responsibilities	5, 48
1. Common Law Duties and Liability to Clients and Third Parties	5, 48
2. Federal Statutory Liability	5, 48
3. Privileged Communications, Confidentiality, and Privacy Acts	5, 48
BUSINESS LAW	
A. Agency	
1. Formation and Termination	32, 33
2. Authority of Agents and Principals	32, 33
3. Duties and Liabilities of Agents and Principals	32, 33
B. Contracts	
1. Formation	10, 11, 12, 13, 14, 15, 43
2. Performance	17
3. Third-Party Assignments	16
4. Discharge, Breach, and Remedies	17, 18
C. Uniform Commercial Code	
1. Sales Contracts	19, 20, 21, 22
2. Negotiable Instruments	24, 25, 26, 27
3. Secured Transactions	29
4. Documents of Title and Title Transfer	49

D. Debtor-Creditor Relationships

    1. Rights, Duties, and Liabilities of Debtors, Creditors, and
        Guarantors   28, 31, 43
    2. Bankruptcy and Insolvency   30

E. Government Regulation of Business

    1. Federal Securities Regulation   42, 43
    2. Other Federal Laws and Regulations (Antitrust, Copyright,
        Patents, Money-Laundering, Labor, Employment, and ERISA)   8, 9, 34, 47

F. Business Structure (Selection of Business Entity)

    1. Advantages, Disadvantages, Implications, and Constraints   36, 37, 38, 39, 40, 41, 42, 43,
                                                       48
    2. Formation, Operation, and Termination   36, 37, 38, 39, 40, 42, 43
    3. Financial Structure, Capitalization, Profit and Loss Allocation,
        and Distributions   39, 42, 43
    4. Rights, Duties, Legal Obligations and Authority of Owners and
        Management   37, 38, 39, 40, 41, 42, 43

CORPORATE GOVERNANCE

A. Rights, Duties, Responsibilities, and Authority of the Board of
    Directors, Officers, and Other Employees   37, 38, 39, 40, 41, 42, 43,
                                             48

B. Control Environment

    1. Tone at the Top—Establishing Control Environment   5, 48
    2. Monitoring Control Effectiveness   5, 48
    3. Change Control Process   5, 48

PREPARATION FOR THE EXAMINATION

Clearly, the best preparation for the examination is a comprehensive review of the examination content. Brief content and skill specification outlines are provided at www.cpa-exam.org and indicate the content and skill areas covered by each portion of the examination.

Another excellent preparation step is to review the sample tests, including the multiple-choice questions and simulations available at the above-cited Web site. By working through these questions, candidates also become familiar with the software used to take the examination.

It is also advisable to view the tutorial provided at the same Web site to see the features of the software and to gain an understanding of the general design and operation of the examination. The tutorial demonstrates the functionality of question types, tools, resources, and navigation found in the Uniform CPA Examination. The software is unique. Candidates will find it most useful to know how to operate the online "Calculator" and other features.

At the Web site, candidates can also find "Frequently Asked Questions" and more information under the topic "Become a CPA/ For Candidates."

A current list of test centers can be found at www.prometric.com/cpa. Test sessions can also be scheduled through this Web site, which is of course available twenty-four hours a day, seven days a week. It may be best to arrange a session at least forty-five days before a preferred test date.

Finally, students who plan to sit for any of the Uniform CPA Examinations should obtain copies of *Uniform CPA Examination Candidate Bulletin* issued by the AICPA.[3]

---

[3] Copies may be viewed at **www.aicpa.org** or obtained by writing to:

American Institute of Certified Public Accountants, Inc.
1211 Avenue of the Americas
New York, New York 10036-8775

Answers

Chapter 1

True-False Questions

1. T
2. F. Legal positivists believe that there can be no higher law that a nation's positive law (the law created by a particular society at a particular point in time). The belief that law should reflect universal moral and ethical principles that are part of human nature is part of the natural law tradition.
3. T
4. T
5. T
6. F. With respect to federal statutes, the U.S. Constitution is the supreme law of the land. A federal statute the conflicts with the U.S. Constitution may be struck as unconstitutional.
7. F. The National Conference of Commissioners on Uniform State Laws drafted the Uniform Commercial Code (and other uniform laws and model codes) and proposed it for adoption by the states.
8. F. This is the definition of civil law. Criminal law relates to wrongs against society as a whole and for which society has established sanctions.
9. T
10. F. A citation may contain the names of the parties, the year in which the case was decided, and the volume and page numbers of a reporter in which the opinion may be found, but it does not include the name of the judge who decided the case.

Fill-in Questions

with similar facts; precedent; permits a predictable

Multiple-Choice Questions

1. D. Legal positivists believe that there can be no higher law than the written law of a given society at a particular time. They do not believe in "natural rights."
2. B. The use of precedent—the doctrine of *stare decisis*—permits a predictable, relatively quick, and fair resolution of cases. Under this doctrine, a court must adhere to principles of law established by higher courts.
3. D. The doctrine of *stare decisis* attempts to harmonize the results in cases with similar facts. When the facts are sufficiently similar, the same rule is applied. Cases with identical facts could serve as binding authority, but it is more practical

A-1

to expect to find cases with facts that are not identical but similar—as similar as possible.

4.   A. An order to do or refrain from a certain act is an injunction. An order to perform as promised is a decree for specific performance. These remedies, as well as rescission, are equitable remedies. An award of damages is a remedy at law.

5.   B. Equity and law provide different remedies, and at one time, most courts could grant only one type. Today, most states do not maintain separate courts of law and equity, and a judge may grant either or both forms of relief. Equitable relief is generally granted, however, only if damages (the legal remedy) is inadequate.

6.   C. The U.S. Constitution is the supreme law of the land. Any state or federal law or court decision in conflict with the Constitution is unenforceable and will be struck. Similarly, provisions in a state constitution take precedence over the state's statutes, rules, and court decisions.

7.   B. In establishing case law, or common law, the courts interpret and apply state and federal constitutions, rules, and statutes. Case law applies in areas that statutes or rules do not cover. Federal law applies to all states, and preempts state law in many areas.

8.   A. Law that defines, describes, regulates, or creates rights or duties is substantive la w. Law that establishes methods for enforcing rights established by substantive law is procedural law. Criminal law governs wrongs committed against society for which society demands redress.

9.   B. In reasoning by analogy, a judge compares the facts in one case to the facts in another case and to the extent that the facts are similar, applies the same legal principle. If the facts can be distinguished, different legal rules may apply. In either case, a judge will ordinarily state his or her reasons for applying a certain principle and arriving at a certain conclusion.

10.   C. A concurring opinion makes or emphasizes a point different from those made or emphasized in the majority's opinion. An opinion written for the entire court is a unanimous opinion. An opinion that outlines only the majority's views is a majority opinion. A separate opinion that does not agree with the majority's decision is a dissenting opinion.

GamePoints

1.   A breach of contract falls, of course, in the area of the law of contracts. Contract law is a part of civil law, in contrast to criminal law. Civil law spells out duties that exist between persons. The remedies available for a breach of contract include money damages, which is the usual remedy at law. If this remedy is unavailable or inadequate, the breaching party might be ordered to perform as promised. Or the contract might be cancelled and the parties returned to the positions they held before the contract's formation.

2.   Sources of law that might afford an opportunity for relief for a breach of contract or warranty, as this problem poses, include statutory law. In particular, the Uniform Commercial Code, which provides a uniform, yet flexible, set of rules governing commercial transactions, is most likely to be brought to bear on this issue. Administrative law is also a possibility, because regulations may affect every aspect of a business operation, including the way a firm makes and sells its products.

Chapter 2

True-False Questions

1.   T

2.   T

3.   F. The decisions of a state's highest court on all questions of state law are final. The United States Supreme Court can overrule only those state court decisions that involve questions of federal law.

4.   T

5.   F. Most lawsuits—as many as 95 percent—are dismissed or settled before they go to trial. Courts encourage alternative dispute resolution (ADR) and sometimes order parties to submit to ADR, particularly mediation, before allowing their suits to come to trial.

6.   F. In mediation, a mediator assists the parties in reaching an agreement, but not by deciding the dispute. The mediator emphasizes points of agreement, helps the parties evaluate their positions, and proposes solutions.

7.   F. If an arbitration agreement covers the subject matter of a dispute, a party to the agreement can be compelled to arbitrate the dispute. A court would order the arbitration without ruling on the basic controversy.

8.   F. The jury verdict after a summary jury trial (SJT) is not binding. SJT is a form of alternative dispute resolution in which the parties' attorneys present their cases to a jury, but no witnesses are called, and the verdict is advisory only.

9.   F. Negotiation typically does not involve a third party. The major difference between negotiation and mediation is that mediation does involve the presence of a third party—a mediator—who assists the parties in reaching an agreement and who often suggests solutions towards that end.

10. T

Fill-in Questions

trial; reviewing; factual issues; the law to the facts; of law but not of fact

Multiple-Choice Questions

1.   A. On a "sliding scale" test, a court's exercise of personal jurisdiction depends on the amount of business that an individual or firm transacts over the Internet. Jurisdiction is most likely proper when there is substantial business, most likely improper when a Web site is no more than an ad, and may or may not be appropriate when there is some interactivity. "Any" interactivity with "any resident" of a state would likely not be enough, however.

2.   D. Mediation is becoming the most popular form of ADR, with participants reporting high rates of satisfaction with the results. The advantages of mediation include lower cost than either arbitration or traditional litigation, the speed with which a dispute can be resolved compared to arbitration or litigation, and resolutions that benefit both sides to a dispute.

3.   A. As noted above, a corporation is subject to the jurisdiction of the courts in any state in which it is incorporated, in which it has its main office, or in which it does business. The court may be able to exercise personal jurisdiction or *in rem* jurisdiction, or the court may reach a defendant corporation with a long arm statute. In the right circumstances, this firm might also be involved in a suit in a federal court, if the requirements for federal jurisdiction are met: a federal question is involved, or there is diversity of citizenship and the amount in controversy is $75,000 or more.

4.   D. An appeals court examines the record of a case, looking mostly at questions of law for errors by the court below. If it determines that a retrial is necessary, the case is sent back to the lower court. For this reason, an appellant's best ground for an appeal focuses on the law that applied to the issues in the case, not questions concerning the credibility of the evidence or other findings of fact.

5.   D. The United States Supreme Court is not required to hear any case. The Court has jurisdiction over any case decided by any of the federal courts of appeals and appellate authority over cases decided by the states' highest courts if the latter involve questions of federal law. But the Court's exercise of its jurisdiction is discretionary, not mandatory.

6.   D. Negotiation is an informal means of dispute resolution. Generally, unlike mediation and arbitration, no third party is involved in resolving the dispute. In those two forms, a third party may render a binding or nonbinding decision. Arbitration is a more formal process than mediation or negotiation. Litigation involves a third party—a judge—who renders a legally binding decision.

7.   D. Neither the amount involved nor the parties' satisfaction is relevant. An arbitrator's award will be set aside if it violates pubic policy. Other grounds on which an award may be set aside arise from the arbitrator's conduct—for example, if his or her bad faith substantially prejudices the rights of one of the parties, or if he or she decides issues that the parties did not agree to submit to arbitration.

8.   C. In a summary jury trial, the jury's verdict is advisory, not binding as it would otherwise be in a court trial. In a mini-trial, the attorneys argue a case and a third party renders an opinion, but the opinion discusses how a court would decide the dispute. Early neutral case negotiation is what its name suggests, involving a third party who evaluates the disputing parties' positions.

9.   C. In the suit in this question, the court can exercise *in rem* jurisdiction. A court can exercise jurisdiction over property located within its boundaries. A corporation is also subject to the jurisdiction of the courts in any state in which it is incorporated, in which it has its main office, or in which it does business.

10.   A. Every state has at least one court of appeals, which may be an intermediate appellate court or the state's highest court. If a federal or constitutional issue is involved, the case may ultimately be appealed to the United States Supreme Court.

GamePoints

1.   You could file a suit against your opponent in this problem in a trial court of general jurisdiction in either the state of your residence or the state of the defendant's home. Because there appears to be diversity of citizenship in the situation set out here, and the amount in controversy could conceivably exceed the jurisdictional amount, a suit might alternatively be filed in a federal district court, which is the equivalent of a state trial court of general jurisdiction.

2.   Even if you meet the requirements for the United States Supreme Court to exercise jurisdiction in your case—there is a federal question at issue, or a federal court of appeals has reviewed your case, or both—the Supreme Court can still refuse to hear your appeal. There is no absolute right of appeal to the nation's highest Court. A party may ask the Court to issue a writ of *certiorari* (this is an order to a lower court to send the Court the record of the case for review), but the Court may deny the request.

Chapter 3

True-False Questions

1. F. Pleadings inform each party of the other's claims and specify the issues. Pleadings consist of a complaint and an answer, not a motion to dismiss.
2. F. In ruling on a motion for summary judgment, a court can consider evidence outside the pleadings, such as answers to interrogatories.
3. T
4. T
5. T
6. F. A losing party may appeal an adverse judgment to a higher court, but the party in whose favor the judgment was issued may also appeal if, for example, he or she is awarded less than sought in the suit.
7. F. The process that involves obtaining access to documents and other materials in the hands of an opposing party prior to trial is the *discovery* process.
8. T
9. F. The plaintiff in a civil case must prove a case by a preponderance of the evidence (the claim is more likely to be true than the defendant's). Some claims (such as fraud) must be proved by clear and convincing evidence (the truth of the claim is highly probable). The standard in a criminal trial is *beyond a reasonable doubt*.
10. T

Fill-in Questions

to dismiss; for judgment on the pleadings; summary judgment

Multiple-Choice Questions

1. D. The considerations for whether to take a case to court involve primarily time and money. Even settling out of court for less than you are owed may be wise in terms of future expenses, time waiting, time lost, and frustration.
2. D. A complaint contains a statement alleging jurisdictional facts, a statement of facts entitling the complainant to relief, and a statement asking for a specific remedy. It is filed with the court that has proper jurisdiction and venue. A copy of the complaint is served, with a summons, on the defendant named in the complaint.
3. A. This is part of discovery. Discovery saves time, and the trend is toward more, not less, discovery. Discovery is limited, however, to relevant materials. A party cannot obtain access to such data as another's trade secrets or, in testimony, an admission concerning unrelated matters. A party is not entitled to any privileged material either.
4. C. A defendant may file a motion to dismiss if he or she is not properly served with the complaint, if the court lacks personal or subject matter jurisdiction, if the venue is improper, if the complaint does not state a claim for which relief can be granted, or other specific reasons.
5. C. If a defendant's motion to dismiss is denied, the defendant must then file an answer, or another appropriate response, or a default judgment will be entered against him or her. Of course, the defendant is given more time to file this response. If the motion is granted, the plaintiff is given more time to file an amended complaint.
6. A. An important part of the discovery process is a deposition, which is sworn testimony. Interrogatories are a series of written questions for which written answers are prepared and signed under oath by the plaintiff or defendant. A pretrial conference involves the plaintiff, the defendant, their attorneys, and judge.
7. A. An appeals court examines the record of a case, looking mostly at questions of law for errors by the court below. If it determines that a retrial is necessary, the case is sent back to the lower court. For this reason, an appellant's best ground for an appeal focuses on the law that applied to the issues in the case, not questions concerning the credibility of the evidence.
8. D. After a plaintiff calls and questions the first witness on direct examination, the defendant questions the witness on cross-examination. The plaintiff may then question the witness again (redirect examination), and the defendant may follow (recross-examination). Then the plaintiff's other witnesses are called, and the defendant presents his or her case.
9. C. After a verdict, the losing party can move for a new trial or for a judgment notwithstanding the verdict. If these motions are denied, he or she can appeal.
10. C. For obvious reasons, a losing party may wish to appeal a judgment. A winning party has the same right to appeal if he or she is dissatisfied with the relief granted.

GamePoints

1. The first option might be to file a motion to set aside the verdict and hold a new trial. This motion will be granted if the judge is convinced, after examining the evidence, that the jury was in error (assuming the trial involved a jury) but does not think it appropriate to issue a judgment for your side. A second option would be to appeal the trial court's judgment, including a denial of the motion for a new trial, to the appropriate court of appeals. An appellate court is most likely to review the case for errors in law, not fact. In any case, the appellate court will not hear new evidence.

2. Your avatar can ask the court to order a sheriff to seize property owned by your corporate nemesis and hold it until the firm pays the judgment. If Canis fails to pay, the property can be sold at a public auction and the proceeds given to your avatar, or the property can be transferred to your avatar in lieu of payment.

Chapter 4

True-False Questions

1. F. A federal form of government is one in which separate states form a union and divide sovereign power between themselves and a central authority. The United States has a federal form of government.
2. F. The president does not have this power. Under the doctrine of judicial review, however, the courts can hold acts of Congress and of the executive branch unconstitutional.
3. T
4. T
5. F. Under the supremacy clause, when there is a direct conflict between a federal law and a state law, the federal law takes precedence over the state law, and the state law is rendered invalid.
6. T
7. F. The protections in the Bill of Rights limit the power of the federal government. Most of these protections also apply to the states through the due process clause of the Fourteenth Amendment.
8. F. Commercial speech (advertising) can be restricted as long as the restriction (1) seeks to implement a substantial government interest, (2) directly advances that interest, and (3) goes no further than necessary to accomplish its objective.
9. F. Due process relates to the limits that the law places on the liberty of *everyone*. Equal protection relates to the limits that the law places on only *some people*.
10. T

Fill-in Questions

states; states; state

Multiple-Choice Questions

1. D. Under Articles I, II, and III of the U.S. Constitution, the legislative branch makes the law, the judicial branch interprets the law, and the executive branch enforces the law. There is no separate "administrative branch."
2. A. Under the commerce clause, Congress has the power to regulate every commercial enterprise in the United States. Recently, the United States Supreme Court has struck down federal laws, to limit this power somewhat, in areas that have "nothing to do with commerce," including noneconomic, criminal conduct.
3. A. State statutes that impinge on interstate commerce are not always struck down, nor are they always upheld. A court will balance a state's interest in regulating a certain matter against the burden that the statute places on interstate commerce. If the statute does not substantially interfere, it will not be held in violation of the commerce clause.
4. A. The First Amendment provides corporations and other business entities with significant protection of their political speech. As another example, a law that forbids a corporation from using inserts in its bills to its customers to express its views on controversial issues would also violate the First Amendment.
5. B. Commercial speech does not have as much protection under the First Amendment as noncommercial speech. Commercial speech that is misleading may be restricted, however, if the restriction (1) seeks to advance a substantial government interest, (2) directly advances that interest, and (3) goes no further than necessary.
6. B. Aspects of the Fifth and Fourteenth Amendments that cover procedural due process concern the procedures used to make any government decision to take life, liberty, or property. These procedures must be fair, which generally mean that they give an opportunity to object.
7. C. Substantive due process focuses on the content (substance) of a law under the Fifth and Fourteenth Amendments. Depending on which rights a law regulates, it must either promote a compelling or overriding government interest or be rationally related to a legitimate governmental end.
8. A. Equal protection means that the government must treat similarly situated individuals in a similar manner. The equal protection clause of the Fourteenth Amendment applies to state and local governments, and the due process clause of the Fifth Amendment guarantees equal protection by the federal government. Generally, a law regulating an economic matter is considered valid if there is a

"rational basis" on which the law relates to a legitimate government interest.

9. D. A federal law takes precedence over a state law on the same subject. Also under the supremacy clause, if Congress chooses to act exclusively in an area in which the states have concurrent power, Congress is said to preempt the area.

10. A. Dissemination of obscene materials is a crime. Speech that harms the good reputation of another, or defamatory speech, is not protected under the First Amendment. "Fighting words," which are words that are likely to incite others to respond with violence, are not constitutionally protected. Other unprotected speech includes other speech that violates criminal laws, such as threats.

GamePoints

1. The First Amendment to the U.S. Constitution guarantees the freedom of speech. The courts interpret this amendment to give substantial protection to commercial speech, including advertising. But this protection is not as extensive as that given to noncommercial speech. Even if commercial speech is not related to illegal activities nor misleading, it may be restricted if a state has a substantial interest that cannot be achieved by less restrictive means. In this problem, the state has a substantial interest in consumers not being misled. This consideration affects what can be said in any product's ads.

2. State governments have the authority to regulate affairs within their borders, in part under the Tenth Amendment, which reserves all powers to the states not delegated to the national government. This authority is known as the states' police power, and under it, the states regulate private activities to protect or promote the public order, health, safety, morals, and general welfare. If these state regulations conflict with federal law, however, they are rendered invalid under the Constitution's supremacy clause.

Chapter 5

True-False Questions

1. T
2. T
3. T
4. F. According to utilitarianism, it is the consequences of an act that determine how ethical the act is. Applying this theory requires determining who will be affected by an act, assessing the positive and negatives effects of alternatives, and choosing the alternative that will provide the greatest benefit for the most people. Utilitarianism is premised on acting so as to do the greatest good for the greatest number of people. An act that affects a minority negatively may still be morally acceptable.

5. T
6. F. In situations involving ethical decisions, a balance must sometimes be struck between equally good or equally poor courses of action. The choice is often between equally good alternatives—benefiting shareholders versus benefiting employees, for example—and sometimes one group may be adversely affected. (The legality of a particular action may also be unclear.)

7. T
8. F. Simply obeying the law will not meet all ethical obligations. The law does not cover all ethical requirements. An act may be unethical but not illegal. In fact, compliance with the law is at best a moral minimum. Furthermore, there is an ethical aspect to almost every decision that a business firm makes.

9. T
10. F. Bribery is also a legal issue, regulated in the United States by the Foreign Corrupt Practices Act. Internationally, a treaty signed by the members of the Organization for Economic Cooperation and Development makes bribery of public officials a serious crime. Each member nation is expected to enact legislation implementing the treaty.

Fill-in Questions

Religious standards; Kantian ethics; the principle of rights

Multiple-Choice Questions

1. C. Business ethics focus on the application of moral principles in a business context. Different standards are not required. Business ethics is a subset of ethics that relates specifically to what constitutes right and wrong in situations that arise in business.

2. B. Traditionally, ethical reasoning relating to business has been characterized by two fundamental approaches—duty-based ethics and utilitarianism, or outcome-based ethics. Duty-based ethics derive from religious sources or philosophical principles. These standards may be absolute, which means that an act may not be undertaken, whatever the consequences.

3. A. Under religious ethical standards, it is the nature of an act that determines how ethical the act is, not its consequences. This is considered an *ab-*

solute standard. But this standard is tempered by an element of compassion (the "Golden Rule").

4. A. In contrast to duty-based ethics, outcome-based ethics (utilitarianism) involves a consideration of the consequences of an action. Utilitarianism is premised on acting so as to do the greatest good for the greatest number of people.

5. C. Utilitarianism requires determining who will be affected by an action, assessing the positive and negatives effects of alternatives, and choosing the alternative that will provide the greatest benefit for the most people. This approach has been criticized as tending to reduce the welfare of human beings to plus and minus signs on a cost-benefit worksheet.

6. A. A corporation, for example, as an employer, commonly faces ethical problems that involve conflicts among itself, its employees, its customers, its suppliers, its shareholders, its community, or other groups. Increasing wages, for instance, may benefit the employees and the community, but reduce profits and the ability of the employer to give pay increases in the future, as well as decreasing dividends to shareholders. To be considered socially responsible, when making a decision, a business firm must take into account the interests of all of these groups, as well as society as a whole.

7. B. Striking a balance between what is profitable and what is legal and ethical can be difficult. A failure to act legally or ethically can result in a reduction in profits, but a failure to act in the profitable interest of the firm can also cause profits to suffer. In any profession, however, there is a responsibility, both legal and ethical, not to misrepresent material facts, even at the expense of some profits. This is a clear ethical standard in the legal profession and in the accounting profession. This question and answer are based on a question that was included in the CPA exam in November 1994.

8. A. In part because it is impossible to be entirely aware of what the law requires and prohibits, the best course for a business firm is to act responsibly and in good faith. This course may provide the best defense if a transgression is discovered. Striking a balance between what is profitable and what is legal and ethical can be difficult, however. A failure to act legally or ethically can result in a reduction in profits, but a failure to act in the profitable interest of the firm can also cause profits to suffer. *Optimum* profits are the maximum profits that a firm can realize while staying within legal and ethical limits.

9. D. The principle of rights theory of ethics follows the belief that persons have fundamental rights. This belief is implied by duty-based ethical standards and Kantian ethics. The rights are implied by the duty that forms the basis for the stan-

dard (for example, the duty not to kill implies that persons have a right to live), or by the personal dignity implicit in the Kantian belief about the fundamental nature of human beings. Not to respect these rights would, under the principle of rights theory, be morally wrong.

10. A. The Foreign Corrupt Practices Act prohibits any U.S. firm from bribing foreign officials to influence official acts to provide the firm with business opportunities. Such payments are allowed, however, if they would be lawful in the foreign country. Thus, to avoid violating the law, the firm in this problem should determine whether such payments are legal in the minister's country.

GamePoints

1. Ethics is the study of what constitutes right and wrong behavior, focusing on morality and the way in which moral principles are derived or the way in which such principles apply to conduct in daily life. Sometimes the issues that arise concern fairness, justice, and "the right thing to do." In the context of this problem, to address these questions, it might be considered what is at stake. If there is a competition with other players or some other situation in which consulting outside sources is questionable, then it is unethical to review the Web sites. If, however, you are playing alone, and you have made your best attempt to advance, it may not be unethical to seek help.

2. The ethics in this situation relate to fairness, justice, "the right thing to do," and personal honesty and integrity. Intentionally lying to a vendor about the condition of goods sold is untruthful, illegal, and unethical. It is a breach of a duty of good faith, without which the social and economic dealings among us all could not continue. To further lie to others about the same issue would compound the breach. None of the approaches to ethical reasoning described in this chapter would support any of the acts set out in the problem.

Cumulative Hypothetical Problem for Unit One—Including Chapters 1–5

1. A. Mediation involves the a third party, a mediator. The mediator does not decide the dispute but only assists the parties to resolve it themselves. Although the mediator does not render a legally binding decision, any agreement the parties reach may be legally binding.

2. D. These state and federal courts would all have jurisdiction over the defendant. The customer's state could exercise jurisdiction over the firm through its long arm statute. The firm's state would have jurisdiction over it as a resident. A federal court could hear the case under its diversity jurisdiction: the parties are residents of different states and the amount in controversy is at least $75,000.

3. A. Damages, or money damages, is a remedy at law. Remedies in equity include injunctions, specific performance, and rescission. The distinction arose because the law courts in England could not always grant suitable remedies, and so equity courts were created to grant other types of relief. The U.S. legal system derives from the English system.

4. C. The power of judicial review is the power of any state or federal court to review a statute and declare it unconstitutional. Courts can also review the actions of the executive branch, which includes administrative agencies, to determine their constitutionality. A statute or rule that is declared unconstitutional is void. The power of judicial review is not expressly stated in the Constitution but is implied.

5. B. A state may restrict commercial speech if the state has a substantial interest that cannot be achieved by less restrictive means. Protecting the interests of consumers is a substantial state interest. Preventing consumers from being misled by certain kinds of advertising is an interest that may arguably not be achievable by any less restrictive means than an outright ban.

Questions on the Focus on Ethics for Unit One—Ethics and the Legal Environment of Business

1. D. Ethics is the study of what constitutes right or wrong behavior. It focuses on the application of moral principles to conduct. In a business context, ethics involves the application of moral principles to business conduct. Legal liability is a separate question and may, or may not, indicate unethical behavior. Profitability is also a separate issue. A reference to the "moral minimum" in the context of ethics refers to compliance with the law as the least a corporation can do to perform ethically.

2. A. If a business firm does not conduct its operations ethically, its goodwill, reputation, and future profits likely suffer. A firm that shows a commitment to ethical behavior often receives benefits greater than any advantages it may have sacrificed to do "what's right." A firm that is perceived as ethical may also attract investors.

3. C. Because of the many stakeholders to whom a business may owe a duty, there are circumstances in which a firm could act socially irresponsible in maintaining a position for its "rightness," particu-

larly if it could be interpreted as "weak." Shareholders are owed a return on their investments, employees are owed jobs and payment for their work, communities need vibrant economies, and so on. None of this would be possible if the business at the core did not make a profit. Of course, there should be at least some basis in truth or rightness for a legal position, or it will ultimately be a losing argument. In that situation, the firm could not meet its obligations.

Chapter 6

True-False Questions

1. T
2. F. A reasonable apprehension or fear of *immediate* harmful or offensive contact is an assault.
3. T
4. F. Puffery is seller's talk—the seller's *opinion* that his or her goods are, for example, the "best." For fraud to occur, there must be a misrepresentation of a *fact*.
5. F. If a party who initiates a suit does so out of malice—and without probable cause—that party may have committed malicious prosecution. But a person who files a suit based on a legally just and proper reason, even with malice, does not commit this tort. Also, to succeed, in some states, a plaintiff must show damages other than the normal cost of litigation.
6. T
7. F. Disparagement of property is a general term for torts that can be more specifically referred to as slander of quality or slander of title.
8. F. This is not misconduct, in terms of a wrongful interference tort. Bona fide competitive behavior is permissible, whether or not it results in the breaking of a contract or other business relation.
9. T
10. F. The federal government and some states have statutes prohibiting or regulating the use of spam. Also, the sending of spam may constitute trespass to personal property, and could be curtailed by private lawsuits. What the government can do to restrict spam may be limited by the First Amendment's protection for freedom of speech, however.

Fill-in Questions

whatever force is reasonably necessary to prevent harmful contact; real danger and apparent danger;

after the danger has passed; never; to defend others or property

Multiple-Choice Questions

1. D. This is a third party's use of predatory methods to end a business relationship between others. Individuals are permitted to interfere unreasonably with others' business to gain a share of the market. Appropriation is the use of another's name or likeness for gain, without permission. Assault concerns the apprehension or fear of immediate harmful or offensive physical contact. Conversion is a tort involving property.

2. A. To delay a customer suspected of shoplifting, a merchant must have probable cause (which requires more than a mere suspicion). A customer's concealing merchandise in his or her bag and leaving the store without paying for it would constitute probable cause. Even with probable cause, a merchant may delay a suspected shoplifter only for a reasonable time, however.

3. D. Advertising is bona fide competitive behavior, which is not a tort even if it results in the breaking of a contract. Obtaining more customers is one of the goals of effective advertising. Taking unethical steps to interfere with others' contracts or business relations could constitute a tort, however.

4. B. The basis of the tort of defamation is publication of a statement that holds an individual up to contempt, ridicule, or hatred. Publication means that statements are made to or within the hearing of persons other than the defamed party, or that a third party reads the statements. A secretary reading a letter, for example, meets this requirement. But the statements do not have to be read or heard by a specific third party. (Whether someone is a public figure is important only because a public figure cannot recover damages for defamation without proof of actual malice.)

5. C. Under the Communications Decency Act, an Internet service provider (ISP) may not be held liable for defamatory statements made by its customers online. Congress provided this immunity as an incentive to ISPs to "self-police" the Internet for offensive material.

6. B. Trespass to land occurs when a person, without permission, enters onto another's land, or remains on the land. An owner does not need to be aware of an act before it can constitute trespass, and harm to the land is not required. A trespasser may have a complete defense, however, if he or she enters onto the land to help someone in danger.

7. D. Trespass to personal property is intentional physical contact with another's personal property that causes damage. Sending spam through an Internet service provider (ISP) is intentional contact with the ISP's computer systems. A negative impact on the value of the ISP's equipment, by using its processing power to transmit e-mail, constitutes damage (the resources are not available for the ISP's customers). Also, service cancellations harm an ISP's business reputation and goodwill.

8. C. An individual who is defending his or her life or physical wellbeing can, in self-defense, use whatever force is reasonably necessary to prevent harmful contact. Although this question does not include this circumstance, a person can also act in a reasonable manner to defend others who are in danger. Of course, force cannot be used once the danger has passed.

9. B. To constitute fraud, a statement of fact must be involved. Reliance on an opinion is not justified unless the person making the statement has superior knowledge of the subject matter. Puffery, or seller's talk, (for example, "this is the best product!") is too subjective.

10. B. Meryl committed a battery and may have committed an assault. For an intentional tort, what matters is the actor's intent regarding the consequences of an act or his or her knowledge with substantial certainty that certain consequences will result. Motive is irrelevant, and the other person's fear is not a factor in terms of the actor's intent.

GamePoints

1. The most likely tort that your opponent committed is assault. This is any intentional and unexcused threat of immediate harmful or offensive contact. In the circumstances described in this problem, your opponent most likely caused you to feel reasonably apprehensive of harmful contact. One arguable issue might be whether any harm was imminent based on Tom's statement "if I lose one more time," implying that the game must be played before any harm occurs. But his snatching the game control from your hands—an act that might constitute battery, conversion, or trespass to personal property—and raising it in a threatening manner likely offsets this interpretation.

2. The most likely torts committed by the party who originated the virus are trespass to personal property and conversion. Trespass to personal property occurs when a party unlawfully harms the personal property of another or otherwise interferes with the owner's right to exclusive possession and enjoyment. The damage caused by the virus to your system certainly qualifies. Conversion exists when personal property is wrongfully taken from its rightful owner and placed in the service of another—any act depriving an owner of personal property without permission or just cause. If trespass to personal property occurs, conversion usually happens as well. These torts are the civil side of theft. Here, the virus has placed your computer in the service of the virus's propagator, depriving you of the use of your system.

Chapter 7

True-False Questions

1. F. One of the elements required to establish negligence is an injury, Of course, there must be a connection between the wrongful act and the injury, The breach of the duty of care must *cause* the injury— "but for" the wrongful act, the injury would not have occurred..
2. T
3. T
4. F. A defendant may be liable for the result of his or her act regardless of intent—that is part of the basis of the doctrine of strict liability. Similarly, it usually does not matter whether the defendant exercised reasonable care. Strict liability is liability without regard to fault or intent.
5. F. In an action based on strict liability, a plaintiff does not have to prove that there was a failure to exercise due care. That distinguishes an action based on strict liability from an action based on negligence, which requires proof of a lack of due care.
6. T
7. T
8. F. The theory of strict liability also applies in some cases involving product liability and bailments. The basis for imposing strict liability to any activity is the creation of an extraordinary risk.
9. T
10. T

Fill-in Questions

1. negligence;
2. assumption of risk
3. comparative

Multiple-Choice Questions

1. A. To satisfy the elements of a negligence cause of action, a breach of a duty of care must cause the harm. If an injury would not have occurred without the breach, there is causation in fact. Causation in fact can usually be determined by the but-for test: but for the wrongful act, the injury would not have occurred.
2. C. To commit negligence, a breach of a duty of care must cause harm. If an injury was foreseeable, there is causation in fact. This can usually be determined by the but-for test: but for the wrongful act, the injury would not have occurred. Thus, an actor is not necessarily liable to all who are injured. Insurance coverage and business dealings are not factors.
3. A. Strict liability is liability without fault. This is imposed on dangerous activities when they (1) involve potentially serious harm to persons or property, (2) involve a high degree of risk that cannot be completely guarded against by the exercise of reasonable care, and (3) are activities not commonly performed in the area. The other choices represent irrelevant factors.
4. B. The standard of a business that invites persons onto its premises is a duty to exercise reasonable care. Whether conduct is unreasonable depends on a number of factors, including how easily the injury could have been guarded against. A landowner has a duty to discover and remove hidden dangers, but obvious dangers do not need warnings.
5. B. Strict liability is applied to abnormally dangerous activities because of their extreme risk. An abnormally dangerous activity is, among other things, an activity not commonly performed in an area in which an injury or damage occurs as a result of the activity.
6. D. The theory of strict liability is a doctrine that is applied to certain activities regardless of fault. This is in part when the activities, like demolition, involve a high degree of risk that cannot be completely guarded against by the exercise of reasonable care.
7. B. An individual with knowledge, skill, or intelligence superior to that of an ordinary person has a higher standard of care than the ordinary person—that which is reasonable in light of those capabilities. Thus, a professional's duty is consistent with what is reasonable for that professional.
8. C. Without an injury—a loss, damage, harm, a wrong, or an invasion of a protected interest—there is nothing to recover in an action based on negligence. The other elements of negligence are a duty of care, a breach of the duty, and the breach's causation of an injury or damage.
9. A. A person who voluntarily enters into a situation, knowing the normal risks involved, cannot recover if he or she is injured by a consequence of those risks. As indicated by the answer to this question, these risks do not include those that are different from or greater than the risks normally involved in the situation.

10. A. In most states, the defense of comparative negligence can reduce the amount of a tortfeasor's liability if the injured person failed to exercise reasonable care. Although some states allow a plaintiff to recover even if his or her fault was greater than the defendant's, in many states, a plaintiff gets nothing if he or she was more than 50 percent at fault.

GamePoints

1. Negligence is the most likely tort that your opponent is committing. The elements are (1) a duty of care, (2) a breach of the duty, and (3) the breach's causation of (4) an injury. In this problem, Your opponent has a duty to exercise a reasonable amount of care within the context of the game. Driving too fast is likely not an exercise of reasonable care. This breach causes crashes, which injure your avatar, or game identity. Assumption of risk is your opponent's best defense. A party who voluntarily enters into a situation—such as, in this question, a race—knows the risk involved and cannot recover if he or she suffers an injury as a consequence. The requirements are knowledge of the risk and a voluntary assumption of it. As a player of the game, you most likely meet both requirements.

2. To recover on the basis of negligence, the injured party—Twyla—must show that the cruiser's owner—the Prince of Peril—owed her, as the plaintiff, a duty of care, that the Prince breached that duty, that the plaintiff was injured, and that the breach caused the injury. In this game situation, the Prince's act (leaving the cruiser running while he leaped from it) most likely breached the duty of reasonable care. The earth shook. The silo collapsed. Its falling on Twyla was the direct cause of her injury, not her own negligence. Thus, liability turns on whether the plaintiff can connect the breach of duty to the injury. This involves the test of proximate cause—the question of foreseeability. The consequences to the injured party must have been a foreseeable result of the defendant's carelessness.

Chapter 8

True-False Questions

1. T
2. F. A copyright is granted automatically when a qualifying work is created, although a work can be registered with the U.S. Copyright Office.
3. T
4. T

5. F. Anything that makes an individual company unique and would have value to a competitor is a trade secret. This includes a list of customers, a formula for a chemical compound, and other confidential data.
6. F. Trade names cannot be registered with the federal government. They are protected, however, under the common law (when used as trademarks or service marks) by the same principles that protect trademarks.
7. F. A copy does not have to be the same as an original to constitute copyright infringement. A copyright is infringed if a substantial part of a work is copied without the copyright holder's permission.
8. F. A trademark may be infringed by an intentional or unintentional use of a mark in its entirety, or a copy of the mark to a substantial degree. In other words, a mark can be infringed if its use is intended or not, and whether the copy is identical or similar. Also, the owner of the mark and its unauthorized user need not be in direct competition.
9. T
10. F. Proof of a likelihood of confusion is not required in a trademark dilution action. The products involved do not even have to be similar. Proof of likely confusion is required in a suit for trademark infringement, however.

Fill-in Questions

70; 95; 120; 70

Multiple-Choice Questions

1. B. A firm that makes, uses, or sells another's patented design, product, or process without the owner's permission commits patent infringement. It is not required that an invention be copied in its entirety. Also, the object that is copied does not need to be trademarked or copyrighted, in addition to being patented.
2. A. The user of a trademark can register it with the U.S. Patent and Trademark Office, but registration is not necessary to obtain protection from trademark infringement. A trademark receives protection to the degree that it is distinctive. A fanciful symbol is the most distinctive mark.
3. D. This is not copyright infringement because no copyright is involved. This is not cybersquatting because no one is offering to sell a domain name to a trademark owner. (It is also unlikely that this violates the Anticybersquatting Consumer Protection Act because there is no indication of "bad faith intent.") Trademark dilution occurs when a trademark is used, without the owner's without permis-

sion, in a way that diminishes the distinctive quality of the mark. That has not happened here.

4. A. Copyright protects a specific list of creative works, including literary works, musical works, sound recordings, and pictorial, graphic, and sculptural works. Although there are exceptions for "fair use," a work need not be copied in its entirety to be infringed. Also, to make a case for infringement, proof of consumers' confusion is not required, and the owner and unauthorized user need not be direct competitors.

5. D. Business processes and information that cannot be patented, copyrighted, or trademarked are protected against appropriation as trade secrets. These processes and information include production techniques, as well as a product's idea and its expression.

6. C. Trademark law protects a distinctive symbol that its owner stamps, prints, or otherwise affixes to goods to distinguish them from the goods of others. Use of this mark by another party without the owner's permission is trademark infringement.

7. B. A certification mark certifies the region, materials, method of manufacture, quality, or accuracy of goods or services. A collective mark is a certification mark used by members of a cooperative, association, or other organization (a union, in this problem). A service mark distinguishes the services of one person or company from those of another. A trade name indicates all or part of a business's name.

8. B. Ten years is the period for later renewals of a trademark's registration. The life of a creator plus seventy years is a period for copyright protection. No intellectual work is protected forever, at least not without renewal. To obtain a patent, an applicant must satisfy the U.S. Patent and Trademark Office that the invention or design is genuine, novel, useful, and not obvious in light of contemporary technology. A patent is granted to the first person to create whatever is to be patented, rather than the first person to file for a patent.

9. D. The Berne Convention provides some copyright protection, but its coverage and enforcement was not as complete or as universal as that of the TRIPS (Trade-Related Aspects of Intellectual Property Rights) Agreement. The Paris Convention allows parties in one signatory country to file for patent and trademark protection in other signatory countries. The Madrid Protocol concerns trademarks.

10. A. Publishers cannot put the contents of their periodicals into online databases and other electronic resources, including CD-ROMs, without securing the permission of the writers whose contributions are included.

GamePoints

1. Different attributes of your game device are protected under different categories of intellectual property law. The name of the product could be protected as a trademark once it is either registered or used in commerce. It might be argued that the name is not sufficiently fanciful or distinctive, but this argument could be countered by pointing out that "The Gem" is not a jewel. The device might obtain patent protection if the conditions for the grant of a patent are met—that the device's invention, discovery, or design is genuine, novel, useful, and not obvious in light of current technology. The software that drives the game might be protected under copyright law. Various other aspects of the production and selling of this product could be protected against appropriation by competitors as trade secrets.

2. No song could be uploaded without the copyright owner's permission. This problem poses an instance of copyright infringement. This use of others' works without the permission of the copyright owners would not be "fair use" because it is not a clearly permissible purpose (criticism, comment, news reporting, teaching, scholarship, or research) and it would not otherwise pass a court's scrutiny—particularly as this use would undercut the market for the copyrighted work.

Chapter 9

True-False Questions

1. T

2. F. Felonies are crimes punishable by imprisonment of a year or more (in a state or federal prison). Crimes punishable by imprisonment for lesser periods (in a local facility) are classified as misdemeanors.

3. F. These are elements of the crime of robbery. (Robbery also involves the use of force or fear.) Burglary requires breaking and entering a building with the intent to commit a crime. (At one time, burglary was defined to cover only breaking and entering the dwelling of another at night to commit a crime.)

4. F. This is an element of larceny. The crime of embezzlement occurs when a person entrusted with another's property fraudulently appropriates it. Also, unlike robbery, embezzlement does not require the use of force or fear.

5. T

6. F. The crime of bribery occurs when a bribe is offered. Accepting a bribe is a separate crime. In either case, the recipient does not need to perform the act for which the bribe is offered for the crime to exist. Note, too, that a bribe can consist of something other then money.

7. F. The recipient of the goods only needs to know that the goods are stolen. The recipient does not need to know the identity of the thief or of the true owner to commit this crime. Thus, not knowing these individuals' identities is not a defense.

8. T

9. T

10. F. A business takes a risk that by electronically storing its customers' credit card numbers, or any personal information, the data may be vulnerable to theft. Cyber thieves have developed ingenuous methods for infiltrating computer networks and "stealing" this information, often without a business realizing that its system has been compromised, unlike the scene of physical break-in. The financial burden imposed by the theft and subsequent use of the data is normally borne by the business, particularly as most credit-card issuers require it.

Fill-in Questions

unreasonable; probable; due process of law; jeopardy; trial; trial by; witnesses; bail and fines

Multiple-Choice Questions

1. C. The elements of most crimes include the performance of a prohibited act and a specified state of mind or intent on the part of the actor.

2. C. Fraudulently making or altering a writing in a way that changes another's legal rights is forgery. Forgery also includes changing trademarks, counterfeiting, falsifying public documents, and altering other legal documents.

3. B. Embezzlement involves the fraudulent appropriation of another's property, including money, by a person entrusted with it. Unlike larceny, embezzlement does not require that property be taken from its owner. Unlike burglary, embezzlement does not involve breaking and entering. Unlike forgery, embezzlement does not require the making or altering of a writing. Unlike robbery, embezzlement does not involve force or fear.

4. A. This is online auction fraud. Fraud is a misrepresentation knowingly made with the intent to deceive another and on which a reasonable person relies to his or her detriment. Fraud can occur online through an auction Web site when a buyer pays for an auctioned item but does not receive it, as in this question, or receives something worth less than the promised article. In either case, it can be difficult to pinpoint a fraudulent seller, who may assume multiple identities.

5. B. This is *phishing*, a form of identity theft. In circumstances such as those set out in this question, once an unsuspecting individual responds to the request by entering the credit-card or other personal information, the phisher can use it to pose as that person or to steal the funds in the person's bank or other account. The crime may begin with a link in a fraudulent e-mail message or a URL provided in an e-mail note. The message or note may ask that the information be submitted to a certain e-mail address or via a Web site that is genuine in appearance but nonetheless false. *Vishing* is a form of phishing involves voice communication—an e-mail requesting a phone call, for example, to relate a bank account number.

6. B. The perpetrator in this set of facts is a *hacker*—someone who uses one computer to break into another. A *Trojan horse* is software, an application, or a program that appears to be legitimate but allows someone to gain unauthorized access to a computer. As with other forms of software, a Trojan horse fits the definition of *malware*, which includes any application or program that is harmful to a computer or its user. A *firewall* is hardware or software designed to prevent unauthorized access.

7. B. In considering the defense of entrapment, the important question is whether a person who committed a crime was pressured by the police to do so. Entrapment occurs when a government agent suggests that a crime be committed and pressure an individual, who is not predisposed to its commitment, to do it.

8. C. A person in police custody who is to be interrogated must be informed that he or she has the right to remain silent; anything said can and will be used against him or her in court; and he or she has the right to consult with an attorney. The person also must be told that if he or she is indigent, a lawyer will be appointed. These rights may be waived if the waiver is knowing and voluntary.

9. C. If, for example, a confession is obtained after an illegal arrest, the confession is normally excluded. Under the exclusionary rule, all evidence obtained in violation of the constitutional rights spelled out in the Fourth, Fifth, and Sixth Amendments normally is excluded, as well as all evidence derived from the illegally obtained evidence. The purpose of the rule is to deter police misconduct.

10. B. A formal charge issued by a grand jury is an indictment. A charge issued by a magistrate is called an information. In either case, there must be sufficient evidence to justify bringing a suspect to trial. The arraignment occurs when the suspect is brought before the trial court, informed of the charges, and asked to enter a plea.

GamePoints

1. The perpetrator in this set of facts—the yeti—appears to have committed several violent crimes. These include the murder of your climbing companion and assault, with a likely impending battery and the attempted murder, of your avatar. These crimes are classified by degree, which depends on the circumstances surrounding the acts. The intent of the perpetrator, whether a weapon was used, and sometimes the level of pain and suffering of the victim, are potential factors.

2. The Internet has expanded opportunities for identity theft and related crimes by providing easy access to private data. This data can be accessed illegally through a number of clandestine methods from virtually anywhere in the world. For example, through an online connection, a hacker might have invaded your computer without your knowledge to install undetected software. This application could have transmitted a copy of your keystrokes to the hacker's computer. The hacker might then have interpreted these strokes to reveal your personal and financial data. This information can be used to impersonate you and thereby spend money as you.

Cumulative Hypothetical Problem for Unit Two—Including Chapters 6–9

1. B. Intellectual property law protects such intangible rights as copyrights, trademarks, and patents, which include the rights that an individual or business firm has in the products it produces. Protection for software comes from patent law and from copyright law. Protection for the distinguishing trademarks on the software come from, of course, trademark law.

2. C. Of these choices, the firm most likely violated tort law, which includes negligence and strict liability, both as distinct torts and as a part of product liability. Negligence requires proof of intent. Strict liability does not. These firms may also have breached their contracts and their warranties, topics which are discussed in the next Unit.

3. B. This is cyber theft. Accessing a computer online, without authority, to obtain classified, restricted, or protected data, or attempting to do so is prohibited by the National Information Infrastructure Protection Act of 1996. Penalties include fines and imprisonment for up to twenty years.

4. A. A corporation can be held liable for the crimes of its employees, officers, or directors. Imprisonment is not possible, in a practical sense, as a

punishment for a corporation. A business firm can be fined or denied certain privileges, however.

5. C. Corporate officers can be held personally liable for the crimes they commit, whether or not the crimes were committed for their personal benefit or on their firm's behalf. Also, corporate officers can be held liable for the actions of employees under their supervision. Furthermore, a court can impose criminal liability on a corporate officer in those circumstances regardless of whether he or she participated in, directed, or even knew about a given crime.

Questions on the Focus on Ethics for Unit Two—Ethics and Torts and Crimes

1. C. The collection, buying, and selling of consumers' personal information may violate the individuals' privacy rights. A business should formulate a privacy policy and inform those whose data the firm collects. Copyrights and trademarks are not infringed in this problem. A business is not protected by the freedom of speech in the buying and selling of personal information.

2. B. This problem presents a cybergriper. A cybergriper uses another's trademark to protest, or otherwise complain about, in good faith and usually without profit, the owner's product or policy. Courts have held that this use of a mark is protected by the freedom of speech. The business's mark is not infringed because the public is not likely to be confused by the cybergriper's use.

3. B. This question presents the issue of the extent to which tort law, in a case involving misappropriation of trade secrets, encroaches on the freedom of speech. A court is not likely to hold that posting computer code that allows its users to de-encrypt and copy copyright-protected DVDs is "pure speech" or a fair use of copyrighted material. The posters could thus be ordered to stop posting the code, and this order would not be violation of a privacy right.

Chapter 10

True-False Questions

1. F. All contracts involve promises, but all promises do not establish contracts. (A contract is an agreement that can be enforced in court.) Contract law reflects which promises society believes should be legally enforced, and assures parties to private contracts that the agreements they make will be enforceable.

2.   T

3.   T

4.   F. A bilateral contract is accepted by a promise to perform. A unilateral contract is formed when the offeree (the party who receives the offer) completes the requested act or other performance.

5.   F. An oral contract is an express contract, which may be written or oral. In an express contract, the terms are fully stated in words. In an implied contract, it is the conduct of the parties that creates and defines the terms.

6.   F. An unenforceable contract is a valid contract that cannot be enforced due to certain defenses. A voidable contract is a valid contract in which one or both of the parties has the option of avoiding his or her legal obligations.

7.   T

8.   T

9.   T

10.   F. A court imposes a quasi contract to avoid the unjust enrichment of one party at the expense of another. Quasi contracts are not true contracts.

Fill-in Questions

objective; objective; did; circumstances surrounding

Multiple-Choice Questions

1.   B. Freedom of contract refers to the law's recognition that most every individual may enter freely into contractual arrangements. This freedom is expressed in Article I, Section 10 of the U.S. Constitution.

2.   B. One party has performed; the other has not. The contract is executed on the one side and executory on the other, and classified as executory. Once the delivered goods are paid for, the contract will be fully executed.

3.   A. In considering an implied-in-fact contract, a court looks at the parties' actions leading up to what happened. If, for example, a plaintiff furnished services, expecting to be paid, which the defendant should have known, and the defendant had a chance to reject the services and did not, the court would hold that the parties had an enforceable implied-in-fact contract.

4.   A. An obligation to pay will be imposed by law to prevent one party from being unjustly enriched at another's expense. This is the doctrine of quasi contract. The doctrine will not be applied, however, if there is a contract covering the matter in dispute. Also, there are some circumstances in which parties will not be forced to pay for benefits "thrust" on them, particularly if this is done over their protest.

5.   B. According to the objective theory of contracts, a party's intent to enter into a contract is judged by outward, objective facts as a reasonable person would interpret them, rather than by the party's own subjective intentions. A reasonable person in the position of a party receiving an offer can know what is in the offer only from what is offered. A court might consider the circumstances surrounding a transaction, and the statements of the parties and the way they acted when they made their contract.

6.   A. An express contract is a contract in which the terms are fully expressed in words, but those words do not necessarily have to be in writing. A contract that is implied from conduct is an implied-in-fact contract. Implied-in-law, or quasi, contracts are not actual contracts but are imposed on parties by courts.

7.   A. The primary purpose of the rules for the interpretation of contracts is to determine the parties' intent from the language used in their agreement and to give effect to that intent. A court will not ordinarily interpret a contract according to what the parties later claim was their intent when they contracted.

8.   D. One of the rules for the interpretation of contracts is that evidence of the parties' course of performance, the parties' prior course of dealing, and any custom and usage of trade in the particular industry may be admitted to clarify the meaning of ambiguous terms. This evidence is given priority (or weight) in that order, with express terms having the highest priority, or greatest weight.

9.   A. A voidable contract is a valid contract that can be avoided at the option of one or both of the parties. If a party with the option chooses to avoid the contract, both parties are released from their obligations under it. If a party with the option elects to ratify the contract, both parties must perform.

10.   D. Like this definition of a promise, a contract can be defined as an agreement to do or refrain from doing some legal act now or in the future. Mutual promises can make up an agreement, and an agreement that can be enforced in a court is a contract.

RockOn

1.   This situation describes a unilateral contract (a contract that includes the exchange of a promise for an act). The notice is the promise, and the musician's performance is the act that completes the contract. Note that the musician was not obligated to perform. If you had hired him to perform, and he had agreed, the contract would have been bilateral. At any rate, because the musician complied with the

conditions of the promise, you are bound to perform as promised—that is, to pay.

2. In the situation set out in this question, you do not have to pay the performer. There is no indication that you offered or promised to pay. All that you offered was stage time, which the performer received. As in the previous problem, the musician was not obligated to perform, so there was no contract on this basis.

Chapter 11

True-False Questions

1. T

2. F. One of the elements for a valid offer is that the terms be definite enough to be enforced by a court. This is so that a court can determine if a breach occurred and, if so, what the appropriate remedy would be. An offer might invite a specifically worded acceptance, which could constitute sufficiently definite terms.

3. T

4. F. Irrevocable offers (offers that must be kept open for a period of time) include option contracts. Other irrevocable offers include a merchant's firm offer and, under the doctrine of promissory estoppel, an offer on which an offeree has changed position in reliance.

5. F. The mirror image rule requires that the terms of an offeree's acceptance must exactly match the terms of the offeror's offer to form a valid contract. Any other response effectively rejects the offer, terminating it. An offeree may, of course, include a counteroffer with his or her rejection.

6. T

7. F. The UETA was drafted by the National Conference of Commissioners on Uniform State Laws and the American Law Institute as a proposal of legislation for the states to enact individually. Most states have enacted the UETA.

8. T

9. T

10. F. Under the UETA, an e-record is considered received when it enters the recipient's processing system in a readable form, even if no person is aware of its receipt.

Fill-in Questions

serious; offeror; reasonably definite; offeree

Multiple-Choice Questions

1. C. When an acceptance is made conditional, it constitutes a rejection, but the conditions state a counteroffer. A counteroffer is both a rejection of an original offer and a simultaneous making of a new offer.

2. A. Generally, an offer may be revoked any time before acceptance. Most offers are revocable, even if they say that they are not, as long as the revocation is communicated to the offeree before acceptance. This may be done by express repudiation or by acts that are inconsistent with the offer and that are made known to the offeree (such as a sale to someone else about which the offeree learns).

3. C. An acceptance is effective if it is timely. Under the mailbox rule, using a mode of communication expressly or impliedly authorized by the offeror makes an acceptance effective when sent. If no mode is expressly stated, the mail is acceptable. Here, the offeror did not specify a certain mode, so the mode that the offeree used to accept was a reasonable means.

4. C. In general, ads are treated as invitations to negotiate, not offers. This question and answer are based on a question that appeared in the CPA exam in May 1981.

5. A. A shrink-wrap agreement is typically between the manufacturer of hardware or software and its user. The terms of a shrink-wrap agreement typically concern warranties, remedies, and other issues. Shrink-wrap agreements have not always been enforced. The most important consideration is the time at which the manufacturer communicated the terms to the end-user. If they are proposed after a contract is entered into, they can be construed as proposals for additional terms, to which the consumer must expressly agree.

6. C. A binding contract can be created by clicking on, for example, an "I agree" button if an opportunity is provided to read the terms before the button is clicked. If the terms are not revealed until after an agreement is made, however, it is unlikely that, as in cases involving shrink-wrap agreements, they would be considered part of the deal. Here, the problem states that the button referred to the terms, meaning the buyer knew, or should have known, what was being agreed to.

7. B. Under the E-SIGN Act, no contract, record, or signature may be denied legal effect solely because it is in electronic form. An e-signature is as valid as a signature on paper, and an e-document is as valid as a paper document. One possible complication is that state laws on e-signatures are not uniform. Most state have enacted the Uniform Electronic Transactions Act (UETA) but with individual modifications.

8. C. To be "sent," an e-record must be properly directed from the sender's place of business to the intended recipient, in a form readable by the recipient's computer, at the recipient's place of business. This location is the recipient's place of business with the closest relation to the transaction. If a party does not have a place of business, the party's residence is used. An e-record is received when it enters the recipient's processing system in a readable form, even if no person is aware of the receipt

9. B. If the parties to a deal subject to the UETA agree to a security procedure and one party does not detect an error because the party did not follow the procedure, the conforming party may be able to avoid the effect of the error. To do so, the conforming party must (1) promptly notify the nonconforming party of the error and of his or her intent not to be bound by it and (2) take reasonable steps to return any benefit or consideration received. If there can be no restitution, the transaction may not be avoidable. (If the parties do not agree on a security procedure, other state laws determine the effect of the mistake.)

10. D. The UETA is like most other uniform acts that apply in the business context. For contracts that fall within its scope, it applies in the absence of an agreement to the contrary. Parties who would otherwise be covered by the UETA can agree to opt out of all or part of the act and agree not to be covered by it, however, or vary any or all of its provisions. The parties must have agreed to conduct their transaction electronically, however.

RockOn

1. No. An offer is terminated when, within its terms, it is rejected by the offeree, which occurred here. An attempt to accept an offer after its termination is an offer to enter into a new contract. There are exceptions to this rule, which will be explained in subsequent chapters. For example, if consideration had been given to hold the offer open for the stated period, the offeree would have had the remainder of the period to change the rejection into acceptance. Also, under the Uniform Commercial Code, a "firm offer" to a merchant might have remained open. But those exceptions do not apply here.

2. These terms are part of a click-on agreement, which is formed when a buyer, completing a transaction on a computer, is required to indicate assent to such terms by clicking on a link that makes the assent clear ("Okay!" in this problem). Under the Uniform Commercial Code (which codifies the law of

sales) and the *Restatement (Second) of Contracts* (which distills the common law), parties can agree to terms by conduct or action that recognizes the contract and shows assent. Here, then, the terms are most likely binding.

Chapter 12

True-False Questions

1. T
2. T
3. F. Promises based on past consideration—that is, promises made with respect to events that have already happened—are unenforceable. They lack the element of bargained-for consideration.
4. T
5. F. A promise does have value as consideration. Consideration may consist of goods, money, performance, or a promise.
6. T
7. F. Unlike a release, a covenant not to sue does not always bar further recovery. If one party does not do what he or she promised, the other party can file a suit for breach of contract.
8. F. When a debt is liquidated, it is not in dispute—it is a preexisting obligation. A preexisting obligation cannot be consideration. For an accord and satisfaction, a debt must be disputed. The consideration is the parties' giving up their legal right to contest the amount of debt.
9. T
10. T

Fill-in Questions

promise; detriment; promisor; promise; enforced; promisee; substantial

Multiple-Choice Questions

1. C. To constitute consideration, the value of whatever is exchanged for the promise must be legally sufficient. Its economic value (its "adequacy") is rarely the basis for a court's refusal to enforce a contract.
2. C. Consideration must be bargained for. Performance or a promise is bargained for if, as in this problem, the promisor seeks it in exchange for his or her promise and the promisee gives it in exchange for that promise.
3. A. Past consideration is no consideration. Promises made with respect to past consideration are not enforceable. This question and answer are

based on a question that appeared in the May 1995 CPA exam.

4. D. The promisee was not legally obligated to undertake the act, and the promisor was not legally obligated to pay the promisee until the performance was completed. Also, consideration must be bargained for. Performance or a promise is bargained for if, as in this problem, the promisor seeks it in exchange for his or her promise and the promisee gives it in exchange for that promise.

5. B. Two parties can mutually agree to rescind their contract, at least to the extent that it is executory. They may also agree to a new contract, which may include whatever new terms they agree to. If the rescission and the making of the new contract are simultaneous, and a dispute later arises, the court may have to decide whether to apply the preexisting duty rule, but that issue would seem unlikely in the circumstances described in this problem.

6. D. Generally, a promise to do what one already has a legal duty to do is not legally sufficient consideration, because no legal detriment or benefit has been incurred or received. This is the preexisting duty rule. Unforeseen difficulties may qualify as an exception to this rule, but an increase in ordinary business expenses, which is a type of risk usually assumed in doing business, does not qualify as an unforeseen difficulty.

7. A. The injured party signed a valid, enforceable release. No fraud was involved. Consideration was given in the form of the uninjured party's promise to pay in return for the injured party's promise not to sue for a larger amount.

8. B. A person who reasonably relies on the promise of another to that person's detriment can recover under the doctrine of promissory estoppel (also called detrimental reliance). There must be (1) a promise, (2) reliance on the promise, (3) reliance of a substantial, definite nature, and (4) justice in the enforcement of the promise.

9. A. This is not an illusory promise, which occurs when the terms of a contract do not bind the promisor to do anything. Such a promise is no promise at all—it is unenforceable due to lack of consideration—but here the notice requirement deprives the promisor of the opportunity to hire someone else for that period. The other answer choices do not make sense.

10. A. In a covenant not to sue, the parties substitute a contractual obligation for some other type of legal action, such as a tort. A covenant not to sue does not always bar further recovery, unlike a release.

RockOn

1. Yes. Under the doctrine of promissory estoppel, a party who makes a promise can be estopped from revoking the promise, and a party who has reasonably relied on the promise can obtain a measure of recovery. For the doctrine to be applied (1) there must be a promise, (2) the promisee must reasonably rely on the promise, (3) the reliance must be substantial and definite, and (4) justice must be better served by the enforcement of the promise. It is reasonable to expect that a charitable organization will incur obligations in reliance on a promise of a donation and that it would be unjust if the promise were not kept. That is what occurred in this problem.

2. No. Under the preexisting duty rule, a party to a contract is not bound to a modification of the contract unless there is additional consideration for the modification. In this case, there was no new consideration for the reduction in the amount paid under the contract, so the assent to the change is not enforceable.

Chapter 13

True-False Questions

1. T

2. T

3. F. A person who enters into a contract when he or she is intoxicated can avoid the contract only if he or she was so intoxicated as to fail to comprehend the legal consequences of entering into the deal. Note, though, that the intoxication does not need to have been involuntary.

4. F. Parents are not ordinarily liable for contracts made by their minor children who were acting on their own. (A minor is also personally liable for his or her torts. In some circumstances, the minor's parents may also be held liable, if, for example, the tort was malicious or committed at the direction of the parent.)

5. T

6. T

7. T

8. F. An illegal contract is void. A court will not enforce it on behalf of any party to it.

9. F. A contract with an unlicensed practitioner may be enforceable if the purpose of the statute is to raise government revenues, but not if the statute's purpose is to protect the public from unlicensed practitioners.

10. F. A covenant not to compete may be upheld if the length of time and the size of the geographic area in which the party agrees not to compete are reasonable. A court may in fact reform these terms to make them reasonable and then enforce them as reformed.

Fill-in Questions

ratification; disaffirm; indicates; ratification

Multiple-Choice Questions

1. C. Ratification is accepting and thus giving legal force to an obligation that was previously unenforceable. Most contracts with minors are not fully enforceable until the minor reaches the age of majority. Similarly, a minor cannot effectively ratify a contract until he or she attains majority. This question and answer are based on a question that appeared in the May 1993 CPA exam.

2. B. If a person was intoxicated enough to lack mental capacity, the contract is voidable at his or her option. Being intoxicated enough to lack mental capacity means being so impaired as not to comprehend the consequences of entering into a contract. Otherwise, the contract is enforceable. Under no circumstances would the contract be void.

3. D. Only a guardian can enter into legally binding contracts on a person's behalf if the person has been adjudged mentally incompetent by a court. Any contract entered by the incompetent person is void. If the person has not been so adjudged, however, a contract may be enforceable if the person either knew it was a contract or understood its legal consequences.

4. C. To disaffirm a contract, a minor must return whatever he or she received under it. In a state in which there is also an obligation to return the other party to the position he or she was in before the contract, the minor must also pay for any damage to the goods.

5. D. The general rule is that an illegal contract is unenforceable. Thus, if an illegal agreement is executory, with the illegal part not yet performed, the party whose performance has not been rendered can withdraw. The person cannot be held in breach, and the contract cannot be enforced.

6. D. This promise (a covenant not to compete) is enforceable, because it is no broader than necessary for the other party's protection. Such promises may be considered contracts in restraint of trade, illegal on grounds of public policy, when they are broader than necessary (particularly in terms of geographic area and time), or are not accompanied by a sale of a business.

7. D. A contract with an unlicensed party is illegal and not enforceable by either party to it if the purpose of the licensing statute is to protect the public from unauthorized practitioners. If the purpose of the statute is to raise government revenues, however, the contract is enforceable.

8. B. The reasonableness of a covenant not to compete, accompanied by the sale of a business or included in an employment contract, is determined by the length of time and the size of the area in which the party agrees not to compete. In some cases, a court might even reform overly restrictive terms to prevent any undue burdens or hardships.

9. A. An exculpatory clause (a contract clause attempting to absolve a party of negligence or other wrongs) is often held unconscionable, especially in a case involving a lease of real property, or in which an employer is attempting to avoid liability for injury to an employee, or in which a business important to the public interest is seeking its enforcement.

10. D. A contract with an unlicensed individual may be enforceable depending on the nature of the applicable licensing statute. If the statute bars the enforcement of such contracts, of course they are not enforceable. They are also not enforceable if the statute's purpose is to protect the public from unlicensed practitioners. Otherwise, if the statute is intended only to raise revenue, such contracts may be enforceable.

RockOn

1. No. A contract entered into for an illegal purpose is not enforceable by any party to it. In fact, an illegal contract is void, it will be deemed not to have existed, and a court will not aid either party in enforcing, rescinding, or recovering under it. This is true even if one of the parties is unjustly enriched as a result of the contract. The reason for this rule is so that the courts are not used to the advantage of a party who broke the law by entering into an illegal bargain.

2. No. A contract between an adult and a minor is voidable by the minor, but not by the adult. For a minor to exercise the option to avoid the contract, he or she needs only to manifest an intent not to be bound. The minor thus avoids the contract by disaffirming it. Of course, the entire contract must be disaffirmed, the disaffirmance must be timely, and the minor must return the goods or pay their reasonable value. An adult has no power to void the contract on the basis of the other contracting party's minority status.

Chapter 14

True-False Questions

1. T
2. F. If the parties to both sides of a contract are mistaken as to the same material fact, either party can rescind the contract at any time. This is a bilateral, or mutual, mistake. Either party can enforce a contract, however, if the mistake relates to the later market value or quality of the object of the contract.
3. T
4. F. Proof of an injury is not needed to rescind a contract for fraud. Proof of an injury is required, however, to recover damages on the basis of fraud.
5. T
6. T
7. F. If the parties to the contract had substantially unequal bargaining positions and enforcement would be unfair or oppressive, the contract will not be enforced. A court may base its decision on the doctrine of unconscionability, or on traditional concepts of fraud, undue influence, or duress.
8. F. A person can misrepresent a material fact without intending to defraud. This is known as innocent misrepresentation. A party who contracts with the person in reliance on the statement may be able to rescind the contract.
9. F. If a defect is serious (such as the risks of a medical procedure), it must be disclosed. The general rule is, however, that neither party to a contract has a duty to speak. Also, if a defect is obvious, a buyer cannot justifiably rely on a seller's representations.
10. F. When both parties to a contract make a mistake as to the market value or quality of the object of their deal, the contract can be *enforced* by either party. Mutual mistakes of *material fact* permit rescission by either party.

Fill-in Questions

value; value; cannot; value

Multiple-Choice Questions

1. A. Generally, a unilateral mistake—a mistake on the part of only one of the parties—does not give the mistaken party any right to relief. There are two exceptions. One of the exceptions is that the rule does not apply if the other party knew or should have known that a mistake was made. This question and answer are based a question that appeared in the CPA exam in May 1995.

2. C. This statement is none of the other choices because it is a statement of opinion, and thus is not generally subject to a claim of fraud or any of the other causes of action listed here. A fact is objective and verifiable. Puffery often involves vague assertions of quality. Affirmatively concealing a material fact, failing to respond when asked, and in some cases failing to volunteer pertinent facts may constitute fraud, however. Taking advantage of a party with whom one is in a confidential relationship to influence their entering into a "good deal" might constitute undue influence. Threats of physical harm may amount to duress.

3. A. When parties contract, their agreement establishes the value of the object of their transaction for the moment. Each party is considered to assume the risk that the value will change or prove to be different from what he or she thought. In this case, the buyer assumed the risk of a drop in the price. If instead the mistake had involved a material fact and had been mutual, the buyer may have been able to avoid the contract (or enforce it).

4. D. Fraud involves misrepresentation that is intended to mislead another. The perpetrator must know or believe that the assertion is not true. Representations of future facts, statements of opinion, and most laypersons' statements about the law are generally not subject to claims of fraud. People are assumed to know the law. An exception occurs when the misrepresenting party is in a profession known to require a greater knowledge of the law than the average person possesses.

5. B. The problem states the elements of fraudulent misrepresentation: misrepresentation of a material fact, intent to deceive, and the innocent party's justifiable reliance on the misrepresentation. The misrepresentation must be an important factor in inducing the party to contract—reliance is not justified if the party knows or should know the truth. The defrauded may elect to rescind or enforce the contract. Damages are recoverable on proof of injury.

6. D. The contract may be avoided on the ground of undue influence. The inexperienced seller is justified, in these circumstances, in assuming that her nephew will not act in a manner inconsistent with her best interests.

7. B. An adhesion contract (which is what a standard form contract often is) may not be enforced if the adhering party (the buyer, in this problem) shows that the parties had substantially unequal bargaining positions and enforcement would be unfair or oppressive. Such a contract may be avoided on grounds of unconscionability (the most likely possibility here), fraud, undue influence, or duress.

8. D. Proof of an injury is required to recover damages on the ground of misrepresentation. Proof of an injury is not generally required to rescind a contract on that basis.

9. B. Normally, a party to a contract does not have a duty to disclose defects. If a serious defect is known to the seller that is not known or could not be reasonably suspected by the buyer, however, the contract may be avoided by the buyer on the basis of misrepresentation.

10. D. Threatening to exercise a legal right, such as the right to sue to enforce a contract, is not duress. It is also not misrepresentation or undue influence.

RockOn

1. No. The buyer's reliance on the simple financial statement was not reasonable. You—the seller—suggested that the buyer hire an accountant to review the statement and the store's records. This should have indicated to the buyer that an accountant's review was required, and his subsequent reliance on the unaudited statement was not justifiable. In other words, when there are means by which the accuracy of a statement can be verified, and it would be reasonable to do this, justifiable reliance requires it.

2. No. You are not liable with respect to the mistakes because the contractor was aware of them. These errors are unilateral mistakes—only one party, you, made them. In such cases, the mistaken party is held to the contract. But if the other party knew or should have known of the mistake, the mistaken party is not held to the contract. Here, the general contractor was aware of your errors, and thus you are not bound to the contract nor are you subject to liability for the mistakes.

Chapter 15

True-False Questions

1. T

2. F. A promise ancillary to a principal transaction and made by a third party to assume the debts or obligations of the primary party must generally be in writing to be enforceable. But there is an exception: an oral promise to answer for the debt of another is enforceable if the guarantor's main purpose is to secure a personal benefit.

3. F. Under the doctrine of promissory estoppel, an oral contract may be enforced if a promisor makes a promise on which the promisee justifiably relies to his or her detriment, the reliance was foreseeable to the promisor, and injustice can be avoided only by enforcing the promise.

4. T

5. F. A contract for customized goods may be enforceable under the UCC even if it is only oral. Also, oral agreements between merchants that have been confirmed in writing may be enforceable.

6. F. The Statute of Frauds requires that contracts for all transfers of interests in land be in writing to be enforceable. Included are sales, mortgages, leases, and other transfers.

7. F. The UCC's Statute of Frauds requires that contracts for sales of goods priced at $500 or more must be in writing to be enforceable. Of course, there are exceptions. Oral contracts for customized goods, for example, may be enforced in some circumstances, as may oral contracts between merchants that have been confirmed in writing.

8. T

9. F. A writing sufficient to satisfy the Statute of Frauds may be an invoice, a confirmation memo, a letter, or a combination of documents, typewritten, imprinted, or handwritten. Generally, such a writing must state the essential terms and be signed by the party against whom the contract is being enforced (although the requirements vary with the type of contract).

10. F. Under the parol evidence rule, if the parties' contract is completely integrated into a writing (which they intend to be the embodiment of their agreement), evidence of their prior negotiations, prior agreements, or contemporaneous oral agreements that contradicts or varies the terms of their contract is not admissible at trial.

Fill-in Questions

ancillary; primary; must; need not

Multiple-Choice Questions

1. A. A contract that cannot be performed within one year must be in writing to be enforceable. This contract could not be performed within one year so it must be in writing, or evidenced by a writing. (The contracts in answer choices *a* and *c* are of uncertain duration and thus could terminate within a year.)

2. C. Either party can enforce this oral contract. A contract that cannot be performed within one year must be in writing to be enforceable. Because the employee was hired to work for six months, the contract can be performed within a year and does not need to be in writing to be enforced.

3. B. Under the parol evidence rule, if a writing that is determined to constitute a contract includes everything that the parties intended, no evidence of prior negotiations, prior agreements, or contemporaneous oral negotiations may be used to change the terms. A later oral agreement is admissible, however. This question and answer are based on a question that appeared as part of the CPA exam in May 1995.

4. C. Under the Statute of Frauds, a contract for the sale of an interest in land must be in writing to be enforceable. A party to an oral contract involving an interest in land cannot force the other party to buy or sell the property.

5. B. This is an exception to the rule that a contract for a transfer of an interest in land is not enforceable unless it is in writing. If a buyer pays part of the price, takes possession, and makes permanent improvements and the parties cannot be returned to their pre-contract status quo, a court may grant specific performance of an oral contract for the transfer of an interest in land.

6. C. The Statute of Frauds requires only a writing signed by the party against whom enforcement is sought. Thus, a signed sales receipt may be enough. A purchase order that is signed only be the party seeking its enforcement, or not signed by either party, would not qualify, regardless of the details that are included on the form.

7. D. Letterhead stationery, and even a business card, might qualify as a signed writing. But neither would be sufficient proof on which to enforce a contract without proof of the necessary terms—parties, subject matter, price, and consideration. In the case of a sale of property, in some states those terms include price and a description of the property.

8. C. Under the UCC, an oral contract for goods priced at $500 or more is enforceable to the extent that the buyer accepts delivery of the goods (or the seller accepts payment). Note that there must be delivery or payment for this exception to the Statute of Frauds to apply.

9. D. A collateral promise must be in writing to be enforceable unless the main purpose of the party making the promise is to secure a benefit for himself or herself. Here, the problem does not include such a purpose. (A collateral promise is a secondary, or ancillary, promise to a primary, or principal, contractual relationship—a third party's promise to assume the debt of a primary party to a contract, for example.)

10. C. If the main purpose of a guarantor in accepting secondary liability is to serve a benefit for himself or herself, the contract need not be in writing to be enforceable. Here, the guaranty is to serve the guarantor's purpose, so it does not need to be in writing to be enforced.

RockOn

1. Yes, the oral agreement is enforceable. A contract that cannot be performed within one year of the date of its formation must be in writing to be enforceable under the Statute of Frauds. The contract in this question allows sixteen months for its performance but it can be performed within one year. Therefore, it is enforceable even though it is oral and not in writing.

2. No. The parol evidence rule excludes evidence of prior or contemporaneous oral agreements that vary the terms of a written contract. It is stated in the problem that the parties agreed the landlord would pay for the utilities, but the written lease provided for their payment by the tenants. Thus, the parol evidence rule will bar the introduction of evidence concerning these parties' oral agreement with respect to who pays the utility bills for the leased property.

Chapter 16

True-False Questions

1. F. Intended beneficiaries have legal rights in contracts under which they benefit. An intended beneficiary is a party whom the contracting parties intended to benefit. Third parties who benefit from a contract only incidentally (incidental beneficiaries) normally do not have rights under the contract.

2. F. In an assignment, the party assigning the rights is the *assignor*. The *obligor* is the party who was originally obligated to perform for the assignor. The party who receives the rights on an assignment is the *assignee* (who may also be the *obligee*). In a delegation, the party delegating the duties is the *delegator* (also the *obligator*) and the party assuming the duties is the *delegatee*.

3. F. A right under a personal service contract cannot normally be assigned. Also, a right cannot ordinarily be assigned if a statute expressly prohibits its assignment, a contract stipulates that it cannot be assigned, or assignment would materially increase or alter the risk of the obligor.

4. F. Rights that cannot be assigned are listed in the answer to the previous question. A right cannot be assigned if (1) a statute expressly prohibits its assignment; (2) a contract stipulates that it cannot be assigned; (3) it is under a contract that is uniquely personal; or (4) assignment would materially increase or alter the risk of the obligor.

5.   T
6.   T
7.   F. An assignment is effective with or without notice. Until the obligor has notice of the assignment, however, the obligor can discharge his or her obligation by performance to the assignor. Also, if the same right is assigned without notice to more than one party, there may be a question as to who has priority.
8.   T
9.   T
10.   T

Fill-in Questions

an assignment; a delegation; assigned; assign

Multiple-Choice Questions

1.   C. An incidental beneficiary cannot enforce a contract between two other parties. An example of such a contract would be a consumer's agreement to buy a new car from an auto dealer. The car's manufacturer would indirectly benefit under this contract, but could not enforce it if, for example, the consumer refused to pay the dealer.
2.   B. The party originally entitled to the payment of the money is the assignor, the party who agreed to pay is the obligor, and the party who receives the right to the payment is the assignee. An assignee has a right to demand performance from an obligor, but the assignee takes only those rights that the assignor originally had, and these rights are subject to defenses that the obligor has against the assignor. The obligor's consent is not necessary for an effective assignment.
3.   A. The rights of an intended third party beneficiary to a contract vest when the original parties cannot rescind or change the contract without the third party's consent. This occurs when the beneficiary learns of the contract and manifests assent to it. This also occurs when the beneficiary changes position in reliance on the contract.
4.   C. A right cannot normally be assigned if the assignment would materially increase or alter the risk of the obligor (the different circumstances represented by different persons with different property alter the risk in this problem). A right under a personal service contract cannot normally be assigned, but this is not a personal service contract, which requires a service unique to the person rendering it (an insurance policy is unlikely to qualify).
5.   D. Delegating a duty does not normally free the delegator of the obligation to perform if the delega-

tee does not do so. Ordinarily, if a delegatee fails to perform, the delegator remains liable to the obligee. Of course, the obligee must accept performance from the delegatee if it is forthcoming. Note that here, this is not a personal service contract, which would prohibit its delegation, nor is its delegation prohibited by any other circumstance.
6.   D. The presence of one or more of any of these factors strongly indicates that a third party is an intended, rather than an incidental, beneficiary.
7.   D. An assignment is not valid if it materially increases or alters the risk or duties of the obligor. An assignment is also invalid if a statute prohibits it, if it involves a contract for personal services, or if, with some exceptions, the contract stipulates that it cannot be assigned. This question and answer are based on a question that appeared in the CPA exam in May 1995.
8.   D. An anti-assignment contract clause is generally effective, but there are exceptions. One of those exceptions concerns the right to receive damages for the breach of a sales contract. The assignment of such a right is valid, even if the contract prohibits it.
9.   A. The effect of an unconditional assignment is to extinguish the rights of the assignor. Such an assignment also gives the assignee a right to demand performance from the obligor. Of course, the assignee's rights are subject to the defenses the obligor has against the assignor.
10.   C. An assignment does not require notice. When an assignor assigns the same right to different persons, in most states the first to receive the assignment is the first in right.

RockOn

1.   Yes, Jack can enforce the agreement between the contracting parties, even though he is not a party to the deal, because he is an intended third party beneficiary of it. That is, the original parties to the contract intended at the time of contracting that their performance directly benefit a third person—Jack. In such a situation, the third person is a beneficiary of the contract and has legal rights with regard to it. He or she can sue the promisor directly to enforce it. Thus, if the group's new management agency does not pay its debts to the old manager Jack, he can sue Mega for breach, even though he was not an original party to the contract.
2.   Yes. You remained liable to the party with whom you originally contracted despite the fact that you delegated you duties under the contract to a third party. A delegation of duties does not relieve the delegator—you—of your obligations under a contract. If, as occurred here, the delegatee does not

perform properly, the delegator is liable to the obligee.

Chapter 17

True-False Questions

1. T
2. T
3. F. A material breach of contract (which occurs when performance is not at least substantial) excuses the nonbreaching party from performance of his or her contractual duties and gives the party a cause of action to sue for damages caused by the breach. A *minor* breach of contract does not excuse the nonbreaching party's duty to perform, however, although it may affect the extent of his or her performance and, like any contract breach, allows the nonbreaching party to sue for damages.
4. F. An executory contract can be rescinded. If it is executory on both sides, it can be rescinded solely by agreement. In any case, the parties must make a new agreement, and this agreement must qualify as a contract. (The parties' promises not to perform are consideration for the new contract.)
5. T
6. T
7. T
8. T
9. F. A contracting party's refusal to perform, before either party is required to do so, constitutes anticipatory repudiation and can discharge the nonbreaching party, who can sue to recover damages immediately. The nonbreaching party can also seek a similar contract elsewhere.
10. F. Statutes of limitations limit the period during which a party can sue based on a breach of contract. UCC 2–725, for example, limits this time to four years.

Fill-in Questions

Rescission; Novation; Substitution of a new contract; An accord; accord

Multiple-Choice Questions

1. A. An accord is an executory contract to perform an act to satisfy a contractual duty that has not been discharged (that is, to provide and accept performance different from what was originally promised). An accord suspends the original obligation. A satisfaction is the performance of the accord. If a party does not perform under an accord, the nonbreaching party can bring an action based on either the accord or the original contract.
2. B. For mutual rescission, the parties must make a contract that satisfies the legal requirements, which include consideration. Promises not to perform as originally agreed can constitute consideration when a contract is executory. If it is executed on one side, however, additional consideration or restitution is necessary.
3. C. Contracts that involve construction need only be performed to the satisfaction of a reasonable person. When a contract requires performance to the satisfaction of a third party, a few courts require the personal satisfaction of the third party (who must act honestly and in good faith). A majority of courts require the work to be satisfactory to a reasonable person. In this problem, if the work would satisfy a reasonable person, it must be paid for, regardless of the subjective motivation of the party to whom performance was rendered.
4. A. A breach of contract entitles the nonbreaching party to damages, but only a material breach discharges the nonbreaching party from his or her duty to perform under the contract. In this problem, the builder has a claim for the amount due on the contract, but the buyer is entitled to have set off the difference in the value of the building as constructed (that is, to subtract the expense to finish the construction).
5. A. Reneging on an employment contract before the employment starts is anticipatory repudiation of the contract and discharges the nonbreaching party from performance. The nonbreaching party can treat the anticipatory breach as a material breach and sue for damages immediately.
6. B. A condition that must be fulfilled before a party is required to perform is a condition precedent. In other words, the condition precedes the absolute duty to perform.
7. C. A novation substitutes a new party for an original party, by agreement of all the parties. The requirements are a previous valid obligation, an agreement of all the parties to a new contract, extinguishment of the old obligation, and a new contract (which must meet the requirements for a valid contract, including consideration).
8. D. Accord and satisfaction, agreement, and operation of law are valid bases on which contracts are discharged, but most contracts are discharged by the parties' doing what they promised to do. A contract is fully discharged by performance when the contracting parties have fully performed what they agreed to do (exchange services for payment, for example).
9. B. This contract would thus be discharged by objective impossibility of performance. On this ba-

sis, a contract may be discharged if, for example, after it is made, performance becomes objectively impossible because of a change in the law that renders that performance illegal. This is also the result if one of the parties dies or becomes incapacitated, or the subject matter of the contract is destroyed. This question and answer is based on a question in the May 1995 CPA exam.

10. D. Contracts that have not been fully performed on either side can be rescinded. The parties must make another agreement (which must satisfy the legal requirements for a contract). The parties' promises not to perform are consideration for the new agreement. A contract that has been fully performed on one side can be rescinded only if the party who has performed receives additional consideration to call off the deal.

RockOn

1. The transaction between these three parties—the bank, the investors, and you—is a novation. There was a previously valid obligation between you and the bank, the three parties in the problem agreed to a new contract, the obligation under the original contract was expressly extinguished by the new contract. Under the new contract, the investors replaced you as a party to the loan from the bank. The investors took on the responsibility and liability for payment of the loan. You were released from liability. Note that under an assignment, in which you might have assigned the rights to the property and delegated the duty to pay the loan to the investors, you would have remained liable if they failed to pay.

2. A party who in good faith performs substantially all of the terms of a contract can enforce the contract against the other party under the doctrine of substantial performance. To qualify as substantial, the performance must not vary greatly from the performance promised in the contract. It must create substantially the same benefits. If the defect in performance can easily be compensated for by an award of damages, the contract will likely be held to have been substantially performed. The measure of damages is the cost to bring the object of the contract into compliance. If that cost is unreasonable, the measure is the difference in value between the performance that was rendered and complete performance. In this problem, the failure to deliver a working voice-recognition (VR) system is a breach of the contract. Assuming that the breaching party acted in good faith and the system otherwise performs as promised, it could be argued that the contract was substantially performed. If a VR system can be acquired elsewhere for a reasonable cost, this could be the measure of the nonbreaching party's damages. If a VR system cannot be had, the measure would instead reflect the difference in value between the system that was promised and the one that was delivered. Joystick would owe Out of the Box the contract price minus this amount.

Chapter 18

True-False Questions

1. T
2. T
3. F. An award of nominal damages, though usually small inn amount, establishes that a breaching party acted wrongfully. Also, nominal damages may be awarded when no actual loss results from a breach of contract (but the breach must still be proved).
4. F. Liquidated damages are certain amounts of money estimated in advance of, and payable on, a breach of contract. *Liquidated* means determined, settled, or fixed.
5. T
6. F. Rescission is available in cases involving fraud, mistake, duress, or failure of consideration. Both parties must make restitution to each other by returning whatever benefit was conveyed in execution of their contract. If the actual item cannot be returned, an equivalent amount in money must be paid.
7. T
8. F. There can be no enforceable contract if the doctrine of quasi contract is to be applied. Under this doctrine, to prevent unjust enrichment, the law implies a promise to pay the reasonable value for benefits received in the absence of an enforceable contract. This recovery is useful when one party has partially performed under a contract that is unenforceable.
9. T
10. F. Damages is the usual on breach of contracts for sales of goods. To obtain specific performance, damages must *not* be an adequate remedy. If goods are unique, or a contract involves a sale of land, damages would not adequately compensate an innocent party for a breach of contract, so specific performance is available.

Fill-in Questions

the contract price and the market price; specific performance; the contract price and the market price

Multiple-Choice Questions

1. A. The failure of one party to perform under a contract entitles the other party to rescind the contract. Both parties, however, must make restitution (return goods, property, or money previously conveyed). Here, on breaching the contract, which entitled the employer to rescind the deal, the contractor did not return the amount of the employer's payment.

2. C. A breach of contract by failing to perform entitles the nonbreaching party to rescind the contract, and the parties must make restitution by returning whatever benefit they conferred on each other, particularly when the breaching party would otherwise be unjustly enriched.

3. C. Under a contract for a sale of goods, the usual measure of compensatory damages is the difference between the contract price and the market price, plus incidental damages. On a seller's breach, the measure includes the difference between what the seller would have been owed if he or she had performed and what the buyer paid elsewhere for the goods.

4. B. The measure of damages on breach of a construction contract depends on which party breaches and when the breach occurs. If, as in this problem, the owner (buyer) breaches during construction, normally the contractor (seller) may recover its profit plus the costs incurred up to the time of the breach.

5. B. On the seller's breach of a contract, the buyer is entitled to be compensated for the loss of the bargain. Here, the buyer will receive what was contracted for, but it will be late. When, as in this problem, a seller knew that the buyer would lose business if the goods were not delivered on time, the loss of the bargain is the consequential damages (the amount lost as a foreseeable consequence of the breach).

6. C. Specific performance is an award of the act promised in a contract. This remedy is granted when the legal remedy (damages) is inadequate. Damages are generally inadequate for a buyer on the breach of a contract for a sale of land, because every piece of land is considered unique. If specific performance is not available, however, as when the land cannot be sold by the contracting seller, damages are possible, and their measure is the benefit of the buyer's bargain (the difference between the contract price and the market price of the land at the time of the breach).

7. A. A quasi contract may be imposed when a party has partially performed under a contract that is unenforceable. (An oral contract, the terms of which cannot be performed within one year, is unenforceable under the one-year rule of the Statute of Frauds.) To obtain quasi-contractual relief, a party must show that (1) he or she conferred a benefit on another, (2) he or she conferred the benefit with the reasonable expectation of being paid, (3) he or she did not act as a volunteer in conferring the benefit, and (4) the party receiving the benefit would be unjustly enriched by retaining the benefit without paying for it.

8. D. The clause is a penalty clause and, as such, it is unenforceable. To determine whether a clause is a liquidated damages clause or a penalty clause, consider first whether, when the contract was made, damages would clearly be difficult to estimate in the event of a breach. Second, consider whether the amount set as damages is a reasonable estimate. Two "yeses" mean the clause is enforceable. One "no" means the provision is an unenforceable penalty. Here, the damages on the seller's breach would not be difficult to estimate, nor is the amount set in the contract a reasonable estimate of those damages.

9. A. Reformation permits a contract to be rewritten to reflect the parties' actual intentions when they have imperfectly expressed their agreement in writing. This often applies in a case of fraud or mutual mistake (in a land sale contract, for example, when the property's legal description is erroneous). To prevent hardship, a court may also reform a covenant not to compete to convert its unreasonable terms into reasonable ones.

10. D. If the clause is determined to be a penalty clause, it will be unenforceable. To determine whether a clause is a liquidated damages clause or a penalty clause, consider first whether, when the contract was made, damages would clearly be difficult to estimate in the event of a breach. Second, consider whether the amount set as damages is a reasonable estimate. Two "yeses" mean the clause is enforceable. One "no" means the provision is an unenforceable penalty. This question and answer are based on a question that was in the May 1993 CPA exam.

RockOn

1. The amount of your recovery for the promoter's breach of its contract with you would most likely include $4,250 in compensatory damages. This is the difference between the value of the breaching party's promised performance under your contract (that is, the $8,000 that the promoter would have paid you) and the value of its actual performance ($0), reduced by the amount of the loss that you avoided (the $4,250 that your band earned performing in a different venue on the contract date).

You might also recover incidental damages—any amount that you spent to find the other job.

2. You can sue the seller who refused to complete the sale for compensatory damages or specific performance. Compensatory damages compensate for the loss of a bargain—for injuries actually sustained and proved to have arisen from a breach—with the amount being the difference between the value of the promised performance and the value of the actual performance. Specific performance is the performance of the act promised in the contract. This equitable remedy may be granted if the subject of the contract is unique, which in this case would most likely be true. Each parcel of land is unique.

Cumulative Hypothetical Problem for Unit Three—Including Chapters 10–18

1. D. An offeror can revoke an offer for a bilateral contract, which is what this offer is, any time before it is accepted. This may be after the offeree is aware of the offer.

2. C. Courts impose an objective, or reasonable, analysis in determining whether or not a contract was made and in interpreting its terms. This is known as the objective theory of contracts.

3. B. A mutual mistake of fact may be a ground for relief, but it is not the only mistake for which relief may be granted. Although a party to a contract is not normally granted relief for a unilateral mistake, if the other party knew, or should have known, of the mistake, the law allows for relief.

4. C. A novation completely discharges a party to a contract. Another party assumes the discharged party's obligations. If a party has assigned his or her rights under a contract, he or she may still be liable in the event the assignee defaults. A *executed* accord would allow a party to avoid liability under a contract, but an *unexecuted* accord does not.

5. A. Damages, the remedy at law, is the usual remedy for a breach of contract. Specific performance is granted only if the remedy at law is inadequate, as it is when, for example, the goods that are the subject of a contract are unique. Courts are also reluctant to award specific performance in cases involving contracts for services.

Questions on the Focus on Ethics for Unit Three—Contract Law and the Application of Ethics

1. A. If a contract is unconscionable, it is so unfair and one-sided as to "shock the conscience" of a court and be unenforceable. Unconscionability, which represents an attempt by the law to enforce ethical behavior, is a common law concept that is not pre-cisely defined. Even UCC 2–302, which adopts the doctrine, does not define the term with specificity. Instead, it is the prerogative of the courts to determine its application in contract cases.

2. D. If, in contracting, an individual fails to look after his or her own interest, the party with whom he or she contracts arguably does not have a responsibility to look after the other's interest. It can be acceptable to take advantage of the circumstance, although if there is a suit, the court might consider the relative bargaining positions of the parties to decide whether the deal is too one-sided.

3. C. In the interests of fairness and justice, a court may estop the subcontractor from denying the existence of a contract, in the circumstances presented in this question. A party who reasonably relies on such a promise to his or her detriment can then obtain some measure of relief for any ensuing injury or damage. Ethical standards underlie this doctrine.

Chapter 19

True-False Questions

1. T

2. T

3. F. If a transaction involves only a service, the common law usually applies (one exception is the serving of food or drink, which is governed by the UCC). When goods and services are combined, courts have disagreed over whether a particular transaction involves a sale of goods or a rendering of service. Usually, a court will apply the law that applies to whichever feature is dominant. Article 2 does not cover sales of real estate, although sales of goods associated with real estate, including crops, may be covered. A contract for a sale of minerals, for example, is considered a contract for a sale of goods if the severance is to be made by the seller.

4. F. Unlike the common law rule that contract modification must be supported by new consideration, the UCC requires no consideration for an agreement modifying a contract.

5. F. A contract will be enforceable, and a writing will be sufficient under the UCC's Statute of Frauds, if it indicates that a contract was intended, if it includes a quantity term, and—except for transactions between merchants—if it is signed by the party against whom enforcement is sought. Most terms can be proved by oral testimony or be supplied by the UCC's open term provisions (for example, price, delivery, and payment terms). A contract is not enforceable beyond the quantity of goods shown in the writing, however, except for output and requirements contracts.

6. T
7. T
8. F. A seller can accept an offer to buy goods for current or prompt shipment by promptly *shipping* the goods or by promptly *promising* to ship the goods. Of course, under the mirror image rule, an offer must be accepted in its entirety without modification, or there is no contract. Under the UCC, additional terms may become part of the contract if both parties are merchants (though not if at least one party is a nonmerchant).
9. T
10. F. Under the UCC, oral contracts for specially manufactured goods may be enforceable. Also, an oral contract for a sale or lease of goods may be enforceable if the party against whom enforcement is sought admits in court pleadings or proceedings that a contract was made. Partial performance of a contract for a sale or lease of goods may also support the enforcement of an oral contract, at least to the extent of that performance.

Fill-in Questions

Course of dealing; Usage of trade; trade; consistent; terms in the agreement

Multiple-Choice Questions

1. D. A sale is defined in the UCC as "the passing of title from the seller to the buyer for a price." The price may be payable in money or in goods, or services. A lease involves the transfer of possession and use, not title, in exchange for rental payments. (Article 2A of the UCC applies to leases.)
2. B. A merchant is a person who acts in a mercantile capacity, possessing or using expertise specifically related to the goods being sold. A merchant for one type of goods is not necessarily a merchant for another type, however. The test is whether the merchant holds himself or herself out by occupation as having knowledge or skill unique to the goods in the transaction.
3. A. Under the UCC, a sales contract will not fail for indefiniteness even if one or more terms are left open, as long as the parties intended to make a contract and there is a reasonably certain basis for the court to grant an appropriate remedy. If the price term is left open, for example, and the parties cannot later agree on a price, a court will set the price according to what is reasonable at the time for delivery. If one of the parties is to set the price, it must be set in good faith. If it is not fixed, the other

party can set the price or treat the contract as canceled.
4. B. A lease involves a lessor who leases (or buys) goods from a supplier and leases (or subleases) them to a lessee. In other words, a lessor sells the right to the possession and use of goods under a lease. Sales are subject to Article 2 of the UCC. Gifts are not subject to the UCC.
5. A. The contract is subject to the Statute of Frauds, and thus should be in writing to be fully enforceable. (Initialed notes, among other things, may constitute a sufficient writing.) A contract that is subject to the Statute of Frauds but is not in writing will be enforceable, however, under the partial performance exception when payment is made and accepted (at least to the extent of the payment actually made). Other enforceable exceptions include admissions in court and contracts for specially made goods (if they are not suitable for sale to others and if substantial steps have been taken toward their manufacture).
6. C. In a transaction between merchants, additional terms in the acceptance of an offer become part of a contract *unless* they fall under one of three exceptions. One exception is the other merchant's objection to the terms within a reasonable time. Another exception exists if the first merchant's form expressly required acceptance of its terms. The third exception occurs when the additional terms materially alter the original contract.
7. A. A contract in writing that was intended to be a final expression cannot be contradicted by evidence of prior agreements or contemporaneous oral agreements. Some evidence outside the contract is admissible, however. Besides the evidence noted in the correct answer, evidence of what the parties did under the contract (their course of dealing and their course of performance) and the usage in their trade (commercial practices) is also admissible.
8. C. A firm offer can only be made by a merchant in a signed writing. The other party does not need to be a merchant. Consideration is not necessary, and no definite period need be specified. This question and answer are based on a question that appeared in the CPA exam in November 1995.
9. A. An unconscionable clause is one that is so unfair and one-sided that it would be unreasonable to enforce it. When considering such a clause, a court can choose among the answers choices in this problem. To assess unconscionability, a court may weigh such factors as a high price, a consumer's level of education, and his or her capacity to compare prices.
10. D. Contracts without specified quantities are not enforceable under the UCC. The UCC includes a number of open-term provisions that can be used to

fill the gaps in a contract. Terms for delivery, payment, and price can be proved by evidence, or whatever is reasonable will be determined. The quantity of goods must be expressly stated, however, or a court cannot award a remedy.

Starbucks Coffee Co. International Sales Contract Applications

1. B. As stated in the "Breach or Default of Contract" clause on the second page, this contract is subject to Article 2 of the UCC. If the parties to a sales contract do not express some of the terms in writing, including the price term, the contract is still enforceable. A sales contract that must be in writing is only enforceable, however, to the extent of the quantity stated in writing. If these parties did not state the amount of product ordered, the contract may not be enforced because if a quantity term is left out, the court would have no basis for determining a remedy.

2. B. When a seller, as a party to a sales contract, states or otherwise expresses what the goods will be, then the goods must be that. The goods must at least conform to the seller's description of them, wherever that descriptions is, whether in the contract, in promotional materials, on labels, by salespersons, by comparison to a sample, etc. A seller's subjective belief is not the standard. The buyer's subjective belief may be the standard if the contract specifies that the goods must personally satisfy the buyer.

3. C. This clause states the terms for payment under this sales contract and indicates that the buyer has two days after the day of tender in which to pay for the goods or will be considered in breach. The "BREACH OR DEFAULT OF CONTRACT" clause sets out what happens "if either party hereto fails to perform." These are all incentives for the buyer to pay on time.

4. A. This clause allows the buyer to reject nonconforming product, although this is limited to a specific number of days. (Note that the buyer' right to reject does not need to be stated in a contract for the buyer to have that right.) This clause details the procedures that the parties may follow if the product does not meet its description. These are incentives for the seller to deliver conforming goods.

5. D. This is a destination contract, as indicated by the "ARRIVAL," "DELIVERY," "INSURANCE," and "FREIGHT" clauses. This means that the seller bears the risk of loss until the coffee is delivered to its destination (a "Bonded Public Warehouse" in Laredo, Texas). Risk of loss is discussed in more detail in the following chapter.

RockOn

1. Yes, you would win a suit to enforce the rain check. This item meets the requirements of a merchant's firm offer. Under the UCC, a firm offer exists if a merchant gives assurances in a signed writing that his or her offer will remain open. This type of offer is irrevocable, even without consideration, for a reasonable period not to exceed three months if no other time limit is stated. In this problem, the employee gave you a signed rain check for the guitar. The merchant is thus obligated to honor it within a reasonable time. Your return in one month is certainly within that time frame.

2. The agreement to deliver the goods on June 1—the modified delivery date—was binding. An oral agreement that modifies a contract for a sale of goods does not need new consideration to be binding. Because the contract in this problem involves a sale of goods for less than $500, it does not fall within the Statute of Frauds, and the oral modification is enforceable. Of course, a modification must be sought in good faith. But there does not seem to be any question here that the change in delivery dates was not sought in good faith.

Chapter 20

True-False Questions

1. T

2. F. Title passes at the time and place at which the seller delivers the goods—unless the parties agree otherwise, which is always an option under the UCC.

3. T

4. F. This is the definition of a sale or return.

5. F. A buyer has an insurable interest in goods the moment they are identified to the contract by the seller. A seller has an insurable interest in goods as long as he or she has title. After title has passed, a seller who has a security interest in goods retains an insurable interest. Thus, a buyer and a seller can both have an insurable interest in goods at the same time.

6. T

7. F. In a sale on approval, the risk of loss remains with the seller until the buyer accepts the goods.

8. F. Generally, a buyer acquires whatever title the seller has to the goods. If a seller (or lessor) stole the goods, he or she has no title, and the buyer (or lessee, who might otherwise acquire a valid leasehold interest) gets nothing. The real owner can reclaim the goods from the buyer or the thief.

9. F. Under a *shipment* contract, title passes at time and place of shipment. Under a destination contract, title passes when the goods are tendered at a certain destination.

10. T

Fill-in Questions

F.O.B.; F.O.B.; F.O.B.; F.A.S.

Multiple-Choice Questions

1. C. These are the requirements for identification. Title and risk of loss cannot pass from seller to buyer until the goods are identified to the contract. Other actions on the part of a seller, such as arranging for shipment or obtaining insurance, do not determine when an interest in goods passes.

2. B. A contract's shipping term is the most important factor in determining when the risk of loss of the goods subject to the contract passes from the seller to the buyer. Under a shipment contract, the risk of loss passes when the seller gives the goods to the carrier. Under a destination contract, the risk of loss passes when the seller tenders delivery of the goods to the buyer. This question and answer are based on a question that appeared in the November 1995 CPA exam.

3. C. When goods are to be picked up by a buyer, if a seller is a nonmerchant, risk passes on the seller's tender of delivery (unless the parties agree otherwise). The goods were tendered before the theft, so the buyer suffers the loss. If the seller is a merchant, the risk of loss passes when the buyer takes possession of the goods.

4. B. If a bailee holds goods for a seller and the goods are delivered without being moved, under a negotiable document of title, the risk of loss passes when the buyer receives the document. If the document is nonnegotiable, however, more is required to transfer the risk: the buyer must also have had a reasonable time to present the document and demand the goods. In either case, the risk can also pass on the bailee's acknowledgment of the buyer's right to possess the goods. In any case, if the bailee refuses to recognize the buyer's right, the loss stays with the seller.

5. C. Under a destination contract, the risk of loss passes when the seller tenders delivery at the specified destination. This agreement—"F.O.B. Omni" (the buyer)—is a shipment contract under which the seller was required to deliver the goods to the buyer. Thus, the destination was the buyer's location, and the goods were lost before they reached that destination. The loss was the seller's. (Of course, the seller will most likely have insurance to cover the loss.) Also, note that "F.O.B." indicates the seller bears the cost of the transport to the specified destination.

6. B. A buyer has an insurable interest in goods as soon as they are identified to the contract, even before the risk of loss passes. A seller has an insurable interest as long as he or she still has title to the goods. More than one party can have an insurable interest at the same time.

7. B. Generally, the party who breaches a contract bears the risk of loss. Here, the seller breached by shipping defective goods. The risk would have passed to the buyer if the buyer accepted the goods in spite of their defects. (If the buyer had accepted the goods and then discovered the defects, the buyer could have revoked its acceptance, which would have transferred the risk back to the seller.)

8. B. Under a shipment contract, if the contracting parties do not specify a time for title to pass, then it passes on delivery of the goods to the carrier.

9. C. Entrusting goods to a merchant who deals in goods of the kind gives the merchant power to transfer all rights to a buyer in the ordinary course of business. The owner of the car has good title against the dealer, but a buyer in the ordinary course of business can acquire, in good faith, good title from the merchant. This title is good against even the original owner. Note that had a thief stolen the car from the original owner and left it with the dealer, the later buyer would not have good title against the original owner.

10. C. When goods are to be picked up by a buyer, if a seller is a merchant, the risk of loss does not pass to the buyer until the buyer takes possession of the goods (unless the parties agree otherwise). The goods were tendered before the theft, but the buyer did not take possession.

RockOn

1. Before the fire, the buyer in this problem did not have title to the trombones. Under the UCC, title passes to a buyer when the seller delivers the goods. Here, the goods were identified to the contract but not delivered—they were not even yet loaded on a truck for delivery when the fire occurred. The identification of the goods did give the buyer the right to obtain insurance on them, however.

2. No, you cannot recover the equipment you ordered because it was not identified to the contract. Before any interest in goods can pass from a seller to a buyer, the goods must be in existence and they must be identified as the specific goods designated in the contract. Here, of course, the goods existed as part of the seller's inventory. But they had not been

separated or otherwise marked, shipped, designated, or distinguished by the seller as the particular goods to pass under this contract.

Chapter 21

True-False Questions

1. T
2. T
3. T
4. F. If the parties do not agree otherwise, the buyer or lessee must pay for the goods at the time and place of their receipt (subject, in most cases, to the buyer or lessee's right to inspect). When a sale is on credit, a buyer must pay according to credit terms, not when the goods are received. Credit terms may provide for payment within thirty days, for example. A credit period usually begins on the date of shipment.
5. F. If a contract does not state where goods are to be delivered, and the buyer is to pick them up, the place for delivery is the seller's place of business (unless the parties know that the goods are elsewhere, in which case the place of their delivery is their location). Shipment and destination contracts are subject to different rules that depend on their terms.
6. F. A buyer or lessee who accepts nonconforming goods can revoke the acceptance, but only notifying the seller or lessor, which must occur within a reasonable time and before goods have, for example, spoiled. If the goods are perishable, the buyer or lessee must follow any reasonable instructions of the seller or lessor regarding the goods. (This is also the case when the buyer or lessee rejects the goods.)
7. F. Before the time for performance, if a buyer or lessee clearly communicates his or her intent not to perform, the seller or lessor can suspend performance and wait to see if the other will perform, or the seller or lessor can treat the anticipatory repudiation as a breach, suspend performance, and pursue a remedy.
8. F. A buyer can reject an installment only if its nonconformity *substantially impairs* the value of the installment and it cannot be cured (in which case, the seller has breached the contract).
9. T
10. T

Fill-in Questions

conforming; and; buyer; receipt; even if

Multiple-Choice Questions

1. C. The parties to a contract can stipulate the time, place, and manner of delivery. In the absence of specified details, however, tender of delivery must be at a reasonable hour and in a reasonable manner. The buyer must be notified, and the goods must be kept available for a reasonable time. This question and answer are based on a question that appeared in the CPA exam in November 1995.
2. B. Replevin is an action to recover specific goods in the possession of a party who is wrongfully withholding them. When a seller (or lessor) refuses to deliver (or repudiates the contract), the buyer or lessee may maintain an action to replevy the goods. The buyer or lessee must show, however, an inability to cover.
3. B. Under the circumstances in this problem, the buyer's best course is to attempt to obtain substitute goods for those that were due under the contract. When a buyer is forced to obtain cover, the buyer can recover from the seller the difference between the cost of the cover and the contract price, plus incidental and consequential damages, less whatever expenses (such as delivery costs) were saved as a result of the seller's breach.
4. A. It is the seller's obligation to tender delivery of goods. Under a shipment contract, a seller must make a reasonable contract for the transportation of goods, tender to the buyer whatever documents are necessary to obtain possession of goods from the carrier, and notify the buyer that shipment has been made.
5. C. If a buyer repudiates a contract or wrongfully refuses to accept goods, a seller can sue for damages equal to the difference between the contract price and the market price at the time and place of tender. The seller can also recover incidental damages, which include the cost of transporting the goods. If the market price is less than the contract price, damages include the seller's lost profits.
6. C. Depending on the circumstances, when a seller or lessor delivers nonconforming goods, the buyer or lessee can reject the part of the goods that does not conform (and rescind the contract or obtain cover). The buyer or lessee may instead revoke acceptance, or he or she may recover damages, for accepted goods.
7. C. A buyer (or lessee) can sue for damages when a seller (or lessor) repudiates the contract or fails to deliver the goods, or when the buyer has rightfully rejected or revoked acceptance of the goods. The place for determining the price is the place at which the seller was to deliver the goods. The buyer may also recover incidental and conse-

quential damages, less expenses saved due to the breach.

8.   C. If a buyer repudiates a contract or wrongfully refuses to accept goods, a seller can cancel the contract, which discharges the seller's obligations, or sue for damages: the difference between the contract price and the market price at the time and place of tender. The seller can also recover incidental damages. If the market price is less than the contract price, damages include the seller's lost profits. This question and answer are based on a question from the November 1995 CPA exam.

9.   B. Unless the contract provides otherwise, a buyer (or lessee) has an absolute right to inspect tendered goods before making payment, to verify that they are as ordered. If they are not as ordered, the buyer has no duty to pay, and the seller cannot enforce any right to payment.

10. A. If, before the time of performance, a party to a contract informs the other party that he or she will not perform, the nonbreaching party can treat the repudiation as a final breach and seek a remedy or wait, for a commercially reasonable time, hoping that the breaching party will decide to honor the contract. In either case, the nonbreaching party can suspend his or her performance.

RockOn

1.   Yes, the seller is in breach of the contract in this problem. The seller did not comply with the perfect tender rule, which requires that goods and their tender not fail in any respect to conform to the contract. The note of accommodation has no bearing on this issue. And because the seller sent the nonconforming goods on the last day to ship the order, there is no time to cure the breach. In this situation, the buyer has the right the reject the goods. Of course, the buyer also has the right to accept the goods, which might be an option in this set of facts.

2.   Here, you can recover the contract price plus incidental damages, which consist of the storage costs—a total of $256,000. This is the remedy when a buyer breaches a contract by refusing to accept conforming, specially manufactured goods and the seller is unable to resell them.

Chapter 22

True-False Questions

1.   T

2.   F. Warranties are not exclusive. A contract can include an implied warranty of merchantability, an implied warranty of fitness for a particular purpose, and any number of express warranties.

3.   F. Unless the circumstances indicate otherwise, the implied warranty of merchantability (and the implied warranty of fitness for a particular purpose) can be disclaimed by such expressions as "as is" and "with all faults." A disclaimer of the implied warranty of merchantability must mention *merchantability*. Express warranties can also be disclaimed.

4.   T

5.   F. An action based on negligence does not require privity of contract. At one time, there was a requirement of privity in product liability actions based on negligence, but this requirement began to be eliminated decades ago. Privity of contract is also not a requirement to bring a suit based on strict product liability.

6.   F. In an action based on strict liability, a plaintiff does not have to prove that there was a failure to exercise due care. That distinguishes an action based on strict liability from an action based on negligence, which requires proof of a lack of due care. A plaintiff must show, however, that (1) a product was defective, (2) the defendant was in the business of distributing the product, (3) the product was unreasonably dangerous due to the defect, (4) the plaintiff suffered harm, (5) the defect was the proximate cause of the harm, and (6) the goods were not substantially changed from the time they were sold.

7.   T

8.   T

9.   F. There is no duty to warn about such risks. Warnings about such risks do not add to the safety of products and could make other warnings seem less significant. In fact, a plaintiff's action in the face of such a risk can be raised as a defense in a product liability suit.

10. T

Fill-in Questions

can; can; can; need not; must

Multiple-Choice Questions

1.   C. An implied warranty of merchantability arises in every sale of goods by a merchant who deals in goods of the kind. It makes no difference whether the merchant knew of or could have discovered a defect that makes a product unsafe. The warranty is that the goods are "reasonably fit for the ordinary purposes for which such goods are used." The efficiency and the quality of their manufacture, and the manufacturer's compliance with government regulations, are not factors that directly influence this determination.

2. A. To disclaim an implied warranty of fitness for a particular purpose, a warranty must be conspicuous, but the word *fitness* does not have to be used. A disclaimer of the implied warranty of merchantability must mention *merchantability*. Warranties of title, however, can be disclaimed only by specific language (for example, a seller states that it is transferring only such rights as it has in the goods), or by circumstances that indicate no warranties of title are made.

3. A. Showing a sample to a customer creates a warranty that the goods delivered to the customer will in fact match the sample. A sample represents a standard that the goods must meet. Warranties of fitness for a particular purpose, merchantability, and usage of trade are implied warranties. This question and answer are based on a question that appeared on the CPA exam in 1997.

4. D. This is a statement of opinion (puffing). Puffing creates no warranty. If the salesperson had said something factual about the vehicle (its miles per gallon, its total mileage, whether it had been in an accident, etc.), it would be more than puffing and could qualify as an express warranty.

5. A. Assumption of risk is a defense in an action based on product liability if the plaintiff knew and appreciated the risk created by the defect and voluntarily undertook the risk, even though it was unreasonable to do so.

6. A. A manufacturer may be held liable if its product is unsafe as a result of negligence in the manufacture or if the design makes it unreasonably dangerous for the use for which it is made. A manufacturer also has a duty to warn and to anticipate reasonably foreseeable misuses. An injury must not have been due to a change in the product after it was sold, but there is no requirement of privity. There is no liability, however, with respect to injuries caused by commonly known dangers, even if the manufacturer does not warn against them.

7. D. In a product liability action based on strict liability, the plaintiff does not need to prove that anyone was at fault. Privity of contract is also not an element of an action in strict liability. A plaintiff does have to show, however, in a suit against a seller, that the seller was a merchant engaged in the business of selling the product on which the suit is based. Note that recovery is possible against sellers who are processors, assemblers, packagers, bottlers, wholesalers, distributors, retailers, or lessors, as well as against manufacturers.

8. C. These choices concern the defective condition of a product that causes harm to a plaintiff. A product may be unreasonably dangerous due to a flaw in the manufacturing process, a design defect, or an inadequate warning.

9. C. All courts extend the doctrine of strict liability to injured bystanders. A defendant does not have to prove that the manufacturer or seller failed to use due care, nor is there a requirement of privity (or "intent" with regard to entering into privity). The defense of assumption of risk does not apply, because one cannot assume a risk that one does not know about.

10. B. If a manufacturer fails to use due care to make a product safe, the manufacturer may be liable for product liability based on negligence. This care must be used in designing the product, selecting the materials, producing the product, inspecting and testing any components, assembling the product, and placing warnings on the product.

RockOn

1. Yes, the seller in this problem has violated an express warranty that the goods will conform to the seller's promise with respect to the ability of the goods to meet the buyer's needs. Such an express warranty is created by an affirmation of fact or other promise that becomes part of the basis of the bargain. It is a question of fact in every case as to whether a seller's representation was made at a time and in a way so as to induce a buyer to enter into a contract. It seems clear in this set of facts, however, that the seller's problem induced the purchase. You would not likely have otherwise bought equipment that was not sufficient for your needs.

2. Yes, you can recover damages without proof of negligence. An injured plaintiff—you, in this case—can sue a seller on a theory of strict product liability if the plaintiff can show that a good was sold in a defective or unreasonably dangerous condition and caused the injuries complained of. The plaintiff does not need to prove fault, wrongdoing, or a breach of due care by the defendant.

Chapter 23

True-False Questions

1. F. According to the principle of comity, however, a nation will give effect to the laws of another nation if those laws are consistent with the law and public policy of the accommodating nation.

2. F. The act of state doctrine tends to immunize foreign nations from the jurisdiction of U.S. courts—that is, foreign nations are often exempt from U.S. jurisdiction under this doctrine.

3. F. As with the act of state doctrine, the doctrine of sovereign immunity tends to immunize foreign nations from the jurisdiction of U.S. courts

4. F. The Foreign Sovereign Immunities Act sets forth the major exceptions to the immunity of foreign nations to U.S. jurisdiction.

5. T

6. F. U.S. courts can exercise jurisdiction over a foreign entity under U.S. antitrust laws when a violation has a substantial effect on U.S. commerce or is a *per se* violation of those laws.

7. F. Legal systems in all nations can be generally divided into *common* law and civil law systems.

8. T

9. T

10. T

Fill-in Questions

An expropriation; A confiscation; an expropriation; a confiscation

Multiple-Choice Questions

1. C. The U.S. Congress cannot tax exports, but it may establish export quotas. In particular, under the Export Administration Act of 1979, restrictions can be imposed on the export of technologically advanced products.

2. C. Under certain conditions, the doctrine of sovereign immunity prohibits U.S. courts from exercising jurisdiction over foreign nations. Under the Foreign Sovereign Immunities Act, a foreign state is not immune when the action is based on a commercial activity carried on in the United States by the foreign state.

3. A. Under the act of state doctrine, the judicial branch of one country will not examine the validity of public acts committed by a recognized foreign government within its own territory. The awarding of a government contract under the circumstances described in the problem meets this criterion.

4. C. U.S. courts give effect to the judicial decrees of another country under the principle of comity, if those decrees are consistent with the laws and public policies of the United States.

5. D. Unlike exports, imports can be taxed. A tax on an import is a tariff (generally set as a percent of the value). Imports can also be subject to quotas, which limit how much can be imported.

6. B. The Civil Rights Act of 1964, and other U.S. discrimination laws, apply to U.S. firms employing U.S. citizens outside (and inside) the United States. U.S. employers everywhere must abide by U.S. employment discrimination laws, so long as those laws do not violate the laws of the countries in which their workplaces are located. But those laws protect only U.S. citizens, not citizens of foreign countries.

7. B. Although increasingly influenced by codified (statutory) law and in some observers' opinions overwhelmed with administrative rules and regulations, common law legal systems are based on judicial decisions and precedent. Despite this general frame of reference, common law courts in different nations have developed different principles.

8. C. Civil law systems are based on codified (statutory) law. Administrative rules and regulations and judicial decisions are, of course, part of the operation of a civil law system. In a civil law system, courts are permitted to interpret the statutes that make up the code and to apply the rules, but unlike a common law system, in which judicial precedent plays a significant role, the courts in a civil law system are not expected to develop their own body of law.

9. A. Generally observed legal principles of international law are violated by a confiscation. Expropriation, which is a taking of property for a proper public purpose and with the payment of just compensation, does not violate these principles.

10. A. A distribution agreement in this context is a contract between a seller and a distributor to distribute the seller's products in the distributor's country. Such an agreement sets out the terms and conditions of the distributorship—price, currency of payment, availability of supplies, method of payment, and so on.

GamePoints

1. The doctrine of sovereign immunity protects foreign nations from review of the legal consequences of their actions in U.S. courts. But there are exceptions set forth in the Foreign Sovereign Immunities Act. A foreign state, or the instrumentality of a foreign state, is not immune when an action is based on a commercial activity carried on in the United States by the foreign state or having a distinct effect in the United States. In the problem, if the firm that reneges on its promise to your avatar is an arm of a foreign state, it is not likely immune from the jurisdiction of U.S. courts because of the effect of its commercial activity. If the firm is not part of a foreign nation, it has no claim to immunity under these principles.

2. Probably not. The government would likely assert the act of state doctrine in any suit that you might file in a U.S. court. Under this doctrine, the judicial branch of one country will not review the validity of public acts by a foreign government within its own borders. Thus, when a government seizes a privately owned business or privately owned goods, the act of state doctrine may prevent any recovery in a U.S. court. Further, together, the act of state doctrine and the doctrine of sovereign immunity tend to immunize foreign nations from the jurisdiction of U.S. courts so that, in general, U.S. firms or individuals who own property overseas have little U.S. legal protection against government actions in the countries in which they operate.

Cumulative Hypothetical Problem for Unit Four—Including Chapters 19–23

1. C. If nothing is stated in a contract about the risk of loss, then the UCC determines when the risk of loss passes. Under the UCC, if there are no contract terms to the contrary, the risk of loss passes on delivery, if the seller is a merchant.

2. C. Under the principle of comity, in an international context, one nation defers and gives effect to the laws and judicial decrees of another nation. The application of this principle is founded on courtesy and respect. The principle is most likely to be applied as long as the laws and decrees of the imposing nation are consistent with the law and public policy of the accommodating nation.

3. C. The modification would not be considered a rejection. Assuming the contract price of the games is $500 or more, this contract is a sale of goods subject to the Uniform Commercial Code (UCC). Under UCC 2–207, a merchant can add an additional term to a contract, with his or her acceptance, as part of the contract, unless the offeror expressly states otherwise. There is no indication in the question that the offeror limited its offer to its terms.

4. D. Of these choices, with respect to the customers, the firm most likely violated product liability law, which includes negligence and strict liability theories for liability and recovery. Negligence requires proof of intent. Strict liability does not. These firms may also have breached their contracts and their warranties, topics that are categorized as contract law and sales law.

5. B. Under UCC 2–709, a seller can demand enforcement of a contract if the buyer breaches, the goods have been identified, and the seller cannot resell the goods for a reasonable price. From the perspective of the seller, recovery of the contract price is specific performance.

Questions on the Focus on Ethics for Unit Four—Domestic and International Sales and Lease Contracts

1. B. Besides good faith, read into every contract is the concept of commercial reasonableness. These two concepts impose certain duties on the contracting parties. Also underlying the application of the UCC provisions are reasonability in the formation, performance, and termination of contracts. To determine what is commercially reasonable, a court may look to the course of dealing, usage of trade, and the surrounding circumstances.

2. C. This doctrine is an application of the concept of commercial reasonableness. Under this doctrine, performance may be excused but only if the nonperforming party has made every effort to meet his or her obligations under the contract.

3. D. In the interests of fairness, even though a party has agreed to a term, it may be held to be so unfair as to be unenforceable. Under this doctrine, a court may decline to enforce the entire contract, enforce the contract without the clause, or limit the enforcement of the clause to avoid an unfair result. The court would look at the circumstances as of the time the contract was made in the context of its commercial background. Ethical standards underlie this doctrine.

Chapter 24

True-False Questions

1. T

2. T

3. T

4. T

5. F. To be negotiable, an instrument must be payable on demand or at a definite time. Instruments that say nothing about when payment is due are payable on demand.

6. F. The length of the extension does not have to be specified if the option to extend is solely that of the *holder*. After the specified date passes, the note becomes, in effect, a demand instrument. The period of an extension must be specified, however, if the option is given to the maker.

7. F. This is an order instrument. Order instruments that meet the requirements for negotiability are negotiable. An instrument that contains any indication that does not purport to designate a specific payee (for example, "payable to bearer") is a bearer instrument. A bearer instrument that meets the requirements for negotiability is also negotiable. When an instrument is not negotiable, it may be transferred by assignment.

8. T

9. T

10. F. To be negotiable, an instrument must be payable in a fixed amount of money. Money includes a "medium of exchange authorized or adopted by a domestic or foreign government as a part of its currency." An instrument payable in an amount stated in foreign currency can be paid in that currency or in U.S. dollars.

Fill-in Questions

drawer; drawee; payee; maker; payee

Multiple-Choice Questions

1. A. One of the requirements of negotiability is that an instrument be payable to order or to bearer. An instrument that is payable to the order of an identified person is an order instrument. An instrument that is payable to bearer is a bearer instrument. A bearer instrument can be negotiated further without a payee's signature. References to other agreements do not affect an instrument's negotiability. Conditioning payment would render an instrument nonnegotiable, however. This question and answer are based on a question from the May 1995 CPA exam.

2. B. An instrument that is not payable to the order of an identified person is a bearer instrument. Although this instrument uses order language, it does not designate a specific payee.

3. A. To be negotiable, an instrument must state with certainty on the face of the instrument a fixed amount of money to be paid when the instrument is payable. When an instrument states simply that it is payable "with interest," the interest rate is the judgment rate of interest, which is fixed by statute.

4. B. A draft is created when the party creating it orders another party to pay money, usually to a third party. The drawee (the party on whom the draft is drawn) must be obligated to the drawer, either by an agreement or through a debtor-creditor relationship, for the drawee to be obligated to the drawer to honor the draft. A trade acceptance is a draft; a check is a draft.

5. B. The drawer is the party who initiates a draft, which orders the drawee (the bank in this problem) to pay. A check orders the payment of a certain amount of money to the holder on demand. The party to whom a check (or any instrument) is made payable is the payee.

6. D. A negotiable instrument that has only two parties is a promissory note: a written promise made by one person (the maker) to another (the payee). A certificate of deposit is a type of note issued when a party deposits funds with a bank that the bank promise to repay with interest. A draft (a check is a draft) involves three parties (drawee, drawer, and payee).

7. D. All of the other answer choices are among the requirements for negotiability. The other requirements are that an instrument must be in writing (on something permanent and portable—a shirt might be acceptable but not, for example, a cow), must state a fixed amount of money, and must be payable to order or to bearer, unless it is a check.

8. A. The location of the maker or drawer's signature does not affect the negotiability of an instrument. Also, a signature may, among other things, be a trade name or may consist of thumbprint, a handwritten statement, or a rubber stamp.

9. A. A promise or order is conditional, and nonnegotiable, if it does what any of the other answer choices state. This instrument, however, only makes a reference to another writing (as it would if, for example, it stated, "this debt arises from the performance of delivery services"), which does not make the instrument conditional. Similarly, a statement that an instrument is payable only from a particular fund or source does not affect its negotiability.

10. A. That an instrument is undated does not affect its negotiability, nor does postdating or antedating an instrument affect negotiability. Also, the omission of the name of the bank on which an instrument is drawn or payable will not render an instrument nonnegotiable.

GamePoints

1. This instrument is a promissory note. A promissory note is a two-party instrument in which a maker promises to pay a payee a certain sum of money. This item fits that definition. Given the assumption noted in the question, the instrument is negotiable even though a payment date is not specified. In that circumstance, it is payable on demand. It is otherwise in writing, signed by the maker, contains an unconditional promise to pay a sum certain in money with no other promise, and is payable to order. (Without the assumption in the question, however, it might not be negotiable, because it is not written on material that lends itself to permanence. It also may not be especially portable, considering the apparatus—a game disk and a game player, at least—needed to display and view it.)

2. This is a trade acceptance. A trade acceptance is a draft drawn by a seller on a buyer and is payable to the seller on a future date. The seller obtains the buyer's acceptance of the draft. As indicated, the seller is both the drawer and the payee on the draft. A trade acceptance is frequently used in sales of goods. Trade acceptances are standard credit instruments in sales transactions.

Chapter 25

True-False Questions

1. T
2. T
3. F. This promise would support a contract but would not satisfy the value requirement for HDC status. Value sufficient to make a holder an HDC includes taking an instrument in payment of, or as security for, a preexisting debt; giving a check in payment for the instrument; and performing the promise for which the instrument was issued.
4. F. Bearer instruments can be negotiated by delivery alone. That is why a bearer instrument is considered payable to whoever is in possession of it.
5. F. To be a holder, a person must have possession and good title. The definition of a holder, from UCC 1–201(20), is "the person in possession if the instrument is payable to bearer, or in the case of an instrument payable to an identified person, if the identified person is in possession."
6. T
7. T
8. F. If a holder is an HDC, all other parties' claims to an instrument and most other parties' defenses against payment on the instrument cannot be successfully asserted against the HDC.
9. T
10. F. A holder who knows or has reason to know of a claim to an instrument or a defense against payment on it cannot become an HDC. Furthermore, such a holder cannot change his or her status by selling the instrument and repurchasing it from a later HDC in an attempt to take advantage of the shelter principle.

Fill-in Questions

can; cannot; cannot

Multiple-Choice Questions

1. A. A party can convert a blank indorsement to a special indorsement "by writing over the signature of the indorser in blank any contract consistent with the character of the indorsement." In other words, the payee can do what is stated in this example.
2. A. Before the payee indorsed the back of the check, it was an order instrument. It could be negotiated further only with the payee's signature (and with delivery). After the check was indorsed, it became a bearer instrument and could be negotiated by delivery alone. If a bearer instrument is lost, it can be payable to whoever finds it.

3. C. The first step in becoming a holder in due course (HDC) is that a party must be a holder. To be a holder, the instrument must be negotiable. The requirements for HDC status are that a party takes the instrument for value, in good faith, and without notice of any claims to it or defenses against payment on it. This question and answer are based on a question that appeared in the CPA exam in May 1995.
4. C. A thief cannot be a holder. A party who takes in good faith and without notice from a thief is an HDC, however. A party in the situation of the drawer of this check might also avoid liability to an ordinary holder by asserting the personal defense of unauthorized completion of an incomplete instrument (discussed in the next chapter).
5. D. A party who takes an instrument with knowledge of one defense that the maker or drawer has against payment on the instrument prevents the party from attaining HDC status as to all defenses. The party does not satisfy the requirement for HDC status that he or she must take the instrument without notice.
6. B. A holder takes an instrument for value when he or she pays cash for it, gives a negotiable instrument for it, or makes an irrevocable commitment to a third person. The holder is an HDC to the extent that he or she gives value for the instrument (and meets the other requirements for HDC status). Here, the value given for the instrument does not include the unperformed part of the agreement. Thus, the seller is an HDC only to the extent for which value has been given at the time that the note is sold.
7. A. A bank can become an HDC when honoring other banks' checks to the extent it has given value. Thus, a bank becomes an HDC when it permits a customer to draw against a credited instrument, but only to the extent that the customer draws on the credit.
8. C. A holder of a time instrument who takes it after its due date is "on notice" that it is overdue. Such a holder cannot become an HDC. Nonpayment by the due date should indicate to any purchaser who is obligated to pay that there is a defense to payment on the instrument.
9. C. An instrument that is payable to the order of a specific payee is negotiated by delivery of the instrument to that payee. The payee negotiates the instrument further by indorsing it and delivering it to the transferee.
10. C. A restrictive indorsement requires the indorsee to comply with certain instructions regarding the funds involved (but it does not restrict the negotiation of the instrument). A blank indorsement specifies no particular indorsee and can be a simple

signature. A qualified indorsement disclaims contract liability on the instrument (for example, an indorser adding "without recourse" to his or her signature is a qualified indorsement). A special indorsement names the indorsee ("pay to Adam") with the signature of the indorser.

GamePoints

1. If Holder knew or had reason to know that Forger did not have the authority to write the check, your avatar cannot become an HDC. Notice of a defense to payment—in this case, notice of a lack of authority to sign the instrument—bars attaining HDC status. As an ordinary holder, your avatar would be subject to the same defenses against payment that could be asserted against the transferor. Here, the transferor is Forger, whom Quiescent could refuse to pay based on the lack of authority to draw the check. Thus Holder could not collect—Quiescent would have a defense good against your avatar and could refuse to pay.

2. With respect to the items that were originally order instruments, when each indorser signed the back of an instrument in blank, he or she converted it to a bearer instrument. Because a bearer instrument can be negotiated by delivery alone, an item that falls into the hands of a thief or an unscrupulous finder could be easily cashed. To avoid such losses, Holder could add a notation to each signature on the back of the items to convert the blank indorsements into special indorsements. For example, Holder might write "Pay to Holder" above the signatures. This would convert each blank indorsement into a special indorsement, which would require Holder's indorsement, plus delivery, for further negotiation.

Chapter 26

True-False Questions

1. T
2. F. Some parties are secondarily liable.
3. T
4. F. All transferors of negotiable instruments, including those who present instruments for payment, make certain implied warranties regarding the instruments. For example, a person who transfers an instrument for payment warrants to any other person who in good faith accepts or pays the instrument, with some exceptions, that the instrument has not been altered.
5. T

6. T
7. F. The loss in such a case falls on the drawer against whom the check is effective if it has been transferred to an innocent party. However, comparative negligence may be available as a defense against liability to a drawee bank, for example, which may thus be partially liable for the amount paid on the instrument.
8. F. Personal defenses can be used to avoid payment to an ordinary holder, but only universal defenses can defeat the claims of all holders, including HDCs.
9. F. An unauthorized signature can be binding, however, if the person whose name is signed ratifies it. The person's negligence may also prevent him or her from denying liability. Usually, when there is a forged or unauthorized indorsement, the burden of loss falls on the first party to take the instrument with the forged indorsement.
10. T

Fill-in Questions

presentment; presenter; presenter; the maker or the drawer; materially altered

Multiple-Choice Questions

1. A. Forgery of the signature of the maker of a note is a real defense and thus good against an HDC. This is only if the person whose signature was forged has not ratified it or is precluded from denying it. The other choices are personal defenses, which are good against ordinary holders but not HDCs. This question and answer are based on a question that appeared in the November 1992 CPA exam.
2. D. If a check has been materially altered and the alteration is clearly visible, a party who takes the check has notice of a defense against payment on it and cannot become an HDC. He or she can recover nothing on the check. (If the alteration was not visible and the party could otherwise become an HDC, he or she could enforce the check according to the original terms.)
3. A. When a drawee fails to accept or pay a draft, including a check, the drawer's (secondary) liability arises. The party holding the draft can then attempt to obtain payment from the drawer.
4. A. All of the parties on a note are discharged if the maker of a note (the party primarily liable on it) pays to a holder the amount due in full. Payment by any other party, however, discharges only that party and later parties, however.
5. D. If a person is deceived into signing a negotiable instrument, believing that he or she is sign-

ing something other than a negotiable instrument, fraud in the execution is committed against the signer, who has a valid defense against payment even if the instrument is negotiated to an HDC.

6. B. Makers of notes and acceptors of negotiable instruments are primarily liable. (Drawers—and indorsers—have secondary liability.) A drawee (the bank in this problem) becomes primarily liable becomes an acceptor, which occurs when, as here, it accepts a check for payment.

7. A. When there is a breach of warranty concerning the underlying contract for which a negotiable instrument (the note) was issued, the maker can refuse to pay the note. This is a personal defense, not good against an HDC, but the party who accepted the note was not an HDC, but the other contracting party who took the note with knowledge of the claim against it. The other choices are also personal defenses, but they do not fit the facts in this problem.

8. B. Based on their signatures on an instrument, a drawer and a payee-indorser have secondary liability. Parties who are secondarily liable promise to pay only if the following events occur: (1) the instrument is properly and timely presented; (2) the instrument is dishonored; and (3) notice of dishonor is given in a timely manner to the secondarily liable party.

9. A. If a drawer believes an imposter to be the named payee at the time the drawer issues an instrument, the imposter's indorsement is effective (not considered a forgery) as far as the drawer is concerned. This is also true when there are other parties between the drawer, the imposter, and the drawee (for example, when the imposter negotiates the check to a third person who presents it to the drawee for payment).

10. B. The issuer of the check in this problem was authorized to use an employer's checks to pay for certain items. Assuming the seller knew of this agency relationship, the principal (the employer) is liable for the amount of the check. There is nothing in the facts here to suggest that the seller had notice of a defense to payment on the check, or notice that the amount of the check was materially altered, either of which would have prevented it from becoming an HDC and changed the liability of the parties.

GamePoints

1. This instrument is a check. No one was primarily liable on it at the time of its issue. The drawer was only secondarily liable. If, however, it is presented for payment to the drawee bank, and the drawee bank indicates its acceptance of the instru-

ment, the bank will become primarily liable. The drawer's liability will remain secondary. If the bank refuses to pay it or to accept it, the drawer's liability will apply. In that situation, the steps required to collect payment on the check are: (1) the instrument must be properly and timely presented for payment, (2) the instrument must be dishonored, and (3) in some circumstances (not present here) timely notice of dishonor must be given.

2. Generally, when there is an unauthorized indorsement on a check, the loss falls on the first party to take the instrument with the indorsement. The loss falls on the drawer, however, under the fictitious payee rule. This concerns the intent of the drawer to issue a check to a payee who has no interest in it. This occurs when a dishonest employee deceives the employer into signing a check payable to a party with no right to it or when a dishonest employee abuses his or her authority to issue an instrument on the employer's behalf. The indorsement is not then treated as a forgery—the employer can be held liable on the check to an innocent holder.

Chapter 27

True-False Questions

1. T

2. F. If a bank pays a check over a customer's proper stop-payment order, the bank is obligated to recredit the customer's account, but only for the amount of the actual loss suffered by the drawer because of the wrongful payment.

3. F. A bank's duty to honor its customer's checks is not absolute (although when a bank receives an item payable from a customer's account, but there are insufficient funds in the account to cover the amount, the bank can choose to pay it and charge the customer's account). Failing to pay an overdraft will not subject the bank to criminal prosecution, though a person who writes a bad check may be prosecuted (and sued).

4. T

5. T

6. T

7. T

8. F. Under the Expedited Funds Availability Act of 1987, there are different availability schedules for different funds, depending on such factors as the location of the bank on which an item is drawn, what type of item it is, the age and activity of an account, and the amount of the item.

9. T

10. F. A forged drawer's signature on a check has no legal effect as the signature of the party whose name is signed. If the bank pays the check, the bank must recredit the customer's account (unless the customer's negligence contributed substantially to the forgery).

Fill-in Questions

drawer; creditor; principal; drawee; debtor; agent

Multiple-Choice Questions

1. D. When a bank pays a check on a drawer's forged signature, generally the bank is liable. This is particularly true when the bank's negligence substantially contributes to the forgery. If the customer's negligence contributed to the forgery, however, the bank may not be liable. The amount of the check does not affect liability.

2. C. Each bank in the collection chain, including the depositary bank, must pass the check on before midnight of the next banking day following receipt. Under the deferred posting rule, a check received after a bank's cutoff hour, can be considered received the next day.

3. D. This is assuming the drawer's state allows oral stop-payment orders. If a drawee bank pays a check over a customer's stop-payment order, the bank is obligated to recredit the account of the customer, but the bank is liable for no more than the actual loss suffered by the drawer.

4. A. A bank that pays a customer's check bearing a forged indorsement must recredit the customer's account or be liable to the drawer customer for breach of contract. A customer has a duty to examine returned checks and corresponding bank statements, however, and must report any forged indorsements within three years.

5. A. The certification of a check by the bank on which it is drawn discharges the drawer, who was secondarily liable on the check. The bank remains primarily liable and has now guaranteed payment. This question and answer are based on a question that appeared in the November 1981 CPA exam.

6. B. A drawee bank's contract is with its customer, not with those who present its customers' checks for payment. Thus, a drawee bank is not liable to a holder who presents a check for payment, even if the drawer has sufficient funds on deposit to pay the check. The holder's recourse is against the drawer, who may subsequently hold the bank liable for a wrongful refusal to pay.

7. A. A bank is not obligated to pay a stale, uncertified check. If the bank decides to pay it, however, the bank might consult the customer first or simply pay it an d charge the customer's account of the amount.

8. C. If a drawee bank cashes a customer's check over a forged indorsement, or fails to detect an alteration on a check of its customer-drawer and cashes the check, the bank is liable for the loss. (The customer's negligence can shift the loss, however.) The bank may be able to recover some of the loss from the forger, if he or she can be found.

9. C. The customer is liable for this amount because the bank was not notified that the card was missing until after the withdrawal. If a customer does not inform the institution within less than two business days after learning of a card's loss or theft, the customer's liability for unauthorized transactions is up to $500.

10. D. An issuer of e-money may be subject to the Right to Financial Privacy Act if the issuer is deemed to be (1) a bank by virtue of its holding customer funds or (2) an entity that issues a physical card similar to a credit or debit card. In other words, accepting customer deposits would be enough, but investigating credit backgrounds would not. (As its name implies, the Right to Financial Privacy Act provides legal safeguards for the privacy of a user of e-money against its issuer.) An entity that does not accept deposits may be subject to other laws, including the Uniform Money Services Act.

GamePoints

1. The drawer's signature on this check is a forgery. A forged signature is not legally effective as the signature of the drawer. If a bank pays a check on which the drawer's signature is forged, the bank generally suffers the loss. The bank may be able to recover some of the amount of the loss from a customer whose negligence contributed to the forgery, from the forger of the check, or from a holder who cashes it. None of these parties are identified in this problem, however, nor are any facts provided to indicate any party's negligence. Under that circumstance, if the bank cashes the check—which is also not indicated—the bank would have to recredit the account of its customer (Jacky).

2. Under the Expedited Funds Availability Act and Federal Reserve Regulation CC, which spell out the availability schedules for various items deposited into a bank account, the entire amount of the funds represented by the check in this problem must be available for withdrawal on the next business day. This is because the depositary and payor banks are branches of the same institution. Under Check 21 (the Check Clearing in the 21st Century Act) the time to process the check would be substantially reduced. This might mean that the funds would be available the same business day, or even immediately on deposit. This is because under Check 21 banks can exchange digital images of checks instead of the original paper versions.

Cumulative Hypothetical Problem for Unit Five—Including Chapters 24–27

1. B. A promissory note is a written promise by one party to pay money to another party. This instrument is not a draft: there is no drawee. Because it is not a draft, it cannot be a sight draft, a check, or a trade acceptance, all of which are drafts.
2. B. This instrument meets all of the requirements for negotiability: it is in writing, it is signed by the maker, it is an unconditional promise to pay a fixed amount of money, it is payable to bearer, and it is payable at a definite time. The extension clause does not affect its negotiability because, although the right to extend is given to the maker, the period of the extension is specified.
3. C. The instrument is negotiable, but it can be negotiated further only by the bank's indorsement, because it was converted from a bearer instrument to an order instrument with the indorsement to pay to the order of the bank. Because it was a bearer instrument, it could have been negotiated by delivery only, without indorsement. The indorsement "without recourse" does not affect the negotiability of the instrument.
4. A. The bank is an HDC because it took the instrument (1) for value, (2) in good faith, and (3) without notice that any person had a defense against payment on it. The party from whom the bank bought the instrument was not an HDC, however, because that party did take the instrument with knowledge of the contract dispute.
5. D. No party to a check has primary liability with respect to payment on it. The drawer is secondarily liable to the payee. If the drawer has sufficient grounds, he or she may sue the drawee for wrongful dishonor, but the payee cannot successfully sue the drawee.

Questions on the Focus on Ethics for Unit Five—Negotiable Instruments

1. A. The maker's reliance on the fraudulent party's assurance that the note was not a note constitutes negligence. UCC 3-305(a)(1)(iii) states that fraud is a defense against an HDC only if the injured party signed the instrument "with neither knowledge nor a reasonable opportunity to obtain knowledge of its character or essential terms." The HDC doctrine reflects the philosophy that when two

or more innocent parties are at risk, the burden should fall on the party that was in the best position to prevent the loss.
2. B. Under UCC 4–402(b), a bank that wrongfully dishonors a customer's check "is liable to its customer for damages proximately caused by the wrongful dishonor of an item. Liability is limited to actual damages proved and may include damages for an arrest or prosecution of the customer or other consequential damages." In other words, on wrongful dishonor, a bank's liability may be considerable.
3. A. Most, if not all, banks verify signatures only on checks that exceed a certain amount, which is typically $2,500 or more. Checks for less than this amount are randomly selected for signature verification. This has proven to be economically efficient for banks—it can be less costly to cover the occasional forged check than to verify all signatures on all checks. Under the UCC, banks are held to the standard of "ordinary care." It may be that this practice, which is standard in the banking industry, could be construed as "ordinary care."

Chapter 28

True-False Questions

1. F. A mechanic's lien involves real property. An artisan's lien involves personal property.
2. F. This is prohibited under federal law. Garnishment of an employee's wages for any one indebtedness cannot be a ground for dismissal of an employee.
3. T
4. F. An artisan's lien involves personal property. A mechanic's lien involves real property.
5. T
6. T
7. TF. Each state permits a debtor at least *part*—but not necessarily *all*—of the family home, free from the claims of unsecured creditors and trustees in bankruptcy. Federal bankruptcy law places a cap on the amount that may be exempted under state law in a bankruptcy proceeding. Some states allow an exemption only if the debtor has a family
8. T
9. F. This is the most important concept in suretyship: a surety can use any defenses available to a debtor (except personal defenses) to avoid liability on the obligation to the creditor. Note, though, that a debtor does need not to have defaulted on the underlying obligation before a surety can be required to answer for the debt. Before a *guarantor* can be

required to answer for the debt of a debtor, the debtor must have defaulted on the underlying obligation, however.

10. T

Fill-in Questions

contract of suretyship; surety; surety; guaranty contract; guarantor

Multiple-Choice Questions

1. B. The cobbler can keep the shoes until the customer pays for the repair. If the customer fails to pay, the cobbler has an artisan's lien on the personal property for the amount of the bill and can sell the items in satisfaction of the lien.

2. B. The creditor in this problem can use prejudgment attachment. Attachment occurs at the time of or immediately after commencement of a suit but before entry of a final judgment. The court issues a writ of attachment, directing the sheriff or other officer to seize property belonging to the debtor. If the creditor prevails at trial, the property can be sold to satisfy the judgment. (A writ of execution can be used after all of the conditions represented by the answer choices in this problem have been met.)

3. D. The creditor can use garnishment, a collection remedy directed at a debtor's property or rights held by a third person. A garnishment order can be served on the employer so that part of debtor's paycheck will be paid to the creditor. This question and answer are based on a question that was part of the CPA exam in 1996.

4. C. The debt is $200,000. The amount of the homestead exemption ($50,000) is subtracted from the sale price of the house ($150,000), and the remainder ($100,000) is applied against the debt. Proceeds from the sale of any nonexempt personal property could also be applied against the debt. The debtor gets the amount of the homestead exemption, of course.

5. B. A guarantor is secondarily liable (that is, the principal must first default). Also, in this problem, if the officer were, for example, the borrower's only salaried employee, the guaranty would not have to be in writing under the main-purpose exception to the Statute of Frauds. A surety is primarily liable (that is, the creditor can look to the surety for payment as soon as the debt is due, whether or not the principal debtor has defaulted). Usually, also, in the case of a guarantor, a creditor must have attempted to collect from the principal, because usually a debtor would not otherwise be declared in default.

6. C. A guarantor has the right of subrogation when he or she pays the debt owed to the creditor. This means that any right the creditor had against the debtor becomes the right of the guarantor. A guarantor also has the right of contribution, when there are one or more other guarantors. This means that if he or she pays more than his or her proportionate share on a debtor's default, the guarantor is entitled to recover from the others the amount paid above the guarantor's obligation. This problem illustrates how these principles work.

7. D. At the request of a creditor who obtains a judgment against a debtor, a writ of execution is issued after the entry of the judgment if the debtor still does not pay. A sheriff, or other officer, executes the writ by seizing the debtor's nonexempt property, selling it, and using the proceeds to pay the amount of the judgment.

8. A. Safe & Stolid can place a mechanic's lien on their customer's property. If the customer does not pay what is owed, the property can be sold to satisfy the debt. The only requirements are that the lien be filed within a specific time from the time of the work, depending on the applicable state statute, and notice of the foreclosure and sale must be given to the customer and property owner in advance.

9. D. A surety agrees to be primarily liable to pay a debtor's debt. If the debtor and the creditor materially alter the terms of their contract without the surety's consent, a surety who agreed to act without being compensated is discharged completely. (A surety who accepted payment is discharged to the extent that he or she suffers a loss under the contract as modified.)

10. C. If a creditor in possession of a debtor's collateral surrenders it without the guarantor's consent, the guarantor is released to the extent of any loss attributable to the surrender. This protects a guarantor who agrees to the obligation only because the debtor's collateral is in the creditor's possession.

GamePoints

1. Creditors who make improvements to real property can place mechanic's liens on the property if the creditors are not paid for their labor, services, or material. Creditors who repair personal property can place artisan's liens on the property for the same reason, but the creditor must have possession of the property. With either lien, the creditor can sell the property to satisfy payment of the debt. The proceeds are used to pay the debt and the costs, with any remainder paid to the debtor. Both a mechanic's lien and an artisan's lien requires the lienholder to give notice of legal action to the debtor before the debtor's property is sold to satisfy the debt.

2. A surety has primary liability on a debt, and on the creditor can seek payment exclusively from the surety. A debtor's adjudication of mental incompetence is a risk that the surety takes and its occurrence does not release the surety from liability on the debt. But if the debtor or a party acting on behalf of the debtor performs all of the requirements of the loan contract—particularly if that debt is paid in full—the surety is discharged. Thus, a co-signing surety is released from his or her obligation to pay a debt if that debt is paid. Here, the debtor's spouse satisfied the debt, thereby releasing the surety—your avatar Knight Light—from liability.

Chapter 29

True-False Questions

1. F. Perfection is the process by which secured parties protect themselves against the claims of third parties who may wish to have their debts satisfied out of the same collateral. In most situations, this process involves filing a financing statement with a state official. That filing may be accomplished by a paper filing or electronically.

2. T

3. F. A security interest in proceeds perfects automatically and remains perfected, in most cases, for at least twenty days after the debtor's receipt of the proceeds.

4. F. The financing statement must include the names of the debtor and creditor, and describe the collateral. Also, to avoid problems arising from different descriptions, a secured party can repeat the security agreement's description in the financing statement or file the two together.

5. T

6. T

7. T

8. T

9. F. A debtor who has defaulted has redemption rights. Before the secured party decides to retain the collateral or before it is disposed of, the debtor can take back the collateral by tendering performance of all secured obligations and paying the secured party's expenses. (Other secured parties have this same right.)

10. F. When more than one creditor claims a security interest in the same collateral, the first interest to be filed takes priority. The first to attach has priority if none of the interests has been perfected.

Fill-in Questions

1. creditor; creditor

2. first; first

Multiple-Choice Questions

1. C. A *financing statement* must provide the names of the debtor and the creditor and describe the collateral covered by the security agreement. Filing a financing statement (which is the most common means of perfecting a security interest) gives notice to other creditors of the secured party's interest. Why the debtor and the creditor entered into the deal is not relevant to others' interests in this context.

2. B. In those cases in which it is otherwise available, the right of self-help repossession can generally be exercised so long as the secured party does not commit trespass onto land, assault, battery, or breaking and entering. Here, the repossession occurred on a public street and did not involve any commission of the other crimes.

3. B. To be effective, a written security agreement must (1) be signed by the debtor, (2) contain a description of the collateral, and (3) the description must reasonably identify the collateral. This meets one of the three requirements for an enforceable security interest. The other requirements are that creditor's giving something of value to the debtor, and the debtor having rights in the collateral. Once these requirements are met, the interest attaches. A security interest is enforceable when attachment occurs.

4. B. A security agreement that provides for the creation of a security interest in proceeds (as well as after-acquired property and future advances) is a floating lien. This concept can apply to a shifting stock of goods—for example, the lien can start with raw materials and follow them as they become finished goods and then inventories and as they are sold, finally becoming accounts receivable, chattel paper, or cash.

5. A. To retain collateral that a secured party repossessed on a debtor's default, the secured party must notify the debtor and (in all cases except consumer goods) any other secured party of whom the party has notice of a claim, as well as junior lien claimants who filed their liens or security interests ten days before the debtor consented to the retention. If the debtor or other secured party objects within twenty days, the collateral must be sold, or otherwise disposed of. If the collateral is sold, the first priority of the proceeds are the fees stemming from the secured party's preparation for the sale.

6. A. A secured party's security interest in collateral includes an interest in the proceeds (whatever is received) from the sale, exchange, or other disposal of the collateral. This interest perfects automatically and remains perfected for twenty days. Ways to extend this period are listed in the answer. It should be noted, too, that the initial effective term of the filing of a financing statement is a period of five years, and this can be extended for another five years by the filing of a continuation statement before the expiration of the original filing.

7. C. The first security interest to be filed or to be perfected has priority over other filed or perfected security interests. Although the first lender was not the first to provide funds to the debtor, it was the first to file its financing statement. Priority between perfected security interests is nearly always determined by the time of perfection (which is usually by filing). Note, though, that perfection may not protect a secured party's interest against the claim of a buyer in the ordinary course of business, and some others.

8. C. A purchase-money security interest (PMSI) is created (1) when a seller retains or takes a security interest in collateral to secure part or all of the purchase price of property serving as collateral, or (2) when some other party (such as a bank) takes a security interest in the collateral to secure the party's advances or other obligation that is actually used by the debtor to acquire rights in or to use the collateral.

9. D. In most states, filing is in a central office (of the state in which the debtor is located). When collateral consists of timber to be cut, fixtures, or collateral to be extracted, a filing in the county in which the collateral is located is typically required. Of course, if perfection is by a pledge (possession), no filing is necessary.

10. B. The filing of a security interest in a corporate debtor's collateral should be done in the state in which the debtor is incorporated. For individual debtors, however, the place of filing is the state of the debtor's principal residence. Of course, the perfection of an interest in some types of collateral, such as negotiable instruments, can only be accomplished by taking possession of the property.

GamePoints

1. Attachment of the security interest occurred when the loan was made and the debtor—the borrowing corporation in this problem—executed the security agreement. The requirements for attachment include (1) the secured party's giving of value to the debtor, (2) the debtor's rights in the collateral, and (3) a written security agreement describing the collateral and signed by the debtor (unless the creditor has possession of the collateral). These requirements are met here—the "value" is the amount of the loan, the borrower has rights in its accounts receivable, and a security agreement was signed by an authorized representative on the debtor's behalf. Filing a financing statement is not necessary for a security interest to attach (although it is needed to perfect the interest).

2. Between these parties, the party who was the first to file a financing statement has priority in the collateral. Perfecting a security interest by filing a financing statement protects the secured party's interest in the collateral against most creditors who acquire a security interest in the same collateral after the filing. Note that a later creditor still acquires a security interest but it has a lower priority. A later secured party's claim of ignorance as to the previous interest is irrelevant—all parties are deemed to have constructive notice of the prior filing.

Chapter 30

True-False Questions

1. F. Any individual can be a debtor under Chapter 7, and any debtor who is liable on a claim held by a creditor may file for bankruptcy under Chapter 7. A debtor does not have to be insolvent.

2. F. The filing of a bankruptcy petition, voluntary or involuntary, automatically stays most litigation and other actions by creditors against the debtor and his or her property. A creditor may ask for relief from the stay, but a creditor who willfully violates the stay may be liable for actual damages, costs, and fees, as well as punitive damages.

3. T

4. T

5. F. A Chapter 13 case can be initiated by the voluntary filing of a petition, but it may also be started by the conversion of a Chapter 7 case. This conversion may occur on a finding of substantial abuse under the "means test," for example. (A Chapter 13 case may be converted to a case under Chapter 7 or Chapter 11 in certain circumstances.)

6. T

7. T

8. F. Under Chapter 11, the creditors and the debtor formulate a plan under which the debtor pays some of the debts, the other debts are discharged, and the debtor is then allowed to continue the operation of his or her business.

9. F. Some small businesses—those who do not own or manage real estate and do not have debts of more than $2 million—can choose to avoid creditors' committees under Chapter 11. Those who choose to do so, however, are subject to shorter deadlines with respect to filing a reorganization plan.

10. F. Bankruptcy is a subject of federal law, and bankruptcy proceedings are held in federal courts. In some cases, a debtor may be required, or may elect, to exempt property from inclusion in his or her estate under state law, but even in those cases, federal law may dictate some limits, particularly with respect to the amount of a homestead exemption.

Fill-in Questions

7; 11; 13; 7; 11; 13; 7; 11; 13

Multiple-Choice Questions

1. C. Under Chapter 11, creditors and debtor plan for the debtor to pay some debts, be discharged of the rest, and continue in business. Under Chapter 13, with an appropriate plan, a small business debtor can also pay some (or all) debts, be discharged of the rest, and continue in business. A petition for a discharge in bankruptcy under Chapter 11 may be filed by a sole proprietor, a partnership, or a corporation; a petition for a discharge under Chapter 13, however, may be filed only by a sole proprietor, among these business entities, subject to certain debt maximums.

2. D. Under Chapter 13, a debtor can submit a plan under which he or she continues in possession of his or her assets, but turns over disposable income for a five-year period, after which most debts may be discharged. When applicable, a Chapter 13 plan must provide for the surrender of collateral to secured creditors. Note, too, that a court may approve a Chapter 13 plan over the objection of a creditor or a trustee if the property to be distributed under the plan is more than the amount of the creditors' claims.

3. B. Under Chapter 7 or Chapter 11, a corporate debtor (or an individual debtor or a partnership, but not a farmer or a charitable institution) with twelve or more creditors can be forced into bankruptcy by three or more of them who collectively have unsecured claims for at least a certain amount. (The amount is periodically increased.) A debtor with less than twelve creditors can be involuntarily petitioned into bankruptcy by one or more of them if the petitioner (or petitioners) has a claim for at least a certain amount.

4. D. Claims that are not dischargeable in bankruptcy include the claims listed in the other answer choices: claims for back taxes accruing within three years before the bankruptcy, claims for domestic support, and claims for most student loans (unless their payment would result in undue hardship to the debtor, as stated in the correct answer choice). There are many other debts that are not dischargeable in bankruptcy.

5. A. Any individual debtor can file a petition for bankruptcy under Chapter 7. The debtor does not have to be insolvent. A court can dismiss a petition, however, if granting it would constitute substantial abuse under the "means test" (which, considering the low amount of the debtor's income in this problem, is unlikely) or if the court finds that the debtor could pay off his or her debts under Chapter 13. Most debtors who are eligible under Chapter 7 could also file under Chapter 11, although the latter is more commonly used by corporate debtors. Under Chapter 11, some of the debts are paid. Chapter 13 is also a possibility under the circumstances described in the problem, but a debtor is more likely to prefer a Chapter 7 discharge, which does not require payment of many debts. Chapter 12 is an option only for certain farmers.

6. C. The first unsecured debts to be paid are domestic support obligations, subject to certain administrative costs, and then other administrative expenses of the bankruptcy proceeding. Among the debts listed in this problem, the order of priority is unpaid wages, consumer deposits, and taxes. Each class of creditors is fully paid before the next class is entitled to anything.

7. A. Other grounds on which a discharge may be denied include concealing property with the intent to defraud a creditor, fraudulently destroying financial records, and refusing to obey a lawful court order. Having obtained a discharge in bankruptcy within the eight previous years is also a ground for denial. The other choices represent individual debts that are not dischargeable in bankruptcy, but they are not grounds for denying a discharge altogether. This question and answer are based on a question from the 1997 CPA exam.

8. C. Other transfers that a trustee can set aside include a transfer made with the intent to hinder, delay, or defraud a creditor; transfers made to an insider within one year before the debtor's filing a petition in bankruptcy; payments within ninety days before the filing of the petition for a preexisting debt; and any reason that the debtor could use to get the property back.

9. B. Most corporations can file for bankruptcy under Chapter 7 or 11. The same principles that govern liquidation cases generally govern reorganizations as well. Corporate debtors most commonly file petitions for bankruptcy under Chapter 11. One important difference between the two chapters is that in a Chapter 11 proceeding, the debtor can continue in business.

10. B. A bankruptcy trustee has the power to avoid preferential payments (preferences), fraudulent transfers, and transactions that the debtor could rightfully avoid (such as transactions founded on fraud or duress). Other transfers that a trustee can set aside include those listed in the answer to question number 8 above.

GamePoints

1. Downloading apps to, and playing video games on, a cell phone are not grounds for denying a discharge in bankruptcy. Unpaid alimony and support debts will not cause a petition to be denied (although neither will be discharged if a discharge of other debts is granted). Attending a credit-counseling briefing is a requirement to obtain a discharge and will not cause a discharge to be denied. But if a debtor cannot satisfactorily explain a loss of assets, he or she will likely be denied a discharge in bankruptcy under Chapter 7. Thus, in this problem, your inability to satisfactorily explain the lack of assets may serve as a ground for the court to deny a discharge.

2. Yes, the accounting firm in this problem can file an involuntary Chapter 11 bankruptcy petition against you. Involuntary petitions are permitted under Chapters 7 and 11 only. An involuntary petition is commenced by its filing with a bankruptcy court. A single creditor may file the petition if the debtor has fewer than twelve creditors and the unsecured portion of the creditor's claim is at least $12,000. These conditions are met by the facts here—you have ten unsecured creditors and the accounting firm has an unsecured claim for $15,000.

Chapter 31

True-False Questions

1. F. This is the definition of loan flipping. Steering and targeting occur when a lender manipulates a borrower into accepting a loan product that benefits the lender but is not the best loan for the borrower.

2. F. This is a definition of a mortgage. A mortgage is also defined as a written instrument that gives a creditor an interest in real property being acquired by a debtor as security for the debt's payment. A recession occurred following the collapse of

the housing market and the financial crisis that accompanied it in the second half of the first decade of the twenty-first century.

3. F. When all disclosures required under federal law are provided, a borrower's right to rescind a mortgage is limited to three business days (not including Sunday) after a loan is finalized. If the lender fails to provide material required disclosures, the borrower has a right to rescind the transaction for up to three years.

4. T

5. T

6. F. This is almost the definition of the average prime offer rate, which is the rate offered to the best, or most qualified, borrowers as established by a survey of potential borrowers. The annual percentage rate, or APR, is the actual cost of a loan on a yearly basis.

7. T

8. F. A Higher-Priced Mortgage Loan, or HPML, is subject to an amendment to Regulation Z enacted by the Federal Reserve Board. A lender cannot make an HPML based on the value of the borrower's home without verifying an ability to repay the loan. Part of the process involves a review of the borrower's financial records, including the borrower's other credit obligations. This is only one of the additional protections that consumers receive under this regulation.

9. F. To initiate foreclosure on a mortgage, the lender records a notice of default, or NOD, with the appropriate county office. The borrower is then on notice that a foreclosure sale is possible and can act to cure the default. If the loan is not paid within a reasonable time after a notice of default, the borrower will receive a notice of sale. This is also posted on the property, recorded with the county, and published in the newspaper.

10. T

Fill-in Questions

a fixed-rate; an adjustable-rate; an interest-only subprime mortgage; hybrid mortgage; home equity loan

Multiple-Choice Questions

1. B. A mortgage is a loan that a lender provides to enable a borrower to buy real property. It is a written instrument that gives the creditor an interest in, or lien on, the property being acquired by the debtor as security for the payment of the debt.

2. A. A fixed-rate mortgage is a standard mortgage with a fixed, or unchanging, rate of interest. Payments in the same amount are due periodically

for the duration of the loan, which normally ranges from ten to forty years. The rate depends on a number of factors, including the borrower's credit rating. With adjustable-rate and interest-only mortgages, the amount of the payments can increase over time.

3. A. Under the Truth-in-Lending Act of 1968, a lender must disclose the terms of a loan in clear, readily understandable language for a potential borrower to make rational choice. Among the terms that must be disclosed is the annual percentage rate (APR). The APR is what the answer says—the annual cost of a loan on a yearly basis. Like other disclosures, the APR must be based on a uniform formula of calculation.

4. D. As the example in this problem illustrates, steering and targeting occur when a lender manipulates a borrower into accepting a loan product that benefits the lender but is not the best loan for the borrower. This a predatory lending practice that is often at the heart of a violation of real estate financing laws.

5. A. Federal law primarily regulates mortgage terms that must be disclosed in writing. Congress and the Federal Reserve Board imposed a number of these requirements on lenders as a consequence of the real-estate financing bubble that occurred in the early years of the twenty-first century. Many of the new disclosures were included in the provisions of the Truth-in-Lending Act of 1968 and the Federal Reserve Board's Regulation Z.

6. D. Recording a mortgage in the appropriate county office perfects the creditor's rights in the property against later good faith purchasers for value and others. If the debtor defaults, a creditor who has *not* perfected his or her interest by recording it may have only the priority of an unsecured creditor. This question and answer are based on a question from the 1995 CPA exam.

7. A. An amendment to Regulation Z that the Federal Reserve Board enacted created a category of expensive loans known as Higher-Priced Mortgage Loans, or HPMLs. To qualify as an HPML, a loan must be secured by the borrower's principal residence and the annual percentage rate, or APR, of the mortgage must exceed the average prime offer rate for a comparable transaction by at least 1.5 percentage points if the loan is a first lien or at least 3.5 percentage points if the loan is a subordinate lien. The average prime offer rate is the rate offered to the best qualified borrowers.

8. C. The Home Affordable Modification Program (HAMP) offers incentives to lenders to change the terms of certain loans. The purpose of HAMP is to modify mortgages to, as the answer states, reduce the monthly payments to levels that borrowers can reasonably afford to pay. This amount is specifically estimated to be no more than 31 percent of an individual's borrower's gross monthly income.

9. C. Foreclosure is a process that allows a lender to repossess and auction the property that secures a loan. A lender has the right to foreclose on real property securing a mortgage if a homeowner defaults, or fails to make the payments on the mortgage. Before a foreclosure sale, the borrower has a right to buy the property by paying the full amount of the debt, plus interest and costs—this is the equitable right of redemption. A short sale is a sale of the property for less than the balance of the mortgage loan, and forbearance is the postponement for a limited time of part or all of the payments on the loan. A lender might opt for either of these choices to avoid foreclosure, which can be expensive and time consuming.

10. A. If the amount on a sale of property in foreclosure is not enough to cover the amount of the loan, a lender can ask a court for a judgment against the borrower for the amount of the debt remaining unpaid. This is a deficiency judgment. The borrower is required to make up the difference to the lender over time. Some states do not permit deficiency judgments for mortgaged residential real estate.

GamePoints

1. The mortgage is a residential loan, and thus the Truth-in-Lending Act (TILA) applies. The loan is a first mortgage but the APR exceeds the interest rate on Treasury bonds of comparable maturity by only 2 points and the fees are not more than 8 percent of the loan. Thus, the Home Ownership and Equity Protection Act (HOEPA)—which covers mortgage loans that carry a high rate of interest or impose high fees on borrowers—does not apply. The mortgage is a first lien secured by the borrower's home, but the APR does not most likely exceed the average prime offer rate for a comparable transaction by 1.5 percentage points or more. Thus, the loan is not a Higher-Priced Mortgage Loan (or HPML). The U.S. Treasury Department's Home Affordable Modification Program (HAMP) encourages private lenders to modify mortgages to lower the monthly payments of borrowers in default. But The borrower is not in default, so the loan is not eligible for HAMP.

TILA imposes disclosure requirements on lenders. When all required disclosures are provided, a borrower's right to rescind is limited to three business days (not including Sunday) after a loan is finalized. If a lender fails to provide material required disclosures, the borrower has a right to rescind the transaction for up to three years. So, if

Blockhead did not give Carlotta all of the required disclosures, her right to rescind extended to three years. Otherwise, she is too late.

2. Blockhead's options include forbearance, a workout agreement, a U.S. Department of Housing and Urban Development (HUD) loan, a short sale, a sale and leaseback arrangement, the U.S. Treasury Department's Home Affordable Modification Program (HAMP), a deed in lieu of foreclosure, and a prepackaged bankruptcy. Foreclosure is also an option.

In these facts, because the market value of Edgar's home has declined, it would be unlikely to bring enough on a short sale or a foreclosure sale to recover the unpaid amount of the loan. A deficiency judgment would be necessary. The best option here, however, would most likely be forbearance or a workout agreement. Blockhead could ask for proof of Edgar's upcoming job and agree to delay Alpha's efforts to collect the next six payments on the mortgage. This option would save both parties time, expense, and the negative consequences of some of the other choices.

Cumulative Hypothetical Problem for Unit Six—Including Chapters 28–31

1. A. A creditor can place a mechanic's lien on real property when a person contracts for labor to repair the property but does not pay. An artisan's lien entitles a creditor to recover from a debtor for the repair of personal property. In both cases, the property can be sold to satisfy the debt, but notice of the foreclosure and sale must first be given to the debtor.

2. D. With the right of subrogation, a surety, or a guarantor, may pursue any remedies that were available to the creditor against the debtor. These rights include collection of the debt. A right of contribution is available to a co-surety, who pays more than his or her proportionate share of a debt, to recover from any other co-sureties. An exemption, in the context of a debt, is property that a debtor can protect from being used to pay the debt. Exoneration is not a term that applies to this circumstance.

3. A. If a buyer in the ordinary course of business does not know that a purchase violates a third party's rights, the buyer takes the goods free of any security interest. This is an exception to the general rule that a security interest in collateral continues even after the collateral is sold.

4. B. Only a debtor can file a plan under Chapter 11, but for the court to confirm it, the secured creditors must accept it. There is another condition that the plan must meet. It must provide that the creditors retain their liens and the value of the property to be distributed to them is not less than the secured portion of their claims, or the debtor must surrender to the creditors the property securing those claims.

5. A. A Chapter 11 plan must provide for the full payment of all claims entitled to priority and the same treatment of each claim within a particular class. After the payments are completed, all debts provided for by the plan are discharged.

Questions on the Focus on Ethics for Unit Six—Creditors' Rights and Bankruptcy

1. A. The opposite of all of the rest of the answer choices is true—self-help repossession is stressful for debtors, because it is often done in the middle of the night or otherwise attempted clandestinely; the repossession can be risky, in part because it may encourage violent confrontations with debtors; and the UCC does not define "breach of the peace," which can add to the complications. That self-help repossession can be done without involving the courts, however, is why it is permitted.

2. C. When the number of bankruptcies—whether or not this is due to lower prices for borrowers' products—creditors suffer higher risks in making loans. To cover their own subsequent increased costs, creditors can (1) increase the interest rates charged to all borrowers, which is the answer here; (2) require additional security, or collateral; or (3) become more selective in making loans. In all of these situations, there are ethical and economic concerns for all of the parties.

3. A. The bankruptcy laws—including the automatic stay provision, and the provisions as to which and how much debt can be discharged—can make a creditor's secured or unsecured obligation worthless, while enhancing the debtor's position by freeing secured assets from the obligations that they secure. This situation and the ease with which debtors can file for bankruptcy underlies the attempt of the bankruptcy laws to make it less easy for debts to be discharged by directing debtors to debt-counseling classes and funneling petitions into Chapter 13 (subject to the "means test"). Under Chapter 13, many debts may be paid according to a five-year plan and a budget imposed on a debtor, rather than going unpaid and being discharged.

Chapter 32

True-False Questions

1. T
2. T

3. T

4. F. This could be a violation of the agent's duty of loyalty to the principal. An agent must act solely for the benefit of the principal, in matters relating to the subject of the agency relation.

5. F. Although anyone can be an agent, a principal must have capacity to contract. Thus, in most states, a minor can be an agent but not a principal.

6. T

7. F. When an agent breaches an agency contract, the principal can choose to avoid the contract.

8. F. If an agent is negligent and harms a third party, the injured third party can successfully sue the principal. In some circumstances, the principal may also sue the agent. The same principles apply when an agent violates a principal's instructions.

9. T

10. T

Fill-in Questions

performance; notification; loyalty; obedience; accounting

Multiple-Choice Questions

1. B. The problem states that the two persons are hired as employees. The employer is the principal. Normally, all employees who deal with third parties are deemed to be agents.

2. D. This is an agency relationship. An agency agreement does not have to be in writing, and an agent does not need to indicate that he or she is an agent. The business of the agent is not a determining factor in whether an agency relationship exists.

3. C. If an agent is not a gratuitous agent (one who does not perform for money), a principal owes the agent compensation for his or her services rendered. In this problem, if nothing had been agreed to, the principal would owe the agent the customary amount for his or her services. Also, payment must be timely. Another of a principal's duties is to reimburse an agent for expenses related to the agency, unless the parties have agreed otherwise. This question and answer are based on a question that appeared in the CPA exam in 1996.

4. B. A failure to disclose material information bearing on an agency relationship is a breach of an agent's duties. In that circumstance, the agency is voidable at the option of the principal. When the principal transfers the property that was the object of the agency, as in this problem, the agency relationship has been voided.

5. A. There is a long list of factors that courts can consider in determining whether an individual is an employee or an independent contractor, and all of the choices in this question are among those factors. The most important factor, however, is the degree of control that the employer has over the details of the work.

6. D. Neither consideration nor a written agreement is required to form an agency relationship. Normally, an agency relationship must be based on an agreement that the agent will act for the principal, but the agreement does not have to be in writing—it can be oral or it can be implied from the parties' conduct.

7. A. An agent's duties to a principal include a duty to act solely in the principal's interest in matters concerning the principal's business. This is the duty of loyalty. The agent must act solely in the principal's interest and not in the interest of the agent, or some other party. It is also a breach of the duty of loyalty to use a principal's trade secrets or other confidential information (but not acquired skills) even after the agency has terminated.

8. B. In performing an agency, an agent is expected to use reasonable diligence and skill, which is the degree of skill of a reasonable person under similar circumstances. If an agent claims special skills, such as those of in this problem, he or she is expected to use those skills.

9. D. If a principal causes a third person to believe that another person is his or her agent, and the third person deals with the supposed agent, the principal is estopped to deny the agency relationship. The third person must reasonably believe that the relationship existed and that the agent had authority. An ordinary, prudent person familiar with business practice and custom would have been justified in making the same conclusion.

10. A. Agency law is essential to the existence of most business entities, including corporations, because without agents, most firms could not do business. A corporate officer who serves in a representative capacity, as in this problem, is an agent. The corporation is the principal. For a contract to be binding on the firm, it needs only to be signed by the agent and to be within the scope of the officer's authority.

GamePoints

1. Game Sportz is a principal. Felicity, Ethan, Desiree, and you are its agents and employees. Cody is an independent contractor.

   In an agency relationship, an agent agrees to act on behalf of a principal. An agent is subject to the principal's control. An employee is subject to an employer's control—an independent contractor is not. A corporation is has contractual capacity but can act only through its agents. As a corporation,

Game Sportz acts through its agents, whom it grants authority to so act. Felicity, Ethan, Desiree, and you act on behalf of Game Sportz. Of course, the authority is different in its extent, but under the facts as stared, each party can bind the firm for certain purposes in deals with third parties. Cody does not have the authority to legally bind the company, however. Felicity, Ethan, and Desiree, are subject to Games Sportz's control through you, and you are subject to the firm through its board. All of you are employees. Because Cody is not subject to the company's control with respect to the physical conduct in the performance of his contracts, he is an independent contractor.

2. Transgressions in these facts include breach of contract and conversion. Thus, possible remedies include the normal contract and tort remedies. Also, when an agent breaches his or her duty to the principal by retaining benefits that belong to the principal—which happened here—a court can impose a constructive trust and declare that the agent holds the benefits for the principal's behalf. A constructive trust may also be imposed when an agent retains profits that belong to the principal. Here, the benefits were the rebate payments, which were paid to Ethan's account.

Chapter 33

True-False Questions

1. T
2. F. An agent is liable for his or her own torts, but a principal may also be liable under the doctrine of *respondeat superior*. The key is whether the tort is committed within the scope of employment. One of the important factors is whether the act that constituted the tort was authorized by the principal.
3. T
4. T
5. T
6. F. Criminal acts by an agent are not the responsibility of the principal, who will not thus be liable to a third party for any consequent harm.
7. F. The parties to an agency may always have the *power* to terminate the agency at any time, but they may not always have the *right*. If a party who terminates an agency does not have the right to do so, he or she may be liable for breach of contract.
8. F. One of the main attributes of an agency relationship is that the agent can enter into binding contracts on behalf of the principal. When an agent acts within the scope of his or her authority in entering a contract, the principal is bound, whether the principal's identity was disclosed, partially disclosed, or undisclosed to the other party to the contact.
9. T
10. F. An e-agent is a semi-autonomous computer program that is capable of executing specific tasks, including responding to e-mail or other electronic communication without review by an individual.

Fill-in Questions

is; an undisclosed; undisclosed; tort injuries; generally does not result

Multiple-Choice Questions

1. D. Implied authority can be conferred by custom, inferred from the agent's position, or inferred as reasonably necessary to carry out express authority. In determining whether an agent has the implied authority to do a specific act, the question is whether it is reasonable for the agent to believe that he or she has the authority.
2. A. Until an agent is notified of the principal's decision to terminate the agency relationship, the agent's authority continues. Similarly, third parties with whom the agent deals must be informed of the termination to end the agent's apparent authority, as regards those third parties. Unless an agency is in writing, in which case it must be terminated in writing, an agent can learn of a termination through any means.
3. C. Under the doctrine of *respondeat superior*, an employer (or principal) is vicariously liable for the wrongful acts of his or her employee (or agent) committed within the scope of employment (or agency).
4. A. Unless an agency is in writing—in which case, it must be terminated in writing—an agent can learn of a termination through any means. Until an agent is notified of the principal's decision to terminate the agency relationship, the agent's authority continues. Similarly, third parties with whom the agent deals must be informed of the termination to end the agent's apparent authority, as regards those third parties.
5. C. When an agent acts without authority and a third party relies on the agency status, the agent may be liable for breach of any contract purportedly signed on behalf of a principal. The agent may not be liable, however, if the third party knew that the agent did not have authority to contract on behalf of the principal. In either case, the principal is not liable, unless he or she ratifies the contract.
6. A. Apparent authority exists when a principal causes a third party reasonably to believe that an

agent has the authority to act, even if the agent does not otherwise have the authority to do so. If the third party changes positions in reliance on the principal's representation, the principal may be estopped from denying the authority. Thus, here, the principal could not hold the customers liable for failing to pay.

7.   C. When an agent acts within the scope of his or her authority to enter into a valid contract on behalf of an undisclosed principal, the principal is liable on the contract. Ratification is not necessary. The agent may also be liable on the contract. This question and answer are based on a question included in the May 1995 CPA exam.

8.   B. An employer is liable for harm to a third party by an employee acting within the scope of employment. Here, the question is whether the employee was acting within that scope. Factors that indicate he was not include that the act (theft) was not authorized, did not advance the employer's interest, is not commonly performed by employees for their employers, and involved a serious crime. The employer might be liable if it knew that the employee would commit a tort or allowed it. In this problem, the employee acted without the employer's knowledge.

9.   C. An agent (or employee) is liable for his or her own torts, whether or not they were committed within the scope of a principal's employment. The principal is also liable under the doctrine of *respondeat superior* when a tort is within the scope of the employment. One of the important factors in determining liability is whether the agent was on the principal's business or on a "frolic of his or her own."

10.   A. When an agent is employed to accomplish a particular objective, the agency automatically terminates when the objective is accomplished.

GamePoints

1.   Of course, an agency relationship can only be created for a legal purpose, and one created for an illegal purpose is unenforceable. Assuming an agency relationship exists, an agent can enter into binding contracts on behalf of the principal. When an agent acts within the scope of his or her authority in entering into a contract, the principal is bound, whether the principal's identity was disclosed, partially disclosed, or undisclosed to the other party to the contact. The agent is also bound if the principal's identity was only partially disclosed or not disclosed to the other party. Thus, in this problem, you are bound to all three contracts and your agent is also bound to the second and third contracts (but not the first).

2.   Under the doctrine of *respondeat superior*, a principal is liable for any harm caused to another through an agent's negligence as long as the agent was acting within the scope of his or her authority at the time of the harmful act. Here, you instructed your agent to "loot the universe," which he was doing when his negligent escape from the asteroid caused an injury to the Cyclops. Thus, the Cyclops could recover from you for the harm.

Chapter 34

True-False Questions

1.   T

2.   F. Employment "at will" means that either party may terminate the employment at any time, with or without good cause. There are many exceptions to this doctrine, enacted by state legislatures and Congress, or created by the courts. These include exceptions based on contract or tort theories, or public policy.

3.   F. Employers are free to offer employees no benefits. Federal and state governments participate in insurance programs designed to protect employees and their families by covering some of the financial impact of retirement, disability, death, and hospitalization.

4.   T

5.   F. A "whistleblower" is one who reports wrongdoing. These statutes protect employees who report their employers' wrongdoing from retaliation on the part of those employers.

6.   F. The Electronic Communications Privacy Act prohibits the interception of telephone (and other electronic) communications. Some courts recognize an exception for employers monitoring employee business-related calls, but monitoring personal conversations is not permitted.

7.   F. It is the central legal right of a *union* to serve as the bargaining representative of employees in negotiations with management.

8.   F. An employer is required to evaluate job applicants, and their documents, fairly and consistently (for example, proof of qualifications or citizenship cannot be asked of some individuals and not others). But it is illegal for an employer to hire for work in the United States a person who is not authorized to work here.

9.   T

10.   T

Fill-in Questions

either; unless; may; Some; A few states; may not

Multiple-Choice Questions

1. A. Child-labor, minimum-wage, and maximum-hour provisions are included in the Fair Labor Standards Act (also known as the Wage-Hour Law), covering virtually all employees. The employer may also be subject to the other laws given as choices in this problem, but those laws concern other rights and duties of employees and employers. This question and answer are based on a question that was included in the May 1995 CPA exam.

2. B. Under the Family and Medical Leave Act (FMLA) of 1993, employees can take up to twelve weeks of family or medical leave during any twelve-month period and are entitled to continued health insurance coverage during the leave. Employees are also guaranteed the same, or a comparable, job on returning to work.

3. C. Under the Consolidated Omnibus Budget Reconciliation Act (COBRA) of 1985, most workers' medical, optical, or dental insurance is not automatically eliminated on termination of employment. The workers can choose to continue the coverage at the employer's group rate, if they are willing to pay the premiums (and a 2 percent administrative fee).

4. C. When an employment relationship is "at will," either the employer or the employee may terminate it at any time—and for any reason. An employment relationship is at will when there is no contract and no law to otherwise restrict its duration or other conditions of its termination.

5. B. Depending on the particular state, and the rulings of the courts in the state, some state constitutions effectively prohibit private employers from testing for drugs. There are also state statutes that restrict drug testing by private employers. Other sources of limitation on the use of such tests include collective bargaining agreements and employee tort actions for invasion of privacy.

6. A. It is illegal to hire for work in the United States a person who is not authorized to work here. The principal responsibility to verify an individual's identity and eligibility to work rests with the employer. The U.S. Citizenship and Immigration Services supplies a form that an employer must complete within three days of hiring an employee (and retain for three years). An employer has some defenses against alleged violations but is otherwise subject to penalties for illegally employing noncitizens.

7. A. Among these choices, an employer may hire a noncitizen who is a lawful permanent resident (as proved by an I-531 Alien Registration Receipt, or "green card"). Subject to certain strict requirements, an employer may apply for a "green card" for a noncitizen. But under no circumstances can an employer legally hire a noncitizen who is in the United States unlawfully. Also, an immigrant employee's ability to stay in the United States and to switch jobs here is limited

8. A. Persons who immigrate to the United States to work include those with special skills, such as the individual in this question. To hire such an individual who is not otherwise authorized to work here, an employer must petition the U.S. Citizenship and Immigration Services, or CIS. The employer can obtain a visa for a person to work in the United States in a highly qualified, specialty occupation as part of the H-1B visa program. ICE is the U.S. Immigration and Customs Enforcement, which enforces immigration laws and rules. RICO is the acronym for the Racketeer Influenced and Corrupt Organizations Act, under which a private individual who claims injury as a result of illegal hiring may sue an employer.

9. D. It is an unfair labor practice for an employer to threaten employees with the loss of their jobs if a union wins a scheduled union election. What can be difficult is determining what constitutes a threat. Explicit statements, such as "if the union wins, you're all fired," are obvious violations. Less clear is whether such a statement as "if the union wins, we will lose business to our competitors" is a violation. The point, however, is that an employer cannot require rejection of a union as a condition of employment. The other choices are, of course, not unfair labor practices.

10. D. An employer can hire permanent replacement workers during an economic strike. After the strike, the replacement workers do not have to be fired to make way for the strikers. Temporary replacement workers may be hired during any strike.

GamePoints

1. The Fair Labor Standards Act requires covered, nonexempt individuals who work more than forty hours in one week to be paid overtime wages of no less than 1.5 times their regular pay rate for the hours worked beyond forty. In two of the weeks noted in this problem—the first and second weeks—you played the game for more than forty hours and would be entitled to overtime pay if, of course, this game-play was work. That you played less than forty hours in the other weeks has no effect.

2. State workers' compensation laws allow compensation to be paid to workers whose injuries occur on the job or in the course of their employment. Under those laws, an employee who receives workers' compensation cannot successfully maintain a suit against his or employer for negligence to recover for the same injury. Thus, in this problem, Derek is entitled to recover workers' compensation because he was an employee of the service, and the injury was accidental and occurred in the course of employment. Derek could not then, however, successfully sue the service on a negligence theory because he was the service's employee and would be recovering workers' compensation.

Chapter 35

True-False Questions

1. T
2. F. An employer may be liable even though an employee did the harassing, if the employer knew, or should have known, and failed to take corrective action, or if the employee was in a supervisory position and took a tangible employment action against the injured employee.
3. F. Just as an employer may be liable for an employee's misconduct, the employer may be liable for harassment by a nonemployee, if the employer knew, or should have known, of the harassment and failed to take corrective action.
4. T
5. T
6. T
7. F. If the Equal Employment Opportunity Commission (EEOC) decides not pursue a claim, the victim can file a suit against alleged violator. The EEOC can pursue a claim in federal district court, however, in its own name against alleged violators (and this is true even if the employee has agreed to submit the dispute to arbitration). The EEOC can also intervene in a suit filed by a private party.
8. F. Title VII covers only employers with fifteen or more employees, labor unions with fifteen or more members, labor unions that operate hiring halls, employment agencies, and federal, state, and local agencies. In other words, small employers are generally exempted from the application of this federal statute.
9. T
10. T

Fill-in Questions

can; may sue if a settlement between the parties is not reached; reinstatement, back pay, and retroactive promotions

Multiple-Choice Questions

1. C. Here, the employer would seem to have a valid business necessity defense. It appears reasonable that administrative assistants be able to type. An employer can insist that, to be hired, a job applicant possess the actual skills required for a job. Except for an applicant's willingness or unwillingness to acquire certain skills, the other answer choices might be legitimate defenses in other circumstances.
2. C. The Equal Pay Act of 1963 prohibits gender-based discrimination in wages for equal work. Different wages are acceptable because of any factor but gender, including seniority and merit.
3. A. The other choices would not subject the employer to liability under the Age Discrimination in Employment Act (ADEA). Discrimination is prohibited against persons forty years of age or older, even if the discrimination is unintentional. Mandatory retirement may be instituted, but not on account of an employee's age, and an employee may be discharged for cause at any age. This question and answer are based on a question that appeared in the CPA exam in 1996.
4. C. An employer who is subject to the Americans with Disabilities Act cannot exclude arbitrarily a person who, with reasonable accommodation, could do what is required of a job. A disabled individual is not required to reasonably accommodate an employer. Also, the standard is not "significant additional costs," to either the employer or the disabled individual.
5. C. Title VII prohibits employment discrimination on the basis of race. This includes discriminating against members of a minority with darker skin than other members of the same minority. Title VII also prohibits using physical characteristics that are typical of some races to distinguish applicants or employees.
6. A. Before filing a lawsuit, the best step for a person who believes that he or she may be a victim of employment discrimination is to contact a state or federal agency to see whether the claim is justified. The appropriate federal agency is the Equal Employment Opportunity Commission. Most states have similar agencies that evaluate claims under state law.
7. C. Title VII prohibits showing a preference for members of one minority over members of another. Title VII also prohibits making distinctions according to the race of a person's spouse, friends, or other contacts. The other laws mentioned in the answer choices prohibit discrimination on the basis of age and disability, respectively, as suggested by their titles.

8.   A. The Age Discrimination in Employment Act (ADEA) of 1967 requires, for the establishment of a *prima facie* case, that at the time of the alleged discrimination, the plaintiff was forty or older, was qualified for the job, and was discharged or otherwise rejected in circumstances that imply discrimination. The difference between a *prima facie* case under the ADEA and under Title VII is that the ADEA does not require a plaintiff to show that someone who is not a member of a protected class filled the position at the center of the claim.

9.   C. The employer's best defense in this problem would be that being able to pass the tests is a business necessity—it is a necessary requirement for the job. Discrimination may be illegal even if it is not intentional, and whether or not all men pass the tests is not relevant to whether there is discrimination against women. If the employer hires some women for the job, it could not argue successfully that gender is a BFOQ for the job.

10.   A. Sexual harassment occurs when, in a workplace, an employee is subject to comments or contact that is perceived as sexually offensive. An employer may be liable even though an employee did the harassing. If the employee was in a supervisory position, as in this problem, for an employer to be held liable, a tangible employment action may need to be proved. Here, the employee's pay was cut.

GamePoints

1.   Under the Americans with Disabilities Act, a disabled person qualified for a given job is protected from employment discrimination on the basis of his or her disability. A disabled person is not unqualified for a job simply because the employer would have to make a reasonable accommodation. In fact, employers are required to reasonably accommodate the needs of persons with disabilities. Thus, here, the employer has apparently engaged in discrimination by choosing not "to make changes to accommodate this guy." For that reason, the disabled person could recover damages.

2.   Title VII of the Civil Rights Act of 1964 prohibits job discrimination against employees on the basis of race. To recover on this ground, the employee must show that (1) the employee is a member of a protected class, (2) the employee applied and was qualified for the position in question, (3) the employer rejected the employee, and (4) the employer continued to seek applicants or hired someone not of a protected class. In this problem, the employee applied and was qualified for the promotion (a year's driving experience and a specific license). The employer clearly rejected the employee on the basis of race ("whites are lazy"). And the em-

ployer most likely continued to seek applicants and may have hired "someone not of a protected class." The chief difficulty in concluding that this problem presents an instance of employment discrimination under these standards is the employee's race. "Whites" have not been historically discriminated against so that Sam could qualify as a member of a "protected class."

Cumulative Hypothetical Problem for Unit Seven—Including Chapters 32–35

1.   D. The Social Security Act of 1935 provides payments for persons who are retired or disabled. The Social Security Administration is a federal agency that also administers the Medicare program. Unemployment benefits, however, are part of a state system created by the Federal Unemployment Tax Act of 1935.

2.   B. The requirements for recovery under state workers' compensation laws include the existence of an employment relationship and an accidental injury that occurs on the job or within the scope of employment. Accepting benefits precludes an employee from suing his or her employer, but it does not bar the employee from suing a third party for causing the injury.

3.   D. One of the agent's fiduciary duties to the principal is the duty of loyalty. This means that the agent must not engage in conflicts of interest, and the agent cannot compete with the principal without informing the principal and obtaining the principal's consent.

4.   A. Title VII of the Civil Rights Act of 1964 covers many forms of discrimination, including discrimination based on gender, race, religion, color, and national origin. But Title VII does not prohibit discrimination based on age, which is the subject of the Age Discrimination in Employment Act of 1967.

5.   D. The Age Discrimination in Employment Act of 1967 prohibits discrimination against persons aged forty or more. This includes mandatory retirement of such individuals. In most circumstances, however, an employer can discharge an employee for cause, regardless of his or her age, without running afoul of this, or any other, federal antidiscrimination law.

Questions on the Focus on Ethics for Unit Seven—Agency and Employment

1.   D. The conduct stated in the answer choices is permitted by legal and ethical considerations. Other actions that may be proscribed by ethics include secretly profiting from the agency relation, and

failing to disclose the agent's interest in property that the principal is buying.

2. C. Agents and principals owe each other fiduciary duties. The law mandates for a principal duties of compensation, cooperation, and reimbursement of agency-related expenses. A principal is not legally bound to a duty of loyalty, however, although a sense of loyalty may be based on ethical obligations.

3. D. When an innocent party must suffer a loss, the party in the best position to prevent the loss is generally held to bear its burden, even if that party was also innocent with respect to the loss. In an employment relationship, that party is the employer, who, when the situation involves an employee and a third party, is in a better position to control the employee. The employer may also have insurance or some other form of "deep pockets" from which to cover a loss or injury.

Chapter 36

True-False Questions

1. F. A sole proprietorship is the simplest form of business organization. In a sole proprietorship, the owner and the business are the same. Anyone who creates a business without designating a specific form for its organization is doing business as a sole proprietorship.

2. T

3. T

4. T

5. F. The parties to a franchise (the franchisor and the franchisee) determine its termination. Generally, the parties provide in the franchise contract that termination is "for cause" and notice is required. Of course, in the case of a dispute, litigation may ensue and the parties may end up in court, which may then have to determine whether or not to terminate the franchise arrangement. That is not the usual course, however.

6. T

7. F. A franchisor can exercise greater control in this area than in some other areas of the business, because the *franchisor* has a legitimate interest in maintaining the quality of the product or service to protect its name and reputation.

8. F. There is state law covering franchises, and it is very similar to federal law on the subject, requiring certain disclosures, limiting termination without cause, and so on. State deceptive practices acts and UCC Article 2 may also apply to franchises.

9. F. Federal laws covering franchises include the Automobile Dealers' Franchise Act of 1965, the Petroleum Marketing Practices Act (PMPA) of 1979, the federal antitrust laws, and the Franchise Rule of the Federal Trade Commission (which requires certain disclosures and a meeting between the parties to a franchise agreement).

10. T

Fill-in Questions

distributorship; chain-style; manufacturing

Multiple-Choice Questions

1. D. There are no limits on the liability of the owner of a sole proprietorship for the debts and obligations of the firm. A sole proprietorship has greater organizational flexibility, however, than other forms of business organization.

2. B. Antitrust laws are most likely to be violated if the franchisor requires the franchisee to purchase exclusively from the franchisor. A franchisor's setting of prices at which products may be sold may also violate antitrust laws.

3. A. Under a contract between the franchisor and the franchisee, the latter may be required to pay a fee for the franchise license, fees for products bought from or through the franchisor, and a percentage of advertising and administrative costs.

4. A. In this type of franchise, a franchisor typically requires a franchisee to pay it a fee for the right to sell its products. The franchisor also usually requires that the franchisee pay the franchisor a percentage of the receipts from the sales of the products.

5. B. Of the choices here, again the franchisor can set the terms. There may be little for a franchisee to negotiate with some franchises, but perhaps the chief advantage of a franchise is that the franchisee is obtaining the opportunity to profit from the sales of a proven product or service.

6. C. Franchise agreements typically provide that the franchisor can terminate a franchise for cause. If no set time for termination is provided, a reasonable time will be implied. A franchisor cannot usually terminate a franchise without notice.

7. A. A franchisee may have some protection under the Franchise Rule of the Federal Trade Commission with respect to what the franchisor must disclose, and how and when the disclosure must be made, before the franchisee invests in a franchise. A franchisee may have additional protection under federal law, depending on the nature of the products or services being sold. State protection, while similar to federal law, may include more protection under deceptive practices acts or Article 2 of the UCC.

8. A. A disadvantage of the sole proprietorship form of doing business is that the ability to raise capital while maintaining control, and retaining the same form, is limited chiefly to borrowing funds. The trade off in this situation is that a sole proprietorship provides greater organizational flexibility—no one needs to be consulted in making business decisions. Bringing in partners would convert the business to a partnership. Issuing stock would require incorporating or establishing another form of business. Selling the business would of course sacrifice all control.

9. C. A franchise is an arrangement through which the owner of a copyright, a trademark, or a trade name licenses others to use it in selling goods or services. Most franchises can also be characterized as distributorships, chain-style business operations, or manufacturing or processing-plant operations.

10. B. A franchisee is a purchaser of a franchise. The seller of a franchise is the franchisor. Although economically dependent, or at least related, these parties are usually otherwise independent of each other.

GamePoints

1. At its inception, a small, undiversified business with few, or no, employees and little profits and is most likely to exist as a sole proprietorship. This is in part because a sole proprietorship is easier and less expensive to start than other forms. As the owner, you can make decisions without consulting others. Taxes are paid on the business's income as the owner's personal income. One advantage to this form is its organizational flexibility—you can operate the enterprise without formality. An important disadvantage is there are no limits to your liability for business debts and obligations. A second disadvantage is the ability to raise capital without losing control. The sole option may be to borrow.

2. A franchisee's failure to meet a franchisor's sales quota can be cause for the termination of the franchise. As the parties to the franchise agreement, you and your franchisor set out what would constitute the basis for a termination of your relationship. Your agreement included a sales quota and stated that termination would be for "cause." If you do not meet the quota, you breach the agreement. This is cause for its termination. Of course, the franchisor must give you notice and reasonable time to wind up the business.

Chapter 37

True-False Questions

1. T

2. F. A general partnership is formed through an agreement among the partners. If this agreement satisfies the definition of partnership, nothing more is needed for a partnership to exist. The partnership agreement does not need to be in writing, except as otherwise required under the Statute of Frauds. Most states, however, require other types of partnerships to file certain information in designated state offices (usually the secretary of state).

3. F. General partners are subject to personal liability for the debts and obligations of a partnership. This is true whether or not they have participated in its management. On the firm's dissolution, its creditors (partners and non-partners) have the highest priority in the distribution of the firm's assets. If those assets are not sufficient to pay the creditors, the general partners are liable for the difference.

4. T

5. T

6. F. Unless it is set out otherwise in the partnership agreement, profits are shared equally, and losses are borne in the same proportion as the profits, under the UPA.

7. F. The death of a limited partner will not dissolve a limited partnership, nor will a limited partnership dissolve on the personal bankruptcy of a limited partner.

8. F. A feature that makes a limited liability partnership attractive is that its partners can avoid liability for any partnership obligation, whether in contract, tort, or otherwise. Of course, each partner is liable for his or her own wrongful acts.

9. F. The liability of the *limited* partners in a limited partnership is limited to the amount of their investment in the firm, but the liability of the *general* partners is the same as that of the partners in a general partnership (unlimited).

10. T

Fill-in Questions

are; one or more; obligation; is not; does not release

Multiple-Choice Questions

1. B. Under a partnership by estoppel theory, a person who is not a partner, but who represents himself or herself as a partner, is liable to a third person who acts in reasonable reliance on that representation. If one of the actual partners had consented to the misrepresentation, however, the firm would also be liable.

2. A. This arrangement for the payment of an employee (a base wage and a sales commission) does not make the employee a partner in the employer's business. There are three attributes of a partnership: sharing profits, joint ownership of a business, and an equal right in the management of the business. None of these are present here.

3. B. A newly admitted partner is liable for previous debts and obligations of the partnership only to the extent of his or her capital contribution to the firm. In other words, as far as a new partner is concerned, existing partnership debts can be satisfied only from the assets of the firm. Previous partners may be fully, and personally, liable, however.

4. C. The dissociation of a partner from a partnership is not necessarily the end of the firm's business, which may be continued by the remaining partners. The partner's interest in the firm must be bought out, however, according to the UPA's rules. Also, to avoid potential liability on a theory of apparent authority, a partnership should file a statement of dissociation in the appropriate state office.

5. C. Partners are jointly and severally liable for partnership obligations, including contracts, torts, and breaches of trust. This means that any or all of the partners may be held liable. This is true even if, as in this problem, they did not participate whatever gave rise to the obligation.

6. B. None of the payments represented by the facts in this problem (a debt to be paid by installments or rent to a landlord) is evidence that a partnership has been created. Even joint ownership of property and the sharing of profits from that property is enough to create a partnership.

7. D. Ordinarily, limited partners are liable for the debts of their limited partnerships only to the extent of their capital contributions to the firms. A general partner, in contrast, may be held personally liable for the full amount of the firm's obligations. Similarly, a limited partner, unlike a general partner does not have a right to control the partnership. This question and answer are based on a question that appeared in the November 1989 CPA exam.

8. D. Limited partnerships may be dissolved by many causes but not by any of these choices. Partners may expressly agree to dissolve their partnership, or dissolution may be caused by the withdrawal, death, or mental incompetence of a general partner (unless the others agree to continue the business). A general partner's death or bankruptcy causes the firm to dissolve, as would an event that makes it impossible to operate the partnership lawfully. Dissolution can also result from a court decree.

9. A. After a partner informs the other partners that he or she is dissociating from the partnership, the withdrawing partner is not liable for contracts entered into by his or her former partners. The parties who sign the contract are, of course, liable, however, as is a partnership that, like the firm in this problem, carries on the business.

10. C. Professionals, and others, who organize as a limited liability partnership can avoid personal liability for the wrongdoing of other partners. In that circumstance, they may have only the same liability as a limited partner in a limited partnership.

GamePoints

1. Agreements to form a partnership can be oral or implied by conduct, but sometimes they must be in writing to be enforceable under the Statute of Frauds. In this problem, the partners agree to pursue their venture for five years, which by this term is to continue for more than one year. Thus it must be in writing under the one-year rule of the Statute of Frauds to be enforceable. Practically speaking, even if the one-year rule did not apply, the agreement might be better in writing to make proof of the profit sharing provision easier. In the absence of proof of an agreement to the contrary, it is assumed that partners agreed to share profits and losses equally.

2. According to the principles discussed in this chapter, your firm is most likely bound to the contract. The chief factor to determining the liability is what the third party knew and when he or she knew it. The apparent authority of a partner to bind a partnership in dealing with a third party cannot be limited by an agreement between the partners of which the third party is unaware. Every partner is an agent of the partnership and can bind the firm to a contract with a third party. Only if the third party is aware that a partner's authority is limited will the liability of the firm be limited. If your firm is bound to this contract, as a partner, you are personally liable to the full extent. At first risk is the amount of your capital contribution. Once the partnership's assets have been exhausted in meeting the firm's obligation, your personal assets may be reached by the firm's creditor to make up any deficiency.

Chapter 38

True-False Questions

1. F. State law applies to the formation of limited liability companies (LLCs). Like the formation of a corporation and other forms of limited liability organizations, the formation of an LLC requires that articles of organization be filed in the state of formation. Otherwise, an LLC will not be held to exist, and its members will not enjoy the features that they wanted.

2. T

3. F. One of the chief advantages of a limited liability company (LLC) is that it offers the limited liability of a corporation. Because an LLC also offers the tax advantages of a partnership, many businesses are using this form of organization.

4. T

5. T

6. T

7. F. A joint venture is an enterprise in which two or more persons combine their efforts or property for a single transaction or project, or a related series of transactions or projects. It resembles a partnership, except that its members have less apparent and implied authority than partners and the death of a member does not affect the venture's continuation.

8. T

9. T

10. F. As a form of business organization, a business trust resembles a corporation.

Fill-in Questions

members; limited liability company; members *or* shareholders; joint stock company

Multiple-Choice Questions

1. B. A limited liability company (LLC) can be taxed as a partnership, a sole proprietorship (if there is only one member), or a corporation, but electing to be taxed as a partnership is often preferable. The income can be passed through to its members without being taxed at the company level. Generally, there is no particular advantage to being taxed as a corporation. In fact, avoiding the double corporate tax is one reason for forming an LLC.

2. B. Normally, the members of a limited liability company are liable for the debts of their company only to the extent of their investment in the firm, like corporate shareholders or limited partners. Sole proprietors and general partners, in contrast, may be personally liable for the full amount of their firms' obligations.

3. C. One of the advantages of the limited liability company (LLC) form of business organization is that its members are not personally liable for the debts of their firm regardless of the extent of their participation in management (unlike a limited

partnership). In fact, unless agreed otherwise, an LLC's management will be considered to include all members. Another advantage is that there is generally no limit on the number of members that a firm can have (unlike an S corporation).

4. D. It is expected that eventually, state laws governing limited liability companies (LLCs) will be made relatively uniform. As for the other choices, the members are not subject to personal liability for the firm's obligations and can participate in the management of the firm to any extent. Also, unlike corporate income, LLC income can pass through the firm and be taxed only once.

5. C. This definition is like the definition of a partnership. A joint venture is similar to a partnership, and is generally subject to partnership law, but unlike a partnership, a joint venture is created in contemplation of a limited activity. A joint venture may have more than two members, and a joint venture is not a corporate enterprise, although its members may be corporations. This question and answer are based on a question that appeared in the November 1989 CPA exam.

6. B. As noted in the answer to the previous question, a joint venture is similar to a partnership, and is generally subject to partnership law, but unlike a partnership, a joint venture is created in contemplation of a limited activity.

7. D. A syndicate may exist as a partnership, a corporation, or no legally recognized form. As in this problem, a syndicate is a group of individuals financing a project.

8. B. A joint stock company is a hybrid of a partnership and a corporation in that it is usually treated like a partnership, but its members are not treated like agents of each other and it has many characteristics of a corporation: (1) ownership by shares of stock, (2) managed by directors and officers, and (3) perpetual existence.

9. A. A business trust is similar to a corporation. Like corporate shareholders, the owners hold shares in the trust and they are not personally liable for the organization's debts and obligations.

10. C. In a manager-managed limited liability company (LLC), the members designate a group of persons (members or not) to manage the firm. These managers owe the fiduciary duties of loyalty and care to the LLC and its members.

GamePoints

1. Unless you and the other party agree otherwise, a joint venture is the most likely form that you will use to undertake this project. A joint venture is an enterprise in which two or more persons combine their efforts or property for a single transaction or project, (or in some cases a related series of transactions or projects). In an agreement, you can set out how profits and losses are to be split. Normally, unless you agree otherwise, however, joint venturers share profits and losses equally. A joint venture resembles and is taxed like a partnership, and the same principles generally apply to both. Each joint venturer has an equal right to manage the business and is liable for its debts and other obligations. But members in a joint venture have less implied and apparent authority than partners.

2. According to the principles discussed in the chapter, the firm would be taxed as a partnership unless it elected to be taxed as a corporation. In other words, the profits would pass through the firm to its owners, who would declare the amounts as personal income and pay taxes accordingly. The members of a limited liability company (LLC) can be its managers, but a non-member can also manage the day-to-day business of the firm. Because an LLC offers its members the limited liability of a corporation—the owners are liable for the obligations of the firm only to the extent of their investment in it—a member of an LLC is not likely to be held fully liable for the acts of another member or employee.

Chapter 39

True-False Questions

1. T
2. T
3. F. A corporation formed in a country other than the United States, but that does business in the United States, is an alien corporation. A foreign corporation is a corporation formed in one state, but doing business in another state.
4. F. Powers set out in corporate documents (and in the laws of the state of incorporation and state and federal constitutions) are express powers. Acts of a corporation that exceed its express and implied powers are called *ultra vires* (which means "beyond the powers"). Legal and illegal acts can be *ultra vires*.
5. T
6. T
7. F. An S corporation has tax imposed only at the shareholder level. Other corporations are subject to double taxation, however, which was one of the reasons for the enactment of the S corporation statute. Only corporations with seventy-five or fewer shareholders can qualify for S-corporation status, although in some circumstances, a corporation can be an S-corporation shareholder.

8. T
9. F. Each state has its own body of corporate law, and these laws are not identical. Most states have adopted, at least in part or at least in principle, the Model Business Corporation Act or its revision, the Revised Model Business Corporation Act. There is still variation among the states, however, some of which do not follow either act.
10. T

Fill-in Questions

promoters; unless; an incorporator; need not

Multiple-Choice Questions

1. D. State incorporation laws vary, so looking for the state that offers the most favorable provisions for a particular firm is important. There are some principles that states commonly observe, however. For example, in all states a firm can have perpetual existence, but cannot do business under the same, or even a similar, name as an existing firm.
2. D. Implied powers attach when a corporation is created. These powers include the power to borrow money, to lend money, to extend credit, and to make charitable contributions. The other powers listed here are typically expressed in state statutes.
3. A. Corporate directors manage the business of a corporation. The directors normally employ officers, who oversee the daily operations. The directors may be initially designated by the incorporators or promoters, but are later elected by the shareholders (the owners of the corporation).
4. A. This firm has the characteristics of a closely held corporation. A closely held corporation is also generally allowed to restrict the transfer of its stock. Firms represented by the other answer choices could also be closely held corporations. To be a professional corporation, a firm must be a corporation formed by professionals (and the firm is designated by "P.A." for "professional association," or some other appropriate abbreviation). S corporations and nonprofits corporations have other requirements.
5. C. All corporations issue bonds (and stocks). Bonds are also known as debt securities. Types of bonds include callable bonds, debentures, and mortgage bonds.
6. C. To obtain capital, a corporation issues securities, principally stocks and bonds. Essentially, a security represents either an ownership interest in a firm or a debt owed by the firm.
7. A. Articles of incorporation serve as a primary source of authority for its organization and functions. The information contained in the articles includes the firm's operating name, its duration, its

nature and purpose, its capital structure (including the value and classes of corporate stock), its registered office and agent (who receives legal documents on the firm's behalf), and the date of its annual shareholders' meeting (which is not likely to appear in the corporation's charter).

8.   A. Common stock represents an interest in a corporation with regard to all of these aspects in proportion to the number of shares owned out of the total number of shares issued. Common stock represents the true ownership of a corporation. Preferred shareholders have priority to the payment of any dividends (they do not have a right to dividends) but may not have the right to vote. Common stockholders are the last to receive payment for their investment, however, on the dissolution of the corporation.

9.   C. The certificate of incorporation is viewed as evidence that the firm has met the requirements for corporate existence. A *de facto* corporation is one as to which there is a defect in complying with state law, but among other things, there was a good faith attempt to comply. A firm that does not have a certificate of incorporation may be held to be a corporation by estoppel when a third party contracts with it and it should not otherwise by allowed to avoid liability.

10   A. Other factors that a court may use to pierce the corporate veil include that a party is tricked or misled into dealing with the firm rather than the individual, that the firm is too thinly capitalized (not overcapitalized), and that the firm holds too few (not too many) shareholders' meetings.

GamePoints

1.   In this problem, the corporation that was formed in good faith despite a failure to follow all of the prescribed procedures is a *de facto* corporation. This means that it would be treated as a corporation despite the defect in formation. Thus the company with which the *de facto* corporation did business cannot avoid their contract on the ground of a defect in incorporation.

2.   An *ultra vires* act is a corporate act beyond the authority granted to the firm under its charter or in the statutes by which it was incorporated. Here the firm had the authority under its articles of incorporation to engage in any activity for "any lawful purpose." If a sale of substantially all its assets is a lawful purpose, the firm can contract for it. Generally, if the sale would profit its shareholders, the contract is allowable and proper.

Chapter 40

True-False Questions

1.   T
2.   T
3.   F. Preemptive rights consist of preferences given to shareholders over other purchasers to buy shares of a new corporate issue in proportion to the number of shares that they already hold. This allows a shareholder to maintain his or her proportionate ownership share in the corporation. Generally, these rights are granted (or withheld) in the articles of incorporation.
4.   T
5.   F. Any damages recovered in a shareholder's derivative suit are normally paid to the corporation on whose behalf the shareholder or shareholders exercised the derivative right.
6.   T
7.   F. Officers and directors owe the same fiduciary duties to the corporations for which they work. They both owe a duty of loyalty. This duty requires them to subordinate their personal interests to the welfare of the corporation.
8.   F. The business judgment rule immunizes directors (and officers) from liability for poor business decisions and other honest mistakes that cause a corporation to suffer a loss. Directors are not immunized from losses that do not fit this category, however.
9.   T
10.   T

Fill-in Questions

but ownership is not; can; recorded as the owner in the corporation's books

Multiple-Choice Questions

1.   B. Dividends may be paid from the other sources listed here. Once declared, a dividend becomes a debt enforceable at law like any other debt. Generally, state law allows dividends to be paid as long as a corporation can pay its other debts as they come due and the amount of the dividend is not more than the net worth of the corporation.
2.   A. There is no such right. This is also not a right of directors, except as specified in the articles of incorporation. The ownership of a corporation by shareholders also does not include rights of actual ownership of specific corporate property.
3.   D. A corporation's board of directors hires the firm's officers and other executive employees and

high-level managers. These employees' contracts with the corporation define the individuals' rights.

4. A. Directors must exercise care in their duties. For example, they are expected to use a reasonable amount of supervision over corporate officers and employees when they delegate work. Their liability for breach of this duty could be grounded in negligence or mismanagement of corporate personnel. They are also expected to be loyal: faithful to their obligations and duties.

5. D. The other choices do not represent proper purposes for which a shareholders' derivative suit may be filed. A shareholder's derivative suit is a claim filed on behalf of the corporation. Such a suit may allege, for example, that officers or directors misused corporate assets. Of course, any damages that are awarded must be paid to the corporation. This question and answer are based on a question that appeared in a CPA exam in 1998.

6. C. Cumulative voting can often be used in the election of directors to enhance the power of minority shareholders in electing a representative. In calculating a shareholder's votes under the cumulative voting method, in this problem, Mary's number of shares is multiplied by the number of directors to be elected.

7. B. Unless a state statute provides to the contrary, a quorum of directors must be present to conduct corporate business, such as the declaration of a dividend. A quorum is a majority of the number of directors authorized in the firm's articles or bylaws. The rule is one vote per director.

8. A. The board of directors hires the company's officers and other managerial employees, and determines their compensation. Ultimate responsibility for all policy decisions necessary to the management of corporate affairs also rests with the directors.

9. C. Directors' main right is their right to participate in board meetings. Directors also have a right to inspect corporate books and to be indemnified in defense of some lawsuits (regardless of the outcome of the suit). Rights that directors do not have include a right to compensation. That is, directors may be compensated for their efforts, but they have no inherent right to it. "Preemption" and "first refusal" are rights in this context.

10. C. Under their duty of loyalty, directors cannot compete with their corporation or have an interest which conflicts with the interest of the corporation. Owning the stock of a competitor would also constitute an interest which conflicts with the interest of the corporation on whose board a director serves.

GamePoints

1. Under the business judgment rule, if a corporate officer or director makes a serious but honest mistake in judgment, he or she is not normally liable to the firm. To avoid liability, the officer or director must have acted in good faith and in a reasonable manner. The officer or director may reasonably rely on information provided by corporate employees. Thus, if there is a reasonable basis for a corporate decision, a court is not likely to interfere even if the firm suffers. Under this rule, it is not likely that the directors of the corporation in this problem would be personally liable for the drop in the price of its stock.

2. A shareholder can sue on a corporation's behalf to redress a wrong suffered by the firm when those in control of it—the directors—fail to sue in the corporate name. To maintain a shareholder's derivative suit, a wrong must have been done to the corporation. This is particularly useful when the wrong is caused by a corporate officer or, as in this problem, a director. In such a case, any damages recovered are paid to the corporate treasury. One likely defense to the suit is the business judgment rule, under which a director or officer is immune from liability when a decision within managerial authority complies within the individual's fiduciary duties.

Chapter 41

True-False Questions

1. T

2. F. Appraisal rights are available only when a statute specifically provides for them. The rationale for appraisal rights is that shareholders should not be forced to become owners of corporations that are different from the ones in which they originally invested

3. F. Shareholder approval is required to amend articles of incorporation (and to undertake other extraordinary business matters, such as selling all of a corporation's assets outside the ordinary course of business).

4. F. Shareholder approval is not normally required to buy all, or substantially all, of another corporation's assets. It is necessary, however, that the selling corporation's shareholders approve the sale of all or substantially all of its assets to another corporation.

5. T

6. F. Dissolution can occur by this means, but there are many other ways to bring about the dissolution of a corporation. Also, liquidation, which is the other step in the termination of a corporation, can be performed without court supervision.

7.   T

8.   F. Ordinarily, a corporation that purchases the assets of another corporation does not assume the other's liabilities. In some cases, however, the purchasing corporation may be held responsible for the seller's liabilities (for example, if the purchasing corporation continues the seller's business with the same personnel).

9.   T

10.   F. In those states that provide for shareholder appraisal rights, they are usually available in sales of substantially all of a corporation's assets. Note that once a shareholder chooses to exercise appraisal rights, he or she loses his or her status (to vote, receive dividends, and so on) in many jurisdictions.

Fill-in Questions

extraordinary; shareholder; before; before; the vote is taken.

Multiple-Choice Questions

1.   A. In a merger or consolidation, the surviving corporation acquires all the assets of both corporations without a formal transfer. In a merger, the surviving corporation's articles of incorporation are considered to be *amended* by the articles of merger, and in a consolidation, the articles of consolidation *replace* the previous corporations' articles.

2.   B. Directors and shareholders must approve a consolidation (or a merger). Corporate officers do not have to approve either a merger or a consolidation. In both cases, a state must also issue a certificate of consolidation or merger. A court approval's is not required, however.

3.   A. In either a merger or consolidation, the surviving corporation acquires all of the assets and assumes all of the debts of its predecessors (the corporations that formed it).

4.   B. Without shareholder approval, one corporation may buy all, or substantially all, of the assets of another corporation. The other choices are actions that a board of directors cannot undertake without shareholder approval. This question and answer are based on a CPA exam question that appeared in a 1997 exam.

5.   D. A corporation's failure to comply with administrative requirements could also result in a court-ordered dissolution. Filing an annual report is an administrative requirement. Dissolution may be ordered if a corporation fails to commence business

operations after forming. Other reasons include obtaining a corporate charter through fraud and abuse of corporate powers. Failure to declare a dividend and failure to earn a profit are not grounds for which a court would order a dissolution, if the directors are otherwise complying with their fiduciary duties

6.   B. This combination is a merger (one, but only one, corporation continues to exist). In a consolidation, an entirely new corporation acquires all of the assets and liabilities of the consolidating, disappearing corporations.

7.   C. In a merger, the surviving corporation assumes all of the debts and liabilities of the disappearing corporation. Of course, the surviving corporation also inherits all of the disappearing corporation's rights. These rights and liabilities include those arising from litigation. (When one firm "absorbs" another, the firm doing the "absorbing" will be the survivor.)

8.   A. This combination is a consolidation (a new entity takes the place of the consolidating, disappearing firms). In a merger, one of the merging entities continues to exist.

9.   C. These articles must first be approved by the corporations' directors and shareholders. If this were a consolidation, the procedure would be the same.

10.   C. A statute must provide for these rights before they can be exercised. If it does, however, and the parties cannot agree on a fair appraisal value, a court will determine it. Note that appraisal rights are usually not available in cases of short-form mergers or sales of substantially all a corporation's assets.

GamePoints

1.   The basic steps in a merger, consolidation, or share exchange are the same. These steps are (1) the board of directors of each corporation approves the plan—the plan must specify the terms and conditions of the corporate combination and how the value of the shares of the firms involved will be determined; (2) each firm's shareholders must vote on the plan at a shareholders' meeting; (3) the plan must be filed in the appropriate state office, usually with the secretary of state; and (4) the state must issue a certificate for the planned combination.

2.   A corporation can merge, consolidate, or exchange shares—or engage in other actions that amount to a corporate combination—and if the transaction would profit the firm, it is allowable and proper. But, as noted in the answer to the previous problem, the corporation must obtain the approval of the board of directors and the shareholders. In

most states, if a shareholder dissents from such a proposal, as in this problem, he or she can demand appraisal rights. The shareholder is then entitled to a payment of the fair value for the number of shares that the shareholder holds on the day of the corporate combination. There are strict procedures to be followed—for example, a written notice of dissent must be filed before the shareholder vote on the proposal—but so far in the facts stated here, the procedure has been followed. Determining the fair value of the shares is the next step.

Chapter 42

True-False Questions

1. T
2. T
3. T
4. T
5. F. Rule 506, issued under the Securities Act of 1933, provides an exemption for these offerings, if certain other requirements are met. This is an important exemption, applying to private offerings to a limited number of sophisticated investors.
6. T
7. T
8. F. *Scienter* is required for liability under Section 10(b) of the 1934 act and under SEC Rule 10b-5. For either criminal or civil sanctions to be imposed under these provisions, the violator must have acted with an intent to defraud or with the knowledge of his or her misconduct. This can be proved by false statements or a wrongful failure to disclose material facts.
9. F. Anyone who receives inside information as a result of an insider's breach of his or her fiduciary duty can be liable under SEC Rule 10b-5, which applies in virtually all cases involving the trading of securities. The key to liability is whether the otherwise undisclosed information is *material*.
10. F. Most securities can be resold without registration. Also, under Rules 144 and 144A ("safe harbor" provisions), there are specific exemptions for securities that might otherwise require registration with the SEC.

Fill-in Questions

prosecution; triple; twenty-five; may

Multiple-Choice Questions

1. A. A corporate officer is a traditional inside trader. The outsider in this problem is a tippee who is liable because the tippee knew of the officer's misconduct. Liability here is based on the fact that the information was not public. Liability might be avoided if those who know the information wait for a reasonable time after its public disclosure before trading their stock.
2. A. This purchase and sale is a violation of Section 16(b) of the Securities Exchange Act of 1934. When a purchase and sale is within a six-month period, as in this problem, the corporation can recover all of the profit. Liability is strict liability—proof of neither *scienter* nor negligence is required.
3. D. Under the Securities Act of 1933, a security exists when a person invests in a common enterprise with the reasonable expectation of profits derived primarily or substantially from the managerial or entrepreneurial efforts of others (not from the investor's own efforts).
4. A. Because of the low amount of the issue, it qualifies as an exemption from registration under Rule 504. No specific disclosure document is required, and there is no prohibition on solicitation. If the amount had been higher than $1 million but lower than $5 million, this offer might have qualified for an exemption under Regulation A, which requires notice to the SEC and an offering circular for investors.
5. D. The amount of this offering is too high to exempt it from the registration requirements except possibly under Rule 506. This issuer advertised the offering, however, and Rule 506 prohibits general solicitation. Thus, without filing a registration statement, the issuer could not legally solicit *any* investors (whatever it may have believed about the unaccredited investors).
6. D. This issue might qualify under Rule 505 except that the issuer advertised the offering, which it cannot do and remain exempt from registration. In other words, the amount of this offering disqualified the issuer from advertising it without filing a registration statement.
7. B. A registration statement must supply enough information so that an unsophisticated investor can evaluate the financial risk involved. The statement must explain how the registrant intends to use the proceeds from the sale of the issue. Also, besides the description of management, there must be a disclosure of any of their material transactions with the firm. A certified financial statement must be included.
8. B. Of course, the offering must be registered with the SEC before it can be sold, and this requires a registration statement. Investors must be given a prospectus that describes the security, the issuing corporation, and the risk of the security.

9. B. Under the Securities Exchange Act of 1934, the Securities and Exchange Commission all of the other duties and more, including regulating national securities trading, supervising mutual funds, and recommending sanctions in cases involving violations of securities laws. This question and answer are based on a question that was included in a 1996 CPA exam.

10. A. Most resales are exempt from registration if persons other than issuers or underwriters undertake the resales. Resales of restricted securities acquired under Rule 505 or Rule 506 may trigger registration requirements, but the original sale in this problem came under Rule 504.

GamePoints

1. If the SEC files a suit against this firm on the basis that its offering was not exempt from registration, the SEC will likely win, and the firm will be required to forebear sanctions. The problem is that the offering complies with all of the requirements for an exemption from registration but one—the offering is advertised to the general public online and the stock is sold to too many unaccredited investors (including, of course, your avatar). A private, noninvestment company offering for less than $5 million in any twelve-month period may be exempt under Rule 505 of Regulation D if it is sold to no more than thirty-five unaccredited investors (any number of accredited investors is okay), it is not generally advertised or solicited, and the SEC is notified of the sales. This offering does not qualify.

2. Minor misstatements or ill-phrased puffery is not of much concern to serious investors. Like others, you and your avatar would most likely want to know only facts that illuminate the business condition of an issuer—such things as fraud, an important change in a firm's finances, or a new discovery or product, as well as a firm's liability, loans to officers or directors, and pending lawsuits. This type of information could affect a decision to invest in the firm. And false statements or omissions of such information could subject the firm to liability under the securities laws. That would be material.

Chapter 43

True-False Questions

1. F. Important considerations in selecting a lawyer include the attorney's knowledge as to what a client needs, the attorney's willingness to investigate the relevant law, the attorney's ability to communicate with the client, and the attorney's perception of what issues are of foremost concern.

2. T

3. F. A business's name must be different from those of other businesses, to avoid, among other things, misleading consumers. A corporation's name should also include the word *corporation, company,* or *incorporated*. To protect a corporate name as a trade name within a state in which the firm does business, the name should be filed with the appropriate state office.

4. T

5. F. By means of what is called a private offering, a limited amount of money can be raised from a limited number of investors without first registering the shares with the Securities and Exchange Commission. The requirements include a limit on how much money can be raised, how many investors are asked to buy, and how sophisticated (knowledgeable about investments) the investors are.

6. T

7. F. A contract *should* be in writing in case of a dispute, and in some cases, a contract *must* be in writing to be enforced. The requirement of a writing comes under the Statute of Frauds, which is part of the basic contract law principles that apply to be business.

8. T

9. F. An employer is bound to its promises of employment. Such promises may even be implied from statements in employment manuals. For this reason—and for the reason that other disputes may arise—all terms of employment should be put in writing, including grounds for termination.

10. T

Fill-in Questions

employees; employees; employees

Multiple-Choice Questions

1. A. The benefits of retaining an attorney at any point in a business relationship, but particularly during the start-up of a business, include the response to this question. Besides providing *legal* advice for a client's situation—which the attorney is bound to keep confidential—a lawyer may be able to direct a new business to potential investors, provide *business* advice, and act as a sounding board for business ideas. Another benefit is the flexibility of payment plans.

2. D. Sole proprietorships, general partnerships, and limited liability companies avoid the formalities of incorporating or of creating a limited partnership, but there is no business form that avoids all legal

requirements. All businesses must meet such requirements as business name registration, occupational licensing, state tax registration, health and
environmental permits, zoning and building codes,
import/export regulations, and laws governing the
workplace.

3.   A. At the initial meeting of a corporation's
board of directors, the directors adopt bylaws, appoint corporate officers, and take other necessary
steps. Those steps do not include the "adoption" of
articles of incorporation, which must be drafted and
filed before a corporation exists, or the selection of a
corporate name, which is also done before a corporation exists (of course, the name can be changed
later). Stock certificates are not usually necessary to
prove the ownership of the shares in a corporation.
Even if they are printed, however, it is not necessary to distribute them at the initial meeting of a
firm's board of directors.

4.   C. Registering a trademark with the U.S. Patent and Trademark Office gives the mark national
protection if it is in use or will be within six months.
Of course, there are other requirements—the mark
must be distinctive, for example, so as not to mislead customers, and must remain in use. The owner
must protest others' use of the mark, and the registration must be renewed after five years (and every
ten thereafter).

5.   A. When an entrepreneur starts a new business, the management of accounts receivable and
accounts payable can be important. Many small
businesses retain professional accountants to perform this service. It can add an expense to the firm's
liabilities, but it can also add to a new business's
credibility with potential investors. Bookkeeping
software is available, but is should not be appropri-
ated from others and it does not add the cachet of a
professional accountant. Errors might provoke litigation, but this is not an advantage—accurate
bookkeeping is thus legally significant.

6.   A. A corporation, or any other limited liability
entity, shields its owners from personal liability in
circumstances such as those described in this question. The business entity is liable for the damages,
but the owners will not normally be liable beyond
the extent of their investment in, or other contributions to, the firm. The corporate business form offers limited liability to its shareholder-owner. This
can be an important consideration in starting a
business and in attracting capital to expand it.

7.   A. If a firm is not organized as a sole proprietorship, anyone who signs contracts or negotiable
instruments (drafts or notes) on the firm's behalf
must do so as an agent to avoid personal liability.
Otherwise, if the contract is breached, or the instrument is not honored or paid, the party may be

held liable on it. This advice applies to corporations
and other limited liability forms of business organizations, as well as partnerships.

8.   A. Partnerships—like limited liability companies, limited liability partnerships, and S corporations—avoid the double taxation that may affect
other types of corporations. The profits are passed
through the business entity to the partners, in n the
case of a partnership. The partners are taxed only
on their individual returns. The business is not
taxed on these amounts. A sole proprietor also pays
taxes on business income as an individual. Clearly,
taxation can be a critical factor to be considered in
choosing a small- business organizational form,

9.   A. With a private offering, a certain limited
amount of money can be raised from a certain limited number of investors without registering the
shares as securities with the Securities and Exchange Commission (SEC). A public offering may
raise a large amount of capital, but the offering
must be registered with the SEC and applicable
state agencies. Registration can be complex. A
shareholder agreement can define relative ownership rights and interests, or define other issues between a company's owners, but it may not address
an attempt to raise capital from other investors.
Key-person insurance is a concept that does not apply here.

10.   C. A buy-sell provision in a shareholder agreement enables shareholders to buy others' shares
and provides for the price to be paid. A shareholder
agreement that includes a right of first refusal prevents the sale of shares to a third party without
first giving the other owners a right to buy. A "take-
along" clause allows an investor to participate in a
sale of shares to a third party. (This clause may provide an incentive for a venture capitalist to invest in
the firm.) A key-person *insurance policy* provides
benefits to a firm if the key person dies.

GamePoints

1.   Although a loan is possible, most businesses
raise capital by exchanging ownership rights (equity) for capital. A plan describing your firm, its
games, and its anticipated performance is presented
to potential investors who examine your books and
assets. Terms of financing, how much ownership
and control an investor will receive, the type and
quantity of stock (if any) the investor will get, and
other issues are part of the negotiations. Depending
on the form of the business seeking the investment,
the investor may be called a shareholder, a partner,
or a member. Depending on the amount of the investment, how that amount is solicited, and what
the investment buys, your firm's attempt to attract

investors may have to be registered with the Securities and Exchange Commission.

2. Creative products, game code, customer lists, pricing policies, and similar intellectual property can be protected. You can require your employee to agree not to divulge trade secrets, for example, if the employee goes to work for a competitor or into business for herself. You can also insist that the employee *not* go to work for a competitor or set up a competing business, in which your trade secrets will likely be disclosed. These latter agreements (covenants not to compete) must, of course, be reasonable in terms of time and geographic limits, or they will not be enforced. As for the potential investor, he should expect, and you can insist, that he sign a confidentiality agreement before you reveal more about your game plan.

Cumulative Hypothetical Problem for Unit Eight—Including Chapters 36–43

1. A. A partnership is an association of two or more persons who manage a business and share profits. Here, the partnership began when the parties combined their assets and commenced business. Before that time, there was no sharing of profits, no joint ownership of a business, and no equal right in the management of a business (because there was no business). The execution of a formal partnership agreement is not necessary, nor is the consent of creditors.

2. B. Unlike general partnerships, which can come into existence even when the parties do not intend to form a partnership, a limited partnership can only be created pursuant to the provisions of a state statute. This statute sets out exactly what partners must do to form a limited partnership, which must include at least one general partner who assumes personal liability for the debts of the firm.

3. D. The information that each state requires to be in articles of incorporation differs somewhat, but the information represented by the choices in this problem is generally required. It is not necessary to name the initial officers in the articles. Other information that might be required includes the number of authorized shares. Other information that is not required includes quorum requirements.

4. D. Other information that must be included in a registration statement, under the Securities Act of 1933, includes a description of the issuer's business, a description of the security, the capital structure of the business, the underwriting arrangements, and the certified financial statements.

5. B. Rule 504 exempts certain stock offerings from the registration requirements of the Securities Act of 1933. To qualify, a non-investment company offering may not exceed $1 million in any twelve-month period, the Securities and Exchange Commission must be notified of the sale.

Questions on the Focus on Ethics for Unit Eight—Business Organizations

1. D. This duty arises from the legal principles of agency, and applies to all corporate officers, managers, and directors. When personal interests conflict with the interests of the corporation, the corporate party must not act against the interest of the corporation. If an officer usurps a corporate opportunity by, for example, setting up a competing firm to take advantage of an opportunity that might have otherwise been utilized by his or her corporation, a successful claim against the individual can result in the individual giving up an interest in the new company to the shareholders of the corporation.

2. D. Corporate directors have a fiduciary duty to exercise care when making decisions that affect their corporations. Fiduciary duties may, in some extraordinary circumstances, be owed to other directors, officers, or the firm's creditors, particularly if a director's corporation is nearly insolvent. In normal situations, however, the duty of care extends chiefly to the corporation's shareholders, and may include a duty to implement a program to uncover and prevent wrongdoing by corporate personnel.

3. A. In almost every set of circumstances, an employee who wants to buy stock in his or her employer's firm on the basis of positive, non-public information should wait at least until a reasonable time has passed after the information has been made public. To make a buy sooner would most likely violate the proscription of insider trading under federal securities law. The Sarbanes-Oxley Act requires attorneys to report material violations of the securities laws to a corporation's highest authority. The Securities and Exchange Commission (SEC) and the American Bar Association allow attorneys to disclose confidential information to the SEC, but in some instances such reporting may violate a state's ethics code for its lawyers.

Chapter 44

True-False Questions

1. T
2. T
3. T

4. F. Agencies formulate and issue their rules under the authority of Congress. These rules are as legally binding as the laws enacted by Congress. It is for this reason, in part, that rulemaking procedures generally include opportunities for public comment, that the rules are subject to review by the courts, and that agencies are subject to other controls by the three branches of government.

5. F. Appeal is not mandatory, and if there is no appeal, the initial order becomes final. Either side may appeal the determination in an agency adjudication, however, to the commission that oversees the agency or ultimately to a federal court.

6. F. Congress can influence agency policy in several ways. These include that Congress can create or abolish an agency, or influence policy by the appropriation of funds for certain purposes. Congress can also revise the functions of an agency.

7. T

8. T

9. T

10. F. In most circumstances, a warrant is required for a search or the agency will be held to have violated the Fourth Amendment. Warrants are not required, however, to conduct searches in businesses in highly regulated industries, in certain hazardous operations, and in emergencies.

Fill-in Questions

Federal Register; anyone; must; *Federal Register*

Multiple-Choice Questions

1. A. Agency powers include functions associated with the legislature (rulemaking), executive branch (investigation), and courts (adjudication). Under Article I of the U.S. Constitution and the delegation doctrine, Congress has the power to establish administrative agencies and delegate any or all of these powers to those agencies.

2. C. Agencies may obtain information through subpoenas or searches. A subpoena may compel the appearance of a witness (a subpoena *ad testificandum*) or the provision of certain documents and records (a subpoena *duces tecum*). In some cases, particularly searches of businesses involved in a highly regulated industry, searches may be conducted without warrants.

3. D. Procedures vary widely among agencies, even within agencies. But under the Administrative Procedure Act, rulemaking typically includes these steps: notice, opportunity for comment, and publication in the *Federal Register* of a final draft of the rule. The notice-and-comment period opens a proposed rule to public comment. The period must be at least thirty days, and it s often longer.

4. C. An agency has the authority to issue subpoenas. There are limits on agency demands for information, however. An investigation must have a legitimate purpose. The information that is sought must be relevant. The party from whom the information is sought must not be unduly burdened by the request. And the demand must be specific.

5. A. This is the "arbitrary and capricious" test under which acts committed willfully, unreasonable, and without considering the facts can be overturned. (The other choices are not legitimate grounds for judicial review.) A court may also consider whether the agency has exceeded its authority or violated any constitutional provisions. Depending on the circumstances, when a court reviews an act of an administrative agency, the court may also determine whether the agency has properly interpreted laws applicable to the action under review, acted in accord with procedural requirements, or reached conclusions that are not supported by substantial evidence.

6. B. The Government-in-the-Sunshine Act requires "every portion of every meeting of an agency" that is headed by a "collegial body" to be open to "public observation." The Freedom of Information Act requires the federal government to disclose certain records to persons on request, with some exceptions. The Regulatory Flexibility Act requires, among other things, analyses of new regulations in certain circumstances. The Small Business Regulatory Enforcement Fairness Act covers several matters important to businesses, including the federal courts' authority to enforce the Regulatory Flexibility Act, but it does not cover the opening of agency meetings to the public.

7. C. The Administrative Procedure Act provides for court review of most agency actions, but first a party must exhaust all other means of resolving a controversy with an agency. (Also, under the ripeness doctrine, the agency action must be ripe for review: the action must be reviewable—which agency actions presumably are—the party must have standing, and an actual controversy must be at issue.)

8. D. The president's veto is a method by which the authority of an agency can be checked or curtailed. The limits listed in the other responses in this question are choices available to Congress to limit the authority of administrative agencies.

9. B. After an agency publishes notice of a proposed rule, any interested parties can express their views in writing, or orally if a hearing is held. The agency must respond to all significant comments by modifying the final rule or explaining, in the statement accompanying the final rule, why it did not modify the rule in response to the comments.

10. B. An administrative law judge (ALJ) presides over hearings when cases are brought to the agency. Like other judges, an ALJ has the power to administer oaths, take testimony, rule on questions of evidence, and make determinations of fact. It is important to note that an ALJ works for the agency but must not be biased in the agency's favor. There are provisions in the Administrative Procedure Act to prevent the bias, and to otherwise promote the fairness, of the ALJs, for example by prohibiting ex parte comments to the ALJ from any party to the proceeding.

GamePoints

1. The Occupational Health and Safety Administration (OSHA) establishes standards that protect employees from exposure to workplace hazards and ensure a safe working environment. OSHA is a federal agency so the employer must be engaged in interstate commerce or an activity affecting interstate commerce. An on-site inspection of a workplace by an OSHA inspector does not need to be conducted after working hours and the employer does not need to be given advance notice of the visit. If an employee requests an inspection, the inspector has probable cause to obtain a warrant. If the employer agrees to an inspection, no warrant is needed. Assuming the warehouse in this problem is a workplace and subject to federal rules, the only objection of the employer that might be valid is the insistence on a warrant.

2. You could respond by filing an answer to the allegation. The case will be heard in a trial-like setting before an administrative law judge. Hearing procedures differ among different agencies. The procedure may be informal (sitting around a table in a conference room, for example) or more formal. The latter resembles a trial, with discovery, the presentation of witness testimony and physical evidence, and such steps as cross-examination. After the hearing, the judge makes a decision and issues an order. If necessary, you will than have an opportunity to appeal to the body that runs the agency or a court.

Chapter 45

True-False Questions

1.   T
2.   T

3. F. Under certain circumstances, consumers have a right to rescind their contracts. This is particularly true when a creditor has not made all required disclosures. A contract entered into as part of a door-to-door sale may be rescinded within three days, regardless of the reason.

4. T

5. F. A consumer can also include a note in his or her credit file to explain any misinformation in the file. Under the Fair Credit Reporting Act, consumers are entitled to have deleted from their files any misinformation that leads to a denial of credit, employment, or insurance. Consumers are also entitled to receive information about the source of the misinformation and about anyone who was given the misinformation.

6. T

7. F. The Fair Debt Collection Practices Act applies only to debt collectors that attempt to collect debts on another party's behalf. Typically, the collector is paid a commission—a percentage of the amount owed or collected—for a successful collection effort.

8. F. The Federal Trade Commission (FTC), the Federal Reserve Board of Governors (Fed), and other federal agencies regulate the terms and conditions of sales. For example, the FTC issues regulations covering warranties and labels, and the Fed regulates credit provisions in sales contracts.

9. F. One who leases consumer goods in the ordinary course of their business must disclose *all* material terms in writing—clearly and conspicuously—if the goods are priced at $25,000 or less and the lease term exceeds four months. The Consumer Leasing Act of 1988 requires this.

10. T

Fill-in Questions

$50; before; prohibits; from billing; if

Multiple-Choice Questions

1. C. Under the Fair Debt Collection Practices Act, once a debtor has refused to pay a debt, a collection agency can contact the debtor *only* to advise him or her of further action to be taken. None of the rest of these choices would be legitimate possibilities.

2. D. The FTC has the power to issue a cease-and-desist order, but in some cases, such an order is not enough to stop the harm. With counteradvertising (also known as corrective advertising), an advertiser attempts to correct earlier misinformation by admitting that prior claims about a product were untrue.

3. B. A regular-size box of laundry soap, for example, cannot be labeled "super-size" to exaggerate the amount of product in the box. Labels on consumer goods must identify the product, the manufacturer, the distributor, the net quantity of the contents, and the quantity of each serving (if the number of servings is given). Other information may also be required.

4. B. Under certain circumstances, consumers have a right to rescind their contracts. In a door-to-door sale, a consumer generally has at least a three-day cooling-off period within which to rescind the transaction. Salespersons are required to give consumers written notice of this right.

5. B. This is required under Regulation Z (which was issued by the Federal Reserve Board under the Truth in Lending Act) and applies to any creditor who, in the ordinary course of business, lends money or sells goods on credit to consumers, or arranges for credit for consumers. The information that must be disclosed includes: the specific dollar amount being financed; the annual percentage rate of interest; any financing charges, premiums or points; the number, amounts, and due dates of payments; and any penalties imposed on delinquent payments or prepayment.

6. D. When contracting parties are subject to the Truth-in-Lending Act (TILA), Regulation Z applies to any transaction involving an installment sales contract in which payment is to be made in more than four installments. Normally, such loans as those described in this problem require more than four installments to repay. In any transaction subject to Regulation Z, the lender must disclose all of the credit terms clearly and conspicuously.

7. C. The Fair Packaging and Labeling Act requires that products include a variety of information on their labels. Besides the information specified in the answer to this problem, manufactures must identify themselves and the packager or distributor or the product, as well as nutrition details, including how much and what type of fat a product contains.

8. B. Under the Smokeless Tobacco Health Education Act of 1986, packages of smokeless tobacco products must include warnings about the health hazards associated with the use of smokeless tobacco similar to warnings contained on cigarette packages.

9. A. The Consumer Product Safety Commission (CPSC) has sufficiently broad authority to remove from store shelves any product that it believes is imminently hazardous and to require manufacturers to report on products already sold. Additionally, the CPSC can ban the make and sale of any product that the CPSC deems to be potentially hazardous. The CPSC also administers other product safety legislation.

10. D. The Truth-in-Lending Act includes rules covering credit cards. There is a provision that limits the liability of a cardholder to $50 per card for unauthorized charges made before the creditor is notified, and exempts a consumer from liability if the card was not properly issued. When a card is not solicited, it is not "properly issued," however, and thus a consumer, in whose name unauthorized charges are made, is not liable for those charges in any amount.

GamePoints

1. No, the lender in this problem has violated the provisions of the Truth in Lending Act (TILA), which requires the disclosure of credit and loan terms to enable borrowers to shop for the best financing arrangements. The TILA applies to those who lend money in the ordinary course of their business, which of course a credit union does. (There is an exception for installment loans of fewer than four payments, but that is an unlikely schedule for an auto loan.) Under the TILA, all of the terms of a credit instrument must be fully disclosed even if "it would take too long."

2. With respect to food, the general legal standard is that it contains no substance that could cause injury to health. Most statutes involving food are monitored and enforced by the Food and Drug Administration and the Food Safety and Quality Service of the U.S. Department of Agriculture. Various federal laws specify safe levels of potentially dangerous food additives—which cannot be carcinogenic—create classifications of food and food advertising, and provide for the inspection of meat and poultry.

Chapter 46

True-False Questions

1. F. Common law doctrines that were applied against polluters centuries ago may be applicable today. These include nuisance and negligence doctrines.

2. T

3. F. There are different standards for different pollutants and for different polluters. There are even different standards for the same pollutants and polluters in different locations. The standards cover the amount of emissions, the technology to control them, the notice that must be given to the public, and the penalties that may be imposed for noncompliance.

4.   F. The Toxic Substances Control Act of 1976 regulates substances that the production and labeling of substances of that potentially pose an imminent hazard or an unreasonable risk of injury to health or the environment. The Comprehensive Environmental Response, Compensation, and Liability Act (CERCLA) of 1980 regulates the clean up of leaking hazardous waste disposal sites.

5.   T

6.   T

7.   F. To penalize those for whom a violation is cost-effective, the EPA can obtain a penalty equal to a violator's economic benefits from noncompliance. Other penalties include criminal fines. Private citizens can also sue polluters. It is generally more economically beneficial for a business to comply with the Clean Air Act.

8.   T

9.   F. Under CERCLA, a party who transports waste to a hazardous waste site may be held liable for any and all of the cost to clean up the site. There is a variety of "potentially responsible parties" who may also be held liable, including the party who generated the waste, and current and past owners and operators of the site. A party assessed with these costs can bring a contribution action against the others, however, to recoup the amount of their proportion.

10.   T

Fill-in Questions

federal; federal; environmental impact that an action will have; environment; an action might cause to the environment; and reasons

Multiple-Choice Questions

1.   A. An environmental impact statement (EIS) must be prepared when a major federal action significantly affects the quality of the environment. An action that affects the quality of the environment is "major" if it involves a substantial commitment of resources and "federal" if a federal agency has the power to control it.

2.   C. Under the 1990 amendments to the Clean Air Act, different standards apply to existing sources and major new sources. Major new sources must use the maximum achievable control technology (MACT) to reduce emissions from the combustion of fossil fuels. Other factories and businesses must reduce emissions of hazardous air pollutants with the best available technology.

3.   D. Sport utility vehicles are now subject to the same standards for polluting emissions as automobiles. If new motor vehicles do not meet the emission standards of regulations issued under the Clean Air Act, the EPA can order a recall of the vehicles and a repair or replacement of pollution-control devices.

4.   C. A polluter can be ordered to clean up the pollution or to pay for the clean-up costs, and other penalties may be imposed. For example, fines may be assessed and imprisonment ordered.

5.   B. Under the Resource Conservation and Recovery Act, producers of hazardous waste must properly label and package waste to be transported. Under the Comprehensive Environmental Response, Compensation, and Liability Act, the party who generated the waste disposed of at a site can be held liable for clean-up costs.

6.   B. Under the Resource Conservation and Recovery Act of 1976, the EPA monitors and controls the disposal of hazardous waste. Under the Comprehensive Environmental Response, Compensation, and Liability Act, the EPA regulates the clean up of hazardous waste sites when a release occurs.

7.   B. An action that affects the quality of the environment is "major" if it involves a substantial commitment of resources. Minor landscaping does not qualify because it does not involve such a commitment. The landscaping in this problem is "federal," however, because a federal agency controls it, and any landscaping can affect the quality of the environment.

8.   C. Under the 1990 amendments to the Clean Air Act, different standards apply to existing sources and major new sources. Major new sources must use the maximum achievable control technology to reduce emissions from the combustion of fossil fuels. Other factories and businesses must reduce emissions of hazardous air pollutants with the best available technology.

9.   B. One of the goals of the Clean Water Act is to protect fish and wildlife. In part, this goal is met by protecting their habitats, such as swamps and other wetlands. Protecting these areas can also protect navigable waters into which wetlands drain and other surrounding resources. Before dredging and filling wetlands, a permit must be obtained from the Army Corps of Engineers.

10.   B. Any potentially responsible party can be charged with the entire cost to clean up a hazardous waste disposal site. Potentially responsible parties include former owners and may, under certain circumstances, include a lender to the owner. Of course, a party held responsible for the entire cost may be able to recoup some of it in a contribution action against other potentially responsible parties.

GamePoints

1.   Under the National Pollutant Discharge Elimination System (NPDES) of the Clean Water Act of 1972, the trash removal service may be able to dispose of some of its waste in the ocean, providing it meets the NPDES requirements. The Marine Protection, Research, and Sanctuaries Act, also known as the Ocean Dumping Act, regulates the transportation and dumping of pollutants in ocean waters, and provides permit programs for some materials. But dumping of chemical warfare supplies and high-level radioactive waste, as well as other radiological, chemical, and biological wastes, into the ocean is prohibited. Civil penalties and criminal fines are possible up to $50,000 each. Imprisonment for up to a year and an injunction may also be ordered. The oil refinery may be liable under the Oil Pollution Act of 1990 for discharging oil into navigable waters or onto the shore. Sanctions include the clean-up costs, which can be considerable, as well as damages for the harm to natural resources, private property, and the local economy.

2.   The Comprehensive Environmental Response, Compensation, and Liability Act of 1980 regulates the clean up of hazardous waste disposal sites. Any potentially responsible party can be charged with the entire cost to clean up a leaking hazardous waste disposal site. Potentially responsible parties include the person who generated the waste, the person who transported the waste to the site, the person who owned or operated the site at the time of the disposal, and the current owner or operator of the site. Sludge most likely qualifies at least as a party who owned or operated Toxin at the time of the disposal, and possibly its leak, and may have been the party who generated or transported the waste, even if Sludge does not own Toxin now. A party who generates only a fraction of the waste can be held liable for the entire clean-up cost. (Of course, whoever is held liable for the cost can bring a contribution action against any other person who is, or who may be, liable for a percentage of the expense.)

Chapter 47

True-False Questions

1.   F. This is a vertical restraint.
2.   F. This is a horizontal restraint.
3.   T
4.   F. Exclusive dealing contracts are those under which a seller forbids a buyer from purchasing products from the seller's competitors.

5.   F. Price discrimination occurs when sellers charge competitive buyers different prices for identical goods.
6.   F. This is a *vertical* merger. A horizontal merger is a merger between firms that compete with each other in the same market.
7.   F. This is a *horizontal* merger. A vertical merger occurs when a company at one stage of production acquires another company at a higher or lower stage in the chain of production and distribution.
8.   T
9.   T
10.   T

Fill-in Questions

A restraint of trade; Monopoly power; monopoly power

Multiple-Choice Questions

1.   A. An agreement to set prices in the manner described in the problem is a price-fixing agreement, which is a restraint of trade and a *per se* violation of Section 1 of the Sherman Act.
2.   C. Conduct that is blatantly anticompetitive is a *per se* violation of antitrust law. This is the most important circumstance in determining whether an action violates the antitrust laws. If an action undercuts competition, a court will not allow a party to undertake it. Such conduct typically includes price-fixing agreements, group boycotts, and horizontal market divisions. The U.S. Department of Justice can prosecute violations of the Sherman Act as criminal or civil violations, but can enforce the Clayton Act only through civil proceedings. The Federal Trade Commission can also enforce the Clayton Act (and has sole authority to enforce the Federal Trade Commission Act). A private party can sue under the Clayton Act if he or she is injured by a violation of *any* antitrust law.
3.   D. Territorial or customer restrictions, like the restriction described in the problem, are judged under a rule of reason. The rule of reason involves a weighing of competitive benefits against anticompetitive harms. Here, the manufacturer's restriction on its dealers would likely be considered lawful because, although it reduces *intra*brand competition, it promotes *inter*brand competition.
4.   D. In applying the rule of reason, courts consider the purpose of the conduct, the effect of the conduct on trade, the power of the parties to accomplish what they intend, and in some cases, whether there are less restrictive alternatives to achieve the same goals.

5.   C. The elements of the offense of monopolization include monopoly power and its willful acquisition. Market domination that results from legitimate competitive behavior (such as foresight, innovation, skill, and good management) is not a violation.

6.   D. Price discrimination occurs when a seller charges different buyers different prices for identical goods. To violate the Clayton Act, among other requirements, the effect of the price discrimination must be to substantially lessen competition or otherwise create a competitive injury.

7.   A. Of course, a U.S. firm is subject to the jurisdiction of a U.S. court. For a U.S. court to hear a case against a foreign entity under U.S. antitrust laws, the entity's alleged violation of the law must have a substantial effect on U.S. commerce (or be a *per se* violation). In other words, foreign and domestic firms may be sued for violations of U.S. antitrust laws.

8.   A. Conduct subject to the rule of reason is unlawful if its anticompetitive harms outweigh its competitive benefits. Conduct typically subject to a rule of reason analysis includes trade association activities, joint ventures, territorial or customer restrictions, refusal to deal, price discrimination, and exclusive-dealing contracts.

9.   B. Similar exemptions from the antitrust laws include cooperative research among small business firms, cooperation among U.S. exporters to compete with comparable foreign associations, and joint efforts by businesspersons to obtain legislative, judicial, or executive action.

10.   A. An important consideration in determining whether a merger substantially lessens competition and hence violates the Clayton Act is market concentration (the market chares among the firms in the market). If a merger creates an entity with more than a small percentage market share, it is presumed illegal.

GamePoints

1.   Contracts, combinations, and conspiracies that restrain trade and monopolize are prohibited under the Sherman Act. Price-fixing is an agreement among makers or sellers to increase or maintain a price level with the purpose of blocking free trade. A price-fixing agreement among competitors is so blatantly and substantially anticompetitive as to be considered *per se* illegal. This is true even if the price is reasonable. In this problem, the agreement among the competitive sellers fits the definition of price-fixing and is thus per se illegal. There is no need to determine whether the agreement actually injures market competition.

2.   Yes. The set of facts in this problem presents an attempt to monopolize. Such an attempt is illegal under the Sherman Act if it (1) is intended to exclude competitors and garner monopoly power and (2) has a dangerous probability of success. Business firms enter into exclusive or favored agreements every day. To have a "dangerous probability of success," the party making the attempt must possess some degree of market power. In this problem, the game maker has and uses its monopoly power to affect competition. The marketplace injury consists of an increase in the prices of the maker's products and the decreasing market shares of the maker's competitors.

Chapter 48

True-False Questions

1.   T
2.   T
3.   F. Compliance with GAAP and GAAS may be required, but it is no guarantee of freedom from liability. Also, there may be a higher standard of conduct under a state statute or judicial decision.
4.   F. The majority view is that accountants are subject to liability for negligence to foreseeable users. In some states, however, the view is to extend liability only to users whose use of, and reliance on, an accountant's statements or report was reasonably foreseeable.
5.   F. Under the securities acts, an accountant may be subject to criminal penalties for willful violations.
6.   T
7.   F. Tax preparers may be subject to penalties if they fail to furnish a taxpayer with a copy of the return.
8.   T
9.   T
10.   F. No, privity is not required. To recover, a plaintiff must prove five elements, including *scienter*, a fraudulent act or deception, reliance, materiality, and causation.

Fill-in Questions

will not; may; may

Multiple-Choice Questions

1.   B. Working papers are the property of the accountant whose work they represent, but working

papers cannot be released without the permission of the client for whom they were accumulated.

2. C. Generally, an auditor can be held liable to a third party for negligence. In most states, however, an accountant is liable only to users whom the accountant knew or should have known about. In some states, privity is required; in others, "near privity" is the requirement. This question and answer are based on a question that appeared in the CPA exam in 1997.

3. D. Under the Securities Act of 1933, an accountant may be liable for any false statement of material fact or omission of a material fact in a registration statement. The other elements indicated in the other choices are not requirements for liability under this statute.

4. C. Under the Securities Exchange Act of 1934, an accountant may be liable for any false statement of material fact or omission of a material fact made with the intent to defraud. An accountant may also be liable for failing to disclose to a client facts that give reason to believe misstatements have been made or fraud has been committed.

5. A. In most states, under a court order an accountant must disclose information about his or her client, including communications between the accountant and the client.

6. A. The client assigned the employee who was committing the wrongful act to assist the accountant, who failed to discover the wrongdoing because the employee covered it up. The client's loss was thus due to the client's own error. This generally reduces or eliminates any potential liability on the part of the accountant.

7. C. Besides the cost to obtain the accountant's contracted-for services elsewhere and the amount of any penalties for failing to meet deadlines, the client may recover other reasonable and foreseeable losses.

8. C. In this problem, the attorney failed to exercise reasonable care and professional judgment, thereby breaching the duty of care owed to clients. If a statute of limitations runs out, a client can no longer file a suit and loses a potential award of damages.

9. B. In a number of states, working papers remain the property of the accountant. These papers may act as crucial evidence in case the accountant needs to defend himself or herself against charges of negligence or fraud. At the same time, because the working papers reflect the client's financial situation, the client has the right of access to them. Also, in some circumstances, audit papers must be retained for as long as five years.

10. C. Another possible defense that an accountant or other professional may assert against a charge of negligence, in a state that allows contributory negligence as a defense, is that the client was negligent.

GamePoints

1. An accountant must comply with generally accepted accounting principles and generally accepted auditing standards, which set out the conventions, rules, and procedures to follow in practicing accountancy. These principles and standards concern professional qualities and judgment. A violation may result in liability to a client for a loss that results. An argument could be made that a reasonably competent accountant would draft a dense financial document, even if it were intended to read and understood by the average consumer, because the consumer would not be the accountant's client—the client is the credit-card issuer—and a simpler document would not be in the client's best interest. You might also argue that "professional qualities and judgment" require the document to disclose all of the financial details, even if they are not phrased in a way easily understood by a non-accountant. Along this line of argument, you could assert that you would be negligent if you did *not* draft the terms in all their complexity.

2. Yes. Applying the standard set forth in Section 552 of the *Restatement (Second) of Contracts,* most courts would hold an accountant liable for negligence to a person whom the accountant "intends to supply the information or knows that the recipient intends to supply it" and persons whom the accountant "intends the information to influence or knows that the recipient so intends." (In fact, some courts would hold an accountant liable to any user whose reliance on the accountant's statement was reasonably foreseeable.) In the circumstances of the game in this question, your avatar the accountant knows that the bank will use the statement you prepare for your corporate client. Thus the bank is a foreseeable user. A foreseeable user is a third party within the class of parties to whom an accountant may be liable for negligence.

Cumulative Hypothetical Problem for Unit Nine—Including Chapters 44–48

1. D. Under the Comprehensive Environmental Response, Compensation, and Liability Act of 1980, any "potentially responsible party" can be charged with the entire cost to clean up a hazardous waste disposal site. Potentially responsible parties include the party who generates the waste, the party who transports the waste to the site, and the party who owns or operates the site.

2. D. Advertising that consists of vague generalities is not illegal. This is also true of advertising that includes obvious exaggerations. Advertising that may lead to sanctions by the Federal Trade Commission is deceptive advertising: advertising that misleads consumers.

3. C. It is price discrimination when a seller charges different buyers different prices for identical products. Price discrimination is a violation of the Clayton Act if the effect of the pricing is to substantially lessen competition or otherwise create a competitive injury.

4. D. The facts in this question do not indicate that the borrowing firm showed the audited statements to the bank nor that the bank relied on the statements in approving the loan. The elements of fraud include misrepresentation of a material fact, *scienter* (knowledge of the charged party that the statement was false), intent to deceive, justifiable reliance on the part of the charging party, and damages. Without reliance, the circumstances in this problem would not amount to fraud.

5. D. A plaintiff does not need to show either intent or reliance to succeed under this law. (Reliance is am element of fraud and is important under the Securities Exchange Act of 1934.) The plaintiff also does not need to show privity. The plaintiff does need to show that he or she suffered a loss. Defenses that the defendant might use in this case is that he or she used "due diligence," he or she used generally accepted accounting principles, the plaintiff knew of the misstatements, the misstatements were not material, there were no misstatements in the registration statement, or there was no connection between the misstatements and the loss.

Questions on the Focus on Ethics for Unit Nine—Government Regulation

1. B. The court is most likely to rule that the "do not call" list requirements are consistent with the First Amendment. The requirements restrict only "core commercial speech," such as sales calls. Also, because the requirements specifically target speech that invades the privacy of the home, there is no breach of First Amendment rights. Furthermore, participation is optional, placing the right to restrict commercial speech in the hands of consumers, not the government. Finally, the list furthers the government's interest in combating abusive telemarketing and inhibiting invasions of privacy.

2. D. When information being disseminated about a consumer by a reporting agency is false, the person may have a basis for a suit against the agency. Under the Fair Credit Reporting Act (FCRA) of 1970, a company that sells consumer information must report it accurately and provide a remedy for consumers who seek to dispute it. If no remedy is provided, the agency is in violation of the FCRA.

3. C. Pollution does not stop at a nation's political border (as illustrated by the federal government's involvement in a problem that was once left to the states). The world is a global community. A single standard for the emission of pollutants might be desirable, but given the competing political and economic interests at stake, it might be nearly unattainable.

Chapter 49

True-False Questions

1. T

2. F. If goods are confused due to a wrongful act, it is the *wrongdoer* who must prove what percentage of the whole belongs to him or her to acquire title to any of the goods. Otherwise, the *innocent party* gets title to the whole.

3. F. The essence of a gift is that it is a voluntary transfer *without* consideration. The elements of a gift are donative intent, delivery, and acceptance.

4. F. If an accession is performed in good faith, ownership depends on the change in the value of the property. The greater the increase in the value of the property, the more likely it will be that the improver will be considered the owner of the property.

5. T

6. F. To constitute a bailment, a delivery must be of possession without any transfer of title and there must be an agreement that the property be returned or otherwise disposed of according to the owner's directions.

7. F. In most cases, a bailee is subject to a reasonable standard of care. Depending on the specific type of bailment, that standard may range from slight care (bailment for the sole benefit of the bailor) to great care (bailment for the sole benefit of the bailee).

8. F. A bailee has *two* basic responsibilities: to take proper care of the property and to surrender or dispose of the property at the end of the bailment.

9. T

10. T

Fill-in Questions

inter vivos; *causa mortis*; *causa mortis*; *causa mortis*; *inter vivos*

Multiple-Choice Questions

1. B. Personal property includes such items as computer software and home pages. Those who produce personal property have title to it. Because the creator of the property produced it, she owns it. There is an exception, however. Employees do not own what they produce for their employers. Here, she was hired to create property for another; the other owns what she created.

2. B. A bailor has a general duty to provide the bailee with goods free from defects that could injure the bailee. In a mutual-benefit bailment, as in this question, a bailor has a duty to inform a bailee of all known defects and any hidden defects that the bailor knows of or could discover with reasonable diligence and proper inspection. (In a bailment for the sole benefit of the bailee, a bailor need notify the bailee only of known defects.)

3. B. The three elements for an effective gift are donative intent, delivery, and acceptance. Here, the giver had the intent, and the recipient clearly accepted, if delivery was effective, which it was. Delivery of the key to the box was constructive delivery of the earrings. Thus, the gift would have been effective even if the giver had died before the recipient had taken them from the box.

4. A. The finder found what appears to be lost property. Generally, the finder of lost property has good title against all *but the true owner*. Therefore, the finder in this problem has title.

5. C. When goods are commingled, and the goods are lost, the owners bear the loss in the same proportion that they contributed to the whole. This is assuming that they can prove how much they contributed to the whole. Thus, the parties take out the same proportions that they put in.

6. D. A bailee must be given exclusive possession and control of the property and knowingly accept it. Here, there is no delivery of possession. Regarding the other choices, money does not need to be involved for a transaction to be a bailment, a car is personal property, and a signed contract is not necessary for a bailment (the bailment agreement may be oral).

7. A. The three elements for an effective gift are donative intent, delivery, and acceptance. Here, the giver had the intent and clearly delivered the object of the gift (by constructive delivery). Thus, the gift would have been effective if the recipient accepted it. Acceptance is generally presumed unless proven otherwise. In the problem, the recipient announced that she did not want the gift and left they key in the possession of the donor. In this case, there was no gift. The property belongs to the donor's heirs.

8. B. The wallet appears to have been placed behind the plant intentionally and thus is classified as mislaid property. The owner of the premises on which mislaid property is found is entitled to possession as against the finder.

9. c. A bailment involves delivery of personal property in such a way that the bailee is given, and knowingly accepts, exclusive possession and control over it. By accepting the coat, the restaurant is given exclusive possession and control over the purse, but it the restaurant does not *knowingly* accepts the purse.

10. B. A common carrier is liable for damage caused by the willful acts of third persons or by an accident when the goods are in the carrier's possession. Thus, the carrier is liable for most of the losses among these answer choices. The other loss is caused by an act of the shipper, however, and thus must be borne by the shipper.

GamePoints

1. The shares of stock and the copyrights are personal property. In this case, the items are intangible personal property, which represents rights or interests but doe not have physical existence. Tangible personal property has physical substance—like a copy of the video game in this problem, or the game player and screen through which it is played. Real property is also tangible, consisting of land and everything permanently attached to it, such as the copyright owner's house.

2. According to the principles covered in this chapter, most courts, including the Court of the Universe, would most likely rule that whatever was recovered from the wreck of the starship rightfully belongs to its owner, Kosmo (or you or the Galaxian Empire). In this question, Kosmo did not abandon the ship. A party who discovers another's property can lay claim to it if it was abandoned. But abandonment requires intent to give title to the property to the first person to discover it. Such an intent is lacking here, because Kosmo planned to return to the drifting vessel and recover whatever could be recovered from the wreck. Kosmo, or you, or the Galaxian Empire, did not intend to pass title to whoever else might have stumbled onto the wreck and "discovered" it. Thus, the owner retained good title to the starship, and Menace would most likely be ordered to return it. If Menace had argued that the property on the *Lightspeed* was mislaid or lost, its case would also most likely have been lost. The starship does not qualify as mislaid or lost. But even if it did, mislaid or lost property must be returned to its owner if the owner comes forward or is found.

Chapter 50

True-False Questions

1. T
2. F. The owner of a life estate has the same rights as a fee simple owner except that the value of the property must be kept intact for the holder of the future interest.
3. F. An easement merely allows a person to use land without taking anything from it, while a profit allows a person to take something from the land.
4. T
5. T
6. F. The government has the power to take private property, but the purposes for which such property may be taken must be *public*.
7. T
8. T
9. T
10. F. A landlord can sell, give away, or otherwise transfer his or her property without affecting a tenant's obligations under a lease, except that the tenant becomes the tenant of the new owner.

Fill-in Questions

warranty; special warranty; quitclaim

Multiple-Choice Questions

1. C. A *profit* is the right to go onto land in possession of another and take away some part of the land itself or some product of the land. In contrast, an easement is a right to make limited use of another person's land without taking anything from the property. A license is a revocable right to come onto another person's land.
2. D. A warranty deed warrants the most extensive protection against defects of title. A quitclaim deed conveys to the grantee only whatever interest the grantor had in the property. A special warranty deed warrants only that the grantor or seller held good title during his or her ownership of the property (the grantor is not warranting that there were no defects of title when the property was held by previous owners). Each of these deeds can have affect a different result if the title to the property is later disputed.
3. A. This action would meet all the requirements for acquiring property by adverse possession: the possession would be (1) actual and exclusive; (2) open, visible, and notorious; (3) continuous and peaceful for the applicable statutory period; and (4)

hostile, against the whole world, including the original owner. The owner's filing a suit would undercut the peaceful and exclusive elements. Occupying the property without the owner's awareness would affect the open and hostile requirements. The state's permission would normally have no effect on this issue.

4. B. The rights that accompany ownership in fee simple include the right to sell the land or give it away, as well as the right to use the land for whatever purpose the owner sees fit, subject, of course, to the law's limitations.
5. D. This is an exercise of the power of eminent domain. The proceeding is known as a condemnation proceeding. The government cannot acquire land in this manner without paying for it, however. A later proceeding is held to determine the fair value of the property. The government pays this price to the owners of the land.
6. A. Besides a legally sufficient description of the property and the price, a valid deed must contain the names of the grantee (buyer) and grantor (seller), words evidencing an intent to convey the property, and the grantor's (and usually the spouse's) signature. This question and answer are based on a question that was included in the CPA exam in November 1995.
7. C. An easement is a right to make limited use of another's real property without taking anything from it. In this problem, it is an easement by necessity—the owner needs access to his property. The right to take something from the property is a profit. A revocable right to come onto the property is a license.
8. C. When a landlord transfers his or her interest in leased property, the tenant becomes the tenant of the new owner. It is to this new owner that the tenant owes rent. Both parties must continue to follow the terms of the lease.
9. A. An assignment does not relieve an assigning tenant from the obligation to pay rent during the original term or during an extension under an option in the original lease. Unlike a lease, an easement does not involve the possession of property. An eviction is when landlord deprives the tenant of possession of the property or interferes with his or her use or enjoyment of it. A sublease is a tenant's transfer of his or her interest in leased property for less than the remaining term of the lease.
10. B. A lease that does not specify how long it is to last but does specify that rent is to be paid at certain intervals creates a periodic tenancy. The tenancy is automatically renewed for each rental period unless it has been properly terminated.

GamePoints

1. An assignment of a lease is an agreement to completely transfer all rights, title, and interest in the lease to another party, the assignee. A tenant has the right to assign the tenant's interest in a lease to another party unless there is a clause restricting or banning the assignment. In this problem, therefore, you as the tenant can assign the lease to someone else. An assignment does not end the tenant's liability under the lease (the rights are assigned but not the duties). Thus, you as the original tenant would not be released from the obligation to pay rent if the assignee did not do so.

2. A landlord can terminate a lease, and evict the tenant, if the tenant uses the property for an illegal purpose. State or local law often stipulates permissible purposes or uses for property. In this problem, counterfeiting video games is illegal, and thus would be a cause for the eviction of Bret the tenant. Failing to maintain a renters' insurance policy, keeping a dog in the apartment, or making repairs to the apartment are generally not grounds for terminating the lease or evicting the tenant, as long as those acts do not violate the terms of the lease.

Chapter 51

True-False Questions

1. T

2. F. Insurance is classified according to the nature of the risk involved.

3. F. A broker is normally the agent of the applicant. If the broker fails to obtain coverage and the applicant is damaged as a result, the broker is liable for the loss.

4. T

5. T

6. F. The application is part of the contract. Misstatements in the application can void a policy, especially if the insurer would not have issued the policy if it had known the facts (although under an incontestability clause, the insurer may have a limited time within which to void a policy on that basis).

7. T

8. F. Coinsurance provisions are standard clauses in fire insurance policies, but they reduce recovery only in cases of *partial* loss and then only if the insured has less insurance than a specified percentage. The dollar amount of recovery is equal to the dollar amount of loss multiplied by the quotient of the dollar amount of insurance and (the total value

of the property multiplied by the specified percentage). In other words, if the specified percentage is 80 percent, the total value of the property is $100,000, the amount of insurance is $40,000, and the loss is $30,000, the amount of recovery is $15,000—$30,000 x [$40,000/ ($100,000 x 80 percent)].

9. T

10. F. An antilapse clause provides a grace period for an insured to pay an overdue premium. A typical period is thirty days, and even then notice may be required to cancel the insurance.

Fill-in Questions

ordinary; nature of the coverage; insurance company; insurance company; is; insurance company

Multiple-Choice Questions

1. D. When applying for insurance, an applicant must disclose all material facts, which include all facts that would influence an insurer in determining whether to charge a higher premium or to refuse to issue a policy altogether. The correct response to this problem requires determining whether the misstatement was material. Under the circumstances stated in the problem, it was not.

2. C. An insurance company evaluates risk factors based on the information in an insurance application. For this reason, misrepresentation can void a policy, especially if the company can show that it would not have extended insurance if it had known the facts.

3. A. The insurable interest in life insurance must exist at the time the policy is obtained. Under a key-person life insurance policy, it will not matter if the key person is no longer in the business's employ at the time of the loss (the person's death).

4. C. To recover for a loss under a property insurance policy, an insurable interest in the property must exist when the loss occurs. It does not make any difference whether or not the property is owned in fee simple, or by an individual, or when an insurance policy is issued. This question and answer are based on a question that was included in the CPA exam in November 1995.

5. C. Property insurance can be canceled for gross negligence that increases the hazard insured against. Other reasons for canceling insurance include nonpayment of premiums, fraud or misrepresentation, and conviction for a crime that, like gross negligence, increases the hazard insured against.

6. C. When a coinsurance clause provides that if an owner insures the property up to a specified percentage of its value (80 percent, in this problem), he or she will recover any loss up to the face amount of the policy. Because, in this problem, the insured's coverage was up to the specified percentage ($160,000), and the loss was for less, the insured can recover the entire amount of the loss.

7. A. If policies with several companies cover the same risk and the amount of coverage exceeds the loss, under a multiple insurance clause the insured collects from each insurer its proportionate share of the liability to the total amount of insurance. If each insurer covers the full value of the property, each insurer's share of the loss will be equal.

8. C. Under an appraisal and arbitration clause, if the insurer and the insured disagree about the amount of recovery (the value of a loss), they can demand separate appraisals. If they still cannot come to terms, the appraisals are assessed and resolved by a third party (called an umpire).

9. B. Liability insurance protects against liability imposed on a company resulting from injuries to the person or property of another. Coverage under a liability policy may also include expenses involved in recalling and replacing a product that has proved to be defective.

10. D. To obtain insurance, one must have a sufficient interest in what is insured. In this problem, the insured had a sufficient interest in the property when the policy was obtained. That is, when the policy was taken out, the insured would have sustained a monetary loss from the property's loss. To collect for a property loss, the insured must likewise have an insurable interest in the property *when the loss occurs*. Here, the insured sold the property *before* the loss.

GamePoints

1. Bernie has an insurable interest in the office building that he occupies as a tenant. Bernie also has an insurable interest in the warehouse that he does not own, but in which he has a lender's, or mortgagee's, interest. For an insurable interest to arise, the insured must derive a pecuniary benefit from the preservation and continued existence of the property—there must be a connection between the insured and the risk so that if the risk insured against takes place, the insured suffers a loss or injury. This includes the possessory interest of a tenant and the interest of a secured creditor. For property, the insurable interest must exist when the specified event happens.

2. A coinsurance clause provides that if the insured does not obtain insurance in an amount equal to a certain percentage of the value of the property, the insured in effect becomes a coinsurer and must pay a proportionate amount of the loss. A purpose of a coinsurance clause is to encourage an insured to obtain a certain amount of property insurance. For example, in this problem, the policy imposed an 80 percent coinsurance clause. This is to encourage Donatello to maintain insurance on the café equal to at least 80 percent of its fair market value. If the owner does not maintain enough coverage, there will not be a recovery of the total amount of a partial loss. Here, the stipulation of the clause is met—the owner has more than the 80 percent amount of required insurance (the café has a fair market value of $350,000 and is insured under a policy for $300,000).

Chapter 52

True-False Questions

1. F. A will is revocable by the testator (or by operation of law) at any time during his or her life.

2. T

3. F. Intestacy statutes regulate how property is distributed when a person dies without a will. These statutes typically provide that after payment of the decedent's debts, the remaining property passes to the decedent's surviving wife, children, or other relatives. If there are no living relatives, the property passes to the state.

4. T

5. T

6. F. A will can appoint a guardian for minor children or incapacitated adults and can also appoint a personal representative to settle the affairs of the deceased.

7. F. The spouse—or child, if a child is born after a will is executed—is entitled to receive whatever portion of the testator's estate that he or she is permitted to take under the state's intestacy laws.

8. T

9. T

10. F. Unless the trust expressly provides otherwise, it will not terminate on the trustee's death. Normally, a trust does specify its own termination date. If its purpose is fulfilled before that date, a court may order termination. If no date is stated, a trust terminates when its purpose is fulfilled, or becomes impossible or illegal.

Fill-in Questions

executor; administrator

Multiple-Choice Questions

1. D. Under a testamentary trust, which is set up in a will, a designated, court-approved trustee would manage the property for the daughters' benefit.

2. B. Under intestacy statutes, each state regulates how property is distributed when a person dies without a will. These statutes attempt to carry out the likely intent of the decedent, setting out rules by which the deceased's natural heirs (such as children, siblings, parents, or other family members) inherit his or her property. This question and answer are based on a question that appeared in the CPA exam in 1997.

3. C. If an express declaration of revocation is missing from a second will, the wills are read together, and if a disposition in the second will is inconsistent with the prior will, the language of the second will controls.

4. C. A surviving spouse usually receives a share of the estate—one-half if there is also a surviving child and one-third if there are two or more children, and the remaining property passes to the children and the children of deceased children.

5. D. When assets are insufficient to pay in full all that a will provides, the gifts of general property, such as sums of money, are reduced proportionately. Thus, the gifts to the testator's daughters will be reduced. This is known as abatement.

6. B. A gift of personal property by will is a legacy (or a bequest)—its recipient is a legatee. A gift of real estate by will is a devise—its recipient is a devisee. Gifts can be specific, general, or residuary (paid out of the assets remaining in the estate after all taxes and bills have been paid, and specific and general gifts have been made).

7. D. On the death of a joint tenant, property held in joint tenancy passes to the surviving joint tenant or tenants without probate. In the other instances, probate is not avoided, and in the case of the trust, ongoing court supervision is required. (Note—property held in joint tenancy is not subject to a will or to probate, but it is subject to estate taxes.)

8. C. Among a trustee's duties is the responsibility to dispose of assets that do not represent prudent investments. A trustee must also distribute the risk of loss from investments by diversification. Thus, when a trustee is granted discretionary investment power, he or she must *not* invest *only* in conservative securities. (If *no* discretion is granted to a trustee, however, most states require conservative investments.)

9. C. A trust's ordinary receipts and expenses, such as rent, are chargeable to trust income (unless the trust provides otherwise). Extraordinary expenses and receipts, such as proceeds from the sale of property, are allocated to principal.

10. B. A durable power of attorney authorizes a person to act on behalf of an incompetent person.

GamePoints

1. A will must meet certain requirements designed to ensure hat the testator understood what he or she was doing at the time the will was made. The testator must have capacity—be of legal age and sound mind. The will must be in writing, the testator must sign it, witnesses must sign it, and sometimes the testator must orally declare that it is his or her will. If the plan of disposition results from another's improper pressure, it may not be valid. In this problem, some of these requirements are met (the document is in writing, and the testator and witnesses signed it) and some are not clear (is the testator of legal age? did the testator "publish" the will?). The chief obstacle to the will's validity, however, is most likely the mental states of the testator and the witnesses. The circumstances might be characterized as evidence of extreme duress, with respect to the testator, and the plan of disposition should be closely scrutinized.

2. The elements of a trust include a designated beneficiary, a designated trustee, a fund sufficiently identified to enable title to the fund to pass to the trustee, and actual delivery by the settlor or grantor to the trustee with the intention of passing title. The trust in this problem meets all of those requirements, and thus your opponent is wrong and you are right. If the settlor or grantor of a trust conveys a farm to a trustee to be held for your benefit, a trust has been created.

Cumulative Hypothetical Problem for Unit Ten—Including Chapters 49–52

1. B. The most important factor in determining whether an item is a fixture is the intent of the owners. Other factors include whether the item can be removed without damaging the real property, and whether the item is sufficiently adapted so as to have become a part of the real property. If removal would irreparably damage the property, the item may also be considered a fixture.

2. C. If a joint tenant transfers his or her interest by deed to a third party, the third party becomes a tenant in common with the remaining joint tenant or tenants. (If there is more than one remaining joint tenant, they are still joint tenants among themselves.)

3. A. The elements for a transfer of real property ownership by deed include the names of the grantor and grantee, the intent of the grantor to convey ownership, the legal description of the property, the signature of the grantor, delivery, and acceptance. Elements that are not required include consideration, the signature of the grantee, a recording of the deed, and a purchase price.

4. A. Under a coinsurance provision, the amount of recovery is the amount of the loss multiplied by the quotient of the amount of insurance and (the total value of the property multiplied by a specified percentage). Here, the specified percentage is 80 percent, the total value of the property is $500,000, the amount of insurance is $300,000, and the loss is $60,000. The amount of recovery is $45,000—$60,000 x [$300,000/ ($500,000 x 80 percent)]. (Note that a coinsurance provision reduces the amount of a recovery only in a case of partial loss and then only if the insured has less insurance than the specified percentage.)

5. B. If a tenant transfers only part of a lease (that is, if the tenant transfer the right to occupy leased premises for less than the whole term) the arrangement is a sublease. (If the transfer is for the whole term, it is an assignment.) In a sublease, the original tenant is still liable to the landlord for the rent and other conditions of the original lease despite the transfer of the right to occupy the property.

Questions on the Focus on Ethics for Unit Ten—Property and Its Protection

1. A. What the local authorities have done is to have effectively confiscated the developer's property. In this developer's case, it does not matter that the surrounding undeveloped property was zoned for use as a nature preserve only. If the developer sues the county, the regulation will likely be held unconstitutional and void unless the county pays for its effective confiscation of the developer's land.

2. A. A finder of lost property can acquire good title to the property against everyone except its true owner. A rightful owner of lost property has rights to the property superior to all others persons. If two non-owners vie for title, the first to possess the property will prevail. There is an exception that applies in cases of abandoned property: if a trespasser finds abandoned property, better title may vest in the owner of the land on which the property was found.

3. C. When a bailment is for the sole benefit of the bailee, as in this problem, a greater standard of care of the bailed property rests with the bailee. The opposite would of course be true if this were a bailment for the sole benefit of the bailor. In all cases, bailees have a duty to exercise at least reasonable care over bailed property, though what constitutes reasonable care depends on the circumstances.